To the Threshold of Power, 1922/33

Origins and Dynamics of the Fascist and Nationalist Socialist Dictatorships

Volume 1

To the Threshold of Power is the first volume of a two-part work that seeks to explain the origins and dynamics of the Fascist and National Socialist dictatorships. It lays a foundation for understanding the Nazi and Fascist regimes – from their respective seizures of power in 1922 and 1933 to global war, genocide, and common ruin – through parallel investigations of Italian and German society, institutions, and national myths; the supreme test of the First World War; and the post-1918 struggles from which the Fascist and National Socialist movements emerged. It emphasizes two principal sources of movement: the nationalist mythology of the intellectuals and the institutional culture and agendas of the two armies, especially the Imperial German Army and its Reichswehr successor. The book's climax is the cataclysm of 1914–18 and the rise and triumph of militarily organized radical nationalist movements – Mussolini's *Fasci di combattimento* and Hitler's National Socialist German Workers' Party – dedicated to the perpetuation of the war and the overthrow of the post-1918 world order.

MacGregor Knox has served since 1994 as Stevenson Professor of International History at the London School of Economics and Political Science. He was educated at Harvard College (B.A., 1967) and Yale University (Ph.D., 1977), and has also taught at the University of Rochester (United States). His writings deal with the wars and dictatorships of the savage first half of the twentieth century and with contemporary international and strategic history. They include *Mussolini Unleashed, 1939–1941* (1982); *The Making of Strategy: Rulers, States, and War* (edited with Williamson Murray and Alvin Bernstein) (1994); *Common Destiny: Dictatorship, Foreign Policy, and War in Fascist Italy and Nazi Germany* (2000); *Hitler's Italian Allies: Royal Armed Forces, Fascist Regime, and the War of 1940–43* (2000); and *The Dynamics of Military Revolution, 1300–2050* (edited with Williamson Murray) (2001). Between his undergraduate and graduate studies he spent three years in the U.S. Army, and served in the Republic of Vietnam (1969) as rifle platoon leader with the 173rd Airborne Brigade.

To the Threshold of Power, 1922/33

*Origins and Dynamics of the Fascist and
National Socialist Dictatorships*

Volume 1

MacGregor Knox
The London School of Economics and Political Science

CAMBRIDGE
UNIVERSITY PRESS

CAMBRIDGE UNIVERSITY PRESS
Cambridge, New York, Melbourne, Madrid, Cape Town, Singapore, São Paulo, Delhi

Cambridge University Press
32 Avenue of the Americas, New York, NY 10013-2473, USA

www.cambridge.org
Information on this title: www.cambridge.org/9780521878609

First published 2007

Printed in the United States of America

A *catalog record for this publication is available from the British Library.*

Library of Congress Cataloging in Publication Data

Knox, MacGregor.
To the threshold of power, 1922/33 : origins and dynamics of the fascist and national
socialist dictatorships / MacGregor Knox.
    p. cm.
Includes bibliographical references and index.
ISBN-13: 978-0-521-87860-9 (hardback)
ISBN-13: 978-0-521-70329-1 (pbk.)
1. Totalitarianism. 2. Fascism – Italy – History.
3. National socialism – Germany – History. I. Title.
JC481.K527 2007
320.53'3–dc22   2007002272

ISBN 978-0-521-87860-9 hardback
ISBN 978-0-521-70329-1 paperback

Per Tina, come sempre
Für Tina, wie immer

Contents

List of Figures and Maps

MAPS

Preface

This is an unfashionable book. The 1960s taught me the necessity of defying the wisdom of the tribe, even the tribe of the intellectuals. The book breaks a number of conventions, most of which I spell out in the introduction. But its mortal sin is to take seriously Thucydides' insistence that human history is the history of power – *dynamis* – and of armed conflict. Much of this first volume may not seem explicitly concerned with warfare, the central feature and supreme purpose of the regimes whose advent, nature, and workings it seeks to explain. But war is ever-present, even in my imprudent excursions into economics, social and political structures, and the realm of ideas. Clausewitz memorably insisted that "the soldier is recruited, clothed, armed, and drilled, [and] sleeps, eats, drinks, and marches, *only for this: that he should fight in the right place at the right time.*" This volume establishes the logistical base and conducts the long approach march toward an understanding of the supremely violent careers of the Fascist and Nazi regimes. Its successor will build on that foundation in analyzing the outcomes, from the respective "seizures of power" in 1922–26 and 1933–34 to common ruin in 1943–45.

This volume's faults are many: it has taken far too long to write, it attempts to do too much, and the larger enterprise of which it is the first instalment is unfinished. But its completion is nevertheless a happy event, for it offers an opportunity for long-overdue thanks to those who have helped along the way. Archives and archivists – the Archivio Centrale dello Stato; the Archivio Storico, Stato Maggiore dell'Esercito; the Politisches Archiv des Auswärtigen Amts; the Bundesarchiv-Militärarchiv, Freiburg im Breisgau and Aachen; the National Archives, London; and the U.S. National Archives, Washington, D.C., and College Park, Maryland – have tolerated my intrusions and, in many cases, my digital cameras. The John Simon Guggenheim Foundation, the Woodrow Wilson International Center for Scholars, the Institute for Advanced Study, and the German Marshall Fund of the United States offered early support of the project of a comparative history of the regimes, and have my abiding gratitude. More recently, the Leverhulme Trust supported two blissful years of research leave that allowed me to explore Italian, German, and U.S. archives in pursuit of material required for the second volume, and to finish much of this one. That is a very great debt indeed, and one that I hope the appearance of this book will at least partially repay.

I thank colleagues and friends, dead and living, old and new, for their long-standing support and encouragement: Sanford Elwitt, Christopher Lasch, and Richard A. Webster; Donald Kagan; Richard Kaeuper, William McGrath, and Perez and Honoré Zagorin; Paul Preston, Mia Rodríguez Salgado, David Stevenson, and Arne Westad; and Richard Bessel, Jürgen Förster, Michael Geyer, Ian Kershaw, Marco Mondini, Williamson Murray, Giorgio Rochat, Thomas Schlemmer, Gil-li Vardi, Cornelius Torp, Hans-Ulrich Wehler, and Hans Woller. I owe particular thanks to Henry Ashby Turner, Jr., for introducing me to the subject of "fascism" and the delights of historical debate in fall–winter 1970, and to his much-missed colleague, Hans W. Gatzke, who directed the resulting Ph.D. thesis with wisdom and forbearance. The editor of my first three books with Cambridge, Frank Smith, and his colleague Lewis Bateman have been profuse with encouragement and support. Lucio Ceva and Brian R. Sullivan have on many occasions given notable help with many issues dealt with in this volume and its sequel, and Isabel V. Hull, Alan Kramer, and Adrian Lyttelton offered detailed incisive comments that improved the manuscript in numerous ways.

Finally, I owe an immense and continuing debt to my father, Bernard M. W. Knox, who fought the soldiers of the German dictatorship in 1944–45 and introduced me to the native soil and language of the Italian one at a time when the rubble left by the Wehrmacht's combat engineers still disfigured the southern approaches to Florence's *Ponte Vecchio*. I likewise owe a growing obligation to my children, Alice and Andrew Knox, biochemist and philosopher, for their cheerfulness and patience. Above all, I am immeasurably beholden to my wife, Tina Isaacs, to whom, in love and gratitude, I once again dedicate a book. Its faults of omission or commission are inevitably mine alone.

London, March 2007
MacGregor Knox

Abbreviations

ADAP	*Akten zur deutschen auswärtigen Politik* (Baden-Baden, Frankfurt am Main, Göttingen, 1950–) (cited as series/volume/document)
AdR	*Akten der Reichskanzlei* (Munich, 1968–) (listed by chancellor and, if pertinent, volume)
AfS	*Archiv für Sozialgeschichte*
AHR	*American Historical Review*
AP	*Atti parlamentari* (Rome, various dates) (cited by chamber, year, page, and date)
APSR	*American Political Science Review*
BA-MA	Bundesarchiv-Militärarchiv, Freiburg im Breisgau
BVP	*Bayerische Volkspartei* (Bavarian People's Party; 1918–33 conservative-particularist Bavarian offshoot of the Catholic Center Party)
Caporetto Inquiry	Commissione d'Inchiesta, *Dall'Isonzo al Piave, 24 ottobre–9 novembre 1917*, vol. 1: *Cenno schematico degli avvenimenti*; vol. 2: *Le cause e le responsabilità degli avvenimenti* (Rome, 1919)
CEH	*Central European History*
Censimento 1921	Istituto Centrale di Statistica, *Censimento della popolazione del Regno d'Italia al 1. dicembre 1921*, 19 vols. (Rome, 1925–28)
CSSH	*Comparative Studies in Society and History*
DAP	*Deutsche Arbeiterpartei* (German Workers' Party; 1919–20 predecessor of the NSDAP)
DDI	*I documenti diplomatici italiani* (Rome 1952–) (cited as series/volume/document)
DDP	*Deutsche Demokratische Partei* (German Democratic Party; 1918–33 successor, in most respects, to the

	Left-Liberals of Imperial Germany, with some National Liberal recruits)
DNVP	*Deutschnationale Volkspartei* (German National People's Party; 1918–33 successor to the Conservatives of Imperial Germany, with some National Liberal recruits)
DRZW	Militärgeschichtliches Forschungsamt, *Das Deutsche Reich und der Zweite Weltkrieg*, 8 vols. to date (Stuttgart, 1979–)
DVP	*Deutsche Volkspartei* (German People's Party; 1918–33 successor, in most respects, to the National Liberals of Imperial Germany, with some Left-Liberal recruits)
De Felice	Renzo De Felice, 1: *Mussolini il rivoluzionario, 1883–1920* (Turin, 1965) 2: *Mussolini il fascista*, I, *La conquista del potere 1921–1925* (Turin, 1966)
ESI	(Einaudi) *Storia d'Italia*, numerous vols. (Turin, 1972–)
Falter, HW	Jürgen W. Falter, *Hitlers Wähler* (Munich, 1991)
Falter, WA	Jürgen W. Falter, Thomas Lindenberger, and Siegfried Schumann, *Wahlen und Abstimmungen in der Weimarer Republik* (Munich, 1986)
GG	*Geschichte und Gesellschaft*
Goebbels	*Die Tagebücher von Joseph Goebbels*, Teil I, *Aufzeichnungen 1923–1941*, ed. Elke Fröhlich, 9 vols. (Munich, 1998–2006)
GSR	*German Studies Review*
GWU	*Geschichte in Wissenschaft und Unterricht*
HJ	*Historical Journal*
HSA	Adolf Hitler, *Sämtliche Aufzeichnungen 1905–1924*, ed. Eberhard Jäckel and Axel Kuhn (Stuttgart, 1980)
HRSA	Adolf Hitler, *Reden, Schriften, Anordnungen: Februar 1925 bis Januar 1933*, 16 vols. and parts (Munich, 1992–2003)
HZ	*Historische Zeitschrift*
IC	*Italia Contemporanea*
JCH	*Journal of Contemporary History*
JEEH	*Journal of European Economic History*
JMH	*Journal of Modern History*
JSS	*Journal of Strategic Studies*
KPD	*Kommunistische Partei Deutschlands* (Communist Party of Germany, 1918–46/90)
Maddison	Angus Maddison, *The World Economy: Historical Statistics* (Paris, 2003)
MGM	*Militärgeschichtliche Mitteilungen*

MIW	Wilhelm Deist, ed., *Militär und Innenpolitik im Weltkrieg 1914–1918*, 2 vols. (Düsseldorf, 1970)
MK	Adolf Hitler, *Mein Kampf*, trans. Ralph Manheim (Boston, 1943)
NA	*Nuova Antologia*
NCO	non-commissioned officer
NSDAP	*Nationalsozialistische Deutsche Arbeiterpartei* (National Socialist German Workers' Party)
OO	*Opera Omnia di Benito Mussolini*, 44 vols. (Florence and Rome, 1951–)
PCI	*Partito Comunista d'Italia* (Communist Party of Italy, 1921–91)
PNF	*Partito Nazionale Fascista* (National Fascist Party, 1919/21–45)
PPI	*Partito Popolare Italiano* (the Catholic mass party, 1919–26)
PSI	*Partito Socialista Italiano* (Socialist Party of Italy, 1891–1994)
Répaci	Antonino Répaci, *La marcia su Roma. Mito e realtà*, 2 vols. (Rome, 1963)
RSHA	*Reichssicherheitshauptamt* (Reich Security Head Office of the SS, 1939–45: internal security, domination of conquered peoples, racial extermination)
RSS	*Rivista Storica del Socialismo*
SA	*Sturmabteilung* (paramilitary mass formations of the NSDAP, 1921–1945)
SC	*Storia Contemporanea*
SGAB	*Sozialgeschichtliches Arbeitsbuch*, 3 vols., various editors (Munich, 1975–82)
SPD	*Sozialdemokratische Partei Deutschlands* (Social Democratic Party of Germany, 1870–)
SS	*Schutzstaffel* (paramilitary elite formations of the NSDAP, with police and military functions after 1933)
SSt	*Studi Storici*
TMPR	*Totalitarian Movements and Political Religions*
UF	Herbert Michaelis and Ernst Schraepler, eds., *Ursachen und Folgen. Vom deutschen Zusammenbruch 1918 und 1945 bis zur staatlichen Neuordnung Deutschlands in der Gegenwart*, 24 vols. (Berlin, 1958–64)
USPD	*Unabhängige Sozialdemokratische Partei Deutschlands* (1917–22; Independent Social Democratic Party of Germany, leftist offshoot of the SPD)
VfZ	*Vierteljahrshefte für Zeitgeschichte*
VSWG	*Vierteljahrschrift für Sozial- und Wirtschaftsgeschichte*

Wehler, DGG   Hans-Ulrich Wehler, *Deutsche Gesellschaftsgeschichte*:
1: *Vom Feudalismus des Alten Reiches bis zur
Defensiven Modernisierung der Reformära
1700–1815* (Munich, 1987)
2: *Von der Reformära bis zur industriellen und
politischen "Deutschen Doppelrevolution"
1815–1845/49* (Munich, 1987)
3: *Von der "Deutschen Doppelrevolution" bis zur
Beginn des Ersten Weltkrieges 1949–1914*
(Munich, 1995)
4: *Vom Beginn des Ersten Weltkriegs bis zur
Gründung der beiden deutschen Staaten
1914–1949* (Munich, 2003)

WIH   *War in History*

INTRODUCTION

Dictatorship in the Age of Mass Politics

[L]ong voluntary subjection under individual Führer and usurpers is in prospect.
People no longer believe in principles, but will, periodically, probably [believe] in
saviors.

– Jacob Burckhardt

Burckhardt, Basel patrician and pessimist, was right. From his university chair
in neutral Switzerland, the nineteenth-century pioneer of the history of culture
saw Bismarck's founding of the German Reich in 1866/71 as the overture to
a "world war" or an "era of wars" that would destroy the cultivated elite
that Burckhardt exemplified. In the "coming barbaric age," mass politics and
industry would create a nightmare world under the domination of vast military-
industrial states whose miserable inhabitants would serve out their regimented
days "to the sound of the trumpet."[1]

The rulers of those states would differ markedly from the dynasties of the
past. Equality, as Burckhardt's contemporary Tocqueville also suggested, could
serve as foundation for wholly new varieties of despotism. In Burckhardt's jaundiced view the egalitarianism of the French Revolution and Rousseau's doctrine
of the inherent goodness of humanity had destroyed all foundation for legitimate authority. The result – from Robespierre and Napoleon to the future of
"terrifying simplifiers" that Burckhardt saw coming upon Europe – was rule by
force in the name of the people. In the "agreeable twentieth century" of Burckhardt's imagination, "authority would once again raise its head – and a fearful
head." Mass politics and the levelling force of the market would compel the
world to choose between the "outright democracy" that Burckhardt disdained
and the "unlimited lawless despotism" that he feared. Despotism might not even

---

[1] Jacob Burckhardt, *Briefe*, ed. Max Burckhardt, 11 vols. (Munich, 1949–94), 5:119, 5:158,
8:276, 5:161; *Jacob Burckhardts Vorlesung über die Geschichte des Revolutionszeitalters*, ed.
Erich Ziegler (Basel, 1974), 19; epigraph: Jacob Burckhardt, *Force and Freedom: Reflections on
History*, ed. James Hastings Nichols (New York, 1943), 41.

be the rule of an individual, as in the past, but rather "the domination of a military corporate body [*die Herrschaft einer militärischen Corporation*]" employing unprecedented terrorist methods. His contemporaries, their wits dulled by the nineteenth century's religion of progress, "might not like to imagine a world whose rulers are utterly oblivious to law, public welfare, profitable labor and industry, credit, and so on, and can therefore rule with the most consummate brutality." But some might live to see it; Burckhardt took perverse pleasure in the thought that the return of "genuine naked force" would transmute the self-satisfaction of the commercial and industrial middle classes he so despised into "pale terror of death."[2]

The agreeable twentieth century proved closer to Burckhardt's forebodings or hopes than to the expectations of other observers of the historical process, from Immanuel Kant, to Georg Wilhelm Friedrich Hegel and Karl Marx, to Richard Cobden. The teleological determinisms of Hegel and Marx – history as the self-realization of the world-spirit or of humanity as a species – were fundamentally optimistic. Hence the sovereign unconcern with which Hegelians and Marxists contemplated the unlucky or weak who perished under the spiked wheel of history. Cobdenite liberalism, the insular Anglo-Saxon successor to the Enlightenment faith in human perfectibility, was more optimistic still. The weak need not perish; free trade would painlessly "[draw] men together, [thrust] aside the antagonism of race, and creed, and language, and [unite] us in the bonds of eternal peace."[3]

After July 1914, millions slaughtered one another in ethnic and ideological massacres, industrialization through terror, and the two greatest wars in history. It required a genuinely heroic belief in Hegel's "cunning of reason" to see at least 100 million dead as advancing the progress of the world-spirit or the self-realization of the species. The "eternal peace" of the Cobdenites receded into the realm of fantasy. And the first of the two world wars led to the revolutionary despotisms that Burckhardt had foreseen, despotisms of mass politics that claimed to rest on the general will that Rousseau had imagined.

The new regimes were anything but uniform in pattern, despite their frequent grouping under the rubric of "totalitarianism" and their shared responsibility for the Second World War. Their single parties under quasi-military discipline and above all their common aspiration to total control of the individual made them appear loosely comparable, but they rested upon radically different political and social foundations. The Soviet regime came to power through revolutionary civil war in a country whose population was three-fourths peasant and whose fiercely authoritarian political culture derived from Byzantium, from the thirteenth-century Mongol conquerors of Moscow and Kiev, and from pitiless autocrats from Ivan the Terrible to Peter and Catherine the Great. By the time the party of Vladimir Ilyich Lenin consolidated its grip on Russia, war and

[2] Burckhardt, *Briefe*, 5:130, 8:290, 9:203, 9:263, 8:115.
[3] Richard Cobden, quoted in Bernard Porter, *The Lion's Share: A Short History of British Imperialism 1850–1983* (London, 1984), 6.

economic collapse had wiped the slate clean. The fragile Western-style civil society – modernity's characteristic web of religious and community groups, voluntary associations, and professional bodies – of nineteenth-century Russia had vanished, and with it any barrier to dictatorship other than the peasantry that Stalin duly crushed.[4]

The dictatorships of west-central Europe, Fascist Italy and National Socialist Germany, arose by contrast in semi-legality within still-functioning industrial societies that despite their many differences shared the Western traditions of public law, limited government, and a civil society largely independent of the state. In Russia, as the dying Lenin apparently feared, a restored "Asiatic" dictatorship was one likely outcome of the collapse of Tsarist autocracy.[5] In Italy and Germany, dictatorship was a less foreseeable consequence of war and upheaval.

From the beginning, one major school of interpretation – in both countries – privileged the unique national characteristics that purportedly produced Fascism and National Socialism. In Italy, the Fascist regime laid jealous and exclusive claim to the heritage of the national movement that had created united Italy from the 1830s to 1870. Anti-Fascist intellectuals in return disparaged Fascism as the "revelation" of that same Italy's deficits in civility and modernity. Once its momentary political utility had passed, Benedetto Croce's famous dismissal of the regime's twenty years in power as a mere "parenthesis" in the triumphant history of a United – and Liberal – Italy won few converts. Italy's trajectory had indeed diverged after 1918 from that of Britain and France, despite common experience of industrial warfare, mass death, and near-defeat. The structural and ideological roots of that divergence clearly extended back far beyond the crises of the Great War and of its aftermath that had produced the Fascist movement.[6] The leaders of that movement, from its origins in 1919–22 to national ruin in 1943–45, were products of Liberal Italy, not visitors from another planet. Understanding Fascism's origins and career inevitably required causal analysis of its specifically national past.

In Germany, the eulogists of Germany's peculiarities, its monarchical-military-Protestant *Sonderweg* – its "eccentric route" to modernity midway between Russian despotism and Anglo-French democracy – held the upper hand until 1945. Thereafter, Germany's unique trajectory "from Bismarck to Hitler" abruptly reversed polarity, and became the foremost answer to the question "How was Auschwitz possible?" That phase held through the early 1980s. In the 1960s the first postwar generation of German historians, with help from a

---

[4] See especially the durable analysis of Martin Malia, *Comprendre la Révolution russe* (Paris, 1980).

[5] Lenin and the specter of an "*Aziatchina*": Karl A. Wittfogel, *Oriental Despotism: A Comparative Study of Total Power* (New York, rev. ed., 1981), 377–79, 393–94, 399–400.

[6] See the persuasive claims – from entirely different perspectives – that Fascism had a lengthy pre-history of Paul Corner, "The Road to Fascism: A Italian *Sonderweg*?," *Contemporary European History* 11:2 (2002), 273–95, and Roberto Vivarelli, *Storia delle origini del fascismo. L'Italia dalla grande guerra alla marcia su Roma*, 2 vols. (Bologna, 1990), especially vol. 2.

few of their elders, discovered Marx, Max Weber, Talcott Parsons, and modernization theory. They fashioned a new "historical social science" *Sonderweg* along which the German people had goose-stepped from the wars of Otto von Bismarck through those of Adolf Hitler.[7] Social formations, politics, and culture had diverged sharply from the democratic West on the one hand, and on the other Germany's tumultuous economic growth had outstripped, by the eve of the Great War, the achievements of the first industrial nation, Great Britain. Prussia's victories, Bismarck's charisma, and political manipulation by the great man and his successors had fortified Prussian-aristocratic domination against industrial modernity and parliamentary democracy well into the twentieth century.

The social-historical *Sonderweg* school designated the Reich's post-1878 tariffs and "negative integration" as the tools that had unified the Prussian-Protestant "state-supporting forces" in a purported "marriage of iron and rye" and in common hatred for the Socialists and Catholics whom Bismarck had damned as "enemies of the Reich." When those remedies proved insufficient, Bismarck and successors had allegedly invoked "social imperialism": colonial, naval, and ultimately continental expansion to preserve the social order and purportedly preempt revolution at home. War in 1914 and the advent of Adolf Hitler were thus desperate bids to stave off domestic reform; the dictator's "stirrup-holders" of 1933 and the monocled nobles who commanded his assault on Soviet Russia in 1941 were merely the final stages of an iron continuity from Königgrätz and Sedan to Auschwitz and the ruined *Führerbunker* of 1945.[8]

Opposing views inevitably arose. British neo-Marxist historians of Imperial Germany mocked the new *Sonderweg* orthodoxy on many counts, but scoffed especially at the democratic credentials of the Western "model" that they themselves ungratefully inhabited. Imperial Germany, in their analysis, figured as a triumphantly modern state ruling a society that had undergone a "successful bourgeois revolution," even if that claim – apart from proposing

---

[7] "Historische Sozialwissenschaft," the school's usual self-description, is not wholly equivalent to "historical social science"; "social-historical *Sonderweg*" will nevertheless have to serve as shorthand for the school's major thesis.

[8] See especially Hans-Ulrich Wehler, *Bismarck und der Imperialismus* (Cologne, 1969), 501 (National Socialism as "extreme social-imperialism"); his *Das deutsche Kaiserreich 1871–1918* (Göttingen, 1973); the fruitful variation on Wehler's continuity theme by a later fierce opponent, Klaus Hildebrand, *Deutsche Aussenpolitik 1933–1945: Kalkül oder Dogma?* (Stuttgart, 1971); and, from the direction of sociology, Ralf Dahrendorf, *Society and Democracy in Germany* (London, 1967); among the elders, the influential refugee from Lenin and Hitler, Alexander Gershenkron, *Bread and Democracy in Germany* (Berkeley, CA, 1943); the German emigré Hans Rosenberg, *Bureaucracy, Aristocracy, and Autocracy: The Prussian Experience, 1660–1815* (Cambridge, MA, 1958) and "Political and Social Consequences of the Great Depression of 1873–1896 in Central Europe," in James J. Sheehan, ed., *Imperial Germany* (New York, 1976), 39–60; and the former SA and NSDAP member Fritz Fischer, *Germany's Aims in the First World War* (New York, 1967); *War of Illusions: German Policies from 1911 to 1914* (New York, 1975); *From Kaiserreich to Third Reich* (London, 1986).

an even cruder linkage between society and politics than that put forward by opponents – left much of pre-1914 German history perplexing. Nor did the allegedly unexceptional bourgeois career up to 1914 that the critics described offer any clue to the sources of the Reich's undeniably exceptional efforts at world conquest from 1914 to 1945 – efforts too broadly supported by Germans from all social groups to pass as contingent phenomena without a past.[9] German scholars of a moderate conservative bent delighted in the British Left's critique, and inevitably exploited it to suggest that Germans should once again aspire to national pride. Others suggested that the *Kaiserreich* had been evolving peacefully toward parliamentary democracy until 1914, or that Germany had succumbed to Nazism in 1933 not from resistance to modernity, but from a surfeit of it, an abrupt overload of overlapping traumatic events – swift and thorough industrialization, total war, humiliating defeat, the sudden advent of genuine mass politics, hyperinflation, and the Great Depression.[10]

Finally, after Soviet collapse and West Germany's annexation of its eastern neighbor in 1989–90, skepticism about the *Sonderweg*'s explanatory power and very existence became general, and embraced not merely the lock-step social-historical concept of the 1960s and 1970s but virtually all suggestions that Germany's pre-1914 past might help explain 1933–45. The Reich's trajectory to and through the era of world wars mutated yet again, into a causally irrelevant German "parenthesis," an unfortunate interlude in the nation's orderly progress toward the stable democracy of the post-1949 and post-1990 eras.

The post-1990 consensus that Germany until 1914 or 1933 was in no significant way peculiar, and that statements to the contrary were quaint throwbacks was itself merely a by-product of generational change and political and historiographical vogue, not of shifts in the underlying evidence. One powerful if faintly indecent objection to the new orthodoxy was that the alignment of Italy and Germany with Western values and political norms, however deep and abiding it might appear from a twenty-first-century vantage point, only dated from 1945. The United States and Great Britain, not indigenous political or social forces, established or reestablished representative democracy in the lands under the bloody footprint of their armies, from Sicily and Normandy to the Elbe. Stalin memorably explained the process, as he himself applied it, in spring 1945: "This war is not as in the past.... Everyone imposes his own system as far as his army can reach. It cannot be otherwise."[11]

The German people nevertheless defended their dictatorship in 1942–45 with such fervor that at least 7 million Germans – up to 10 percent of the

---

[9] See above all Geoff Eley's portion of idem and David Blackbourn, *The Peculiarities of German History: Bourgeois Society and Politics in Nineteenth Century Germany* (Oxford, 1984) (quotation, 144); and the unrepentant "Interview With David Blackbourn and Geoff Eley," *German History* 22:2 (2004), 229–45. For a mildly embarrassed effort to explain later events, Eley, "What Produces Fascism?," in idem, *From Unification to Nazism* (Boston, 1986), 254–82.

[10] Manfred Rauh, *Die Parlamentarisierung des Deutschen Reiches* (Düsseldorf, 1977); Detlev J. K. Peukert, *The Weimar Republic: The Crisis of Classical Modernity* (New York, 1992).

[11] Milovan Djilas, *Conversations with Stalin* (New York, 1962), 114.

population – died. Half of Germany's 5.3 million military dead perished after July 1944 – when the imminence of total defeat was apparent to the meanest intellect. And those who led and many who followed in that suicidal struggle, the entire top and middle management of National Socialist Germany and of its armed forces, and well over half the Germans alive in 1945, had received their intellectual furnishings and political socialization under the *Kaiserreich*.[12] Contingency after 1918 clearly played some role in their behavior, but scarcely explains a cohesion and fanaticism more deadly, to themselves and to others, than those of the warriors of Imperial Japan – whose rulers surrendered pusillanimously, largely from fear of domestic upheaval, after a mere 2.7 million dead.[13]

Yet even Germany's extreme behavior after 1933 did not necessarily rule out general interpretations that grouped it with other contemporary regimes. The common western European character of the Fascist and Nazi dictatorships struck most contemporaries as more salient than the resemblances of either to Soviet Russia. The term *totalitario*, which Liberal opponents of Benito Mussolini coined in 1923–24 and the dictator merrily plagiarized, only became popular as a sweeping "ism," a putative generic phenomenon embracing Moscow, Rome, and Berlin, in the 1940s.[14] Not so "fascism" (lower case), which originated in the Communist International in the months after Benito Mussolini's victory in 1922, over a decade before a second discernibly "fascist" regime arose. By the advent of Hitler in 1933 the term was long-established as the generic designation for the non-communist dictatorships that Marxists chose

---

[12] Except the dictator, whose Austrian origins often figure implausibly in efforts to attenuate German responsibilities. Numbers calculated from base data in *Die Bevölkerung des Deutschen Reichs nach den Ergebnissen der Volkszählung 1939*, 4 vols. (*Statistik des Deutschen Reichs*, vol. 552) (Berlin, 1941–43), 2:6–7: roughly 65 percent of Germans alive in 1939 were born in 1905 and before, as were perhaps 57 percent of Germans alive in 1945 (assuming – given the sketchiness of civilian casualty data – that the dead of 1939–45 documented in note 13 were distributed relatively evenly by age group). See in addition the acute generational analyses of Peukert, *Weimar*, 14–18, and Bernhard R. Kroener, "Strukturelle Veränderungen in der militärischen Gesellschaft des Dritten Reiches," in Michael Prinz and Rainer Zitelmann, eds., *Nationalsozialismus und Modernisierung* (Darmstadt, 1991), 272–79.

[13] German military dead (from a population of about 76 million): 4,923,000, plus a further 395,000 ethnic Germans, Alsace-Lorrainers, and others, according to the fundamental work of Rüdiger Overmans, *Deutsche militärische Verluste im Zweiten Weltkrieg* (Munich, 1999), 219, 228; civilian casualties from air bombardment and Red Army atrocities taken from Overmans, "Die Toten des Zweiten Weltkriegs in Deutschland," in Wolfgang Michalka, ed., *Der Zweite Weltkrieg* (Munich, 1989), 859; Japanese dead (from a 1941 population of 74 million): John Dower, *Embracing Defeat: Japan in the Wake of World War II* (New York, 1999), 45. On the much-disputed sources of Japanese surrender, see above all the account, based in large part on decrypts and Japanese-language sources, of Richard B. Frank, *Downfall: The End of the Imperial Japanese Empire* (New York, 1999), chs. 18–19, and especially 293–95, 310, 345–46.

[14] Jens Petersen, "La nascita del concetto di 'Stato totalitario' in Italia," *Annali dell'Istituto storico italo-germanico* 1 (1976), 143–68; Meir Michaelis, "Giovanni Amendola interprete del fascismo" NA 2158 (1986), 180–209; Leonard B. Schapiro, "Totalitarianism," in C. D. Kernig, ed., *Marxism, Communism, and Western Society*, 8 vols. (New York, 1972–73), 3:188–89.

to describe as "capitalist," and whose leaders were purportedly "agents" of malefactors of great wealth.[15]

The concept of fascism lived down its origins and its implausible identification – in Comintern orthodoxy – with a "monopoly capitalism" whose timorous representatives clearly did *not* rule in Rome or Berlin. In the late 1950s and early 1960s the archives of the interwar period slowly opened; the popularity of the concept of totalitarianism waned as Stalin's successors replaced mass terror with calculated selective repression. Ernst Nolte's *Three Faces of Fascism* (*Der Faschismus in seiner Epoche*, 1963) caught the new mood, and led an explosive wave of research into the putative "fascist phenomenon." With the enthusiasm of entomologists let loose in virgin rain forest, scholars created taxonomies of the interwar "fascist" movements. Paperback volumes sampling a bizarre variety of groups and regimes – one chapter per country – poured from the presses.

The taxonomists soon found themselves in difficulty: they were unable to define fascism convincingly and thus delimit it as a "genus." Nolte, who made the most valiant attempt at definition, described fascism as an "anti-Marxism" that had arisen in response to Bolshevism after 1917. But anti-Marxism was scarcely the most salient feature of Mussolini's *Fascismo* or Hitler's National Socialism.[16] Barrington Moore, Jr., in his 1966 epic, *Social Origins of Dictatorship and Democracy: Lord and Peasant in the Making of the Modern World*, derived fascism not from Marxism-Leninism but from feudalism: "fascism and its wars of aggression" were "the consequence of modernization without a real revolution" under the direction of agrarian elites, a claim that implausibly stretched a monocausal economic-determinist variant of Prussia-Germany's *Sonderweg* to cover the Italian and Japanese cases.[17]

Others avoided the task of definition by simply listing or "modelling" fascism's presumed attributes – the "fascist syndrome" – without offering persuasive rationales for selecting one attribute or set of attributes rather than another. The "cases" furnished the characteristics that made up the social-science "model." That model, with impeccable circularity, then confirmed the author's choice of cases. The geographic and chronological limits of fascism varied notably from author to author, and few proponents of the concept agreed on causal hypotheses about fascism's origins, dynamics, or goals. No single

[15] Theo Pirker, *Komintern und Faschismus* (Stuttgart, 1966), 45 and Ernst Nolte, "Vierzig Jahre Theorien über den Faschismus," in idem, ed., *Theorien über den Faschismus* (Cologne, 1967), 21–23.

[16] MacGregor Knox, *Common Destiny: Dictatorship, Foreign Policy, and War in Fascist Italy and Nazi Germany* (Cambridge, 2000), 54–55; also Chapter 4, note 260.

[17] (Boston, 1966), especially 447–52, 506; for Italian anticipations of this notion, see Emilio Sereni, *Il capitalismo nelle campagne (1860–1900)* (Turin, 1968 [1947]), 312, and Giuliano Procacci, "Appunti in tema di crisi dello Stato liberale e di origini del fascismo," SSt 6 (1965), 225 ("blocco di potere di tipo prussiano"); but see also the suggestion of Giampiero Carocci, *Storia d'Italia* (Milan, 1975), 13–19, that Italy's trajectory so combined elements of the English, French, and Prussian roads that "coherent development" was lacking.

conceptual mold fit the "fascisms" of industrialized Germany and of agrarian
eastern Europe or Iberia, much less the putative "emperor-fascism" of distant
Japan. Many historians divided even the seemingly close Italian and German
"cases." Some of the "ideological and moral roots of *Fascismo*" allegedly "grew
from the soil of the French Revolution"; Italy's dictator ostensibly "believed in
the idea of progress." The Hitler movement, by contrast, was purportedly an
atavistic "radicalism of the Right," a twisted product of the German *Sonderweg*.[18] At a subjective level, it emerged that Italian and German "fascists" had
failed dismally to find common ideological ground in efforts to found a "fascist
international" in the early 1930s.[19]

By the mid-1970s, proponents of the concept were in considerable embarrassment. The taxonomists sought to divide fascism into two or more fascisms, or resorted to involuntarily revealing adjectives: pre-fascist, proto-fascist,
quasi-fascist, semi-fascist, neo-fascist, fascistic, and fascistoid. Some scholars
attempted to define fascism by connecting it – like the German *Sonderweg*
itself – to the problematic social-science notion of modernization.[20] Others
innocently continued to assume that generic fascism was a thing rather than a
concept, and analyzed its presumed social bases in a variety of interwar European societies.[21] But the inability of its supporters to define it cleanly, to divide
fascist movements and regimes convincingly from merely "authoritarian" ones,
to explain its rise coherently, and to agree on whether it ended in 1945 provoked
increasing skepticism.

Former believers chronicled the "deflation" of the concept: "we have agreed
to use the word without agreeing on how to define it."[22] Skeptics argued that
the common link between fascisms was mere style, the aesthetic of the violent

[18] Renzo De Felice, *Intervista sul fascismo* (Bari, 1976), 54, 74, 100, 106; De Felice apparently
derived this left-right distinction from Jacob L. Talmon, *The Origins of Totalitarian Democracy*
(London, 1952); for a catalogue of differences between all three regimes, see Bernd Martin,
"Zur Tauglichkeit eines übergreifenden Faschismus-Begriffs," VfZ 29 (1981), 48–73; on Japan's
distinctiveness see also Peter Duus and Daniel I. Okimoto, "Fascism and the History of Pre-War
Japan: The Failure of a Concept," *Journal of Asian Studies* 39:1 (1979), 65–76.

[19] Michael Ledeen, *Universal Fascism. The Theory and Practice of the Fascist International, 1928–
1936* (New York, 1972).

[20] Taxonomy: Eugen Weber, *Varieties of Fascism* (Princeton, NJ, 1964); Alan Cassels, *Fascism*
(New York, 1975); Stanley Payne, *Fascism: Comparison and Definition* (Madison, WI, 1980)
and *A History of Fascism* (Madison, WI, 1995) remain the best. Modernization: Henry Ashby
Turner, Jr., "Fascism and Modernization," *World Politics* 24 (1972) 547–64 (548 for adjectival
proliferation, including "fascistoid"); on the theoretical pitfalls, Dean C. Tipps, "Modernization
Theory and the Comparative Study of Societies: A Critical Perspective," CSSH 15:2 (1973), 199–
226, remains vital. For a recent exhumation of the concept, pleading for a "weak version" of the
theory (a "simple authoritarian regime" cannot "*over the long term* maintain control . . . over
an increasingly economically developed society"), see Sheri E. Berman, "Modernization in Historical Perspective: The Case of Imperial Germany," *World Politics* 53:3 (April 2001), 431–62.

[21] See especially Stein Ugelvik Larsen et al., eds., *Who Were the Fascists? Social Roots of European
Fascism* (Bergen, 1980).

[22] Gilbert Allardyce, "What Fascism Is Not: Notes on the Deflation of a Concept," AHR 84:2
(1979), 367–88.

political deed.[23] Yet others suggested that the social-Darwinist pseudo-science and the genocidal deeds of "German fascism" were indeed unparalleled – except perhaps in Stalin's Soviet Russia, with its pseudo-scientific dogma of class struggle and its up to 30 million dead.[24] Scholars continued to turn out slim volumes on theories of fascism, but with diminishing conviction. The most persuasive recent effort has largely confined itself to the history of ideas, defining fascism as a "genus of political ideology whose mythic core...is a palingenetic form of populist ultranationalism." But such definitions contribute little to understanding the regime dynamics and differing outcomes of the various putative cases of generic fascism.[25]

Historical interest in the meantime shifted to the peculiarities of the movements and regimes themselves. A "new social history" – *Alltagsgeschichte* in its German variant – of everyday life "from the bottom up" duly emerged. A postmodernist "cultural history" viscerally hostile to the analysis of a putatively imaginary historical process followed. Youthful scholars professing the new genres promised to color in many totally blank areas in the recent history of Europe. But contempt for high politics engendered at least two perilous liabilities. First, the "new social historians" of Nazi Germany often focused on minor episodes of non-conformism among the population. They failed to show much interest in how the regime demonstrably inspired fanatical belief and reduced recalcitrant individuals and groups to obedience. Some even implied that the non-political rhythms of everyday life overrode even the most violent forms of political change, a strangely innocent attitude in a century in which high politics had killed, maimed, dispossessed, or displaced hundreds of millions, and had divided Germany for forty-five years. Second, the new emphases on particularity, on history from the "bottom," and on evanescent and often trivial cultural phenomena to the exclusion of the commanding heights of government, armed forces, and industry led to a proliferation of works whose authors actively denigrated synthesis. Large-scale efforts to explain historical change became – in voguish jargon – "master narratives" or "metanarratives" suspect or convicted a priori of sinister political or cultural agendas. The consequence, as the mills of academic specialization ground steadily and the stream of Ph.D. dissertations,

[23] See especially Armin Mohler, "Le 'style' fasciste," *Nouvelle École* 42 (1985), 59–86.
[24] On the parallels between *völkisch* racism and Marxism-Leninism, see among others Karl Dietrich Bracher, *Zeit der Ideologien* (Stuttgart, 1983), ch. 3; also p. 347 in this volume. The clamorous "*Historikerstreit*" of the 1980s over the comparability of National Socialism unfortunately revolved around Ernst Nolte's absurd thesis that the "so-called annihilation of the Jews by the Third Reich was a reaction [to] or distorted copy" of Stalin's camps, and the debate was too intertwined with West Germany's bitter academic and political feuding to shed much light on the historical issues; the best summary is Charles Maier, *The Unmasterable Past* (Cambridge, MA, 1988). For the numbering of Stalin's victims – a subject of impassioned dispute – see above all Steven Rosefielde, "Stalinism in Post-Communist Perspective: New Evidence on Killings, Forced Labour and Economic Growth in the 1930s," *Europe-Asia Studies* 48:6 (1996), 959–87, and Michael Haynes, "Counting Soviet Deaths in the Great Patriotic War: A Note," ibid. 55:2 (2003), 303–09.
[25] Roger Griffin, *The Nature of Fascism* (London, 1991), especially 26.

monographs, journal articles, conference volumes, and essay collections on the era of the world wars widened relentlessly, was an increasing and apparently irremediable fragmentation of knowledge.

If self-referential analysis of national *Sonderwege* is inadequate, if theoretical and practical perplexities have deflated the generic concept of fascism, and if academic specialization and the histories of "everyday life" and of "culture" threaten to dissolve historical knowledge into disjointed particulars, little hope may exist for understanding the twentieth-century dictatorships that Burckhardt had imagined. Yet generalization is an inescapable duty. Fragments are not historical knowledge. Erudition without synthesis illuminates only minute disconnected portions of the past and contributes nothing to understanding the present. Synthesis without erudition, without ruthless testing of generalizations against the widest possible spread of evidence, replaces incoherence with hollow formulas. Perhaps the career of generic fascism in particular is a cautionary tale about how not to frame a concept. Perhaps fascism, from its Comintern origins in 1922 to its re-elaboration by historians in the 1960s and 1970s, sought to cover too broad a range of too disparate phenomena.[26]

Successful concepts also exist. The ideal-types that Weber helped pioneer have proven indispensable for analyzing significant characteristics of historical phenomena, from *domination*, whether *traditional*, *legal*, or *charismatic*, to *bureaucracy* and *the state*.[27] Generalizing abstractions ("isms") with apparently well-understood origins and histories have likewise helped mightily to order the historical evidence, just as the changing meanings of those abstractions are themselves vital evidence. Few but the most recalcitrant empiricists or mocking skeptics would dismiss notions such as "absolutism," the organizing drive of the early modern monarchical state toward internal and external power. *Nationalism* is for most working historians the passionate urge to merge ethnicity and state invented in the decades surrounding 1789 and spread murderously across Europe and the world.[28] *Communism*'s corpus of sacred books, historical development from the Bolshevik Revolution through the Third International, and Leninist-dictatorial practice – enduring in its remaining outposts around the globe – make it a concept of uncommon solidity. *Capitalism*'s origins, nature, and relationship to politics have aroused fierce debate, but few historians would dispense with the term. *Democracy*, despite appropriation by

---

[26] For intriguing discussion of this pitfall, see Giovanni Sartori, "Concept Misformation in Comparative Politics," APSR 64:4 (1970), 1033–53.

[27] Perez Zagorin, *Rebels and Rulers, 1500–1660* (Cambridge, 1982) is a particularly successful example of the use of ideal-types in comparative history; Wolfgang J. Mommsen, *The Age of Bureaucracy* (New York, 1974); Fritz Ringer, *Max Weber's Methodology* (Cambridge, MA, 1997) and "Max Weber on Causal Analysis, Interpretation, and Comparison," *History and Theory* 41:2 (2002), 163–78, provide admirable introductions to Weber's ideas, their context, and their continuing usefulness. "Charisma": pp. 300–01 in this volume.

[28] See the splendid – and involuntarily complementary – discussions of Elie Kedourie, *Nationalism* (London, 1960) and Ernest Gellner, *Nations and Nationalism* (Ithaca, NY, 1983).

every known form of modern dictatorship, nevertheless has a modern history that stretches back to the English and French revolutions and a set of core values – popular sovereignty and rights *against* the state – that define the phenomenon and delimit it from other types of regime. *Liberalism* and *conservatism*, although increasingly awkward to define as the distance from their origins in the American, French, and industrial revolutions increases, are concepts ingrained in the very texture of nineteenth-century Western history.

Even *totalitarianism* has its uses. The concept's opponents initially damned it, with decreasing plausibility, as Cold War rhetoric that did an injustice to Stalin's purportedly humanist and progressive Marxism-Leninism by coupling it with Hitler's inhuman and allegedly backward-looking racism.[29] Others disparaged the notion as hollow and reductionist because no known regime was in fact "total," or plausibly complained that the concept's usual form, a syndrome or model, failed to illuminate its origins, development over time, and ultimate goals.[30] Yet totalitarianism is at least capable of clean definition as that form of dictatorship or dictatorial movement, inconceivable before the age of mass politics, that seeks total control over the individual in the name of an idea. Alternatively, as a scholar of the Cold War era, Martin Drath, suggested with breathtaking parsimony, totalitarianism was the outcome of a political movement's attempt "to impose, against the prevailing value-system of a given society, an entirely different system of values." In Drath's concept, all other aspects of totalitarian regimes derived from that "primary phenomenon" of forced value change, and "[o]nly the resistance to a totalitarian system that springs up – or is expected – from within existing society makes the system genuinely total." Either definition allows a neat distinction between totalitarian and authoritarian regimes; in Drath's words, "while authoritarianism is generally conservative, totalitarianism is rather...decisively revolutionary."[31]

---

[29] See especially p. 347. On a subjective level, neither Stalin nor Hitler seems to have seen the proposed distinction clearly, at least in private. Stalin remarked regretfully after June 1941 that "together with the Germans we would have been invincible!" Hitler's wistful verdict on his former quasi-ally was "a beast, yet also a notable man [*eine Bestie, aber immerhim von Format*]" (Svetlana Alliluyeva, *Only One Year* [New York, 1969], 392; Adolf Hitler, *Monologe im Führerhauptquartier 1941–1944*, ed. Werner Jochmann [Hamburg, 1980], 363; see also 336). The instant mutual comprehension between the two systems in August 1939 suggests that their resemblance – despite the ideological divide – was more than skin-deep. Their subjectively felt kinship is not necessarily decisive in validating the concept of totalitarianism – other levels of analysis exist. But opponents of the concept nevertheless need to confront squarely both that sense of kinship and Mussolini's high praise for Stalin's system as "a sort of Slavic Fascism" (Galeazzo Ciano, *Diario 1937–1943* [Milan, 1980], entry for 16 October 1939).

[30] For the classic "syndrome" approach and its admitted weakness in explaining origins, Carl J. Friedrich and Zbigniew K. Brzezinski, *Totalitarian Dictatorship and Autocracy* (Cambridge, MA, 2nd rev. ed., 1965), 19, 21–22.

[31] "Totalitarismus in der Volksdemokratie," introduction to Ernst Richert, *Macht ohne Mandat: Der Staatsapparat in der sowjetischen Besatzungszone Deutschlands* (Cologne, 1958), xxiv, xxix; see also Werner J. Patzelt's illuminating discussion of Drath's ideas: "Wirklichkeitskonstruktion

Framing the concept as the unfolding of the will to total power of the bearers of an ideology that – in Hannah Arendt's words – "pretend[s] to know the secrets of the historical process" builds the dynamics of the movements and regimes into the definition itself. The futile although much-argued issue of whether any given regime actually approached "total" control thus becomes irrelevant. Despite the rambling confusion of Arendt's *Origins of Totalitarianism*, a work that helped popularize the concept almost as much as Mussolini, Hitler, and Stalin, her analysis of the dynamics peculiar to Nazism contained flashes of stunning prescience. Her description of the central role of the "will of the Führer" in the German dictatorship and in its accelerating radicalization, and of that will's reciprocal relationship to the "planned shapelessness" of Nazi rule offered a still-persuasive means of reconciling the schools of interpretation later known to generations of undergraduates as "intentionalism" and "functionalism."[32]

Finally, the putrescence of Marxism-Leninism and the fall of the first Marxist empire in 1989–91 desanctified the concept of *revolution* and freed it for wider use. From their beginnings, the Italian and German regimes intermittently described themselves as revolutionary – a claim that provoked scorn and derision from virtually all political opponents and most later scholars. The enthusiastic social-science analysts of revolution of the 1960s and 1970s invariably defined their subject, with a circularity rivalling that of many fascism theorists, as upheavals from the Left and "below."[33] Yet even supposedly "popular" revolutions come "from above": only charismatic authority and political organization can convert riot or *jacquerie* into revolution. And even in the epochal pseudo-revolutionary year 1968, a relatively value-free definition of the concept was possible: "a rapid, fundamental, and violent domestic change in the dominant values and myths of society, [and] in its political institutions, social structure, leadership, government activity, and policies."[34]

The Italian and German regimes undeniably fit that template, with the possible exception of changes in social structure – an issue for consideration in due course. But the tentative admission of Fascism and Nazism to the charmed circle of revolutions is no end in itself: it makes possible an understanding of their

im Totalitarismus," in Achim Siegel, ed., *Totalitarismustheorien nach dem Ende des Kommunismus* (Cologne, 1998), 235–44.

[32] Arendt, *The Origins of Totalitarianism* (New York, 1966 [1951]), 348–49, 398–400, 402–05; for a sympathetic yet critical analysis of some of Arendt's gaps and inconsistencies, see particularly the account of Friedrich Pohlmann, "Der 'Keim des Verderbens' totalitärer Herrschaft. Die Einheit der politische Philosophie Hannah Arendts," in Siegel, ed., *Totalitarismustheorien nach dem Ende des Kommunismus*, 223–24; for an introduction to the intentionalist-functionalist dispute, Ian Kershaw, *The Nazi Dictatorship: Problems and Perspectives of Interpretation* (London, 2000), ch. 4.

[33] For still-unsurpassed introductions to these issues, see Eugen Weber "Revolution? Counterrevolution? What Revolution?," JCH 9:3 (1974), 3–47, and Perez Zagorin, "Theories of Revolution in Contemporary Historiography," *Political Science Quarterly* 88:1 (1973), 23–52.

[34] Samuel P. Huntington, *Political Order in Changing Societies* (New Haven, CT, 1968), 264.

dynamics derived from the study of other revolutions. Or of one revolution in particular: the first and greatest European secular revolution, the upheaval of 1789–1815. By 1791 the French Revolution had created what Lenin, much later, memorably described as "dual power" – an anomaly Lenin ended by coup d'état. In the France of 1791, the unsatiated revolutionary factions of the *Assemblée Nationale* and their supporters in the streets as yet lacked the capacity or will to seize power by force. They also lacked the preeminent organizational tool of later professional revolutionaries, Lenin's centralized, conspiratorial, implacable "party of a new type."[35] But they nevertheless laid siege to France's post-1789 constitutional monarchy and to its ministers. And they found, step by step, debate by impassioned debate, a road to power. The road they found was war.

From autumn 1791 onward the revolutionaries proclaimed the necessity of a "war of peoples against kings" both foreign and domestic; the Revolution had erased the traditional boundary between home and foreign affairs. France sat upon "a volcano of conspiracies about to erupt"; it was "surrounded by snares and perfidy"; "all nobles, aristocrats, and those dissatisfied with the Revolution have united against equality; all the kings of the earth are leagued against us." The revolutionaries inevitably preached preemptive attack on the "party of despotism" within and without: "Free France [was] on the point of fighting against enslaved Europe."[36] Jacques-Pierre Brissot de Warville, factional leader and ideocrat-in-chief, proclaimed in January 1792 that war was "a good thing [*un bienfait*]; it overthrows the aristocracy who fears it; it thwarts the [royal] ministers who endure it after pretending that they willed it (applause); *it consummates the revolution.*" War, Brissot's comrade Maximin Isnard had already announced, was "*indispensable* for consummating the Revolution"; it might also, he added with sinister equanimity, "set all Europe ablaze."[37] Only popular mobilization and battlefield triumph could sweep away the remaining shreds of absolutism, and change forever the lives of all humanity. A "general rising of all the peoples" would found "universal liberty" and the salvation

35 Lenin to Alexandra Kollontai, 17 March 1917; "The Dual Power" (April 1917); "What Is To Be Done? Burning Questions of our Movement" (1902), in Lenin, *Collected Works*, 45 vols. (Moscow, 1960–70), 35:297–99, 24:38–41, 5:464–67.

36 Maximin Isnard, in *Archives Parlementaires de 1787 à 1860* (Paris, 1862–), 35:442 (29 November 1791); 39:416 (6 March 1792); 34:541 (31 October 1791); 37:88 (5 January 1792). A lecture by Timothy Blanning at Princeton University in April 1989 on "Nationalism and the French Revolution" introduced me to the astonishing sources quoted; see also his *The Origin of the French Revolutionary Wars* (London, 1986); for some of the background, Carol Blum, *Rousseau and the Republic of Virtue* (Ithaca, NY, 1986); François Furet, *Interpreting the French Revolution* (Cambridge, 1981); idem, "Les Girondins et la guerre," in idem and Mona Ozouf, *La Gironde et les Girondins* (Paris, 1991), 199–205; and Talmon's still indispensable *Origins of Totalitarian Democracy*.

37 "[La guerre]...consomme la révolution" (my emphasis): Brissot, *Archives Parlementaires*, 37:471 (17 January 1792); see also his exposition of the case for war on 29 December 1791, especially 36:607; Isnard ("guerre indispensable pour consommer la Révolution"), ibid., 37:85 (5 January 1792) (my emphasis).

of "France and [of] the human race." Secular apocalypse would answer the driving need – also deeply felt in later revolutions – for an end to the revolutionary process that would harmonize internal and external worlds: "We need a *dénouement* to the French Revolution (applause)."[38] The war of 1792–1815 granted *dénouement* indeed: it consumed the monarchy, the aristocracy, the revolutionaries who forced the monarchy to launch it, the dictator who extended and perfected it, and 1.8 million Frenchmen.

The example that France's revolutionary fanatics had set lay dormant for a long century. But a new revolutionary age might easily revive the structural conditions – the incompleteness of revolutionary breakthrough and the burning universal ambitions – that had impelled the men of 1791–92 to "consummate" their revolution through the conquest of Europe. Burckhardt's agreeable twentieth century provided a promising field for such experiments. And along with at least some of the abstractions already outlined, empirical study of the patterns and regularities that provide the underpinnings for concepts, and of the irregularities and discontinuities that mark the limits of those concepts, might be of service in understanding the resulting catastrophe.

That study is called comparative history. It has existed since the Greeks of the fourth and third centuries B.C.E. sought to grapple with their own variegated political forms – from monarchy through aristocracy to tyranny and democracy. Its modern fathers have been Max Weber, Marc Bloch, and Otto Hintze. Its purposes have been essentially two: to clarify the unique causes and consequences of historical phenomena by comparing them to apparently similar phenomena, and to derive general patterns and potential explanations for those patterns from the analysis of groups of comparable cases. The two procedures are not mutually exclusive; they complement one another.[39]

The comparative method unfortunately offers little guide to the selection of phenomena or cases for comparison.[40] That requires practiced intuition, knowledge that crosses the fiercely defended frontiers of academic specialization, and languages that the historian may not initially possess. Those who successfully overcome those barriers then face the need to invent unusual multi-dimensional forms of organization. They must strike a balance between chronological narrative and structural analysis, a task far harder when covering two or more subjects than in a typical single-threaded monograph. They must cope with the often severe imbalances between their cases in the quantity and quality

38 Isnard, *Archives Parlementaires*, 37:547 (20 January 1792); Marguerite Élie Guadet, ibid., 36:382 (25 December 1791); Brissot, ibid., 36:600 (29 December 1791); Anacharsis Cloots, ibid., 36:79 (13 December 1791); "dénouement": Isnard, ibid., 35:67 (14 November 1791).

39 For Bloch, see his "Pour une histoire comparée des sociétés européennes," *Revue de Synthèse Historique* 46 (1925), 15–55; Hintze: *The Historical Essays of Otto Hintze*, ed. Felix Gilbert (Oxford, 1975). William H. Sewell, "Marc Bloch and the Logic of Comparative History," *History and Theory* 6 (1967), 208–18 and Theda Skocpol and Margaret Somers, "The Uses of Comparative History in Macrosocial Inquiry," CSSH 22:2 (1980), 174–97, usefully delineate some applications and pitfalls of the method.

40 Sewell, "Marc Bloch," 213.

of sources. They cannot afford the luxury of ambiguity or doubt: comparison demands clarity and decisiveness in describing the characteristics of the cases being compared. They must brave accusations of reductionism and distortion, for comparison is impossible without compressing and truncating complex realities, without focusing on issues pertinent to the historian's purpose, and without imposing on all cases compared common conceptual frameworks that inevitably seem perverse to specialists. Worst of all, the comparative historian cannot fully know before writing whether comparison will illuminate individual cases or yield much in the way of a generalizing argument.

Some historical phenomena nevertheless demand comparison. The long history of the concepts of fascism and totalitarianism, whatever the merits of the concepts themselves, suggests that the great dictatorships of the interwar era were fundamentally comparable. And historians of those regimes have indeed frequently compared or contrasted them to one another. In the case of the Italian and German dictatorships, the postwar national historians on either side of the Alps have tended to emphasize dissimilarities – on the basis of deep knowledge of one case and a few references to secondary literature on the other. The main exceptions to this consensus on the uniqueness of one's "own" dictatorship have been the proponents of a generic fascism, from Italian Marxists or voices on the left of the German historical profession to Ernst Nolte on its far right. A few sophisticated attempts at comparison of the regimes' structures have given weight to similarities as well as differences, yet without force-fitting the evidence into generic "models."[41] But only a systematic multi-dimensional dissection of the origins, ideologies, structures, dynamics, and ultimate goals of the two movements and regimes can clarify the degree and levels of uniqueness and similarity of the two cases. Only comparison can clear the way for explanatory frameworks or theories that might at last give content to concepts such as fascism – or transcend them, approaching the understanding of the historical process through exacting titration of the causal factors of two closely related historical cases, from their distant and often disparate origins to their common ruin.

---

[41] See the exemplary articles of Wolfgang Schieder, "Fascismo e nazionalsozialismo. Profilo di uno studio strutturale comparativo," *Nuova Rivista Storica* 54 (1970), 114–24 and "Das Deutschland Hitlers und das Italien Mussolinis. Zum Problem faschistischer Regimebildung," in Gerhard Schulz, ed., *Die grosse Krise der dreissiger Jahre* (Göttingen, 1985), 44–71, and Gustavo Corni, "La politica agraria del fascismo: un confronto fra Italia e Germania," SSt 28 (1987), 385–421.

PART I

THE LONG NINETEENTH CENTURY, 1789–1914

I

Latecomers

Historical outcomes in retrospect seem foreordained, the product of constricting structures and harsh necessities. But the past is also the province of chance and free will. The territories now known as Italy and Germany were not predestined to suffer the dictatorships of 1922–43 and 1933–45. Yet those dictatorships nevertheless had deep historical roots. The trajectories of the two societies through the "long nineteenth century" from the French Revolution to the First World War were parallel in vital ways, and significantly different from the paths of the two great powers of western Europe, France and Great Britain. And the Italian and German *Sonderwege* also differed significantly from one another in ways that affected the nature, goals, and fate of the two regimes that ultimately ruled in Rome and Berlin.

I. PECULIARITIES OF THE OLD ORDER

At the highest level of abstraction, Italy and Germany in 1789 were "belated nations" that had suffered crushing setbacks while the powers of western and northern Europe had pressed forward. The Ottoman Turks largely closed the eastern Mediterranean to trade, just as the discovery of the New World slowly shifted the center of gravity of the European economy to the Atlantic. Simultaneously, the "military revolution" of gunpowder and ruinously expensive standing armies condemned to impotence all who failed to follow the example of Spain, France, and the other large territorial states.

The brilliant civilization of northern and central Italy had led Europe in art, technology, and commerce. But it succumbed to French and Spanish conquest after 1494, in large part because the very vitality of its city-states had prevented the unification of the peninsula against outsiders. Two centuries of relative political, economic, and intellectual decline followed, under the domination of a Spain that had itself entered a long downward spiral.[1] Germany's

---

[1] See especially Guido Quazza, *La decadenza Italiana nella storia europea* (Turin, 1971), and the remarks of Fernand Braudel in ESI 2/2:2233–48.

medieval patchwork of territorial states, free towns and cities, Church principalities, and noble domains was even less well-equipped than Italy for the
new age. And the Protestant Reformation soon fractured Germany anew along
religious as well as social and political lines. The militant Catholic reaction, the
Counter-Reformation, generated conflicts that culminated between 1618 and
1648 in the bloodbath of the Thirty Years' War. Spain, Sweden, and France intervened in Germany, as France and Spain had done in Italy. Germany required
almost a century to recover from devastation and depopulation; in Italy, the
Counter-Reformation's burning determination to eradicate all new ideas reinforced Spanish domination. By the late seventeenth century Italy and Germany,
like Spain but without Spain's vast empire, had become "backward" through
immobility or regression relative to nimbler, freer, and better organized rivals:
England, France, and the Dutch Republic.[2] By 1789 that backwardness was
gradually lifting, but it bequeathed a resentful consciousness of inferiority that
persisted into the twentieth century.

    Yet the differences between Italy and Germany were at that point more sig-
nificant than their similarities. Both were fragmented, but in different ways and
to different degrees. Italy had one historic divide, which lay and still lies between
North and South. The North, from the Alps to southern Tuscany, was linked
politically and culturally – from the Carolingian empire of the ninth century
to the end of Habsburg rule in 1859–66 – to central and western Europe. The
South and the islands, from the Norman conquest in the eleventh century at
the earliest or from the domination of Spain (1282 in Sicily, 1326 in Sardinia,
1442/58 in Naples) at the latest, was a realm apart.[3] The North developed into
a land of city-states in which a patriciate largely descended from bankers and
merchants set the tone; the South and islands remained a land of theocrats and
monks, lords and *contadini*, courtiers and parasitic *lazzaroni*, in which few
beside clergy, nobles, and bureaucrats possessed the written word. Geography
reinforced political, social, economic, and cultural divisions: the North had a
disproportionate share of Italy's small stock of well-watered flatlands; much of
the South consisted of jagged eroded mountains.[4] These were two utterly different societies whose principal common ties were the Roman Catholic Church

---

[2] I have tried to use the term "backward" in a relative and subjective sense, not a teleological one;
    quotation marks should henceforth be understood.
[3] On the disputed chronology, nature, and even existence of Southern backwardness, see – from an
    enormous literature – Giuseppe Galasso, *Il Mezzogiorno nella storia d'Italia* (Florence, 1977),
    79–80 and David Abulafia, *The Two Italies* (Cambridge, 1977); Rosario Villari, "L'economia
    degli Stati italiani dal 1815 al 1848," in Luigi Bulferetti et al., eds. *Nuove questioni di storia
    del Risorgimento e dell'Unità d'Italia*, 2 vols. (Milan, 1961), 1:634–35; Sereni, *Capitalismo nelle
    campagne*, 135–75, 309–11; Luciano Cafagna, *Dualismo e sviluppo nella storia d'Italia* (Padua,
    1989), 187–220; the depressing survey of the South's condition at unification in Vera Zamagni,
    Dalla periferia al centro. La seconda rinascita economica dell'Italia 1861–1990 (Bologna, exp.
    ed., 1993), 37–44, 100; and the pointed remarks of Galasso, "The nation and Sicily, modernity
    and the Mezzogiorno," *Modern Italy* 7:1 (2002), 75–84.
[4] See the striking hydrographic and terrain data in SVIMEZ, *Un secolo di statistiche italiane. Nord
    e Sud 1861–1961* (Rome, 1961), 2–4.

and the literary language of their elites. One of those societies – the North – created both united Italy and the Fascist movement and regime. The other – the South – played little active role in either outcome.

Germany by contrast had not one but two deep divides, and all its regions played essential parts in Germany's twentieth-century upheavals. The first divide was social and regional. The eastward thrust of German colonization from the eleventh century onward created a broad belt of new settlement from Elbe to Vistula. Free peasants and landless younger sons of the nobility wrested farmland from Slavs, woods, and bogs. By the fifteenth century the growth of an export trade in grain from the Baltic ports had begun to convert the German nobles of the new areas into assiduous agricultural entrepreneurs, farming their estates directly. Their resulting search for reliable labor led them to force their peasantry gradually into serfdom, a medieval institution that was decaying in western and southern Germany. The absence of restraint – strong towns or territorial states – gave the eastern nobles victory. The "second serfdom" they imposed had by 1600 divided Germany along the line of the Elbe. Germany's west and south remained a land of cities and towns where much of the nobility, as in Italy, was content with an opulent urban existence founded upon the rents and dues of peasant tenants. In west and south, landowning peasants and urban middle classes competed with the nobility; the east became a land in which lord dominated both serfs and free peasants.[5]

Germany's second and equally deep division was inevitably religious. The Reformation and the ensuing Catholic counteroffensive had nearly destroyed the dilapidated structure of the medieval Reich – the "Holy Roman Empire of the German Nation." But both Reformation and Counter-Reformation had gotten stuck halfway. The peace of exhaustion that ended the Thirty Years' War in 1648 did not merely confirm princely power over the confession of the subject: *cuius regio, eius religio*. It also froze a religious map fragmented at every level. Lutheran and Calvinist north and east faced Catholic south and west. Protestant Prussia confronted Catholic Austria and Bavaria. Protestant cities and towns had Catholic counterparts, some of them under the rule of prince-bishops. Protestant towns and villages often looked out upon Catholic ones as close as the next hill or valley. And in the Reich's "free cities" in which toleration was the rule, individual Protestants, Catholics, and Jews – a minority that had first settled in Germany under the Romans – coexisted uneasily.

Italy and Germany were likewise different in two further vital respects: the nature of their social hierarchies and the strength of their aristocracies relative to their middle classes and peasantries. Urbanized, mercantile north Italy had never developed the rigid "society of orders" – clergy, nobility, and "third estate" – so conspicuous in France. Birth might confer citizenship and political or economic rights in a city-state or a guild, but exercise of those rights or privileges depended above all upon wealth. Wealth and status, in north Italy,

---

[5] See in general F. L. Carsten, *The Origins of Prussia* (Oxford, 1954), chs. 8–11, and the summary in Wehler, DGG, 1:71–73.

coincided to a far greater extent than in France or Germany. Clergy and nobility still enjoyed tax and judicial privileges in some regions or states, but in the thirty years before 1789 the reforming Habsburg bureaucracies largely swept them away in Tuscany and Lombardy; even the fossilized Venetian republic expropriated Church lands. The guilds, with few exceptions, had by 1789 fallen victim to the reforming state or to economic decay.[6] And Italy's social language had no vocabulary suitable for a society of orders. The closest Italian equivalent to "order" was "*ceto*" ("stratum"), a flexible term; *ceti* might have corporate existence and clearly defined boundaries, but needed neither.

Germany's hierarchy and the notions that reinforced it were very different: status and wealth often diverged widely, and status lines were both more numerous than those of France or Italy and more rigidly drawn. Custom initially defined those lines, and the absolutist state redrew them to its convenience. Nobility, *Bürgertum* or middling city population, and peasants formed the three primary *Stände* or "estates." Within those strata ran further fiercely defended lines that divided high nobility from low, merchant patricians from guild masters, guild masters from apprentices, and fragmented the peasantry through distinctions of almost infinite subtlety. The state created for its service a series of *Stände* that in part cut across the lines of custom: officers, soldiers, bureaucrats, jurists, professors, and clergy. *Stand* was hereditary, except for the "artificial *Stände*" created by the state, whose members' offspring nevertheless inherited a mighty status advantage. *Stand* also gave satisfaction to all levels of the hierarchy above beggars and laborers. The mighty could and did indulge in *Standesdünkel*, the blimpish conceit of the highborn. The more humble had the reassurance of knowing their place in a settled world and the keen pleasure of viewing their social inferiors with precisely calibrated disdain. Enshrined both in language and in social reality, *Stand* was a tenacious force for immobility, but its decay and overthrow might yet unleash – as in Revolutionary France – destructive forces of enormous power.[7]

The balances between the various social forces in Italy and Germany were likewise as different as the respective languages of social demarcation. Except in the South, the Italian aristocracy was weak. Spanish domination ended the political competition and sapped the cultural vitality of the Italian city-states, but not the ascendancy of their urban patriciates, which in the Middle Ages had absorbed or defeated the rural military aristocracy and had fastened the domination of the towns upon the countryside. From the fifteenth to the seventeenth century, as Italy's relative economic and political decline accelerated, the great patrician families fled risk. They recalled their capital from their branch offices

[6] See Luigi Dal Pane, *Il tramonto delle corporazioni in Italia* (Milan, 1940).
[7] For a description of Germany's eighteenth-century social structure, see Diedrich Saalfeld, "Die ständische Gliederung der Gesellschaft Deutschlands im Zeitalter des Absolutismus. Ein Quantifizierungsversuch," VSWG 67:4 (1980), 457–83; on the bureaucracy as "artificial *Stand*" (in the phrase of Wilhelm Heinrich Riehl), Hansjoachim Henning, *Die deutsche Beamtenschaft im 19. Jahrhundert. Zwischen Stand und Beruf* (Stuttgart, 1984), 9.

in London or Nuremberg, and bought ever-larger country estates. Merchant aristocracies mutated into powerful "landed patriciates."[8]

These groups enjoyed considerable success in preserving and expanding their wealth; by one estimate, in the eighteenth century they owned half of the cultivated land of north-central Italy, against a corresponding figure of 20 to 25 percent for the French nobility and of a mere 10 percent for the nobility of western and southern Germany.[9] But the power of the patriciates was nevertheless brittle: they lacked a grip on the state. Except in the surviving republics, Venice, Genoa, and Lucca, they no longer ruled. Elsewhere they sometimes took a role in the princely bureaucracies, but with decreasing aptitude and effectiveness as the eighteenth century drew on. As municipal oligarchs in formerly self-governing cities that chafed under the rule of Italy's territorial states, they tended to define themselves by separateness from rather than symbiosis with those states. Their mercantile origins and their location in states that were Habsburg dependencies or military nullities largely foreclosed the profession of arms, fundamental to the modern state and mainstay of the German and French nobilities.[10] The patriciates' fierce exclusiveness also worked against them; in Venice and Genoa their reluctance to coopt new forces from below and consequent numerical decline lessened their hold upon society. Finally, the patriciates normally resided in the cities, cut off from direct exercise of power over the *contadini* who worked their estates through sharecropping or leasing. Below the patriciate, as the eighteenth century progressed, a variety of intermediate groups both in city and countryside gained in prosperity and social weight.[11]

The northwest corner of Italy was an exception to this pattern. The Piedmontese aristocracy remained largely rural, as in France. But as in France it faced a partially independent landowning peasantry. Piedmontese nobles also

---

[8] For the phrase, Salvatore F. Romano, *Le classi sociali in Italia dal medioevo all'età contemporanea* (Turin, 1977), 115; see also Enrico Stumpo, "I ceti dirigenti in Italia nell'età moderna. Due modelli diversi: Nobiltà piemontese e patriziato toscano," in Amelio Tagliaferri, ed., *I ceti dirigenti in Italia in età moderna e contemporanea* (Udine, 1984), 151–97.

[9] For north Italy and France, Carlo Capra, "Nobili, notabili, élites: dal 'modello' francese al caso italiano," *Quaderni Storici* 13 (1978), 24; for Germany and France, Eberhard Weis, "Ergebnisse eines Vergleichs der grundherrschaftlichen Strukturen Deutschlands und Frankreichs vom 13. bis zum Ausgang des 18 Jahrhunderts," VSWG 57:1 (1970), 9–14, which is noteworthy for its attempt to accurately compare the differing forms of land tenure in France and Germany west of the Elbe.

[10] See especially Gregory Hanlon, *The Twilight of a Military Tradition: Italian Aristocrats and European Conflict, 1560–1800* (London, 1998).

[11] For the north Italian patriciates, see above all James C. Davis, *The Decline of the Venetian Nobility as a Ruling Class* (Baltimore, MD, 1962); R. Burr Litchfield, *Emergence of a Bureaucracy. The Florentine Patricians, 1530–1790* (Princeton, NJ, 1986); Franco Arese, "Nobiltà e patriziato dello stato di Milano," in Silvia Pizzetti, ed., *Dallo stato di Milano alla Lombardia contemporanea* (Milan, 1980); Stumpo, "I ceti dirigenti"; and Galasso, "Le forme del potere, classi e gerarchie sociali," ESI 1:470–71, on the lack of connection with the state of both elites and masses.

served a military absolutism that was remarkably uninhibited about ennobling middle-class administrators and officers. The result was an aristocracy both larger in proportion to population and less exclusive than the landed patriciates of Milan, Florence, Genoa, or Venice, and more closely tied to the state, although little stronger than the other northern elites in relation to the peasantry and the growing middle classes.

Only in the South and islands did Italy possess a landed ruling class whose weight crushed all other social groups. By the end of the eighteenth century, 650 lay and ecclesiastical magnates commanded roughly 60 percent of the income of the continental South, and a mere 90 of these *baroni* controlled two-thirds of the population.[12] The lords maintained their power through the savagery of their armed retainers, the exercise of wide-ranging judicial powers, the exaction of numerous "feudal" dues, and the direct ownership of roughly 30 percent of the land in the form of great estates (*latifundia*). But even this seemingly firm domination rested upon insecure foundations. In the capital, administration and the law fostered oligarchic groups that were potential opponents of the nobility. The monarchical state increasingly sought to curtail noble power – in self-defense if rarely from reforming zeal. With ever greater frequency the *baroni* themselves preferred the delights of Naples or Palermo to the ennui of their estates. Absentee landlords were not improving landlords, and thus weakened themselves economically over the long term. Absentee landlords inevitably delegated the administration of their estates to agents, and thus themselves helped to create the cadres of a new agrarian middle class. And absentee landlords gradually forfeited much of the ascendancy over their *contadini* that had rested on face-to-face domination. Even in the South, the nobility was far from secure as the eighteenth century ended.

Germany had no parallel to the aristocracies out of urban patriciates of north Italy. Its nobilities fell into two rough patterns, one of which had weaknesses that resembled those of its north Italian counterpart. Much of the rural nobility (*Landadel*) of the territorial states of western and southern Germany, although "feudal" rather than mercantile by origin, shared with the aristocracy of north Italy a preference for city over estate life and for assured rents over the profits and risks of direct cultivation. By contrast, the *Junker* nobility east of the Elbe resolutely enjoyed face-to-face domination – *Herrschaft* – over its peasantry. The *Junkers*, descendants of the "young lords" (*Jungherren*) of the medieval era of settlement, farmed their "knight's estates" (*Rittergüter*) directly through the labor of an enserfed or dependent peasantry. They policed the villages within the boundaries of their estates and dispensed their own justice in their own courts. They chose, from the thin strata of landowning peasants, village officials to supervise the work and conduct of serfs and landless laborers. They appointed the village pastor, who preached obedience to their authority. They enjoyed,

[12] Zamagni, *Dalla periferia al centro*, 37, and Adrian Lyttelton, "Landlords, Peasants and the Limits of Liberalism," in John A. Davis, ed., *Gramsci and Italy's Passive Revolution* (London, 1979), 120–22.

along with the few landed peasants, a monopoly of land ownership, forbidden by law to non-noble city-dwellers. And unlike the *baroni* of the southern Italy, they displayed a fierce drive toward agricultural efficiency in the service of increasingly distant markets. Finally, the *Junkers* and their state – the Prussian power-state – had since the seventeenth century evolved a unique relationship that mightily fortified both.[13]

That state was merely one of the many contrasts between Italy and Germany in the realm of politics, contrasts both striking and heavy with consequences. Italy after 1494 was a victim of great-power rivalries, not a participant. In the early eighteenth century it exchanged the domination of a weakened Spain for that of another foreign master, the Austrian Habsburgs. The ten principal Italian states of the late eighteenth century – from the Habsburg and Habsburg-Lorraine dependencies of Lombardy and Tuscany through the ramshackle and corrupt Papal States to the decayed Spanish Bourbon Kingdom of Naples – were weak states. The seeming compactness and homogeneity of their territories, compared to the bizarre kaleidoscope of Germany's states and microstates, imperfectly papered over fierce rivalries between the former city-states and disparate regions within them. Internal division had its counterpart in external impotence; Italy's states were equally incapable of aggression or self-defense. Only the diminutive kingdom of Savoy (Piedmont-Sardinia from 1720) maintained a militarily respectable though small army. But the Piedmontese state, despite centralizing reforms in the early eighteenth century, lacked the administrative rationality of late-eighteenth-century Habsburg Lombardy or Tuscany. And its proud aristocratic officer corps indignantly rejected the thought of creating an army library, and as late as 1778 quashed proposals for teaching its members subjects as unchivalric as mathematics, map-making, or the art of fortification.[14] A unique source of immobility and backwardness dominated Central Italy: the theocratic papal territories, whose ruler also claimed supreme religious authority over Italy and the world. Nor did the Italian states share a common political organization; "Italy" was a geographical expression and increasingly a cultural one, but had no political reality whatsoever. Finally, Italy's states lacked deep roots in society; even in the north, where a civic culture based upon the husks of the medieval city-states persisted, fierce and narrow loyalties to family took precedence over the claims of states whose characteristic misrule – and rule by a foreign occupying power – inspired the deepest mistrust.

Germany was very different. First and most important, from the mid-eighteenth century it was the home of not one but two great powers, a dualism

---

[13] See especially Otto Hintze, "The Hohenzollern and the Nobility," in Hintze, *Historical Essays*; Carsten, *Origins of Prussia*, and Robert M. Berdahl, *The Politics of the Prussian Nobility* (Princeton, NJ, 1988).

[14] Lucio Ceva, "Il problema dell'alto comando in Piemonte durante la prima guerra d'indipendenza," *Il Risorgimento* 37:2/3 (1985), 147; also Walter Barberis, *Le armi del principe. La tradizione militare sabauda* (Turin, 1988), ch. 3.

that began and ultimately ended in war. Upstart Protestant Prussia challenged Catholic Austria in 1740 and made good that challenge, thanks to the military brilliance of Frederick the Great (1740–86) and the solidity of the army and administrative machine that his predecessors in the house of Hohenzollern had built. Prussia was not merely "an army with a state," as one of Frederick's ministers put it. It was an army with a society. The *Junker* monopoly of power over land and peasants was not simply due to *Junker* pertinacity. It was also the product of a symbiosis between military state and nobility that had evolved from the reign of the Great Elector (1640–88) to that of Frederick the Great. The monarchical-military state confirmed and strengthened the nobility's power on the land in return for two principal concessions. The nobility grudgingly surrendered its corporate privilege of approving new taxes. Landless nobles or younger sons with no prospect of inheriting the family estate manned the army's officer corps and the remarkably efficient and relatively honest bureaucracy that taxed and administered to support that army. Mutual mistrust gave way, especially after the accession of Frederick the Great, to increasingly wholehearted collaboration between centralizing state and rural nobility.

By the late eighteenth century, army, bureaucracy, and nobility formed a unique interlocking structure that molded society to military requirements. Nobles served the Prussian state and only the Prussian state; they could not leave Prussia without the king's consent. Conscripted peasants served their landlords ten months a year, and for the remaining two did active duty under officers sometimes related to their landlords. Prussia's towns were garrison towns; Prussia's state industries produced for the army. Prussia's countryside, where much of the population wore cast-off uniforms, furnished the agricultural surplus and the peasant conscripts and reservists that supported both garrisons and industries. By 1740 Prussia was thirteenth among European states in population, but maintained Europe's fourth-largest army.[15]

Habsburg Austria, Prussia's rival, responded to the Prussian challenge with the reforms of Maria Theresa (1740–80) and of her son and co-ruler Joseph II (1765–90). Austria lacked the single-minded military emphasis of its rival, but centralization, rationalized taxation, partial expropriation of the Church, and army reform nevertheless helped. The monarchy's polyglot character, bewildering structure, and far-flung possessions offered both strengths and weaknesses. It had considerable territorial depth and its population in 1740 outnumbered Prussia's by a factor of nine to one. But it also faced potential threats in widely separated theaters or potential theaters of war: Italy, Germany, the

---

[15] Wehler, DGG, 1:246–48; Hans Rosenberg, *Bureaucracy, Aristocracy, and Autocracy*; Otto Büsch, *Militärsystem und Sozialleben in alten Preussen* (Berlin, 1962); for an unpersuasive challenge to Büsch's conceptual framework, and to the related notion that Prussian and German military arrangements were in some sense peculiar, see Peter H. Wilson, "Social Militarization in Eighteenth-Century Germany," *German History* 18:1 (2000), 1–39; C. B. A. Behrens, *Society, Government and the Enlightenment. The Experiences of Eighteenth Century France and Prussia* (New York, 1985) provides useful context.

Low Countries, and the Danube. The core territories of Prussia were by contrast a single theater.

As well as harboring two great powers locked in constant struggle, Germany diverged from the pattern of the Italian state system in other decisive respects. The Frankish and medieval German empires to which the Habsburg empire traced its descent had claimed north Italy, even though their centers of gravity had lain in the north. But even after the loss of Italy, the Reich had failed to weld itself into a medieval national monarchy. The Habsburgs, who captured the imperial throne in the course of the fourteenth and fifteenth centuries, ruled their hereditary Austrian lands but also reigned impotently over the Holy Roman Empire's colorful assortment of princely states and territories, free cities and towns, ecclesiastical mini-states, and knight's estates. The Reich constitution, confirmed and strengthened by the Habsburg failure to re-Catholicize Germany by force in the Thirty Years' War, guaranteed self-government (*Libertät*) and independence under the Reich to 1,789 political units that included 314 sovereign or partly sovereign states, cities, and towns. An archaic representative institution, the *Reichstag*, and a body of Reich law and custom guaranteed that *Libertät*. And Catholic preponderance in the Reich's political institutions balanced Protestantism's numerical advantage.

The mid-sized states of Bavaria, Saxony, Württemberg, and Hanover were comparable in size and efficiency to the larger states of north and central Italy, but Germany's territorial fragmentation denied them the neatly delineated boundaries of their Italian counterparts. Lesser German states bore distant resemblances to smaller Italian units such as the duchies of Modena or Parma. The free cities of Germany's north and west were smaller in territory than Italy's major surviving city-state republics, Venice and Genoa, but were similar in their closed oligarchic governments. The ecclesiastical principalities of the Rhineland, Westphalia, and Thuringia shared a common theocratic root with the Papal States, but were far smaller. They had a variety of rulers, rather than a single one who was also head of the Roman Catholic Church. And they existed as an integral part of the framework of the Reich, whereas the Pope recognized no earthly overlord. Italy lacked counterparts to the free towns of the German southwest, the guild-fossilized "German home towns" of the Empire that gave that region its peculiarly static quality.[16] Nor did anything in Italy even remotely resemble the dusting of princely micro-states and Imperial Knights' estates that covered the map of central and southwestern Germany. On the scales of size and power, Italy's states clustered in the middle. Germany's ran to extremes. Unlike Italy, Germany also existed as an independent political reality, however bizarre, decrepit, and paralyzed by Austro-Prussian conflict: the medieval structure of the "Holy Roman Empire of the German Nation." Finally, Germany's larger and more efficient states rested upon a compact between state and society, and enjoyed the confidence of their subjects to an extent unknown

---

[16] See Mack Walker's wonderful *German Home Towns: Community, State, and General Estate, 1648–1871* (Ithaca, NY, 1971).

in Italy. Luther had commanded obedience to the secular arm while joining it to the spiritual in a "union of throne and altar" not found in Catholicism except in the ecclesiastical principalities and the Papal States. The Thirty Years' War, which surpassed in devastation the Italian wars of the sixteenth and seventeenth centuries, made even harsh authority seem preferable to none. The subsequent decades of relative peace had consolidated the *Obrigkeitsfrommheit* – reverence for authority, a word without Italian or English counterparts – of grateful peasants and *Bürger*.

Despite common membership in the civilization of western and central Europe, Italy and Germany had inevitably developed entirely different political mythologies and intellectual traditions.[17] On the eve of the French revolutionary upheaval Italian traditions were on the whole either municipal or universal; notions of nation and nation-state had a short history and shallow roots. Dante had proclaimed the cultural and linguistic unity of the peninsula, but in politics he had sustained the universal claims of the Holy Roman Emperors from beyond the Alps.[18] Machiavelli and Guicciardini had invoked the freeing of "*Italia*" from the French and Spanish barbarians, but utterly without practical effect. Some eighteenth-century Italian intellectuals, in a desperate search for a national past, followed the Neapolitan philosopher-historian Giambattista Vico in substituting the mysterious Etruscans, who had allegedly first unified the peninsula, for Rome.[19] Yet that recondite myth of origin never developed a mass following.

The "hundred cities of Italy" likewise offered examples of greatness suitable for appropriation as national glories, from the Florence of Petrarch, Dante, Brunelleschi, Machiavelli, and the Medici bank to the seaborne empires of Venice and Genoa. But the mutual jealousies of the city-states made their traditions unsuitable as foundation of a unitary national myth. Nor did Rome's two universal traditions offer precedent for an Italian state. The Roman republic had leapt to Spain, Greece, North Africa, and Asia Minor before it had unified the peninsula politically or administratively. An "*Italia*" with roughly the boundaries of the later Italian state had been a province under the empire, but that unity – as the core territory of a universal empire – had proved transitory. The megalomaniacal usurper and "tribune" of the Roman people, Cola

---

[17] I use the terms "political mythology" or (political) "myth" without theoretical pretensions, to mean a story imbued with symbolic meaning that serves as a focus for group loyalties. That literate societies have – and require – myths to an extent as great or greater than pre-literate ones is a point that scarcely needs belaboring.

[18] The authors of the Fascist *Enciclopedia italiana*, 36 vols. (Milan, 1929–39) consequently tied themselves in knots in attempting to claim Dante as a herald of Italian political unity (12:337); for the implausibility of "Italy" as a political concept before the sixteenth century, contrast the *Enciclopedia*'s sketchy and embarrassed discussion of "Italia" (19:694) with its long essay on the "Idea di Roma" (29:906–28).

[19] Emiliana Noether, *Seeds of Italian Nationalism, 1700–1815* (New York, 1951), 78–85, 163–66; Alberto Mario Banti, *Il Risorgimento italiano* (Rome, 2005), 69 (Gioberti and Vico).

di Rienzo, had during his brief dictatorship over the city in 1347 proclaimed himself *"zelator Italiae"* and had declared all inhabitants of Italy to be Roman citizens. But he had also insisted, all too typically, that Rome was capital not simply of Italy but of the world.

The Church had risen from the ruins of the Roman Empire. It had reinforced the Roman myth by its own claim to universality, backed by more than fifteen hundred years of organizational continuity. Its very existence was a mighty obstacle to unity for the peninsula. Papal territories stretched from Bologna to the border of the kingdom of Naples. Extensive land ownership gave it a presence in the remainder of Italy unmatched by any other institution. Its grip on popular and elite loyalties, especially in the countryside, remained unshaken throughout Italy despite eighteenth-century efforts by Viennese bureaucrats and Italian reformers to reduce it to obedience.[20] The creators of an Italian national mythology would thus have to seek to push aside or bend to their purposes two anti-national myths – one of them embodied in Italy's most tenacious and deep-rooted institution – that dominated the Italian landscape through the stones of their monuments.

Germany's intellectuals fashioned a far more deeply rooted mythology of the nation, and a far more serviceable universal myth. The German humanists, thanks largely to the rediscovery of the *Germania* of Tacitus, had worked off some of the inferiority once felt toward their Italian counterparts. The greatest of Roman historians had celebrated the barbaric virtues of the humanists' alleged ancestors: the "pure blood," relative indifference to money, improbably strict sexual mores, forthrightness and trustworthiness, and abiding enthusiasm for spears "stained with the blood of a defeated enemy." Luther had adapted this cult of German "simplicity" to his battle against the alien "Papacy of Rome, founded by the Devil," thus lending to the myth the weight of the immense authority he acquired. He had reinforced traditions of veneration for the German language, which his Bible and his forceful writings did so much to create. He had helped to identify the Holy Roman Empire, that "nation" of princes, noble ecclesiastics, and patrician-ruled towns, with the German people. And Luther's sometime partisan, the humanist and warrior Ulrich von Hutten, had proclaimed the people the "natural rulers of the world [*weltherrschendes Volk*]."[21]

The humanists, Luther, and the Empire also provided figures to incarnate the unity of that *Volk*. Hutten's contribution was to found the cult of Arminius – Hermann the Cheruscan – who had broken three of Augustus's legions in the

---

[20] For the eighteenth-century struggle of the reformers to shake the Church's grip on society, see especially Franco Venturi, *Settecento riformatore* (Turin, 1969–76), 2; on the Church's strengths, Galasso, "Le forme del potere," ESI 1:466–68.

[21] See Léon Poliakov, *The Aryan Myth. A History of Racist and Nationalist Ideas in Europe* (New York, 1974), 80–85, still the best comparative account of the various nationalist "myths of origin"; Eugen Lemburg, *Geschichte des Nationalismus in Europa* (Stuttgart, 1950), 146–48 remains useful on the uses to which German humanists put Tacitus.

Teutoburger forest in A.D. 9.[22] Luther contributed his own person, at least
to German Protestants: religious leader of the *Volk* in an age in which religion
was politics, he offered subsequent generations a model for charismatic national
leadership in the service of an idea. The Reich provided the medieval Hohenstaufen emperors, especially Frederick I Barbarossa (1152–90) and Frederick
II (1210–50), who had given rise to a tenacious mythology that once again
had no lasting Italian counterpart. The figures of the two emperors became
entwined with apocalyptic prophecies that ultimately derived from the works
of Joachim of Fiore (ca. 1135–1202), a Calabrian abbot who had read into the
Book of Revelation the prophetic stage-theory of history later secularized by
Hegel and Marx. In south Italy the resulting myth – of a Frederick II asleep
under Mount Etna but fated to return to redeem the world – soon lost its hold
on the popular imagination. The emperor of the legend was no Italian, and no
Italian was available upon whom to fasten other such legends; Caesar and
Augustus seemed impossibly remote. The corresponding German legend had
far greater durability. Frederick II or Frederick Barbarossa slept in the Black
Forest or under Kyffhäuser mountain in Thuringia; his reappearance as savior
at a moment of supreme crisis would inaugurate a universal German empire.[23]
The mystical savior of the Kyffhäuser offered later Germans a model for leadership with intriguing possibilities. Its link to a political unit that was both an
outline for a German nation-state *and* an empire with universal claims was also
potentially explosive.

As well as contributing to the foundation of Germany's national mythology,
Luther also cut at the power of the chief rival and obstacle to that mythology, the Roman Church. The Church, already far weaker in Germany than in
Italy, emerged from the Reformation and Thirty Years' War ruling extensive
principalities, but claiming neither Vienna nor Berlin. Its anchor was above all
the Reich's ramshackle constitutional structures rather than the new territorial states. By contrast, Lutheranism and especially Calvinism, as Max Weber
was not the first to point out, were associated both with breaking down the
medieval abhorrence of money and profit, and with the economic integration
of large territorial units. Above all, Protestantism reinforced rather than sapped
the territorial state, especially the Prussian power-state. Both the union of
"throne and altar" and the Pietist sect that attached itself to Prussia during the

---

[22] For later developments, see Hans Peter Hermann, "Arminius und die Erfindung der Männlichkeit
in 18. Jahrhundert," in idem, Hans-Martin Blitz, and Susanna Mossmann, *Machtphantasie
Deutschland: Nationalismus, Männlichkeit und Fremdenhass im Vaterlandsdiskurs deutscher
Schriftsteller des 18. Jahrhunderts* (Frankfurt am Main, 1996), 160–91, and Horst Callies,
"Arminius, Held der deutschen," in Günther Engelbert, ed., *Ein Jahrhundert Hermannsdenkmal
1875–1975* (Detmold, 1975), 33–42.

[23] See Norman Cohn, *The Pursuit of the Millennium: Revolutionary Millenarians and Mystical
Anarchists of the Middle Ages* (New York, rev. and exp. ed., 1970), 108–13, 119–26, 143–47,
and the detailed discussion of Franz Kampers, *Die Deutsche Kaiseridee in Prophetie und Sage*
(Munich, 1969 [1896]), part B.

reign of Frederick the Great's father strengthened monarchical obedience. The contribution of the Pietists and of their neo-Pietist successors throughout the early nineteenth century was an ethic of duty toward the common good, a heatedly enthusiastic style that carried over from religion into politics, and a quaint belief that history was a process of revelation leading to an imminent Last Judgment.[24] That apocalyptic style and Protestantism's intimate connection with the national mythology, with the secular state, and with the spread of the literacy that Protestantism demanded and fostered had no Italian counterparts.

Finally, Italy and Germany were very different in the extent and nature of their participation in the great intellectual movement of the age, the Enlightenment. The Italian intellectual revival that began in the 1690s produced a number of thinkers of European stature, above all Vico – whose work remained largely unread until the nineteenth century – and the Milanese penologist Cesare Beccaria. But much of the Italian Enlightenment was a response to the gradual penetration of the advanced thought of France and Britain. Italian intellectuals were self-consciously determined to rejoin western European civilization, and not too proud to adopt French or even English models.[25] And to the skepticism of their fellow citizens toward the state they added their own discontents: with the exception of the Habsburg domains, and then only within narrow limits, Italian states before 1789 were neither bold nor particularly enlightened in their reforms.

Germany, from the 1750s onward, had an Enlightenment entirely its own, sustained by a level of literacy throughout Germany west of the Elbe that outstripped the remainder of continental Europe, and surpassed even France's advanced northeast. Germany's writers and philosophers, from Johann Wolfgang von Goethe and Friedrich Schiller to Johann Gottfried Herder and Immanuel Kant, overshadowed their French contemporaries in penetration of thought. And the German Enlightenment soon gave birth to a reaction against France itself of a sort that never developed in Italy. In part that development was a product of social resentments as well as German self-regard. The German literary elite that arose after 1770 was overwhelmingly Protestant, and almost exclusively middle class and proud of it – unlike their French counterparts, many of whom were either noble or aspired to become so; Voltaire and Beaumarchais bought titles. The worthy *Bürger* across the Rhine viewed such behavior with contempt and ridiculed their own court aristocracies for aping French fashions, manners, language, and morals. "Spew out the ugly slime of the Seine / Speak German, O you German!" thundered Herder, the virtual inventor of German cultural nationalism. At a more fundamental level than mere cultural and social criticism, Herder also damned the Roman Church as an oppressive colonizing force that had erased the "spirit of the Nordic peoples" along with

---

[24] See Carl Hinrichs, *Preussentum und Pietismus* (Göttingen, 1971), 11 and, in general, chs. 1–2.
[25] See Stuart J. Woolf, *A History of Italy, 1700–1860. The Social Constraints of Political Change* (London, 1979), 75–84.

their primordial pagan rites and customs.[26] Correspondingly, the rationalism of Descartes, Newton, and Locke never enjoyed the overwhelming prestige it gained in France and Britain. By the 1790s German Romanticism was still a literary movement, but one with powerful political implications.

Enlightened Germans also took a different attitude toward their states, especially Prussia, than did the *philosophes* and at least some of their Italian counterparts. In France the Enlightenment acted as a corrosive force upon the Old Regime, whose apparent obscurantism, arbitrariness, incompetence, and incapacity for reform it helped expose. In Italy, Enlightenment thinkers never quite ceased to hope for reform from their states, but owed foreign dynasties or closed city-state oligarchies little abiding loyalty. In Germany, despite frequent complaints that the Frederician state treated individuals as cogs in a soulless machine, the Enlightenment worked for rather than against the state. The German princes and the Prussian administration inspired a loyalty approaching reverence in intellectuals as well as common subjects. The levelling rationalizing state of the late eighteenth century appeared the only force for the free development of the individual in an otherwise largely static society. And because society was static, Germany's *literati* lacked the backing of a broad and prosperous middle class such as those of France or England; instead, they owed their living largely to the German states that so many of them served as professors, jurists, and bureaucrats.[27] In the coming revolutionary century, German state-reverence and satisfaction with the old order proved a precious asset to the German princes and a powerful influence upon Germany's future.

2. REVOLUTIONS FROM ABOVE, 1789–1871: POLITICS, SOCIETY, MYTHS

Politics, war, and ideas made Italy and Germany, not glacially slow social processes or the alleged structural imperatives of a non-existent or still feeble industrial capitalism. "In the beginning was Napoleon"; at the end, Camillo Benso di Cavour and Otto von Bismarck.[28]

---

[26] Literacy, and the role of Protestantism and confessional rivalry in its spread: Etienne François, "Alphabetisierung und Lesefähigkeit in Frankreich und Deutschland um 1800," in Helmut Berding, Etienne François, and Hans-Peter Ullmann, eds., *Deutschland und Frankreich im Zeitalter der Französischen Revolution* (Frankfurt am Main, 1989), 409–17; Herder views and remarks: Kedourie, *Nationalism*, 59; George S. Williamson, *The Longing for Myth in Germany: Religion and Aesthetic Culture from Romanticism to Nietzsche* (Chicago, 2004), 75, 99, 110.

[27] On the differing effects of the Enlightenment on France and Prussia, see the perceptive remarks of Behrens, *Society, Government, and the Enlightenment*, 152–85, as well as Henri Brunschwig, *Enlightenment and Romanticism in Eighteenth Century Prussia* (Chicago, 1974), 15–21; for the origins of the fateful association of the German absolutist state with freedom, Leonard Krieger, *The German Idea of Freedom* (Chicago, 1972), 21–45; for the social position of eighteenth-century German intellectuals, ibid., 41–44; also Wehler, DGG, 1:210–17, and Charles W. Ingrao, "A Pre-Revolutionary Sonderweg," *German History* 20:3 (2002), 279–86.

[28] "Am Anfang war Napoleon": Thomas Nipperdey, *Deutsche Geschichte 1800–1866. Bürgerwelt und starker Staat* (Munich, 1990), first sentence. For an unintentional reductio ad absurdum of

I. War and Politics

French conquest brought to Italy and Germany Napoleon's "idea that ha[d] found bayonets," a revolution that made subjects of princes into citizens of nation-states. The Revolution proclaimed the abolition of the society of orders; individuals, not orders, had rights. Those individuals, the revolutionaries insisted, were equal members of a new political unit, the *nation*.

In the decade after 1796 the conquerors turned the Italian states upside down, sometimes with the help of "Jacobin" minorities inflamed with hopes of renewing both humanity and Italy with French support. From the debris Napoleon ultimately fashioned a "Kingdom of Italy" embracing much of the peninsula. The temporal power of the Papacy, a tradition stretching back at least a thousand years, collapsed. The fossilized republics of Venice and Genoa vanished. *Départements* replaced provincial or city-state boundaries. Written constitutions founded on French models, French administrative techniques, and the Napoleonic civil code permanently marked Italian conceptions of public law and politics. Codified law and centralized administration fit too well with the traditions of Italian enlightened absolutism for the dynasties restored in 1814–15 to do more than tinker with Napoleon's legacy.

Not the revolutionary General Bonaparte but the Emperor Napoleon I conquered Germany, with a correspondingly milder direct impact except in the Rhineland territories already seized in the 1790s and in the principalities carved from western Germany for Napoleon's relatives.[29] The emperor sought, above all, troops, money, and obedience, and tolerated German dynasties willing to supply them. Yet the consequences of French influence were as deep or deeper as those of direct rule upon Italy. Four years of revolution from above, from 1803 to 1807, altered the map of Germany at the local level in a manner that even France's gerrymandering of Italy did not match.

The Reich and its variegated mini-states, its multifarious layers of rights, liberties, and customs, dissolved. In its place Napoleon and the German princes between them brought the modern state to southern and western Germany. Bavaria rounded out its territories with relish. In Württemberg, Baden, Hesse, and the Bonaparte-ruled "Kingdom of Westphalia" and "Grand Duchy of Berg," centralizing bureaucratic absolutisms rode roughshod over previously independent nobles, cities, towns, and villages. Almost 60 percent of all Germans changed rulers. And this "princes' revolution" also destroyed the religious balance that had held since 1648. The disappearance of sixty-six ecclesiastical

the thesis that economics drove the making of Prussia-Germany, see Helmut Böhme, *Deutschlands Weg zur Grossmacht: Studien zum Verhältnis von Wirtschaft und Staat während der Reichsgründungdzeit 1848–1881* (Cologne, 1966).

[29] For the vicissitudes of the territories the French occupied earliest and most thoroughly, see T. C. W. Blanning, *The French Revolution in Germany. Occupation and Resistance in the Rhineland, 1792–1802* (Oxford, 1983); for the consequent abiding differences in public and private law between the Rhineland and the rest of Germany, see Elizabeth Fehrenbach, *Traditionelle Gesellschaft und revolutionäres Recht* (Göttingen, 1974).

principalities, the exclusion of Austria, and the end of the Reich was the last great victory of the Reformation. It made German Catholics a minority in their own land and left the Church at the mercy even of Catholic princes.[30]

Yet not all German states bore the French yoke gladly. Prussia, drubbed at Jena-Auerstädt and Eylau in 1806–07 and shackled by a peace settlement that temporarily halved the kingdom in size and population, in desperation gave power to bureaucratic and military reformers who had long recognized that 1789–93 had "given the French amid bloodshed and upheaval entirely new energies." Prussia could only win back its freedom as a state by setting loose those same energies.[31] Subjects (*Untertanen*) must become citizens (*Staatsbürger*) with equality of rights. All male citizens must become soldiers – an aspiration soon embodied in Prussia's pioneering short-term military service law. The *Wehrgesetz* of 1814 made the army the "foremost school [*Hauptbildungsschule*] of the whole nation for war"; over the following century universal conscription stamped, far more deeply and indelibly than under the *ancien régime*, a military character upon Prussian and ultimately upon German society. All qualified by education and talent should become officers, breaking the nobility's virtual monopoly over military leadership. Concurrently, the officer corps purged itself of incompetents with breathtaking ruthlessness; barely half the officers of the defeated army of 1806–07 shared in the victories of 1813–15.[32]

In society at large, the abolition of serfdom, the end to prohibition on middle-class estate ownership, the coming of freedom of trade and occupation, mass education, elected municipal government, and Jewish emancipation aimed to create both the reformers' independent-minded *Staatsbürger* and an economic upswing that would fund the reconstruction of army and state despite French exactions and the devastation of the countryside by war. To combat Napoleon, the reformers fashioned a peculiar mixture of Adam Smith, the France of 1793, and the Prussia of Frederick the Great.[33] Their variant of the bureaucratic-military revolution from above that France had inspired throughout Germany saved Prussia – and gave it a unique if still half-acknowledged claim to national leadership.

The Vienna Settlement of 1814–15 restored much of Italy's map to the position of 1789, but the memory of the Kingdom of Italy persisted and French

---

[30] See Karl Otmar Freiherr von Aretin, *Vom deutschen Reich zum Deutschen Bund* (Göttingen, 1980), 108–09.

[31] Baron von Hardenberg to King Frederick William III, "On the Reorganization of the Prussian State," 12 September 1807, in Georg Winter, ed., *Die Reorganisation des Preussischen Staates unter Stein und Hardenberg*, 2 vols. (Leipzig, 1931–38), 1:305; background: Karen Hagemann, "Occupation, Mobilization, and Politics: The Anti-Napoleonic Wars in Prussian Experience, Memory, and Historiography," CEH 39:4 (2006), 58–61.

[32] For the purge and its context, Knox, *Common Destiny*, 197–98.

[33] "Die preussische Beamtenschaft hatte bewusst für Adam Smith gegen Napoleon optiert, um den einen durch den anderen zu vertreiben" (Reinhart Koselleck, *Preussen zwischen Reform und Revolution. Allgemeines Landrecht, Verwaltung und Soziale Bewegung von 1791 bis 1848* [Stuttgart, 2nd ed., 1975], 14).

constitutional thought remained a model for Italian jurists and intellectuals.[34] The German territorial states swollen by the "princes' revolution" reasserted their sovereignty within the framework of a new German Confederation of thirty-nine states established at Vienna. The pre-1789 patchwork of almost 1,800 entities was irretrievably gone, and a newly emboldened Prussia fell heir to much of western Germany. Only the power of Austria and the tenacious will to self-perpetuation of Germany's mid-sized states upheld the German and European settlement against challenges from rogue great powers or from the growing national movements that the French example had inspired.

Those movements gradually spread. In Italy, a network of shadowy secret societies with up to 600,000 members, the *Carbonari* ("charcoal-burners"), led the way. Nationalist and constitutionalist revolts in 1820–21 and 1830–31, from Piedmont to Sicily, by officers and *Carbonari* ended in predictable disaster and numerous executions. In each case, Austrian armies based on Lombardy-Venetia restored Italian rulers to power or helped them to crush resistance. Thereafter, a young Genoese, Giuseppe Mazzini, took the lead in the *Risorgimento*, the cultural-political revival that demanded and ultimately created an Italian nation-state. His novel conspiratorial sect, *Giovine Italia* ("young Italy"), founded in Marseille in summer 1831, was perhaps the earliest political movement to exploit a generational divide; Mazzini had contemplated barring anyone over forty. *Giovine Italia* demanded the unification of all Italy under a democratic republic founded by "a provisional, dictatorial authority, concentrated in a small number of men."[35] Italy's established rulers regarded that program as anarchy and terrorism, and in 1833–34 duly put down in blood Mazzini's first feeble insurrectionary efforts. In Germany, police repression at first sufficed to calm the agitation of nationalist student groups, the *Burschenschaften*, which had culminated in a boisterous 1817 commemoration, complete with torchlight parades and anti-Semitic "German-Christian" overtones, of Luther's defiance of the Papacy and of Napoleon's fatal 1813 defeat at Leipzig. The first widespread anti-Semitic riots in Germany since the Middle Ages, the "Hep! Hep!" violence of 1819, responded to Jewish emancipation with an all-too-literal translation into street mayhem of Jahn's injunction that "hatred of everything foreign was the German's duty."[36] By the 1830s nationalism had reemerged as a mass movement, especially in southwestern

---

[34] See Carlo Ghisalberti, "Der Einfluss des napoleonischen Frankreich auf das italienische Rechts- und Verwaltungssystem," in Armgard von Reden-Dohna, ed., *Deutschland und Italien im Zeitalter Napoleons* (Wiesbaden, 1979), 41–56, and his *Dall'antico regime al 1848: le origini costituzionali dell'Italia moderna* (Bari, 1974).

[35] Mazzini (1831), *Scritti politici*, ed. Franco Della Peruta, 3 vols. (Turin, 1976), 1:68.

[36] Stefan Rohrbacher, "The 'Hep Hep' Riots of 1819: Anti-Jewish Ideology, Agitation, and Violence," in Christhard Hoffmann, Werner Bergmann, and Helmut Walser Smith, eds., *Exclusionary Violence: Antisemitic Riots in Modern German History* (Ann Arbor, MI, 2002), 23–42 (Jahn, 34; for the pervasiveness of anti-Jewish press agitation, 33–36); the editors' introduction, 4, suggests a German chronological primacy in modern anti-Semitic violence: the first major outbreaks in Russia, classic land of the pogrom, dated from the 1880s.

Germany and the Rhineland, the areas most affected by French laws and ideas, nearest in social structure to the post-revolutionary France of peasant proprietors, and closest to the threat of French occupation. In 1840 a Near Eastern crisis in which France momentarily challenged the powers produced the first mass mobilization of German opinion. "They shall not have it, the free German Rhine" became the refrain of innumerable patriotic singing societies. Nationalist opinion, promoted by the rapid spread of literacy and less and less shackled by press censorship, was henceforth a powerful political force that Germany's princes and bureaucrats ignored at their peril.[37]

Austrian power at last began to crumble in the chain reaction of urban revolutions, from Palermo to Paris, Vienna, Berlin, Milan, and Venice, of spring 1848. The ensuing quarter-century of inter-state turmoil opened the road for Piedmont and Prussia, the Italian and German monarchies whose traditions, military power, and ambitions predisposed them to expansion. In 1848–49 Charles Albert of Savoy and Frederick William IV of Prussia conceded parliamentary institutions at least partly to fortify their claims to national leadership. But in the end they preferred defeat by Austria or humiliating inaction to invoking the full power of their peoples. Their liberal-democratic rivals, from Mazzini and Giuseppe Garibaldi – whose volunteers had defended the short-lived Roman Republic with unparalleled skill and valor – to the south German radicals who proposed to democratize Germany with a portable guillotine, conspicuously failed. By summer 1849, a resurgent Austria, a newly confident military-monarchical Prussia, and a conservative French republican regime under the great Napoleon's erratic nephew had brought Piedmont to heel at Custoza and Novara, had destroyed democratic republics from Rome and Venice to Baden, and had scattered the democrats beyond redemption.

The next generation of Piedmontese and Prussian leaders were both sterner and more flexible than the men of 1848. Cavour had made his political debut in spring 1848 by warning Charles Albert that he must choose war or revolution: hesitation in attacking Austria might "make the ancient throne of the Savoyard monarchy crumble."[38] Cavour's own war of aggression against Austria in 1859 harnessed the army of Napoleon III and the enthusiasm of the Italian national movement – which provided up to 24,000 volunteers, half the strength of the Piedmontese regular army – to a carefully limited monarchical revolution from above embracing Lombardy and central Italy. Then the unplanned and unforeseeable spring–summer 1860 successes of Garibaldi's "Thousand" – which soon grew to 20,000 volunteers – destroyed the Bourbons and imposed upon Cavour the gift of the South.[39] A radical-democratic "Duce" of red-shirted irregulars, hailed by the southern populations as a saint and astride a third of Italy as

[37] Hagen Schulze, *Der Weg zum Nationalstaat. Die deutsche Nationalbewegung vom 18. Jahrhundert bis zur Reichsgründung* (Munich, 1985), 80–83; Jörg Echternkamp, *Der Aufstieg des deutschen Nationalismus (1770–1840)* (Frankfurt am Main, 1998), ch. 6; Wehler, DGG, 2:398–99.

[38] Quoted in Rosario Romeo, *Dal Piemonte sabaudo all'Italia liberale* (Bari, 1974), 124.

[39] Numbers: Banti, *Risorgimento*, 107, 113.

"Dictator of the Two Sicilies," was diplomatically hazardous and domestically intolerable.[40] The Piedmontese army thus accepted with haste and scorn Garibaldi's willing surrender of his conquests to Charles Albert's jovial and feckless son and successor, Victor Emmanuel II. Bismarck's three victorious wars, against Denmark in 1864, Austria and the lesser German states in 1866, and France in 1870–71 preempted "people's war" with "royal war" to an even greater degree than had Cavour. Yet the militant and military-minded nationalism of Bismarck's Prussian Liberal adversaries, fifty years of conscription, and the "old Prussian spirit" ensured a measure of popular participation far exceeding that of the *Risorgimento*. Bismarck made good his threat or boast of 1866: "If there is to be revolution, we would rather make it than suffer it."[41]

This seemingly parallel transformation of two "geographic expressions" into frameworks for nation-states produced outcomes far different in vital respects. Italy, contrary to the proud 1848 slogan of the wretched Charles Albert, did not "make itself." Piedmont's post-1815 army remained a well-ordered *ancien régime* force, not a Prussian-style "school of the whole nation for war." Repeated purges, relentless political surveillance in the 1820s and 1830s, and a cult of blind obedience and barrack-square routine under clerical supervision stunted its already weak impulse toward learning from the Napoleonic experience. It went to war in 1848 without a warplan or functioning high command; the minister of war confessed to Piedmont's Chamber of Deputies that he had unsuccessfully advised Charles Albert to remedy the inadequacies of Piedmont's senior generals by hiring a French marshal.[42] In the war of 1859, France provided most of the forces and did most of the fighting. In the Piedmontese-Italian army's next independent campaign, in 1866, the same command and staff failures revealed two decades earlier led to renewed disaster at Custoza, despite considerable fighting power displayed at regimental level and below. The navy simultaneously incurred a humiliating and never fully avenged débâcle at Lissa in the Adriatic.[43]

---

[40] On Garibaldi's charismatic appeal, see especially Della Peruta, *Realtà e mito nell'Italia dell'ottocento* (Milan, 1996), 92–93, and Banti, *La nazione del Risorgimento. Parentela, santità e onore alle origini dell'Italia unita* (Turin, 2000), 172–74, 189, 98–99 figure 10 (an 1850 portrait of Garibaldi as Jesus Christ).

[41] For the Prussian Liberals' notable bellicosity (and rifle clubs), see Franz Lorenz Müller, "The Spectre of a People in Arms: The Prussian Government and the Militarisation of German Nationalism, 1859–1864," *English Historical Review* 122:395 (2007), 82–104; Nikolaus Buschmann, *Einkreisung und Waffenbruderschaft. Die öffentliche Deutung von Krieg und Nation in Deutschland 1850–1871* (Göttingen, 2003); and Dietmar Klenke, "Nationalkriegerisches Gemeinschaftsideal als politische Religion," *HZ* 260 (1995), 395–448. Quotation: Otto Pflanze, *Bismarck and the Development of Germany*, 3 vols. (Princeton, NJ, 1963–90), 1:306.

[42] On the army in the Napoleonic era and its lack of resemblance to that of Prussia, see especially Barberis, *Le armi del principe*, ch. 4; for its performance in 1848, Ceva, "Il problema dell'alto comando," 150–53.

[43] Ceva, *Le forze armate* (Turin, 1981), ch. 4, still offers the best brief analysis of the "third war of independence."

The Prussian army conceded nothing to that of Piedmont in monarchical obedience. But unlike Piedmont's it was a thinking obedience, and one scarcely confined to the officer corps alone, as the workings of the *Wehrgesetz* and the efforts of Prussian schoolmasters over an entire century extended military expertise and literacy downward throughout society. The reformers of the Napoleonic era broke – in this as in other ways – with the traditions of Frederick the Great, who detested *"Raisonneurs"* in his army. The general staff, refounded in 1808 and based in due course on competitive selection of the most brilliant junior officers for rigorous specialized training and eventual positions as chiefs of staff to senior commanders, provided a unique central nervous system for the control of mass armies. One of the staff system's founders, the philosopher-general Carl von Clausewitz, memorably summed up a central feature of the institutional culture the reformers created in his famous description of war as the realm of "chance and probability within which the creative spirit is free to roam."[44]

By the 1860s a Prussian prince could write with conscious pride that *"there is a stronger desire for independence from above and for taking responsibility upon one's self than in any other army."* A Bavarian observer, with a touch of professional envy, noted later the extent to which nineteenth-century Prussia had promoted – rather than punished or cashiered, as in Bavaria – those whose "self-will at times overstepp[ed] the normal bounds of leadership and initiative... harsh and pitiless personalities inclined to excess in their handling of both subordinates and superiors." That practice, the Bavarian remarked, was "not coincidental, but a carefully considered and implemented system."[45] Prussia's system rested increasingly upon the principle of *Auftragstaktik* or "mission tactics," as later ages and other armies described it: superiors set tasks (*Aufträge*), but were obligated to allow subordinates the choice of methods for their accomplishment. As the swift growth in firepower, battlefield scale, and army size from the Napoleonic age to the twentieth century made centralized command less and less possible, the general staff system and the cult of initiative – *Selbständigkeit* – and of creative freedom gave the Prussian army an ever-increasing tactical and operational edge over all rivals.[46]

---

44 "[A] paradoxical trinity – composed of primordial violence, hatred, and enmity...; of the play of chance and probability within which the creative spirit is free to roam, and of its element of subordination, as an instrument of policy, which makes it subject to reason alone": Karl von Clausewitz, *On War*, ed. and trans. Michael Howard and Peter Paret (Princeton, NJ, 1989), 89 (book I, ch. 1, section 28).

45 Prince Frederick Charles (1860) (emphasis in original), in Karl Demeter, *The German Officer-Corps in Society and State 1650–1945* (New York, 1965), 260; Ludwig von Gebsattel (Bavarian Military Plenipotentiary in Berlin) to Bavarian Minister of War, 23 November 1905, quoted in Hermann Rumschöttel, "Bildung und Herkunft der bayerischen Offiziere 1866 bis 1914," MGM 2 (1970), 123 ("die Schätzung und Förderung von Offizieren, die, an sich leistungsfähig und durchaus tüchtig, durch einen die Grenzen der normalen Selbständigkeit zuweilen überschreitenden Eigenwillen schwer zu behandelnde, nach oben und unten gleich schroffe und rücksichtslose, zu Übergriffe neigende Persönlichkeiten").

46 On the genesis and consequences of the "Prussian idea of freedom," see especially Knox, *Common Destiny*, ch. 5.

The army's leaders, from anonymous line officers and ministry bureaucrats to Helmuth von Moltke the Elder, chief of the Great General Staff from 1857, were equally clear-sighted in other ways. In the 1840s and 1850s they bet heavily on repeating rifles, telegraphs, and railroads. William, Regent of Prussia from 1857 and king after 1861, single-mindedly forced the virtual doubling in size of Prussia's line army in the early 1860s, amalgamating much of Prussia's *Landwehr* or reserve formations with the line, increasing the army's intake of conscripts, and lengthening the term of service from two to three years.[47] The system nevertheless retained one of its greatest strengths, the close association over decades between each regiment and a given recruitment area – guaranteeing a rare degree of unit homogeneity, cohesion, and tradition. The resulting military instrument and the officer corps' professional independence of mind and swiftness in learning tactical lessons backed Bismarck's daring diplomacy with the battlefield victories denied to Cavour and his successors.

The triumphs of Bismarck and Moltke, and the military disasters of Charles Albert and his son and successor, Victor Emmanuel II, were the single most important force upon the divergent political paths that Italy and Germany travelled for the remainder of the century, and in part thereafter. But ideas also played a role: the far greater influence in Italy of French enlightenment models and of French public law also shaped the Italian state. The swift dilution of Piedmont's personnel and institutions through an almost five-fold expansion of territory from 1859 to 1870 weakened the absolutist element at Piedmont's core – whereas Prussia's size and tenacious desire to remain itself, and the relative vitality, compared to their Italian counterparts, of the lesser German states made Prussia-Germany pseudo-federal, preserving both Prussia and the major federal states as strongholds of royal and princely prerogative. Yet it was battlefield failure, above all else, that parliamentarized Italy. Charles Albert's abdication after defeat in 1849 and the disasters of 1866 did not formally restrict the royal prerogative in foreign affairs and war enshrined in the constitutional *Statuto* granted in 1848. The monarch preserved broad extra-parliamentary powers and the capacity to intervene decisively in the event of deadlock. Defeat nevertheless made government the affair of the prime minister, the cabinet, and the amorphous parliamentary majority of the center that Cavour formed in the 1850s and that governed Piedmont and Italy thereafter.[48]

---

[47] Dennis E. Showalter, *Railroads and Rifles: Soldiers, Technology, and the Unification of Germany* (Hamden, CT, 1975); Gordon A. Craig, *The Politics of the Prussian Army 1640–1945* (Oxford, 1955), ch. 4; Michael Geyer, *Deutsche Rüstungspolitik 1960–1980* (Frankfurt am Main, 1984), 24ff.; Manfred Messerschmidt, *Die politische Geschichte der preussisch-deutschen Armee (Handbuch zur deutschen Militärgeschichte, 4:1, Militärgeschichte im 19. Jahrhundert)* (Munich, 1975), 177–84.

[48] Howard McGaw Smyth, "Piedmont and Prussia: The Influence of the Campaigns of 1848–1849 on the Constitutional Development of Italy," *AHR* 55:3 (1950), 479–502 is eloquent on the consequences of Piedmontese defeats in contrast to Prussian victories – although Smyth assumes the two states and societies were more alike than they actually were, and neglects ideological factors.

Prussian conquest of Germany and German victory over France had very different consequences. The immense prestige earned in 1866–70, along with German liberalism's greater deference to the Hegelian state and Prussia's greater relative weight in Germany than Piedmont's in Italy, gave the Prusso-German military-monarchical executive almost as broad a sphere of action in the new Reich of 1871 as it retained in Prussia. Prussian liberalism had almost paralyzed the royal government in the constitutional conflict of the early 1860s by exploiting parliament's power of the purse to seek an unwelcome voice in William's military reforms. William and Bismarck had fought that claim, and had won their war in 1866 without and against the Prussian lower house. Then Bismarck had halted the Prussian armies short of Vienna and had barred the road to the creation of the unitary state embracing all German-speakers that many liberals sought. The new Reich's pseudo-federal structure retained most of the German princely houses, and marooned outside the new Reich the 9 million–odd Germans who formed the increasingly beleaguered ruling minority of the Habsburg empire. Yet the defeat of the liberals was not total. Bismarck and the king recognized the new Reichstag's budgetary powers, and their "lesser Germany" without Austria scarcely stilled abiding ambitions for a greater Germany stretching far to the south and east. The wars of 1866–71 deferred decisions as well as imposed them. The monarchical-military "revolution from above" that founded the Reich pre-judged only some of the new state's future.[49]

II. Societies and Economies, Continuity and Change

Politics and war led the way; society followed. Not until well after 1815 did economics – that other revolution in the mines and mills of north England – strike even Germany with any force, and that revolution's protagonists long remained subordinate to the military-monarchical state. The Napoleonic domination of Italy destroyed the settled habits of centuries. French administration and law, backed by bayonets ruthlessly employed, gripped society with far greater force than the timid reforms of the eighteenth-century Italian states. The *Code Napoléon*, imposed in Italian translation, gave the peninsula its first uniform body of civil law. In the long term, the Code's insistence on equality before the law and on the division of inheritances was a powerful levelling force against the patriciates of the North and the baronage of the South, which had preserved their social domination through primogeniture and entails.[50] In the short term, ever-growing French exactions dictated the swift sale of many

---

[49] See especially Wolfgang J. Mommsen, "Das deutsche Kaiserreich als System umgangener Entscheidungen," in Helmut Berding et al., *Vom Staat des Ancien Regime zum Modernen Parteienstaat. Festschrift für Theodor Schieder* (Munich, 1978), 239–65; and, despite characteristic perversity, Carl Schmitt, *Staatsgefüge und Zusammenbruch des Zweiten Reiches: Der Sieg des Bürgers über den Soldaten* (Hamburg, 1934), especially 11–14, 19, 20, 23, 25, 36, 39.

[50] Napoleon, as he explained to his brother Joseph in 1806, saw the civil code – and the ruler's discretionary power to allow the nobility to nevertheless establish entails – as a powerful engine

Church lands that had escaped the Habsburg reformers. In France, the sale of the assets of Church and *emigré* aristocracy after 1790 had benefited the urban middle classes but also mightily reinforced the landowning peasantry. In Italy the aristocracy had not fled and the landowning peasantry was weak. Confiscation and sale of Church land therefore benefited Italy's aristocrats and urban elites about equally, and largely left the peasantry out. Land sales and the *Code Napoléon* began to fuse patricians and middle-class magnates into that *classe proprietaria* defined by land ownership rather than birth that henceforth dominated Italy's countryside.[51] In the South, thanks to the abolition of "feudal" dues and jurisdictions, middle-class groups in the countryside gradually asserted themselves alongside the *baroni*; Sicily and Sardinia, protected from Napoleon by the British fleet, nevertheless retained much of the old order. In the North, recruitment for the new Napoleonic bureaucracies created an administrative and judicial elite that outlived the Napoleonic era and henceforth formed a vital component of Italy's upper middle class.

Germany's social structures and administrative, legal, and intellectual traditions were far less adaptable to French models than those of Italy. Many of the emperor's new vassal states adopted versions of the *Code Napoléon*. But they imposed that code on a society of *Stände* that still enjoyed – or suffered under – almost infinitely varied and complex noble land tenures, rights, and privileges, institutions that had only existed – if at all – in an attenuated form in north Italy and had vanished in France without compensation in 1793. The result in Germany was confusion and delay, modifications and innumerable exceptions; no German state fully abolished peasant obligations until 1848, although the west and south German states gradually phased them out in a manner that protected peasant rights. Napoleon himself promised to preserve some privileges of the high nobility or *Standesherren*, the former Imperial Knights whose south and west German lands had been fiefs of the Holy Roman Empire. And some states, most notably Saxony and the *Junker*-dominated Mecklenburgs, made no attempt at reform whatever. Germany's large Jewish minority, freed in the reforms from vexatious restrictions, benefited only gradually from the equality promised to it. The society of *Stände* gave way only haltingly to a civil society of free individuals equal before the law. The Napoleonic revolution in western and southern Germany freed – or created – states far more than *citizens*.

Prussia's reforms, which ensured Prussia's survival and expansion, and determined the character of its influence on the other German lands, inevitably had effects less far-reaching than the reformers had hoped. The reforms sat

for consolidating Bonaparte power: "no great houses will remain except those you [Joseph] erect into fiefs" (quoted in Fehrenbach, *Traditionelle Gesellschaft und revolutionäres Recht*, 26). Napoleon's exemptions were transitory; the levelling effect of the code remained.

51 Capra, "Nobili, notabili, élites," and Renato Zangheri, "Gli anni francesi in Italia: Le nuove condizioni della proprietà," SSt 20 (1979), 5–26, provide useful preliminary summaries of this development. In the best studied area, Bologna, middle-class holdings rose from 26 percent in 1789 to 36 percent in 1804 and 54 percent by 1835 (ibid., 22; also Zangheri, *La proprietà terriera e le origini del Risorgimento bolognese*, vol. I, 1789–1804 [Bologna, 1961]).

uneasily within the framework of previous Prussian practice, especially the General Law Code or *Allgemeines Landrecht* of 1794, which catalogued in loving detail the differing rights of and legal boundaries between the various *Stände*. The nobility inevitably fought the erosion of its privileges, while the Prussian *Bürgertum* of the Napoleonic era was neither sufficiently prosperous, politically conscious, nor unified to offer the reformers support. Yet the prohibition on middle-class acquisition of *Rittergüter* did fall away, and by 1885 nobles owned less than 60 percent of Prussia's major estates, although they continued to hold almost all very large ones.[52] Fierce noble resistance largely preserved the judicial, police, and local political powers of the estate owners until 1848 and beyond, whereas peasant emancipation from serfdom came slowly and largely at peasant expense. In effect though not in intention, the reform freed serfs from the land but not from the estate owner, whom many continued to serve as landless laborers.

And Prussian bureaucratic traditions themselves, as much as the resistance of the nobility or the apathy of the middle classes, preserved well into the mid-nineteenth century many aspects of the society of *Stände*: differentiation in everything from marriage law to punishments for criminal offenses.[53] The reforms of the Napoleonic era also accentuated the tendency, already present in the *Allgemeines Landrecht*, to define *Stand* in terms of functional relationship to the state. The officer corps, in particular, received in the reform era a twofold gift. First, the reformers offered, from the mouth of the king himself, a solemn promise of a French revolutionary "career open to talent" that in theory banished social privilege from the battlefield:

> From now on knowledge and education [*Bildung*] shall give claim to officer positions in peacetime, and in war outstanding bravery and presence of mind. Therefore all individuals from the entire nation who possess these qualities may lay claim to the highest posts of honor in the army. All previously exercised precedence based on social status [*Vorzug des Standes*] in the army ceases utterly herewith, and all have equal duties and equal rights.[54]

Yet along with the ringing statement of August 1808 came a fateful redefinition of the officer corps as a *Stand* within the state possessing special rights and its own codified conception of "honor." The survivors of the 1806–07 débâcle had demonstrated a unique capacity for self-government and self-criticism through their merciless purge of incompetents; the reforms then gave them full control

---

[52] See the statistics of J. Conrad, "Die Latifundien im preussischen Osten," *Jahrbücher für Nationalöknomie und Statistik* 50 (1888), 138–41.

[53] See the numerous examples in Koselleck, *Preussen zwischen Reform und Revolution*, 52–147.

[54] Article 2 of "Krieges-Artikel für die Unter-Offiziere und gemeinen Soldaten," 3 August 1808, printed in Eugen von Frauenholz, *Entwicklungsgeschichte des deutschen Heerwesens*, vol. 5, *Das Heerwesen des XIX. Jahrhunderts* (Berlin, 1941), 101–13; regulation on officer recruitment issued by Frederick William III, 6 August 1808, in Messerschmidt and Ursula von Gersdorff, eds., *Offiziere im Bild von Dokumenten aus drei Jahrhunderten* (Stuttgart, 1964), 171. For the influence of the French model, see Knox, "Mass Politics and Nationalism as Military Revolution," in Knox and Williamson Murray, eds., *The Dynamics of Military Revolution 1300–2050* (Cambridge, 2001), 57–73.

over officer recruitment and thus over their own collective future. Officers entered the army as officer candidates and passed competitive written examinations before being coopted, subject only to royal approval, by the officers of their regiment.[55]

The military reforms thus fused expertise, guaranteed through the recruitment of talented commoners, with noble conceptions of *Stand* honor, decentralized corporate self-selection, and the officer corps' direct personal relationship to its supreme commander, the king. This peculiarly Prussian mixture had political and social consequences well into the twentieth century. In creating the new *Offiziersstand*, the reformers reshuffled the society of *Stände* into two groups rigidly defined by *military* function. On one side stood those whose birth – and increasingly education, the *Bildung* of the reformers and of the highly literate middle classes – made them capable of becoming officers: the nobility and upper middle classes. On the other stood those who served in the ranks of the new universal service army.

The officer corps after 1808 coopted rather than merely accepted commoners; social prestige born of noble exclusiveness, of the victories of Frederick the Great, and of Prussia's eminent part in the triumph over Napoleon in 1813–15 ensured a continuing supply of middle-class talent. The desire to be coopted began the slow task of molding middle-class mores and politics to military standards. In return, competition with commoners compelled noble officers and officeholders in the state bureaucracy to make their way by achievement as well as by birth. Over the next century competition gradually raised the educational standards imposed on officer candidates and on the officer corps as a whole – for the "First *Stand*" could not fall too far behind the free professions and the civilian bureaucrats in *Bildung* without losing its social preeminence.[56] In the very long term the new standards of military-bureaucratic efficiency and the system of universal military service imposed in 1813–14 had mutually contradictory effects. Brilliant military or bureaucratic careers for commoners transmuted the natural leaders of protest from below into fervent supporters of the state, while universal military service and battlefield sacrifice helped inspire the masses to press for equal political rights and for release from the bondage of *Stand*.[57]

By mid-century, the blind forces of demography and economics that more than doubled western Europe's population between 1800 and 1913 and multiplied its production by a factor of six had also begun to move both societies.[58] Demographic growth and economic development were inevitably uneven; Italy,

[55] Ernst Rudolf Huber, *Deutsche Verfassungsgeschichte seit 1789* (Stuttgart, 1957–91), 1:232–38.

[56] See, for example, the comments of an unnamed commanding general (1862), quoted in Demeter, *The German Officer-Corps*, 285; likewise, 289 (1909); and, in general, ibid., chs. 10–12.

[57] See Huber, *Verfassungsgeschichte*, 1:238–39; and Geyer's trenchant dismissal of the Erich von Stroheim image of the "feudal" Prussian officer corps that pervades the literature: "The Past as Future: the German Officer Corps as a Profession," in Geoffrey Cocks and Konrad H. Jarausch, *German Professions, 1800–1850* (Oxford, 1990), 185–91, 194–95, and 210 note 43.

[58] Colin McEvedy and Richard Jones, *Atlas of World Population History* (London, 1978), 18; Paul Bairoch, "Europe's Gross National Product, 1800–1975," JEEH 2:5 (1976), 276.

along with most of southern and eastern Europe, proved less dynamic than
Germany. Between 1811 and 1851 Italy's population only increased by 32 percent (from 18.7 to 24.7 million), roughly the European average.[59] That was
enough to strain existing economic structures, but not to produce a breakdown
of political order. Agriculture, which accounted for more than 60 percent of
all production, remained largely stagnant. Despite the freeing of the market in
land in the Napoleonic upheaval, great estates in Sicily and some parts of the
continental South, and sharecropping (*mezzadria*) in much of the North and
all of central Italy, remained the fundamental pattern.

But in north Italy, the section climatically and socially closest to western and
central Europe, change was perceptible even before mid-century. In Lombardy
and some areas of Piedmont, the dynamic regional economy that later drove
Italy's industrialization began a slow advance during the economic upturn that
stretched from the late 1820s to the mid-1840s. The techniques of northern
Europe's "agricultural revolution" were readily adaptable to the wet and fertile
Po Valley, where entrepreneurial traditions had survived the "centuries of decadence."[60] From the eastern edge of Piedmont across Lombardy and southward
to Bologna and Ferrara, the urban *signori* who owned the flatlands gradually
ceased to be satisfied with assured rents, and sought with increasing aggressiveness to expand production and markets. By 1900 Po Valley agriculture was
raising 30 percent of Italy's crops by value on a mere 13 percent of the nation's
arable and forest lands.[61]

Agrarian capitalism, as elsewhere, was a precursor and prerequisite for industrialization. But until after mid-century only a precursor: Italy was not blessed
with coal and iron, the key materials of the "first industrial revolution": tex-
tiles, steam power, and railroads. Factory production, even in silk (Italy's leading
export throughout the century) and cotton, was slow to develop except in parts
of Lombardy and Piedmont. The industrial and artisanal production of north
Italy as a percentage of total production did not begin gaining substantially
on that of agriculture until the 1880s. Italy's states were also slow to promote
growth. Technical talent remained in short supply. Customs barriers, wretched
roads, the peninsula's ever-present mountains, and the economic incompatibility of North and South stood in the way of the development of anything
resembling a national market. Speech in the Tuscan dialect officially designated
"Italian" was probably confined in 1861 to around 10 percent of the peninsula's
population. Literacy, a vital factor in increasing productivity, grew only slowly;
most Italian states were too weak to promote it and too backward to desire
it. Piedmont and Lombardy led: by 1861 up to 45 percent of their populations
over age 6 could read. But for north-central Italy as a whole the corresponding
figure was 33 percent, and a mere 12.9 percent in the South and islands. Italy's

[59] SVIMEZ, *Nord e Sud*, 11.
[60] See particularly Domenico Sella, *Crisis and Continuity. The Economy of Spanish Lombardy in
the Seventeenth Century* (Cambridge, MA, 1979).
[61] Sereni, *Capitalismo nelle campagne*, 313.

overall economic performance reflected these conditions: between 1820 and 1870 annual per capita GDP grew from an estimated $1,117 to $1,499.[62]

United Italy thus remained strikingly divided. Cavour and the liberal "moderates" had won against astonishing odds: the might of Austria, the recalcitrance of the lesser states, the embittered resistance of the Roman theocracy and of its mass following, the initiative and wrathful disdain of the democrats, and the indifference or outright hostility of the peasantry that made up 65 percent of the population. The North-South divide shocked the *moderati*, and compounded the centuries-old contempt of Italy's city-dwellers for rustic barbarism; a Cavour proconsul famously summarized in 1860 the Piedmontese elite's developing view of the South: "Anything but Italy; this is *Affrica*. The Bedouin, compared to these ignorant boors [*cafoni*], are [the very] flower of civic virtue."[63] Cavour and associates, invoking largely non-existent foreign pressures, instantly centralized and monopolized power throughout the South. The Piedmontese generals scornfully sent home Italy's only successful army between Napoleon and 1915–18: Garibaldi's 50,000 battle-tested volunteers, three-fifths of whom were Southerners. These ill-considered steps, wholly characteristic of the jealous exclusiveness of the *moderati* and the envy and traditionalist zeal of the army hierarchy, created a power vacuum in the countryside and helped trigger and prolong a decade-long anarchic peasant war: Bourbon-clerical "brigandage" against Piedmontese-Italian conscription and taxes on the one hand, and the exactions and encroachments of land-owning classes old and new on the other. Victory required the commitment of almost half of the new Royal Italian Army, villages burned to the ground, and at least five thousand executions and rebel combat deaths.[64] In the North, tax rebellions against the hated *macinato*, levied on the grinding of grain, likewise convulsed the countryside; as in the South, army and "moderates" answered with martial law and summary executions.[65] Garibaldi returned periodically from retirement, to fight Austria with his customary brilliance in 1866 and to challenge vainly in 1862 and 1867 the Italian, French, and papal forces defending

[62] North and South: Cafagna, *Dualismo e sviluppo*, 187–220; Zamagni, *Dalla periferia al centro*, ch. 1, and 100–01, 164–65; Literacy: SVIMEZ, *Nord e Sud*, 795; Italian-speakers in 1861: Tullio De Mauro, *Storia linguistica dell'Italia Unita* (Rome, 1991), 43 (2.5 percent of population) and Arrigo Castellani, "Quanti erano gli italofoni nel 1861?," *Studi linguistici italiani* 8:1 (1982), 24 (between 9 and 12.6 percent, if illiterates are included). Per capita GNP (purchasing-power parity: 1990 international Geary-Khamis dollars), Maddison, 58–59.

[63] Farini (on the inhabitants of the Naples area) to Cavour, quoted in Banti, *Nazione*, 200; for the extent and persistence of urban and northern scorn for "cafoni," Della Peruta, *Realtà e mito*, 81.

[64] For the heavy burden of counterinsurgency commitments, see Pierluigi Bertinaria, "Lo stanziamento dell'esercito italiano in età liberale, 1869–1910," in *Esercito e città dall'Unità agli anni trenta*, 2 vols. (Rome, 1989), 1:7–8; the best analysis of the insurrection remains Franco Molfese, *Storia del brigantaggio dopo l'Unità* (Milan, 1964); 362–64 for "brigand" and army/Carabinieri dead (which may have totalled several thousand).

[65] For the extent and geography of Italian peasant violence throughout the century, see Della Peruta, *Realtà e mito*, 165–81.

the truncated Church dominions around Rome. Mazzini remained in wrathful exile, pouring scorn on Liberals, monarchy, and a "royal army ready for armistice, capitulation, and fraudulent mediations [*raggiri di mediazioni*]," as he had put it as early as 1848. His partisans jeered that no *moderato* had ever "been hanged for the Italian cause."[66] The Papacy damned united Italy from the outset. And above all else, territorial unity failed to bridge the gap between city and countryside, between a peasantry at or below the edge of subsistence and the patriots, soldiers, and city-dwelling *signori* who had made Italy. Mazzini had despaired of reaching the *contadini*; pamphlets could not indoctrinate the illiterate, and as he noted in 1834, outside the cities "the apostolate of the spoken word [led] to the gallows."[67] Yet he also failed to perceive that attracting the peasantry to the cause and eventual reality of an Italian nation-state might require material incentives – the sacrifice of some of the *classe proprietaria*'s land. The *moderati*, men of property all, were unlikely agrarian reformers. The unhealing wound that thus divided "real" from "official" Italy persisted into the late twentieth century.[68]

Germany was by contrast far more dynamic and less regionally disparate than Italy. Population grew almost 40 percent between 1817 and 1848, from 25 to 34.8 million, faster than the European average.[69] Agriculture, from the *Junker* entrepreneurs of East Elbia to the prosperous peasantry of northwestern Germany, was increasingly capital-intensive and productive. Industry, stirring since the 1820s, took wing in the 1840s. In Saxony, Berlin, and Silesia, textile, mechanical, and mining firms grew with startling speed. The Rhine provinces, which the powers at Vienna in 1814 had pressed upon Prussia to force it to confront a potentially resurgent France, proved to have assets the diplomats had not suspected: immense quantities of coal and iron. The application of steam power to mining and transport brought together the coal and iron of the Ruhr valley and the surrounding regions, and ultimately gave Prussia economic mastery in central Europe.[70] The Prussian state also helped itself, by promoting a customs union or *Zollverein* that after 1834 offered the German states an embryonic national market. In Italy, Austria maintained a degree of economic as well as political hegemony through its control of Lombardy-Venetia; in Germany it lost economically to Prussia, which retaliated against Vienna's political predominance by resolutely excluding the Habsburg domains from the *Zollverein*. And in one vital respect the Prussian reformers' work went forward triumphantly: by the 1820s the Prussian bureaucracy had created

---

[66] *Ai giovani. Ricordi* (November 1848), quoted in Banti, *Nazione*, 92; Della Peruta, *Realtà e mito*, 87.

[67] Quotation: Banti, *Risorgimento*, 66.

[68] Lyttelton, "Landlords, Peasants and the Limits of Liberalism," offers persuasive analysis of the constraints on reform, as well as (128–30) dissection of Gramsci's famous – and utopian – notion that recasting the *Risorgimento* as peasant revolution would have set Italy firmly on the path to modernity.

[69] SGAB, 1:27–28 (Reich borders of 1871); Wehler, DGG, 2:7–24.

[70] See the exemplary analysis of Wehler, DGG, 2:64–139, 614–40.

the world's first effective system of universal primary education. By the mid-1860s over 99 percent of the Prussian army's German-speaking recruits had attended school, and by 1871 overall adult illiteracy in Prussia's two-thirds of Germany had sunk to an average of 13.7 percent, with far lower values across the western provinces. That unique achievement – the Prussian state's most striking contribution to the creation of its own civil society – paid handsomely on the battlefield and in the factory.[71] Germany's estimated annual per capita GDP, at $1,077, had been slightly below that of Italy as a whole in 1820. By 1870 it had grown to $1,839, compared to $1,499 for Italy.[72] The new German nation-state thus inherited surprisingly solid social and economic foundations.

III. Crystallization and Diffusion of the National Myths

Finally, the force of ideas, whether borne on bayonets or surreptitiously filtering across state and linguistic boundaries, molded Italy and Germany in divergent ways. The reaction of Italian educated opinion to French domination was remarkably mild; the only irreducible ideological opposition to the new order came from the Church and the social groups most tied to it. Disappointed Italian Jacobins, the ancestors of the democratic radicals of the *Risorgimento*, indeed plotted against France – because French military domination betrayed revolutionary France's proclaimed principles of liberty and independence for all. Moderates such as Vincenzo Cuoco damned the Neapolitan Jacobins of 1799, in whose regime Cuoco had briefly served, for seeking in doctrinaire fashion to impose abstract and alien models on a population steeped in tradition. But Cuoco, the most influential Italian political thinker of the revolutionary era, was not Burke. Although deploring French excesses after 1792, he rejected neither the French Revolution itself nor the principle of popular sovereignty. His solution to the gap between the Jacobins of 1799 and the people was a paternalist gradualism characteristic of later Italian moderates – the exploitation of tradition by reforming elites seeking to educate the people "to do spontaneously that which you want."[73] Cuoco and others like him thus chose to serve Napoleon's new regime. They acted not from opportunism but from a genuine belief in the modern centralizing state. And Napoleon gave them much of what they sought; he created the first kingdom in history that bore the name of Italy, a kingdom with a bureaucracy manned by Italians and a written, if authoritarian constitution. He gave Italy a national army with a green-white-red tricolor flag and a tradition of victories – in French service – against the troops of first-class

---

[71] François, "Alphabetisierung und Lesefähigkeit," 411–12; Wehler, DGG, 2:478–91; SGAB, 1:232, table b.

[72] Maddison, 58–59.

[73] Cuoco, *Saggio storico sulla rivoluzione napoletana* (Turin, 1975), 183 (ch. 19); on Cuoco, see *Dizionario biografico degli italiani* (Rome, 1960–), 1:388–402 and Banti, *Risorgimento*, 19–21, 30–31.

powers.[74] He involuntarily transformed Italian unity from literary myth into political issue.

In Germany, national consciousness came to politics *against* rather than through French conquest – an immense difference at the origin of much later suffering. The great Austrian and Prussian defeats of 1805–07 immeasurably intensified the reaction against French culture gathering force in Protestant Germany since the 1770s. Irritation at the levelling rationalism of the Enlightenment came naturally to the society of *Stände*. French victories and depredations – Prussians for generations remembered "the time of the French" after 1806 – transmuted that irritation into fierce Teutonizing hatred. Germany's stratified society, as it faced a revolutionary age, provided a ready audience for ideologues seeking to shore up traditional authority with new doctrine. The French did make disciples, especially among the officials and lawyers of the mid-sized states that collaborated with Napoleon. But the new centralized bureaucracies and rationalized law codes ran against the grain of the societies upon which they descended.

The collision of French bayonets and French ideas with the German body politic helped create three intertwined political-intellectual movements: German nationalism, German conservatism, and German liberalism. German nationalism combined a fiercely exclusive "anthropology," a fervent quasi-religious style, and historical myths that posed universal claims.[75] The greatest of the nationalist prophets of the Napoleonic era, Johann Gottlieb Fichte and Ernst Moritz Arndt, drew on Herder's notion of language as the determinant of national identity. But they discarded Herder's intermittent insistence that all nations and tongues were equally close to God. The German princes had lost on the battlefield, but the German *Volk*, its language and its *Geist*,[76] was nevertheless deeper, more authentic, more original than all others, especially the frivolous rationalist French.

Both in style and in the persons of its chief representatives, German nationalism was the product of Protestant Germany. Protestant intellectuals evidenced a unique, precocious, and enduring fascination with myth that culminated in the creation of a uniquely powerful German national mythology. Protestant apocalyptic traditions furnished Arndt with his weapons against Napoleon, that "prince of darkness" and "Devil on his hellish throne." The Holy Ghost became the German *Volksgeist* moving through history, a notion that within a generation dovetailed seamlessly with Hegel's stage-theory of history, which assigned to the Protestant Reformation and Prussian state a central role in the

---

74 See especially Della Peruta, *Esercito e società nell'Italia napoleonica* (Milan, 1988).
75 On early nationalist anthropologies, see Kedourie, *Nationalism*, chs. 4–5; Poliakov, *Aryan Myth*; and Williamson, *Myth*, ch. 3.
76 Attempts to translate *Geist* ("spirit," "mind," and too much more) into English – or Italian – are futile; the term and its multifarious usage in nineteenth- and twentieth-century Germany indeed testify to one peculiarity of the German *Volksgeist* heavy with consequences, the language's capacity for emotion-laden abstraction.

self-realization of the world-spirit. Arndt and others secularized the Judaeo-Christian Last Judgment and brought it into German contemporary history as "vengeance's sweet day," the "bloody sword" of German revenge. The poet Heinrich von Kleist commanded the extermination of the enemy in apocalyptic tones: "Strike him dead: the Last Judgment will not ask your reasons!" And Fichte, in the same vein, proclaimed flatly in 1808 the mission of installing "this [German] *Geist* in the world domination for which it is destined [*die ihm bestimmte Weltherrschaft*]."[77]

Logically enough in view of its sources and expectations, the German national cult was also uncompromisingly total in its claim on the individual. Fichte projected a system of national education that would render the young literally incapable of willing anything that the nation (or its rulers?) did not want. The new nationalism's choice of unifying myths revealed and thereafter reinforced its authoritarian bent. Fichte demanded a Germanic anti-Napoleon, an apocalyptic *"Zwingherr zur deutschheit."* Poets such as Max von Schenkendorf called for the mystical *Kaiser* to waken, rescue his *Volk*, and exact bloody vengeance:

> Deutscher Kaiser! Deutscher Kaiser!
> Säumst Du? Schläfst Du? Auf, erwache!
> Komm' zur Sühne, komm' zur Rache.[78]

By 1817, the Barbarossa ballad of Johann Friedrich Rückert had put the myth into the form that saturated the popular mind through countless school and household anthologies in the coming century:

> Der alte Barbarossa
> Der Kaiser Friederich
> Im unterird'schen Schlosse
> Hält er verzaubert sich
>
> . . . .
>
> Er hat hinabgenommen
> Des Reiches Herrlichkeit
> Und wird einst wiederkommen
> Mit ihr, zu seiner Zeit[79]

---

77 On all this, see Williamson, *Myth*, chs. 2–3; Klaus Vondung, *Die Apokalypse in Deutschland* (Munich, 1988), 26–27, 138–39, 158–61, 173; Vondung, "Geschichte als Weltgericht: Genesis und Degradation einer Symbolik," in idem, ed., *Kriegserlebnis* (Göttingen, 1980), 62–84; Wehler, *DGG*, 1:513–25; also Fichte, *Werke. Auswahl in Sechs Bänden*, ed. Fritz Medicus (Leipzig, 1908–12), 5:607; and Arndt, "Vaterlandslied" (1812), in his *Gedichte* (Halle, n.d.), 86–87. For Hegel, the Reformation, and the Prussian state, Kurt Kupisch, *Zwischen Idealismus und Massendemokratie. Eine Geschichte der evangelischen Kirche in Deutschland von 1815–1945* (Berlin, 1955), 44.

78 "German emperor! German emperor! / Are you slothful? Are you sleeping? Up, awaken! / Come [to demand] atonement, come [to exact] vengeance."

79 "The aged Barbarossa / The Emperor Frederick / Down under in his castle / Enchanted there he sits. . . . Down with him he has taken / The glory of the Reich / And with it shall return / When his time shall come."

The emperor, in magical sleep, awaited the great crisis that would summon him forth from the Kyffhäuser.

Arminius, who had crushed the legions of an earlier Latin empire and had figured as an anti-French symbol in the literary revival of the 1770s, likewise enjoyed new fame in the war against Napoleon. Kleist delivered himself of a long verse drama, *Die Hermannschlacht*, whose unlovely hero personified bloodlust and righteous treachery in the national cause. Any *good* Romans – or French – must suffer "revenge's thunderbolt" first, for the good ones were most dangerous of all. Arndt's grimly vengeful *Vaterlandslied* of 1812 and numerous other patriotic effusions likewise called the German people to a new *Hermannschlacht*.[80] In a yet more famous ballad ("*Des Deutschen Vaterland*") of 1813 Arndt also sought to give Germany a shape – "as far as the German tongue resounds" – that was as yet mercifully vague, but if interpreted literally promised to redraw the map of Europe in blood.

German nationalism thus possessed a certainty in its claims to world primacy that eluded rivals both in Italy and elsewhere. German misgivings about Enlightenment rationalism had as yet few Italian counterparts except among clericals. And Germany's intellectuals developed, long before the coming of Darwin, an increasing exclusiveness based on blood and a definition of the nation inextricably intertwined with hatred of Europe's oldest minority. Cultural critics from Herder onward, and practitioners of the philological analysis in which Germany led the world, gradually cut Protestant Germany loose from its biblical foundations, rendering even Luther's sonorous rendition of the Hebrew Bible "more distant, more foreign, and in a sense, more 'Jewish.'" That which was German became that which was not Jewish.[81] Expectations of the German-national apocalypse, enthusiastic commitment to the total subordination of the individual, myths of charismatic leadership, megalomaniacal external claims, and hatred of ethnic enemies both external and internal constituted a uniquely explosive mixture.

But despite the potential disruptiveness of its ideas, German nationalism remained as yet relatively ineffectual even during the 1813–14 "War of Liberation" against France; a specifically Prussian patriotism founded on hatred for the occupying French proved at least as powerful a mobilizing force.[82] No ready alternative to the existing German dynasties existed, and many German intellectuals were as yet less convinced than their Italian counterparts of the feasibility or desirability of a unitary nation-state. Social ambivalence complemented political confusion. German nationalism was a creation of the literate

[80] Kampers, *Die deutsche Kaiseridee*, 165, 161–62; Kleist, *Sämtliche Werke und Briefe*, 2 vols. (Munich, 1952) 1:608–09; Craig, "German Intellectuals in Politics, 1789–1815: The Case of Heinrich von Kleist," CEH 2:1 (1969), 8–10; Arndt, *Gedichte*, 86–86.

[81] Quotation: Williamson, *Myth*, 34; Paul L. Rose, *German Question/Jewish Question: Revolutionary Antisemitism in Germany from Kant to Wagner* (Princeton, NJ, 1990), especially 41.

[82] Hagemann, "The Anti-Napoleonic Wars," 594–609; Echternkamp, *Nationalismus*, especially 216–18.

middle classes, the Protestant *Bildungsbürgertum*, whose neoclassical ideal of intellectual cultivation explicitly challenged Germany's Frenchified or brutishly provincial nobility. Arndt, son of a Swedish-Pomeranian ex-serf, harbored a violent hostility to privilege, but many others celebrated as Germany's greatest glory the society of *Stände* that accorded the *Bildungsbürgertum* an honored place, if not one as yet entirely appropriate to its inner worth.

Celebration of the society of *Stände* in turn intersected with German conservatism, which like German nationalism was in part a reaction against the Enlightenment that became fiercely political thanks to French conquests and reforms.[83] The romantic mythology of nature (*Die Natur*, inevitably identified with German forests and mountains), its historical and political counterpart, the myth of the perfect organic union of medieval state and society developed by ideologues such as Adam Müller, and the thundering of legal scholars such as Friedrich Carl von Savigny against the artificial code law of the French and of their German imitators held powerful appeal for *Bildungsbürger* and *Junker* alike. But not all conservatives were political Romantics; the movement remained split between bureaucratic absolutists in the tradition of Frederick the Great, and those nostalgic for the *Stände* as they had purportedly existed before the absolutist state had bent the nobility to its service.

Bureaucratic absolutism also shaped German liberalism. The Prussian reformers were liberal in their economic theory and in their attempts to abolish legal restraints on mobility between *Stände*. But they were above all servants of the state, and the function of the civil society that they sought to create and mobilize was to support that state. The liberal tradition they helped found thus had none of that individualist distrust of state power found among those nurtured on Locke. And the principal philosophical shapers of that tradition, Kant and Hegel, reinforced German liberalism's dependence on the state. Kant insisted that the state served the transcendent moral purpose of realizing individual freedom. But in the final analysis he accepted as a vehicle to that end the existing monarchical states, whose goal was naturally a freedom antithetical to that of their subjects, their own. Hegel went beyond the "virtual political paralysis" visible in Kant. He explicitly subordinated the freedom of the individual to that of the state, which was "that form of reality in which the individual has and enjoys his freedom; but on the condition of his recognizing, believing in, and willing that which is common to the Whole." German liberalism, child of bureaucratic absolutism, marked by Napoleonic conquest, imbued with Kant's ambiguities and Hegel's potential for state-idolatry, carried birthmarks that distinguished it sharply from its neighbors to the west and south.[84]

---

[83] For German conservatism before French conquest, see Klaus Epstein, *The Genesis of German Conservatism* (Princeton, NJ, 1966); Berdahl, *Prussian Nobility*, chs. 4–5, is incisive on the connections between Prussian society and Prussian conservatism after 1807.

[84] On the influence of Kant and Hegel, see the lucid discussion of Krieger, *German Idea of Freedom*, 86–138; quotations from 124, 132.

Even more than in Germany, the post-1815 restoration south of the Alps proved the formative period of the national mythology that attached itself to the coming Italian state. Literature, as in Germany, offered a refuge from censorship and police surveillance, a distant land in which a united Italy of the mind might flourish. The *Patria* – fatherland – that Italy's *literati* created, freely appropriating imagery and rhetoric from the Roman Church, had suffered for centuries the oppression of foreign tyrants. Its manifold internal divisions had been the root of repeated disasters. Its honor – freely identified with the *Madonna*-like purity of Italian womanhood – had been debased and profaned. Its military prowess was the subject of universal mockery.[85] And all efforts at national redemption by Italy's heroes had as yet proved vain, largely through the evildoing of Italian traitors. The Christ-hero or national "martyr," the traitor Judas, and the Austrian tyrant and his barbarous Croat mercenaries formed a persuasive seamless whole. And as in Germany, if with less jealous exclusiveness, descent defined the nation: "RACE [*RAZZA*] [is] the expression of an identity of origins and of blood," in the words of a later foreign minister of united Italy.[86]

Mazzini inevitably proved the most influential national ideologue. The redemption of a *Patria* "sullied by centuries of disunion, servitude, materialism, and individualism" belonged to the "initiates of the religion of martyrdom," the "few, privileged to feel and suffer for an entire generation . . . to live as prophets and to die as martyrs." That heroic chosen band had "ten centuries of outrages to avenge; . . . a slavery of five centuries to obliterate." The resulting "*united, independent, free, and republican*" Italy, from Nice to Trieste to the Ionian sea, along with Sicily, Sardinia, and Corsica ("the islands declared Italian by the tongue of their inhabitants") was destined to "accomplish a mission . . . within humanity."[87] Mazzini in due course derived that mission from the glories of the Roman empire. He proposed a Rome-centered stage-theory of history that like its Germanocentric counterparts was a distant descendant of the medieval ruminations of Joachim of Fiore: Italy had progressed from the Rome of the Caesars to the Rome of the Papacy. The "third Rome," that of the Italian people, was coming and with it an age in which Italy would give "a new and more powerful Unity to all the nations of Europe." That "third and still vaster Unity" would not erase national distinctions within the harmonious future "Europe of the Peoples" of Mazzini's imagination. Yet Rome would nevertheless be its center.

85 For one famous characterization – ascribed to the French – of Italians as fit "only to contrive treacheries, and not for war," see Massimo d'Azeglio, *Ettore Fieramosca, ossia la disfida di Barletta* (1833), quoted in Banti, *Nazione*, 96.

86 See the brilliant exhumation of the "*Risorgimento* canon" by Banti, *Nazione*, especially 77–78, 97, 129, 139–40, 177; for the "genial, creative parasitism" with which the *Risorgimento* borrowed Church language, imagery, and narratives, 119–39, 199; 163 for "RAZZA" (typography in original: Pasquale Stanislao Mancini [1851], later architect of Italy's position in the Triple Alliance, and a founder of Italy's African empire).

87 Banti, *Nazione*, 189; 64 for Mazzini on Corsica, assigned to Italy by God; Mazzini, *Scritti politici*, 1:82, 81, 77, 70, 63, 66 (italics in original).

Mazzini was wholly unable to imagine the extent to which nationalisms might conflict.[88] Nor did he suspect that inducing Italy's neighbors to accept the primacy of the "third Rome" would require all the naked ferocity of the "first Rome"'s legions. He was equally blind to the consequences for liberty of his notion that political convictions must be a *fede*, a fanatical system of belief. The myth of Italy's world mission would necessarily overstrain any eventual Italian state. And since failure could only be a result of disunity or treason – a paranoid touch borrowed from the men of 1793 and ultimately from Rousseau – *fede* would inevitably dictate the annihilation of traitors at home: the national community was and must be "*one*, indivisible."[89] The "genuine radicalism and totalitarianism" of Mazzini's theory of politics had perilous long-term implications.[90]

Mazzini was not alone, even if talk of national unity, constitutionalism, railroads, and customs unions was in the 1830s and 1840s still the affair of small urban elites living off a predominantly agricultural economy. The elites themselves were inevitably divided. Liberal nobles and the propertied and professional middle classes initially sought the restoration of traditional city-state self-government – the government of the local *classe proprietaria* – rather than a north Italian or unitary Italian state. The Jacobin undertones of Mazzini's republican extremism horrified these *moderati*. They and their counterparts in the German *Bildungsbürgertum* had learned a simple lesson from France's peasant revolt of 1789 and Terror of 1793–94: the illiterate masses entered the political arena only to take the lives and property of their betters. Italy's *moderati* therefore inclined toward monarchy – a limited, "representative," parliamentary monarchy that would rule through themselves – as the best guarantee of social stability.

And after the publication of Vincenzo Gioberti's *Del Primato morale e civile degli italiani* in 1843, many *moderati* were able to delude themselves that the Papacy might reconcile itself to their cause, thus removing the second great obstacle, after Austria, to greater unity for the peninsula. Gioberti later admitted that his "neo-Guelph" project of a federation of Italian states on the German Confederation pattern, under the leadership of a liberal Papacy, was an exercise

---

[88] See for instance his claim (*Dei doveri dell'uomo*, quoted in Banti, *Nazione*, 64) that Europe's kings and "privileged classes" were the sole source of enmity between peoples – a notion shared with the men of blood of 1791–92 who sought to "set all Europe ablaze" (p. 13 in this volume).

[89] See Banti's analysis of Italian nationalism's "paranoid" inclination to ascribe failure to treason (*Nazione*, 177); "*una*, indivisibile": Mazzini, in ibid., 80 (italics in original).

[90] "[I]l vero radicalismo e totalitarismo mazziniano": a democratic liberal, writing under Fascism: Luigi Salvatorelli, *Il Pensiero politico italiano* (Turin, 1935), 229. Efforts to rescue Mazzini from responsibility for his ideas tend to stress his indisputably democratic beliefs – without grappling with the implications, given the inevitability of the ethnic conflict he failed to comprehend or anticipate, of his totalizing conception of the national faith, his notion of martyrdom, and his territorial claims. See for instance Alessandro Levi, *La filosofia politica di Giuseppe Mazzini* (Naples, 1967 [1916]), ch. 8, and Salvo Mastellone, *Il progetto politico di Mazzini (Italia-Europa)* (Florence, 1994), ch. 14.

in deliberate wishful thinking. But Gioberti fulfilled a vital political role in offering a scenario, however implausible, that would allow moderate liberals and nationalists to reconcile their political aspirations with their religious beliefs and with the political fact of the Church's massive presence in Italian life. Yet Gioberti, despite his credentials as a moderate, also vehemently reinforced one vital element of Mazzini's national cult, the megalomaniacal claim to an Italian *primato* and world mission in all fields of human endeavor – claims parallel to those that German nationalists had pressed since the Napoleonic era.

Compared to the fantasies of Mazzini and Gioberti, German nationalist aspirations by the 1840s were far less disproportionate to the nation's potential strength. And thanks to the promotion of literacy by the German states, German nationalism did not long remain the property of narrow elites, as was the case in Italy until virtually the end of century. The leaders of the mass opinion that emerged in the 1830s and 1840s erected and elaborated national myths with at least as much gusto as Mazzini and Gioberti. The philologists, in common with counterparts in France and England but not Italy, equipped Germany with a new, non-biblical pedigree stretching back into a putative "Indo-Germanic" or "Aryan" past. The brothers Jacob and Wilhelm Grimm exhumed German folklore and myth, assembling an alternative and largely non-Christian national past.[91] Germanic tribalism enjoyed new vogue, thanks to scholarly efforts to disinter the *Nibelungenlied*, a medieval epic of slaughter and treachery revolving around the hero Siegfried, his murderer Hagen, and (with noteworthy historical confusion) Attila the Hun. Enthusiasts hailed it as the "German Iliad."[92]

Commemoration of the Napoleonic wars provided an occasion to erect between 1838 and 1875 a *Hermannsdenkmal*, a massive monument to Arminius as "rescuer and founder" of the German nation.[93] Historians, to public acclaim, revived Frederick Barbarossa and Frederick II of Hohenstaufen as primordial symbols of national unity. Even Greece, Germany's precursor – in the minds of the classically trained *Bildungsbürger* – in its world cultural leadership and manifold political divisions, inspired a German political mythology. The historian Gustav Droysen's widely read history of Alexander the Great (1833), perhaps against the initial intentions of its author, gained renown as a thinly veiled

[91] For useful surveys of these complex developments, Poliakov, *Aryan Myth*, chs. 4–5, 9, 10 and Williamson, *Myth*, chs. 2–3; on the unfolding of German nationalism to 1848, Wehler, DGG, 2:394–412 and Echternkamp, *Nationalismus*; for the later contributions of Germany's academics, Hedda Gramley, *Propheten des deutschen Nationalismus. Theologen, Historiker und Nationalökonomen* (Frankfurt am Main, 2001).

[92] Williamson, *Myth*, 34; for the fate of the *Nibelungenlied* in modern Germany, Otfried Ehrismann, *Das Nibelungenlied in Deutschland: Studien zur Rezeption des Nibelungenlieds von der Mitte des 18. Jahrhunderts bis zum Ersten Weltkrieg* (Munich, 1975), especially ch. 5 ("Das Nibelungenlied in der Schule") on its century-long career as a tool of patriotic indoctrination, and Klaus von See, "Das Nibelungenlied – Ein Nationalepos," in Joachim Heinzle and Anneliese Waldschmidt, eds., *Die Nibelungen* (Frankfurt am Main, 1991), 43–110.

[93] Thomas Nipperdey, "Nationalidee und Nationaldenkmal in Deutschland im 19. Jahrhundert," HZ 206 (1968), 567–73.

allegory on Prussia's mission in Germany and Germany's mission in Europe and beyond: the armies of the half-barbaric Macedonian border kingdom, under the leadership of a uniquely great individual, imposed order on Greece's patchwork of city-states, and went on to found a world empire.[94] Nor did Droysen confine himself to Macedon; his massive Hegelian history of the Prussian state, issuing majestically from the presses from 1855 on, suggested at the outset that the Hohenstaufen Reich was one expression of the German nation's "position as world ruler [*weltherrschenden Stellung*]." The popular poet Emanuel Geibel, in a phrase with a future, proclaimed a German mission to "heal the world" ("*Und es mag am deutschen Wesen / Einmal noch die Welt genesen*"). Geibel also sought stern leaders: "a Man, a Nibelungen grandson, / To break the crazed racehorse of our times / With brazen fist and brazen thigh," and saw in external conflict Germany's salvation from internal fragmentation: "War! War! Give us war to heal the quarrels / That scorch the marrow of our bones!"[95] Historians and ideologues also began to address in concrete territorial terms the question that Arndt had posed in 1813, "What is the German's fatherland?" Their answers, thanks to the far-flung borders of the old Reich, the thrust of medieval German colonization as far east as Russia, and the mixed pattern of settlement of central Europe, promised conflict with *all* of Germany's neighbors.

The revolutionary storms of mid-century inaugurated that conflict. The German radical and liberal leaders who emerged in spring 1848 displayed an external megalomania more concrete in its aims and infinitely more ruthless in its expression than that of Mazzini. From Marx and Engels on the left fringe of the democratic movement to figures such as Wilhelm Jordan of Berlin on its right, German radicals ranted about Germany's "world mission" and the need to assess with "healthy national egotism" the claims "of puny little nationalities" such as the Czechs.[96] More respectable liberal figures were scarcely less ambitious. Max von Gagern, brother of the later speaker of the abortive revolutionary national assembly at Frankfurt, aggressively lobbied King Frederick William IV of Prussia for a German-national war with Russia to save Germany "from anarchy and dissolution." Prussia's first liberal ministry unsuccessfully sought an offensive alliance with France against Russia. The liberals' pretext for war was to be the restoration of Poland, a cause dear to the French; the result the overthrow of the 1815 settlement and the creation of a mighty German national state.

In the Frankfurt assembly, leaders such as the aged and celebrated Arndt expressed with passionate intensity a "yearning" for possession of Holland,

94 Schulze, *Weg zum Nationalstaat*, 107; see also the analysis of Felix Gilbert, *Johann Gustav Droysen und die preussisch-deutschen Frage* (Berlin, 1931) (HZ, Beiheft 20), 25–35.

95 Droysen, *Geschichte der preussischen Politik*, vol. I (Leipzig, 2nd ed., 1868 [1855]), 5; also noteworthy are the remarks on 3–4 about the "historical necessity" underlying Prussia and its "calling [to unite] the whole [Beruf für das Ganze]." Geibel: *Werke*, ed. Wolfgang Stammler (Leipzig, n.d.), 2:220 (1861), 1:210–11 (1844).

96 Wehler, DGG, 2:743 (Marx and Engels); Lewis Namier, *1848: The Revolution of the Intellectuals* (Garden City, NY, 1964), 147 (Jordan).

Belgium, Switzerland, and "world mastery by sea." Germany's mission, proclaimed a liberal Austrian noble, was to create "a gigantic Reich of 70 millions, and if possible of 80 or 100 million, and plant the standard of Arminius in that Reich, to stand there armed against east and west, against the Slavic and Latin peoples, to wrest mastery of the seas from the English, and to become the most powerful nation [*Volk*] on this earth – *that* is Germany's future!"[97] Representatives of the German professoriate, the cream of the *Bildungsbürgertum*, offered learned rationales for excess. *History* decreed rule over non-Germans in Schleswig, Bohemia, Poland, and on the southern borders of Austria. *Language* enjoined borders that stretched "as far as the German tongue resounds."

The German Fatherland of the Frankfurt assembly consequently stretched from Strasbourg to Riga and from the northern border of disputed Schleswig – homeland of Cimbri and Teutones, as Jacob Grimm, father of German philology, reminded the assembly – to Trieste. If the European powers, on the basis of the 1815 treaties or their own interests should presume to challenge Germany's alleged territorial rights or impugn its "national honor," the result (in the words of one overheated Left-Liberal) would be "a German national rising...of a sort the world has perhaps never yet seen."[98] But no great war and *deutsche nationale Erhebung* came. No Barbarossa emerged from under the Kyffhäuser, despite fiery invocations by figures such as Max von Gagern. The German *Mitteleuropa* with a world-spanning fleet of the Frankfurt assembly's imagination remained a "sweet academic pipe-dream."[99]

The national states that ultimately emerged between 1859 and 1871, Cavour's prosaic Piedmontese-*moderato* parliamentary monarchy and Bismarck's triumphant "small-German" Reich, thus represented a thwarting of the wilder aspirations of both national movements. Both new states lacked the full range of territories inhabited by Italians and Germans, or claimed as their historic right. War in 1870 against the "ancestral enemy" of 1813, the national

---

[97] Namier, *Revolution of the Intellectuals*, 66–67; Ludwig von Pastor, *Leben des Freiherrn Max von Gagern 1810–1889* (Munich, 1912), 234; and the courageous work of Günter Wollstein, *Das "Grossdeutschland" der Paulskirche: Nationale Ziele in der bürgerlichen Revolution 1848–49* (Düsseldorf, 1977), passim and 248 (Arndt); "Riesenreich": Count Friedrich Deym, in *Stenographischer Bericht über die Verhandlungen der deutschen constituirenden Nationalversammlung zu Frankfurt am Main* (Leipzig, 1848–49), 4:2882.

[98] The painful similarity of some Frankfurt speeches to twentieth-century German radical nationalist rhetoric comes through best in the original: "Wir haben keine Rücksicht zu nehmen, als auf die Ehre Deutschlands! [Bravo auf den linken] Möge es Russland, möge es Frankreich, möge es England wagen, uns hineinzureden in unsere gerechte Sache! Wir wollen ihnen antworten mit anderthalb Millionen bewaffneter Männer. Ich sage ihnen, nicht Russland, nicht Frankreich und nicht England werden es wagen, und ich will ihnen sagen warum...; deshalb,...weil sie wissen, dass, wenn sie einen ungerechten Angriff auf Deutschland unternehmen, dies eine deutsche nationale Erhebung herbeiführen würde, wie sie vielleicht die Weltgeschichte noch nicht gesehen hat." (Heinrich Simon, Breslau, speaking on Schleswig-Holstein: Wollstein, *'Grossdeutschland' der Paulskirche*, 70; for Grimm on Schleswig, ibid., 47.)

[99] In the words of a Danish critic (Wollstein, *'Grossdeutschland' der Paulskirche*, 334 note 73); for Gagern on Barbarossa, Pastor, *Gagern*, 241.

war that poets such as Geibel hailed apocalyptically as a "Last Judgment," gave Germany Strasbourg – capital of newly annexed Alsace-Lorraine.[100] But by Bismarck's design, Vienna, Trieste, and Riga remained outside the new German Reich. The fortunes of Italy's wars and statecraft likewise left Trento, Trieste, and the formerly Venetian cities of Dalmatia under the Habsburg yoke. Garibaldi's home city of Nice, ceded as compensation to France in 1860, Corsica, relinquished to France by Genoa in 1768, and Britain's outpost at Malta likewise lay "unredeemed" in the eyes of Italian nationalists. Nor did the internal regimes of the new nation-states fulfill the dreams of their national movements. Unification in and through military defeat had made a monarchical Italy wracked with internal war and social and factional strife, not the "*one*, indivisible" republic of Mazzini's Rousseauvian fantasy. The peasant question festered irremediably; the very existence of post-1860 political divisions offended the horror of faction embedded in the intellectual DNA of the nationalist *fede*.[101] As Gramsci, in Mazzini's footsteps, memorably described it, the *moderati*

> claimed that they sought to create a modern state in Italy, and instead produced a bastard. They sought to constitute a broad and energetic governing class, and they failed. [They sought] to situate the masses within the structure of the state, and they failed. The paltry political life from 1870 to the twentieth century, the elemental and endemic rebelliousness of the popular classes, the niggardly and stunted existence of a skeptical and cowardly governing elite are the consequence of that failure.[102]

Bismarck, seemingly infinitely more successful, might address the Reichstag in cuirassier uniform and pass for the mystic hero of Teutonic tradition. But even he descended frequently to the political squabbling that so horrified *Bildungsbürger* seeking to heal or overlook Germany's religious, social, regional, and political divisions; the new Reich soon wore an air of venomous anti-climax. Despite their very different political, social, and economic structures, both states suffered from powerful and supremely dangerous unfulfilled expectations.

---

[100] Geibel, *Werke*, 2:243–44: "Ein Weltgericht ist dieser Krieg."

[101] See especially the comments of Banti, *Nazione*, 204 on the national movement's "holistic, compact, organic" concept of the nation, and on its consequences; also idem, *Risorgimento italiano*, 11.

[102] Gramsci, *Il Risorgimento* (*Quaderni del carcere*, vol. 3) (Turin, 1974), 94–95.

2

Italy and Germany as Nation-States, 1871–1914

The two newly minted nation-states followed economic and social trajectories that initially diverged, until the industrialization of north Italy began to close the gap. Their core institutions, and above all the armies that underwrote the state's solidity and promised further expansion, continued to differ in their centrality to society, their degree of independence within the state, and – most fateful of all – in their internal cultures. Yet as Italy and Germany crossed the threshold of mass politics in the decades before 1914, their parliamentary systems came to mirror in parallel ways the divisions within their societies. In both countries the quasi-autocratic power of the executive withstood and thwarted the claims of twin mass forces: socialism and organized Catholicism. And the national myths, although differing in virulence and penetration, nevertheless proved similarly if not equally disruptive to domestic and European order.

1. ECONOMIC EXPANSION, SOCIAL AMBITION

The quasi-contemporaneity of Italian and German territorial unification partially masked differences fundamental to the two societies' roles in the coming century. The economic primacy in continental Europe that Germany achieved by 1913 through coal, steel, and its possession of the largest, most literate, and most highly skilled population in Europe gave it a power potential that seemingly authorized the far-reaching goals its intellectuals had long conceived. Italy's modest achievements, its relative poverty in energy and other resources, and above all the burden of the South made progress fitful and intermittent until the end of the century. Germany's economic dynamism nevertheless merely undermined, without overthrowing, the barriers of *Stand*, whereas Italy's more permeable social divisions offered less resistance to social ascent – even if the distance between the living conditions and mentalities of the Southern peasantry and those of the city-dwellers of the North remained greater than any gap between social groups north of the Alps. The two societies' economies and social structures, the nature of their elites, and their patterns of social aspiration and ascent offer a first approach to understanding their respective itineraries.

I. The Unevenness of Economic Growth

Marx's "economic base," as always, is essential evidence, even if its relationship with politics, society, and ideas is far less unidirectional and infinitely more complex than the master implied. Italy's territorial unification failed to bring the swift growth the liberals had postulated, and upon which national power and status depended. Italy's regions had traded with Britain, France, or Central Europe, not one another. Even the rapid extension of a railway network in the 1860s and 1870s, bought almost at the cost of state bankruptcy, gave Italy a national market only slowly. North and South, it emerged after 1860, were neither complementary nor compatible. The South was too resource-poor to serve either as a supplier of industrial raw materials or as a market for the North's industries. The North remained both too agricultural and too poor in its own right to offer much of an outlet for the luxury export crops – oranges, lemons, almonds, wine, and olive oil – of the South's few intensively cultivated enclaves, from the "golden bowl" around Palermo to the coastal hills of Campania.[1] The South's landed classes, the decayed baronage and the blinkered new men who had begun their rise during the Napoleonic upheaval, for the most part imitated their social superiors in preferring assured rents pressed from a wretched peasantry to the risks and profits of agricultural improvement.

By the late 1870s and early 1880s the economic climate began to turn further against the South's elites. World production in both industry and agriculture swelled as railroad and steamship brought together coal, iron, grain, and markets, and opened up the vast plains of southern Russia, the United States, and Argentina. Prices fell rapidly in and after the worldwide crash of 1873. Cheap grain from the Black Sea and the Americas threw agricultural Europe into crisis. One solution to that crisis, in Italy as in most of Europe, was protectionism. The stiff Italian tariff of 1887 slowed the impact of the world market and helped freeze in place the South's backwardness, checking the growth of luxury exports and saving from extinction the primitive extensive agriculture of the *latifundia* and the millions of proprietors of tiny uneconomic scraps of land. Grain, largely cultivated by half-starved peasants equipped with hoes and wooden ploughs at costs above the world market price, remained the South's major crop. Italy's aggregate per capita economic growth virtually stagnated between 1861 and 1900, as population rose and development lagged.[2]

---

[1] See especially Cafagna, *Dualismo e sviluppo*, 187–220; Zamagni, *Dalla periferia al centro*, 100–01, 164–65; Zamagni, "Ferrovie e integrazione del mercato nazionale nell'Italia post-unitaria," in *Studi in onore di Gino Barbieri*, 3 vols. (Pisa, 1983), 3:1635–49; and Banti, *Nazione*, 19–24.

[2] Maddison, 58, 60: Italy's PPP GDP per capita, 1861: $1,447; 1900: $1,785; Germany's: $1,583/$2,985.

The North predictably followed a different path. Italy's lack of coal and high-grade iron ore slowed the development of heavy industry. A massively state-subsidized and tariff-protected steel complex, placed for strategic reasons at Terni in central Italy in the 1880s, produced Italy's first industrial steel and armor-plate for the merchant marine and navy – at grossly inflated prices. Then the new technology of electric power generation and transmission harnessed the "white coal" of the Alpine torrents to the industrialization of north Italy, while the upturn in the world economy after the mid-1890s expanded Italy's export opportunities. The machine-building, metal-working, electrical, and chemical firms of the "industrial triangle" stretching from Milan to Turin and Genoa led a startling ascent that almost doubled Italy's industrial production and more than doubled its exports between 1897 and 1908. By the turn of the century, new plants exploiting the iron ore of Elba even gave Italy a small modern steel industry. By 1911, the economic and social gulf that divided Lombardy, Piedmont, and Liguria (with an aggregate private sector per capita income of 136 percent of the Italian average) from Calabria, Sicily, Basilicata, and the Abruzzi (the four poorest regions, at 68 percent of the national average) had grown even deeper than it had been in 1860. And the industrial triangle alone contained as much industry – whether measured by employment or by energy consumption – as the entire remainder of Italy.[3]

North Italy's "big push" even allowed it to almost keep pace with Germany after 1900, even as the per capita level of industrialization of Italy as a whole declined slightly relative to that of Germany between 1860 to 1913.[4] There the expansion of industry that had accelerated in the 1850s continued with uncanny steadiness, despite the so-called "Great Depression" between the crash of 1873 and the world economic upswing after 1896.[5] Steel, pig-iron, coal, chemicals, electricity, and machine-building clustered in the Ruhr, Silesia, Saxony, Berlin, and lesser industrial centers. With the exception of the agricultural flatlands of

---

[3] Figures from Franco Gaeta, *La crisi di fine secolo e l'età giolittiana* (Turin, 1982), 113 and Zamagni, *Industrializzazione e squilibri regionali in Italia* (Bologna, 1978), 206. For north Italy's "big push," see especially Romeo, *Breve storia della grande industria in Italia (1861–1961)* (Bologna, 1961), 65–114; Bruno Caizzi, *Storia dell'industria italiana dal XVIII secolo ai giorni nostri* (Turin, 1965), 355–410; and Valerio Castronovo, "La storia economica," ESI 4/1:99–206.

[4] 1860: Italy: Germany = 10:15; 1913: Italy: Germany = 26:85, in per capita levels of industrialization expressed as percentages of Britain in 1900 (Bairoch, "International Industrialization Levels from 1750 to 1980," JEEH 11:2 [1982], 281).

[5] For this characterization of a period of dramatic industrial expansion, and for the Great Depression's presumed political and social effects, see above all Hans Rosenberg, *Grosse Depression und Bismarckzeit. Wirtschaftsablauf, Gesellschaft und Politik in Mitteleuropa* (Berlin, 1967) (summarized in his "Political and Social Consequences of the Great Depression of 1873–1896 in Central Europe," in Sheehan, ed., *Imperial Germany*, 39–60). Shulamit Volkov, *The Rise of Popular Anti-Modernism in Germany. The Urban Master Artisans, 1873–1896* (Princeton, NJ, 1978), 10–13, offers useful qualification: the 1880s were "a quiet period of recovery, slow at first and then accelerated." For an incisive comparative analysis of the pattern of German development, see Hartmut Kaelble, "Der Mythos von der rapiden Industrialisierung in Deutschland," GG 9 (1983), 106–18.

East Elbia, German industry was comparatively even in its distribution.[6] The developed and rapidly developing regions of Germany thus contained three-fourths of its population by 1910 – an economic and social structure that offered a sort of inverted mirror-image of Italy, where in 1911 slightly more than half the population lived in the relatively backward Center, South, and islands. By 1914 the German economy had surpassed even that of Britain, and Germany's steel production was 15 times, its pig-iron 32 times, and its coal production a staggering 207 times that of Italy.[7] In terms of industry's share of GDP, Italy as a whole lagged perhaps forty years behind Germany throughout the early twentieth century (see Figures 2.1, 2.2, and 2.3).[8]

But Germany's lead over the Milan-Turin-Genoa industrial triangle and over northern Italy was less impressive. The region that drove Italy's development was in some vital respects economically similar to Germany as a whole, if far from level with Germany's most highly industrialized regions. The rate of increase of Italy's industrial workforce between 1901 and 1910, at roughly 1 percent per year, was notably higher than that of Germany either in that period or earlier. Italy's production of electric power, concentrated overwhelmingly in the North, had by 1913 passed that of France and amounted to a quarter of Germany's. Northern Italy, from predominantly agricultural Venetia, Emilia, and Tuscany to Lombardy, Piedmont, and Liguria, had nevertheless placed only 29.6 percent of its workforce in industrial occupations by 1911. Comparable German and French aggregate figures were 41.0 (1907) and 33.5 percent, although the German figure included the 5 percent of Germany's workforce that mined coal, an energy source infinitely more labor-intensive than Italy's hydroelectric power (see Figure 2.4). Agriculture nevertheless remained at the center of economy and society even in the North. And Italy's principal and enduring social cleavage, coinciding in part with the chasm between North and South, was the divide between the peasantry on the one hand and the *signori* and workers of the towns on the other.

Characteristic of that divide was the urban North's increasing literacy, motor and yardstick of economic development. By 1911 roughly 87 percent of the population of school age or older in the Lombardy-Piedmont-Liguria "industrial triangle" had command of the written word, far closer than forty years earlier to

---

[6] See the regional GNP per capita figures in W. G. Hoffmann and J. H. Müller, *Das deutsche Volkseinkommen 1851–1957* (Tübingen, 1959), 20 (which unfortunately does not split Prussia into its provinces), and the remarks on Germany in Jeffrey G. Williamson, "Regional Inequality and the Process of National Development," *Economic Development and Cultural Change* 13:4/2 (1965), 1–84.

[7] Germany compared to East Elbia: figures from SGAB, 2:41–42, 47 (East Elbia: Mecklenburgs, Pomerania, Brandenburg without Berlin, Silesia, and East and West Prussia; in terms of area the East made up two-fifths of the Reich); steel, iron, coal: Brian R. Mitchell, *European Historical Statistics, 1750–1975* (New York, 2nd rev. ed., 1981), 421, 414, 383–84.

[8] The forty-year gap vis-a-vis Germany was perceptible by the 1890s to contemporaries such as Werner Sombart (see Idomeneo Barbadoro, *Storia del sindacalismo italiano dalla nascita al fascismo*, vol. I, *La Federterra* [Florence, 1973] xl–xli).

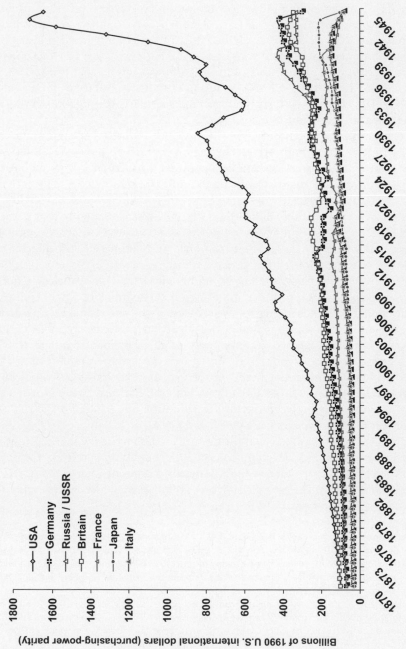

FIGURE 2.1. GDP of the Powers, 1870–1945 (in billions of 1990 U.S. international dollars [purchasing-power parity])

Base data: Maddison, 48–51, 98, 170, 172.

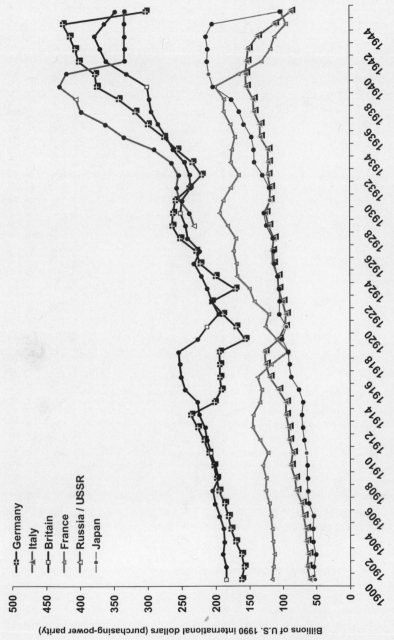

FIGURE 2.2. GDP of the European Powers and Japan, 1900–1945 (in billions of 1990 U.S. international dollars [purchasing-power parity]).

Base data: Maddison, 48–51, 98, 170, 172.

Legend:
- Germany
- Italy
- Britain
- France
- Russia / USSR
- Japan

Y-axis: Billions of U.S. 1990 international dollars (purchasing-power parity)

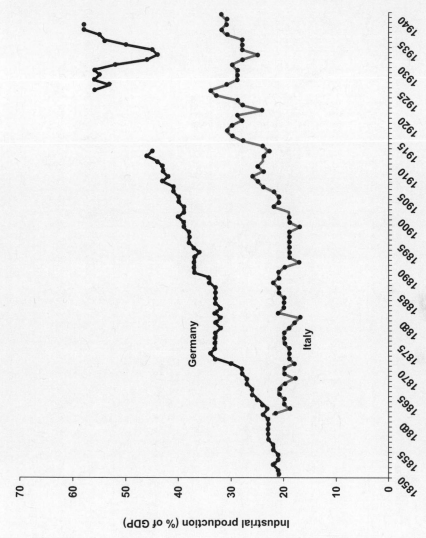

FIGURE 2.3. The German Lead: Industrial Production as Percentage of GDP, 1850–1940.
Base data: Brian R. Mitchell, *European Historical Statistics, 1750–1970* (New York, 1976), 799, 801–02, 808, 811.

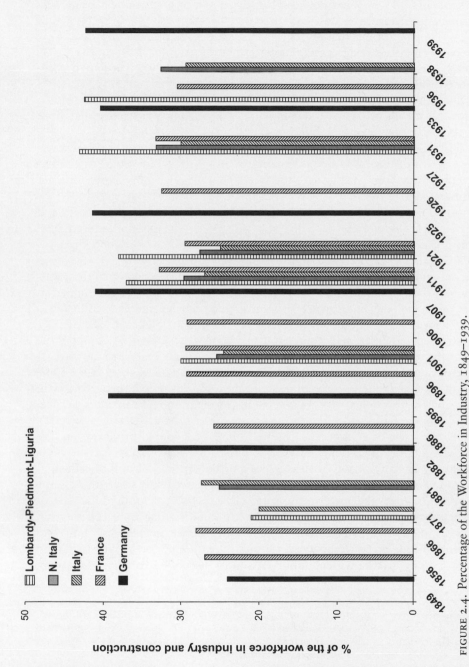

FIGURE 2.4. Percentage of the Workforce in Industry, 1849–1939.

Base data: Mitchell, *International Historical Statistics: Europe 1750–2000* (Basingstoke, 2003), 149–50; SVIMEZ, *Nord e Sud,* 51–52; *Censimento 1921,* 19:242; Wolfram Fischer, ed., *Handbuch der europäischen Wirtschafts- und Sozialgeschichte,* vol. 5 (Berlin, 1985), 126.

the virtually total adult literacy that was the historic achievement of Germany's bureaucrats and schoolmasters. And measured in terms of local per capita purchasing power, northwest Italy had surpassed Germany as a whole by 1913, and far outstripped German regions such as East Prussia (Germany's poorest at 63.4 percent of the Reich aggregate), Silesia (78.7 percent) and Bavaria (82.1 percent).[9] The industrial triangle of northwest Italy, despite the continued dominance of its agriculture, at 45.8 percent of the workforce against industry's 37.1 percent (1911), was nevertheless well along the road to becoming an industrial society, with structures and complaints that in some ways resembled those of its German neighbor (see Figure 2.5).

The rise of industry, despite its different timing and extent in the two countries, produced broadly similar consequences. And it intersected with that second driving force of the age, the worldwide demographic explosion that increased Germany's population by a staggering 67.5 percent and Italy's by almost 34 percent between 1871 and 1914. That difference in growth reflected the disparities between the two new states in speed and extent of industrialization, as did their very different emigration histories. Almost 3 million Germans departed, mostly before 1890, and the agrarian overpopulation and structural unemployment that particularly afflicted the South drove out 13 million Italians, of whom more than 4 million never returned; the exodus culminated in 1913 with the staggering figure of almost 900,000 departures.[10] Cities also swelled swiftly, absorbing some of the increase. Milan tripled in size from 1871 to 1911. Genoa, Turin, and Rome doubled. Naples, Italy's largest city until the 1920s, increased by one and a half times. Italy's already extensive network of smaller cities and large towns thickened; between 1870 and 1910 the proportion of Italians living in cities of more than 20,000 people had swelled from 11 to 29 percent, compared to 35 percent in Germany and 26 percent in France. In the two critical decades between 1890 and 1910 the urban share of Italy's population grew at an annual rate of 2.7 percent. German urbanization, the alleged brutal swiftness of which often passes for explanation for the mass appeal in Germany of anti-Semitism and antimodernist "cultural pessimism," was in reality – at 2.4 percent annually – less rapid than Italy's over those same decades. And over the longer term, from 1870 to 1910, the rate of increase of the urban population was identical in the two countries, at 2.5 percent a year, well ahead of Britain's 1 percent and France's 1.2 percent per year. Italy had nothing to compare with the immense agglomeration of Berlin, with 2 million inhabitants in 1910, or with Hamburg at almost one million, but Naples, Milan,

---

[9] Workforce: Kaelble, "Mythos von der rapiden Industrialisierung," 111. Electricity: Mitchell, *European Historical Statistics 1750–1975*, 500–01. Income per capita: Walther G. Hoffmann, Josef H. Müller, *Das deutsche Volkseinkommen 1851–1957* (Tübingen, 1959), 20; Richard Bessel, "Eastern Germany as a Structural Problem in the Weimar Republic," *Social History* 3 (1978), 207; Zamagni, *Dalla periferia al centro*, 60.

[10] Maddison, 36; SGAB, 2:38–39; Commissariato Generale dell'Emigrazione, *L'emigrazione italiana dal 1910 al 1923*, 2 vols. (Rome, 1926), 1:4; net figures: Sereni, *Capitalismo nelle campagne*, 353.

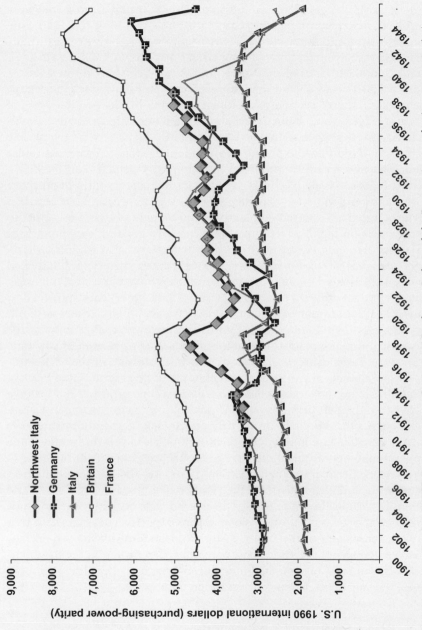

FIGURE 2.5. Per Capita GDP, 1900–1945: Germany, Northwest Italy, and the Powers (at purchasing-power parity).
Base data: National data, Maddison, 58–65 (1990 international Geary-Khamis PPP dollars); northwest Italy extrapolated from the 1911–1928–1938 values in Vera Zamagni, *Dalla periferia al centro*, 58.

Rome, and Turin, clustered loosely around the half-million mark, were similar in size to Germany's second-rank cities: Munich, Dresden, Leipzig, Cologne, and Breslau.[11]

With the exceptions of Naples and Rome, home respectively to a colorfully half-employed underclass and to the central government's indolent bureaucratic legions, these cities and many of their lesser neighbors were increasingly industrial. By 1914 the new industrial working classes made up as much as a third of the population of the cities of the North, and in northern Italy formed almost as large a proportion of the working population as in France (see Figure 2.4). But the northern Italian economy developed a sharper bifurcation than that of Germany or even France. Industry's share of the workforce rose, but agriculture's decline came slower and later than in France, much less Germany. The freedom to sell land and the pressure to divide inheritances instituted under Napoleon had over a century produced in Italy the result that the Revolution achieved in France: a small peasantry. By 1911 more than two-fifths of northern Italy's agricultural population consisted of landowning or long-lease peasants and farmers, ranging from the desperately poor owners of dwarf hill-plots to the prosperous and highly entrepreneurial large farmers and lease-holders of the Po Valley flatlands. Those with a stake in the land also included share-croppers (*mezzadri* or *coloni*), the dominant rural category in Central Italy and also widespread along the southern fringes of the Po Valley, and small numbers of resident contract laborers (*salariati fissi, obbligati, boeri*) with some degree of security. At the bottom of the rural social pyramid, vast armies of landless day-laborers – *braccianti* – toiled and suffered: more than a third of the North's agricultural population, half of the South's, and 65 percent of Sicily's.[12] In the South and islands, their prevalence was an expression of the backwardness in social relations and agricultural technique of great estates and peasant micro-holdings, and the eroded hills, thin soils, endemic drought, and massive overpopulation that left penury as the sole alternative to emigration. The *braccianti* of the North, especially in Po Valley areas where they dominated the workforce, were likewise in part a product of population pressure – and of the concomitant inability of Italian industry to absorb excess agricultural labor as effectively as its German or English counterparts. Yet their status at the bottom of rural society, especially from the rice-growing flatlands of Novara and Vercelli in western Piedmont to the southeastern fringe of the Po Valley where their concentration was greatest, was of a different quality and origin than that of the wretched masses of the South. In the Po delta lands of the province of Ferrara reclaimed from the 1870s onward, and generally across the neighboring flatlands, capitalist farming had introduced irrigation, chemical fertilizers, machines, and sugar beet, hemp, and rice monocultures. The force of the market

---

[11] Kaelble, "Mythos von der rapiden Industrialisierung," 117; Fischer, ed., *Wirtschafts- und Sozialgeschichte*, 43. As Kaelble points out, Germany's urbanization was also no faster than that of Sweden, Norway, and Switzerland.

[12] Figures (1911): Arrigo Serpieri, *La guerra e le classi rurali italiane* (Bari, 1930), 368.

had broken forever age-old production methods, ownership structures, and face-to-face relationships of dependency and deference. The *braccianti*, who by 1901 constituted more than half the working-age agricultural population of provinces such as Ferrara, neighboring Rovigo, or Vercelli, were thus in Marxist terms more "modern" and class-conscious than their industrial counterparts in Milan and Turin.[13] In ways that initially surprised Italy's Socialists, capitalism had produced a rootless class-conscious *agricultural* "proletariat" driven by the very fanaticism of desperation that Marx had vainly predicted as the foremost outcome of urban industrial development. The plight of the *braccianti* was especially acute in the new Po delta lands – for the heavy work of reclamation had lured migrants in, then stranded them in a landscape divided among large agricultural enterprises that required a mere fraction of their labor.[14]

Other Italian groups grew or shrank more slowly. The lower middle class of private sector office workers, a characteristic by-product of industrialization elsewhere, did not begin to appear in sizable numbers even in north Italy until the 1920s. Artisans declined swiftly and catastrophically in the South, less rapidly in the North, where they levelled off after 1900 at a proportion similar to that in Germany, around 6 percent of the working population; their annual rate of decline, at about 4.2 percent per year from 1881 to 1901, far outdid the 2.1 percent per year of their German counterparts over roughly the same period. Italy's small retailers, the second pillar of the lower middle classes, grew steadily if unspectacularly by 1.7 percent per year, in contrast to their stagnation or slight regression in Germany. Finally, in marked contrast to Germany, Italy had little in the way of religious or ethnic minorities. Its Jews, emancipated by the French after 1796 or – in the case of Rome – by the Italian state's belated destruction of the papal theocracy in 1870, numbered fewer than 33,000 at the 1911 census, less than a tenth of one percent of Italy's population.[15]

The structure of German society as the nineteenth century ended was significantly different from that of northern Italy in four vital respects. First, Germany's independent peasantry had risen gradually in absolute numbers but had shrunk markedly as a proportion of the workforce. By 1907, landowning or long-lease peasants made up a mere 8.9 percent of Germany's working population, in stark contrast to their 38.8 percent share in northern Italy (1901). Second – and in consequence – Germany's landless agricultural laborers, at 25.9 percent (1907), formed rather more of the workforce than in northern Italy (19.1 percent in 1901). Third, industrial wage labor made up 30.6 percent

---

[13] See the enthusiastic endorsement of Giuliano Procacci, "Geografia e struttura del movimento contadino della Valle padana nel suo periodo formativo (1901–1906)," SSt 5:1 (1964), 92, but also note 47 in this chapter.

[14] See Sereni, *Capitalismo nelle campagne*, 341–43; and the exemplary analyses of Anthony L. Cardoza, *Agrarian Elites and Italian Fascism: The Province of Bologna, 1901–1926* (Princeton, NJ, 1982), ch. 1, and Paul Corner, *Fascism in Ferrara, 1915–1925* (London, 1975), 1–6; also Procacci, "Geografia e struttura del movimento contadino," 46–51.

[15] Kaelble, "Mythos von der rapiden Industrialisierung," 113; Renzo De Felice, *Storia degli ebrei italiani sotto il fascismo* (Turin, 1961), 6 (practicing Jews); SVIMEZ, *Nord e Sud*, 13.

of Germany's workforce, in contrast to 20.4 percent of that of northern Italy in
1901. Germany's population enjoyed a standard of living comparable to that
of northern Italy, but proportionately fewer Germans were economically independent and more of them were industrial wage laborers. Religious and ethnic
minorities occupied positions that as yet had no Italian counterparts: 615,000
professing Jews, more than 3.5 million Poles, 1.8 million Alsace-Lorrainers,
and 200,000 Danes (roughly 0.95, 5.5, 2.7, and 0.3 percent of the population respectively). Almost 6 percent of the 1912 Reichstag vote went to ethnic
parties.[16] Finally, the language of social divisions cut deeper in Germany than
in Italy. The notion of *Stand*, of a relatively immutable social status tied to
occupation, still permeated the language of an increasingly mobile, urban, and
industrial society – creating immense pressures and resentments, and twisting
the ambitions of individuals into curious shapes largely unknown elsewhere.

II. Hierarchies and Aspirations

The summits of the two social pyramids differed even more than their bases:
nobility and middle classes held entirely different shares of wealth and political
power and were themselves divided in different ways. In Italy, the collapse of the
nobility that began under absolutism and accelerated mightily under Napoleon
had by the late nineteenth century transformed Italy's elites. Patrician families
in northern Italy and *baroni* in the South still held land, but far less than earlier,
and the *contadini* and urban middle classes proportionately more. The urban
classe proprietaria that owned as much as half of the cultivated surface of the
Po Valley was by 1900 overwhelmingly non-noble.

Above all, patrician or noble elements held ever fewer positions of power
in the state. The blinkered officer corps of restoration Piedmont had admitted commoners through the military academy, but also through the promotion
of the non-commissioned officers who after 1853 made up at least a third –
and on occasion almost two-fifths – of each year's newly commissioned lieutenants. That system narrowed the horizons of the officer corps yet further,
while skimming off talent that might otherwise have remedied the perennial
and disastrous weaknesses of the Piedmontese-Italian non-commissioned officer (NCO) corps.[17] By 1858–59, on the eve of Piedmont's expansion and of a
consequent further massive dilution, less than 30 percent of the Piedmontese
officer corps was noble. According to the most widely cited figures, which may
however overstate the nobility's decline, as early as 1887 only a third of all

[16] SGAB, 2:47, 175; Dieter Langewiesche, ed., *Ploetz – Das deutsche Kaiserreich* (Würzburg, 1984),
128; Wolfgang Petter, "'Enemies' and 'Reich Enemies.' An Analysis of Threat Perceptions and
Political Strategy in Imperial Germany 1871–1914," in Wilhelm Deist, ed., *The German Military
in the Age of Total War* (Leamington Spa, 1985), 33.

[17] See the pioneering insights of Lucio Ceva, "Riflessioni e notizie sui sottufficiali," NA 2182,
April–June 1992, 331–53; for the figure of two-fifths (39 percent, in 1899–1900), Rochat, "Gli
ufficiali italiani nella prima guerra mondiale," in idem, *L'esercito italiano in pace e in guerra.
Studi di storia militare* (Milan, 1991), 115 note 2.

generals, fewer than a fifth of all general staff officers, fewer than an eighth of all cavalry officers, and a derisory 3.1 percent of the entire officer corps of the Royal Italian Army – the *Regio Esercito Italiano* – were noble. Those proportions were far closer to the 8 percent of Second Empire France than to those of Prussia-Germany.[18] Italy's state apparatus, with the partial exception of the higher reaches of the diplomatic service, was even more middle class than the army. By 1900 Italy's parliamentary governing elite was likewise overwhelmingly middle class even at the summit. The northern Italian and often noble *moderati* who had presided over unification faded rapidly once their grouping, the *Destra* or "Right," lost control of parliament and administration to the more plebeian *Sinistra* or "Left" in 1876. Thereafter the remnants of the *Destra* increasingly failed to win election whereas the nobles of the South largely held to their contemptuous rejection of the new state. From 1876 to 1903 nobles made up only 16 percent of Italy's ministers.[19]

The nobles' successors were above all the members of the learned professions, who made up almost three-fifths of those same ministers, and the government bureaucrats, who furnished a further fifth. But Italy's middle classes scarcely formed a unified elite. Its many deep cleavages included but were scarcely limited to municipal and regional jealousies, the North-South divide, and organized Catholicism's passionate rejection both of Italy's "unjust, violent, null and void" annexation of Rome and of the notion that "the Roman Pontiff can and ought to reconcile himself and come to terms with progress, liberalism and modern civilization" (last and most heinous of the eighty transgressions meticulously registered in the *Syllabus Errorum* of 1864).[20] Nor – even in Italy – was wealth the sole determinant of social distinction. Since the Napoleonic period the administrative bureaucracy had offered a promising upward route to ambitious and educated members of the urban middle and lower middle classes. In the stagnant South, the classical secondary education of the *liceo* led to a university degree in law or medicine and then to the bureaucracy or officer corps, and for those with influential *amici* perhaps even the Chamber of Deputies. The fierce and often vain hope for social ascent was the root of the most startling southern paradox, a supply of lawyers (1.5 per thousand of population in 1911) more than ten times that of Prussia, side-by-side with an illiteracy rate that approached 60 percent.[21]

---

[18] Ceva, "Forze armate e società civile dal 1861 al 1887," in Istituto per la storia del Risorgimento italiano, *1861–1887: Il processo d'unificazione nella realtà del paese. Atti del L congresso di storia del Risorgimento italiano* (Rome, 1982), 283–86 and William Serman, *Les origines des officiers français 1848–1870* (Paris, 1979), 305–06; for the possibility that the Italian estimates need upward revision, Marco Mondini, *Veneto in armi. Tra mito della nazione e piccola patria* (Gorizia, 2002), 65–66, 91 note 34.

[19] Ministers: Paolo Farneti, *Sistema politico e società civile* (Turin, 1971), 180.

[20] *Syllabus Errorum* (1864), error 80; *Respicientes* (1870), point 12; and – for the authority behind these statements – the First Vatican Council's proclamation of papal infallibility (1869).

[21] Massimo Barbagli, *Disoccupazione intellettuale e sistema scolastico in Italia (1859–1973)* (Bologna, 1974) (figures: 38 [Prussia, 1901], 63); SVIMEZ, *Nord e Sud*, 795 (illiterates as a

But whereas bureaucratic and military careers might offer escape from death-in-life among the seared naked hills of the South, they conferred infinitely less social prestige than their German counterparts. With the partial exception of Piedmont and of the conspicuous military vocation of Italy's small Jewish community, the Italian upper middle classes resolutely denied their sons, whether as regular or reserve officers, to the *Regio Esercito*.²² In Venetia, where Austrian occupation from 1815 to 1866 had interrupted an already weak native military tradition, local notables and clergy viewed the officers of the local garrisons with icy disdain until the last years before 1914.²³ The shock of a further battlefield disgrace yet more stinging than Custoza, the triumph of Ethiopian feudal armies over a disorganized and ill-led Italian expeditionary force at Adowa in 1896, reinforced these deep-seated traditions and trapped the *Regio Esercito* in the vicious circle that persisted throughout its existence. Victory required the highly intelligent – if not necessarily intellectual – soldiers whose recruitment was only possible through the wholehearted backing of Italian society. Conversely, recurring battlefield humiliation and the absence of strong regional military traditions outside Piedmont helped ensure that for decades society sent to the army the "stupidest sons of the family," the "black sheep and half-wits," as Liberal Italy's greatest statesman, Giovanni Giolitti, despairingly observed in assessing the Italian generals of 1915–18. That the military elite itself incessantly lamented the tightfistedness of the Liberal state, as the pay and allowances of the army's higher echelons gradually fell behind those of their civilian counterparts, scarcely increased the social attraction of the career of arms or the battlefield effectiveness of Italy's army.²⁴

Germany's broader and more disruptive growth inevitably eroded the far stronger positions of its nobles. But growth neither hoisted the German *Bürgertum* into the saddle in its own right nor erased the regional, religious, and status distinctions that fragmented it. The industrial revolution scarcely loosened the grip of that most crucial of *Stand* barriers, a model for lesser

percentage of the population over age 6); on the South's rapidly growing contribution to the officer corps – especially the infantry officer corps – after the 1890s, see Piero Del Negro, "Ufficiali di carriera e ufficiali di complemento nell'esercito italiano della grande guerra: la provenienza regionale," in Gérard Canini, ed., *Les fronts invisibles: nourrir–fournir–soigner* (Nancy, 1984), 285.

²² For the marked over-representation of Jews in the pre-1915 army officer corps (5.4 percent in 1901, against roughly 0.1 percent of the population), Mondini, "L'identità negata: materiali di lavoro su ebrei ed esercito dall'età liberale al secondo dopoguerra," in Ilaria Pavan and Guri Schwartz, eds., *Gli ebrei in Italia tra persecuzione fascista e reintegrazione postbellica* (Florence, 2001), 152.

²³ Mondini, *Veneto in armi*, ch. 3; similarly, Marco Meriggi, "L'ufficiale a Milano in età liberale," in *Esercito e città*, 1:273–96.

²⁴ Giolitti, in Olindo Malagodi, *Conversazioni della guerra (1914–1919)*, 2 vols. (Milan, 1960), 1:58 and 199–200 ("i discoli e i deficienti"); Vincenzo Caciulli, "La paga di Marte. Assegni, spese e genere di vita degli ufficiali italiani prima della Grande Guerra," *Rivista di storia contemporanea* 22:4 (1993), 569–95.

distinctions between the lower orders, the line between the nobility and the rest. Above all, economic growth had little effect upon the all-pervasive role of the Prusso-German state in conferring or recognizing social distinction. West of the Elbe, Germany's nobles defended their positions as regional elites despite encroachment from the industrial middle classes. The high nobles or *Standesherren* of the defunct Holy Roman Empire fiercely maintained their exclusiveness even against the lesser nobility, and secured continuing protection from the state. The otherwise levelling German Civil Code of 1900 preserved the rights of *Standesherren* to dispose of their properties and control the marriages of their dependents in accordance with family custom, not civil law. East of the Elbe, the "knight's estate" or *Rittergut* remained the dominant form of agricultural enterprise and social power. By the 1880s, despite the circulation of landed wealth permitted under the Prussian reform of 1808, nobles still held almost 70 percent of estates of more than 1,000 hectares in Prussia's eastern provinces, and 97.2 percent of the 1,027 estates of more than 10,000 hectares. Entails, which Prussian law actively encouraged, by 1900 froze the ownership of roughly 6 percent of Prussia's surface area.[25] The steady growth of cities and industry lessened the *Junkers'* economic and social weight within Germany while imported grain – staved off only partially through tariffs after 1878–79 – threatened their solvency. But despite the growing hollowness of their position in the Reich as a whole, down to 1914 the *Junkers* nevertheless gripped firmly their backward quarter of Germany east of the Elbe.

Yet noble power on the land was weak indeed beside the Prussian nobility's main strength: its position in the state. The royally appointed and overwhelmingly noble Prussian House of Lords was the foremost symbol of that position. The Reich diplomatic service was a museum of the aristocracy: in 1914 its members included eight princes, twenty-nine counts, twenty barons, fifty-four lesser nobles, and a mere eleven *Bürgerliche*. Only posts as reputedly dismal as Peru, Venezuela, Colombia, and Thailand had non-noble heads of mission. Even after the turn of the century Prussia's key local and regional administrators remained predominantly noble: eleven of the twelve provincial governors, two-thirds of all county administrators, and more than half of all *Landräte* or district commissioners. The nobility's share of the Prussian officer corps declined from 65 percent in 1860 to 30 percent in 1914. Yet even in 1914 all of Germany's eight army commanders and twenty-five corps commanders, and the majority of officers from the rank of colonel upward, were noble. The army's intellectual elite, the Great General Staff, was evenly split.[26] Only the key personnel of the

---

[25] Conrad, "Die Latifundien im preussischen Osten," 141, 143–45, and Christof Dipper, "L'aristocrazia tedesca nell'epoca borghese. Adattamento e continuità," *Quaderni Storici* 21:2 (1986), 362–92.

[26] Figures: John Röhl, "Beamtenpolitik im Wilhelminischen Deutschland," in Michael Stürmer, ed., *Das kaiserliche Deutschland. Politik und Gesellschaft 1870–1918* (Düsseldorf, 1970), 302, 292; Demeter, *The German Officer-Corps*, 28–29.

central Reich ministries, the governments of Germany's cities, the officer corps of the south German states, and the leadership of the great navy built after 1897 as Germany's first *national* armed force were solidly middle class.

The German middle classes continued the process of fragmentation already marked at mid-century. By 1914 the wealth of the new elites of industry and banking had long outshone that of the older *Bürgertum* of property, education, and state service; industrialization had vastly widened the range and types of non-noble riches. The plutocratic villas of the Krupps and of many lesser magnates spoke an unmistakable language: proud corporate groups such as the university professors and upper bureaucrats were no longer of necessity the first members of the *Bürgerstand*. Practitioners of law and medicine, those other strongholds of the *Bildungsbürgertum*, found themselves outnumbered by the technical and supervisory professions of an increasingly industrial and bureaucratized age. Chemical engineering drove out Protestant theology. Jews, thanks to the formal emancipation begun in the Napoleonic era and completed throughout Germany by 1871, entered the liberal professions and journalism – the only middle-class careers other than banking and commerce open to the unbaptized – in numbers strikingly disproportionate to their roughly 1 percent share in the population, and with a conspicuous success that aroused enduring vehement envy and spite.[27]

Region, religion, and the state likewise segmented the middle classes. Former free cities such as Hamburg or even the Frankfurt am Main that Bismarck had vengefully annexed to Prussia had middle-class leaders far more self-conscious and less deferential toward Prussian royal and aristocratic authority than the good *Bürger* of Berlin. The Rhineland and Ruhr annexed in 1814–15 and the south and central German states coerced in 1866–71 maintained middle-class traditions of entrepreneurship and heartfelt regional loyalties. The creation of a Protestant Prusso-German Reich initially helped deepen rather than heal Germany's Protestant-Catholic cleavage. The collapse of the old Reich had dismantled German Catholicism's constitutional rights and guarantees. The new Reich did not merely make Catholics a minority, one-third to two-thirds; it made them second-class citizens if not – in Bismarck's stinging slogan – "enemies of the Reich." The economic backwardness of largely Catholic south Germany, although not of the Catholic Rhineland, in part derived from the confessional divide and reinforced it in the consciousness of both Protestants and Catholics.

Finally, the Prusso-German state itself acted to fragment both middle classes and aristocracy. It controlled admission to the law – the decisive middle-class profession – and regulated the conduct of lawyers with a rigor unknown in

---

[27] See Werner E. Mosse, *Jews in the German Economy: The German-Jewish Elite 1820–1935* (Oxford, 1987); Peter G. J. Pulzer, *The Rise of Political Anti-Semitism in Germany and Austria* (New York, 1964), 9 (512,000 or 1.25 percent of Reich population in 1817; 0.95 percent in 1910); and Hans-Günter Zmarzlik, "Antisemitismus im deutschen Kaiserreich 1871–1918," in Bernd Martin and Ernst Schulin, eds., *Die Juden als Minderheit in der Geschichte* (Munich, 1981), 250–51.

France or Italy. It offered to selected members of the upper middle classes a profusion of honorific ranks and resplendent decorations that ranged from the eminence of *Kommerzienrat* or *Medizinalrat* to the giddy if rarely achieved height of a newly minted title of nobility. Ranks, decorations, and titles generally admitted the bearer to court and bound him to the monarchy. Ranks, decorations, and titles cut the state's middle-class servants, the administrative bureaucrats, professors, and officers, off from middle-class origins.[28] Membership in the *Offiziersstand* and higher *Beamtenstand* conferred, through association with the state, a distinction rivalling that of mere wealth. Germany's "first *Stand*," the active officer corps, owed loyalty not to the Prussian or Reich constitution but to the monarch's person – a link often styled "feudal," but in reality a legacy of the absolutism of Frederick William I and Frederick II. In return for a loyalty that was in theory total and unconditional, the monarch conferred signal privileges and personally supervised officer commissioning, promotions, postings, pay, punishments, pardons, and dismissals through his military cabinet. Every officer from the most junior *Leutnant* upward automatically enjoyed access to court. The *Offiziersstand* was partially exempt from civil law and possessed its own peculiar jurisdiction, honor courts charged with the investigation and punishment of offenses against the *Stand*'s code of honor.

Above all, and especially after 1866–71, the *Offiziersstand* enjoyed by general consent higher prestige than any other group in Prussia – and increasingly throughout south Germany as well. The "king's coat" and officer's epaulettes marked a man out from his fellows.[29] It made him the object of all manner of special courtesies. Railway clerks dropped their habitual surliness; civilians had to address him as "*Hochwohlgeborener*" – "noble sir" – an honorific otherwise reserved for the aristocracy. The *Leutnant*, a commodity much sought after in the marriage market, was the preeminent object of feminine enthusiasm. Prussia-Germany's foremost historian of ideas, Friedrich Meinecke, summed up: "the Prussian lieutenant made his way through the world like a young god, and the middle-class reserve lieutenant did so as at least a demigod"[30] The army's extraordinary social distinction guaranteed it the pick of the best brains of Germany's nobility and upper middle classes; that in turn promised to further improve the army's battlefield performance, social prestige, and prospects of recruiting talent.

Deification of the *Offiziersstand* inevitably extended to its part-time members, the "demigods" of the reserve officer corps. The corps had existed since the reformers' military law of 1814, but William I and his generals had radically

[28] See in general Kaelble, "Französisches und deutsches Bürgertum 1870–1914," in Jürgen Kocka, ed., *Bürgertum im 19. Jahrhundert. Deutschland im europäischen Vergleich* (Munich, 1978), 127–32.

[29] As a satirical verse quoted in Hartmut John, *Das Reserveoffizierkorps im deutschen Kaiserreich 1890–1914* (Frankfurt am Main, 1981), 292, put it: "Niemals erreicht ein Zivilist, / Und sei's der schneidigste Jurist, / Den vollen Glanz des ersten Stand / Die Eleganz des Leutenants."

[30] Meinecke, *Die deutsche Katastrofe*, in *Werke*, vol. 8, *Autobiographische Schriften* (Stuttgart, 1969), 336.

changed its character in virtually doubling Prussia's war strength army in 1860–
61. Prussia's original reserve officers had been the determinedly middle-class
Landwehr officers selected from "one-year volunteers" whose education and
income qualified them for a striking privilege: service of one year in the ranks
of the active army rather than the otherwise obligatory two or three. William
I had savagely reduced the size of the despised *Landwehr* in favor of the line,
but had kept the institution of the one-year volunteer. After further alterations
in 1874 it served as the source of a new type of reserve officer modelled on the
"young gods" of the active officer corps and destined to serve alongside them
in the units of the wartime line army.

The success of William's neo-absolutist experiment was scarcely assured, for
it depended upon the intensity of the military aspirations of the Prusso-German
middle classes. Yet as early as the 1850s middle-class resentment against universal military service had begun to mutate into ambition. The sons of Rhineland
industrialists increasingly sought one-year service with exclusive regiments.
Then, in the words of an officer who served in the Rhineland in the early 1870s,
came the wars: "The Rhinelander scarcely turned into an old-Prussian, but certainly became a first-class German. It was thus quite natural that the press to
enter upon an officer's career became more intense – the fame-bedecked insignia
of 1864, '66, and '70–71 had a magical effect upon educated youth."[31] That
magic, let loose when bloody victories at last slaked the middle-class nationalism frustrated in 1848, henceforth made the right to place "LdR" – *Leutnant
der Reserve* – upon a visiting card the summit of male middle-class happiness. Professors, higher bureaucrats, and businessmen felt incomplete without
a reserve commission. Professional success might depend on it. Especially in
Prussia but even in the more relaxed atmosphere of south Germany, middle-
class men without reserve commissions lacked "the decisive element of social
standing" and formed a "second class within the educated *Stand.*"[32] But – to
the army's profit – even middle-class men who failed this decisive social test
could console themselves with reserve NCO status.

The military institutions of the Prusso-German state thus proved "stronger
than society."[33] They were the source of one of Prussia-Germany's most decisive social cleavages, a line that ran through rather than between the nobility and the middle and lower middle classes, in apparent contradiction to the
monarchy's 1808 promise of military careers open to talent. On one side of
the line stood those entitled to serve as one-year volunteers and thus theoretically capable of joining the *Offiziersstand*; on the other, the rest. Candidates for

---

[31] Friedrich Zunkel, "Industriebürgertum in Westdeutschland," in Wehler, ed., *Moderne deutsche
Sozialgeschichte* (Cologne, 1973), 321; Franz von Lenski, *Aus den Leutnantsjahren eines alten
Generalstabsoffiziers* (Berlin, 1922), quoted in John, *Das Reserveoffizierkorps*, 48.

[32] Karl von Wartenburg, "Der Reserveoffizier, ein Revolutionär," in *Deutches Wochenblatt* (1899),
1008, quoted in John, *Der Reserveoffizierkorps*, 304; also the testimony of Gerhard Ritter,
Staatskunst und Kriegshandwerk (Munich, 1954–68), 2:128–31.

[33] For this notion, see especially Wittfogel, *Oriental Despotism*.

one-year privilege, reserve officer commission, and active officer corps had to pass through a series of filters that were not purely social: educational achievement, military bearing and competence, and political opinions figured alongside income. The resulting cleavage was a bureaucratic construct that did not correspond to any preexisting set of social distinctions. Increasingly some segments of the "new *Mittelstand*," the lower administrative and technical professions that industrialization had created, proved capable of ascent into the *Offiziersstand*, while even nobles whose *Bildung*, income, bearing, military capacity, or political attitudes the active officer corps deemed wanting failed to achieve commissions. Ambition to join the *Offiziersstand* indeed pressed upon the middle classes a code of honor ultimately derived from the nobility, complete with an assiduously enforced duelling code that placed its adepts in mortal danger, and outside – or above – the law.[34] But neither the inherited view of the reserve officer mechanism as vehicle for an ominous antimodernist "feudalization" of the *Bürgertum*, nor the implication that it was part of the alleged triumph of the German bourgeoisie captures its true impact. The aristocratic airs, duelling scars, and "late-absolutist privileges" of the active and reserve officer corps were above all *symptoms* of the division of Prussian society by *military* function, and of the abiding death-grip of military enthusiasms upon an entire society.[35]

---

[34] See Ute Frevert, *Ehrenmänner: das Duell in der bürgerlichen Gesellschaft* (Munich, 1991), ch. 4, for the Prussian army as the preeminent "bastion" of nineteenth-century German duelling; ibid., 119–32 for the duel's spread among the middle classes through the reserve officer institution, with assistance from the sado-masochistic fraternity culture of the German university (ibid., 133–77). Frevert (ibid., 16) claims that the "*Ehrenzweikampf*" was not a product of middle-class "feudalization efforts" or an element of a putative "German *Sonderweg*" determined by the relative "backwardness" of the German "bourgeois class," since duelling was common during the same period in England, the United States, Austria, France, and Italy. That conclusion appears to involve at least two orders of misconception: that duelling elsewhere had much in common either in lethality or in staying power over time with the German short-range pistol duel, and that Germany's peculiarities, if they existed, would of necessity be a function of class (a notion shared both by social-historical *Sonderweg* theorists and their adversaries). Outside Germany, things *were* different: British duelling died in the 1840s; the U.S. Civil War eliminated both the institution and its foremost American practitioners, the slave-owning Confederate gentry – only the informal frontier gunfight inevitably survived; and French and Italian duellists normally fought with swords and ceased soon after first blood: see Kevin McAleer, *Dueling: The Cult of Honor in Fin-de-Siècle Germany* (Princeton, NJ, 1994), ch. 6, for France (fatalities, late in the century, as low as two per year); Italian duels in the same period killed a mere twenty men (0.5 percent of the available sample): Jacopo Gelli, "Il duello in Italia nell'ultimo ventennio (1879–1899)," NA 1901:1, 159. As Frevert's sample (*Ehrenmänner*, 270) of 353 archivally documented duels demonstrates, the nineteenth-century German duel was utterly different: one *or more* fatalities in 28.9 percent of duels in Prussia (1800–1914) and 22.9 percent in Bavaria (1821–1912). Such encounters apparently became more lethal as the century drew on; the army's predilection for pistols became widespread except among students, and pistol reliability and accuracy improved markedly. For Italian duelling culture and the 1850s Lombard fashion of demonstrating Italian valor by provoking Austrian officers, see especially Banti, *Nazione*, 141–47, 183–86, 190.

[35] For the wider debate, Introduction, notes 8 and 9. For the now-famous "Kehr thesis," central to the orthodox social-historical interpretation of the German *Sonderweg*, see Eckart Kehr, "The

Even those with military talent whose birth and education barred them from aspiring to officer status could nevertheless become career or reserve NCOs, with the added attraction that after twelve years' service, career NCOs could graduate to a guaranteed job in the state administration. The army's immense prestige, the sharp social cleavage between the "officer-material *Stände*" and the rest, and the twelve-year NCO career-track gave Prussia-Germany a large and superlatively trained and motivated corps of NCOs whose further careers intensified the already marked military flavor of state and society. An additional and even more weighty consequence in the long term was that the exclusion of the lower *Stände* from officer careers created a mighty head of steam of frustrated lower- and lower-middle-class ambition.

The victories of 1864–71 thus enabled the Prusso-German state to partially redefine *social* status as *military* status. That was a phenomenon utterly without parallel in Italy, much less in Britain or France. Fateful success in fusing an already vehement middle-class nationalism with military elitism and social ambition, and the blockage to lower-class ambitions embodied in the officer corps' steep educational and social requirements, marked German society in ways that long outlived the "late-absolutist" Hohenzollern monarchy.

2. THE POLITICS OF STUNTED PARLIAMENTARISM

As the long nineteenth century ended, the convergence between the new nation-states was most marked in the realm of politics. Italy and Germany remained dramatically distinct, but those distinctions inevitably lessened as both entered the age of the masses.

I. Liberal Italy and the Threat of Mass Politics

At the summit, united Italy remained a parliamentary system operating through an uneasy "diarchy" of the monarch and of a prime minister whose power rested upon the Chamber of Deputies. The monarchy failed to regain the prestige that Charles Albert and Victor Emmanuel II had shattered through military defeat. Yet the *Statuto* of 1848 still reserved to the monarchy a decisive voice in foreign and military policy, formal control over declaring war and making peace, and the power to "approve" legislation passed by parliament. Once Bismarck turned toward formal peacetime alliances at the end of the 1870s in order to consolidate Prussia-Germany's position against the threat of French resurgence, the Italian monarchy, as in the 1860s, found the road to Berlin. The Triple Alliance of 1882 linking Germany, Austria-Hungary, and Italy, periodically renewed until 1914, neutralized the foremost potential adversaries of united Italy: France through German prowess and Austria-Hungary through alliance. The ever-vengeful Vatican lost the support of the Habsburgs for its

Genesis of the Royal Prussian Reserve Officer" in his *Economic Interest, Militarism, and Foreign Policy*, ed. Gordon A. Craig (Berkeley, CA, 1977), 97–108.

claims on Italy, and Italy gained in Protestant Prussia-Germany an ally viscerally hostile to the Papacy's temporal aspirations.

In the late 1880s, Umberto I, son of Victor Emmanuel II, briefly increased the monarchy's political weight further by backing as prime minister the charismatic Francesco Crispi, an ex-Mazzinian firebrand sympathetic in later years to Bismarck, whose ruthlessness he admired and sought feebly to emulate. In accordance with *Risorgimento* tradition, Crispi had long believed that "the unification of Italy will be useless unless it brings us power and greatness."[36] He therefore exhausted his authority and that of the Liberal regime in pursuit of the twin great-power fashions of the age, high tariffs and expansion in Africa. The tariff of 1887 worsened the agricultural crisis to which it was a response; French retaliation stunted Italy's agricultural exports, the only potentially dynamic sector in the economy of the South. Crispi crushed with troops the resulting movements of protest, then failed to force through a recalcitrant Chamber of Deputies the land reform with which he had planned to raise the South's fortunes. That defeat foreclosed Liberalism's last best chance of reinventing itself as a modern party with a mass following.[37] And Crispi's attempt to expand Italy's first colony, an enclave on the Red Sea acquired in 1882, ended in battlefield fiasco at Adowa. He fell amid popular tumult and the open hostility of Italy's embryonic industrial interests and regions, whose persistent aversion to African adventure strikingly disconfirmed later theorizing about industry as the driving force of Italian imperialism.[38] In the spring of 1898 the indecisive right-Liberal government that followed crushed with cannon fire urban Italy's last seasonal *ancien régime* bread riots at a cost of more than eighty dead – and then itself collapsed. Umberto thereupon appointed a forceful Savoyard general, Luigi Pelloux, as prime minister with the mission of dominating both the streets and parliament. But Umberto lacked an idea in whose name he could rule by force.

When the left-opposition and disenchanted Liberals paralyzed by filibuster Pelloux's attempts to defend the Liberal state by making it a police state, the king lacked the nerve to shatter the constitution and coerce the Chamber of Deputies. Italy's "constitutional conflict" of 1898–1900 therefore ended with the defeat of the king's men in general elections. For once, the country dictated to the executive; radicals, republicans, and Socialists markedly increased their seats. Then Umberto's assassination by an anarchist seeking revenge for army and police repression placed on the throne his stunted and pedantic son, Victor Emmanuel III. The new king took to heart his father's political failure and violent death; throughout a reign that lasted until 1946 he sought to hide from responsibility behind the *Statuto*. The monarchy nevertheless retained powers

---

[36] Quoted in Ernesto Ragionieri, "La storia politica e sociale," ESI 4/3:1825; in general, Christopher Duggan, *Francesco Crispi, 1818–1901: From Nation to Nationalism* (Oxford, 2002).

[37] Duggan, *Crispi*, 667–69.

[38] Ibid., 708–09; Nicola Labanca, *In marcia verso Adua* (Turin, 1993), 361–65; Fausto Fonzi, *Crispi e lo "Stato di Milano"* (Milan, 1965), especially 527–28, 533–34.

in both war and peace that could well prove decisive in moments of crisis; the "diarchic" nature of Italy's executive remained a powerful source of ambiguity and conflict.

In normal times, given the monarchy's repeated failures and the example of Cavour, the prime minister nevertheless served as united Italy's executive – so long as he commanded a majority in the Chamber of Deputies. In the wake of the fin-de-siècle crisis the prime minister strengthened against both monarch and parliament his own position and that of the administrative bureaucracy that he controlled. The army retreated backstage. Giolitti, prime minister for most of the 1903–14 decade, shrank the already weak powers of the Senate further by appointing the remarkable total of 225 senators.[39] Yet the power of Giolitti, although the opposition frequently described it as a parliamentary dictatorship, rested not on party discipline but on an amorphous Liberal majority glued together with "favours received or indiscretions detected and overlooked."[40]

Nor was Liberal Italy's fragility confined to its executive; parliament's own social roots remained correspondingly shallow. The men of the *Destra* were no more partisans of universal suffrage than their German, French, or English liberal counterparts. They were nevertheless aware of the need to expand united Italy's narrow base, an electorate of 2 to 2.2 percent of the population of which slightly more than half turned out to vote. Yet the South's backwardness and the "brigand" revolt that forcefully expressed that backwardness deterred them after 1861 from widening the franchise, and shocked them into abandoning plans for the administrative decentralization that Cavour himself had favored. Instead, from the peasant war of the 1860s through Crispi's travails and the fin-de-siècle crisis to the eve of the Great War and beyond, martial law, summary courts, and internal exile periodically imposed "public security" upon troubled areas, especially in the South.[41]

Enfranchising illiterate rural masses and loosening the grip of Piedmont-Italy's proconsuls, prefects, and soldiers seemed likely to produce at best a massive bloc of papal and Bourbon deputies, and at worst Italy's dissolution. The *Sinistra* was both more southern and less socially exclusive than the *Destra*; in 1882 it dropped the voting age from twenty-five to twenty-one, lowered the wealth threshold established in 1848, and exempted from the wealth qualification males capable of reading and writing. This "widened" franchise still encompassed only 6.9 to 9.8 percent of Italy's population, and endured until the belated enfranchisement in 1912 of illiterate males who had done military service or reached the age of thirty raised the electorate to 24.2 percent of the

[39] Carlo Ghisalberti, *Storia costituzionale d'Italia, 1849–1948* (Bari, 1974), 288.

[40] In the British ambassador's memorable words: Simon M. Jones, *Domestic Factors in Italian Intervention in the First World War* (New York, 1986), 36.

[41] See especially Luciano Violante, "La repressione del dissenso politico nell'Italia liberale: stati d'assedio e giustizia militare," *Rivista di storia contemporanea* 5:4 (1976), 481–524 and Giovanna Tosatti, "La repressione del dissenso politico tra l'età liberale e il fascismo: l'organizzazione della polizia," SSt 38:1 (1997), 217–31. For the extent of endemic rural violence, Della Peruta, *Realtà e mito*, 165–81.

population. Yet only 60.4 percent of potential voters, or 14.1 percent of the population, turned out in 1913 – a result achieved by Imperial Germany in the 1870s.[42] Italy's parliamentary politics well into the twentieth century thus remained an affair of narrow elites, the more narrow through the absence of Italy's clerical forces – until the perceived Socialist threat dictated the attenuation from 1905 onward of the stern 1874 papal order (*"non expedit"*) forbidding participation in national elections (see Figure 2.6).

Piedmont's electoral law, derived from a French model and extended to united Italy, simultaneously reinforced that narrowness and inhibited the creation of parliamentary mass parties. It provided for single-member electoral districts with second-round run-off elections if no candidate achieved a first-round majority. That mechanism, now well known as a force responsible for the rise and persistence of the fragmented multi-party systems of nineteenth- and twentieth-century continental Europe, remained in effect until 1919 except for a brief experiment in party list voting from 1882 to 1892. It lessened the influence of Italy's already discouraged voters by allowing each district's notables, especially in the South, to decide elections through cozy run-off bargaining among themselves. Worse still, its relative efficiency in registering the votes of minorities, compared to the rough justice of the Anglo-Saxon first-past-the-post plurality system, helped make the Chamber of Deputies a too-faithful mirror of the fragmentation of Italian society.[43]

Administrative centralization further reinforced the effects of the electoral law. After the accession of the *Sinistra* the government habitually "made" the elections through its prefects, who bolstered deputies or candidates by lavishing favors upon their districts and brokering their run-off bargains. In much of the North, administrative tutelage and the rule of the notables gave way after the widening of the franchise in 1882 to an embryonic system of organized parties. But in the South the function of the voters remained that of ratifying the choice that notables, prefect, and interior minister imposed through *clientelismo*, bribery, threats, and violence. In consequence, and contrary to constitutional theory, parliamentary upheavals such as the fall of the *Destra* in 1876 normally *preceded* rather than followed Liberal Italy's electoral shifts. Nor

---

[42] See Figures 2.6 and 2.8, and their source notes; Ghisalberti, *Storia costituzionale*, 185 and appendix, table 2; and Ugo Giusti, *Le correnti politiche italiane attraverso due riforme elettorali dal 1909 al 1921* (Florence, 1922), 10.

[43] It is no accident that Great Britain and the United States have stable two-party systems and single-member constituencies in which the winner needs only a plurality rather than an absolute majority. The plurality system, arrived at by luck and preserved by tradition, *forces* the creation of broad coalition parties capable of governing; no other electoral system does. For the effect of run-off voting (and for the causal relationship between the Anglo-Saxon single-member-constituency plurality voting system and two-party government), see Maurice Duverger, *L'influence des systèmes electoraux sur la vie politique* (Paris, 1950) and William H. Riker, "The Two-Party System and Duverger's Law: An Essay in the History of Political Science," APSR 76:4 (1982), 753–66. Giuseppe Maranini, *Storia del potere in Italia 1848–1967* (Florence, 1967) argues the decisive importance of the electoral law in preventing the creation of a mass party of the middle classes in Italy.

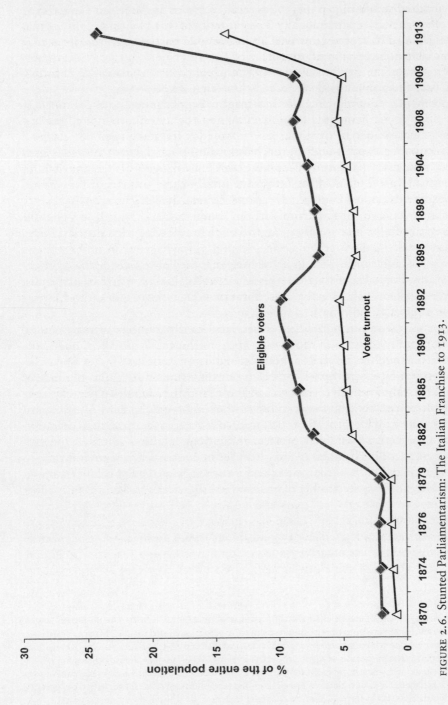

FIGURE 2.6. Stunted Parliamentarism: The Italian Franchise to 1913.

Base data: Eligible voters: Giusti, *Le correnti politiche*, 10; turnout: Serge Noiret, *La nascita del sistema dei partiti nell'Italia contemporanea: La proporzionale del 1919* (Bari, 1994), 292 note 684; population: Maddison, 36.

could any prime minister after 1876 dispense with the bloc-vote of the almost two hundred southern deputies whose fear of return to the South should they lose office guaranteed their loyalty. The existence of that bloc and of the society that it claimed to represent proved an insuperable barrier to the creation of a system of genuinely national mass parties.

The South, the narrowness of the franchise, the mechanism of the electoral law, and Rome's grip on local politics thus combined to freeze in place Cavour's "pseudo-parliamentary" system of ruling through an amorphous parliamentary center composed of individuals and cliques linked by personal ties to the prime minister. In 1876 that time-honored practice acquired a new name: *trasformismo*, coined to describe the *Sinistra*'s ambition to absorb into the capacious bosom of its majority all deputies, regardless of origins or ideology, willing to be thus "transformed." The disciplined parliamentary mass parties that had evolved in Britain and Germany by the 1890s remained conspicuously absent. The narrowness of the franchise and the Southern bloc-vote encouraged the Liberals to rule without a party – and when they ultimately came to need one, it was too late.[44]

Two mass movements, the Socialist Party of Italy (PSI) and the forces of organized Catholicism, did ultimately emerge. But unlike France, which provided the model for Italy's administrative centralization and run-off elections and which likewise suffered the rule of a shapeless parliamentary center, in Italy those forces emerged outside parliament. France had first attempted virtual universal male suffrage in the revolutionary year 1792; the Second Republic of 1848 had reinstated it, and the Third Republic had reaffirmed it after 1871. Nor was the French state's bitter quarrel with the Church as envenomed as the corresponding struggle in Italy. France's socialists could vote, and French monarchist-clericals briefly dominated a parliament many of them despised. In Italy, by contrast, the absence of universal suffrage and the anathemas of the Vatican against the Italian state that had dispossessed it meant that Socialists and Catholics emerged from the mid-1880s onward as powerful extra-parliamentary mass movements fiercely opposed both to the system and to one another. And unlike Germany, where a degree of regional and confessional segregation limited competition and acrimony between Catholic Center and the largely Protestant Social Democratic Party of Germany (SPD), the Italian mass forces were from the beginning mortal enemies at the local level. Their organizations, from industrial and agricultural unions to workers' cooperatives to agricultural credit banks, constituted closed universes, islands of socialism or integral Catholicism within an increasingly

---

[44] On the origins and effects of Liberal Italy's "pseudo-parliamentary" system see Maranini, *Storia del potere* (who privileges the consequences of the electoral law) and Farneti, *Sistema politico e società civile*, who emphasizes above all the effects of the North-South and Church-state divides, which made the formation of national parties impossible and helped discourage any widening of the narrow franchise; narrowness in turn allowed Liberal Italy's principal subcultures to organize themselves outside parliament, and deprived the liberals of the effective opposition within the system that would have forced them to constitute themselves as a mass party.

capitalist and lay society. Their politics, and especially those of their agricultural labor unions, largely developed as a "politics of the *piazza*" against an existing order that still felt compelled to reply with police and army firepower.

The new forces established regional strongholds, battlegrounds between the new mass politics and the old liberalism. The industrial triangle remained Italy's only zone of relative pluralism, where Socialists, Catholics, and left, center, and right-Liberals coexisted. Then came the two embryonic mass parties' citadels: Venetia, Bergamo, and Brescia for organized Catholicism, and the "red belt," republican and anarchist until the 1890s and predominantly Socialist until 1921–22, stretching across Italy from Tuscany to Emilia-Romagna and the Marche.[45] Both *Destra* and *Sinistra* had attempted to preserve the fragile unitary state by excluding the masses from parliament. That exclusion preserved the fragility of the state and gave new form to Italy's regional fragmentation.

With the coming of the new century Giolitti sought to bring Socialists and Catholics into parliament as junior partners. He understood far better than most of his fellows that in the age of the irresistible "ascent of the popular classes," the system had to change in order to remain the same. As minister of the interior or prime minister throughout most of the 1901–14 period, he "made" the three general elections of 1904, 1909, and 1913. He wooed both the moderate "reformist" Socialist leadership and the conservative Catholic forces that inevitably mobilized against the "red threat" manifest in great strike waves that culminated provisionally in 1907. To the Socialists he offered the beginnings of social insurance and for the first time the freedom – in the North if not the South – to organize unions and strike without immediately facing police and troops. From the Catholics he silently accepted votes for right-Liberal candidates. Above all, he preempted the demands of both movements for the universal suffrage that the Socialist reformists hoped would foreshadow the peaceful demise of capitalism, and that organized Catholicism expected would harness the peasant masses against Socialism and the lay state.

Implicit in Giolitti's attempt to tame the new mass forces through a renovated *trasformismo* was his inflexible resistance to any notion that Liberalism itself should become a disciplined mass party. A Liberal party organization would limit his own domination, exercised through an increasingly powerful and uncontrollable state bureaucracy operating from the center, and through *clientelismo*, manipulation, and force at the periphery.[46] A party machine and program would impede attempts to entice non-liberal newcomers into his majority in the Chamber, and might furnish a base to challengers such as his austere and pedantic right-Liberal rival, Sidney Sonnino. Tone-deaf to ideology, Giolitti presumed the same of others. His matter-of-fact style was a relief after the rhetorical inflation of Crispi. But Giolitti's common sense was ultimately a weakness, for it led him to assume that Socialism was merely an economic protest movement, and that organized Catholicism simply aspired to defend

---

[45] For the boundaries of Italy's regional subcultures, see Farneti, *Sistema politico e società civile*, 202–08.

[46] Giolitti's aims and methods: Vivarelli, *Origini*, 2:42–48, 62–74.

the social order. He gambled that he could defuse the one by economic concessions and tame the other through appeals to its innate conservatism – and that a parliamentary majority created and ruled through disreputable bargains with the notables and clienteles of the South would somehow also be capable of enacting fundamental reforms.

He was wrong on all counts. Italian Socialism, unlike its German counterpart, was as much a rural as an urban movement The local and regional organizations or *leghe* of the Po Valley agricultural day-laborers, banded together in the National Federation of the Workers of the Soil (*Federterra*), infused the party with an insatiable radicalism born of depths of misery unparalleled in the industrial cities, and of the Socialist movement's exploitation of rustic naiveté through an all-too-this-worldly adaptation – the "socialization of the land" – of the dogmatic eschatological message of the Roman Church.[47] The fury of the *braccianti* broke forth repeatedly in Socialist and anarcho-syndicalist agricultural strikes, and in an abortive though widely observed general strike in 1904. The rise of the *leghe* prolonged and intensified Italy's endemic rural overpopulation; "class struggle" appeared to offer an alternative to emigration, and in the areas in which *leghe* flourished, especially Emilia and Apulia, emigration before 1914 was notably below the national average, and far below that from Sicily and the continental South.[48] Overpopulation in turn reinforced the quasi-religious zeal of organizers and followers: only absolute coercive control of labor could prevent strikebreakers from neighboring areas from depriving *lega* members of the means of life. The PSI's agricultural unions were thus conspicuous in their jealous exclusiveness, will to dominate all other rural groups, and immemorial suspicion of city folk, including the urban Socialists who nevertheless gave the movement its political voice and its connection to regional and national politics.[49]

In the South and islands, rural violence by the landless peasantry was likewise endemic throughout the long nineteenth century. But the aspiration of the

---

[47] For the Catholic-rural contribution to PSI radicalism, ibid., 2:394–95, 399–410, and, from a wholly different perspective, Renato Zangheri, ed., *Lotte agrarie in Italia. La Federazione nazionale dei lavoratori della terra (1901–1926)* (Milan, 1960), especially lxxvii; socialization: *Federterra* 1901 program, 68. Zangheri concedes the movement's "cultural backwardness" (xxi) despite the modernity (for Marxists) of the Po Valley day-laborers as products of capitalist development. Contrary to the view of Salvatore Adorno, "La ricerca di Vivarelli e le origini del fascismo," *SSt* 34:2–3 (1993), 702–03, socioeconomic modernity is in no sense incompatible with primitive mentalities.

[48] See the careful statistical analysis of J. S. MacDonald, "Agricultural Organization, Migration and Labour Militancy in Rural Italy," *Economic History Review* 16:1 (1963), 61–75. In strict observance of Marx's anti-Malthusian dogma, Sereni (*Capitalismo nelle campagne*, 304–05, 348–50) ascribes Po Valley overpopulation to capitalism. Socialism appears more deeply implicated, and Giuseppe Are, following MacDonald, has suggested that the masses of organized braccianti constituted "a pathological element in Italian economic development" ("Pensiero economico e vita nazionale in Italia (1890–1922). Considerazioni preliminari," *SC* 2:2 [1971], 358–62).

[49] See especially Procacci, "Geografia e struttura del movimento contadino," 55–64, and Zangheri, *Lotte agrarie*, xxvi–lviii.

southern peasantry to a scrap, however minuscule, of land gave little scope for
the creation of the mass movements that served to focus and channel protest,
however destructively, in the North.[50] Strikes Giolitti's state now permitted, but
demonstrations anywhere in the peninsula that appeared to threaten "public
order" it repressed in time-honored fashion with rifle fire. Socialist indignation at the resulting "massacres of proletarians" combined with the apocalyptic expectations of the Socialist agricultural base to undermine those same
reformist leaders upon whom Giolitti hoped to rely in parliament. And in any
case, agrarian overpopulation and the resulting ever-present threat of strikebreakers ensured that *leghe* led by PSI reformists were as ruthless in practice as
those controlled by extremists.

Then Giolitti, obedient to the "historical necessity" of maintaining Italy's
great-power status, a myth no Italian government dared flout, launched a hastily
improvised landing operation to seize Libya in September 1911. The resulting
war with Turkey and with Libya's recalcitrant Arabs allowed political Catholicism to complete the transformation begun when it had rallied against the
Socialist threat. Once a force that denied the legitimacy of the Italian state,
it now advanced a quasi-theocratic claim to lead Italy's God-given mission of
civilizing the infidel; solemn high masses marked the October 1911 anniversary
of the battle of Lepanto in 1571. Even more ominously, the war unleashed
within the Socialist movement the revolutionary "maximalists," professional
"preachers of redemptive violence." Prominent among the *massimalisti* was
Benito Mussolini, party journalist and son of a blacksmith; his brutal oratory
spurred the maximalist conquest of the party and the expulsion of prominent
reformists at the tumultuous congress of Reggio Emilia in July 1912.[51]

Giolitti thus lost the Socialists for good. The tacit Liberal-Catholic electoral
alliance in the 1913 elections, the "Gentiloni Pact," nevertheless gave Liberal
Italy a temporary lease on life that lasted through the coming Great War. Yet
the *maestro* did not thereby gain the docile majority to which he aspired; his
apparent concessions to Catholic religious and political demands inspired the
most determinedly lay forces to parliamentary revolt in early 1914. Giolitti
took the occasion to resign in the expectation that he would return once the
new Chamber tired of the successor he designated, the right-Liberal Antonio
Salandra.

But the revolt against *giolittismo*, Giolitti's prosaic compound of pragmatic
compromise, cautious piecemeal reform, bureaucratic fiat, and Southern *clientelismo* and violence had now become general. The agrarian elites of the Po
Valley and the new industrial leadership, suddenly bereft of the customary

---

[50] Procacci, "Geografia e struttura del movimento contadino," 47, 49, 55–58; Sereni, *Capitalismo
nelle campagne*, 334–35.

[51] See Luigi Ganapini, *Il nazionalismo cattolico. I cattolici e la politica estera in Italia dal 1871
al 1914* (Bari, 1970), ch. 4; "Predicatori della violenza redentrice," Filippo Turati's apt phrase,
quoted in Gaeta, *Età giolittiana*, 227. For the nature and long-term influence on Italian Socialism
of Mussolini's "irrationalist *sovversivismo*," see particularly Vivarelli, *Origini*, 2:374–82.

army backing against strikers and agitators, viewed Giolitti's concessions to the Socialists as spineless capitulation. Especially in combative Emilia-Romagna, the strike waves after 1900 and the apparent "abdication" of the state led to the swift growth of landlord self-help organizations with a *politica della piazza* of their own: bands of armed strikebreakers. In the cities, the industrialists emerged on the national political scene demanding incisive measures to safeguard their rights and interests; they founded Italy's first effective national economic lobby, the *Confindustria*, in 1910.

More explicitly political discontents found a voice in increasingly insistent pressure groups. The disreputably republican and Mazzinian irredentist movement that had issued from the *Risorgimento* turned from the 1880s onward toward political respectability and an ever more imperious disregard of the claims of the Slovenes, Croats, and Germans who lived within the "natural frontiers" of the far grander Italy (*"la più grande Italia"*) of the future. The innocuously named Dante Alighieri Society (1889) was in reality an unsubtle reference to Dante's delimitation of Italy's eastern border as the Kvarner (Carnaro), the gulf east of Istria on which Rijeka (Fiume) lies. No sharp – and comforting – historical line divided Mazzinian irredentism committed to self-determination for Slavs as well as Italians from an imperialism that sought to dominate non-Italians in the name of historic rights and strategic necessity. A Navy League (1897) and an Italian Colonial Institute (1906) also emerged, pledged to make Italy great through naval armaments and scraps of Africa. Unlike their German counterparts, these semi-official groups appealed to the elites rather than to both elites and masses. And with the exception of the anti-Slav extremists from Trieste who had absorbed all the ethic intolerance of the Dual Monarchy, the pressure groups normally refrained from challenging the government's command of foreign policy.[52]

Not so the authoritarian avant-garde that coalesced to form the Italian Nationalist Association in 1910–11.[53] The *nazionalisti* flayed Giolitti's *"borghesia* that rules and governs" for "its fear which summons up boldness in its attackers, its flight so much swifter than their pursuit," and its "exaggerated compassion for the weak and humble, [its] obliviousness to the heights of human achievement, [its] sneering at heroism...."[54] The Nationalists' sneers were merely an extreme symptom of the widespread disenchantment of Italy's elites – and especially of their younger generations – with Giolitti's prosaic achievements. Democratic intellectuals such as the combative and influential Gaetano Salvemini damned the *maestro* as "minister of the underworld" who

---

[52] See above all Giovanni Sabbatucci, "Il problema dell'irredentismo e le origini del movimento nazionalista in Italia," SC 1:3–4 (1970), 469–82, and Richard J. B. Bosworth, *Italy, the Least of the Great Powers: Italian Foreign Policy Before the First World War* (Cambridge, 1979), 51–67; for the "mentalità austriaca" of Trieste-style Italian nationalism, Giuseppe Prezzolini, quoted in Vivarelli, *Origini*, 1:176–77 note 45.

[53] Henceforth "Nationalists" (uppercase).

[54] Enrico Corradini, *Discorsi politici* (Florence, 1923), 10 (from the program of *La Voce*, 1903).

controlled parliament through southern corruption and violence. And in the "Red Week" of June 1914, the Socialist, syndicalist, and anarchist agrarian and small-town base, from Ancona far into the Romagna, rose against the Liberal state in confused and bloody pursuit of the millennium until subdued by army firepower.

Giolitti had tried to renovate and broaden the "pseudo-parliamentary" system he had inherited through the traditional method of cooption. But his decisive step, the concession of virtual universal suffrage in 1912–13, came too late. Socialism and organized Catholicism had set in a mold of extra-parliamentary ideological rigidity. Bringing them into parliament risked transferring the unbridgeable ideological, social, and regional fractures of Italian society to a Chamber of Deputies already riven by personality conflicts and factional disputes. Giolitti's refusal to compete organizationally with the two mass forces through a disciplined Liberal party completed this recipe for paralysis. Socialists and Catholics proved unable to make their full electoral weight felt in 1913, but they could scarcely fail to do so when Italy next voted.[55] No Liberal prime minister, however cunning or charismatic, would then command a stable majority. Parliamentary arithmetic would dictate a power vacuum at the top; the slightest stress might unleash chaos in the *piazza* below, as the new mass forces challenged the Liberal order.[56]

II. The German Reich: Warrior State – Enfranchised Masses – Radical Nationalism

Imperial Germany, that "best-administered, worst-governed state" in Europe, achieved similar results by a different route. It too possessed a "diarchy" at the summit, but one weighted heavily in favor of the military monarchy rather than the civilian Reich chancellor. The king of Prussia and German emperor was by Bismarck's constitution "Supreme Warlord" of all German forces in war and commander-in-chief of all except Bavarian forces in peacetime. He appointed on his own authority the Reich chancellor, the minister-president and ministers of Prussia, and the secretaries of the Reich departments. Chancellor and ministers remained constitutionally "responsible" to him, rather than to majorities in the Reichstag or Prussian chamber. Generations of jurists and historians, along with the Reichstag representatives of all parties except the SPD, celebrated these peculiar arrangements, then and later, as "German constitutionalism," the nation's unique third way between Anglo-French parliamentarism and Russian despotism.[57]

---

[55] See especially Maria Serena Piretti, *Le elezioni politiche in Italia dal 1848 a oggi* (Rome, 1995), chs. 8–9.

[56] I owe the essentials of this analysis to Paolo Farneti's *Sistema politico e società civile* and "La crisi della democrazia italiana e l'avvento del fascismo: 1919–1922," *Rivista Italiana di Scienze Politiche* 5:1 (1975), 45–82.

[57] For continuing celebration of this aspect of the German *Sonderweg* even after 1945, Huber, *Verfassungsgeschichte*, passim; for the almost unanimous preference of the Reichstag parties

The immemorial Prussian traditions consolidated by Frederick the Great had made land warfare the personal province of the Prussian sovereign; no "German" war minister could therefore arise. The Prussian minister of war nevertheless increasingly answered to the Reichstag on military affairs. Only Prussia's navy evolved into a Reich institution, while remaining equally firmly in the Kaiser's hands. The army, which the minister of war had dominated until the 1850s, became after Prussia received a constitution and especially from the early 1880s a many-headed hydra: the corollary of the Prussian war minister's distasteful duty of answering Reichstag questions was the final escape from war ministry control of the Great General Staff and of the Kaiser's "military cabinet," or officer personnel office.[58] By 1914 almost forty officers, including the twenty-five army corps and military district commanders, were directly subordinate to the Kaiser in person; the navy followed suit. The chancellor for his part served at the Kaiser's pleasure, had no formal voice in military affairs, and required the Kaiser's approval for all major departures in both domestic and foreign policy.

Only the Kaiser had the power to coordinate all aspects of state policy, a role cut for a Frederick the Great. Neither William I, who reigned until 1888, nor his grandson William II, who ascended the throne later that year after his father, Frederick III, died prematurely of cancer, could fill it. William I in later years delegated much of his power to Bismarck. William II took that power back after rancorously dismissing Bismarck in 1890, but proved too indolent and unstable to exercise it effectively. He succeeded nevertheless in launching Prussia-Germany upon a "new course" aimed at what he described in 1891 as "a sort of Napoleonic supremacy" in Europe.[59]

His instrument, after a series of struggles with uncooperative ministers and a recalcitrant Reichstag, was the great battle-fleet inaugurated in the two navy laws of 1898 and 1900. In conscious imitation of his grandfather's military revolution in the 1860s that gave Prussia domination of Germany, William II sought to create an instrument with which Germany could break through into the charmed circle of world powers, alongside the British Empire, Russia, and the United States. Abroad, the navy designed exclusively for combat power "between Helgoland and the Thames" would threaten Britain's jugular; a "high-seas fleet action fought through to the end" would raise Germany to world hegemony. At home, the fleet undermined the Reichstag; William's navy secretary after 1897, Alfred Tirpitz, secured approval for the automatic replacement of obsolete ships, a procedure that in the long run promised a navy that

---

for German "constitutionalism" over foreign "parliamentarism," see the detailed analysis of Mark Hewitson, "The *Kaiserreich* in Question: Constitutional Crisis in Germany before the First World War," JMH 73:4 (2004), 655–83.

[58] For details (along with a whimsical effort to claim Imperial Germany was more "constitutional" than it really was), Huber, *Verfassungsgeschichte* 4:527–34.

[59] See Röhl, "A Document of 1892 on Germany, Russia and Poland," HJ 7:1 (1964), 144; the Kaiser added hopefully that he proposed to pursue that supremacy "in the peaceful sense."

would be even more the monarchy's private instrument than was the army.[60] But also the instrument of the rising German nation: long before Lenin, naval officer corps and "fleet-professors" proclaimed that industrialization meant war. A German collision with "England" was inherent in the fabric of the modern world.

Yet the British refused to yield gracefully in the naval cold war that the Kaiser and Tirpitz had launched. It soon became clear to London that the parity or superiority that Germany sought in the North Sea threatened Britain's existence, not simply its world position. To prevent German command of the sea, London would shrink from no sacrifice of treasure and lives. And William himself collapsed under the pressures of office and the weight of Germany's leadership myths. The strain of the 1905–06 Morocco crisis, which his Foreign Office had conscripted him to launch and had then bungled; public allegations of homosexuality against members or former members of his entourage; and the 1908 uproar in both Germany and Britain over his bizarre claim to the London *Daily Telegraph* that he had masterminded Britain's victory over the Boers exhausted his limited stock of self-confidence.

William II's failure to fill the role assigned him was in part a consequence of psychological frailty. But it also was a measure of the difficulties inherent in the role: the conflicting and countervailing pressures that limited monarchical power in Bismarck's system and the increase of those pressures as Germany hesitantly crossed the threshold of mass politics. Prussia's domination of the Reich government and its possession of roughly three-fifths of Germany's land area and population did not preclude resistance from the other states, especially those of Catholic south Germany. Only the states, under the constitution, could levy direct taxes, and the Reich government depended in part upon their voluntary contributions. The federal structure gave particularism a continued constitutional expression, and in Württemberg and Baden offered the remnants of democratic liberalism a share of power in the legislatures.

Most limiting of all was the universal suffrage Reichstag, equipped with budgetary powers the government was compelled to respect, and focus of a genuinely national politics that gradually overshadowed the federal states. Bismarck had created the Reichstag to neutralize the liberals through the votes of the masses. The liberals had accepted it primarily as a tool for forging a unified national market and legal system, and for taming rather than supplanting the monarchical executive.[61] Neither was happy with the result. The early

---

[60] Tirpitz quotations ("durchgeschlagene rangierte Hochseeschlacht"): Volker Berghahn, *Der Tirpitz-Plan. Genesis und Verfall einer innenpolitischen Krisenstrategie under Wilhelm II* (Düsseldorf, 1971), 109, 185; also idem, "Zu den Zielen des deutschen Flottenbaus unter Wilhelm II," HZ 210 (1970) 62–75; and idem and Wilhelm Deist, eds., *Rüstung im Zeichen der wilhelminischen Weltpolitik: grundlegende Dokumente 1890–1914* (Düsseldorf, 1988), especially 109, 116–17, 122, 127.

[61] For the Prussian liberals' lack of enthusiasm, even in the 1848–71 period, for "parliamentarism" in the sense of an executive designated by and responsible to the legislature, see Hewitson, "*Kaiserreich*," 731–32.

Reichstag elections helped congeal Germany's characteristic "five-party system" in the form held until 1929–33 (see Figure 2.7).

Conservatives, National Liberals, and Left-Liberals had existed in a variety of regional shadings since 1848. Catholics, Socialists, and the Poles, Danes, and Alsatians unwillingly included within the new borders found a political voice through the electoral system, even if voting did not save the Poles of the Prussian East from the ever-harsher repressive laws of Bismarck and his successors. Yet despite discrimination of various kinds and the absence of reapportionment that resulted in an ever-greater under-representation of the swiftly growing cities, the subjects of the authoritarian German Reich voted in relative freedom, unaffected by the bureaucratic tutelage, corruption, and widespread violence characteristic of Liberal Italy's elections. The Reich electoral system did resemble Liberal Italy's in one crucial respect: the requirement of a run-off between the first and second-place candidates if no one received an absolute majority on the first ballot. That helped perpetuate the political fragmentation derived from Germany's preexisting social, religious, and ethnic divisions, and aggravated by urbanization and the chancellor's machinations.

The Liberals, with the assistance of a Bismarck viscerally hostile to Catholicism and gleeful at the chance to inflame antagonisms that might fracture and discredit the Reichstag parties, made a further mighty contribution to fragmentation through their head-on attack on the Church after 1872. They cast their *Kulturkampf* or "struggle of cultures" as a contest between Counter-Reformation darkness and the light of nineteenth-century liberal Protestant principles, and as a mortal struggle over the essence of the German nation itself. The onslaught of the Liberals and of Bismarck's state gratuitously alienated potential Liberal allies – and voters – in Catholic Germany. It helped transform the Catholic Center Party from a powerful Rhineland pressure group into a formidable national mass party with a disciplined bloc of ninety to one hundred seats that soon came to hold the balance in the Reichstag. And the forced intermingling of Catholics and Protestants as industrialization rendered German society increasingly mobile inflamed and perpetuated the confessional divide.[62]

Those tendencies Bismarck grimly exploited in his 1878–79 turn toward agricultural and industrial tariffs, a step aimed in part at remolding the parties into mere economic lobbies representing mutually hostile interest groups incapable of forming Reichstag majorities without government leadership.[63]

---

[62] See above all Helmut Walser Smith, *German Nationalism and Religious Conflict: Culture, Ideology, and Politics, 1870–1914* (Princeton, NJ, 1995), chs. 1–3.

[63] Bismarck's turn to protectionism played a central role in the social-historical *Sonderweg* interpretations of the 1960s (see note 8), as one of several stratagems promoting the "rallying [*Sammlung*]" of "state-supporting forces" that purportedly prolonged Prussian-aristocratic domination into the twentieth century. For the threadbare nature of the concept, see especially Otto Pflanze, "'Sammlungspolitik' 1875–1886; Kritische Bemerkungen zu einem Modell," in his *Innenpolitische Probleme des Bismarck-Reiches* (Munich, 1983), 153–93; on protectionism as the quasi-universal international response to the post-1870 collapse of transport costs and

FIGURE 2.7. The German "Five-Party System," 1871–1918: Parties, Votes, and Reichstag Seats

Reichstag election	Conservatives[a]			National Liberals[b]			Left Liberals[c]			Center			SPD			Others[d]			Total seats	Electoral participation (% of eligible voters)
	Seats	% of seats	% of vote	Seats	% of seats	% of vote	Seats	% of seats	% of vote	Seats	% of seats	% of vote	Seats	% of seats	% of vote	Seats	% of seats	% of vote		
1871	94	24.6	23.0	155	40.6	37.3	47	12.3	9.3	63	16.5	18.6	2	0.5	3.2	21	5.5	8.6	382	50.7
1874	55	13.8	14.1	158	39.8	30.7	50	12.6	9.0	91	22.9	27.9	9	2.3	6.8	34	8.6	11.4	397	60.8
1877	78	19.7	17.6	141	35.5	29.7	39	9.8	8.5	93	23.4	24.8	12	3.0	9.1	34	8.6	10.1	397	60.3
1878	116	29.3	26.6	109	25.5	25.8	29	7.4	7.8	94	23.7	23.1	9	2.3	7.6	40	10.3	9.0	397	63.1
1881	78	19.7	23.7	47	11.9	14.7	115	30.3	23.1	100	25.2	23.2	12	3.0	6.1	45	11.3	9.1	397	56.1
1884	106	26.8	22.1	51	12.9	17.6	74	18.7	19.3	99	25.0	22.6	24	6.1	9.7	43	10.9	8.7	397	60.3
1887	121	30.5	25.0	99	25.0	22.3	32	8.1	14.1	98	24.7	20.1	11	2.8	10.1	36	9.2	8.4	397	77.2
1890	93	23.4	19.1	42	10.6	16.3	76	19.1	18.0	106	26.7	18.6	35	8.8	19.8	40	11.4	8.3	397	71.2
1893	100	25.2	19.2	53	13.4	13.0	48	12.2	14.8	96	24.2	19.1	44	11.1	23.3	56	14.2	11.2	397	72.2
1898	79	19.9	15.5	46	11.6	12.5	49	12.3	11.1	102	25.7	18.8	56	14.1	27.2	65	16.4	13.9	397	67.7
1903	75	18.9	13.5	51	12.9	13.9	36	9.1	9.3	100	25.2	19.8	81	20.4	31.7	54	13.7	12.1	397	73.3
1907	84	21.2	13.6	54	13.6	14.5	49	12.4	10.9	105	26.5	19.4	43	10.9	28.9	62	15.7	12.7	397	84.3
1912	57	14.4	12.2	45	11.3	13.6	42	10.6	12.3	91	22.9	16.4	110	27.7	34.8	52	13.2	10.6	397	84.5

[a] Konservative, Reichspartei (Freikonservative).

[b] Nationalliberale, Liberale (1871, 1874, 1877, 1878).

[c] Deutsche Fortschrittspartei, Deutsche Volkspartei, Liberale Vereinigung/Freisinnige Vereinigung, Freisinnige Volkspartei.

[d] Guelphs, Poles, Danes, Alsace-Lorrainers, Anti-Semites, miscellaneous.

Source: Adapted from SGAB, 2:173–75.

Finally, the rise of Social Democracy, the party of the urban workers, allowed Bismarck to further fragment Liberalism and to divide Germans by class as well as by religion and economic interest. He replied to the SPD in 1878 with laws restricting the Socialist right to organize politically, while offering state accident and health insurance to the SPD's constituents and tariffs to industrialists and agrarians. His proposals forced Liberals to choose between cherished principles – equality before the law and laissez-faire – and cherished goals, the blunting of Socialist threat and of foreign competition. In the end, Bismarck secured enough National Liberal votes to govern with Conservative support and the acquiescence of a Center Party intent, after the waning of the *Kulturkampf* in the late 1870s, on proving its loyalty to the Reich and giving scope to its own social conservatism.

Bismarck's own most durable legacy to German internal politics derived from his efforts to freeze through conflict the balance between government and Reichstag enshrined in the constitution. If from 1864 to 1871 he had run domestic policy "on the steam-power of foreign affairs," he ruled at home thereafter through the diplomatic technique that his sometime British opposite number Lord Salisbury aptly described as "employing his neighbors to pull out each other's teeth."[64] The domestic counterpart to the "coalition nightmare" that haunted Bismarck's foreign policy was the specter of a stable Reichstag majority independent of the government. To preclude its formation he seconded the Liberal attack on the Catholics and persecuted Socialists and Poles. He made enmity between the Protestant nationalism that had emerged victorious from his wars and the Catholic and worker subcultures the most deeply felt of the new Germany's many political divisions.

But Bismarck's perpetuation of those enmities was more than the mere attempt to unify the Protestant Prussian in-group, the German-national majority culture, by the "negative integration" once decried by the social-historical *Sonderweg* school.[65] The absolutist executive's promotion of internecine hatred resulted above all from the structural impasse at the heart of "German constitutionalism" in the age of mass politics: the Reichstag's universal-suffrage electorate and budgetary veto perpetually threatened to thwart government policy, unless ministers could maintain and even exacerbate the German people's

commodity prices, rather than as an indicator or source of German peculiarity, see the theoretically astute perspective of Cornelius Torp, "Weltwirtschaft vor dem Weltkrieg: Die erste Welle ökonomischer Globalisierung vor 1914," HZ 297:3 (2004), especially 592–609, and his pioneering *Die Herausforderung der Globalisierung. Wirtschaft und Politik in Deutschland 1860–1914* (Göttingen, 2005), especially 365–70.

[64] Hermann Oncken, in Wehler, *The German Empire 1871–1918* (Leamington Spa, 1985), 24; Salisbury: Raymond J. Sontag, *Germany and England. Background of Conflict, 1848–1894* (New York, 1969), 218.

[65] See p. 3; Wolfgang Sauer, "Das Problem des deutschen Nationalstaates," in Wehler, ed., *Moderne deutsche Sozialgeschichte*, 430–31; Wehler, *German Empire*, 90–03; the nuanced treatment in DGG, 3:889–907 ignores the concept.

preexisting and future divisions.[66] The domination over a recalcitrant society that Liberal Italy's establishment ensured by exclusion, Imperial Germany secured primarily by fragmentation. In 1878–79 Bismarck consequently also splintered the Liberals, the vital component of his own post-1870 majority. After winding down the *Kulturkampf* he merrily allied himself with the Center whenever occasion offered. He deliberately wrecked his own coalition of "in-groups," the Conservative-National Liberal *Kartell* majority of 1887, in a vain effort to make himself forever indispensable to the new master, William II.[67] And the lack of responsibility for government that his constitution imposed upon the parties left them free to indulge their already strong traditions of ideological narrow-mindedness, while displaying reckless intransigence even upon the material issues with which he urged them to busy themselves.

The resulting system soon evolved in directions far different than those Bismarck sought, leaving him prone in moments of crisis to contemplate its overthrow by a *Staatstreich*, a monarchical-military coup d'état against the Reichstag and constitution that he had created. His splitting of the National Liberals over tariffs and anti-Socialist laws indeed completed the process of Liberal disintegration begun when he had stolen their nationalist cause in the 1860s. The Liberals' failure thereafter to make the leap from the politics of notables to machine-politics and effective competition with the mass parties was in part a result of a central element in north-German Protestant nationalist majority culture, often misleadingly described as apolitical, that deplored parties as a threat to the unity of the German *Volk*.[68] Yet for a time, closeness to the monarchical state and a growing commitment to *völkisch* notions that were also popular further right helped draw potential supporters and masked the Liberals' slow decline.[69]

Bismarck's persecution of the Socialists also helped make the SPD the disciplined and nominally Marxist party it became; the lapse of the anti-Socialist laws in 1890 and the gathering force of urbanization then permitted an explosion of the Socialist vote, from 10.1 percent in the 1887 Reichstag elections to 31.7. in 1903. Political Catholicism slowly shrank from 27.9 percent of the

---

[66] See the trenchant analysis of Hugo Preuss, architect of the Weimar constitution that involuntarily perpetuated Germany's lack of "identity between *Volk* and state": *Das deutsche Volk und die Politik* (Jena, 1915), 9–10, and especially 194–95.

[67] See John Röhl, "The Disintegration of the Kartell and the Politics of Bismarck's Fall from Power, 1887–90," HJ 9:1 (1966), 77–89.

[68] For introductions to the concept, see Fritz Stern, "The Political Consequences of the Unpolitical German," in his *The Failure of Illiberalism* (New York, 1972); Rudy Koshar, *Social Life, Local Politics and Nazism: Marburg 1880–1935* (Chapel Hill, NC, 1986), especially 6–7, 45–59; and Stanley Suval, *Electoral Politics in Wilhelmine Germany* (Chapel Hill, NC, 1985), 242–43.

[69] On liberal failure, see Sheehan, *German Liberalism in the Nineteenth Century* (Chicago, 1978), chs. 10–16 and Thomas Nipperdey, *Die Organisation der deutschen Parteien vor 1918* (Düsseldorf, 1961), chs. 3–4; on their increasingly *völkisch* inclinations, which offer additional support to the notion that German was indeed peculiar, see Eric Kurlander, "Nationalism, Ethnic Preoccupation, and the Decline of German Liberalism: A Silesian Case Study, 1898–1933," *The Historian* 65:1 (2002), 95–121.

vote in 1874, at the height of the *Kulturkampf*, to 16.4 percent in 1912. Urbanization gradually but unmistakably led some Catholic city-dwellers to vote in accordance with new surroundings rather than their old religion. The Conservatives profited from the embarrassment of laissez-faire liberals at the onset of the agricultural crisis; conservatism captured and thenceforth held East Elbia, a miniature German counterpart to the Italian South in its retarding effects on politics and the economy. The Conservative vote reached 25 percent of the national total in 1887, Bismarck's most successful election, then declined to the vicinity of 12 percent by 1912 (see Figure 2.8).[70]

Malapportionment and fragmentation meant that Reichstag seats did not fully reflect the movement of voters toward the SPD. That circumstance and the countervailing effect of the wealth-graded suffrage laws of Prussia and Saxony partially masked Socialist growth and delayed its full impact. The SPD suffered most, Conservatives and Center least, from the failure to redraw the electoral districts to match the massive population increase of the cities. The run-off system privileged the National Liberals and the Center, who could ally most easily with parties to their left or right in the second round of voting, and most damaged the SPD, which all "*bürgerlich*" parties held in fear and contempt; the SPD won few run-offs. Finally, the three-class franchise in Prussia and its similarly restrictive counterparts in Saxony and in some of the minor states gave the Conservatives, National Liberals, and Center unassailable regional bastions. The combined effect of malapportionment, political fragmentation, and regionalism were analogous to, although less severe than, the franchise restrictions that hobbled Italy's mass electorate until 1913. Although the German parties, despite *Kulturkampf* and anti-Socialist laws, learned from the beginning the rules of the electoral and parliamentary game rather than those of the *piazza*, the German system's stability nevertheless depended on the partial disenfranchisement of some Germans. That disenfranchisement, along with the Reichstag's relative powerlessness against chancellor and monarch, insulated Conservatives, liberals of all stripes, and even the Center from the full force of mass politics until 1918.

A further source of potential instability was the Reich's multifarious extra- and antiparliamentary interest groups and single-issue lobbies. Proverbially, three Germans together are a duly constituted association (*Verein*), and Germany was undeniably swift in developing an underbrush of *Vereine* and *Verbände* surpassing in luxuriance anything found in northern Italy, or even in France and Britain. The "Great Depression" of 1873–96, sometimes invoked despite its worldwide impact as explanation for the German peculiarities that ended in Hitler, undeniably helped launch the high-tariff crusaders of the Central Organization of German Industrialists (1876).[71] It likewise gave resonance

---

[70] Voting trends: Suval, *Electoral Politics in Wilhelmine Germany*; see also Gerhard A. Ritter and Merith Niehuss, *Wahlgeschichtliches Arbeitsbuch* (Munich, 1980) and Ritter's fine interpretive essay, *Die deutschen Parteien 1830–1914* (Göttingen, 1985).

[71] See p. 60 and Introduction, note 8.

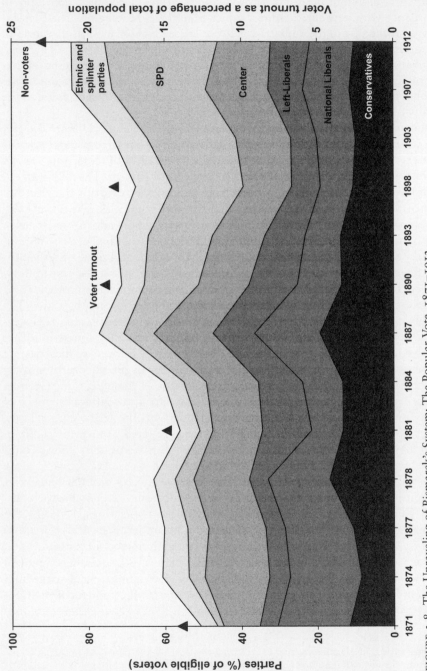

FIGURE 2.8. The Unraveling of Bismarck's System: The Popular Vote, 1871–1912.
Base data: SGAB, 2:173–75, 22–23.

to the propaganda of the Colonial League (1882/87) and of the rural anti-Semitic splinter parties that arose in the 1880s to consign modernity – Jews, bankers, industrialists, and city-dwellers – to perdition.

But other vitally important *Vereine* developed out of Germany's own histori-cal circumstances, or as a normal appurtenance of a complex society and polity. At least some of Germany's wildly popular veterans' groups – symptomatically dubbed *Kriegervereine*, "warrior leagues," and utterly without an Italian coun-terpart – dated as far back as the 1830s. The victories of Bismarck and Moltke and the workings of universal military service, not the 1873–96 "Great Depres-sion," made their national federation, the Kyffhäuser League, into Imperial Germany's mightiest mass organization, encompassing in 1913 some 2.8 mil-lion members, or better than one in every seven adult male Germans.[72] The cohesion of the Catholic and worker subcultures depended on Center Party and SPD, religion and Marxist ideology, but also on thick webs of associated or affiliated organizations that ranged from the Center Party's mighty *Volksverein für das Katholische Deutschland* with its more than 850,000 members by 1914 to humble local groups devoted to song and beer or to that most patriotic of sports, riflery.[73] Even the National Liberals, despite their character as a party of notables who claimed to represent the whole of society rather than narrow inter-ests, enjoyed the support of combative interest organizations of the new *Mittel-stand* such as the fervently nationalist German-National Shop Clerks' League (*Deutschnationaler Handlungsgehilfenverband*), with more than 120,000 mem-bers in 1911.

Yet the event that provoked the founding of Germany's most virulent extra-parliamentary organizations was political not economic: Bismarck's fall in 1890. Bismarck's departure roughly coincided with a slow rise in political par-ticipation driven largely by the expansion of the SPD and by the more or less successful efforts of the other parties to compete with the Socialist and Cen-ter mass organizations. Almost simultaneously, German industry outstripped agriculture's share of the national product (1889–90) and German steel pro-duction surpassed that of Britain (1893) – events that fostered a growing sense

---

[72] See Hansjoachim Henning, "Kriegervereine in den deutschen Westprovinzen," *Rheinische Vier-teljahrsblätter* 32 (1963), 430–58, on the genesis, social composition, and relative egalitarianism of these groups, at least in western Germany; Klaus Saul, "Der 'Deutsche Kriegerbund.' Zur innenpolitischen Funktion eines 'nationalen' Verbandes im kaiserlichen Deutschland," MGM 6 (1969), 95–130 (2,837,944 members, against the 2,483,661 members of the SPD trade unions); SGAB, 2:23 gives the male population twenty years old or older as 17,757,000 (1911); Dieter Düding, "Die Kriegervereine im Wilhelminischen Reich und ihrer Beitrag zur Militarisierung der deutsche Gesellschaft," in Jost Dülffer and Karl Holl, eds., *Bereit zum Krieg: Kreigsmentalität im wilhelminischen Deutschland 1890–1914* (Göttingen, 1986), 99–121; and Thomas Rohkrämer, *Der Militarismus der "kleinen Leute": die Kriegervereine im Deutschen Kaiserreich, 1871–1914* (Munich, 1990).

[73] For vivid description of the *Verein* network of one small town in a later period, see William Sheridan Allen, *The Nazi Seizure of Power. The Experience of a Single German Town, 1922–1945* (New York, rev. ed., 1984), 17–19.

that German industrial prowess both justified and made possible far-reaching power claims.

Under these circumstances, and given William II's eccentricities, Bismarck's departure left an ever more apparent leadership vacuum into which a variety of vociferous nationalist organizations sought to step. Of these, the most significant was the Pan-German League (*Alldeutsche Verband*, 1891–94), founded expressly to scourge the great man's pygmy successors. The Pan-Germans, often hastily dismissed as a marginal group with little influence on government, were in effect the distilled essence of the politically committed *Bildungsbürgertum*.[74] Their fluctuating membership peaked at more than 22,000 in 1901, declined abruptly when the League frontally attacked the Reich government, but then slowly rose again to 18,000 by the eve of war. They attracted, at various points in their prewar career, figures that ranged from savants such as Max Weber to the foremost National Liberal leaders, Ernst Bassermann and Gustav Stresemann. They also laid claim to the Austrian Germans whom their hero Bismarck had marooned amid the "ethnic chaos" of the Habsburg empire, and to the millions of ethnic Germans of southeastern and eastern Europe. Increasingly, as Austrian anti-Semitism and the nationality struggle between German and Czech intensified in the 1890s, some "Germans abroad" responded to that call, although Catholicism and the Habsburgs together reduced Austria's most extreme racist agitator, the covert neo-pagan Georg Ritter von Schönerer, to political impotence.[75]

The Pan-Germans' increasingly insistent claims to embody the national will deeply influenced all sectors of the national camp, from conservatives to liberals. The *Alldeutsche* and like-minded groups gave voice to an increasingly powerful radical nationalism, a fanaticism in the name of the overriding claims of *Volk* and race that increasingly undermined and attacked traditional authority, deriding government and emperor for their feebleness in defending the German *Volk*. The German Society for the Eastern Marches (*Deutsche Ostmarkenverein*, 1894) preached the forcible "Germanization" of Prussia's large Polish minority with a vehemence that put the German state's already harsh anti-Polish measures in the shade. The Navy League (*Flottenverein*, 1898) grew under Tirpitz's supervision into a true mass organization with more than 250,000 members and perhaps as many as 900,000, counting those in affiliated organizations. But it broke loose from tutelage in 1905–08, when its radical wing rounded savagely on government and navy for failing to drive forward forcefully enough the expansion of the fleet. The *Wehrverein* or Army League of 1912 laid siege to government and war ministry with ever-greater vehemence in defense of a "Germandom" allegedly threatened with annihilation, and in

---

[74] See especially Roger Chickering, *We Men Who Feel Most German: A Cultural Study of the Pan-German League, 1886–1914* (Boston, 1984), 114–15 and, in general, chs. 4–6; also Rainer Hering, *Konstruirte nation: Der Alldeutsche Verband 1890 bis 1939* (Hamburg, 2003), especially ch. III.2.

[75] See Pulzer, *Rise of Political Anti-Semitism*, chs. 17, 20.

support of the forced-pace expansion and modernization of the army without regard for social or international consequences.[76]

Even among the interest lobbies, Bismarck's departure occasioned a further radicalization with weighty implications. Bismarck's immediate successor, Chancellor Georg Leo von Caprivi, drew the logical conclusion from the triumph of industry over agriculture: Germany must either export goods, or men. He consequently lowered tariffs in the teeth of the last phase of the "Great Depression" and partially opened Germany's markets through bilateral treaties that secured reciprocity for German exports. Germany's agrarian interests reacted vehemently. Caprivi's treaties gave the *Junker* entrepreneurs of East Elbia who founded the Farmers' League (*Bund der Landwirte*, 1893) the chance to mobilize a peasant electorate that reached well into south Germany. The *Bund* deployed the armory of racist abuse and mass meetings of the anti-Semitic parties, but reached a far wider audience. It provoked emulation by the south German rural organizations of the Center Party. It gave the Conservatives the grass-roots organizational underpinning and the mass vote that braked their decline, while injecting new notes of violent radicalism into German politics.[77]

The future clearly belonged to the mass parties, above all the SPD. Logically enough, given the left-right polarization that mass politics had brought, all other parties except the Left-Liberals opposed electoral changes that might increase the SPD share of Reichstag seats. In other words, until 1918 the overwhelming majority of Germany's parliamentary elite firmly opposed further democratization of German politics. Nor did the *bürgerlich* parties show much enthusiasm for the essence of parliamentary government itself, the capture of the executive by parliament. Despite much later discussion of Germany's purported "silent parliamentarization" in the years before 1914, the system's principal characteristic was a growing potential for ungovernability.[78] The Kaiser held power by prerogative but was decreasingly able to exercise it. Chancellors after Bismarck, especially Bernhard von Bülow (1900–09) and Theobald von Bethmann Hollweg (1909–17), faced a Reichstag that the growth of the SPD and the mutual antagonisms of the other parties rendered less and less manageable. The parties gained and held their voters by incarnating or exploiting the many fissures within German society; their deliberate cultivation of the quarrels through which they prospered lamed their capacity for eventually exercising

---

[76] On the "*nationale Verbände*" and the new nationalism "from below," see above all Eley, *Reshaping the German Right. Radical Nationalism and Political Change after Bismarck* (New Haven, CT, 1980) and Chickering, "Der 'Deutsche Wehrverein' und die Reform der deutschen Armee 1912–1914," MGM 25 (1979), 7–33 ("Germanentum": 14).

[77] See Hans-Jürgen Puhle, *Agrarische Interessenpolitik und preussischer Konservatismus im wilhelminischen Reich (1893–1914)* (Hannover, 1966), ch. II.2, and Blackbourn, *Populists and Patricians* (London, 1987), ch. 8.

[78] See, against the claims of Rauh, *Parlamentarisierung des Deutschen Reiches*, the arguments of Dieter Langewiesche, "Das deutsche Kaiserreich – Bemerkungen zur Diskussion über Parlamentarisierung und Demokratisierung Deutschlands," AfS 19 (1980), 628–42.

power. Years of persecution, an officially Marxist posture, and the visceral hostility of all other parties and of the monarchical-military state debarred the greatest of the mass forces, the SPD, from sharing in government – although only figures on its left fringes such as Rosa Luxemburg shared the utopian enthusiasms of Italy's *massimalisti*. Nor could the Center, political arm of a religious minority, speak convincingly for Protestant Prussia-Germany. The Conservatives represented little more than East Elbia, some of the peasant clientele of the Farmers' League, sectors of the Prussian bureaucracy, and the officer corps. Liberals of all stripes indeed claimed to speak for the whole, but their lack of mass support gave that claim the lie. As the Reich steered into rising internal and external storms after 1905, extra-parliamentary attacks on the government for its alleged lack of national spirit gained an increasing audience within the dominant culture of north-German Protestantism. In the end, the stability of the Reich, like that of Liberal Italy, would depend on the ability of that culture to master belatedly the challenges of mass politics.

3. THE INSTRUMENTS OF WAR

Tirpitz's great navy failed utterly. By 1912 even its creator conceded that the High Seas Fleet would not foreseeably acquire the relative numerical strength needed to justify its existence by ensuring an "authentic chance of victory" over Britain in the North Sea. Italy's *Regia Marina* grew under the shadow of Lissa into a second-rank force focused vainly on battle with its ostensible Triple Alliance partner, Austria-Hungary. Neither the German Imperial Navy nor the Royal Italian Navy fit into anything resembling a national command structure or strategic concept. Neither Kaiser nor king of Italy nor chancellor nor prime minister could have created or operated such a structure, nor enunciated such a concept – for which the respective utopias of the naval officer corps, maritime world mastery and Adriatic domination, were no substitute. And above all, in terms of their political and social impact both before and after 1914, both navies were almost infinitely inferior to their senior services: armies that could mobilize millions of men.

The German army, the victor of 1870–71, inevitably led the way – in Europe and the world. The renewed and transformed Prusso-German military culture that emerged from Bismarck's wars, swiftly permeated the south German states, and powerfully influenced the nascent German navy had four salient and mutually reinforcing characteristics.[79] First, that culture was even more self-referential than that of most armies; direct subordination to the monarch,

---

[79] For the "military culture" of Imperial Germany, and much of what follows, see the ground-breaking work of Isabel V. Hull, *Absolute Destruction: Military Culture and the Practices of War in Imperial Germany* (Ithaca, NY, 2004), part II, and the summary in idem, "Military Culture, Wilhelm II, and the End of the Monarchy in World War I," in Annika Mombauer and Wilhelm Deist, eds., *The Kaiser* (Cambridge, 2003), 239–45; for the origins of Prussian tactical virtue and the cult of Selbstständigkeit, Knox, *Common Destiny*, 187–94, and Stephan

proven organizational effectiveness, and the charisma of victory largely insulated the officer corps from lay criticism after 1871. In accordance with Prussian tradition, internal discussion was remarkably free by the standards of other armies of the day. Yet debate meant above all tactical debate; even the exhaustive training of general staff adepts focused increasingly on problems at divisional level and below. Nor could the officer corps as a group question the primacy of the "German sword" in ensuring Germany's greatness and security – even if the great Moltke had concluded after 1871 that "the next war" would be a total war – a *Volkskrieg* – not merely between armies but between entire nations that might last for seven or even thirty years and be unwinnable by military means.[80] Worse still, the primacy of battle meant battle against Prussia-Germany's immediate continental neighbors: this was a military establishment scarcely suited by worldview and logistical-strategic education to seizing and exercising the world domination that officer corps and *Bildungsbürgertum* viewed as Prussia-Germany's right.

Second, the army's authentic virtues at the tactical level of warfare determined its responses to virtually every question it confronted. The Prussian cult of initiative demanded of the individual a rare combination of qualities: a controlled and rational amalgam of boldness, will to victory, and murderous implacability: "*Kühnheit*" – "*Siegeswille*" – "*Vernichtungswille*." The officers of the Prussian and federal armies, bound by a code of honor that mandated short-range pistol duels that killed up to a third of those engaged, were in any event predisposed by upbringing and training to view caution as cowardice.[81] Their model was the tactical "wholehearted decision [*ganzer Entschluss*]," but scaled up to embrace operations, strategy, and life. Wagering one's existence – or that of the nation – on the steadiness of the individual trigger-finger or on an entire society's throw of the "iron dice" of war was so self-evidently the preferred course of action that Prusso-German officers almost invariably derided as feeble even the few alternatives their blinkered vision did perceive.[82]

The third fundamental characteristic of the mental world of the Prusso-German "first *Stand*" was a totalizing notion of war as a merciless limitless

---

Leistenschneider, *Auftragstaktik im preussisch-deutschen Heer 1871 bis 1914* (Hamburg, 2002), chs. 2–4.

[80] Dennis E. Showalter, "Goltz and Bernhardi: The Institutionalization of Originality in the Imperial German Army," *Defense Analysis* 3 (1987), 305–18; Antulio J. Echevarria II, "A Crisis in Warfighting: German Tactical Discussions in the Late Nineteenth Century," MGM 55 (1996), 52–68; Moltke on future war (1890): Stig Förster, "Der Deutsche Generalstab und die Illusion des kurzen Krieges, 1871–1914: Metakritik eines Mythos," MGM 54 (1995), 66.

[81] For the character and salience of army duelling, Frevert, *Ehrenmänner*, ch. 4 and 270 (also note 34 in this chapter); both Frevert and McAleer, *Dueling*, 84, recognize the central role of the "first *Stand*" in making duelling, and especially the lethal pistol duel, the norm throughout the German upper classes, but persist in trying to force-fit German duelling into class categories – "bourgeois" or aristocratic – that fail to do justice to the autonomous role, in this and other respects, of the officer corps as a state-created professional *Stand*.

[82] "Ganzer Entschluss": Hull, "Military Culture" (citing Groener's praise of Schlieffen's style), 243.

struggle for national existence, derived from the Napoleonic experience and from the encounter with France in 1870–71, and reinforced by misunderstood Darwinism. That Bismarck had by preference sought decision by more subtle and controllable methods than battle – "Many paths led to my goal. I had to try all of them...the most dangerous at the end" – completely escaped those who had executed his strategy with striking tactical élan.[83] Clausewitz's evident enthusiasm for war's "absolute perfection" as the total struggle practiced by the French revolutionaries and Napoleon inspired the learned Prusso-German soldiers of later decades. Yet the later Clausewitz's analytical distinction between the "complete, untrammeled, absolute manifestation of violence" inherent in his philosophical ideal-type or "pure concept" of war, and the effects of chance, friction, politics, and perhaps even moral misgivings that constrained "real war," wholly eluded his successors.[84] Under their stewardship, Clausewitz's ruling concept of battlefield annihilation ("*Vernichtung*") of enemy forces as the "first-born son of war" mutated into something infinitely more sinister. The army's attitude toward enemy civilians, in particular, hardened radically in 1870–71. In the face of French partisan attacks against its supply columns and trains, the army had used civilians as human shields, had seized and executed hostages, had shot both males and occasionally women deemed hostile, and had ruthlessly destroyed houses and farms. Postwar reflection further hardened German doctrine on the treatment of partisans ("*franc-tireurs*"), uncooperative enemy civilians, and civilian property. Irregular armed resistance in any form was "war-rebellion [*Kriegsrebellion*]." Deception of army units or supplying information to enemy forces was "war-betrayal [*Kriegsverrat*]." The punishment for both was death.[85]

In the new century the general staff gloatingly celebrated, in its official history of Germany's 1904–06 war against native insurrection in Southwest Africa, the army's "ruthless energy" in seeking the "annihilation [*Vernichtung*] of the Herero *Volk*" – a proud public tribute to genocide that suggests the extremist dynamism of the army's belief system.[86] Negotiation even with a beaten enemy was unacceptable because it would represent a success that was less than total, an outcome that mortally threatened the army's institutional prestige, essence, and role in life. Instead, the German army came to prefer *Vernichtung* in a

---

[83] Quoted in Pflanze, *Bismarck*, 1:91.

[84] Clausewitz, *On War*, 591–93 (book VIII, ch. 3); 87 and 119, and 76, 77, 78, 119 (Book I, ch. 1, sections 23, 3, 6, and ch. 7); on the "two Clausewitzes," see especially Beatrice Heuser, *Reading Clausewitz* (London, 2002), ch. 2; for later German army misreadings, ibid., 105–07.

[85] For regulations and practice in 1870–71, see Mark R. Stoneman, "The Bavarian Army and French Civilians in the War of 1870–1871: A Cultural Interpretation," *War in History* 8:3 (2001), 271–93; for later developments, Grosser Generalstab, *Kriegsbrauch im Landkriege* (Berlin, 1902), 50–52, and Hull, *Absolute Destruction*, 119–30.

[86] Grosser Generalstab, *Die Kämpfe der deutschen Truppen in Südwestafrika*, 3 vols. (Berlin, 1906–07), 1:207; for context and brilliant analysis, Hull, *Absolute Destruction*, part 1, and "Military Culture and the Production of 'Final Solutions' in the Colonies: The Example of Wilhelminian Germany," in Robert Gellately and Ben Kiernan eds., *The Specter of Genocide: Mass Murder in Historical Perspective* (Cambridge, 2003), 141–62.

literal sense, if as yet only in the colonies: "Within the German border every male Herero, armed or unarmed, ... will be shot to death." The army pursued the survivors of battle to their deaths in the waterless wastes of the Omaheke desert, and imprisoned the few remaining Hereros on German territory in lethal concentration camps. The outcome – a mere 15,000 mostly female survivors from an ethnic group that had originally numbered more than 80,000 – was not wholly exceptional by contemporary Belgian or French standards, and was dwarfed by a contemporaneous although less publicized German scorched-earth campaign in East Africa that cost up to 300,000 native lives. But the German army's peculiar pride in mass murder was abnormal even in the annals of European colonialism, as was the related and virtually total absence of civilian restraint on the army's actions.[87]

Fourth, these tendencies both nourished and fed upon a radical and potentially totalitarian notion of "military necessity" that trampled on moral and legal restraints and soon came to ignore or deride political considerations.[88] Emperor William II, who had succeeded to the throne in 1888, was in some respects more moderate than his entourage and officer corps. Yet he passionately reflected their deepest convictions in his private dismissal ("[I] shit on all their resolutions") of the 1899 Hague Conference aimed at limiting the savagery of war. His famously impolitic 1900 exhortation to his troops to emulate "the Huns under their king Attila" – yet another echo of the *Nibelungenlied* – and take no prisoners was likewise in line with his army's values. The general staff's 1902 manual on the "usages of land warfare" that guided the German army in the war of 1914–18 was almost equally explicit in its scorn of "humanitarian attitudes that frequently degenerate into sentimentality and pathetic emotion-mongering [*weichlicher Gefühlsschwärmerei*] ... in complete contradiction *to the nature and ultimate purpose of war*."[89]

The resultant of these forces was a cultural dynamic that consistently – long after Imperial Germany's resulting demise in 1914–18 – inspired German decision-makers, both military and civilian, to regard enemy civilians and

---

[87] Quotation: Generalleutnant von Trotha's proclamation to the Hereros, 2 October 1904, in Hull, "'Final Solutions' in the Colonies," 155; East Africa: ibid., 155–57, and Detlef Bald, "Afrikanischer Kampf gegen koloniale Herrschaft. Der Maji-Maji-Aufstand in Ostafrika," MGM 19 (1976), 23–50. As Hull suggests ("Final Solutions," 141–44), German army culture and practice is the crucial link, left uncommonly vague by Hannah Arendt in her *Origins of Totalitarianism*, between European colonialism and the most salient example of modern European genocide.

[88] For an early manifestation, see the celebration of "military realism" and of the sovereignty of "military necessity" in Julius von Hartmann, "Militärische Notwendigkeit und Humanität: Ein kritischer Versuch," *Deutsche Rundschau*, 13–14 (1877–78), 13:111–28, 14:71–91, especially 13:120–21 and 14:89–91, and, in general, Messerschmidt, "Völkerrecht und 'Kriegsnotwendigkeit' in der deutschen militärischen Tradition seit den Einigungskriegen," GSR 6 (1983), 237–43.

[89] For the *"Hunnenrede,"* to troops embarking to help suppress the Boxer Rebellion, Hull, *Absolute Destruction*, 135; Hague conference marginal note: Johannes Lepsius, Albrecht Mendelssohn Bartholdy, and Friedrich Thimme, eds., *Die grosse Politik der europäischen Kabinette, 1871–1914*, 40 vols. (Berlin, 1922–27), 15:306; and Grosser Generalstab, *Kriegsbrauch im Landkriege*, 3 (my emphasis).

property as wholly and unconditionally subject to "military necessity," to escalate implacably in the face of failure, and to select or accept the most extreme or high-risk course from any given set of options. Phrases such as "all or nothing" and "victory or *Untergang*" were not slogans, but a central strand of the intellectual DNA of the Prusso-German elites. In the language of baccarat used by all concerned, civilians included, Germany's habitual play was "*va-banque.*" The resulting dynamic was nowhere more in evidence than in German military planning from the 1890s onward.

The elder Moltke's assessment that the adoption of universal-service armies and modern communications and weapons by Russia as well as France nullified Germany's chances of a victory as swift and total as in 1871 was flatly unacceptable to his successors and to the officer corps as a whole.[90] The result, during the 1891–1905 tenure of Count Alfred von Schlieffen as chief of the Great General Staff, was an ever more desperate search for expedients that might offer the decisive victory that the belief system of the officer corps demanded. Institutional wisdom dictated that only a *ganzer Entschluss* could save Germany. Innumerable map exercises and staff rides fortified Schlieffen in that predetermined conclusion. Attack was the sole option; all-out offensive alone promised the swift decisions of 1866 and 1871. And only in the western theater did terrain, rail network, and surfaced roads offer the prospect of decision – if the overwhelming majority of German forces could crush France before the Russians reached Berlin.

Schlieffen, faced with a progressive increase in unit firepower and army size from the 1890s onward, framed his western offensive by simply scaling up the one tactical technique that seemed to answer the escalating lethality of the frontal assault and the difficulty of finding open flanks at the tactical level: envelopment.[91] His later fascination with Hannibal's devastating double envelopment of a Roman army at Cannae in 216 B.C.E., the "perfect battle of annihilation" to which he devoted a series of essays during his retirement, was not coincidental.[92] His final concept for a German war for continental hegemony, solemnly bequeathed in February 1906 to his successor, a nephew of the great Moltke, famously proposed to envelop and crush the French army in one gigantic battle. A great wheeling right wing deploying two-thirds of the entire German

---

[90] See Stig Förster, "Illusion des kurzen Krieges," especially 79–80.

[91] The suggestion that Schlieffen simply scaled up one particular tactical remedy – envelopment – into the wholly different realms of operations and strategy derives in large part from Shimon Naveh, *In Pursuit of Military Excellence: The Evolution of Operational Theory* (London, 1997), especially 92–95 – but see Schlieffen's own insistence, with particular regard to encirclement, on the virtual identity of tactics and strategy: Robert T. Foley, "Preparing the German Army for the First World War: The Operational Ideas of Alfred von Schlieffen and Helmuth von Moltke the Younger," *War and Society* 22:2 (2004), 15. I owe a heavy debt to Gil-li Vardi for long and fruitful discussions about the existence, or non-existence, of German operational thought.

[92] For persuasive analysis of the indirect relationship between Schlieffen's war planning and his Cannae studies, see Terence M. Holmes, "Classical Blitzkrieg: The Untimely Modernity of Schlieffen's Cannae Programme," *Journal of Military History* 67:3 (2003), 745–72.

field army would crash through the low countries and trap the French against the south German border. That invading Belgium and the Netherlands would infallibly convert a two-front continental war into global conflict scarcely troubled Schlieffen: British sea-power with its dwarf-army could scarcely thwart the army's victory.[93]

The younger Moltke introduced into Schlieffen's "legacy of the secret of victory in a three-front war" some limited flexibility, reinforcing the German left wing in Lorraine for a possible breakthrough counteroffensive once the expected French attack there failed.[94] Moltke also chose to leave Holland uninvaded, as an economic "wind-pipe" for Germany – a change to Schlieffen's grand design that betrayed both uneasiness about the war's duration and fatal underestimation of British ruthlessness in the face of German aggression.[95] But in other more vital respects, Moltke multiplied the plan's already astounding risks. His decision to skirt Dutch territory so narrowed his attack corridor that the possession – intact – of the vital Belgian rail junctions at Liège became a precondition for the plan's unfolding. Moltke's response was to add a hair-trigger, with the help of his fanatical (and ostentatiously non-noble) chief of mobilization planning, Erich Ludendorff: German forces would seize Luxembourg and Liège by surprise attack upon the outbreak of war. In 1913, Moltke also broke precedent dangerously by declining to update the deployment plan for an offensive against Russia that offered the sole alternative to Schlieffen's concept: the limitless eastern spaces appeared to rule out swift decision. In both cases the general staff planned in deepest secrecy, without consulting Kaiser, chancellor, or other Reich or even army authorities. Nor did the sketchy information the political leaders received about the great plan cause them to question

---

[93] Acrimonious dispute over the existence and nature of Schlieffen's "plan" and its relevance to the German attack on Belgium and France has on balance confirmed the traditional view of the plan's existence, inflexibility, radicalism, and execution in 1914. See on the one hand the arguments of Terence Zuber, "The Schlieffen Plan Reconsidered," WIH 6:3 (1999), 262–305; "Terence Holmes Reinvents the Schlieffen Plan," ibid. 8:4 (2001), 468–76; *Inventing the Schlieffen Plan: German War Planning 1871–1914* (Oxford, 2002); "Terence Holmes Reinvents the Schlieffen Plan – Again," ibid. (2003) 10:1, 92–101; "The Schlieffen Plan Was an Orphan," ibid. 11:2 (2004), 220–25; and Hew Strachan, *The First World War*, vol. I, *To Arms* (Oxford, 2001), 165 note 4, 166, 169; and on the other those of Holmes, "The Reluctant March on Paris: A Reply to Terence Zuber's 'The Schlieffen Plan Reconsidered,'" WIH 8:2 (2001), 208–32; "The Real Thing: A Reply to Terence Zuber's 'Terence Holmes Reinvents the Schlieffen Plan,'" ibid. 9:1 (2002), 111–20; "Asking Schlieffen: A Further Reply to Terence Zuber," ibid. 10:4 (2003), 491–92; Foley, "The Origins of the Schlieffen Plan," ibid. 10:2 (2003), 222–32; and the trenchant and persuasive contribution of Mombauer, "Of War Plans and War Guilt: The Debate Surrounding the Schlieffen Plan," JSS 28:5 (2005), 857–85.

[94] Quotation: General Wilhelm Groener (1920), in Jehuda Wallach, *Das Dogma der Vernichtungsschlacht. Die Lehren von Clausewitz und Schlieffen und ihre Wirkungen in zwei Weltkriegen* (Munich, 1970), 107.

[95] For Moltke's schizophrenic attitude toward a general war's likely duration, see Stig Förster, "Illusion des kurzen Krieges," 83–90, 93, and Mombauer, *Helmuth von Moltke and the Origins of the First World War* (Cambridge, 2001), 211, 285, 287–88; for British planning, Avner Offer, *The First World War: An Agrarian Interpretation* (Oxford, 1989), 270–99.

the overall necessity of violating Belgian neutrality and thus fighting Britain as well as France and Russia. The absence of overall strategic coordination, which the Kaiser failed to provide, not least because his subordinates did not trust him with the necessary top secret information, meant that the general staff's essentially tactical warplan failed to mesh either with what passed for naval planning, or with the sketchy to non-existent long-war preparations of the war ministry and the civilian authorities.[96]

If – when – Germany went to war, its sole remaining option after 1913 was a supreme "*ganzer Entschluss*": lightning surprise attack in the West – and global war – even before international tension reached breaking point. The slightest delay in seizing Liège might otherwise hobble the right wing's deployment, with catastrophic results. Nor did the general staff's radicalism end there. To raise the numbers their warplan increasingly required, Moltke, prodded by Ludendorff, besieged the Prussian war ministry, demanding the enlargement of the officer corps and the additional units that the plan required. *Military necessity* threatened – not for the last time – to tear down even the cherished social barriers that delimited Prussia-Germany's "first *Stand*."[97]

Italy's *Regio Esercito Italiano* travelled a different road after its foundation in 1861. The supreme humiliation of June 1866 at Custoza struck an army disorganized by the rapid expansion of the early 1860s and sorely tried by its demoralizing counterinsurgency commitment in the South. The navy's débâcle at Lissa the following month compounded the blow to national and military confidence and prestige.[98] The army officer corps remained for several decades starkly divided on regional lines between Piedmontese traditionalists, grudgingly admitted officers from central Italy and the former Bourbon army, and Garibaldi's unwelcome volunteers. The retention of Piedmont's tradition of commissioning long-service NCOs for their presumed political reliability scarcely enhanced either the army's social cachet or the homogeneity and mutual confidence of its officers. The jealousies and petty hatreds of branch and specialty common to all armies appear to have been particularly divisive, with the added peculiarity that the "muddy-boots" infantry enjoyed a pariah status inversely related its battlefield centrality.[99]

The outcome of this unfortunate if hardly coincidental conjunction of military disaster and organizational dysfunction was the exact converse of the social magic that Prussia's long-standing traditions and mid-century victories had wrought. Not until the indecisive victories of the Libyan War of 1911–12 that served as prelude to twenty years of unexpected but predictable Arab

---

[96] See particularly the pioneering work of Lothar Burchardt, *Friedenswirtschaft und Kriegsvorsorge. Deutschlands wirtschaftliche Rüstungsbestrebungen vor 1914* (Boppard, 1968).

[97] See Berghahn and Deist, eds., *Rüstung im Zeichen der wilhelminischen Weltpolitik*, ch. 9.

[98] Mondini, "Guerra, nazione e disillusione. Custoza e l'antimito dell'Italia imbelle," in *L'Italia chiamò: memoria militare e civile di una regione* (Sommacampagna, 2003), 63–80.

[99] "Scarponi" as pariahs: Banti and Mondini, "Da Novara a Custoza: culture militari e discorso nazionale tra Risorgimento e Unità," in ESI, *Annali*, vol. 18, *Guerra e pace*, 443; cleavages within the officer corps: Mondini, *Veneto in armi*, 95–97.

insurgency did the *Regio Esercito* begin to enjoy even the conditional approbation of Italy's elites.[100] Behind the officer corps whose leaders Giolitti had
described in 1914–15 with somber contempt stood only masses of ill-treated
and largely if decreasingly illiterate peasants, subject to universal service only
from the 1870s, in sharp contrast to the long military apprenticeship of Prussian society before and after 1814. Italy's conscripts were also frequently at
odds both with their comrades and their surroundings – for fear of regional
revolt dictated throughout most of the *Regio Esercito*'s existence the recruitment of each regiment or brigade from several widely separated regions, its
stationing in yet another, and its perpetual rotation from garrison to garrison,
again in sharp contrast to the German army's stable local recruitment.[101] Nor
did Italy's officer corps and political class appreciate the necessity, much less
accept the expense, of the large, expert, and comparatively youthful combat-
arms NCO corps that gave the German army so much of its company-level
fighting power. Tentative *Regio Esercito* efforts to replicate the German twelve-
year-NCO failed; the civil administration simply ignored the law requiring it
to set aside posts for ex-sergeants.[102] Attempts to create reserve officer "demigods" on the Prusso-German pattern likewise fell short miserably, amid general
indifference. Italy's middle classes saw one-year service exclusively as an escape
from the full rigors of conscription; in the decade after 1900 barely 3 percent
of those who happily accepted that class privilege chose to become reserve officers of the *Regio Esercito*, compared to the roughly one-fifth of Germany's
one-year volunteers who ultimately received their long-coveted commissions
after a gruelling apprenticeship.[103]

The organizational culture of an army so constituted and recruited was likely
to be largely incapable of reform without catastrophic external shock. Prussia's
victory over Austria in 1866 had saved Italy from further disasters after Custoza. Yet neither the humiliations of 1866 nor the even deeper scar of Adowa
produced – or could produce – anything like the revolutionary effects of 1806–
07 in Prussia. Professional creativity and the ability to learn from experience
remained both rare and deeply suspect; in the words of a preeminent student
of the *Regio Esercito*'s career, Italian military memoirs give "the impression
that initiative and the proclivity to observe and emulate [other armies] indeed

[100] See the telling example of the border region of Venetia: Mondini, *Veneto in armi*, ch. 3.
[101] See Rochat, "Strutture dell'esercito dell'Italia liberale: i reggimenti di fanteria e bersaglieri,"
and Bertinaria, "Lo stanziamento dell'esercito italiano," in *Esercito e città*, 1:21–60, 5–19.
[102] John Gooch, *Army, State and Society in Italy, 1870–1915* (New York, 1989), 103.
[103] Italy: Giorgio Rochat and Giulio Massobrio, *Breve storia dell'esercito italiano dal 1861 al
1943* (Turin, 1968), 88–89: only 622 – 3.26 percent – of Italy's 19,034 one-year volunteers
between 1900 and 1910 received commissions; the others "either were incapable of passing
the necessary examination or preferred to leave active duty as NCOs or privates, in the expectation that they would thus run fewer risks in the event of war." Germany: tables in John,
Das Reserveoffizierkorps, 148, 155, 264–66; my estimate that roughly a fifth of all one-year
volunteers received commissions rests on John's figure of 18.3 percent for Bavaria in 1906; the
other federal armies appear to have been slightly less selective.

existed [in the Italian army], but as forces striving against the current and almost constituting breaches of discipline," even when displayed by senior officers.[104]

The creation in 1867–74 of a *Scuola di guerra* to train staff officers, and of a general staff in 1881–82, further divided an already fractured officer corps, but failed to concentrate the army's limited collective intellect on effective preparation for war. Nor did the chief of the general staff or the army as a whole enjoy the organizational sovereignty of their German counterparts. The chief of staff remained at least formally subordinate to Italy's minister of war, and – more destructively – not necessarily designated as field commander in the event of war.[105] The minister of war in turn was a subordinate member of the government; he might even, as briefly in 1907–09, be a civilian – an outcome unthinkable in Prussia-Germany.

The army's extensive responsibilities for controlling civilian unrest debilitated and demoralized its cadres, whereas the German army, despite possession of draconian martial law powers entirely free from civilian oversight, appears to have killed a grand total of two civilians between the 1880s and 1914.[106] Above all, the stultifying routine of the *Regio Esercito*'s barracks, offices, fortresses, and drill-grounds swiftly deflated even the most inquiring and professionally ambitious young officers. Tactical training consisted largely of drill, and the officer corps viewed the ability to "utter the word of command and to get good results in a series of complicated close-order movements" as definitive proof of leadership skill.[107] Battlefield initiative, when it existed, tended in the absence of doctrine, training, and brainpower to produce disasters such as Adowa, where ragged, dispersed, ill-supplied Italian columns, outnumbered by more than five to one and equipped with obsolete rifles, proceeded independently without maps over unfamiliar terrain until encircled and virtually exterminated by the Ethiopians.[108] As for the elite "learned arms" of artillery and engineers, they adjusted grudgingly to the accelerating technological changes that transformed

---

[104] Ceva, "Riflessioni e notizie sui sottufficiali," 347–48; also the works cited in note 107.

[105] The best account of the extraordinary – and in part deliberate – confusion surrounding the chief of staff's role and powers is Ceva, "Comando militare e monarchia costituzionale italiana (1848–1918)," in idem, *Teatri di guerra* (Milan, 2005), 54–62.

[106] Ernst-Heinrich Schmidt, *Heimatheer und Revolution 1918. Die militärischen Gewalten im Heimatgebiet zwischen Oktoberreform und Novemberrevolution* (Stuttgart, 1981), 258–59, note 631: on only nine occasions from the 1880s to 1914 did troops intervene to support the police; see also Anja Johansen, "Policing and Repression: Military Involvement in the Policing of French and German Industrial Areas, 1889–1914," *European History Quarterly* 34:1 (2004), 73.

[107] See the depressing tale of Eugenio De Rossi, *La vita di un ufficiale italiano sino alla guerra* (Milan, 1927), and for a stunning exemplar of the army's dominant mentality, Emilio De Bono, *Nell'esercito nostro prima della guerra* (Milan, 1931) (quotation, 321); also the analysis of Mondini, *Veneto in armi*, 95–116, and of Paolo Langella, "Cultura e vita dell'ufficiale italiano (1878–1911)," in *Esercito e città*, 1:201–18.

[108] Italian casualties were approximately 50 percent of the force of roughly 15,000 men committed, but exact numbers are unknown because the Italian commands failed to maintain unit rosters. For the mentalities and policies that produced the débâcle, see particularly Labanca, *Adua*, (logistics, rifles, casualties, and rosters, 327–41, 359, 379); the most compelling narratives

warfare from the 1870s to 1914–15. But at no time before 1915 – or indeed before 1945 – did the Italian army eagerly embrace machines.[109]

Under these circumstances, the general staff neither filled the army's doctrinal vacuum, nor provided warplans that offered guidance on what was to follow mobilization and deployment against one of united Italy's twin adversaries, France and Austria-Hungary.[110] Italy's tradition of defeat, and its weakness in mobilizable forces, logistical infrastructure, and industry inclined Italian planners before 1914–15 toward defensive deployments, with the exception of a hare-brained but persistent scheme to deploy an army on the extreme left of the German front in a war against France.[111] The chief of general staff's lack of organizational independence and of assured command in the event of war likewise inhibited forward planning.[112] This was an army for which the drumbeat of military necessity beat weakly indeed; its conspicuous political weakness, relative battlefield ineffectiveness, divided leadership, and lack of unit-level cohesion limited its impact both on Italian society and on Italy's adversaries.

4. THE NATIONAL MYTHS

The myths that defined the two new nations and might serve to fortify charismatic national leadership were profoundly different. Equally contrasting was the extent to which those myths had the power to move masses.

I. Italy: "The Necessity of Violence"

Italy's national mythology was notably less compelling and pervasive than its German counterpart. In part that deficit was a reflection of the already described unsuitability for nationalist purposes of the myths of Rome. Yet it also reflected Italy's lag in spreading the blessings of literacy and universal military service to the masses. The weaknesses of Italy's national myths derived as well from the culture's inborn skepticism toward secular authority, and from the strength of Italy's mutually antagonistic ideological subcultures, Catholicism and socialism. The national myths that did prosper inevitably were the

---

remain Roberto Battaglia, *La prima guerra d'Africa* (Turin, 1958) and Angelo Del Boca, *Gli italiani in Africa orientale*, vol. 1, *Dall'unità alla marcia su Roma* (Bari, 1976).

[109] For the 1918–45 period, see particularly Knox, *Hitler's Italian Allies* (Cambridge, 2000), ch. 3, and Antonio Sema, "La cultura dell'esercito," in Gabriele Turi et al., *Cultura e società negli anni del fascismo* (Milan, 1987), 91–116.

[110] For the vacuum, see Gooch, "Clausewitz Disregarded: Italian Military Thought and Doctrine, 1815–1943," in Michael I. Handel, ed., *Clausewitz and Modern Strategy* (London, 1986), 309–10.

[111] Gooch, *Army, State and Society*, 48–49, 125–26, 149–55.

[112] Gooch, *Army, State and Society*, 132, 150–51; Fortunato Minniti, "Perché l'Italia non ha avuto un piano Schlieffen," in Società italiana di Storia Militare, *Quaderno 1999* (Naples, 2003), 5–29.

product of thin strata of lay political leaders and intellectuals, of an *intelligentsia* defined – like those of eastern Europe – largely by possession of the written word.

That *intelligentsia* sought to integrate the masses into the nation while preserving its own leading role; like their *Bildungsbürger* counterparts, Italian Liberals looked on with horror as democratic mass politics emerged in the 1890s. Indeed the very notion of "political myth" was in part a product of that emergence, and of their tenacious resistance against it. The economist and sociologist Gaetano Mosca had explained in the 1880s that politics was no more than rule by elites who cloaked their power with convenient ideologies, described with a detachment bordering on sarcasm as "political formulas." Mosca remained a Sicilian right-Liberal who looked to the state bureaucracy, unelected and uncontaminated by the masses, to save liberal values in the emerging era of mob rule. But against the background of the Europe-wide reaction against positivism and the upsurge of mass parties after 1890, less liberal theorists such as Gustave Le Bon, Georges Sorel, and Vilfredo Pareto turned Mosca's disenchanted insight to use. They proclaimed the sovereignty of emotion. For Le Bon, the "feminine" crowd of the age of universal suffrage and mass half-education thirsted not for freedom, but for bondage to mighty leaders, political formulas made flesh. For Sorel, not Marx's fallacious analysis of capitalist economics but his apocalyptic myth of world redemption through savagery moved the revolutionary masses. Pareto, while violently debunking socialist mythology, emphasized the power of myth to inspire politically useful emotions. These notions, which either originated in Italy or swiftly crossed the Alps from Paris, served as welcome inspirations for the political formulas of the generation whose formative experience was humiliation at Adowa.[113]

The most pervasive of united Italy's myths were two, well established by 1890: that the new Italy was incomplete (a claim with drastic consequences) and that it must be – if not the epochal and universal "Third Rome" of Mazzini's fevered imagination – at least an honored and feared European great power. The *moderati* had been fully conscious of Italy's backwardness and fragility. They had tended to reject attempts to harness the policies of the new Italian state to the literary cult of Roman antiquity, and inclined instead to a common-sense belief in gradual national progress back toward socioeconomic parity with northern Europe. Yet in the long run their successors could not escape the national duty to claim Trento and Trieste. And their aspiration to raise the "least of the great powers" to nominal equality with the greatest had made demands almost as far beyond Italy's resources as the ambition to become the

---

[113] It is worth noting that Sorel's long association with Pareto dated from 1897, and that Le Bon – whose *Psychologie des foules* (1895) Sigmund Freud later described as "justly famous" – built on work by Scipio Sighele, professor at the University of Pisa and later prominent among the *nazionalisti* (Freud: Zeev Sternhell, *La droite révolutionnaire. Les origines du fascisme français, 1885–1914* [Paris, 1978], 148–49, note 3).

"Third Rome." It had also left them open to attack when events disconfirmed the new Italy's great-power status.

Their rival Mazzini, who with the help of the equally eccentric Gioberti had created the unitary faith that had imposed on Piedmont-Italy the dubious present of the South, had hastened to explain why united Italy had seemingly turned out badly. Diplomatic subterfuge, foreign arms, and royal Piedmontese annexation had made the new Italy. It had claimed Rome as its capital but lacked a Roman idea. Above all, the people "had been absent." The national revolution was unfinished. Territorially unfinished, through the omission of Trento, Trieste, and Nice. Unfinished in its wider mission as cultural-political beacon for Europe and – an addition of the late Mazzini – as civilizing force across *"mare nostrum"* in North Africa.[114] Above all, the revolution was unfinished in its paramount task of national integration.

In that task, the "making Italians" of which Cavour's colleague and rival, Massimo d'Azeglio, had almost despaired, only one shortcut was visible: war.[115] Bismarck's last war had apparently won south Germany for Prussia in 1870–71. The Italian elites, mortally stung by Custoza and Lissa, had thereafter been hypnotized by the prospect of creating national unity – erasing disgrace, and giving the new Italy the status of great power to which it laid claim – through warfare. The *moderati* themselves had not been immune, although with them the myth of violent national integration took on a cautious and conservative cast. "Italy will never be truly welded together, the prestige of authority will never be founded on bases of impregnable solidity, except through a great war against France," one prominent Savoyard diplomat had noted – in elegant French – shortly after the Franco-Prussian war. Pasquale Turiello, a pioneer in the analysis of the South's backwardness, had written in the early 1880s of the need for "a great and renewed virile resurgence, a second trial of arms and blood" to give Italy the vigor and unity hitherto lacking. Those further leftward showed equal lack of restraint, even in the cause of Italy's great-power status. Felice Cavallotti, orator-in-chief of the parliamentary *estrema* until a conservative editor skewered him in a duel in 1898, had exhorted his fellow deputies to keep in mind that only a "bloody baptism" could give Italy its due position among nations.[116]

Alfredo Oriani, an eccentric recluse of the Romagna who wrote from the 1870s until his death in 1909, offered the most influential fusion of Mazzini's

---

[114] Mazzini on Africa: "Politica internazionale" (1871), quoted in the marvelous work of Federico Chabod, *Storia della politica estera italiana dal 1870 al 1896*, vol. I, *Le Premesse* (Bari, pbk. ed., 1971), 1:328.

[115] "Having made Italy, we must [now] make Italians": the most famous invented quotation in Italian history. For what d'Azeglio actually wrote, Banti, *Nazione*, 203, and Simonetta Soldani and Gabriele Turi, eds., *Fare gli italiani. Scuola e cultura nell'Italia contemporanea*, 2 vols. (Bologna, 1993), 1:17.

[116] Edoardo De Launay, Italian minister in Berlin, quoted approvingly in Chabod, *Politica estera italiana*, 1:33; Turiello and Cavallotti: ibid., 1:31.

myth of failed revolution with that of Italy's unfulfilled great-power destiny. In Oriani's *Risorgimento*, product of "the heroic tyranny of a minority," the masses "had remained inert." Battles had been few, and "almost always decided by the preponderance of [our] allies." After 1866, under the baneful levelling influence of industrialism, "the martyrs had turned into clerks." But a new "idealist revolt" and a new elite was coming to sweep away Liberal Italy, and perhaps even the unworthy house of Savoy. That coming national revolution that Mazzini had not lived to see was inextricably bound up with war:

> War is an inevitable form of the struggle for existence, and blood will always be the best warm rain for great ideas.... The future of Italy lies entirely in a war which, while giving it its natural boundaries, will cement internally, through the anguish of mortal perils, the unity of the national spirit.[117]

Indeed all the "centuries-long efforts of Italy to constitute itself as a nation, the blood of its heroic enterprises" aimed it toward overseas expansion. The purported fact that "our revolution did not triumph through our *virtù* as a people" in turn imposed the duty of thereafter making "a greater Italy." For that duty, according to Oriani, Roman precedents were unsuitable. Rome itself, "great in the rhetoric of the ages, was now merely the least productive city of Italy after Naples." Italy must become a "great modern nation" in rivalry with the other European and world powers:

> To be strong to become great, that is our duty: expand, conquer, spiritually, materially, through treaties, through commerce, through industry, through science, through art, through religion, through war. We cannot withdraw from the struggle; therefore prevail we must. The future belongs to those who do not fear it; *fortuna* and history are women, and love only lusty fellows capable of taking them by force....[118]

Oriani's principal successors as the guardians of the national myths proved to be Gabriele D'Annunzio and the *nazionalisti*, the most aggressive opponents of Giolitti within the Italian establishment. Where Oriani had spoken nostalgically for the rural Italy he inhabited, lamenting the disruption of its settled order and hierarchical values, his successors gleefully embraced the machine age.[119] D'Annunzio, poet-dramatist-novelist-warrior-dandy-aesthete and national seer, celebrated industrial Italy's future upon the waves and beyond

[117] Oriani, *La rivolta ideale*, ed. and preface by Benito Mussolini (Bologna, 1926 [1906]), 70, 46; in this remarkably turgid and obscure work Mazzini, "a lyrical and tragic nature" who inspired a "a lyrical and tragic minority," operates within the framework of Hegel's stage-theory of world history (75, 71, 15); idem, *Fino a Dogali* (Bari, 1918 [1889]), 126.

[118] Oriani, *Fino a Dogali*, 268; *La rivolta ideale*, 81–82, 95, 73, 109, 121, 278.

[119] For this contrast between Oriani and his successors, see Norberto Bobbio, *Profilo ideologico del novecento italiano* (Turin, 1986), 58–60; Bobbio seeks – not wholly convincingly, but nevertheless instructively – to identify an "Italian ideology" serving as counterpart to the notions described in George L. Mosse's *The Crisis of German Ideology. Intellectual Origins of the Third Reich* (New York, 1964).

them: "Ship of steel, straight swift vibrant / splendid as a naked sword," and bent upon revenge for Lissa. Ship whose

> Fearsome prow, steering toward the domination of the world
> Took the shape of a plowshare
> *Italia! Italia!*
> . . . .
> So may you one day see the Latin sea covered
> With the slaughter of your war
> And for your crowns your laurels and myrtles bent.

So ran his "On a Torpedo-Boat in the Adriatic" of 1893 and his "Augural Song for the Chosen Nation" of 1901. Yet *"il Poeta"* had hardly begun to exploit his talent for nationalist excess. When Italy's invasion of Libya in 1911 led the editor of Italy's most influential newspaper, the right-Liberal *Corriere della Sera*, to ask D'Annunzio for verse appropriate to "our landing on those historic coasts," the Poet was all too ready:

> *Italia*, rise once more, rise up!
> Sing again your song of lands beyond the sea
> as you know how, with all your power
> as when above the sea there rose
> in blood and fire one savage cry:
> "Board! Board!" and the waves trembled.
> . . . .
> Raise with a shout your radiant face
> And by land and sea hold fast your war.[120]

As for the Nationalists, their origins as a Florentine literary clique around the periodicals *Leonardo* (1903–07) and *Il Regno* (1903–06) endowed them with a sort of dual citizenship. They were simultaneously modernist rebels against the purported cultural mediocrity of Liberal Italy and the most voraciously extremist of the establishment's foreign policy pressure groups. Cultural protest bound them to the avant-garde or would-be avant-garde, to the Nietzschean-vitalist-Futurist celebration of force and change, of the overriding right of exceptional beings and nations to crush the weak, of which D'Annunzio was the foremost Italian prophet. In politics, they offered a sharply defined alternative to Giolitti's fitful efforts to adapt Liberal Italy to the age of mass politics by accommodation and cooption. Giovanni Papini and Giuseppe Prezzolini, before leaving the Nationalists in favor of a more purely cultural radicalism, specialized in articulating the contempt for parliamentarism and democracy ever more characteristic of the younger Italian *intelligentsia*. They pioneered the Nationalist

[120] Paolo Alatri, ed., *Scritti Politici di Gabriele D'Annunzio* (Milan, 1980), 95, 113–15 (my translations); Luigi Albertini, *Epistolario 1911–1926*, 4 vols. (Milan, 1968), 1:14, 16; Richard A. Webster, "La vocazione messianica di Gabriele D'Annunzio," NA 2194 (1995), 88–101, is also instructive.

denunciation of the "vacuous poverty of Italian politics," of the "parliamentary lie," of the "lachrymose effusions of effeminate humanitarianism." "Necessary massacres" suffused the modern world; "industrial civilization, like [the] warrior civilizations [of the past], feeds upon corpses." And war was "a swift and heroic route to power and riches."[121]

Together with Enrico Corradini, the Nationalists' foremost rhetorician if not their profoundest thinker, Papini and Prezzolini accepted the challenge of socialism with defiance. *Nazionalismo*, in Corradini's words, was to be "our nation's socialism [*il nostro socialismo nazionale*]," a doctrine of class struggle against socialism both for the as yet "avaricious and inept" middle classes and for the nation against its rivals in the arena of world politics. For Corradini, Italy was a "proletarian nation," economically and intellectually dependent, as rich in population as it was poor in resources, doomed to emigration and to the consequent loss of its most enterprising members. To compete with the "conqueror states" of northwestern Europe, Italy must industrialize ever more intensively. That would ultimately close off emigration by giving the masses work, promote "the development of the imperialist spirit," and provide the sinews of war. In the present, Italy faced three choices: birth control, which was "cowardly"; emigration, which was "servile"; and conquest. Corradini unhesitatingly chose conquest as outlet for Italy's population and as a source of "national discipline": "[T]hen let there be war! And may *nazionalismo* arouse in Italy to the will to victorious war." Alfredo Rocco, Corradini's younger and ultimately more influential ally, likewise described war as "armed emigration" to free a nation of 42 million confined to territories both "narrow and poor." War, in the nationalist lexicon, was as essential to nationalism as revolution to socialism; for aggressive war and revolution were both imperialisms, the one external, the other internal.[122]

For Corradini and Rocco the precondition for victory was a "revolutionary reform" of the liberal state, which in its present pathetic condition could neither integrate the ever-skeptical masses nor assert Italy's external claims. A new "national consciousness" required as its counterpart a new "national state." United Italy's creation, Corradini argued, was too intertwined with the principle of individual freedom, and not sufficiently with that of the freedom of the state, which alone could reconquer the masses from socialism or rescue them from apathy.[123] This "myth of the new state," which Rocco soon endowed with authoritarian legal and constitutional theories, was nevertheless

---

[121] Giovanni Papini and Giuseppe Prezzolini, *Vecchio e nuovo nazionalismo* (Rome, 1967 [1914]), 2, 75, 13; Papini, in Emilio Gentile, "Il futurismo e la politica. Dal nazionalismo modernista al fascismo (1909–1920)," in De Felice, ed., *Futurismo, cultura e politica* (Turin, 1988), 114.

[122] Corradini, *Discorsi*, 86 (1909), 100 (1910), 109–14 (1911); *L'ombra della vita. Costume-letteratura e teatro-arte* (Naples, 1908), 288–90: "Tutto il mondo è imperialista o all'esterno o all'interno; e c'è oggi un imperialismo de' proletarii che si chiama socialismo"; Rocco, *Scritti e discorsi politici (1913–1934)*, 3 vols. (Milan, 1938), 1:22, 86; Rocco's statistics were optimistic: Italy's population did not reach 42 million until the 1930s.

[123] Corradini, *Discorsi*, 131, 114, 231ff. ("Stato liberale e Stato nazionale"), 242.

anything but the exclusive property of those *nazionalisti* who yearned to hang "democretins" from lamp posts, or proclaimed with Francesco Coppola that "the immortal principles of the French Revolution turn my stomach."[124] Born from liberal disorientation in the new world of mass politics, the myth gripped even anti-Giolittian liberals of the younger generations such as Giovanni Amendola, who ended after 1922 as a fierce opponent of the Fascist "new state." The myth drew its increasing force from liberal revulsion at the new Socialist and Catholic mass forces, and from the contrast between the heroic days of unification and the present desert of bureaucratic lethargy, parliamentary corruption, and estrangement of the masses from the state. It also fed upon the savage rejection of the distant and recent past pioneered by Futurists such as Filippo Tommaso Marinetti, sworn to demolish the existing Italy of monuments, museums, and "antiquarian gutlessness," and to expunge in blood the "tedious memory of Roman greatness."[125]

What the "new state" lacked was a serviceable mythology of leadership. The monarchy inspired loyalty in its officer corps and, perhaps more surprisingly, in much of peasant Italy. Yet Charles Albert and Victor Emmanuel II had failed to find on the battlefield the victories or even the glorious defeats needed to create a role of national leader for subsequent monarchs to fill. Other precedents were unpromising; the Caesars distant, Cola di Rienzo and Cesare Borgia disqualified by failure. Cavour's almost Giolittian calculation and Mazzini's otherworldliness meant that the *Risorgimento*, along with its numerous "martyrs," offered only one model of successful heroism: Garibaldi. But Garibaldi had wisely given the South away rather than trying to rule it. His was the role of swashbuckling "*duce*" of irregulars, not of national military-political leader, and the army's jealousy foreclosed the role of charismatic leader of volunteers. Nor did the drab post-*Risorgimento* offer models other than the unfortunate Crispi, that "hero and martyr" to whose African "dreams and intentions, in a land in which even dreams and intentions are feared when they depart from the commonplace" the Nationalists erected a modest cult.[126]

Leadership vacuum thus gave D'Annunzio an opening for his chief contribution to the national mythology, his personal adaptation of Nietzsche's *Übermensch* to the demands of mass politics. D'Annunzio shared with the Nationalists and their liberal fellow travelers the contempt of parliament and its "dwarfish masticators of financial arithmetic" that had become widespread by the 1890s. He proposed instead the heroic individual as national leader. The

---

[124] "Io sono uno cui gli immortali principî della rivoluzione francese fanno schifo." (Coppola at the 1912 Nationalist congress, quoted in Bobbio, *Profilo ideologico*, 58; ibid. for "I democretini à la lanterne.")

[125] Gentile, *Il mito dello Stato nuovo dal antigiolittismo al fascismo* (Bari, 1982); for Amendola, see especially 73. Marinetti: Luciano De Maria, ed., *Per conoscere Marinetti e il Futurismo* (Milan, 1973), 6–7, 36, 37 ("vigliaccheria passatista"), 153, 222, and John A. Thayer, *Italy and the Great War: Politics and Culture* (Madison, 1964), 239.

[126] Corradini, "Commemorazione della battaglia d'Adua," in his *Discorsi*, 254; Papini, "Crispi" (1904), in *Vecchio e nuovo nazionalismo*, 102.

"young king," Victor Emmanuel III, might perhaps be the "hero we await / the shepherd of the fruitful race," but D'Annunzio presciently warned the king that "if decay and shame endure / you shall see among the rebels / even he who today salutes you." The hero might also be a commoner seeking to make himself dictator, as in D'Annunzio's play *La Gloria* (1899):

> The necessity of violence presses us, dogs our heels.... Once the central power in our hands, war on the borders and the seas will follow war in the streets: a far greater trial of strength. An entire race [*stirpe*] that once more struggles for its existence....

Yet D'Annunzio, while accurately delineating the political role he himself sought to fill in 1914–15 and after, also reflected the pervasive influence of Mosca and Pareto and the horror of mass politics characteristic of Italian liberalism. Like Papini, Prezzolini, Corradini, Rocco, and other prophets of the "new state," he saw salvation coming less from an individual leader than from an entire new elite of *superuomini* that would tame the "rage of the drunken slaves." A "new oligarchy, a new reign of force" would ultimately crown the smoking ruins of parliament. The state "erected on the basis of universal suffrage and equality and cemented by fear" was fortunately "not merely ignoble but also rickety"; "the herd always remain slaves, having an inborn desire to stretch out their wrists to be shackled."[127] That oligarchic thrust toward the creation of a steely new *classe dirigente* had effects far beyond literary and Nationalist circles. It reached downward to the literate lower middle classes and leftward to the anarcho-syndicalists and to figures such as Benito Mussolini on the violent extreme of the Socialist Party. Mussolini's "socialism for supermen" – as Emilio Gentile has well described it – looked as early as 1908 to the advent of "a new species of 'free spirits' fortified in war, in solitude, in great danger...."[128]

The guardians of Italy's national myths also lacked a theory of history that could engender fanatical belief. Unlike the Panglossian liberalism, sentimental socialism, and "Nazarene sheepism" they derided, their worldview tended to be cyclical rather than teleological. Peoples, states, and elites competed in a savage Darwinian universe in which war, as Marinetti gleefully put in celebrating the conquest of Libya, was "the sanitation of the world [*guerra, sola igiene del mondo*]."[129] Externally, the latest stage of that competition was the late-nineteenth-century colonial division of the world and the race for industrial power that had provoked it and made it possible. Internally, it was the class struggle that had likewise issued from the rise of industry. But Corradini and his fellows were neither Hegelians nor even genuine social Darwinists. Their *socialismo nazionale* merely called a new elite to rise up and create a shining

---

[127] D'Annunzio, *La gloria* (Milan, 1899), 47, 52; Alatri, ed., *Scritti Politici di Gabriele D'Annunzio*, 66, 104, 105.

[128] Gentile, *Le origini dell'ideologia fascista* (Bari, 1975), 6–16; OO, 1:181.

[129] Quoted in Mario Isnenghi, *Il mito della grande guerra da Marinetti a Malaparte* (Bari, 1970), 30.

modern Italy, overcoming the nation's late start in the race for empire and its Mediterranean encirclement by France – a literary complaint the Nationalists transformed into a durable element in Italy's great-power claims. Their class struggle for the nation did not promise an apocalyptic end to history. Their proclaimed "realism" offered no esoteric keys to its interpretation. Nor were they pessimistic "social imperialists" seeking expansion to preempt a revolution they deemed otherwise inevitable at home: Italy's Socialists stirred Corradini and associates to scatological vituperation, not fear; nationalism, not socialism, was the wave of the future. Finally, despite financing in due course from some sectors of industry, the Nationalists were in no sense appendages of economic interests, but rather – like their counterparts the Pan-Germans – an illustration of the intoxicating power of ideas.[130]

As for Darwin's heirs in Italy, they confined themselves on the whole to biology; perhaps Custoza, Lissa, and Adowa enjoined discreet silence about the national destinies of "favored races." Darwin's empiricism, which had commended him to Italy's luckless positivists, likewise lessened his influence after the turn of the century. Nevertheless, a broad spectrum of Italian anthropologists, historians, public health experts, eugenicists, and demographers from the late nineteenth century onward explored the implications of the notion of race. The result was a bizarre hybrid, a "Latin" and Catholic racism that dwelt on an alleged spiritual commonality of a putative unitary "Italic race" that fused populations – from the Alps to the islands – with startlingly and demonstrably disparate cranial indices. Italian theoreticians of race, with virtual unanimity, thus rejected the pseudo-biological determinism popular north of the Alps, and frequently scoffed at German-Aryan pretensions to racial purity.[131]

Italy's most widely respected pre-1918 approximation to political biology was thus the population theory of Corrado Gini, widely respected professor of statistics and precocious member of the Italian Nationalist Association. His *Demographic Factors in the Evolution of Nations* (1912) offered a cyclical determinism by which peoples and elites, as evidenced by their birth rates, passed from vigorous growth to maturity to "senile decadence." That life cycle, in Gini's view, was a disproof of the Malthusian and Darwinian assumption of limitless population growth. Nor did Gini seek in pseudo-Darwinian fashion to identify nations with purported sub-species of humanity. He followed the craniological conventions of the anthropology of his day: all European peoples were mixtures of three "fundamental races," the "dark-haired southern dolichocephalic race," the "blond northern dolichocephalic race," and the

---

[130] Geography: Corradini, "Dall'italianismo al latinismo," *Il Regno*, 1 May 1904, 2, and Giovanni Pascoli, "La grande proletaria si è mossa," November 1911, in Rochat, ed., *Il colonialismo italiano* (Turin, 1974), 88; Corradini's claim to realism and his muddled rejection of teleological theories: his *L'ombra della vita*, 287–88, 284. For the contingent and essentially irrelevant nature of the industrial connection, see for instance Romain H. Rainero, ed., *Da Oriani a Corradini* (Milan, 2003), and especially 241–56 (Michela Minesso, "Le élites milanesi e il nazionalismo").

[131] See the accomplished analysis of Roberto Maiocchi, *Scienza italiana e razzismo fascista* (Florence, 1999), chs. 1–3.

"central and eastern brachycephalic race." He made little attempt – at least until the 1930s – to ascribe superiority to a particular "fundamental race." And he registered noncommittally the absorption of presumably superior conquering peoples by the conquered. The source of his wistful fatalism was not race, but the inexorable demographic cycle that governed the aging of populations and might decree "that the European nations are destined for extinction." Gini did see the First World War, when it came, as the ultimate consequence of the "intense demographic pressure" that had impelled a "young" and prolific Germany to challenge both the aging nations to its west and the encroaching Slavic hordes to its east. He also espoused, as did a variety of other Italian scholars, the eugenic notions then popular even in Britain and the United States, and deplored "the systematic defense of the weak and degenerate, which prolongs their life and allows them to reproduce." But his writings were scarcely a call to racial battle.[132]

The absence of a credible Italian mythology of ethnic purity and the minuscule size of the Jewish population likewise discouraged anti-Semitic theorizing, which was a marginal phenomenon in pre-1915 Italy compared to the salience of its enthusiastically pseudo-biological German counterparts.[133] Corradini and some of his fellows regarded Italy's Jews as anti-national and contaminated by association with freemasonry and socialism, but only Catholic organs such as the Jesuit journal *Civiltà Cattolica* attacked them with much fervor, although with little political effect.[134] Only in Africa, where racial differences were everyday reality rather than craniology or theology, did Italians draw drastic racist conclusions. Ferdinando Martini, man of letters and governor of Eritrea after Crispi's misadventure, insisted in 1896 that talk of an Italian civilizing mission in Ethiopia was "lies or idiocy. We must substitute race for race: either that or nothing." It was Italy's mission to "help [the native] to disappear" in the fashion of the red-skinned population of the United States; eventually only one would remain – to celebrate the whites for having abolished the slave trade by destroying its victims.[135] But Martini, despite an influential role in the colonial and foreign policy elite, neither aspired to create a racist theory of history nor succeeded in translating bloodthirsty talk into action in the manner of Germany's "annihilation of the Herero *Volk*."

While the *nazionalisti* heartily approved of struggle and frequently employed terms such as *razza* and the more or less synonymous *stirpe*, they proposed no

---

[132] Gini, *I fattori demografici dell'evoluzione delle Nazioni* (Turin, 1912), 34, 32–33, 107, 139; idem, *Problemi sociologici della guerra* (Bologna, 1921), 8–9, 20–29 (1915); idem, *The Contributions of Demography to Eugenics* (London, 1913), 85. On Gini and Giorgio Mortara, another prominent anti-Malthusian until his forced emigration thanks to Mussolini's racial laws, see especially Maiocchi, *Razzismo fascista*, 83–97, 102.

[133] Maiocchi, *Razzismo fascista*, 187.

[134] De Felice, *Storia degli ebrei*, 26–45; Maiocchi, *Razzismo fascista*, 187–88; Angelo Ventura, "La svolta antiebraica nella storia del fascismo italiano," *Rivista Storica Italiana* 113:1 (2001), 61–65.

[135] Ferdinando Martini, *Nell'Affrica Italiana. Impressioni e ricordi* (Milan, 1896), 61; for Italy's pre-1915 ethnographers on Africa and the "negro race," Maiocchi, *Razzismo fascista*, 157–58.

deterministic theories of history as race struggle. *Razza* or nationality remained "a spiritual matter, not a physical phenomenon," even in the thought of the fierce anti-Slav chauvinists of Trieste.[136] Nor did other possible foundations for an Italian nationalist *fede*, the new Italy's alleged imperial Roman heritage and the Mazzinian cult of the Italian people's "Third Rome," offer a theory of how history worked that was capable of moving masses. That proved a weakness in the twentieth century's savage ideological arena.

II. Germany: "The *Volk* Needs a War"

German myths, as the long nineteenth century ended, were more luxuriant, of far sterner material, and far more widely and deeply rooted in the popular imagination than their Italian counterparts. By 1914 national integration had progressed notably further than in northern Italy, much less Italy as a whole. Prussia and Prussia-Germany's schoolmasters, pastors, and drill sergeants had brought Prusso-German myths to their increasingly literate charges along with Luther's Bible and the manual of arms. Their efforts sapped the independence of Germany's particularisms and subcultures. The dynasties of the federal states gradually lost much of their grip upon popular loyalties. The Hohenzollern, especially after the advent of William II, filled the role of a national monarchy rather than that of a Prussian dynasty; Prussian court ceremonial seemed increasingly hollow and irrelevant even to participants.[137] The Catholics, after the waning of the *Kulturkampf*, sought to win nationalist credentials, even if Bülow turned on them in a 1907 election fought against their allegedly anti-national criticism of German colonial massacres. The Socialists, after 1891, subscribed in theory to revolutionary Marxism while in practice replicating the Prusso-German state with massive party structures that rooted both Social Democratic Party and its constituency to the status quo. Revolution would risk the workers' organizations, not their chains. And despite the hostility of middle-class Germany, a not insignificant portion of the SPD's leaders and led shared in national pride and its accompanying sense of mission.[138]

Yet to many of Germany's most articulate group, the *Bildungsbürgertum*, the new Reich seemed to be fusing too slowly, or even disintegrating. The relative loss of importance of mere learning in the new industrial age, the rise of a mass party of the workers, the emigration or collapse of the peasantry, and

---

[136] Rocco, *Scritti*, 1:238; on the influence of Trieste, see especially Dennison Rusinow, *Italy's Austrian Heritage* (Oxford, 1965), 20–31, and Sabbatucci, "Il problema dell'irredentismo," 488–92.

[137] For a case study of the decline of Wittelsbach ritual in Bavaria, Werner K. Blessing, "The Cult of Monarchy, Political Loyalty and the Workers' Movement in Imperial Germany," JCH 13 (1978), 357–75; for Prussia, Isabel V. Hull, "Prussian Dynastic Ritual and the End of Monarchy," in Carole Fink, Isabel V. Hull, and MacGregor Knox, eds., *German Nationalism and the European Response, 1890–1945* (Norman, OK, 1985), 13–41.

[138] See especially Roger Fletcher, *Revisionism and Empire. Socialist Imperialism in Germany 1897–1914* (London, 1984), and Hans-Christoph Schröder, *Gustav Noske und die Kolonialpolitik des deutschen Kaiserreiches* (Berlin, 1979).

the migration of Polish workers to the Ruhr and of Jews from Poland and Russia to Germany's cities seemed omens of degeneration and downfall. Yet the new Reich, for all its defects, also still held the promise that had electrified the liberals of 1848: of playing a world role as mortal rival to Great Britain. It was precisely the conjunction of *Bildungsbürger* unease – with much of what has prematurely become known as modernity – with the might and optimism that German modernity generated that proved explosive.

These conditions helped give myths of Germany's world mission new impetus in the 1890s, just the widening of the European great-power system into a world system stimulated German aspirations. As in Italy, unity seemed pointless unless the new nation-state was to serve as a prelude to far greater things. The new Germany's cultural mission, like Mazzini's notion of the "Third Rome," was universal in scope; the poet Geibel's jingle about Germany's calling to heal the world was "all too often quoted" in the years before 1914.[139] United Germany's world prowess in *Kultur*, its leadership in fields as disparate as philosophy, philology, history, science, technology, and industry, gave it a far more credible claim to world domination than did united Italy's as yet modest achievements. Nor did the prophets of the supremacy of the German *Geist* neglect power. "We must recognize that the unification of the Reich was a youthful frolic that the nation... should have avoided, if it should merely prove to be the conclusion rather than the starting-point of a German world power policy," thundered Max Weber – unconsciously echoing Crispi – in his perhaps too notorious Freiburg inaugural address of 1895. The savant, old boy of a Heidelberg "fighting fraternity" and Prussian reserve lieutenant, was not alone.[140] The myth that Prussia's mission, now accomplished in Germany, mandated in good Hegelian fashion a German mission in the world was the central belief of the all-dominating Prusso-German historical school whose father was Droysen and whose shrillest voice was Heinrich von Treitschke. It also came to be the central belief of many who attended Treitschke's Berlin lectures between 1874 and the 1890s or read his *History of Germany in the Nineteenth Century*, from Bülow, to Alfred Tirpitz of later naval fame, to the colonial maniac Carl Peters, and to Heinrich Class, chieftain after 1908 of the Pan-German League.[141]

[139] Ludwig Dehio, "Ranke and German Imperialism," in his *Germany and World Politics in the Twentieth Century* (New York, 1967), 55; see for instance Treitschke, quoted in Walter Bussmann, "Treitschke als Politiker," HZ 177:2 (1954), 274, and Heinrich Class (pseud. Daniel Frymann), *Wenn ich der Kaiser wär'. Politische Wahrheiten und Notwendigkeiten* (Leipzig, 1914 [1912]), 187.

[140] See Frevert, *Ehrenmänner*, 11–12 (including Weber's later propensity to challenge fellow academics to duel with sabers).

[141] Weber: Wolfgang J. Mommsen, *Max Weber und die deutsche Politik 1890–1920* (Tübingen, 2nd rev. ed., 1974), 74. On "borussianisches Geschichtsdenken" from Droysen to Treitschke and Lenz, see especially Wolfgang Hardtwig, "Von Preussens Aufgabe in Deutschland zu Deutschlands Aufgabe in der Welt," HZ 231:2 (1980); for Treitschke's audience, see Class, *Wider den Strom* (Leipzig, 1932), 14–16 ("Mir war Treitschke der Meister, der mein Leben bestimmte") and Peter Winzen, "Treitschke's Influence on the Rise of Anti-British Nationalism in Germany,"

It was Treitschke who offered the most compelling recipe for the fulfillment of the Prusso-German mission: a "final settling of accounts with England" that would substitute a world balance of power for Britain's allegedly intolerable "maritime world mastery." Under that banner (in the words of Ludwig Dehio) "the majority of our historians marched, credulously and in close formation, from the turn of the century until the end of the [1914–18] war."[142] The sweeping continental goals that the Pan-Germans simultaneously proclaimed likewise harked back to the giant Reich "armed against east and west" of the 1848 liberals.[143] That securing the "necessities of life" for the "Germanic race" might end "the [national] existence, worthless as it was to civilization, of inferior little peoples [*minderwertige Völkchen*] such as Czechs, Slovenes, and Slovaks" was immaterial.[144] War, the "iron dice" that Bismarck had thrice rolled victoriously, also came to seem increasingly necessary to recreate a nation imperfectly integrated in 1866–71 and increasingly fragmented by industrialization thereafter. The aged Treitschke consoled himself over Germany's lamentable state with the happy thought – expressed in a letter in the mid-1890s to the same Helmuth von Moltke the Younger who ultimately led Germany's armies to the Marne – that "nevertheless at last a turning-point will come and the old Germany, mighty in arms, will once more rise up in all its splendor [*das alte waffengewaltige Deutschland sich wieder in seiner Herrlichkeit erheben wird*]."[145]

Figures such as Class of the *Alldeutsche* were less reticent: "Many enemies, much honor," rang the epigraph of his modestly titled and wide-selling *If I Were the Kaiser: Political Truths and Necessities*, a 1912 philippic against the flabbiness of the Reich leadership and all its deeds and policies, foreign and domestic. Class had no doubts about the necessary remedy: "Whoever loves his nation and seeks to hasten our present illness to its crisis, will yearn for war, the awakener of all the good, healthy, robust forces in the *Volk*." War was the "doctor of our souls" – a German-idealist counterpart to Marinetti's "*sola igiene del mondo*."[146] And even a less aggressive sprig of the *Bildungsbürgertum* than Class, a man such as Kurt Riezler, who as confidant and counselor to Chancellor Bethmann Hollweg after 1909 complained guardedly of German nationalism's naive "faith in violence," noted in his diary as early as 1911 the widespread "authentically German idealistic (and correct) conviction that the

in Paul Kennedy and Anthony Nicholls, eds., *Nationalist and Racist Movements in Britain and Germany Before 1914* (London, 1981), 155–56, 161–63.

[142] Bussmann, "Treitschke als Politiker," 263–69, 275 note 3; Dehio, "Ranke and German Imperialism," 60.

[143] See p. 55.

[144] Mitteleuropa, "Germanic race," and lesser breeds (Ernst Hasse and others, 1897): Alfred Kruck, *Geschichte des Alldeutschen Verbandes, 1890–1939* (Wiesbaden, 1954), 43–44.

[145] Letter of 1895, quoted in Bussmann, "Treitschke als Politiker," 279.

[146] Class, *Wenn ich der Kaiser wär'*, 53, 182–83; for similar sentiments in a military accent, see above all the widely read work of Friedrich von Bernhardi, *Deutschland und der Nächste Krieg* (Stuttgart, 6th ed., 1913 [1912]), especially 36, which quotes Treitschke's *Politics*: "The living God will ensure that war, that fearful medicine for humankind, will recur perpetually."

Volk needs a war." "This conviction," Riezler significantly added, "Bethmann likewise shares."[147]

The accomplishment of Germany's world mission, with or without war, clearly required the same sort of ruthless leadership that had given Prussia the mastery of Germany. Indeed many strands of Prussia-Germany's history and political culture predisposed its subjects to expect and yearn for an iron hand: the bloodthirsty schoolbook ditties summoning the Hohenstaufen hidden Kaiser ("*Auf, erwache! / Komm' zur Sühne, komm' zur Rache*"); the sardonic driving presence of Frederick the Great ("you dogs, do you want to live for ever!"); Fichte's Germanic anti-Napoleon; the savage Teutonic heroes crystallized in the popular imagination in the cult-operas that Richard Wagner created from the *Nibelungenlied*; and the ever-present booted and spurred images of Bismarck.

The office of Kaiser was the natural focus of such loyalties and aspirations. Before 1871 historically minded supporters of the Prussian monarchy such as Heinrich von Sybel, Droysen, and Treitschke had opposed the title of Kaiser as a quaint *grossdeutsch* antique, anti-national due to its associations with Hohenstaufen and Habsburg mastery of Italy or the Balkans and historically phony, a mere literary invention of Schenkendorf, Rückert, and Geibel. But thanks to the German schoolmaster, the Kyffhäuser cult despite its recent origins was by the 1870s too deeply rooted to despise; it cried out to be exploited. The vain Hohenstaufen struggle against the medieval Papacy ultimately offered a welcome way to appropriate the Barbarossa of universal empire for Protestant Prussia: an invented tradition that welded the medieval Reich, Martin Luther, and William I into a single national and imperial myth. After 1871 the imperial office thus performed the role of "mythological symbol of German power and splendor" in schoolbooks, household anthologies, patriotic speeches, innumerable statues of William I, and a shrine on top of the Kyffhäuser sponsored by the *Kriegervereine* – although the imperial institution, as mocking Left-Liberals pointed out, was no older than the Reichstag.[148]

But the *Kaisertum* was not alone. As political participation expanded in the 1890s and after, its claim to symbolize the nation came under increasing attack – a development visible even in the stones of Germany's monuments. The ponderous temple to Arminius in the Teutoburger forest, begun in the 1830s, set the example for other later non-dynastic memorials to national leaders and to the nation itself. From the mid-1890s onward a sturdy middle-class cult disfigured

---

[147] Kurt Riezler: *Tagebücher, Aufsätze, Dokumente*, ed. Karl Dietrich Erdmann (Göttingen, 1972), 180; for Riezler on German nationalism, see his *Grundzüge der Weltpolitik in der Gegenwart* (pseud. J. J. Ruedorffer) (Stuttgart, Berlin, 1914), 111–12; suggestions that the surviving diary excerpts covering the period before August 1914 suffered later alterations designed to conceal German responsibility for the war seem unlikely to apply to remarks as damning as the one quoted (see in general Bernd F. Schulte, *Die Verfälschung der Riezler-Tagebücher* [Frankfurt am Main, 1985]).

[148] Elizabeth Fehrenbach, *Wandlungen des deutschen Kaisergedankens* (Munich, 1969), 27–34, 107–09, 131.

German hilltops with squat "Bismarck-towers" that celebrated the great man as symbol of the nation's "faithfulness unto death." The gigantic memorial dedicated at Leipzig on the hundredth anniversary of the 1813 victory over Napoleon was in the intentions of its builders an act of *self*-glorification: "the hero of the monument is the entire German *Volk*."[149] Monarchical loyalties were gradually yielding to what a right-wing and fiercely loyal Social Democrat happily described as "national self-deification."[150]

Yet as Friedrich Meinecke suggested in a celebratory speech in 1913, Germans were "not content with the notion of our nation as a great spiritual corporate body [*geistige Gesamtpersönlichkeit*]; for we long for a *Führer* for the nation, a *Führer* for whom we can march through fire."[151] As the increasing politicization and "nationalization of the masses" eroded the monarchical myth, it indirectly threw into stark relief the gulf that yawned between dynastic reality and public expectations of mythic leadership. The Kaiser's instability and indolence, varied and often bloodthirsty enthusiasms, and fierce desire to rule in person prevented the already improbable emergence of a new Bismarck. And the emperor's attempt to rule as navalist *Volkskaiser* "returned from the Kyffhäuser," emperor of Germany's world mission as his grandfather William I had been the emperor of Prussia's German mission, drove Germany and *Kaisertum* into a perilous dead end by 1908.[152] Stormy press and Reichstag criticism of the "All-Highest" in person testified to the collapse of William II's version of the imperial myth. That and the ever more manifest failure of the navy to dominate the North Sea, as Britain grimly outspent and outbuilt Tirpitz after 1905–06, lamed all other political projects anchored on the monarchy, such as the Left-Liberal Friedrich Naumann's notions of a parliamentary social-imperial *Volkskaisertum*.[153]

Into the resulting vacuum, already prefigured since the 1890s, strode the Pan-German "national opposition." The Pan-Germans saw the fleet's failure as a failure of nerve. They took as a call to arms the increasing "encirclement" that

[149] Quotations and analysis from Nipperdey, "Nationalidee und Nationaldenkmal in Deutschland," 542–46, 567–73, 578–82; Mosse, *The Nationalization of the Masses. Political Symbolism and Mass Movements in Germany from the Napoleonic Wars Through the Third Reich* (New York, 1975), chs. 2–3, is also useful.

[150] Karl Leuthner, quoted in Fehrenbach, *Wandlungen*, 215; on Leuthner, see Fletcher, *Revisionism and Empire*, 82ff.

[151] Quoted in Fehrenbach, *Wandlungen*, 91.

[152] Kyffhäuser quotation: Fehrenbach, *Wandlungen*, 179; for Wilhelm's peculiarities and their consequences, see especially Hull, *The Entourage of Kaiser Wilhelm II 1888–1918* (Cambridge, 1982), ch. 1, and John C. G. Röhl, "The Emperor's New Clothes: A Character Sketch of Kaiser Wilhelm II," in Röhl and Nicolas Sombart, eds., *Kaiser Wilhelm II: New Interpretations* (Cambridge, 1982), 23–61.

[153] On the Kaiser's vicissitudes, see Hull, *The Entourage of Kaiser Wilhelm II*, and Paul Kennedy, "The Kaiser and German *Weltpolitik*"; Terence F. Cole, "The *Daily Telegraph* Affair and Its Aftermath: The Kaiser, Bülow and the Reichstag, 1908–1909"; and Elizabeth Fehrenbach, "Images of Kaiserdom: German Attitudes to Kaiser Wilhelm II," all in Röhl and Sombart, eds., *Kaiser Wilhelm II*.

Germany's bullying of its neighbors had summoned up. And after 1911 when Germany's second Morocco crisis ended in what they considered humiliation, they damned the monarchy and its incumbent in startling terms. "One can scarcely dare deny... that the manifold errors of the Crown and the persistent incompetence [*dauernde Untüchtigkeit*] of its bearers may lead our *Volk* to ask itself why it should further tolerate a form of government that compels it to suffer a weakling [*unbrauchbares*] chief of state," fulminated Class in his 1912 "Kaiser-book." The Pan-Germans remained conservatives by provenance and milieux. But their convictions increasingly made them revolutionaries.

The *Volk*, not the monarchy nor even the state on which much German middle-class reverence still centered, was the hero of Pan-German mythology. As Class recalled in his memoirs, long conversations with an old revolutionary of 1848, a "south German democrat of the first water," had taught him the capital lesson that being "an enthusiastic son of one's *Volk*" did not in the least preclude being "a resolute foe of its governments."[154] Externally, that *Volk* extended far beyond the reach of those governments. The *Alldeutsche* claimed the Austrian Germans and the eastern European diaspora for an entirely new sort of *grossdeutsch* myth, an ethnic and racist loyalty cut loose from the Habsburgs and egalitarian in its implications. Internally, that egalitarianism was strikingly visible in Class's version of the origins of the monarchy, sprung from a nation whose "equal *Volk*-comrades [*gleichberechtigten Volksgenossen*]" had in the distant past chosen kings by thunderous acclamation, by hoisting upon their shields the bravest man in their assembled host.[155]

Class and *Volksgenossen*, in their radicalism, thus demoted the monarchy to a mere agent of the *Volk*'s world mission. And with relentless logic, Class did not shrink from the ultimate conclusion: if the monarchy itself could not defend the *Volk* and accomplish that mission, the emperor or his advisors must choose a champion, a national Führer.[156] The model proposed in Class's "Kaiser-book," which swiftly became a sort of breviary for the national opposition, was ostensibly Bismarck. The League's propaganda had long pictured the great man as the *"Zwingherr zur Deutschheit"* who had prefigured a coming Pan-German *"Zwingherr zur Alldeutschheit."*[157] And Tirpitz was the Führer whom Class apparently had in mind to lead the coup d'état from above that would cripple the universal suffrage Reichstag, demote Germany's Jews to resident aliens, and rescue monarchy and *Volk* from impending doom. But Class also offered a

---

[154] Class, *Wider den Strom*, 19–20.

[155] The term *Volksgenosse*, much heard after 1933, is untranslatable into English (or Italian); hence the clumsiness of my attempt. *Nation* and *nazione* lack the Wagnerian depths of *Volk*, and the Western notion of "citizen" (German: *Staatsbürger*) is a pale legalism beside the organic sense of belonging that *Volksgenosse* conveys.

[156] Class, *Wenn ich der Kaiser wär'*, 219–20; Bruno Thoss, "Nationale Rechte, militärische Führung, und Diktaturfrage in Deutschland 1913–1923," MGM 42 (1987), 27–77, gives an excellent discussion of the further development of these notions.

[157] *Alldeutsche Blätter*, 4:2, 7 January 1894, quoted in Karl Lange, "Der Terminus 'Lebensraum' in Hitlers 'Mein Kampf,'" VfZ 13 (1965), 428.

remarkable prophecy that put even Bismarck's role in the shade. In the event of defeat in the coming inevitable and yearned-for war, "the present internal fragmentation [*innere Zerrissenheit*] will lead to such chaos that only the mighty will of a dictator will be able to bring order once more."

That the leader of an organization as well connected throughout monarchical Prussia-Germany as the *Alldeutsche* could before 1914 foresee the monarchy's potential replacement by a dictator come, like the hidden Kaiser, to rescue and revenge, was symptomatic of the intensity of middle-class "expectation of a Führer."[158] That sentiment and its intensity had little Italian counterpart. Figures such as Corradini and Rocco never graduated, as did the Pan-Germans amid war and revolution, to a radical nationalism that defined itself not by preservation of the existing order but by its destruction so that the *Volk* might live. Class foreshadowed and helped inaugurate a development with consequences that ultimately proved world-shattering: the emancipation of German nationalism from the monarchy and Prusso-German tradition, and its mutation into a limitless subversive radicalism bent on world mastery or destruction.

The myths of Germany's mission and of the longed-for Führer linked with and reinforced an understanding of the historical process far more structured, dogmatic, and widely rooted than anything found in Italian nationalist circles. German Romanticism's idolatry of nature, its application of organic metaphors to society, its celebration of the alleged natural purity of German *Volk* and language, and its political mythology of war-tempered lords in eternal harmony with sturdy peasants formed a subsoil unavailable in Italy. Hegel contributed to that subsoil both his philosophy of history as the progressive self-realization of a *Geist* apparently incarnate in a Prussian state rooted in the Reformation, and his indifference to the lamentations of those crushed under the wheel of history. He offered a deterministic vehicle derived in part from religion, from the tenacious stage-theory of Joachim of Fiore, and now applied to the all too this-worldly kingdom of the German *Volk*.

This mental universe was characteristic even of German liberalism, and delimited it sharply even before the 1860s from its Western counterparts. Then Bismarck and Darwin together worked a unique black magic. *The Origin of Species* appeared in German in 1860 and immediately met with acclaim even in non-biological spheres such as linguistics. Then came Bismarck's apparent demonstration in the inter-state arena of the "preservation of favored races in the struggle for life." Within a few months of Königgrätz prescient commentators had begun to celebrate Prussia's victory as a consequence of the laws of nature: "An animal exists to exterminate other animals; nations and states crowd their fellows out." A distinguished Hegelian, Adolf Lasson, published the untranslatably titled *Das Culturideal und der Krieg* in 1868; reprinted cheaply after 1900, it became a sort of "political bible for the half-educated." For Lasson, as for the officer corps, international law was a form of servitude;

---

[158] Tirpitz as dictator: Chickering, *We Men Who Feel Most German*, 288; "In Erwartung des Führers": Class, *Wenn ich der Kaiser wär'*, 263.

mortal hatred against outsiders was evidence of "healthy *Volk* life"; and as Hegel had also taught, foreign war was a road to domestic peace and national integration.[159]

German social Darwinism thus owed some of its peculiar power to its conformity with preexisting German intellectual patterns and its coincidence with Bismarck's dazzling violence. But its widening influence was above all a result of its virtual identity with the tradition of German Darwinian biology. That conjunction was absent in Italy; nor did it exist even in Britain or the United States, home to other forceful but ultimately less consequential strains of social Darwinism.[160] Ernst Haeckel, professor of biology at Jena from 1862 to 1909, was not merely the German T. H. Huxley, a first-rank biologist and indefatigable champion of Darwin in Germany.[161] He was also an influential founding member of the Pan-German League, inventor of a biopolitical cult that he baptized Monism, and author of Germany's widest selling anti-Christian tract, *The Riddle of the Universe* (1899). Haeckel claimed to be empirical and materialist, but his Darwinism was German Romantic nature-worship disguised as biology. Darwin had situated humanity in nature; Haeckel deified the cosmos and subjected humanity to its laws, for humanity and *Die Natur* were one – hence "Monism." From that fundamental claim, with an admixture of the notions of racial inequality and Aryan descent for which Europe's foremost nineteenth-century racist prophet, Count Joseph Arthur de Gobineau, had found a relatively small market in his native France, Haeckel constructed a philosophy of history endowed with all the authority of science. Neither Hegel's *Geist* nor Marx's economics was the driving force of the human past; history properly understood "join[ed] what is called the history of the world to the stem-history of the vertebrates." History – which Haeckel equipped with derisive quotation marks – was biology. Science allegedly disclosed that the human species was hierarchically organized, its component "branches" distinguishable by their greater or lesser deviation from the "common primary form of ape-like man." The Germans were naturally the most highly evolved form, identified by the long-headed blue-eyed blondness that Gobineau, the antimodernist cultural

---

[159] See the examples of Karl-Georg Faber, "Realpolitik als Ideologie. Die Bedeutung des Jahres 1866 für das politische Denken in Deutschland," HZ 203 (1966), 25–28, and (for Lasson and Hegel) Messerschmidt, "Völkerrecht und 'Kriegsnotwendigkeit,'" 238–39; for the popularity of Lasson's book, Adolf Gasser, *Preussischer Militärgeist und Kriegsentfesselung 1914* (Frankfurt am Main, 1985), 92–93.

[160] Italian Darwinism largely failed to make the leap from science to ideology before 1914: see in general Maiocchi, *Razzismo fascista*.

[161] For what follows, see Daniel Gasman, *The Scientific Origins of National Socialism. Social Darwinism in Ernst Haeckel and the German Monist League* (London, 1971), especially 35–42, 63, 126. Richard J. Evans, "In Search of German Social Darwinism. The History and Historiography of a Concept," in Manfred Berg and Geoffrey Cocks, eds., *Medicine and Modernity* (Cambridge, 1997), 55–79, offers an introduction to Darwin's involuntary influence on German politics.

critic Julius Langbehn, and Teutomaniacal historical novelists such as Felix Dahn had made into the post-1871 German ideal.[162]

Further evolution depended upon pitiless application of the laws of nature, for politics was applied biology. Sparta had shown the way: "all newborn children were subject to careful examination or selection" and those who were "weak, sickly, or affected with any bodily infirmity were killed"; thus only strong children "propagated the race." Haeckel's biopolitics similarly enjoined negative eugenic measures for undesirable adults. The "indiscriminate destruction of all incorrigible criminals" was humanitarianism, biologically understood. "Incurables" and "lunatics" should likewise – after suitable medical-bureaucratic deliberation – be liberated "from their indescribable torments by a dose of morphia." Conversely, Haeckel's theory gave the state the duty of breaking down all artificial barriers to the rise and propagation of the fit; "the career open to those of greatest talent [*der Bahn frei für die tüchtigsten*] in all fields" was the slogan of Johannes Unold, vice-president of Haeckel's "German Monist League."[163]

Haeckel's biopolitics and its variants found followers even among German pacifists, many of whom saw the extermination of peoples deemed racially inferior as a salutary exception to their abhorrence of war. As developed by numerous disciples and supporters in scholarly journals such as the *Politico-Anthropological Review* and the *Archive for Racial and Social Biology*, Haeckel's ideas also intersected with the literary and philological mythology of Aryan origins and with the exuberant growth of the popular "*völkisch*" racism that by the 1870s, amid accelerating change and economic crisis, had seized upon the freshly emancipated Jews as the cosmic enemy. That racist subculture, which had no counterpart in Italy, fell into two principal strands. The populist tendency included beery agrarian agitators such as Otto Böckel and Hermann Ahlwardt, leaders of the anti-Semitic splinter parties that flourished in the 1880s

---

[162] Haeckel, *The History of Creation* (New York, 1879), 2:310, 321, 323–24, 332; *The Wonders of Life* (New York, 1905), 461–62; Erich Biehahn, "Blondheit und Blondheitskult in der deutschen Literatur," *Archiv für Kulturgeschichte* 46 (1964), 309–33.

[163] Haeckel, *History of Creation*, 1:170–74; *The Wonders of Life*, 21, 118–20. Alfred Kelly's otherwise useful work, *The Descent of Darwin: The Popularization of Darwinism in Germany 1860–1914* (Chapel Hill, NC, 1981), suggests (113) that Haeckel did not "advocate" Spartan-style artificial selection. But Haeckel's remarks on Sparta in his *History of Creation* (1:170–71) – a work that by Kelly's account (25) went through nine editions before 1900 and was "the layman's starting point for a study of evolution" – are unambiguously approving. Haeckel went on (1:173–74; see also *The Wonders of Life*, 21, 118–20) to condemn contemporary "humane civilization" for its abhorrence not merely of Spartan-style eugenics, but also of capital punishment and forcible euthanasia. Unold: quoted in Gasman, *Scientific Origins of National Socialism*, 93. For useful surveys of the many proponents of similar views, Hellmuth Auerbach, "Nationalsozialismus vor Hitler," in Wolfgang Benz, Hans Buchheim, and Hans Mommsen, eds., *Der Nationalsozialismus. Studien zur Ideologie und Herrschaft* (Frankfurt am Main, 1993), 15–18, and Richard Weikart, "Progress through Racial Extermination: Social Darwinism, Eugenics, and Pacifism in Germany, 1860–1918," GSR 26:2 (2003), 273–94.

and 1890s, and publicists such as the indefatigable Theodor Fritsch, founder of the journal *Hammer* (1902–) and of the anti-Semitic sects *Reichshammer-bund* and *Germanen Orden* (1910/12–). It had Austrian counterparts in the underbrush of anti-Semitic organizations that prospered amid the ethnic struggles in Vienna and the Czech lands, from racist extremists such Georg Ritter von Schönerer of the Austrian Pan-German movement to the less vehement "Christian-social" demagogy of the lord mayor of Vienna from 1895/97 to 1910, Karl Lueger. After 1900 Germany's populist anti-Semites lost much of their mass constituency to the Farmers' League and the Center Party, which stole their anti-Jewish and anti-urban appeals. That development, rather than circumscribing the effects of anti-Semitism, was evidence of the extent to which it had come to saturate German politics at the mass as well as at the elite level.[164]

Far above the vulgar agitators, figures such as Treitschke lent their authority to denunciation of the Jews, "our misfortune." *Bildungsbürger* hostility to the machine age welled forth in the works of cultural pessimists such as Paul de Lagarde and Langbehn, who mingled wide-ranging imperial aspirations with Teutomaniacal ancestor-worship, yearning for a "secret emperor," high-minded proposals for the reform of German education and art, and vilification of the Jewish "trichinae and bacilli." Wagner had long inveighed against "Judaism in Music." After his death in 1883, his cult at Bayreuth fell under the dictatorship of his formidable widow Cosima, and purveyed Germanic neo-paganism and an anti-Semitism scarcely less intense, if more genteel, than that of the agitators. Increasingly, the public that made figures such as Langbehn into striking publishing successes interpreted such notions as "idealism."[165]

Out of the Bayreuth circle but also influenced by long residence amid the savage nationality struggles of Vienna came the most influential exponent of elite anti-Semitism, the transplanted Englishman Houston Stewart Chamberlain. His *Foundations of the Nineteenth Century* (1899) was an immediate thundering success, admired equally by William II, Heinrich Class, and the lower-middle-class ranks of the German-National Shop Clerks' League. *Foundations* translated the doctrine that history was *race* history into a sweeping narrative stretching from the ancient world to the end of the eighteenth century. Chamberlain's concept of race was carefully tailored to the needs of his audience, many of whom were uneasy with Darwinian positivism and abhorred Haeckel's combative irreligion. As with the mainstream of Italian racial theory, race for Chamberlain existed simultaneously and ambiguously in the realms of biology *and* of the spirit. "Teutonic *Geist*" as well as "Teutonic blood" was

[164] Ibid.; Richard S. Levy, *The Downfall of the Antisemitic Political Parties in Imperial Germany* (New Haven, CT, 1975); for the Center Party's use of anti-Semitism, Blackbourn, *Populists and Patricians*, ch. 8. On Fritsch, Reginald H. Phelps, "'Before Hitler Came': Thule Society and Germanen Orden," JMH 25 (1963), 247–50, remains useful.

[165] Fritz Stern, *The Politics of Cultural Despair. A Study in the Rise of the Germanic Ideology* (New York, 1965), parts I–II; quotation, 93.

the motive force of history; struggle in the world of actions and ideas could either reinforce or counteract the remorseless forces of biology. And on one vital point – ironically a notion he shared with Haeckel and with the scurrilous pamphleteers of popular anti-Semitism – Chamberlain was unambiguous: Christ was no Jew, but an Aryan. That dogma and Chamberlain's search for the alleged Teutonic essence of Christianity drew on and dovetailed with existing tendencies among Germany's liberal Protestant theologians and biblical critics, who in the 1880s and 1890s evolved a fiercely contentious stance toward Judaism and the seeming perversity of its adherents in resisting conversion. Above all, Chamberlain, unlike the lugubrious Gobineau or the cultural pessimists who mourned an imagined past, was an optimist. *Foundations* was almost Hegelian in relentlessly driving history toward a triumphant conclusion in the world mission of the Teutonic spirit incarnate in the Prusso-German Reich. Chamberlain had created a racist bible for a Protestant majority too attached to Christianity to embrace Wotan or Monism. He had also hit by accident upon the same explosive mixture of determinism and voluntarism that distinguished that other great twentieth-century ideology of apocalyptic conflict, Marxism-Leninism.[166]

The external political corollaries of such visions were inevitably far-reaching, and intersected with the neo-Rankean musings of the German professoriate. The post-1890 age of world politics seemed to fulfill the prophecies that figures such as Tocqueville had made in the 1830s and 1840s: Russia and the United States, new powers of continental scale, were coming to dominate the world. The British empire, effortlessly paramount until the 1860s, had the required size but lacked the necessary large homogeneous population, as its own statesmen and commentators increasingly recognized. Germany, despite its late start, thus had a brief opportunity to replace Britain in the charmed circle of world powers by victory in the struggle foreseen by Treitschke and christened the "War of the English Succession" by Max Lenz of the University of Berlin.[167]

The underpinnings of the professors' "theory of the three world empires" received their most rigorous formulation at the hands of yet another Monist and Pan-German professor, Friedrich Ratzel of the University of Leipzig. Ratzel,

---

[166] For all this, see Martin Woodruffe, "Racial Theories of History and Politics: The Example of Houston Stewart Chamberlain," in Kennedy and Nicholls, eds., *Nationalist and Racist Movements*, 143–53; Geoffrey G. Field, *Evangelist of Race. The Germanic Vision of Houston Stewart Chamberlain* (New York, 1981), chs. 5–7; Uriel Tal, *Christians and Jews in Germany. Religion, Politics and Ideology in the Second Reich 1870–1914* (Ithaca, NY, 1975), especially 191–222; and Williamson, *Myth*, 286–87.

[167] See especially the analysis and testimony of Dehio: "Ranke and German Imperialism" and "Thoughts on Germany's Mission 1900–1918," in his *Germany and World Politics in the Twentieth Century*, 38–108. Lenz, *Die grossen Mächte* (Berlin, 1900), 150, used the phrase without direct reference to an Anglo-German war, but went on to compare the struggle of the Boers to that of Hermann and the Cherusci, and asked "What then, if England is now truly compelled to fight, not merely for its position in Africa, but for its world position?"

remembered as the father of geopolitics, called his creation bio-geography. In *Politische Geographie*, a lengthy 1897 meditation on the "geographical foundations of political power," and in his 1901 essay, "*Lebensraum*. A Biogeographical Study," Ratzel applied to foreign policy the same biological determinism that Haeckel had fastened upon internal politics: "the much misused and still more misunderstood expression 'struggle for existence' means first and foremost struggle for space [*Kampf um Raum*]."[168] The history of peoples – or at least the history of peoples with aptitude for *Kampf* – moved teleologically "from narrower to broader spaces." It involved constant struggle for the "adjustment of *Raum* to population," those twin "political-geographic constants to which all other political factors . . . must be related." The occupation of wide "living space" offered protection from interbreeding and was thus necessary for the creation and preservation of distinct species and subspecies; "the blond race" of Aryans around the Baltic, where Neolithic skulls and those "in yesterday's graves" were allegedly identical, was apparently a product of such broad spaces. True *Realpolitik* was thus the art of securing "for [one's] growing *Volk* the indispensable soil for the future"; borders and treaties were transitory artificial restraints. Expansion by sea – for Ratzel also served in the front ranks of the "fleet-professors" – was the true school of world powers. The sea was "the bearer of progress in history"; Ratzel knew his Thucydides and his Mahan.[169] Yet on land Ratzel displayed a degree of modesty, despite occasional mention of Germany's lack of *Raum*. In noting the Reich's failure to assimilate or swamp the Alsatians seized in 1871, he conceded that "Europe's fragmentation is not to be healed through conquest."[170]

Yet in the hands of others his "bio-geographic" premises combined with other German traditions and swiftly overwhelmed that relative moderation, as the fate of the "Herero *Volk*" demonstrated. And even before 1914 Germany's elites had ready at hand a fateful example of the struggle for *Raum* closer to home than Southwest Africa: the conflict of German against Pole in Posen and West Prussia. The steadily intensifying if unsuccessful efforts to Germanize Prussia's Poles were originally political in inspiration, even if Bismarck privately raged about eliminating Polish noble "trichinae." Yet by 1900 Bülow could already propose privately a remedy almost biological in its rigor: to exploit the opportunity that an eventual war would offer to "expel the Poles from our Polish areas *en masse*."[171] The Pan-Germans, with characteristic verve, extrapolated from that remedy. They openly demanded the seizure of vast tracts of the

168 *Politische Geographie* (Munich, 1897), vol. 1, 343 ("die Biogeographie"); idem, *Der Lebensraum. Eine Biogeographische Studie* (Tübingen, 1901), 51; see also Lange, "Der Terminus 'Lebensraum,'" 429–30.

169 The rise of Greece as the history of naval power: Thucydides, book I, 4–15; Alfred Thayer Mahan, *The Influence of Sea Power upon History, 1660–1783* (Boston, 1890).

170 Ratzel, *Das Meer als Quelle der Völkergrösse* (Munich, 1904), 5, 54; idem, *Politische Geographie*, 9, 360, 383, 388, 389–90, 603; *Der Lebensraum*, 67–71.

171 See Wehler, "Polenpolitik im Deutschen Kaiserreich 1871–1918," in his *Krisenherde des Kaiserreichs 1871–1918* (Göttingen, 1970); quotations, 110–11.

European continent and the application of colonial methods tested in Africa to the lesser European nationalities, Poles, Czechs, Jews – and Italians. Their remedies horrified some members of the governing elite; the Kaiser himself remarked presciently that the Pan-German prescription for the "Jewish Question" would banish Germany "from the ranks of civilized nations [*Kulturnationen*]."[172] But should the iron dice roll once more, the visions of the pan-Germans and the broader radical nationalist consensus in which they played a central role might easily acquire a mass following.

5. FATEFUL PECULIARITIES: THE VIEW FROM 1914

National histories are unique; all societies travel their own *Sonderwege*. But by the end of the long nineteenth century Italy and Germany, despite their many and varied differences, had evolved common features not shared with their eastern or western neighbors. Russia, despite its swift and tumultuous economic ascent in the two decades after 1890, remained a turbulent peasant society with a thin veneer of bureaucrats, intellectuals, and state-supported entrepreneurs. Over it all, a unique autocracy that blended Byzantine, Tartar, and Western absolutist traditions perched with increasing precariousness. That autocracy, its army and police, ultimately mastered the revolution that defeat at the hands of Japan unleashed in 1905; Russia's thin and hesitant liberalism failed its one slim chance for a classic nineteenth-century western European revolution. But unlike the failure of the German liberals in 1848, the defeat of the 1905 revolution was no prelude to victories by Russian Bismarcks and Moltkes, and to a constitutional compromise weighted toward the autocracy but capable of integrating the masses into the state. The triumph of the autocracy merely poised it for final catastrophe in a second and far greater war.[173]

To the west, the societies and polities of Britain and France likewise differed from those of Italy and Germany in ways that help explain later events. Britain had by 1914 become the world's first mature industrial society. More than three-fifths urban, it possessed neither unruly peasants nor toiling urban masses in thrall to the Marxist gospel. Its aristocracy and middle classes had succeeded, despite occasional crises such as that attending the Reform Bill of 1832, in composing their differences without bloodshed. Britain's monarchy and parliamentary system enjoyed the legitimacy born of age and external success. Parliament, not the as yet tiny bureaucracy, nor the small professional army stationed mainly outside Britain, nor even the great navy that secured Britain's global position, was its political center of gravity. The booted and spurred Cromwell, quartering cavalry in England's cathedrals and ruling by

---

[172] See Hartmut Pogge von Strandmann, "Staatsstreichpläne, Alldeutsche und Bethmann-Hollweg," in idem and Imanuel Geiss, *Die Erforderlichkeit des Unmögichen: Deutschland am Vorabend des Ersten Weltkrieges* (Frankfurt am Main, 1965).

[173] For this view of the relationship between 1905 and 1917, see Malia, *Comprendre la Révolution russe.*

military decree, had long since taught the dangers of great leaders and of force uncontrolled by representative government.

The two major parties, largely consolidated before the full impact of mass politics and under an electoral law that compelled the formation of a few large groupings, were uniquely capable of reducing the electorate's inchoate aspirations to coherent policy. Whereas the enlargement of the electorate by 1884 to something approaching universal male suffrage did not give representation swiftly enough to head off all extraparliamentary protest, it effortlessly tamed the workers' movements that after 1900 coalesced to form the Labour Party. Only the Catholic and increasingly nationalist population of Ireland, England's first and most recalcitrant colony, remained permanently unreconciled.

Finally, Britain's religious and mythological landscape offered little raw material for the erection of violent cults. Locke's notion – bizarre by continental standards – that politics should serve the happiness of the individual occupied the same place in British political culture as the all-consuming *nation* of the French revolutionaries, the state-idolatry of Hegel, or the self-deification of the German people. No ethnic-linguistic mythology of the sort Fichte and so many others had developed out of Herder could flourish in a land of mixed population speaking a patchwork of Anglo-Saxon, Norman French, Latin, and Greek. In Britain neither race nor nation-state figured as primary source of individual self-fulfillment. No statesmen addressed parliament in cuirassier uniforms. And Britain's world mission, which enthusiasts proclaimed and in which much middle opinion actively or subliminally believed, was after 1815 an accomplished fact rather than a call to battle. The Boer War indeed brought home to the public what had long been obvious to "reluctant imperialists" in Whitehall: the empire was too far-flung and its subjects too numerous and unruly to dominate in comfort.

The left wing of the Liberal Party, despite increasing evidence that the world did not conform to the naive faith of Cobden and Bright, remained an influential purveyor of pacific reasonableness and social reform, luxuries appropriate to an imperially satiated island state with the world's largest navy. That example the nascent Labour Party largely followed. Anglicanism, that smooth and skeptical English version of the "union of throne and altar" that had such a different career in Prussia-Germany, helped immunize British elites, from county bloodsport hearties to Protestant Ulster *Junkers*, against stronger infections. Nonconformist Protestantism, with its pacifist undertones and its deep influence on the working classes, was an even firmer barrier to anything resembling continental fanaticism.

Anti-Semitism remained a religious and social prejudice that was extraordinarily mild by European standards. That Disraeli, a baptized Jew proud of his origins, could become leader of a party that called itself conservative – and eventually prime minister – was a source of puzzlement and of endless conspiracy theories south and east of the Channel. Racist pseudo-science failed to achieve the lodgments in the universities that it secured in Germany. No schools of biopolitics arose. Darwin's cousin, the eugenicist Francis Galton, found the

British climate of opinion relatively hostile to his theories, which had led him into affiliation with Haeckel.[174]

The dawning realization of the relative decline of Britain's economy, the shock of initial military humiliation at the hands of Boer backwoodsmen, and the German naval threat to Britain's own independence led to nothing more drastic than a larger naval budget and ineffectual campaigns for "national efficiency" or conscription by a variety of Conservative and Liberal Imperialist "ginger groups."[175] Despite the 1909–11 constitutional crisis over the veto of the House of Lords, the uproar over women's suffrage, the rebelliousness of Ulster's Protestants, the consequent disaffection of a segment of the officer corps, and the threat of a paralyzing general strike by coal miners, railwaymen, and transport workers, Britain by 1914 was by continental standards a profoundly stable and settled society and polity.

France, for all its seven regimes between 1792 and 1870 and its colorful succession of crises thereafter, achieved a not dissimilar result. Socially, it remained far more rural than Germany, and its proportion of city-dwellers, at 26 percent, did not match even that of Italy. But its industrial growth rate was level with Germany's for the 1890–1910 period and its rate of shrinkage of agricultural employment was only slightly less than that of Germany. The rate of decline of its artisans, a trend that in Germany purportedly helped create legions of lower-middle-class losers in the modernization process ready to embrace anti-Semitism and dictatorship, was if anything swifter than Germany's.[176] France's Jewish community, at just under two-tenths of a percent of the total population in 1897, was scarcely larger than Italy's. But its overwhelming concentration in Paris and surroundings (home of 64 percent of France's Jews by the 1890s) and the capital's all-dominance in politics and culture ensured that the achievements and wealth of France's Jews would gall the envious almost as much as those of their far more numerous German counterparts.[177]

Yet politically France had crossed the threshold of mass politics in the 1790s, after the United States but before Britain. By 1871 universal manhood suffrage was a principle accepted even by the royalists, who sought to profit from it. Thereafter the conservative electorate of landholding peasants and urban republican lower middle classes provided a broad and stagnant reservoir of votes for a shapeless parliamentary center that ruled effectively despite the apparent chaos of its ever-changing ministries. The Republic resisted threats from the Right, in the 1877 crisis that emasculated the presidency and ensured the dominance of the Chamber of Deputies, during the Parisian agitation surrounding General

---

[174] See Poliakov, *Aryan Myth*, 291–98.

[175] For the contrast between aims, methods, and breadth of appeal of British and German chauvinist groups, and between the relative strength of British pacifism and its German counterpart, see especially Kennedy, *The Rise of the Anglo-German Antagonism, 1860–1914* (London, 1980), 369–81, and the essays in Kennedy and Nicholls, eds., *Nationalist and Racist Movements*.

[176] See Kaelble, "Mythos von der rapiden Industrialisierung," 113.

[177] Numbers: Doris Bensimon and Sergio Della Pergola, *La population juive de France: socio-démographie et identité* (Paris, 1984), 26.

Georges Boulanger in the late 1880s, and in the climactic confrontation between Catholic royal France and lay republican France at the turn of the century, the affair of Captain Alfred Dreyfus. The Republic defied the Church and cut it loose from the state. As German pressure increased after 1905, the Republic defied Germany as well.

And despite its status as the pioneer of political nationalism and its checkered history before 1871, France's mythological landscape was unconducive to the creation of imperial anthropologies or dictatorial leadership-myths. The Revolution had created the political nation. The blood-drenched origins of French nationalism were inextricably bound up with republican symbols: the tricolor, the Marseillaise, and the Declaration of the Rights of Man and the Citizen. Those symbols, after the defeat of the first Napoleon and the 1.8 million dead of his wars had chastened France, helped redefine France's external mission as predominantly cultural: France was the center of *civilization*. Then the trauma of defeat and territorial amputation in 1870–71 gave French nationalism a defensive tone not overcome even on the eve of war in 1914.[178]

Race in France was originally the banner of gloom-ridden aristocrats such as Gobineau, obsessed with defeat at the hands of the revolutionaries of 1789–94; France's most prominent theorist of race preferred to divide the French rather than unite them. Nor did the evidence of ethnography, of the exceedingly mixed nature of the French population, encourage racist appeals. France's greatest nineteenth-century historian and preeminent prose-poet of populist nationalism, Jules Michelet, insisted that "France was not a race as Germany was, but a nation." Ernest Renan, the dominant Parisian master-thinker from the 1860s through the 1880s, indeed accepted Gobineau's conception of race and the German Romantic notion that the Germans, unlike the French, had "clung to their primordial roots and speak a language that has its origin in itself." But Renan had to concede that "France does not believe overmuch in race."[179] That disbelief found reflection even in the pre-1914 cult of "the soil and the dead" of Maurice Barrès and the anti-republican Right, a cultural rather than a pseudo-biological myth, despite implausible efforts to equate it with the racist notions of "blood and soil" from east of the Rhine.[180]

The few French race theorists to take up Gobineau's cause explicitly thus remained isolated figures.[181] Georges Vacher de Lapouge, France's most

---

[178] See especially Jean-Jacques Becker, *1914. Comment les français sont entrés dans la guerre* (Paris, 1977), chs. 1–2.

[179] Michelet: Theodore Zeldin, *France 1848–1945. Intellect and Pride* (Oxford, 1980), 14 (see, in general, Zeldin's entire chapter, "The National Identity"). Renan: letter to Gobineau, 1856, quoted in Poliakov, *Aryan Myth*, 206–07. "Amalgam": Jacques Bainville, in ibid., 272.

[180] See the careful analysis of Linda L. Clark, *Social Darwinism in France* (University, AL, 1984), 95–105, of the positions of Barrès, Maurras, and associated figures, none of whom espoused Haeckel's equation between biology and politics. Even at the literal level, *la terre et les morts* is different in emphasis than *Blut und Boden*.

[181] On their place in French thought, see Clark, *Social Darwinism in France*, 143–54, which suggests that Sternhell, *La droite révolutionnaire*, exaggerates both the coherence and the influence of French racist theory.

prominent craniologist and for William II "the only great Frenchman," indeed surpassed his German contemporaries in stunning insight into the final consequences of the racist faith:

> I am convinced [he wrote in 1887] that in the next century people will slaughter one another by the millions because of a degree or two of difference in the cephalic index. It is by this sign, replacing the Biblical *shibboleth* and linguistic affinities, that nationalities will be identified. Only it will no longer be, as today, a question of pushing back a few kilometers of frontier; the superior races will substitute themselves by force for the human groups retarded in evolution, and the last sentimentalists will be able to witness copious exterminations of peoples.[182]

But unlike his German opposite numbers in whose *Politische-Anthropologische Revue* he sometimes published, Vacher de Lapouge failed as dismally as had Gobineau to fashion a pseudo-biological foundation for French nationalism. A theory that insisted that the Revolution had been a racial struggle in which the "dolicho-blonds" of the nobility had succumbed to France's majority of brachycephalic "born slaves" had its limitations as a tool of mass politics. Nor did Lapouge, a librarian confined by his eccentricities to provincial universities such as Montpellier, Rennes, and Poitiers, enjoy the prestige and power of German racists and eugenic enthusiasts. "Determinism, inequality, selection" failed to command the audience of "liberty, equality, fraternity." His career was that of an embittered outsider, and his final publication, fittingly enough, explained to the readers of a German racist journal "how anthroposociology was throttled in France."[183]

If "anthroposociology" lacked influence, religious and socioeconomic anti-Semitism did achieve wide currency in popular works such as Edouard Drumont's *La France juive* (1885). But it aroused far more forceful opposition in France than in Germany. The differences in this respect between the two societies before 1914 revealed in the Dreyfus affair, that showpiece of French anti-Semitism, are so obvious that they are normally overlooked. Dreyfus, a practicing if not notably devout Jew, had not only received a regular army commission – already unthinkable in Germany, although common in Italy – but was assigned to the holy of holies, the general staff. Ten French generals and hundreds of regular army officers were also Jewish; the *affaire* was as much or more about the army's reputation and autonomy as it was about anti-Semitism.[184] And in the end, although the army hierarchy and Catholic France threw their

---

[182] Vacher de Lapouge, "L'Anthropologie et la science politique," (1887), quoted in Clark, *Social Darwinism in France*, 145; also Jennifer Michael Hecht, "Vacher de Lapouge and the Rise of Nazi Science," *Journal of the History of Ideas* 61:2 (2000), 287.

[183] Quotations: Poliakov, *Aryan Myth*, 269–70; Vacher de Lapouge, "Wie die Anthroposoziologie in Frankreich erdrosselt wurde," *Die Sonne: Monatschrift für Rasse, Glauben und Lebensgestaltung* 13 (1936), 193–95, cited in Clark, *Social Darwinism in France*, 249.

[184] See Eugen Weber, "Reflections on the Jews in France," in Frances Malino and Bernard Wasserstein, eds., *The Jews in Modern France* (Hanover, NH, 1985), 22–25; also Patrice Higonnet, "On the Extent of Anti-Semitism in Modern France," ibid., 207–13; the otherwise vital essay of Shulamit Volkov, "The Written Matter and the Spoken Word: On the Gap Between Pre-1914 and Nazi Anti-Semitism," in François Furet, ed., *Unanswered Questions* (New York, 1989),

entire weight into the battle to maintain Dreyfus's fraudulent conviction for treason, the Republic belatedly exonerated him.

Given the relative unserviceability of racialism and even anti-Semitism, France's anti-parliamentary Right sought other myths. Bonapartism had touched earth under the Second Empire, even before Sedan had reversed the verdict of Jena-Auerstädt. Boulanger, the man on horseback who challenged the Republic in 1888–89, was both republican by conviction and sadly irresolute in action. France seemed strangely lacking in the great leaders of the feminine crowd that Le Bon had described.[185] Boulanger's fiasco left intact only monarchism, upon which the most successful prophet of the Right, Charles Maurras, fastened as foundation for an anti-republican ideology of "integral nationalism." But like the purported racial struggle between the nobility and the inferior masses to which royalist ideology was linked, monarchism divided rather than united France. Maurras and his cohorts in the *Action Française* movement failed to attract anything approaching a mass following except in Paris and in the Catholic subculture still linked sentimentally to the *ancien régime*. Inexorably, the conservative Catholicism of that constituency overcame the anti-republican radicalism of the organization's origins. And far more important, the Republic's own vitality and the growing external threat ensured that the *Action Française* had far less success than the *nazionalisti* and the Pan-Germans in their respective efforts to monopolize the national cult. A republic that could wield the symbols of republican nationalism, mobilize opinion for increased armaments and lengthened military service in 1912–13, and produce *chefs* of the stature and ruthlessness of Georges Clemenceau and Raymond Poincaré need not fear monarchist agitation.[186]

Italy and Germany, despite their differences, were in a separate category. Both states failed to integrate adequately the massive Catholic and Socialist subcultures – for which the German term *Lager*, or armed camp, seems peculiarly appropriate – bequeathed to them by their religious histories or generated by industrialization. United Italy, understandably given the greater unevenness of its economic and social development, was least successful in managing the two new mass forces. Italian Catholics, despite their initial defiance of a state that had overthrown the Papacy's temporal rule, did move guardedly to shore up Giolitti's system against the Socialists. The Libyan War proved a watershed; Catholic nationalism, a phenomenon unthinkable forty years earlier, revealed itself as a mighty force. Yet political Catholicism entered Giolitti's system under a cloud of ambiguity. He saw the Catholics as Liberalism's junior partners; they

33–53, passes over a key asymmetry between French and German anti-Semitism; German anti-Semitism was integral to Prussia-Germany's most powerful institution.

[185] Especially significant are Barrès's difficulties in finding suitable heroes (see Philip Ouston, *The Imagination of Maurice Barrès* [Toronto, 1974], ch. 8). Joan of Arc was clearly no adequate rival to Bismarck or the "hidden Kaiser."

[186] See in general Eugen Weber, *Action Française. Royalism and Reaction in Twentieth-Century France* (Stanford, CA, 1962) and *The Nationalist Revival in France, 1905–1914* (Berkeley, CA, 1969).

saw themselves as its heirs. And the Libyan War that offered the Catholics a chance to demonstrate their newfound national solidarity inflamed the Socialists' rural constituency and unleashed the eloquence of preachers of redemptive violence such as Benito Mussolini. Whereas in Germany the Marxist myth of violent revolution gripped a small and powerless minority within the SPD, in Italy after 1912 it dominated both Socialist leadership and masses.

Germany, despite greater success at taming its subcultures, nevertheless exemplified that "inner *Zerrissenheit*" for which Heinrich Class and others had long prescribed war. German Socialists, despite persecution by the state and their own public commitment to a Marxist millennium, had by 1914 begun their slow transformation into a political pressure group like any other. It was above all the refusal of state, *Junker*, and *Bürger* to accept the SPD that made for the party's isolation and uniqueness. On the religious front, by 1914 Protestant Prussia-Germany commanded the loyalties of its Catholic subjects to an extent inconceivable forty years before. Nevertheless, the Catholic-Protestant divide, reinforced by the regional split between Prussia and south Germany with which it partially coincided, remained one of the two deepest cleavages in German politics. And as in Italy, only with far more powerful consequences, the national camp itself increasingly divided into conservatives loyal to the existing order and radical minorities that sought to destroy or remodel that order in the name of nation or race.

Other features of the two systems reinforced the disruptive potential of these cleavages. The dominant "national" political cultures – Italian liberalism and north-German Protestant nationalism – failed to create mass parties to shore up and supplement the power they held through their states. Italian liberalism, until the coming of virtual universal suffrage in 1913, could dominate parliament with ease without a party organization. German liberalism was notably authoritarian and stridently nationalist, had splintered into two or more parties, and had to divide Protestant votes with the advancing SPD on the one hand and the conservatives of East Elbia on the other. Once both states crossed the threshold of mass politics, their electoral laws ensured that parliament would mirror with ever-greater precision their societies' regional, social, and – in the German case – religious and ethnic conflicts. The narrowness of the Italian suffrage until 1913 and the military-monarchical executive, impotent Reichstag, and drastically unrepresentative Prussian legislature had roughly similar effects: they repressed and turned against the system forces that if left to play themselves out freely in parliamentary government might well have proven innocuous.

Even more dangerously, the myths immanent in the two dominant cultures were substantially more explosive than anything found further west. In July 1914 a British observer noted condescendingly but accurately that "Signor Marinetti's glorification of war, violence and cruelty is like Kipling at fourteen writing in a school magazine, if you could imagine Kipling emancipated from religion and belief in British law and order...." The "make-up exam" of the Libyan War – as the young nationalist historian Gioacchino Volpe christened it – was not enough to expunge the shame of Custoza, Lissa, and Adowa.

The thirst among Italian intellectuals for Oriani's great war to at last make Italy whole was if anything more acute after 1911–12 than before. Even Amendola, who ended his political career in the 1920s as the foremost democratic opponent of militant dictatorship, saw "the warrior, even with all his excess and brutality, [as] a type infinitely superior to the crafty sybarite who finds in the cult of peace the best expression of his pleasure-seeking worldview."[187] Yet despite D'Annunzio's best efforts Italy still lacked myths of leadership appropriate to the age of violence to which the *intelligentsia* aspired. The new elite fated to replace the corrupt and timorous foot soldiers of *giolittismo*, and the oligarchic "new state" supposedly destined to capture at last the loyalty of Italy's masses provided an inadequate focus for nationalist fanaticism. Nor did theories of race offer a potentially egalitarian alternative to that state. The national cult nevertheless increasingly corroded Liberal Italy: for the *literati* and a widening circle of literate Italians, the moderation of Giolitti and of the parliamentary order was a betrayal of a national mission that demanded blood sacrifice.

Germany's mythology was simultaneously more deterministic than anything south of the Alps, more tightly focused upon the figure of a national Führer, far broader in its appeal thanks to its inherent egalitarianism and to the efforts of the Prussian schoolmaster in spreading the blessings of literacy, and less intrinsically unreal than Italy's myths of national destiny. Moderate *Bildungsbürger* hewed to Hegelian bedrock: history as revealed through Bismarck's victories proclaimed Prussia-Germany's world mission. Freer spirits believed that biology was morality, and that it mandated a world mission of the Teutonic branch of the Aryan "race," expressed through the colonial domination of *Raum* in Europe as well as overseas. Virtually all sought Meinecke's "Führer for whom we can march through fire" and failed to find him in William II. Those notions and aspirations extended far down into lower middle classes and the literate peasantry, to which *völkisch* racism offered the "career open to talent." The countervailing myths of the Catholic and Socialist *Lager* were weak indeed compared to their Italian counterparts.

Finally, in the world of action the uniqueness of Germany was incontestable, and heavy with consequences for the entire world. By 1914 German arms and German industry dominated Europe as never before. The "power-dreams of German patriots," in Gerhard Ritter's memorable if embarrassed phrase, rested upon firm foundations. And the men foremost in wielding the "German sword" – the army officer corps – carried within them a unique value system and operational code. Once freed of peacetime restraints, their repertoire would inevitably dictate "*va-banque*" plays with Germany as the stake, and their annihilational goals and autistic notions of "military necessity" would

---

[187] *The New Statesman*, quoted in E. L. Woodward, *Great Britain and the War of 1914–1918* (Boston, 1967), xxx; "esame di riparazione" and great war: see the essential works of Giovanni Belardelli, *Il mito della "nuova Italia." Gioacchino Volpe tra guerra e fascismo* (Rome, 1988), ch. 1 (quotation, 19); Isnenghi, *Mito della grande guerra*, chs. 1–5 (Amendola: 24); and Thayer, *Italy and the Great War*, chs. 8–9.

impose limitless implacable escalation. That radicalism was a fitting complement to the ideologies of radical nationalism with which – in key individuals such as Erich Ludendorff – it eventually merged.

Yet the fissures and contradictions of the two political systems, the disruptive potential of the two national mythologies, and the institutional fanaticism of the German army did not necessarily dictate disaster. In neither Italy nor Germany was war a predetermined *"Flucht nach vorn,"* a "flight forward" by despairing noble elites or a plot by capitalist interests that even in Germany were no more chauvinist than other segments of the ruling classes. In peacetime the inherent caution of Italy's establishment and the strategic vice that gripped Italy between France and Austria-Hungary gave little scope for D'Annunzian posturing and Nationalist agitation. Even limited war in Libya strained Italy's ever-precarious finances and poorly led army. Another few years of peace might have partially pulled the teeth of the Catholics, and returned the Socialists to sanity; Italian liberalism might even have exploited the resulting brief respite to constitute itself as a mass party.

Nor did parliamentary impasse or *Junker* resistance to modernity force Germany inexorably into "social imperialist" adventure in 1914. Bismarck's system was in its origins a compromise with German liberalism, and despite its undeniable rigidities it was capable of gradual if painful evolution.[188] The forces for war within were not products of political impasse; the Reich's domestic structures could easily have accommodated peaceful outcomes. Even as late as 1914, time was arguably on Germany's side. Why not wait to buy Europe rather than conquer it? It was the conjunction of ebullient economic growth, the perceived deterioration of Germany's *external* position between 1906 and 1914, and the manic self-confidence, ingrained gambling instinct, and strategic autism of *both* the German middle classes *and* the officer corps that ultimately made the war. And once launched, war imposed its unique logic on individuals and structures alike, distorting the societies and crumbling the political systems of Italy and Germany, and unleashing the full power of the ideas and forces stored up in the course of the long nineteenth century.

---

[188] For the most trenchant statement of the *"Flucht nach vorn"* thesis, the orthodoxy of the German historical profession from the 1960s to the 1980s, see above all Wehler, *German Empire*, ch. 8; for the later and far more sophisticated version, Wehler, DGG, 3:1152–68.

PART II

FROM WAR TO DICTATORSHIP, 1914–1933

3

The Synthesis of Violence and Politics, 1914–1918

> In the beginning was the deed.
> Heinrich Class,
> after Goethe's *Faust*, 1912

Burckhardt's "pleasant twentieth century" descended upon Europe in August 1914. The Great War, as Europeans soon named it, opened the age of war and revolution that burned away much of the wealth and most of the optimism accumulated in the long peace. The "era of wars" that Burckhardt had foreseen killed a far smaller proportion of the population than the fourteenth-century Black Death. Yet war, aftermath, and renewed war after 1939 savaged at least some of the societies it struck as thoroughly as its seventeenth-century forerunner and the associated "little ice age" of climate-induced famine and epidemic. In absolute numbers it was the greatest catastrophe in Europe's long history. And this Second Thirty Years War – the 1914–45 German War of global hegemony – was entirely man-made.[1]

The first round of the larger struggle, the Great War of 1914–18, was Europe's first full-scale industrial war. It established conclusively what shrewd consideration of the U.S. Civil War had suggested: that French collapse in 1870–71 had been a happy exception, the product of ineptitude in exploiting railroad and telegraph for mobilization and concentration. After 1914 it became increasingly clear that industrial wars did not end until one adversary or coalition had battered the other into submission. War was no longer – if it had ever been – simply a momentary clash of warrior elites, but a test of the strength and staying power of entire societies. Geographic configuration, economic might, political

---

[1] For the long view, see the graphs in Colin McEvedy and Richard Jones, *Atlas of World Population History* (London, 1978), 18, 28. Europe's upward population curve since 400 B.C.E. has four notches: the Barbarian invasions, the Black Death, the "seventeenth-century crisis," and the first half of the twentieth century.

and military leadership, and political and social cohesion determined the fates of the great powers after August 1914.[2]

Britain and above all the United States, blessed with the seas as their moat, could in theory take as much or as little of the war as they wished. The land-locked powers, Germany, Austria-Hungary, and even Russia, had no such con-solation – and their adversaries swiftly cut them off from indispensable outside resources. France and Italy occupied intermediate positions: cursed with land frontiers, yet open to help from the oceans and aligned with the powers that controlled those oceans.

The mature industrial economies, Britain, Germany, and the United States – which rivalled Europe as a whole in total industrial power by 1914 – met the test of industrial war best. France, with much of its mining and manufacturing in German hands after September 1914, fared less well but survived thanks to battlefield doggedness and the support of its allies. Italy and Austria-Hungary, with industrial economies still smaller in proportion to population than those of their western and northern neighbors, suffered accordingly, although Italy ben-efited decisively from external help. Russia, imprisoned by the Danish straits, the Dardanelles, and the Siberian wastes, and with an industrial economy grow-ing chaotically amid a society that remained three-fourths peasant, fared worst of all.

As in the past, political and military leadership was also decisive to the outcome. The essential tasks of the politicians in this first European war fought under virtually total mobilization were two: to brand upon the masses the conviction that the national cause was both just and ultimately victorious, and to match political ends with economic and military means. The performance of the United States and Britain in both areas was adequate for final victory, despite Britain's blood-drenched tactical fiascos on the Somme and in the Flanders mud. France's leaders had little difficulty in the first task: German invasion spoke persuasively of the justice of self-defense.[3] As for the second, France did the essential thing: by military staying power and shrewd diplomacy it secured and kept the allies without which it would have gone under. Italy's leaders largely failed, until disaster at Caporetto in 1917 and German-Austrian invasion of Venetia, to persuade the masses of the necessity of war. Nor did those leaders ever devise a strategy for applying Italy's limited resources to best effect. Germany's leaders succeeded brilliantly at persuading the masses that Germany had fallen victim to a ring of diabolical enemies, but failed equally spectacularly at matching their limitless goals to Germany's finite means. Austria-Hungary and Russia fared worst in all respects; the war in the East was a race toward

---

[2] For a suggestive comparative treatment of some determinants of national performance that concentrates on Germany and Russia, see Gottfried Schramm, "Militarisierung und Demokratisierung. Typen der Massenintegration im Ersten Weltkrieg," *Francia* 3 (1975), 476–97; David Stevenson, *The First World War and International Politics* (London, 1988), offers the best introduction to the diplomacy and strategy of the war.

[3] Becker, *Comment les français sont entrés dans la guerre*, part 3 and 580.

destruction by ill-led ramshackle empires. Russia, deprived of the help of its allies by geography, won that race by a year.

War scarcely tried the political and social cohesion of the United States. Britain's class society held to the end; the willingness of the elites to tax themselves and die at the front counteracted in some measure the demoralizing effects of deaths, privation, pacifist propaganda, and the manifest tactical-operational incompetence of many of Britain's generals. France's peasant-bourgeois order likewise proved equal, amid immense sacrifice, to the task of national defense; repression and concessions together averted near-collapse in the army mutinies of 1917. Italy entered the war far less united politically and far more fractured socially than France and Britain; it emerged from the Caporetto disaster in 1917–18 in a condition worse than that of France. Germany, despite multiple cleavages of *Stand* and class, preserved enough cohesion to hang on until 1917–18 in the expectation of final victory. But when disillusion came, government although not the social order collapsed. Austria-Hungary's cleavages were above all those between nationalities. But Entente refusal or failure to exploit those cleavages until 1917–18 and Austrian success in pitting the empire's nationalities against their respective external hereditary enemies slowed the empire's breakdown. In Russia, the autocracy swiftly ran through its remaining capital of inherited loyalty to the "little father," Nicholas the Last. Military disaster and administrative collapse unleashed the fierce resentments of the urban workers and toppled the precariously balanced rural order.

Geography, economics, leadership, and cohesion or its absence thus interacted to produce a startling range of outcomes. The United States emerged unscathed. It was too insulated by distance and entered too late to suffer invasion or feel the full weight of casualties; in economic terms its war was less a strain than an opportunity for expansion into markets that Europe had dominated. Britain emerged shaken but – thanks also to geography – with no worse result from the viewpoint of its elites than daunting casualty rolls, crushing taxation, diminished economic vitality, and two ineffectual Labour governments in 1924 and 1929–31. France, with the highest per capita losses, suffered the mortal wound to its self-confidence revealed in 1940, but its tenacious social system and even its less durable Third Republic remained standing. Italy, facing smaller proportionate losses with far less cohesion under blinkered leadership and in a cause foreign to the masses, suffered damage to the Liberal regime that swiftly proved fatal. Germany, with losses second proportionately only to France and under severe strain from the Allied "hunger-blockade," collapsed after exertions that would have shattered most of its adversaries, but preserved civil society and its will to power largely intact. Austria-Hungary dissolved into its component nationalities, but again without large-scale destruction of existing social relationships. Only Russia suffered both political-military collapse and the physical annihilation of an entire social order, a unique outcome with terrifying consequences. Yet the two powers in the middle, Germany and Italy, also succumbed through war and in war's long aftermath to the rule of "terrifying simplifiers." Understanding that result requires meditation on the differing ways in which their leaders, elites, and masses interpreted the war, on the economic and social transformations that it brought, and on the processes through which the Liberal and Imperial regimes eroded and crumbled.

1. THE MEANING OF THE WAR: THE INNER CIRCLE FROM EUPHORIA TO RESENTMENT

In the meaning given the Great War lies one key to its perpetuation until Germany's interim destruction as a state in 1945. For all their many differences, the leaders of both Italy and Germany in 1914–15 stood united in one essential respect. They both willed war.

I. Germany: "Even If We Go Down in Ruin..."

The Germans inevitably willed it more decisively and on a larger scale than the leaders of any other power. The Kaiser and Bethmann Hollweg tipped the balance in Vienna in favor of crushing Serbia in July 1914 with veiled threats to leave Austria-Hungary to its fate if it failed to act. When the expected continental war threatened, they plunged ahead.[4] Germany's "leap in the dark, and heaviest duty," as Bethmann Hollweg described it on 14 July, was ostensibly a reply to the supposedly undeserved "encirclement" that Germany's annexation of Alsace-Lorraine, naval threat to Britain's jugular, and bullying of France and Russia after 1905 had summoned up, and to the rotting away of Austria-Hungary, Germany's sole great-power ally.[5] Action had been in the official mind since December 1912, when a warning from London that Germany could not crush France without facing war with Britain had provoked the irate Kaiser to summon an impromptu "council of war."

---

[4] Szögyény to Berchtold, 5 July 1914; Berchtold to Tisza, 8 July 1914, in Imanuel Geiss, ed., *July 1914. The Outbreak of the First World War. Selected Documents* (New York, 1967), 77, 102. The interpretation offered in Fritz Fischer, *Germany's Aims* and *War of Illusions* has on balance stood up against criticism from those who blame the war on a failure of "crisis management," on the alliance systems, on inflexible military planning, or on the European *Zeitgeist* (see especially James Joll, *The Origins of the First World War* [New York, 1984]). Also useful for what follows are Gasser, *Preussischer Militärgeist*, and John C. G. Röhl, "Admiral von Müller and the Approach of War, 1911–1914," HJ 12:4 (1969), 651–73; idem, "An der Schwelle zum Weltkrieg. Eine Dokumentation über den 'Kriegsrat' vom 8. Dezember 1912," MGM 21 (1977), 77–134; idem, "Der militärpolitische Entscheidungsprozess in Deutschland am Vorabend des Ersten Weltkriegs," in his *Kaiser, Hof und Staat. Wilhelm II und die deutsche Politik* (Munich, 1987); Holger Afflerbach, *Falkenhayn: Politisches Denken und Handeln im Kaiserreich* (Munich, 1996), ch. 5; and Mombauer, "A Reluctant Military Leader? Helmuth Von Moltke and the July Crisis of 1914," WIH 6:4 (1999), 417–46.

[5] Bethmann: Riezler, *Tagebücher*, 185. The portions of this source covering the July crisis were recopied at a later date and apparently suffered patriotic deletions or alterations (see especially the bitter charges of Schulte, *Verfälschung der Riezler-Tagebücher*). The passages of the surviving text that suggest a German war of aggression are thereby all the more credible.

There Helmuth von Moltke the Younger had spoken for the army: war was "inevitable, and the sooner the better." Moltke nevertheless had undisclosed qualms. The army as yet lacked the immense forces that Schlieffen's plan required; the Prussian ministry of war's fierce resistance to further dilution of the officer corps prevailed until 1911–12. And even assuming Schlieffen's planned lighting victory in the West, Moltke feared "a long [and] exhausting struggle" involving Britain as well as France and Russia, and lasting perhaps two years.[6] Yet the ever-growing relative strength of Germany's putative adversaries and Russia's rapidly expanding railway network on Germany's eastern border threatened to checkmate Schlieffen's concept. After 1916 the Russians might well mobilize swiftly enough to seize Berlin before the Germans crushed France.

Both the officer corps' claim to be Germany's "first *Stand*" and the middle-class world power aspirations that had propelled German policy since the 1890s were at risk. The precedents of 1866 and 1870 alone made confession that the army could not win decisively unthinkable for the pre-1914 generation of general staff officers. For the individual, such a confession meant professional suicide; for the officer corps, the end of its unique social position as the foremost servants of the state and giddy pinnacle of Prusso-German society. And once Germany's threats against France, Russia, and Britain had completed Germany's "encirclement" between 1905 and 1911, the army could argue – since its culture dictated that the Entente must be as predatory as itself – that the Reich's last hope was preemption before 1916–17. That same logic applied with even greater force to the external aspirations of the German middle classes: the navy had by 1912 clearly failed. Only the army could hack a path to continental domination and world power status, and only if it acted soon.

Moltke and his subordinates therefore demanded and received increases that raised the peacetime strength of the army by a quarter in 1911–13, in defiance of *Junker* resistance to taxes, dilution of the officer corps with non-nobles, and conscription of urban workers alongside politically reliable peasants. In the eyes of the new men – such as Moltke's obsessive mobilization chief, Ludendorff, and the wrathful chieftains of the Army League – the stake was the survival of the *Volk* rather than that of the ruling classes or of the existing German state.[7] Once Moltke had eliminated the alternative of deploying primarily against Russia, all that remained was to find an occasion for what the general repeatedly described as "preventive war" to destroy France – although the perceived threat to the Reich was scarcely immediate and far from certain. Moltke and the Kaiser assigned to the civilians the task of finding an occasion for war that would

---

[6] Fischer, *War of Illusions*, 161–64; for Moltke's long-war fears, Stig Förster, "Illusion des kurzen Krieges," 61–95; Mombauer, *Moltke*, 211, 285, 287–88; and Burchardt, *Friedenswirtschaft und Kriegsvorsorge*, 24–26.

[7] For Ludendorff's quasi-*völkisch* worldview and resulting war aims, see the letters printed in Egmont Zechlin, "Ludendorff im Jahre 1915," HZ 211 (1970), especially 334–37, 340–41, 346–53.

ensure mass support. The age of "cabinet wars," Moltke – echoing his great namesake – insisted in December 1912, was long over. But Germany could nevertheless go to war confidently if it succeeded "in so formulating the *casus belli* that the nation unanimously and fervently takes up arms." In May 1914 Moltke stressed once more to the chief of the foreign office the need for "an early war." To Bethmann Hollweg after Sarajevo he showed the self-assurance of a good company commander preparing to assault a hill: "Yes! We will do it."[8] And in the final week Moltke's pressure for war was decisive; his shining faith in Schlieffen's concept coexisted uneasily with the recognition that war would prove long, gruelling, and perilous.[9]

Bethmann Hollweg, the diplomats, and the Kaiser wavered between a "localized" Austro-Serb war that would split the Entente and give Germany domination of the continent, and the "impending... race-war between the Teutons and the newly overbearing Slavs" (as the Kaiser had described it in 1912) that all viewed with fatalism or anticipation. Bethmann Hollweg – once thought "the 'good German,' impotent to arrest the march of German power, deploring its consequences, yet going along with it" – thwarted William II's fitful efforts to avoid escalation, and aimed for a continental war despite justified fear that it meant the "overthrow of everything that now exists."[10]

Bethmann Hollweg's hopes in the final crisis were three: to keep Britain neutral while Germany crushed France and Russia, to prevent the ever-wavering Kaiser from rescinding his decision for war, and to saddle Russia with responsibility for "world conflagration" in order to dupe Germany's Social Democrats into supporting Germany's war of aggression. In the event he secured only the last two objectives. Brief confusion on 1 August about the position of Britain, and thus of France, caused the Kaiser to countermand the occupation of Luxembourg and ask for deployment against Russia instead – leaving

---

[8] Moltke 1912 quotations from Röhl, "An der Schwelle zum Weltkrieg," 118; see also the Kaiser on "constructing" provocations, December 1912: Lepsius et al., eds., *Die grosse Politik*, 39:11 note 6 (doc. 15560); for army pressure for war in 1914, Fischer, *War of Illusions*, 402–03; Riezler, *Tagebücher*, 275 ("Er sagte eben ja!, wir würden es schaffen."); Hermann von Eckardstein, *Lebenserinnerungen*, 3 vols. (Leipzig, 1920–21), 3:184, quoted in Gasser, *Preussischer Militärgeist*, 87 (Moltke, 1 June 1914: "[W]e are ready; for us, the sooner the better"), and the Foreign Office figures (including Riezler) quoted in the diary of the chief editor of the *Berliner Tageblatt*, Theodor Wolff (Gasser, ibid., vi).

[9] See especially Mombauer, "Moltke and the July Crisis."

[10] "Rassenkampf": William II to Albert Ballin, 15 December 1912, in Röhl, "An der Schwelle zum Weltkrieg," 113; Bethmann the "good German": A. J. P. Taylor, *The Struggle for Mastery in Europe, 1848–1918* (Oxford, 1954), 460; Bethmann on war: Riezler, *Tagebücher*, 183 (7 July 1914); for the chancellor's predilection for continental war, see Bethmann Hollweg's now-famous remark of 8 July (184): "If war comes from the East, so that we must go to war for Austria-Hungary rather than Austria-Hungary for us, then we have the prospect of winning. If war does not come, if the Tsar does not want it or if France, appalled, counsels peace, then we *nevertheless* have the prospect of splitting the Entente through this initiative [so haben wir *doch noch* Aussicht, die Entente über diese Aktion auseinanderzumanoeuvrieren]" (my emphasis); also Mombauer, "Moltke and the July Crisis," 431.

an already frantic Moltke in "tears of despair." But British and Russians soon relieved the army leadership of its momentary embarrassment, and the chief of the Kaiser's naval cabinet could happily note: "The mood is brilliant. The government has been very skillful in making us appear to be attacked." The enthusiasm of the Berlin crowds hailing Kaiser, army, and war inspired the austere and saturnine war minister, Erich von Falkenhayn, to utter a remark Bethmann later judged frivolous, but which summarized well the army's reckless driving spirit: "Even if we go down in ruin, it was beautiful."[11]

Germany's "*ganzer Entschluss*" launched far more than a mere "preventive war" to break a perceived encirclement. From the beginning, German war aims included virtually all of the post-1890 fantasies of Germany's *literati* and officials.[12] By the third week in August army, navy, foreign office, Bethmann Hollweg, the Kaiser, and even the king of Bavaria and the lesser federal princes had begun to explore the carving up of Germany's Franco-Belgian booty and the new shape that German power would impose on European and world politics. By early September Bethmann Hollweg and his assistant Kurt Riezler had drawn up a provisional list of annexations and conditions designed to provide "security for the German Reich for all imaginable time" by reducing neutral Holland to vassalage, erasing or truncating Belgium, emasculating France, and erecting a German-dominated *Mitteleuropa* as the core of Germany's new world-power position. In the East, Bethmann Hollweg had assured a German-Balt professor as early as mid-August, Russia would "be pushed off into Asia." To that end the German foreign office and army had already launched, with the cooperation of activists from the right wing of the SPD, a campaign to foment social revolution in Russia's Muscovite core and nationalist revolt among the peoples on the empire's periphery.[13]

German victory would mean the complete overthrow of the existing world order – the end of the British "maritime world mastery" at which Treitschke had railed, and the creation of a world (im)balance in which Germany would figure as a "world power" alongside Britain and the United States. Within that new framework, German command of Eurasia would – in Riezler's words – mean German "world mastery." Nor were these notions passing fancies born of the enthusiasms of August 1914. Two years later Riezler was still musing on the war's "three-fold meaning – defense against the France of today; preventive war

[11] Müller diary, quoted in Röhl, "Admiral von Müller," 670 and note 99; Riezler, *Tagebücher*, 228 ("Wenn wir auch darüber zu grunde gehen, schön war's doch!"). On the army's decisive role in launching war, see especially Afflerbach, *Falkenhayn*, 153–71, and Mombauer, "Moltke and the July Crisis."

[12] See the remarkable concession (cited in Gasser, *Preussischer Militärgeist*, 73) of this crucial point in 1970 by the Wilhelmine conservative historian Hans Rothfels, author of works such as *Ostraum, Preussentum, und Reichsgedanke* (Leipzig, 1935); for war aims in the German press before 1914, Klaus Wernecke, *Der Wille zur Weltgeltung. Aussenpolitik und Öffentlichkeit im Kaiserreich am Vorabend des Ersten Weltkrieges* (Hamburg, 1970).

[13] Fischer, *Germany's Aims*, 103–06, 132–54; *War of Illusions*, 526–28.

against the Russia of tomorrow (as such too late); struggle for *Weltherrschaft* with England."[14]

But as Riezler also noted later, "the entire original calculation came unstuck through the battle of the Marne."[15] France fought on. Britain intervened with immediate effect, and helped to halt the German advance by marching the small army that the Germans foolishly held in contempt into the gap that opened between the two German armies on the far right wing. Germany remained encircled, despite the operational triumphs of Ludendorff and Paul von Hindenburg over the Russians at Tannenberg and the Masurian Lakes in East Prussia. Falkenhayn, the Kaiser's choice as successor to the broken Moltke, shattered much of the army in October–November 1914 in reckless attempts to break through the British in Flanders, then subsided onto the defensive. The navy confessed sheepishly that British superiority in battleships, and the Royal Navy's canny decision to blockade from Dover and the Scotland-Norway gap, rather than endanger its big ships in close blockade of the mine- and submarine-infested waters off the German coast, nullified Tirpitz's vision of decisive battle "between Helgoland and the Thames."

German victory now required driving one of Germany's three enemies from the war before the superior resources of the Entente ground Germany down. Bethmann Hollweg ignored Falkenhayn's entirely reasonable if unexpected suggestion of November 1914 that Germany must now seek a negotiated peace with at least one adversary, preferably Russia, even if that meant renouncing annexations. Bethmann thereupon unsuccessfully sought the general's removal. Troop and civilian morale, the fate of the monarchy and – most important to the officer corps – of the army itself were at stake. Until autumn 1918 no German leader dared tell the public that the war had come "unstuck."[16] The military culture shared equally by army and civilians – for even Bethmann Hollweg was a major of the reserve – dictated that the sole answer to impasse was further escalation; Falkenhayn's brief moment of strategic insight stemmed from his dramatic failure in Flanders. Yet he and the Reich leadership soon found ways to harness Germany's shrinking resources to the human, technological, and geographic expansion of violence.[17]

Beginning on 5 August 1914, German troops had shot Belgian and French civilians of both sexes and all ages, along with numerous French, Belgian, and

---

[14] Riezler, *Tagebücher*, 200 (21 August 1914) ("The difficulty that the German has in becoming accustomed to the face of world mastery that he *must* show after victory. Modesty has been in our blood for centuries!") and 368 (1 August 1916). For Bethmann's "September Program" and associated August–September 1914 war aims, see especially Fischer, *Germany's Aims*, 103–06, and *War of Illusions*, 516–41.

[15] Riezler, *Tagebücher*, 275 (25 May 1915).

[16] See Karl-Heinz Janssen, *Der Kanzler und der General. Die Führungskrise um Bethmann Hollweg und Falkenhayn (1914–1916)* (Göttingen, 1967), 49–70; on official disinformation about the Marne, Karl Lange, *Marneschlacht und deutsche Öffentlichkeit 1914–1939. Eine verdrängte Niederlage und ihre Folgen* (Düsseldorf, 1974), chs. 4–7.

[17] See especially Hull, *Absolute Destruction*, chs. 9, 10.

British prisoners of war. German units had acted with the express approval of commanders at all levels, in reprisal for imaginary *franc-tireur* attacks that were simply projections of German doctrine, of the codified experience of 1870–71. By one wholly plausible estimate, half the German regiments deployed in the West in summer–autumn 1914 committed at least one atrocity involving the death of ten or more civilians. The supremacy of "military necessity" thus destroyed at the very outset at least 6,000 civilians through casual shootings, organized executions, machine-gunning in town squares, and use as human shields – a tactic permitted by German regulations and unit procedures but in flagrant violation of the Hague conventions upon which the Kaiser had vented his scatological disdain, but which Germany had nevertheless signed and ratified.[18]

But far worse was to come. Unlike the Italians after their delayed entry into the war in 1915, Germany's armies occupied progressively larger spaces until the very eve of defeat in 1918 – from Belgium and northern France to the Baltic lands, Ukraine, and Caucasus. Throughout those spaces, "military necessity" imposed ever-harsher burdens and penalties on civilians, from forced labor by both men and women applied in Belgium, France, Poland, and Russia impartially and with little regard for racist ideology, to mass deportations, pitiless requisitions of crops and livestock that slowly starved entire populations, ruthless seizure of industrial assets and raw materials, scorched-earth destruction of villages and towns, and beatings, executions, and shootings at the least sign of resistance. And in the eastern territories of Germany's Turkish ally, "military necessity" provided the preeminent justification for Germany's acquiescence and complicity in the murder by Turks and Kurds of 1.5 million Armenians in 1915–17.[19]

[18] John Horne and Alan Kramer, *The German Atrocities of 1914: A History of Denial* (New Haven, CT, 2001), chs. 1–2 and especially 74–78; idem, "War Between Soldiers and Enemy Civilians, 1914–1915," in Chickering and Stig Förster, eds., *Great War, Total War* (Cambridge, 2000); Hull, *Absolute Destruction*, 208–12; for high-level knowledge of German atrocities, Riezler, *Tagebücher*, 216–17.

[19] For 1914–18 occupation policy, and a nuanced and archivally based reconstruction of Germany's role in the Armenian genocide, Hull, *Absolute Destruction*, chs. 10–11. Michael Geyer, "Rückzug und Zerstörung 1917," in Gerhard Hirschfeld, Gerd Krumeich, and Irina Renz, eds., *Die Deutschen an der Somme 1914–1918. Krieg, Besatzung, Verbrannte Erde* (Essen, 2006), 163–79, offers a vivid case study of operation ALBERICH, named for Wagner's malevolent dwarf: the army's all-too-successful efforts to perfect, through individual initiative and painstaking organizational labors, the total destruction of the Somme area from which it withdrew, in order to economize forces, in March 1917. For Germany's eastern "military utopia" and continuities with later events, Vejas Gabriel Liulevicius, *War Land on the Eastern Front: Culture, National Identity, and German Occupation in World War I* (Cambridge, 2000); idem, "Von 'Ober-Ost' nach 'Ostland'?," in Gerhard P. Gross, ed., *Die vergessene Front. Der Osten 1914/15: Ereignis, Wirkung, Nachwirkung* (Paderborn, 2006), 295–310; and Johannes Hürter, ed., *Ein deutscher General an der Ostfront. Die Briefe und Tagebuchblätter des Gotthard Heinrici 1941/42* (Erfurt, 2001), especially 18–19. Ulrich Herbert, "Zwangsarbeit als Lernprozess. Zur Beschäftigung ausländischer Arbeiter in der Westdeutschen Industrie im Ersten

Science and technology, now increasingly coming into its own as a tool of war, likewise offered escalatory prospects. From September 1914, and without knowledge of concurrent French experiments with tear gas, the German army invented chemical warfare. The driving force, alongside the army's anxieties about Germany's situation, was Fritz Haber, the great German-Jewish chemist whose nitrogen fixation process contemporaneously secured for Germany the high explosive for four long years of war after the British Royal Navy cut off Germany's imports of nitrates. When the high command asked whether the Allies could swiftly counter German use of war gases, Haber proudly answered in the negative. The army first unleashed Haber's wonder-weapon ineffectually against the Russians, and then used it more convincingly to punch temporary holes in the Allied lines around Ypres in late April 1915. But chlorine, and later German refinements such as phosgene, hydrogen cyanide, "mustard" blister agent, pin-point delivery with gas shells, and simultaneous "variegated fire" of nausea gas and lethal agents offered only tactical advantage. The enemy promptly falsified Haber's naive prediction. And the west-to-east prevailing winds across the western front, a factor the Germans had characteristically failed to weigh sufficiently, made gas delivery far easier for the Allies.[20]

The navy also produced a wonder-weapon, the submarines that Tirpitz had disdained until the British had rendered the High Seas Fleet strategically pointless. Yet Germany began the war with a mere 25 ocean-going boats, a number that rose slowly to roughly 120 by the end of 1916. Its sinking of civilian vessels without warning, as the U-boat's extreme vulnerability on the surface appeared to require, thus merely provided Britain with a convenient pretext for itself cutting off German food imports, in defiance of an international agreement – the 1910 Declaration of London – which it had signed but not ratified.[21]

Throughout 1915–16 Falkenhayn backed the navy's delusional claims of the new weapon's effectiveness – which the navy failed to match with a corresponding build-up in U-boat numbers. The protests and threats of President Woodrow Wilson, after the U-20 sank the Cunard liner *Lusitania* in May 1915 and killed 128 U.S. civilians, nevertheless gave the U-boat skeptics led by Bethmann Hollweg the upper hand for a time. Escalation by land thus seemingly remained the only method of driving one of Germany's three antagonists from the field. Falkenhayn lurched eastward, then west. The great German breakthrough in Galicia in May 1915 that Falkenhayn, August von Mackensen, and his brilliant *chef*, Hans von Seeckt, organized sent the Russians reeling back for an entire long summer. Yet German planning throughout 1915–16 for the annexation of

Weltkrieg," AfS 24 (1984), 285–304, and Geyer, "Rückzug und Zerstörung," 167–72, offer forward-looking introductions to Germany's 1914–18 forced-labor apprenticeship.

[20] See especially Rolf-Dieter Müller, "Total War as the Result of New Weapons? The Use of Chemical Agents in World War I," in Chickering and Stig Förster, eds., *Great War, Total War*, 95–111.

[21] For the inadequacies both of German planning and of postwar assessments, see Philip K. Lundeberg, "The German Naval Critique of the U-boat Campaign, 1915–18," *Military Affairs* 27:3 (1963), 105–18.

Poland or of a Polish "frontier strip" cleared of Poles and Jews in Pan-German fashion precluded a status-quo peace with Russia – had Russia been willing.[22]

Despite his underlying pessimism, Falkenhayn thereupon once again overestimated Germany's strength, and staked its limited manpower and materiel a second time on crushing France; Russia's vast spaces still seemed to promise protracted indecisive conflict. Operation GERICHT – "execution place" – the limited 1916 offensive against the fortified city of Verdun that Falkenhayn ordered to "bleed France's forces white," did likewise for Germany. The field commanders received insufficient instruction in the subtleties of Falkenhayn's initial concept, which was to pulverize the French with artillery while exposing relatively few Germans; attrition was to force French political collapse or open the way for later German breakthroughs. Worse still, Falkenhayn's initial desire to husband German manpower led him – against the advice of most of his subordinates – to restrict the attack frontage to the east bank of the Meuse. Initial German successes thus brought German units under ever more intense fire from artillery on and behind the French-held heights of the west bank. Falkenhayn, as in Flanders in 1914, then escalated to the limits of Germany's limited capabilities: he abandoned his original concept and threw in division after division in delusional efforts to drive the enemy from Verdun. Even Wilhelm Groener, the affable Württemberger in retrospect reputed the most rational senior figure on the general staff, persisted – as German military culture dictated – in seeing Verdun as a contest of mind against matter that Germany could not and must not lose: "the army with the stronger resolve [*Wille*] will win in the end."[23] By mid-summer 1916 both materiel and *Wille* were clearly on the side of the French.

This second ruinous failure of "Falkenhayn the gambler" at last opened the road for Ludendorff and Hindenburg to emerge as Germany's third supreme command of the war – and escalate further. Bethmann Hollweg had long courted the victors of Tannenberg as counterweights to Falkenhayn. He helped to hoist them into the saddle in August 1916 in the crisis provoked by Britain's great offensive on the Somme – backed by the weight of its fully mobilized industrial firepower – and Rumania's imprudent intervention against the Central Powers. Bethmann Hollweg was confident that the "boundless trust" inspired by two years of eastern victories would "electrif[y] army and *Volk*," and might insulate the monarchy from criticism in the event of defeat.[24] The Hindenburg-Ludendorff name and future successes would help the chancellor to fend off the growing clamor for revenge for the British blockade with the submarines

[22] For German border plans, see Imanuel Geiss, *Der polnische Grenzstreifen 1914–1918* (Lübeck, 1960).

[23] Groener diary, 29–30 June 1916, in Wilhelm Groener, *Lebenserinnerungen: Jugend – Generalstab – Weltkrieg* (Göttingen, 1957), 550–51; Afflerbach, *Falkenhayn*, 360–75, 405–09; Hull, *Absolute Destruction*, 220–21; Foley, *German Strategy and the Path to Verdun: Erich von Falkenhayn and the Development of Attrition, 1870–1916* (Cambridge, 2005), chs. 8–9.

[24] Gerhard Ritter, *The Sword and the Scepter. The Problem of Militarism in Germany*, vol. 3 (Coral Gables, FL, 1972), 188 (my translation).

that Tirpitz propaganda and mass credulity had designated as Germany's latest "secret of victory."

Ludendorff and Hindenburg soon drew up the balance sheet of the great *Materialschlachten* of 1916. The ever-increasing "influence of the machine" meant that even the unquestionable "spiritual superiority [*geistige Über-gewicht*]" of the German soldier was not enough. Superiority in cannon, muni-tions, and machine guns was also increasingly required. Germany must there-fore double its munitions and triple its artillery and machine gun production by spring 1917.[25] To carry out this "Hindenburg Program," Ludendorff and a key assistant, Lieutenant Colonel Max Bauer, demanded the mobilization of Germany's last reserves of manpower through the conscription of civilians for war industry; army and heavy industry soon added the rounding up of hundreds of thousands of Belgians for forced labor in Germany. The battle of materiel nevertheless still privileged *Wille*. To steel German will, the supreme command also ordered intensified indoctrination of the troops, and demanded increased propaganda efforts on the home front and freedom for war aims agitation. The expectation of booty would purportedly inspire superhuman effort.

Yet Germany still lacked a warplan, a road to victory. Ludendorff retained Schlieffen's faith in decisive battle, seemingly confirmed by Germany's great victories in the East. Decision in the West was improbable until Germany had the necessary materiel, and by 1916 the endurance of Austria-Hungary, Turkey, and Bulgaria was ominously limited. In December–January 1916–17 Luden-dorff and Hindenburg therefore placed their immense authority squarely behind the harebrained naval claims that U-boats could "force England to its knees" within months by sinking Britain's grain supply. The United States had long since made clear that any resumption of unrestricted submarine warfare meant adding to the Triple Entente a power demonstrably capable of swiftly arming millions, supporting them and its new allies with the world's largest economy, and inclined – as in 1861–65 – toward fighting to a finish.[26] But as with the Schlieffen Plan's provocation of Britain in 1914, the supreme command placed its faith in lightning tactical-operational victory. "I scoff at *Amerika*," was Ludendorff's commentary on Germany's second strategic "*ganzer Entschluss*" of the war, the gamble that decided the conflict. Riezler saw more clearly: the U-boat campaign indeed meant "victory or ruin."[27]

[25] Hindenburg to Bethmann Hollweg, 2 November 1916, in UF, 1:15–16; on the Hindenburg program, see Gerald D. Feldman, *Army, Industry and Labor in Germany 1914–1918* (Princeton, NJ, 1966), 150ff.

[26] Peyton C. March, chief of staff, U.S. Army, best described the resulting U.S. commitment: "We are going to win the war if it takes every man in the United States" (*The New York Times*, August 1918, quoted in Irving Coffman, *The Hilt of the Sword: The Career of Peyton C. March* [Madison, WI, 1966], 91).

[27] "Ich pfeife auf Amerika," which is perhaps slightly more rude than my translation (quoted in Holger Herwig, *Politics of Frustration: The United States in German Naval Planning, 1889–1941* [Boston, 1976], 121); Riezler, *Tagebücher*, 401.

The navy demanded the unleashing of its submarines – and war with the United States – when it did because its experts claimed the U-boats must strike before Britain's 1917 harvest. Yet with consummate irony the Triple Entente at last cracked little more than a month later, opening the prospect of German continental victory and the command of Eurasia. In mid-March 1917 Tsarism disintegrated, and by autumn Russia had left the war in fact if not yet in name. That merely encouraged Ludendorff and Hindenburg to press successfully for still-larger eastern annexations. The failure of the submarines to produce the promised swift decision, along with a final paroxysmal Russian offensive in July 1917, had as its incongruous result the removal of the chancellor who had opposed war with the United States. Bethmann Hollweg succumbed in mid-July 1917 to a concentric assault by the Conservatives, National Liberals, and supreme command on one flank and a Reichstag majority that had begun to doubt victory on the other. His successors were shadow-chancellors balanced uneasily between the supreme command and a gradually more assertive Reichstag.

Ludendorff now pressed forward in the East to create a chain of vassal states from Finland in the north to the grain, iron ore, manganese, and oil of the Ukraine and Caucasus in the south. The Russian empire lost more than a quarter of its territory and three-quarters of its iron and coal production. The treaty of Brest-Litovsk of 3 March 1918 that imposed those terms was indeed a settlement – as William II exultantly remarked – "whose significance only our grandchildren will truly appreciate"; some grandchildren indeed lived to see its realization, although not under German auspices, after the collapse of Soviet Russia.[28] The peace with Rumania, the treaty of Bucharest of May 1918, similarly reduced that land to semi-colonial dependency.[29] In the West, Ludendorff recognized as early as August 1917 that "if we give Belgium back, we can have peace at any time."[30] Yet he would not make the solemn public pledge to restore Belgium needed to shatter British morale and leave Germany with the domination of Eurasia. The navy's demand for the Flanders coast – its principal war aim, along with a megalomaniacal catalog of coveted bases from Faeroes and Azores to Madagascar and Tahiti – stood in the way, along with Ludendorff's own geostrategic fixation on holding much of Belgium and the French ore-fields of Briey-Longwy to deprive the Entente of continental "sally-ports" and assure German autarky in the *next* war.[31]

---

[28] Comparison of the 1918 map in Fischer, *Germany's Aims,* 547, and a post-1991 map of eastern Europe suggests the full extent of Wilhelm's prescience.

[29] Fischer, *Germany's Aims,* 507, 515–23.

[30] Reichsarchiv, *Der Weltkrieg, 1914 bis 1918,* 14 vols. (Berlin, 1925–44), 13:16.

[31] As Bruno Thoss has pointed out ("Diktaturfrage," 42) this geo-strategic element in German war aims is not reducible to the categories of economic or "social imperialism" that German historians prized as all-explanatory from the 1960s to the 1980s. Navy demands: Herwig, "Admirals versus Generals: The War Aims of the Imperial German Navy, 1914–1918," CEH 5 (1972), 216–20, and Gerhard Granier, *Magnus von Levetzow, Seeoffizier, Monarchist und Wegbereiter Hitlers* (Boppard, 1982), 227–29.

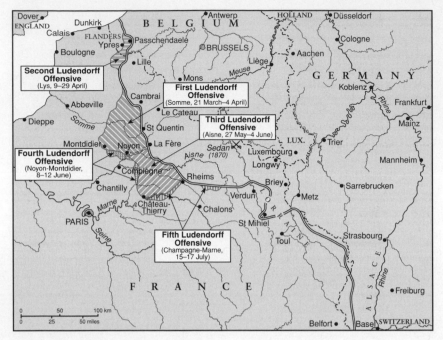

MAP 1. The Western Front, 1918.

As always, the sharp German sword made diplomacy seem unnecessary. Ludendorff had implied as early as January 1917 that he was contemplating a war-winning offensive in the West. The troops set free by Russian collapse now allowed him to mount Imperial Germany's third and last great strategic gamble, a massive series of spring 1918 blows against British and French (see Map 1). At the front, tactics swallowed both operations and strategy, in the final development of Schlieffen's logic. Ludendorff proposed simply to "hack a hole" and take the strategic consequences on faith; to "pulverize" the western allies would be enough. An observer detected "the daring [*Wagemut*] of a leader ... who [was] in the end ready to stake all on a single card." When asked what would happen if the offensive failed, Ludendorff replied unblinkingly: "Then Germany is finished."[32] German military culture and traditions dictated that peace without total annihilational victory on all fronts was defeat. Only total victory could preserve the officer corps as the first *Stand*, the pinnacle

---

[32] Ludendorff offensive intentions, January 1917: Fritz von Lossberg, *Meine Tätigkeit im Weltkriege 1914–1918* (Berlin, 1939), 275; "Das wort 'Operation' verbitte ich mir. Wir hauen ein Loch hinein. Das weitere findet sich": Rupprecht, Kronprinz von Bayern, *Mein Kriegstagebuch* (Munich, 1929), 2:372 note; "[M]an ... trägt sich mit Zerschmetterungsideen": Albrecht Philipp, ed., *Die Ursachen des deutschen Zusammenbruches im Jahre 1918*, vol. 2 (Berlin, 1928), 110; "Dann muss Deutschland eben zugrunde gehen": Max von Baden, *Erinnerungen und Dokumente* (Stuttgart, 1968), 242–43.

of German society; defeat, as an assistant of Ludendorff's put it in autumn 1918, meant a world in which German officers would "eke out their existence impoverished and but little regarded."[33] That was unthinkable. Therefore it was impossible.

The British and the French ultimately held, from native obstinacy and hope that the "Yanks" would belatedly arrive. Ludendorff for his part destroyed the German army. By July 1918 his offensives had cost almost 900,000 casualties; Germany's last manpower reserves vanished on the battlefield or leaked away through desertion, as troops sent west from Russia jumped from the trains on the long slow journey across the Reich.[34] Yet the Reich leadership still disdained negotiation. Germany's loss of the initiative paralyzed Ludendorff's will. Immediately after the first mass surrenders of German troops on the "black day" of 8 August 1918, the Kaiser, with belated wisdom, insisted that "we are at the limits of our capabilities; the war must be ended." But Hindenburg soothed the resulting crown council of 14 August with the bland assurance that German troops would "succeed in holding on French soil, thus in the end compelling the enemy to do our will." Toward the end of September repeated British-Australian-Canadian breakthroughs in the West, the crumbling of Turkey and Austria-Hungary, the collapse of Bulgaria, and the appearance at the front of thirty-eight United States divisions, "each [one] twice as strong as one of ours," at last forced Ludendorff to a conclusion: only a breathing space, an immediate armistice, would forestall catastrophe.[35]

Yet he still sought to dictate the war's meaning, even while surrendering control to the diplomats – who had ready a plan to play Woodrow Wilson against the Entente – and to the politicians. Once the Reichstag parties took power, as he now demanded, Ludendorff's defeat would be theirs, but past victories would still belong to the supreme command. "They shall now eat the soup they have cooked for us," he told his staff darkly on 1 October. The officer who noted his words already saw the double-chinned Ludendorff as a tragic *Nibelungenlied* "hero-figure," a "Siegfried with the death-wound from Hagen's spear in his back." Ludendorff for his part secretly hoped that Wilson's terms would prove "insufferable," giving the pretext for a *levée en masse* without revolution, an outbreak of "*furor teutonicus . . .* that would give us the ability to fight on albeit into annihilation," as a subordinate suggested

---

[33] Albrecht von Thaer, *Generalstabsdienst an der Front und in der OHL. Aus Briefen und Tagebuchaufzeichnungen 1915–1919* (Göttingen, 1958), 240 (9 October 1918), also 251.

[34] Wilhelm Deist, "Der militärische Zusammenbruch des Kaiserreichs. Zur Realität der 'Dolchstosslegende,'" in Ursula Büttner, ed., *Das Unrechtsregime*, vol. 1 (Hamburg, 1986), 111–13, 117; dead, wounded, and missing (with increasing incidence of the latter from August onward): *Der Weltkrieg 1914 bis 1918*, vol. 14 (Berlin, 1944), Beilage 42; also note 146.

[35] Bernhard Schwertfeger, *Die politischen und militärischen Verantwortlichkeiten im Verlaufe der Offensive von 1918* (Berlin, 1927), 223, 229–30; Ludendorff, in Thaer, *Generalstabsdienst*, 233–34, and in Granier, *Levetzow*, 229–30 (Seekriegsleitung war diary); MIW, 2:1290, 1297; and the careful analysis of Geyer, "Insurrectionary Warfare: The German Debate about a Levée en Masse in October 1918," JMH 73 (2001), 464–74.

to an enthusiastic Ludendorff on 29 September.[36] *Endkampf* also licensed the army's ruthless scorched-earth retreat from France and Belgium – which failed in its aim of total devastation primarily through troop exhaustion, labor shortages, and close Allied pursuit of a beaten enemy, not the belated counter-orders of the Reich civilian authorities.

The navy offered its own contribution to Imperial Germany's developing strategy of national suicide, with a Tirpitzian twist and a characteristic lack of coordination with Germany's senior service. As the army's defeat approached, the newly centralized naval high command – formed in August 1918 under Admiral Reinhard Scheer as the navy's answer to Hindenburg and Ludendorff – faced the prospect of ruin. Defeat by land would foreseeably entail the bloodless surrender of Germany's immensely costly fleet before it could justify its existence to the nation. Wilson's demand for an end to submarine warfare and the acquiescence to that demand by Imperial Germany's otherwise indecisive last chancellor, Prince Max of Baden, thus provoked a covert admirals' rebellion against government and monarch. "An honorable battle…, even if it bec[ame] a death-struggle," would guarantee the rebirth of a "German fleet of the future." In the present, a long-shot operational victory or even a hard-fought draw might perhaps topple the despised new parliamentary government and ignite the German people's *Endkampf*.[37]

Last but not least, the Kaiser's officer corps designed a starring role for the monarch in this pageant of national self-immolation: a Hohenzollern death-ride, surrounded by officers of the high command, into the artillery and machine-gun fire of the advancing Allied armies. The foremost proponent of this bizarre notion was no self-styled Prussian feudal retainer, but the reputedly astute and thoughtful Groener, a commoner and Württemberg officer. The equally non-noble naval staff similarly deliberated over whether to invite the "All-Highest" to share the fleet's doom. But suicide in defeat as national strategy, collective endeavor, and individual fate was ahead of its time in 1918.[38] Ludendorff's *Endkampf*, as well as the civilian variants pressed by German parliamentarians and by luminaries such as the Jewish industrialist and organizer

[36] Thaer, *Generalstabsdienst*, 234 ("Eine wahrhaft schöne germanische Heldengestalt…mit der tödliche Wunde im Rücken von Hagens Speer"); Ernst von Eisenhart-Rothe, in conversation with Ludendorff, 29 September 1918, quoted in Geyer, "Insurrectionary Warfare," 473–74, who provides the most extensive dissection of the numerous projects for *Endkampf*; likewise, with emphasis on the Kaiser's projected deathride, Hull, "Military Culture," 251–58.

[37] See Wilhelm Deist, "Die Politik der Seekriegsleitung und die Rebellion der Flotte Ende Oktober 1918," VfZ 14 (1966), 352–53; Leonidas E. Hill, "Signal zur Konterrevolution? Der Plan zum letzten Vorstoss der deutschen Hochseeflotte am 30. October 1918," VfZ 36 (1988), 13–29; and Gerhard P. Gross, "Eine Frage der Ehre? Die Marineführung und der letzte Flottenvorstoss 1918," in Jörg Düppler and idem, eds., *Kriegsende 1918. Ereignis, Wirkung, Nachwirkung* (Munich, 1999), 349–65.

[38] That time came: Bernt Wegner, "Hitler, der Zweite Weltkrieg und die Choreographie des Untergangs," GG 26:3 (2000), 493–518; for 1918, see especially Hull, "Military Culture," and Siegfried A. Kaehler, "Vier quellenkritische Untersuchungen zum Kriegsende 1918," in idem, *Studien zur Deutschen Geschichte des 19. und 20. Jahrhunderts* (Göttingen, 1961), 280–302.

of Germany's wartime raw materials supply, Walther Rathenau, soon fizzled out. The surviving troops and the undernourished urban masses for the most part wanted only an end to the war. And Ludendorff himself provoked his own removal. On 24 October, in a fiery order of the day sent over Hindenburg's signature, he branded Wilson's third note, which had advanced a scarcely veiled demand for the removal of Germany's "military masters and monarchical autocrats," as evidence of the "will to extermination on the part our enemies which [had] unleashed the war in 1914." The army must fight on. Yet in the ensuing struggle for control of German policy between supreme command and Max von Baden's government, the Kaiser at last backed the civilians. Germany's impending defeat allowed William to accept the resignation that Ludendorff defiantly and for once imprudently offered.[39]

Within days, as British, Australians, and Canadians shunted Germany's crumbling armies back across France and Belgium toward the Reich, the navy brought Imperial Germany to its inglorious end. When Scheer and his advisers – circumventing both Kaiser and government – ordered Germany's dreadnoughts on 29 October to raise steam for their death-ride, the result was fleet-wide mutiny. The sailors' rebellion swiftly spread ashore, triggering revolution along Germany's coasts and in a Munich unnerved by fear of Allied invasion through Tyrol and Bohemia as Austria-Hungary left the war. By 6 November, an American breakthrough north of Verdun threatened a front already unhinged by the relentless British advance. Groener, Ludendorff's replacement, received the Kaiser's authorization to beg the Allied command for immediate ceasefire: an irrevocable confession of German defeat.[40] But the Allies' naive willingness to concede an armistice saved the German army from that supreme humiliation, and preserved for the future a threadbare illusion of invincibility.

On 9 November 1918 revolution reached Berlin. The Kaiser fled to Holland – a gesture that foreclosed, even in the minds of his loyal military vassals, all prospect of monarchical revival. The lesser German dynasties dissolved. Two days later Germany signed an armistice that precluded resumption of the war. It was left to Groener to brief the general staff the following spring – not without a further measure of self-deception – on the meaning of the war and an explanation for its shocking outcome: "We unconsciously strove for world domination... *before* we had made our continental position secure."[41]

---

[39] See especially Thaer, *Generalstabsdienst*, 243–46; Ludendorff, *Die Urkunden des Obersten Heeresleitung über ihre Tätigkeit 1916–18* (Berlin, 1920), 576–78; and Geyer, "Insurrectionary Warfare," 506–07.

[40] See the reports of Max von Gallwitz, the army group commander opposite the U.S. sector, 2–7 November 1918, in Department of the Army, *The United States Army in the World War, 1917–1919*, vol. 11, *American Occupation of Germany* (Washington, D.C., 1948), 463, 469–70, 471–72; Groener, *Lebenserinnerungen*, 450; and the trenchant analysis of Llewellyn Woodward, *Great Britain and the War of 1914–1918* (London, 1967), 430–31.

[41] Groener situation briefing, 19–20 May 1919, in Heinz Hürten, ed., *Zwischen Revolution und Kapp-Putsch. Militär und Innenpolitik 1918–1920* (Düsseldorf, 1977), 121 (also Fischer, *War of Illusions*, frontispiece).

II. Italy: From *guerra nostra* to Mutilated Victory

The aims of Italy's leaders were more modest, as befitted the "least of the great powers." The German War surprised Salandra and the foreign minister inherited from Giolitti, the astute and devious Marquis Antonino di San Giuliano. Italy's Triple Alliance allies deliberately neglected their treaty obligations to consult Rome – nor did the war they had launched fit the alliance's stipulation that signatories "be attacked." But such niceties, although they later figured prominently in the defense of Italy's reputation, were not the key to Di San Giuliano's policy. Whatever its obligations – and it had in 1902 secretly pledged Paris its neutrality if Germany attacked France – the situation both domestic and strategic left neutrality as the only option. Public opinion, a force Di San Giuliano and Salandra now reluctantly accepted as a decisive limit on policy, barred mobilization for a war alongside the hated Austrians – upon pain of disturbances that would make the Red Week insurrection of June 1914 seem a minor incident. And should Italy's leaders be insane enough to mobilize against Britain and France, the peninsula's coastal cities lay open to naval bombardment, the colonies were defenseless, and nine-tenths of Italian imports came by sea: grain vital to maintaining order in the cities, almost all Italy's fertilizer, two-thirds of Italy's iron, and 90 percent of the roughly 11 million tons a year of imported coal that fuelled Italian industry.[42] By September it also emerged that the army was incapable of swift mobilization; continuing Arab resistance in Libya, administrative sloth, and massive shortages of cadres, machine guns, artillery, uniforms, and winter clothing precluded action in 1914.[43]

Di San Giuliano, strong in the authority born of experience and insight, therefore swiftly chose neutrality. Salandra, the king, and the army followed. But the logic of Italy's position and of its foreign policy traditions made that choice provisional and galling. For all of Di San Giuliano's tortuous attempts to conciliate Berlin and Vienna, Italy's refusal to march with its allies was in effect a bet upon the Entente. The simultaneous defeat of Austria *and* France – which Di San Giuliano proposed with his characteristic black humor as the ideal outcome for Italy – was improbable. Italy must nevertheless have at least the defeat of the Central Powers, upon pain of an Austrian war of revenge and Austro-German overlordship.[44] But if the Entente defeated Austria and Germany without Italy's help, Salandra and his colleagues knew they would face both international "isolation, hatred, and contempt" and the implacable wrath of elites reared on the myth of Italy as a great power: "The country would

---

[42] See Simon M. Jones, *Domestic Factors*, 128–30; and Martini, *Diario 1914–1918* (Milan, 1966), 7, 11, 17.

[43] See Rochat, "L'esercito italiano nell'estate 1914," in idem, *L'esercito italiano in pace e in guerra*, 74–112; Martini, *Diario*, 7, 17, 38; Sidney Sonnino, *Diario 1914–1916* (Bari, 1972), 16–19; for this and what follows, I have also relied heavily on Brunello Vigezzi, *L'Italia di fronte alla prima guerra mondiale*, vol. I, *L'Italia neutrale* (Milan 1966), 3–140, and Bosworth, *Least of the Great Powers*, ch. 11.

[44] Martini, *Diario*, 26, 49–50; Malagodi, *Conversazioni*, 1:18–19, 20, 31.

never forgive us for allowing Europe to change its political outline without the slightest gain for us." By September a growing press outcry for war against Austria appeared to threaten the monarchy itself, should Italy fail to strike: "war or revolution."[45]

The clamor was superfluous. Di San Giuliano, most skeptical, cautious, and farsighted of the inner circle, drew up Italy's terms for intervention as early as 11 August: Trieste, Trento, and the Tyrol (with its quarter-million ethnic Germans) to the Brenner watershed, and a "fair share" of any war indemnity and of the Mediterranean provinces of Turkey should the Ottomans enter the war against the Entente. Six weeks later Di San Giuliano made explicit the demand for Italy's "natural frontiers," which now included Istria and its Slavs to the Carnaro "as a minimum," possible annexations in Dalmatia, and colonial compensations from Entente booty in Africa.[46] Di San Giuliano, despite an unquestionable devotion to insulating foreign policy from the vagaries of domestic politics, also built into his project a *casus belli* that would justify an Italian attack on Austria both at home and abroad: the British and French fleets and the Serbs must strike Austria decisively in the Adriatic and the Balkans. That would commit Italy's western allies-to-be to Austria's destruction, help fracture Austria-Hungary along ethnic lines, and make an unanswerable domestic case for war. Italy's cause would be immediate self-defense against chaos and "Slav encroachment" upon its borders, and security for the future against Austria-Hungary's Slav successors.[47]

Once Germany's defeat on the Marne seemed to promise ultimate victory to the Entente, Di San Giuliano leaned unhurriedly toward eventual intervention. The war would be long and Italy's hour would come. Salandra by contrast was intermittently impatient: "We cannot hesitate: if I thought that I had once had a chance to restore Trento and Trieste to Italy and had missed it, I would have no peace in this life...."[48] Then Di San Giuliano's death from gout and heart failure in mid-October placed Salandra, a far less subtle mind, in uncontested command. Salandra in turn called to the foreign ministry his political friend and former patron Sidney Sonnino, the reputed conscience of right-Liberalism and one of the few political leaders to urge war in August alongside the Central Powers. Close-mouthed, supremely obstinate, and – in the king's words – with "blinkers like horses," Sonnino reinforced Salandra's drift toward decisively narrowing the war aims and methods Di San Giuliano had sketched. The new look of Italian policy excluded direct cooperation with the western allies, unquestioningly assumed a short war, improbably presumed that a chastened

---

[45] Salandra, with Martini's agreement, in Martini, *Diario*, 39; also 26, 96, 124; likewise Malagodi, *Conversazioni*, 40; "o la guerra o la rivoluzione" (Martini and Sonnino): Martini, *Diario*, 99, 216; isolation: ibid., 159.

[46] DDI 5/1/201, 803; Martini, *Diario*, 218–24.

[47] DDI 5/1/803 and Vigezzi, *L'Italia neutrale*, 106–08, 106–07 note 1.

[48] Salandra, in Martini, *Diario*, 106 (17 September 1914); likewise ibid., 192, 228; see also Sonnino, *Diario*, 15–19.

Austria-Hungary would somehow survive, and focused narrowly on territorial "guarantees" that included most of the Dalmatian coast, a demand that Di San Giuliano had foreseen would arouse implacable Slav enmity. The war of Sonnino and Salandra was to be a jealously safeguarded "*guerra nostra*," an Italo-Austrian cabinet war within the framework of the larger conflict but painstakingly insulated from it. And Salandra himself gave the world a memorable symbol for this eccentricity in the stunningly impolitic phrase, "a *sacro egoismo* for Italy," with which he described the essence of his policy two days after Di San Giuliano's death.

With the exception of Giacomo de Martino, Di San Giuliano's and Sonnino's chief subordinate at the foreign ministry, and Ferdinando Martini, Salandra's minister of colonies and confidant, other individuals, groups, and institutions had virtually no influence on this most fateful project in Liberal Italy's history. The great social forces, most notably the industrial establishment often touted as the motor of Italian imperialism, were divided or belated in their conversion to war.[49] Victor Emmanuel III, despite his prerogatives in foreign and military affairs, normally greeted the reports of his prime minister with sphinx-like reserve while undertaking to support the course his ministers chose.[50] The peacetime armed forces were utterly unlike their German counterparts in their resentful subordination to civilian authority. The navy, when asked, offered in November 1914 a list of islands and territories the annexation of which would ensure the "supremacy in the Adriatic" that Sonnino and De Martino demanded.[51] The army, the service soon to be called to carry the weight of the war, scarcely counted in the decision to launch it. Once the chief of staff, General Luigi Cadorna, had given the government assurances that the army would be ready to attack by spring, Salandra and associates virtually ignored him. In May 1915 Cadorna discovered three weeks before the deadline that Italy was pledged to enter the war on the Entente's side – but only because he went to Salandra and asked.

In accordance with tradition only the prime minister and foreign minister made policy under the oversight of the king. "We two alone" – "*noi due soli*" – as Salandra put it to Sonnino in mid-March 1915, held the power to make Italy's war. "We two alone" could not at that point break openly with the Central Powers. The army would not be ready until May, Sonnino had only just opened conversations with London, and the Entente had not yet endorsed Italy's demands. Yet Salandra also made clear that the two "could do without" the open assent of the king or the approval of country and parliament.[52] He was as good as his word. By the Treaty of London of 26 April 1915, the two

---

[49] On the industrialists and war, see especially the conclusions of Ragionieri, "La storia politica e sociale," ESI 4/3:1972–73.

[50] See Martini, *Diario*, 104, 385.

[51] De Martino to Salandra, 31 October 1914; Viale (Navy) to Sonnino, 15 November 1914, in Sonnino, *Carteggio 1914–1916* (Bari, 1974), 61–67

[52] Salandra to Sonnino, 16 March 1915, in Sonnino, *Carteggio*, 289.

ministers secretly committed Italy to declare war on the Central Powers within a month. The prospective success of Britain's Dardanelles landings, begun on 25 April, the mirage of taking Austria in the rear with Rumanian intervention and a Russian spring offensive, and the expectation – perverse in view of the stalemate in France since October 1914 and the mountains in Cadorna's path – of a swift war of movement against Austria all combined to hasten Salandra's decision.

Yet Salandra knew from polling the prefects in April that the immense majority of the country and of its elites as yet supported continued neutrality. The parliament and Giolitti, architect of Salandra's majority, were equally opposed. To the public, Giolitti had insisted that armed negotiations might secure "a great deal [*parecchio*]" – a phrase seized on as cowardly and mercantile by the partisans of war. In private, Giolitti displayed prescience and black pessimism: the war would be long and Italy might lack the necessary political and economic endurance; an Italian war would not be a mere duel with Austria-Hungary, but would also involve Germany; German forces in turn might drive the Italian army "back behind the Po," take Milan, and provoke revolution; and Germany might well win the wider war. Italy should rather go to war only "after Austria had fallen, for the legacy."[53]

Salandra and Sonnino feared above all the fury that would descend upon the ministry that failed to complete the *Risorgimento* by seizing Trento and Trieste, and that proved unable to assert Italy's great-power status by grasping Adriatic supremacy and Ottoman and colonial booty. Increasingly they and the king feared that a monarchy legitimized by its association with the national cause would not survive a conspicuous failure to advance that cause. Cavour had played on that fear in 1848 and had in turn acted on it in 1859–60, striking south as much to contain Garibaldi as to make Italy. Now it was the turn of Cavour's self-designated successors.[54]

Salandra, an Apulian notable with an elegant pen but averse to flattering the mob – "I don't . . . go to the *piazza*; it isn't my sort of place" – indeed viewed the war as an occasion to cement right-Liberalism in power even in the age of universal suffrage, shaking off Giolitti's tutelage in new elections once the army had entered Trieste in triumph.[55] But that petty calculation paled in importance beside the growing conviction of some in the inner circle, enraged by contacts between Giolitti and the German ambassador, that neutralism was treason. The coming war was "a holy war: necessary [and] inevitable to save the future of the country, to save its dignity, its freedom." Internal and international motivations were inextricably intertwined, as Martini noted on 7 May, after Salandra and

53 Alberto Monticone, "Salandra e Sonnino verso la decisione dell'intervento," in idem, *Gli italiani in uniforme 1915–1918* (Bari, 1972), 67–87; Vigezzi, *Da Giolitti a Salandra* (Florence, 1969), 321–401; Malagodi, *Conversazioni*, 28, 37, 39, 45, 53; Salandra, *Il diario di Salandra* (Milan, 1969), 26–27, 34–35, 36–37.

54 For hints of the King's attitude, see the exchange between Avarna and Bollati (ambassadors at Vienna and Berlin), 19–24 September 1914, DDI 5/1/749, 791.

55 Salandra, in Martini, *Diario*, 534; Giolitti ("Salandra wanted [war] to reestablish government by conservatives; he'll see it differently by war's end"), in Malagodi, *Conversazioni*, 71.

Sonnino confronted the cabinet with the twin faits accomplis of the Treaty of London and the annulment of the Triple Alliance. Italy's choices were "to be a Great Power or not to be one; to remain monarchical or – with the fall of the monarchy – to place in danger even its [territorial] unity; to be masters in our own house, in *mare nostrum*, or condemned to centuries of servitude."[56]

When Giolitti threatened in mid-May 1915 to block war through his control of parliament, just as the Germans crashed through the Russian front at Gorlice-Tarnow and the British advance at Gallipoli petered out, Salandra meekly resigned. That threatened Italy's foreign policy and army with chaos – for with his policy in ruins, Salandra despairingly ordered Cadorna to halt mobilization and deployment. Victor Emmanuel III had already briefly and uncharacteristically exposed himself politically, by backing Salandra and war. He had told Giolitti that he would abdicate rather than see his – and Italy's – still-secret commitments to the Entente dishonored. Giolitti in turn quailed at the responsibility of removing a king. He may also have held back in fear of the revenge the partisans of war would exact for the repudiation of Italy's pledge to the Entente, a step that Martini and his fellows damned as placing Italy "below Mexico and Venezuela." Salandra remained in office, while immense crowds of interventionist demonstrators – a touch foreign to Salandra's and Sonnino's intended cabinet war – chanted "death to Giolitti."[57]

War duly began on 24 May 1915 in an atmosphere of civil war, with the Giolittian parliament cowed into voting war powers and the Socialists silent. Those who launched Italy's war proceeded with Jacobin self-assurance and sense of mission. Martini now understood the passions of the French Revolution, he wrote: "for the enemy of the fatherland, for any Italian who would greet with joy the defeat of our arms (some would, some would), no mercy.... Woe to us if we are beaten, but, by God!, woe to *them* first."[58] As the "radiant May" of interventionist demonstrations drew on into summer and autumn and Italy's armies seized border villages at immense cost before hanging on the wire of the main Austrian line along the Isonzo river, that ruthlessness was ever more needed.

Nor was it absent, for only offensives by land could achieve Italy's war aims: Austria-Hungary's fleet, although numerically inferior, held the *Regia Marina*

[56] Sonnino, *Diario*, 18; Malagodi, *Conversazioni*, 31–32, also 46; Martini, *Diario*, 444 (7 June 1915), 407. Italian historians have also long debated passionately the meaning of this war: whether it was (i) the last and greatest of the *Risorgimento*, as the democratic interventionists claimed, or (ii) Italy's most wholehearted imperialist venture, an interpretation on which Nationalists and Socialists or Communists have concurred, despite diametrically opposed attitudes toward war and empire. The two views are mutually exclusive only if the aspiration to great-power status and empire was utterly foreign to the *Risorgimento* tradition (but see pp. 79, 112, and Chabod, *Politica estera italiana*, ch. 2, especially 1:293).

[57] Salandra, *Diario*, 36–37; Giorgio Candeloro, *Storia dell'Italia moderna*, vol. 8 (Milan, 1978), 106–09; Martini, *Diario*, 414, 418, 421; for the order to stop mobilization, Gianni Rocca, *Cadorna* (Milan, 1985), 68.

[58] Martini, *Diario*, 441 (2 June 1915); for a neutralist view of the spreading "Jacobin contagion" of intolerance, see Albertini, *Epistolario*, 1:328. "Atmosphere of civil war" is the phrase of Vincenzo Morello, a journalist with *La Tribuna*.

to three years of stalemate in the Adriatic. And by launching the war the politicians had unintentionally placed themselves in the hands of Italy's Ludendorff, Luigi Cadorna, a Piedmontese aristocrat of clerical background, a man of "low and slanting brow, prominent eyes, strong jaw...of passion and willpower to the point of obstinacy."[59] He had initially inclined toward a lightning war alongside the Central Powers that – as he retrospectively lamented in 1918 – would purportedly have yielded Nice, Corsica, Tunisia, and Mediterranean preeminence. He had three simple ideas, none of them notably susceptible to modification by experience. Frontal attack, not envelopment, was the supreme form of war. "Extreme measures of coercion and repression" were the essential means of motivating armies largely composed of illiterate *contadini*. And in wartime, total control over the conduct of the war was his prerogative as chief of staff: "Let [the politicians] send me away if and when they want, but while I am here, *I* am in command."[60]

His first idea led Cadorna to ignore reports of the tactical stalemate that reached him in 1914–15 from his attachés in Paris and Berlin, and to project a Napoleonic advance on Vienna for which his armies possessed neither leaders, training, firepower, nor logistical support, and which if successful would in any case have overshot Sonnino's limited objectives by destroying Austria-Hungary.[61] When Cadorna's plan failed bloodily, he took refuge in the notion that the war would only end through the exhaustion of the enemy. And his own lack of tactical imagination and failure to concentrate his army's limited firepower on one objective at a time guaranteed that the attrition would be mostly Italian.

Cadorna's second idea impelled him to drive his army onto the Austrian wire with all the sadistic relish of an eighteenth-century drill sergeant: "Superior officers have the sacred authority to immediately execute recalcitrants and cowards.... Whoever attempts to ignominiously surrender or retreat will be struck down, before he disgraces himself, by summary justice – lead from the trenches behind him or from the military police posted to watch the backs of the troops – unless he has first been dispatched [*freddato*] by his commanding officer."[62] That thirst for blood had the full backing of the Liberal governing class; Sonnino and Cadorna also sought grimly to inhibit desertion to the

---

59 In the words of Malagodi, *Conversazioni*, 33; should what follows seem unnecessarily harsh, see the contemporary (junior officer) critique of Cadorna's leadership by Novello Papafava dei Carraresi, *Appunti Militari 1919–1921* (Ferrara, 1921), 3–41.

60 Rocca, *Cadorna*, 53, 69; Piero Melograni, *Storia politica della grande guerra 1915/1918* (Bari, 1969), 201. Other high military figures deplored in similar terms Italy's choice of the Entente: see Angelo Gatti, *Caporetto. Dal diario di guerra inedito (maggio–dicembre 1917)*, ed. Monticone (Bologna, 1964), 41 (the Duke of Aosta, commander of 3rd Italian Army) and Martini, *Diario*, 991 (the count of Turin).

61 For the attaché reports, Rochat, "La preparazione dell'esercito italiano nell'inverno 1914–15 in relazione alle informazioni disponibili sulla guerra di posizione," *Il Risorgimento* 13 (February 1961), 10–32, and Papafava, *Appunti*, 4–7.

62 Attrition: Rocca, *Cadorna*, 103; "summary justice": Cadorna circular, September 1915, in Barbadoro, "La condotta della guerra: strategia, tattica e scelte politiche," in Paolo Alatri et al., *Storia della società italiana*, vol. 21, *La disgregazione dello stato liberale* (Milan, 1982), 44.

enemy by refusing to organize food aid for its starving prisoners of war in Austro-Hungarian hands.[63]

Finally, Cadorna's notion of military supremacy over the conduct of the war meant that as its strain grew he made ever-fiercer demands upon the government for total mobilization and for police measures against Italy's Socialists, on whose feeble attempts to maintain contact with the war-weary masses he came to blame his own defeats. His jealous suppression of possible successors among the generals, his covert persuasion of the press that he incarnated the national cause, and the vagueness of his position under the constitution – he was in theory chief of staff to the king as nominal commander-in-chief – in effect made him untouchable so long as the king's tacit support lasted. When an Austrian "punitive expedition" descended wrathfully from Tyrol in May–June 1916 and almost reached the plains west of Venice to cut off Italy's armies along the Isonzo, Salandra not Cadorna paid. Parliamentary defeat rewarded Salandra for the general's bloody failures, for having trampled the now-vengeful Giolittians in 1915, for his own less than energetic conduct of the war, and for his claim to a right-Liberal "monopoly" over it.[64] Despite retrospective doubts over the haste with which he had committed Italy to the Entente, he had resolutely held to the domestic political design chosen in expectation of swift victory, and refused to admit to the cabinet enough representatives of other groups to buy off his opponents.

Italy's new prime minister was Paolo Boselli, chosen at age 78 as senior member of the chamber for his inability to cause offense; a cartoonist had summed him up a generation earlier by picturing him as a rabbit. Sonnino remained in office as guarantee to the Entente of Italy's faithfulness. He defended his exclusive command of his sphere as fiercely as Cadorna, and held unyieldingly to the Adriatic aspirations enshrined in the Treaty of London and to his *guerra nostra* distinct from the wider conflict. British offers to send troops and artillery to the Italian front, panic-stricken Austro-Hungarian peace feelers, and proposals to attack the Habsburg empire by exploiting Czech and Yugoslav aspirations were all unwelcome, for they might diminish Italy's sacred treaty rights.

Nor did Sonnino see the point of propaganda abroad for Italy's cause, or of other undignified concessions to the age of the masses. His only obeisance to the realities of industrial coalition warfare was to push his timid colleagues to belatedly declare war on Germany in August 1916 – because of Entente intimations that failure to do so would count at the peace table and would affect the allocations of grain, coal, and of the Allied loans that contributed

---

[63] Giovanna Procacci, *Soldati e prigionieri italiani nella grande guerra* (Turin, 2000), and the even-handed analysis of Kramer, "Italienische Kriegsgefangene im Ersten Weltkrieg," in Hermann J. W. Kuprian and Oswald Überegger, eds., *Der Erste Weltkrieg im Alpenraum* (Innsbruck, 2006), 247–58.

[64] As Orlando, a cabinet member and a beneficiary of the policy, unkindly put it (Martini, *Diario*, 774).

an irreplaceable 13.2 percent of Italy's wartime expenditure.[65] A Giolittian from the South, Gaspare Colosimo, replaced Martini as minister of colonies, and formulated a grand design to surround Ethiopia with Italian territory and strangle it, and to extend Libya south into Chad toward the Gulf of Guinea. Those aspirations were widely shared. An expert on the Italian South, colonial enthusiast, and long-standing friend of Sonnino's, Senator Leopoldo Franchetti, presented Boselli and the foreign minister with a gargantuan war-aims catalog – following the custom established in Germany in 1914–15 – over the signatures of some three thousand luminaries of Italian politics, journalism, science, and the arts, including D'Annunzio and Mussolini. In addition to Italy's Adriatic and African claims, Franchetti demanded no mere concession in Turkey, but "maritime and continental Asia Minor, with all its coasts and islands."[66] Yet a reformist leader whom the PSI had expelled in 1912, Leonida Bissolati, had also joined the new cabinet to oppose Sonnino on the Adriatic; the Treaty of London if scrupulously applied promised endless war with Austria-Hungary's Slav successors, and was utterly unsustainable in the new world of revolution and self-determination that the Petrograd Soviet and Woodrow Wilson proclaimed in spring 1917. The PSI maintained its sullen opposition.

The crisis of Italy's war, the equivalent of Germany's downward spiral of defeat and exhaustion from August to October 1918, left Sonnino in place but changed the political landscape beyond recognition. Cadorna's eleven offensives on the Isonzo ended in August–September 1917 with a last paroxysmal attempt to crack the Austrians before the collapse of Russia freed Habsburg forces from the East to face Italy. By autumn 1917 Italy had sacrificed more than 300,000 dead and missing to achieve a maximum penetration of 20-odd kilometers from the 1915 border.[67] When seven German divisions and picked Austrian units broke through exhausted and poorly deployed Italian units on either side of Caporetto, north of the Bainsizza, on 24 October, they unhinged the entire front. One of Italy's two armies on the Isonzo disintegrated. Cadorna preserved some measure of sangfroid and collected the army's remnants on the Piave–Mt. Grappa line, barely east of Venice (see Map 3, p. 309).

The chamber had been about to unseat Boselli in order to replace him with a more Giolittian ministry, perhaps in view of a compromise peace effort that would have marked the rout of the bold minority that had taken Italy to war. But Caporetto instead improbably cast Boselli's ductile successor Vittorio Emanuele Orlando as Italy's Clemenceau. The ancestral enemy had invaded Italy – and, it was soon clear, could not break the desperate resistance of the army's remnants.

[65] 1915–18 loans: Massimo Legnani, "Sul finanziamento della guerra fascista," in Francesca Ferratini Tosi, Gaetano Grassi, and Massimo Legnani, eds., *L'Italia nella seconda guerra mondiale e nella resistenza* (Milan, 1988), 304.

[66] Robert L. Hess, "Italy and Africa: Colonial Ambitions in the First World War," *Journal of African History* 4:1 (1963), 105–26; Saverio Cilibrizzi, *Storia parlamentare politica e diplomatica d'Italia da Novara a Vittorio Veneto*, 8 vols. (Milan, 1923–49), 6:347–48; 334–49 offers a useful panorama of 1916–17 war aims discussion in the Italian press.

[67] Figures: Caporetto Inquiry, 2:434–35, graph 32.

Orlando had taken office on condition that Cadorna be replaced. But only defeat gave the politicians the courage and the chance to depose the general at last, and then only after British and French prodding.[68] The new army leadership, Armando Diaz, Pietro Badoglio, and Ugo Cavallero, had learned enough from Cadorna's and their own mistakes to hold Grappa and Piave unaided. They rebuilt the army while eleven British and French divisions stiffened or backed the front. And they smothered Austria-Hungary's final despairing attack in July 1918. The new high command offered the army relief from Cadorna's relentless "pushes," better food and more leave, and – in belated homage to the new age – propaganda to shore up morale that included illusory promises to the peasant infantry of "land to the *contadini*."

Among the civilians, Sonnino too helped save Italy. This once his fierce obstinacy fitted the hour; in the face of catastrophic reports from the front, he overawed the cabinet on 9 November 1917 by damning as treason any course except fighting to the end. Orlando – although not averse to exploring what peace terms Vienna might offer – likewise insisted that Italy must hang on, "more than for territorial gain,... for its affirmation as a great nation." A democrat of Giolittian origins, Francesco Saverio Nitti, took over finance and overseas supply, the American connection upon which economic survival and military victory now depended. For Nitti as well as for Orlando, Italy's increasing economic dependence on the quaintly idealistic Americans made Sonnino's fixation on Dalmatia dangerous. But Nitti also had frequent bouts of pessimism, and during much of early 1918 appeared to be positioning himself to lead a future Giolittian ministry in the search for a compromise peace, perhaps with Vatican assistance.[69] Bissolati and Orlando together imposed, despite Sonnino's obduracy, the concessions to Czech and Yugoslav nationalism needed to wield at last the weapon of subversion against Austria-Hungary, as Germany had done since 1914 against Russia. After the defeat of Austria-Hungary's last offensive Orlando hesitantly pressed Diaz, against Nitti's resistance, for an Italian attack to retake Venetia. Italy must not suffer once again the humiliation of 1866, of receiving that territory through the victories of its allies.

In the end, Diaz acted in time. Beginning – by accident – on 24 October 1918, the anniversary of Caporetto, the army and the Allied contingents broke the exhausted and half-starved Austro-Hungarians in the four days of hard fighting later known as the battle of Vittorio Veneto. The ensuing rout of the Habsburg armies intersected with the dissolution of the Habsburg state. A landing force seized Trieste and Italian troops occupied the areas claimed under the Treaty of

---

[68] Isnenghi and Rochat, *La Grande Guerra 1914–1918* (Milan, 2000), 384–85.

[69] Sonnino, in Colosimo minute of cabinet meeting: Raffaele Colapietra, "Documenti dell'Archivio Colosimo in Catanzaro," *Storia e Politica* 20:3 (1981), 590; Orlando on resistance: Malagodi, *Conversazioni*, 252; Orlando, Nitti's ambiguities, and peace feelers through the Vatican: ibid., 269–70, 315, 349; Monticone, *Nitti e la grande guerra* (Milan, 1961), 258–62; Leo Valiani, *La dissoluzione dell'Austria-Ungheria* (Milan, 2nd rev. ed., 1985), 341–42, 347–48, 423–24 and notes.

London after an armistice on 3–4 November 1918. Yet the defeat and dissolution of Austria-Hungary could not still Orlando's doubts. Italy's initial attack, across the Grappa massif, had failed bloodily, and the later thrust across the Piave from 26 October onward had begun as the Austro-Hungarian rear areas were beginning to dissolve. That two British divisions had seized a decisive bridgehead had not helped.[70] Publicly Orlando proclaimed a *vittoria romana* to Roman crowds; privately he directed Diaz to "back-date" the beginning of the decisive blow to 24 October in the high command's bulletins, and feared that the enemy's wretched state and sudden collapse might cast doubt upon the authenticity of Italy's victory.[71] Far worse was to come.

2. THE MEANING OF THE WAR: "AUGUST DAYS" AND "RADIANT MAY"

Outside the inner circles responsible for policy, the war passed through three phases. First came initial euphoria and sweet anticipation of redrawing the map of Europe. Then came death, disillusion, and increasing domestic fragmentation and strain. Finally, amid exhaustion, defeat, and humiliation, new and potent myths arose to challenge or reinforce those under which Germany and Italy had made their separate wars.

I. Germany: War as Apocalypse

Germany's August 1914 was an experience that changed forever the way in which educated Germans – and many others – saw their own people.[72] Riezler had foreseen that "when war comes and the veils fall, the whole *Volk* will follow, driven by necessity and peril." Yet in August he too noted with amazement "the most unforgettable thing of all, the *Volk* itself: all truly joyful at the singular experience of being caught up in a great cause. And the inarticulate utterly unquestioning trust [in Germany's leaders]." Heinrich Class hailed "the holy hour" of national redemption through blood. An obscure Austrian emigré

---

[70] Which does *not* mean that the British rather than the Italians "won" Vittorio Veneto (but see James E. Edmonds and H. R. Davies, *Military Operations: Italy, 1915–1919* [London, 1949], iii, 284–96, 303–04, 354–58).

[71] Orlando, *Discorsi per la guerra e per la pace* (Foligno, 1923), 271 (see also 282); Orlando telegrams of 29 October and 9 November, in Melograni, *Storia politica*, 550–53 ("È inutile che spieghi l'importanza di tale retrodata della nostra offensiva in rapporto all'incalzare delle notizie di un prossimo armistizio"); and OO, 12:188–91 for Mussolini's indignant and detailed 1919 efforts to refute Yugoslav scoffing.

[72] See especially Peter Fritzsche, *Germans into Nazis* (Cambridge, MA, 1998), ch. 2, and particularly 21–28, and Jeffrey Verhey, *The Spirit of 1914* (Cambridge, 2000); the modish tendency to debunk the "August experience" as superficial and class-specific is incompatible with Germany's subsequent very real staying power against heavy odds. John A. Moses, "The Mobilisation of the Intellectuals 1914–1915 and the Continuity of German Historical Consciousness," *Australian Journal of Politics and History* 48:3 (2002), 336–52, helps to situate the effusions quoted in the following pages.

in Munich, a painter of scenes for postcards, later recalled that he too had greeted war with "stormy enthusiasm[;] I fell down on my knees and thanked Heaven from an overflowing heart for granting me the good fortune of being permitted to live at this time." Max Weber, with fewer illusions than most about Germany's prospects, nevertheless wrote to a friend that "*however* it turns out, *this war is great and wonderful.*" Thomas Mann, the archetypal literary *Bildungsbürger*, wrote that the poets knew it: war meant "purification, liberation, and an immense hope." What inspired them was not the prospect of victory "but the war itself, as divine visitation, as moral necessity." The poets indeed worked overtime: by one perhaps extreme contemporary estimate the German people produced 1.5 million war poems in August 1914, an average of 50,000 a day.[73]

The enthusiasm of the masses was more measured; working-class districts and the countryside lacked the jubilant crowd scenes of central Berlin. But their reservists also reported promptly for duty. The huge crowds that did assemble were a wholly new phenomenon, a display of national sentiment that sprung the bounds of the authoritarian particularist states dividing the "German Fatherland."[74] And for the intellectuals, July–August 1914 was the last great intoxicating hour of the *Bildungsbürgertum*'s guardianship of the national cult. Protestant Germany's *literati*, professors, schoolmasters, and pastors outdid themselves in giving meaning to world conflagration. To that task they brought all the national self-deification of the long nineteenth century, the peculiar compound of Herder, Fichte, Arndt, Hegel, Treitschke, and Protestant Prusso-German theology. *Geist* not matter moved the world; German *Geist* was the highest stage so far reached in the development of Mind. And the intellectuals' understanding of the war emerged under the conditions laid down by Moltke the Younger and Bethmann Hollweg, who had been so successful in "formulating [a] *casus belli*" that camouflaged as self-defense Germany's drive for world mastery.

The "ideas of 1914," as they soon became known, consisted of three principal elements. The first was inevitably the defensive nature of the struggle – a conviction essential for Germany's resistance and all the deeper and more powerful for being objectively bogus. The Kaiser provided the basic text on 31 July: "Envious rivals everywhere drive us to legitimate defense. The sword has been forced into our hand." On 4 August, at an emotional Reichstag meeting, he solemnly proclaimed – in a speech which the eminent liberal Protestant theologian Adolf von Harnack had helped to draft – that "no lust of conquest drives us on."[75] On this theme the *Bildungsbürgertum* and virtually all other literate Germans played innumerable variations. This was a "war of the Germans against French

---

[73] Riezler, *Tagebücher*, 185, 193; Class, "Waffensegen!," *Alldeutsche Blätter*, 3 August 1914, quoted in Verhey, *1914*, 176; similarly 18; MK, 161; Wolfgang J. Mommsen, *Max Weber*, 206 (emphasis in original); Mann, *Friedrich und der Grosse Koalition* (Berlin, 1915), 14–15; 1.5 million poems: Vondung, *Apokalypse in Deutschland*, 193.

[74] See Fritzsche, *Germans into Nazis*, for 1914 as a critical stage – as it were – in the self-realization of the German *Volk*.

[75] Ralph H. Lutz, ed., *The Fall of the German Empire, 1914–1918*, 2 vols. (Stanford, CA, 1932), 1:4, 8.

thirst for revenge, Muscovite presumption, [and] English envy." Germany was Christ persecuted; "They hated me without a cause" (John 15:25) recurred in Protestant war sermons. What one pastor described as "Caiaphas-work of England against Germany" was especially incomprehensible given the two nations' shared "Christian-Germanic" makeup. British claims to have declared war over Germany's invasion of Belgium were shameful hypocrisy, a cover for "blood-guilt" incurred in a treacherous "long-planned attack on the German Reich."[76] Ernst Lissauer – whom a Viennese Jewish friend later described sadly as "perhaps the most Prussian or Prussian-assimilated Jew I ever knew" – summed up prevailing sentiment in his wildly popular "*Hassgesang* [hymn of hate] Against England," which sibilantly spat mortal enmity: "*Hass* by water and *Hass* by land / *Hass* of the head and *Hass* of the hand." Britain's "Slav and Gallic accomplices" received slightly less fire from *Bildungsbürger*, but in the tradition of Marx and Engels the SPD took up with enthusiasm the struggle against the "Cossack bestialities" and "collapse, annihilation, and nameless misery" that threatened from the Muscovite despotism to Germany's east.[77]

The inevitable corollary to the defensive nature of Germany's struggle was the national unity it had created. Here also the Kaiser and Harnack provided the fundamental text on 4 August: "I know no more parties; I know only Germans." The "peace within the fortress" or *Burgfrieden* that the Kaiser thereby proclaimed was the outward political expression of a widely held longing for national integration. War had brought the nation in all its quarreling institutions, parties, *Stände*, confessions, and regions together. Social Democrats could at last gratefully "join with a full heart, a clean conscience, and without a sense of treason in the sweeping, stormy song, '*Deutschland, Deutschland, über alles.*'" War inspired to enthusiasm even Thomas Mann's anti-monarchical and anti-militarist brother Heinrich: "under military dictatorship, Germany has become free!" War had swept away what Thomas Mann himself described as the "wolfish-mercantile" materialism, the "can-can-shimmy morality," and the "cockroaches of the spirit" of industrial society. War, wrote the great sociologist of religion Ernst Troeltsch, had engendered a "wave of the supernatural" that had revealed to the German people their organic unity.[78] The militant *Volk*-community, the *Volksgemeinschaft* of August 1914, had joined the pantheon of

76 Quotations: Dr. Weidenmüller, Oberlehrer at Flensburg, October 1914, in Kurt Jürgensen, "Deutsche Abende – Flensburg 1914," GWU 20 (1969), 8; John 15:25: Arlie J. Hoover, "God and Germany in the Great War: The View of the Protestant Pastors," *Canadian Review of Studies in Nationalism* 14:1 (1987), 70; Hauptpastor Heinrich Kähler, in Jürgensen, "Deutsche Abende," 11; Ernst Haeckel, "England's Blutschuld am Weltkriege," *Das monistische Jahrhundert* 3 (1914–15), 541, 548.

77 Quotations: Lissauer, and Stefan Zweig's memoirs on Lissauer: Hans Weigel et al., *Jeder Schuss ein Russ, Jeder Stoss ein Franzos* (Vienna, 1983), 17–18; Otto von Gierke, Germany's greatest legal historian, cited in Koppel Pinson, *Modern Germany* (New York, 1954), 315; Friedrich Stampfer of the SPD, 30/31 July 1914, in Susanne Miller, *Burgfrieden und Klassenkampf. Die deutsche Sozialdemokratie im Ersten Weltkrieg* (Düsseldorf, 1974), 54.

78 Conrad Haenisch of the SPD, quoted in Eric J. Leed, *No Man's Land: Combat and Identity in World War I* (New York, 1979), 50; Mann, *Friedrich*, 12–14; the "radikale Literat" cited is clearly his brother; Troeltsch in Hoover, "God and Germany," 66.

German national myths. Only tiny minorities of dissident Socialists and middle-class pacifists stood outside or against the *Volk*-community. But in 1914 they had no influence whatsoever, and little enough thereafter.

The third major element of the "ideas of 1914" was the long-standing conviction of Germany's world mission, now radicalized and focused by events.[79] The widespread *Bildungsbürger* belief in Germany's moral and systemic superiority made the war, from the very first shot, a war of ideologies, of *Weltanschauungen*. German "heroes," proclaimed Werner Sombart, Germany's foremost political economist, fought British "hucksters." For those who preferred their Hegel straight, the philosopher's intimation that each stage in the development of *Geist* belonged to a particular *Volk* whose task it was to consummate that stage legitimated Germany's claims to mastery. World history, in words of Schiller that Arndt and Hegel had taken up, was the Last Judgment ("*Die Weltgeschichte ist das Weltgericht*").[80] Protestant-Hegelian orthodoxy, sometimes colored by the categories of Houston Stewart Chamberlain, reached the same result. German history was *Offenbarungsgeschichte*, the revelation of God's will through the German *Volksgeist*. God had summoned the Hohenzollern to north Germany in 1415 – an anniversary much celebrated in 1915 – as he had ordered Abraham from Ur to Canaan. God had raised up German Protestantism through Luther, created a German Protestant Reich through Bismarck, and had now through this "holy war" given the entire German people the task of writing a "third act." Germany's aim was "not to abandon the struggle until the power of England to lead nations astray is broken and the German *Volk* has clambered upward to the victorious power position that will allow it, responsible to God alone, to fulfill the world mission granted to the Germanic race for the welfare of the peoples." The majority of articulate Protestant Germans was unique – within Germany and outside it – in seeing the war from the outset as the apocalypse, as a last judgment to be carried out by the *Volk* itself in God's service. For although German Catholics did not yield to the Protestants in patriotic enthusiasm, as a rule they did not claim the war as the culmination of German or world history.[81]

Protestant Germany's fanatical determinism also precluded cool assessment of the likely outcome. *Geist must* defeat matter; even Germany's formidable war machine, its army and fleet, were to the learned Hegelian a "power of the

[79] For Germany's mission and related themes in 1914 and after, see the fundamental work of Vondung, *Apokalypse in Deutschland*, 132–49, 189–207, and idem, "Geschichte als Weltgericht"; also Klaus Schwabe, *Wissenschaft und Kriegsmoral. Die deutschen Hochschullehrer und die politischen Grundfragen des Ersten Weltkrieges* (Göttingen, 1969), ch. 2; and Wilhelm Pressel, *Die Kriegspredigt 1914–1918 in der evangelischen Kirche Deutschlands* (Göttingen, 1967), especially 108–74. Following quotations from Hoover, "God and Germany," 67–70 and Jürgensen, "Deutsche Abende," 11.

[80] See Vondung, "Geschichte als Weltgericht," 70–73

[81] Quotations from Vondung, *Apokalypse in Deutschland*, 195; Hoover, "God and Germany," 67–69; Kähler, in Jürgensen, "Deutsche Abende," 11. For the Catholics, see Heinrich Missalla, *"Gott mit uns." Die deutsche katholische Kriegspredigt 1914–1918* (Munich, 1968).

spirit."[82] The Entente and its colonies had a population in 1914 of just under 765 million; the Central Powers a mere 130 million. But as one East Prussian pastor thundered, "nations are not numbers and God is not bound by the laws of arithmetic."[83] The power of materiel and numbers was a delusion of the western Enlightenment, of the shallow rationalist "*Zivilization*" of the French, of what *Bildungsbürger* from Meinecke to Riezler described with pious horror as the "homogenized, soulless and mindless" world of "hollow meaningless Anglo-American banality." "Mathematical necessity" was powerless against faith, against a *Volksgeist* that had brought forth heroes and geniuses such as Arminius, Luther, Leibnitz, Bach, Frederick the Great, Kant, Fichte, Schleiermacher, Hegel, Goethe, Schiller, Stein, Bismarck, Moltke the Elder, Wagner, Krupp, and Zeppelin. "A nation like this can defy a world of enemies and still triumph" was the almost universal verdict. Belief in German victory, Thomas Mann exulted, was "contrary to all reason"; victory itself would be "a thing contrary to expectation, a wonder utterly without parallel, a victory of the soul against overwhelming numbers."[84] Long after the fervor of mobilization, the universal admiration for its stunning efficiency, and the euphoria of Germany's initial victories had passed, the *Bildungsbürgertum*'s championship of *Geist* – not always the winning strategic card in the new century of machines and masses – dictated its understanding of the war.[85]

And if victory was predetermined, so was its shape. Germany had not merely trampled Belgium from a necessity that "knows no law," as Bethmann Hollweg had half-sheepishly professed to the Reichstag on 4 August. It had done so in fulfillment of its historic mission. Friedrich Naumann, the soul of Protestant liberal imperialism and prophet of *Mitteleuropa*, proclaimed that history taught "that the general progress of human culture is impossible except through the crushing of the national freedom of small peoples."[86] Germany's world mission, liberal professors and Pan-Germans alike hastened to proclaim, required the creation of a central European empire that would reduce western neighbors to political and economic vassalage, drive Russia back into Asia, deport millions of Poles and Jews eastward, and plant peasant settlers from what soon became known as the *Altreich* – the artificial and temporary "old Reich" of 1871–1914 – in Baltic annexations. Some neo-Rankeans argued, and some may even have believed, that Germany's mission was simply to break Britain's "absolute

[82] Adolf Lasson ("Geistesmacht ist auch unser Heer und unsere Flotte"), in Vondung, *Apokalypse in Deutschland*, 204.

[83] Chaplain Reetz of Bromberg, quoted in Hoover, "God and Germany," 75.

[84] Population figures: Reichsarchiv, *Der Weltkrieg*, 1:40. Quotations: Meinecke, *Die deutsche Erhebung von 1914. Vorträge und Aufsätze* (Stuttgart, 1914), 34 ("uniformiert und entgeistet"); Riezler, *Tagebücher*, 271; Hoover, "God and Germany," 68–69, 75–76; Pressel, *Kriegspredigt*, 84; Jürgensen, "Deutsche Abende," 10; Mann, *Friedrich*, 16.

[85] On the social significance of "*Geist* over matter," see the suggestions of Vondung, *Apokalypse in Deutschland*, 204–05; also Meinecke, *Strassburg-Freiburg-Berlin 1901–1919*, in *Werke*, 8:223, on August 1914 as the "Euthanasie des deutschen bürgerlichen Zeitalters."

[86] Quoted in Gasser, *Preussischer Militärgeist*, 67 note 131.

maritime supremacy" and assure "the freedom of all peoples" in the world balance of power of the future. That, claimed the great historian Otto Hintze, was the meaning of the poet Geibel's phrase about Germany healing the world.[87] But Britain's defeat and German hegemony in Eurasia would clearly bring far more than the status of one "world power" among several.

II. Italy: War as Civil War

The aspirations that made Italy's "radiant May" of 1915 were inevitably more modest, and less widely shared throughout society than their German counterparts. Italy's embarrassing position as "least of the great powers" forced upon it a quest for parity, not universal hegemony. Italy's national mythology lacked functional equivalents to the Hegelian-Protestant apocalyptic tradition. "[I]narticulate utterly unquestioning trust" in the national leadership was notably absent. Above all, the majority of Italy's population and elites entered the war without benefit of "necessity and peril," and of the virtuous glow of self-defense that drove the Germans. Italy's "radiant days of May" were thus notably different from their German analogue in significance and consequences.

The coming of European war in July–August 1914 shocked Italian opinion. No encirclement propaganda, no middle-class military ethos, no professors preaching the sanctity of force had prepared it to face European conflagration. The professional officer corps, as Salandra lamented to the king in September, had tended to conceive of its calling as "a modest career undertaken more to assure one's daily bread than in the expectation of a war that few considered probable." Yet some nevertheless greeted the war with the glee of prophets vindicated or as creator of new worlds of opportunity. The Nationalists mocked the collapse of working-class internationalism and of the pathetic faith in progress of Socialists and Liberals. Benito Mussolini, most prominent of the Socialist extremists, privately gloated in mid-September of the "immensity and suddenness of events that reformist and even non-reformist socialism had exiled from history."[88]

By mid-August the war had begun to open new cleavages that cut through and increasingly paralyzed the traditional groups and parties, from syndicalists, Socialists, and republicans to democrats, radicals, Catholics, Giolittians, and right-Liberals.[89] Most of the political spectrum supported the continuance of neutrality with greater or lesser enthusiasm: the majority of Catholics, the vast majority of Giolittians and Socialists, and – at least initially – most

---

[87] See Friedrich Meinecke, "Kultur, Machtpolitik und Militarismus," and Otto Hintze, "Der Sinn des Krieges," in Hintze, Meinecke et al., eds., *Deutschland und der Weltkrieg* (Leipzig and Berlin, 1915), 643, 678–79, 685–86.

[88] Salandra, *La neutralità italiana* (Milan, 1928), 333; Mussolini to Amadeo Bordiga, 25 September 1914, OO, 38:69.

[89] For what follows, I have sacked Brunello Vigezzi's monumental and wonderful *L'Italia neutrale*, and his *Da Giolitti a Salandra*, 111–200.

right-Liberals. Yet within "neutralism," as it soon became known, a further paralyzing cleavage developed between those, principally Giolittians, Catholics, and right-Liberals, willing to threaten war or fight to secure territory from Austria, and those who remained partisans of unconditional neutrality.

A disparate assortment of combative minorities pressed in turn for Italian intervention.[90] The *nazionalisti* were second to none in thirst for war: first for war alongside Germany and Austria in pursuit of vast Mediterranean and colonial ambitions, then, once that was clearly impossible, for a "national and imperial war" – the last of the *Risorgimento* and Italy's first as a great power – to smash Austria-Hungary and seize Adriatic supremacy. That outcome would free Italy to checkmate France in the western Mediterranean and position the nation for the final struggle, possibly in alliance with a Germany detached from Austria, against Britain for domination of *mare nostro*.[91] As war against Austria-Hungary began to seem Italy's only possible war, the anti-Slav rancor of the border areas gained ever-greater influence within the Nationalist movement. Intransigent prophets of ethnic struggle whom *nazionalismo*'s earlier support of the Triple Alliance had alienated returned to the fold. Conspicuous among them was the Venetian Giovanni Giuriati, leader of the irredentist "Trento and Trieste" association, whose father and grandfather had fought the Austrians in 1848–49.[92]

Corradini especially wielded effectively the irredentist myth of the incomplete *Risorgmento*, of Italy's mission to "reunite its last sons," Trento, Trieste, and Dalmatia, to their common mother. Yet it was Alfredo Rocco, seconded by Coppola, who emerged as the movement's most ruthless spokesman. Externally, this war had nothing to do with principles, whatever the Entente or the Germans or Italy's democratic *interventisti* might claim; Rocco sought with success to scandalize by brazenly proclaiming it a war for domination, a "*lotta di nazionalità, lotta di razza*" pitting the Germanic peoples against the Slavs in coalition with Anglo-Saxons and Latins. Failure to join the struggle meant abdication both as a great power and as a people. Italy could not act as a "large Belgium or a greater Switzerland," or be content with acquisitions "without effort and without glory" like that of Venetia in 1866. Only war could avert universal contempt for "our collective cowardice" and parry Austro-German hatred for "the most shameful form of betrayal, that provoked by fright." Only war could refute the wounding taunt that "*les Italiens ne se battent pas.*"[93]

---

[90] I am much indebted to the analysis of *interventismo* of Vittorio De Caprariis, "Partiti politici e opinione pubblica durante la Grande Guerra," in Istituto per la storia del Risorgimento italiano, *Atti del XLI congresso di storia del Risorgimento italiano* (Rome, 1965), 85–94; see also Vigezzi, *L'Italia neutrale*, passim.

[91] Francesco Coppola, in Gaeta, ed., *La stampa nazionalista* (Rocca San Casciano, 1965), 63; Rocco, *Scritti*, 1:144, 147–49, 212.

[92] See Gentile's introduction to Giuriati, *La parabola di Mussolini nei ricordi di un gerarca* (Rome, 1981), ix–xiv.

[93] Corradini, *Discorsi*, 276, 286–89; Rocco, *Scritti*, 1:146, 151–54, 242, 167.

Domestically, as Oriani had preached, war was at least equally imperative. Corradini and Coppola explained in early October 1914 that

> Italy in its recent national life has hitherto lacked a great war, a genuine war that could make her truly sacred in the eyes of her sons and truly admired in the eyes of foreigners; for war alone is the blazing crucible in which the national soul retempers its essential virtues, and exalts itself through the purification of grief and sacrifice until it shines forth both at home and in the sight of the world.[94]

War, Rocco insisted in a more specifically Nationalist vein, would reestablish "national discipline, reinforce the authority of the state, silence all special interests," purge Italians of their congenital "disintegrative individualism," and bury the memory of Red Week. War alone could create "the military spirit that we have lacked for so many centuries" and give Italy the confidence for further expansion. And war abroad meant war at home: as early as October 1914 Rocco proclaimed the Nationalist right – in the face of a "dilapidated and impotent state" – to raise the *piazza* against neutralists and Socialists.[95]

The avant-garde, the Futurists and the literary journals on the Nationalist fringe, likewise took their stand. Derision, not the self-proclaimed realism of the Nationalists, was their weapon; "neutralists, pacifists, and eunuchs" their target; and war an aesthetic delight, a supreme *festa*. "We needed, in the end, a hot bath of dark blood after so many clammy luke-warm sousings of motherly milk and brotherly tears. . . . The siesta of cowardice, diplomacy, hypocrisy, and peace-mongering is over. . . . Let us love war and savor it like epicures so long as it lasts," ranted Giovanni Papini. War, Marinetti announced yet again, would sweep away the old Italy of "diplomats, professors, philosophers, archaeologists, critics, obsession with culture, Greek, Latin, history, senility, museums, libraries, and [the] tourist industry." War, wrote contributors to *Lacerba*, the point journal of avant-garde *interventismo*, would roll back "the excremental tide that rises" around the foreign ministry and destroy the Giolittian governing elite: "Cowardice has placed you on high but nature has made you low, low, low – and we shall bury you." Italy's choice was "war against the *tedeschi* or revolution."[96]

But it was Gabriele D'Annunzio who personified the thirst of the *literati* for redemptive war at home and abroad. And despite his consummate theatricality, D'Annunzio's thirst was both genuine and not easily slaked. Later, while partaking eclectically of combat on land, at sea, and in the air, he ranted with total conviction that the war was "a baptismal font to purify [Italy] of the filth, pusillanimity, and cowardice of centuries." "[A]n immense slaughter"

---

[94] Coppola, in Gaeta, ed., *Stampa nazionalista*, 63; see also Corradini, quoted in Vigezzi, *L'Italia neutrale*, 659.

[95] Rocco, *Scritti*, 1:172–73, 243, 188–89.

[96] Quotations: De Maria, ed., *Per conoscere Marinetti*, 156, 159; Isnenghi, *Mito della grande guerra*, 102–05, 110 (Papini, Fernando Agnoletti, Ardengo Soffici).

was "necessary to reinvigorate [Italy], to give it a steel-like unity. . . . The Italians must be driven by fury to seek nourishment from the brains of their enemies."[97]

Partly thanks to that fierceness of conviction, D'Annunzio's return in May 1915 from his debtor's refuge in France became an explosive celebration of the national cult. His liturgical speech of 5 May near Genoa in commemoration of the 1860 departure of Garibaldi's "thousand" for Sicily was close to a declaration of war on Austria. His tumultuous reception and violent harangues in Rome from 12 May onward were the central events of the "radiant days." He invoked, as did the Nationalists, a Dalmatia that was Italian "by divine and human right" and a "far grander Italy." He too tweaked his audience's ever-sensitive self-regard; without war, "Italian will be a name to blush at, a name to hide, a name to burn the lips." But he added a violent edge foreign to the Nationalists, men of order for all their daring talk of raising the *piazza*. For the "internal enemy" that threatened to defraud Italy of its war was the first target of D'Annunzio's *guerra nostra*. The poet gleefully took full responsibility for inciting violence against Giolitti's treasonous "handful of pimps and swindlers," among whom was "a heavy-breathing licker of dirty Prussian feet . . . for whom death by stoning and flames, instantly resolved and carried out, would be a genuinely light penalty." He called upon the huge crowd to swear vengeance, and urged it, for Italy's salvation, to hunt down Giolitti and his followers and administer "corporal punishment." The crowd, especially Rome's numerous and enthusiastic students, obliged the Poet. Only cordons of military police and cavalry saved Giolitti's house from being sacked, and repulsed the crowd that broke into the Chamber of Deputies. Giolittian parliamentarians and other prominent neutralists suffered beatings across Italy.[98]

Violence both verbal and physical against Giolitti, his parliamentary followers, the Socialists he had sought as allies, and parliament itself had thus by mid-May become the thread that bound the disparate strands of *interventismo* together. Alongside the Nationalist men of order stood the men of Red Week, Italy's "subversives": the republican, anarchist, syndicalist, and revolutionary socialist *interventisti*.[99] The republicans and Garibaldi's son and grandsons had moved first, quaintly sending volunteers to die for France, plotting expeditions to Dalmatia, and demanding war or revolution at home. That agitation, along with the frenetic bellicosity of *Lacerba* and its fellows, in turn made far easier the passage toward war of adventurous anarchists, syndicalists, and Socialists

---

[97] Quoted from Tommaso Gallarati Scotti, "Idee e orientamenti politici e religiosi al Comando Supremo: appunti e ricordi," in Giuseppe Rossini, ed., *Benedetto XV, i cattolici e la prima guerra mondiale* (Rome, 1963), 513; the grisly language argues strongly for the accuracy of Gallarati Scotti's memory.

[98] Alatri, ed., *Scritti Politici di Gabriele D'Annunzio*, 139–44; idem, *Nitti, D'Annunzio e la questione adriatica, 1919–1920* (Milan, 1959), 352–63; and the analysis in Isnenghi, *Mito della grande guerra*, 100–01.

[99] See the graphic account of Marco Cuzzi, "Il nazionalismo militante: gli antesignani delle 'camicie azzurre,'" in Rainero, ed., *Da Oriani a Corradini*, 96–115.

such as Mussolini. Red Week had failed. But war – fought or evaded, victorious or miscarried – offered new and far grander opportunities to attack the Liberal order.

The revolutionary *interventisti* at first inevitably called for war against "Austro-Prussian militarism" for the interests of the proletariat, for a world safe for democracy, and for the ideals of the French Revolution. But the extreme Left soon showed it could wield Italy's national myths as readily as the Right. Cesare Battisti, the Garibaldian socialist from Trento who symbolized the unredeemed city – and died there on an Austrian scaffold in 1916 – appealed to the king for a war of liberation. "Neutrality is for *castrati*," thundered the "syndicalist archangel," Filippo Corridoni, upon emerging from the jail term received for his part in Red Week.[100] By October 1914 Mussolini too had begun to insist that the unconditional opposition to war that he had doubtingly imposed on the PSI was a perilous blind ally. When the party failed to follow him in an about-face, Mussolini resigned as director of *Avanti!* and founded a new paper, *Il Popolo d'Italia*, with Napoleon's motto on its masthead: "The revolution is an idea that has found bayonets." The Socialists expelled him.[101]

Mussolini followed Corridoni and the rest in equating war with youth and national virility. Neutrality was pusillanimous, "eunuchoid," "worthy of people beneath history," and its proponents were "prophets of national cowardice" and "pussy-paunches [*panciafichisti*]." Socialist protests were a "propaganda of cowardice" that threatened to load upon future generations the "heavy burden of a nameless shame." "A people old with fifty centuries of history and young with fifty years of national life" could not behave as "a nation of rabbits." War must destroy "the ignoble legend that Italians do not fight, it must wipe out the shame of Lissa and Custoza, it must show the world that Italy can fight a war, a great war; I say again: *a great war*." No longer would foreigners see Italy as a land "of travelling mandolin-players, of peddlers of statuettes, of Calabrian *banditi*." And only war could fulfill the mission that Alfredo Oriani had assigned Italy: "the unalterable enemy, Austria; *mare nostro*, the Adriatic." Either war, "or let us finish with this *commedia* of [claiming to be] a great power."[102]

Either war, or revolution against an "unwarlike monarchy": the republicans and Mussolini unerringly discerned and pitilessly exploited the greatest fear of inner circle and establishment. Italy's radical nationalists, heirs of Oriani and counterparts to the Pan-Germans in their damnation of monarchical ineptitude and establishment cowardice, came in large part from the Left. To the faithful of the impromptu *"fasci"* – or seditious political groups – for

[100] Vigezzi, *L'Italia neutrale*, 389, citing Yvon De Begnac, *L'archangelo sindicalista (Filippo Corridoni)* (Milan, 1943).

[101] See OO, 6:405–06 and, for Mussolini's passage from socialism to *interventismo*, De Felice, 1, chs. 9–10; Francesco Perfetti, "La 'conversione' all'interventismo di Mussolini nel suo carteggio con Sergio Panunzio," SC 17:1 (1986), 139–70; and especially Paul O'Brien, *Mussolini in the First World War: The Journalist, the Soldier, the Fascist* (Oxford, 2005), ch. 2.

[102] Quotations, in order: OO, 7:15, 57, 386, 96, 6, 75, 70, 197, 418, 253–55, 147.

"revolutionary action" that Mussolini and other warlike ex-Socialists, syndicalists, and anarchists formed across north Italy between December 1914 and January 1915, Mussolini proclaimed the unity of war and revolution. "[T]oday it is war; tomorrow it will be revolution"; "war too can be a means of revolution"; "the day Italian bayonets pass the Ringstrasse in Vienna, the Vatican's death-knell will toll." Salandra's plan to fight a "state war" in the age of the masses Mussolini presciently dismissed as a delusion. Once mobilized for war, as Giolitti also saw, the masses might well escape from right-Liberal tutelage and even from the grasp of the state. And from the Socialists as well, as Mussolini warned a tumultuous November 1914 party meeting in Milan: "Despite all your whistles and protests, the war will flatten the lot of you."[103] Mussolini's 1914–15 equation of war with revolution later met with mockery from historians for whom revolutions were either the locomotives of human progress or not revolutions, and from those determined to deny the despot all coherence or foresight. But events unhappily bore out the shrewdness of his wager on a *guerra rivoluzionaria*. The great war to "consummate the revolution" had consumed the Parisian fanatics of 1791–92; the great war into which Mussolini helped plunge Italy hoisted him into power.

The third major component of the interventionist front was the democratic radicals and the reformist socialists of Bissolati and Ivanoe Bonomi, whom Mussolini had expelled from the party in 1912. The majority branch of the Masonic order and most radical democrats, except for parliamentary figures tied to Giolitti, turned toward war by September 1914. Gaetano Salvemini, suspended between an idiosyncratic socialism and the literary avant-garde hostile to Giolitti, urged war for "the cause of nationality and democracy" as early as 7 August 1914. But it was Bissolati who proved the most influential prophet of democratic war of liberation against the aggressive "feudal" empires attempting the "assassination of European civilization." The democrats publicly challenged Nationalist ambitions in Dalmatia on behalf both of the Mazzinian brotherhood of peoples and of practicality; like Di San Giuliano, they saw that conciliation of the Slavs served Italy's security better than annexations. But they too were not without aspirations that went far beyond self-determination for Italians. Salvemini, who had first opposed the Libyan War and then insisted that Italy must fight it worthily, now advanced the project of gaining Tunisia from France in compensation for French conquests along the Rhine and British colonial annexations. Bissolati in turn aspired to Djibouti, the key to Ethiopia, as well as Tunisia, and called for Italy to assert itself in rivalry with France as the Balkan "tutelary power, freely hegemonic." The Mazzinian thrust of Italy's democratic "international mission" engendered ambitions that might yet mock the brotherhood of peoples.[104]

---

[103] War and revolution: OO, 6:411, 7:139–41, 147, 182, 221, 314, 394, 38:85; "[Salandra] si illude di poter fare una guerra di Stato": 7:341; for Giolitti, Malagodi, *Conversazioni*, 71; Mussolini to the PSI: OO, 7:429.

[104] On the movement of literate opinion, Vigezzi, *L'Italia neutrale*, part 2; Salvemini: ibid., 230 note 1; Bissolati: Raffaele Colapietra, *Leonida Bissolati* (Milan, 1958), 209 (a policy of Balkan

A final indispensable component of *interventismo* was the press, in this first political struggle waged in Italy with modern propaganda methods. The Austrian embassy estimated at the end of 1914 that of Italy's fifty-odd established newspapers, thirty favored war.[105] Uncontested leader both of the press and of press *interventismo* was the *Corriere della Sera* of Milan. Its editor, Luigi Albertini, aspired to and largely secured for his paper a national position analogous to that of the London *Times*. Albertini insisted with all the weight of his immense authority, both publicly and in his frequent contacts with Salandra, that Italy must fight. In European terms, he saw the war unblinkingly – then and later – as a German bid for hegemony.[106] War against the Central Powers, he argued in parallel with Bissolati, Salvemini, and the *interventisti* of the Left, was thus a duty toward Western civilization. But Albertini likewise spoke the language of the anti-Giolittian right-Liberalism of which he was a pillar. Italy could not absent itself and remain a great power; it was "unworthy to expect from diplomatic guile the salvation we must achieve through our own strength"; "days of disenchantment and lamentation" awaited Italy and its leaders if it remained neutral. Finally, Albertini helped serve as impresario of D'Annunzio's appearance at Genoa. As for the *Corriere*'s influential Roman correspondents, Andrea Torre and Giovanni Amendola, they pressed even more fiercely than Albertini for a war for "Adriatic domination."[107] In the campaign for war the *Corriere* led the press, goaded the government, linked together all strands of respectable *interventismo*, and spoke cogently to the upper and middle strata and industrial interests of the North and Center.

Those against war lacked both the fierce determination and the relative cohesion of the *interventisti*. Between government and neutralists lay the pale and wandering undecided, many of them Catholics. As the press bayed for Trento, Trieste, and more, and the *interventisti* branded Giolitti as a traitor with all the vehemence of the prophets of the *Risorgimento*, the Catholics moved toward the government to preserve the national credentials acquired since the Libyan War.[108] For "relative neutrality" – Italian inaction conditional on Austrian surrender of territory – stood doubting "friends" of Salandra, the Giolittians,

"supremacy"), 215 and note 15, 219–21, 223 note 24. Colapietra, despite sympathy for his subject, describes Bissolati as a "democratic imperialist" (in quotation marks in original, 215).

[105] And perhaps ten papers were friendly toward the Central Powers: William A. Renzi, *In the Shadow of the Sword. Italy's Neutrality and Entrance into the Great War, 1914–1915* (New York, 1988), 109.

[106] And after his forced retirement at Mussolini's hands in 1926 wrote what remains, when supplemented with new material that surfaced in and after the 1960s Fritz Fischer debate, the most discerning large-scale account of the war's outbreak: *The Origins of the War of 1914*, 3 vols. (London, 1952).

[107] Ottavio Barié, *Luigi Albertini* (Turin, 1972), 293–99; Vigezzi, *L'Italia neutrale*, 537; "il dominio dell'Adriatico": Albertini, *Epistolario*, 1:261 (Amendola), 295 (Torre); D'Annunzio: ibid., 332, 337–38, 346, 349–53.

[108] For the traitor-figure in *Risorgimento* mythology, pp. 52, 53, 218; on political Catholicism and war, see especially Pietro Scoppola, "Cattolici neutralisti e interventisti all vigilia del conflitto," in Rossini, ed., *Benedetto XV, i cattolici e la prima guerra mondiale*, 95–149.

some radical democrats, and much of political Catholicism. Only Socialists, a few intransigent Catholics, and isolated figures from other camps stood for "absolute neutrality."

That formula, which after May 1915 mutated into the Socialist Party's even more ambiguous "neither support nor sabotage," had two major advantages. It was the one position that could unite the PSI's "maximalist" leadership with the reformist minority and its trade unions. And it kept the party firmly anchored to the often inarticulate neutralism of its peasant and worker constituencies – a vital anchor if the war went badly. But it also had fatal defects. As Mussolini had predicted, it gave the initiative to Salandra and to Socialism's enemies, while threatening to isolate the party from the masses soon to be in uniform. It also made impossible the alliance with Giolitti against war that some reformists sought. For "absolute neutrality" could never be the policy of a liberal government, even a neutralist one. Only at gunpoint, if at all, would Austria yield the minimum aims of the Liberal elite, the Habsburg empire's remaining Italian-speaking territories and Adriatic hegemony.[109]

Unbridgeable disunity and Giolitti's abdication overdetermined neutralism's defeat at the center. But it lost equally on the periphery. When the Socialists launched modest non-violent demonstrations against war to give themselves courage, their traditional command of the *piazza* often failed them – a singular humiliation for a party that claimed to represent the masses. The violent minorities seeking war beat them down, with the help of friends in the security forces applying the draconian measures that Salandra had ordered lest public tumult vex the serene preparation of his cabinet war. Only in the capital of neutralism, Turin, did the forces against war largely rule the streets in the "radiant days of May." Pockets of neutralist protest and violence also emerged across Tuscany and Emilia-Romagna; reservists left for their units amid wildcat strikes and demonstrations crying "down with war, up with social revolution." But only the resolute leadership the neutralists so conspicuously lacked could have converted sporadic outbreaks of discontent into a mass challenge to the government's course. As in Germany, by far the largest crowds – approaching 100,000 in Milan and Rome – turned out for war. And the South's cities likewise stood for Salandra from generic governmental loyalty, pride in a native son, and infatuation with *Risorgimento* rhetoric, while the peasant masses remained largely silent.[110] Like Germany's August 1914, the "radiant days" were from the beginning a powerful exercise in national myth-making. But in Italy's myth the transcendent unity of the nation in the face of external threat took second

---

[109] On this crucial point, see especially the cogent analysis of De Caprariis, "Partiti politici e opinione pubblica," 99–100; for a brilliant sketch of the complexities of PSI attitudes toward war in 1914–18, see Gaetano Arfè, "I socialisti," in Alberto Caracciolo et al., *Il trauma dell'intervento: 1914–1919* (Florence, 1968), 205–34.

[110] For public opinion in spring 1915, see (despite divergences of interpretation), Monticone, "Salandra e Sonnino verso la decisione dell'intervento," 67–86; Vigezzi, *Da Giolitti a Salandra*, 111–200 (Southern rhetoric: 144–55), 321–401; and Paolo Spriano, *Torino operaia nella Grande Guerra* (Turin, 1960), ch. 4.

place – from the very outset – to war against the "internal enemy," the traitors and accomplices of "the foreigner" that *Risorgimento* tradition marked for death.

3. THE MEANING OF THE WAR: FRAGMENTATION, DEFEAT, DENIAL, WRATH

The euphoria of August 1914 and of "radiant May" 1915, however widely or narrowly shared, swiftly passed. Both societies increasingly fractured under the strain of war along the lines of their inherited cleavages, and along new fault lines created by a war of unexpected and unprecedented magnitude and duration.

I. Germany: From Peace Within the Fortress to Stab-in-the-Back

The widespread initial faith in an innate solidarity between Germany's home and fighting fronts presumed an "identity between *Volk* and state" that was incompatible for long both with the manifold bitter divisions in German society and politics, and with the absolutist executive that had helped to create and had lovingly cultivated those divisions.[111] The unprecedented nature of the war and the novel effects of Britain's "hunger-blockade" soon blunted the edge of German *Geist*. The party truce began to unravel publicly by summer–fall 1915. By 1917 Germany's classes and *Stände*; regional, religious, and political subcultures; and front and rear had reopened old hostilities and incubated new ones in an atmosphere of increasingly apocalyptic conflict.

At the front, the conditions of this war proved a far greater shock than those of 1870–71 or 1939–45. Abundant communications and mobility behind the front – telephones, motor vehicles, and railroads – and ever-increasing weight of industrial firepower on the battlefield itself nailed the combatants to their waterlogged shell-holes and caved-in dugouts. Technology overdetermined the war's pattern of immense sacrifice for scarcely visible gain. The Germans at least enjoyed early spectacular victories against poorly equipped Russians and Serbs in 1914–15. Then catastrophic offensive failure at Verdun temporarily shattered German morale. Even defense on the Somme against British attacks conducted with a large and ever-growing firepower superiority proved immensely bloody and demoralizing; a few infantry units briefly refused obedience. The aura of Hindenburg and Ludendorff, the swift destruction of Rumania in fall–winter 1916, and the autumn rains in Flanders brought relief, but not from the slim rations of turnips imposed by the British blockade. The officer corps' brilliance in conceiving and organizing ever more effective methods of defensive battle, further great offensive victories against Italy and Russia, and the high quality of the army's junior officer and NCO leadership nevertheless carried the

---

[111] See Preuss, *Das deutsche Volk und die Politik*, especially 194–95, and pp. 93–94 in this volume.

battered German infantry through 1917.[112] Despite disquieting symptoms such as a steady increase in desertion and occasional fusillades from troop trains, it retained the faith in its leaders needed for one last supreme effort.

The army's rear echelons and the surface navy suffered less terror but more boredom than the front. They were also far more exposed than the front to the petty everyday irritations generated by the exaggeration of *Stand* distinctions that remained a stock-in-trade even of the much expanded and diluted wartime officer corps.[113] When in contact with the enemy, company officers ate what their men ate; a few kilometers rearward, shared danger and shared rations ceased. Officers and NCOs might not draw more food per head for their separate rear-area messes than their men, but they had the power – if they chose to use it – to get the least decayed portions, and the power and money to procure additional food and strong drink from the occupied French. Tales of officers' scandalous high living increasingly enraged soldiers and sailors condemned to inactivity or irritating make-work on a diet of turnips and adulterated bread enlivened with cabbage, dabs of anonymous fats, and an occasional scrap of stringy meat or poorly preserved fish. Assertions of privilege such as the ever-present rear-area shops and brothels earmarked for officers or NCOs likewise grated. Home leaves, although liberally granted – an average of 5 percent of the field army was on leave at any one time – sometimes were or appeared the results of favoritism. Disguised failure in May 1916 at Jutland, the navy's belated Marne, led to increasing despair and a first premonitory wave of naval unrest in early summer 1917. The drawing off of ever more talented officers and petty officers for the submarine offensive and the insatiable demands of the front on the army's rear echelon made both High Seas Fleet and army rear ever more brittle as 1917 ended.[114]

---

[112] For the close connection between "the visible superiority of German leadership" and the German infantry's continuing high performance in 1916–17, see G. C. Wynne, *If Germany Attacks. The Battle in Depth in the West* (London, 1940), 256–57. Wynne, Timothy T. Lupfer, "The Dynamics of Doctrine: The Changes in German Tactical Doctrine During the First World War," *Leavenworth Papers* 4 (1981), the account of 1916–17 by Germany's greatest master of defensive battle, Fritz von Lossberg, *Meine Tätigkeit im Weltkriege*, 215–310, and Geyer, "Von massenhaften Tötungshandeln, oder: Wie die deutschen das Krieg-Machen lernten," in Peter Gleichmann and Thomas Kühne, eds., *Massenhaftes Töten* (Essen, 2004), especially 122–42, explore the nature and dimensions of German intellectual and practical superiority at the tactical level.

[113] "[A]s is well known, in the army you become human only from the rank of lieutenant upward" (Reinhold Maier, *Feldpostbriefe aus dem Ersten Weltkrieg 1914–1918* [Stuttgart, 1966 (1917)], 149).

[114] See Erich Otto Volkmann, *Soziale Heeresmissstände als Mitursache des deutschen Zusammenbruchs von 1918* (Berlin, 1929); the internal army documents in Martin Hobohm, *Soziale Heeresmissstände als Teilursache des deutschen Zusammenbruchs von 1918* (*Die Ursachen des deutschen Zusammenbruches im Jahre 1918*, vols. 11.1 and 11.2); and the anonymous "Die Zermürbung der Front," *Süddeutsche Monatshefte* 16 (October 1918–March 1919), 176–92. For the navy, see Deist, "Die Unruhen in der Marine 1917/18," *Marine-Rundschau* 68 (1971), 325–43. Officers' brothels: Liulevicius, *Eastern Front*, 188.

Finally, conditions on the home front grew increasingly grim after spring–summer 1915. Pre-1914 Germany imported 19 percent of its dietary calories, 27 percent of its protein, and 42 percent of its fats; German experts estimated in late 1914 that careful management of domestic production and the use of substitutes would provide 90 percent of prewar calories and 85 percent of prewar protein indefinitely.[115] What were lacking were the fats in the preferred German diet, laced with butter and *Wurst*, a distribution system that guaranteed uninterrupted supplies, and money for the families of those under arms – whose monthly pay amounted to around a twentieth of a metal-worker's wages and whose government family allowances could not sustain life. The countryside and the rich or well-connected had first call on food, then the army and navy, then the miners and heavy munitions workers, and finally Germany's hapless city-dwellers. Rationing began in earnest in winter 1915–16. But ration cards only guaranteed a place on ever-lengthening shop or soup kitchen queues, not steady supplies, nor prewar quality, nor the money to buy at official prices, which doubled between 1914 and 1918, or at black market rates, which soared by 300 to 700 percent.[116]

Shortages inspired the first food riots in autumn 1915. In the critical months of June and July 1916, before the new harvest, housewives, workers, and boys too young for the war sacked food shops and fought the police in cities and towns across Germany.[117] Industrial strikes provoked largely by rising prices likewise increased, despite martial law and the imprecations of the Right. The subsequent nationalization of distribution failed to prevent a steady reduction in rations throughout the terrible "turnip winter" and spring of 1916–17. Wits came to fear not sausage made with rat, but the prospect of "rat substitute." By July 1917, the war's worst month, the official ration was down to 1,100 calories a day, barely more than one-third of the theoretical standard of 3,000 required to support a full-grown man. The meat ration dropped to 11.8 percent of average prewar consumption in summer–fall 1918. Actual wartime consumption was probably rather higher than the ration, for by the end of the war the illegal market was providing about one-third of all civilian food. But all except country-dwellers and the rich suffered from this most punishing form of forced social levelling. What an American expert retrospectively described in 1916 as the "familiar obesity of the Germans" melted away; by one contemporary

---

115 Eltzbacher commission report, cited in Offer, *First World War*, 25; I have borrowed liberally from Offer's analysis (chs. 1–5) of the German wartime food situation.

116 Prices: Gerd Hardach, *The First World War, 1914–1918* (Berkeley, CA, 1977), 200; also the indices in Jürgen Kocka, *Klassengesellschaft im Krieg. Deutsche Sozialgeschichte 1914–1918* (Göttingen, 1973), according to which the overall cost of living tripled (1914=100; 1918=313). Military pay, metal-workers' wages: Hobohm, *Soziale Heeresmissstände*, 111 (15.90 M. per month); Gerhard Bry, *Wages in Germany 1871–1945* (Princeton, NJ, 1960), 434, 202 (12.94 M. per day, 1918; highly specialized metal-workers in the Berlin area earned 50 to 60 M. per day).

117 See for instance the vivid account in Volker Ullrich, *Kriegsalltag. Hamburg im Ersten Weltkrieg* (Cologne, 1982), 51–56.

estimate, Germany's roughly 55 million civilians lost more than half a million tons of "human mass."[118]

By mid-1919 almost a half million more adults and children than would have died in peacetime had perished. Shortages of coal for heating – resulting from logistical ineptitude and the demands of war industry – and undernourishment made common diseases more virulent, and the great influenza pandemic that fittingly accompanied the war's final year killed 250,000–300,000 of the half-million; traditional estimates of 700,000 and more "hunger deaths" thus appear notably exaggerated.[119] The battlefield was inevitably preeminent: more than two out of five of those called to arms died or suffered serious wounds. A total of more than 2 million men, or almost one in seven in uniform and about 3 percent of Germany's 1914 population, died (see Figure 3.1). Their passing registered daily in black-rimmed newspaper death-notices that the censors dared not ban.

Politics followed the pattern set through the population's increasing desperation over food and losses. The "peace within the fortress" crumbled slowly and inexorably over two interrelated complexes of issues: war aims, the conduct of the war, and peace negotiations on the one hand, and Prussia-Germany's internal order on the other. The war aims question was of supreme importance, for the claim that Germany fought in self-defense was the foundation on which the party truce rested. From August–September 1914 on, prominent individuals, economic pressure groups, and the parties of the center and Right, led or inspired by an increasingly zealous professoriate and the Pan-German League, preached extreme aims to a secretly converted Bethmann Hollweg. The non-Socialist parties in the Reichstag formed a phalanx for massive annexations, a "war aims majority" that endured, with a brief interruption in summer 1917, almost to the bitter end. Security against treacherous attacks – such as those invented by the German government in 1914 – required annexations from Liège and Antwerp to Riga. Justice required them as a fitting judgment on the iniquity of Germany's enemies. And only annexations could repay the German people's immense sacrifices in blood and treasure, while (in the fond hope of the Right) smothering in glory and booty all demands for democratization at home. Shadings of opinion existed; some Prussian Conservatives and much of middle academic opinion at first dissented from the *völkisch* thirst for land "free of people" of the Pan-Germans and the German-Balt agitators. But even moderate figures, from the Center Party and right-wing Social Democrats to

[118] For rat substitute, "familiar obesity," and the "human mass" estimates, see Offer, *First World War*, 54, 31, 33; the ration as a percentage of prewar consumption in Kocka, *Klassengesellschaft*, 20.

[119] Jay Winter, "Surviving the War: Life Expectation, Illness, and Mortality Rates in Paris, London, and Berlin 1914–1919," in idem and Jean-Louis Robert, eds., *Capital Cities at War: Paris, London, Berlin 1914–1918* (Cambridge, 1997), 517–18 note 34, and David K. Patterson and Gerald F. Pyle, "The Geography and Mortality of the 1918 Influenza Pandemic," *Bulletin of the History of Medicine* 65:1 (1991), 14. For the traditional estimate, Gerhard Hirschfeld, Gerd Krumeich, and Irina Renz, *Enzyklopädie Erster Weltkrieg* (Paderborn, 2004),664–65; also 566 (800,000).

FIGURE 3.1. The Hammer of War: Armies and Peoples on Trial, 1914–1919

	France	Germany	Italy	Austria-Hungary	Great Britain	Russian Empire	USA
Total population (millions)	39.6	67.8	36.6	58.6	41.6	167.0	98.8
Men mobilized (millions)	7.9	13.2	5.0	9.0	5.7	15.8	4.3
Men mobilized (% of population)	19.9	19.5	13.7	15.4	13.7	9.5	4.3
Dead of military causes, including POWs (millions)	1.33	2.04	0.65	1.10	0.72	1.81	0.11
Dead of military causes (% of men mobilized)	16.82	15.43	13.00	12.22	12.54	11.46	2.67
Dead of military causes (% of population)	3.35	3.00	1.78	1.88	1.72	1.08	0.12
Excess civilian deaths, including 1918 influenza (millions)	0.50	0.48	0.63	0.70	0.29	1.50	0.55
Total war-related dead (millions)	1.83	2.52	1.28	1.80	1.01	3.31	0.66
War-related dead (% of population)	4.61	3.71	3.50	3.07	2.42	1.98	0.67

Base data: (All figures are approximate.) Boris Z. Urlanis, *Wars and Population* (Moscow, 1971), 209, 267–68; Mario Isnenghi and Giorgio Rochat, *La Grande Guerra, 1914–1918* (Milan, 2000), 228; Giorgio Mortara, *La salute pubblica in Italia durante e dopo la guerra* (Bari, 1925) 107, 120, 522; Jay Winter, "Surviving the War: Life Expectation, Illness, and Mortality Rates in Paris, London, and Berlin 1914–1919," in idem and Jean-Louis Robert, eds., *Capital Cities at War: Paris, London, Berlin 1914–1918* (Cambridge, 1997), 517–18 note 34; David K. Patterson and Gerald F. Pyle, "The Geography and Mortality of the 1918 Influenza Pandemic," *Bulletin of the History of Medicine* 65:1 (1991), 15.

the well-known Berlin military historian Hans Delbrück, stood for annexations that would make Germany supreme in Europe.[120]

Against the "war aims majority" stood – at least in theory – the SPD, which from the beginning had sought by calculated ambiguity and invocation of the party's legendary discipline to keep its left wing within the *Burgfrieden*. Karl Liebknecht, standard-bearer of the far Left, nevertheless cast the Reichstag's first solitary vote against war credits in December 1914. But it was the semi-public barrage of war aims memoranda from Pan-Germans and economic interest groups in spring 1915 that ended all hope of truce within the Social Democratic Party. By mid-summer the evidence that Germany fought for "imperialist" booty led to public schism. The increasing restiveness of the urban population from spring 1916 further swelled the ranks of the SPD's dissidents. When the majority expelled them rather than lose its place "within the fortress," they constituted themselves as an independent Reichstag group in March 1916 and then as the Independent Social Democratic Party (USPD) in April 1917. The tiny "Spartacus Group" around Liebknecht and Rosa Luxembourg took up station on the extreme Left. The war's splintering of Socialist unity both mirrored and accelerated the splintering of German society and politics. The majority of the SPD and its trade unions nevertheless held to the line of 4 August 1914, and collaborated loyally and effectively with army and industry in operating the war economy.[121] Germany's war was a war of national defense. It might even be a war for the self-determination of the suffering peoples under the Russian yoke, although – in the view of Philipp Scheidemann, the chief parliamentary figure of the majority SPD – decidedly not of Germany's Alsatians and Lorrainers.[122]

As food vanished and casualty rolls lengthened, the conduct of the war likewise provoked acrid debate. In February–March 1916 the "war aims majority" and Pan-German fanatics in the press sought to force unrestricted submarine warfare on Bethmann Hollweg even at the price of war with "*Amerika*." Germany's mortal peril demanded use of its "sharpest weapon" without regard for consequences. Behind the agitation stood Tirpitz, whose forced resignation from the Reich Naval Office in mid-March 1916 had freed him to attack the government publicly. Economic pressure groups took up the call in September

---

[120] See the marvelous collection of S. Grumbach, *Das annexionistische Deutschland: Eine Sammlung von Dokumenten, die seit dem 4. August 1914 in Deutschland öffentlich oder geheim verbreitet wurden* (Lausanne, 1917); Fischer, *Germany's Aims*, ch. 5 and passim; Klaus Schwabe, "Ursprung und Verbreitung des alldeutschen Annexionismus in der deutschen Professorenschaft im Ersten Weltkrieg," VfZ 14 (1966); on the wartime conflict between traditional *Junker* interest politics and *völkisch* nationalism, see Abraham J. Peck, *Radicals and Reactionaries: The Crisis of Conservatism in Wilhelmine Germany* (Washington, D.C., 1978), 149–50, 154, 164, 183, 220–21.

[121] See Feldman, *Army, Industry and Labor*.

[122] Miller, *Burgfrieden und Klassenkampf*, 234, 219 (190–240 provides a discerning analysis of SPD war aims; see especially 219 for Scheidemann's aversion to self-determination for Alsatians and Lorrainers, despite – or because of – his recognition of their overwhelming desire for union with France).

1916, and the war aims majority voted in October to support Hindenburg and Ludendorff should they decide to act, isolating Bethmann, the Kaiser, and other remaining doubters. At the moment of decision in January 1917, the chief of the navy accurately summarized the public mood: "*Volk* and army howl for unrestricted submarine warfare."[123]

Then Russia erupted in revolution and the Petrograd Soviet called for immediate peace "without annexations or indemnities," the United States joined Germany's world of enemies, and the U-boats failed to bring relief from the hungriest months of the war. The example of Petrograd and Germany's first major wave of wartime strikes in April 1917 widened the latent cracks in Prussia-Germany's internal order into a fundamental political crisis. The urban crowds of Germany's Socialist subculture seemed to threaten the *Volksgemeinschaft* of 1914 and the war effort. At Easter the Kaiser therefore hesitantly proclaimed that equality in the face of death at the front must ultimately entail reform of Prussia's wealth-graded franchise. But the Kaiser's message neither promised equal suffrage nor immediate reform, for only the existing three-class suffrage could guarantee the Conservative–National Liberal majority in Prussia and the long-term political stability of Bismarck's Reich. Bethmann's stock-in-trade, the "policy of the diagonal" that attempted to pacify the Left with promises so equivocal that the Right could not attack him, was now unsustainable.[124] By 1917 the Reich's situation demanded radical choices.

The crisis culminated in June–July 1917. The failure of the submarines and the prospect of another winter of war impelled Matthias Erzberger of the Center Party – long an annexationist of no small appetite – to advocate a negotiated settlement while Germany could hope to preserve its gains. With the support of Left-Liberals and SPD, he pushed through the Reichstag a resolution proclaiming support for a negotiated peace without "forced territorial acquisitions" – a formula, as Erzberger was well aware, that in no way prohibited the erection of vassal states or annexations ostensibly blessed by self-determination.[125] The war aims majority of all parties except SPD and USPD thus gave way to a new Center–Left-Liberal–SPD "peace resolution majority." But rather than producing a working coalition determined to force both negotiation *and* domestic reforms, Erzberger's stroke simply superimposed a new set of divisions and ambiguities on Germany's existing party cleavages. National Liberals and Conservatives opposed the new majority as "defeatist." The USPD for its part damned Erzberger's resolution as a fraud. That alignment of zealous extremes

---

[123] See especially Ritter, *The Sword and the Scepter*, vol. 3, chs. 5, 8, and Tirpitz, *Politische Dokumente*, vol. 2, *Deutsche Ohnmachtspolitik im Weltkriege* (Hamburg, Berlin, 1926), part III; Epstein, *Matthias Erzberger and the Dilemma of German Democracy* (Princeton, NJ, 1959), 159–60; Fischer, *Germany's Aims*, 292–93; "howl": UF, 1:146 (Holtzendorff).

[124] For this apt description of Bethmann's policy, Dieter Grosser, *Vom monarchischen Konstitutionalismus zur parlamentarischen Demokratie. Die Verfassungspolitik der deutschen Parteien im letzten Jahrzehnt des Kaiserreiches* (The Hague, 1970), 106–07.

[125] See Epstein, *Erzberger*, 203–04.

against a beleaguered center helped paralyze the Reichstag in the present, and foreshadowed the future instability of the Weimar Republic.[126]

Nor – in contrast to a notion that has bewitched historians since 1917–18 – was this crisis a vital step in polarizing Germany into two great camps, of downtrodden masses yearning for a "Scheidemann peace" and reform, and of domineering elites baying for a "Hindenburg peace" and social reaction.[127] Far Right and left-center, enemies in virtually all else, joined in destroying Bethmann Hollweg. Conservatives, National Liberals, and supreme command sought his scalp for his lack of energy and charisma, his opposition to U-boat warfare, his relative moderation on war aims, and his hesitant demand for equal suffrage in Prussia to hold the masses behind the war effort. Erzberger and much of the Center felt that the Belgian blood on Bethmann Hollweg's hands disqualified him from negotiating a peace settlement. Some Left-Liberals and especially the SPD resented his resistance to parliamentarization, to the bringing of chancellor and army under the authority of the Reichstag majority.[128]

In the continuing public debate on war aims, virtually all shades of opinion except Spartacists, USPD, and much of the SPD still supported annexations if feasible. Much of the Center, despite Erzberger's fatherhood of the peace resolution, regarded it without enthusiasm. Most National Liberals and much of the Center opposed any Prussian franchise reform that would destroy or weaken their long-defended strongholds in the Prussian Chamber; Left-Liberals, SPD, and USPD correspondingly sought to democratize Prussia. Yet after Bethmann Hollweg's dismissal, the Left hesitated to demand that any new chancellor be responsible to the Reichstag. The USPD lacked clear constitutional aims; the Spartacists derided all forms of "parliamentary cretinism." The SPD feared that a Reichstag majority capable of governing would be a majority of the Right. The Left-Liberals refused to stray far from the National Liberals, who remained stalwart for a chancellor responsible to the emperor rather than the Reichstag. Finally, the most energetic National Liberal leader, Gustav Stresemann, had since early 1916 espoused parliamentarization and Prussian franchise reform

---

[126] See Grosser, *Vom monarchischen Konstitutionalismus*, 215; Friedrich Naumann anticipated this danger as early as October 1918 (ibid., 165–66).

[127] The most influential statements of the polarization thesis have been – for politics – Arthur Rosenberg's classic, *Imperial Germany. The Birth of the German Republic 1871–1918* (Boston, 1964 [1928]) and – for social history (despite methodological disclaimers) – Kocka, *Klassengesellschaft*. For the notable lack of fit between Kocka's "klassengesellschaftlich-dichotomische Modell" of Imperial Germany and the evidence, see especially ibid., 96–105, 131–36, 140–41; Gottfried Schramm, "Klassengegensätze im Ersten Weltkrieg. Zu Jürgen Kockas Gesellschaftsmodell," *Geschichte und Gesellschaft* 2 (1976), 244–60; and Robert G. Moeller, "Dimensions of Social Conflict in the Great War: The View from the German Countryside," CEH 14 (1981), 142–68.

[128] In this and the following paragraph, I have relied heavily on the brilliant analysis of Grosser, *Vom monarchischen Konstitutionalismus*, part 2; on Bethmann's fall, see especially Epstein, *Erzberger*, 193ff., and Wolfgang J. Mommsen, "Die deutsche öffentliche Meinung und der Zusammenbruch des Regierungssystems Bethmann Hollweg im Juli 1917," GWU 19 (1968), 656–71.

ever more openly in an attempt – in common with a few perceptive Left-Liberals – to give annexationism a mass base. Not polarization but a dramatic increase in Germany's inherited political and social fragmentation – that *"innere Zerrissenheit"* that the Right so lovingly denounced – was the fruit of 1917.

The reaction of the vast majority of Prussia-Germany's bedrock, the dominant north-German Protestants, scarcely diminished that fragmentation. As their religious leaders celebrated the four hundredth year since Luther had nailed his theses to the door at Wittenberg, most saw black Romish conspiracy in the coincidence of the Reichstag "peace" resolution of the Catholic Erzberger with the much-publicized August 1917 peace initiative of Pope Benedict XV. The Kaiser's October 1917 appointment of a Catholic, the Bavarian prime minister Georg von Hertling, to the chancellorship and Prussian minister-presidency – with Reichstag approval – soon added injury to insult.[129] Even before that, Protestant Germany had struck back. In celebration of Sedan Day – 2 September 1917 – Tirpitz, croaking with hatred, led a group of luminaries of the Right in founding a "German Fatherland Party [*Vaterlandspartei*]" to steel the home and fighting fronts for final victory. The war was a "life or death struggle" to decide whether Germany could defend "the liberty of the continent of Europe... against the all-devouring tyranny of Anglo-Americanism," or whether Germans would sink to be mere "ethnic fertilizer [*Völkerdünger*]" for others. Protestant pastors drunk on Hegel and raving of "victory or downfall," parish notables and anti-Semitic agitators, patriotic middle-class ladies, and fanatical members of the German-National Shop Clerks' League enraged at the high wages of munitions workers joined or supported the *Vaterlandspartei* in numbers that dwarfed the SPD's war-shrunken 243,000 members. By 1918 Tirpitz's up to 800,000 followers constituted the largest wartime mass organization in Germany. As the "unity party" of Fatherland, it sought to "rekindle the burning enthusiasm of August 1914" while damning the self-interest of the Reichstag parties for the Reich's "splintering [*Zersplitterung*]" under pressure. It celebrated Bismarck's "titanic battle against the ruinous spirit of faction." It hailed the "German freedom" to do one's duty and damned the "inauthentic democracy" of the hypocritical West. In countless leaflets and speeches it hammered home its message; at this culminating moment of the war the sole hope of Germany's enemies was Germany's own internal disunity: "Germany Awake! [*Deutschland erwache*] Thine hour of destiny has arrived." The *Vaterlandspartei* was the first great mass movement of German nationalism. Its combination of unconditional will to final victory and SPD mass propaganda technique briefly put adherents of a "Scheidemann peace" and the *Bildungsbürgertum*'s few moderate elements in the shade. It offered to Germany's war-anguished middle classes and to all non-combatant Germans

---

[129] See Missalla, *"Gott mit uns,"* 43–44, and especially Gottfried Mehnert, *Evangelische Kirche und Politik 1917–1919* (Düsseldorf, 1959), 43–56.

who defined themselves as *national* a first chance to transmute sentiment into concerted political action.[130]

War also widened beyond measure the cleavage between German Christians and German Jews. Germany's Jewish community had shared the fervent enthusiasms of 1914; Houston Stuart Chamberlain himself had testified in 1915 to the Jews' faithful discharge of their "duty as Germans in the face of the enemy or at home." Yet the encounter of German troops with the alien-seeming "*Ostjuden*" of Poland in 1915–18; the transport of 35,000 Polish Jews to work in Germany; the German Jewish role as retail middlemen and leaders of the liberal press; and the anti-Semites' fierce efforts to exploit the war to advance their cause soon gave the "Jewish question" a salience it had not enjoyed even in the golden age of the anti-Semitic parties before 1900. From spring 1916 characters such as Theodor Fritsch of the *Reichshammerbund* and Konstantin von Gebsattel, second-in-command of the Pan-Germans, showered the Kaiser, the princes, and the politicians with petitions spurring them to roll back "Jewish influence" in Germany. Allegations of Jewish predilection for wartime hoarding and black market profiteering spoke powerfully to a hungry population largely innocent of the workings of supply and demand.[131] That the great Jewish-owned or Jewish-managed organs of the liberal and Socialist press – the *Berliner Tageblatt, Frankfurter Zeitung*, and SPD *Vorwärts* – were hostile to ruthless use of U-boats and Zeppelins and friendly to the peace resolution was proof positive, to Fritsch and the Pan-Germans, of an international "pan-Jewish" conspiracy against German victory. The war itself was thus a struggle, as Gebsattel put it, not merely between German heroism and "debased Anglo-American mammonism," but between the Aryan and Jewish races. And Germany's Jews, claimed the agitators, were shirking combat service in order to commit their treason from safe billets in the army rear or at home. A Prussian war ministry sympathetic to these "complaints from the *Volk*" ordered a wildly popular census of Jews serving in the army in October 1916. Then it held the result secret, encouraging the false rumor that the figures had been "devastating" for the Jews.[132] In thus singling out its Jews, the Second Reich endorsed the

---

[130] Tirpitz speech at Königsberg, 2 (actually 3) September 1917, in Fischer, *Germany's Aims*, 432 (an eerie sound recording also exists); *Vaterlandspartei* founding proclamation in UF, 2:48–50; manifesto of the Brandenburg branch, 3 November 1917, in Lutz, ed., *Fall of the German Empire*, 1:371; on Prussian Protestantism as the party's core, see Günther Brakelmann, *Der deutsche Protestantismus im Epochenjahr 1917* (Witten, 1974), 18 and Mehnert, *Evangelische Kirche und Politik*, 57–59 ("Sieg oder Untergang!," 54). *Vaterlandspartei* and SPD membership figures: Heinz Hagenlücke, *Deutsche Vaterlandspartei. Die nationale Rechte am Ende des Kaiserreichs* (Düsseldorf, 1997), 180–83.

[131] The role of anti-Semitism in the "moral economy" of the German crowd deserves a monograph all to itself.

[132] On all this, see Werner Bergmann and Juliane Wetzel, "Antisemitismus im Ersten und Zweiten Weltkrieg: Ein Forschungsüberblick," in Thoss and Hans-Erich Volkmann, eds., *Erster Weltkrieg / Zweiter Weltkrieg. Ein Vergleich* (Paderborn, 2002), 439–48; Saul Friedländer, "Die

agitation of the anti-Semites and took the first governmental step toward reversing Jewish emancipation in Germany.

The political breakout of the urban masses, the fanatical counter-mobilization of the Protestant-nationalist majority culture, and the explosive spread of anti-Semitism were merely one set of symptoms of the crisis of the Second Reich and of German society that opened in 1917. State and monarchy began to lose their grip on the public imagination. The bureaucracy, saddled with apportioning scarcity and harder hit in pocket and stomach by wartime inflation than most other groups, suffered a swift decline in morale and in the public's trust. The German people for their part had to break the law daily to live; war ended the Reich's career as a well-ordered society. Rationing and scarcity soon made theft – individual and collective, by private citizens and by state employees, for survival or for profit – the order of the day. Those with money or goods to barter bought or sold on the black market. Those without stole. All defied the laws and regulations of the state.[133]

As for the monarchy, the advent of Hindenburg and Ludendorff was final evidence of its irreversible failure as a source of mythic leadership. Even William II's own, the officer corps, despaired of its Supreme Warlord's obvious incompetence. It soon needed reminding of its personal tie to William and its duty to do battle "for Kaiser and king" regardless of the mass army fighting "for Germany" that it led. Machine warfare for Germany indeed brought to the fore a new kind of officer, prefigured by the prewar *Wehrverein* fanatics: narrowly military-technical, explosively energetic, and ferociously nationalist. Ludendorff, prototypical in this and much else, summed up as early as 1915 the credo of the new species and the gulf that separated it from its forebears. "The Field-Marshal," he remarked, "still says Kaiser," but the word he himself preferred was "Fatherland." And to later reproaches that he lacked monarchical deference, he replied defiantly that "the German *Volk* means more to me than the person of the Kaiser." Amid bloodshed and suffering, German radical nationalism and a new kind of officer – the technocratic-fanatical military Führer – were taking leave of the broken shell of aristocratic-monarchical Prussia-Germany.[134]

---

politischen Veränderungen der Kriegszeit und ihre Auswirkungen auf die Judenfrage," and Werner Jochmann, "Die Ausbreitung des Antisemitismus," in Werner E. Mosse, ed., *Deutsches Judentum in Krieg und Revolution 1916–1923* (Tübingen, 1971), particularly 35–39, 415–16, 425–27, 432; Uwe Lohalm, *Völkischer Radikalismus. Die Geschichte des Deutschvölkischen Schutz- und Trutz-Bundes 1919–1923* (Hamburg, 1970), 46–51, 62–66, 71–76 (Gebsattel quotation, 47); and Werner T. Angress, "Das deutsche Militär und die Juden im Ersten Weltkrieg," MGM 19 (1976), 77–144. Egmont Zechlin, *Die deutsche Politik und die Juden im Ersten Weltkrieg* (Göttingen, 1969), part 2, is useful on the ambiguities of German policy toward the Jews of eastern Europe.

133 See the despairing reports of the authorities in Kocka, *Klassengesellschaft*, 133–35, and Karl Ludwig Ay, *Die Entstehung einer Revolution. Die Volksstimmung in Bayern während des Ersten Weltkrieges* (Berlin, 1968), ch. 6 ("Das Ende der Staatsautorität").

134 Wild von Hohenborn speech to officers, January 1917, in MIW, 2:661; Ludendorff, in Thoss, "Diktaturfrage," 69 note 19 and 56. On these issues see especially Hull, *The Entourage of Kaiser Wilhelm II*, 268–69; Geyer, "German Strategy in the Age of Machine Warfare, 1914–1945,"

Yet insofar as German nationalism remained identified with Prussia, war also weakened the mutual ties of the German "tribes." War and privation without victory inevitably drove south – and largely Catholic – Germany away from the Protestant North. The immense smoking cesspit of Berlin, symbol in the south of Prussianism, socialism, and industrial "mammonism," soon provoked the wrath of the South's rulers, shopkeepers, peasants, and workers. Berlin's monopoly of political decision-making, its efforts to centralize the war economy, and its insatiable appetite for Bavaria's lovingly husbanded agricultural surplus aroused fear that regardless of national victory or defeat, Bavaria's independence was doomed. The war's seeming prolongation for the aims of a Protestant Prussian Reich leadership, widely believed rumors that the Prussian supreme command saved the most dangerous missions for Bavarians, and traditional Prussian slurs at alleged south-German slovenliness likewise corroded morale.[135]

The North-South divide also coincided in part with the growing gulf between cities and countryside. Against the foraging and requisitioning cities, all rural classes and *Stände* from *Junker* to peasants and laborers stood in unshakable unity. Fierce traditional mistrusts and the countryside's newfound sense of power as the sole source of food quickly expressed itself in "malicious pleasure that the city-folk must come to beg." The city-folk returned hatred for malice, and soon discovered that as "robber bands" and "troops of fifty or one hundred" they could steal with quasi-impunity what they could not buy. The countryside retaliated – on occasion with the approval of the authorities – with violent self-help. And both groups simultaneously turned their fury on the state, the country-dwellers because it had sought to repeal the law of supply and demand, the city-dwellers because it had failed to do so.[136]

Finally, the war had by 1916–17 opened a gulf between front and rear, a gulf of experience and of generations. With full mobilization of the opposing coalitions' industrial power, fire increased to intensities hitherto unimaginable. Yet except for the slight danger of air attack, only those within five to eight kilometers of the front risked their lives. And of the combat arms, the much-tried infantry – Germany's best and youngest men – inevitably suffered up to nine-tenths of Germany's casualties. The experience of being shelled for days, of being thumped by blast and shredded by whirring razor-sharp steel splinters,

in Peter Paret, ed., *Makers of Modern Strategy from Machiavelli to the Present* (Princeton, NJ, 1986), 538; Thoss, ibid., 39, 44–45, 48; and Riezler, the consummate (and untranslatable) *Bildungsbürger*: "Die im Kriege hinaufgekommenen Tüchtigen, wie Ludendorff, Groener, Bombenenergie, krasseste Unbildung...schliesslich doch ein amerikanisierter Typus – enge" (*Tagebücher*, 401–02).

[135] See the diatribe of Crown Prince (and army group commander) Rupprecht of Bavaria to Hertling, 19 July 1917, in UF, 1:393–98; Feldman, *Army, Industry and Labor*, 282, 421–24; and Ay, *Entstehung einer Revolution*, especially 87–89, 108–09, 119–22, 134–47.

[136] See especially Moeller, "Dimensions of Social Conflict in the Great War," and the reports of the martial law commanders quoted in Kocka, *Klassengesellschaft*, 99–103, 133–35 (quotations, 102, 133, 135).

of the omnipresence of annihilation by unseen enemies in that "kilometer-wide zone behind the foremost lines where explosives held absolute sway," created the German war's most powerful myths and hatreds.[137]

The "storm of steel" bound together the new warrior elite of *Frontsoldaten*. A chosen band, drawn faces shadowed by the new steel "Siegfried-helmets" whose medieval-modern silhouette all Europe came to dread, shielded Germany's western border through their "Watch on the Somme." Not weight of materiel, but the faithfulness unto death, the "Siegfried-loyalty" of the front-soldier was decisive.[138] The impersonal wrath of industrial battle had perhaps extinguished chivalry – on this most participants agreed – but not valor or human intelligence.[139] Machine warfare, by isolating the soldier in a terrifying sea of fire and mud, had in fact heightened the role of the individual. Ernst Jünger, with fourteen wounds and Germany's highest decoration (*Pour le mérite*, 1918) personified the myth and had no doubts: "machines cannot win battles, even if battles are won with machines – a very great difference." The heavier the fire, the more exacting the test: "Here every day proves that the will knows no impossibilities." And those who embodied *Wille* were above all the elite within an elite, the men of the *Stosstruppen* or picked assault units formed under the aegis of Max Bauer at the supreme command – an "entirely new race" of "jugglers with death, masters of the flame and of high explosive, magnificent beasts of prey" born from the thunder of the *Materialschlacht*.[140]

The roots of myth lay in experience: in the very great cohesion of German infantry units, founded on regional recruitment and justified faith in the skill of their leaders; in the exceptionally sharp division between front and rear imposed by 1914–18 technology; in the inevitable envy, hatred, and contempt of the infantrymen of all armies for everyone else; and, in the end, in a defeat that seemed the work of the home front and of political leaders defined by age and cowardice: the "old gang."[141] Even before November 1918, the result was a chasm deeper than distinctions of class and *Stand*. On one side stood the

---

[137] Ernst Jünger, *In Stahlgewittern* (Berlin, 1920), 59.

[138] See Otto Riebicke, *Ringen an der Somme und im Herze* (Magdeburg, 1917) and Ernst von Wolzogen, "Die Wacht an der Somme (1917)," both quoted in Gerd Krumeich, "Le soldat allemand sur la Somme," in Becker and Stéphane Audoin-Rouzeau, eds., *Les sociétés européennes et la guerre* (Paris, 1990), 368–71. Note the dates: this was no postwar myth.

[139] For the 1914–18 emergence of the "new heroic individual" of machine warfare, see particularly Omer Bartov, "Man and the Mass: Reality and the Heroic Image in War," *History and Memory* 2 (1989), 110–22.

[140] Jünger, *Das Wäldchen 125. Eine Chronik aus den Grabenkämpfen 1918* (Berlin, 1926), 56, 59, 210; idem, *Der Kampf als inneres Erlebnis* (1922), in *Sämtliche Werke*, 22 vols. (Stuttgart, 1978–2007), 7:72–73, 37. Bruce I. Gudmundsson, *Stormtroop Tactics: Innovation in the German Army, 1914–1918* (Westport, CT, 1989) and the works cited in note 112 make clear the extent to which the German army's edge over its opponents, proven by its favorable kill ratios in both attack and defense, was an edge in brains and leadership.

[141] Hatred of the rear was hardly peculiar to Germany: "I'd like to see a Tank come down the stalls / Lurching to rag-time tunes, or 'Home, sweet Home,' / And there'd be no more jokes in Music-halls / To mock the riddled corpses round Bapaume" (Siegfried Sassoon, "Blighters," in

warriors, the grim helmeted aristocracy of *Frontkämpfer*. On the other stood the staffs, the "rear-echelon swine" of the army rear, the political class and its attendant capitalist "swindlers and profiteers," and an industrial workforce that wallowed in warmth and safety at ten or twenty times the warrior's pay.[142]

Yet Germany's splintering did not bring the Reich down. Defensive successes in France and great German victories – Caporetto in October–November 1917 and the Bolshevik coup and armistice plea in November–December – shored the home front up. Up to 500,000 munitions workers in Berlin and perhaps one million more throughout the Reich struck in January 1918 against the apparent prolongation of the war – now that the Bolsheviks had offered peace – by supreme command and *Vaterlandspartei*. But the strikers, the USPD, and the SPD leaders who addressed the crowds to avoid isolation from the urban masses found themselves isolated in turn from country and army. The great strikes collapsed swiftly. The authorities sent ringleaders to the front. Patriotic SPD figures such as Friedrich Ebert henceforth bore the stigma of treason in the eyes of the political center as well as the Right. The SPD sheepishly abstained in late March 1918 when the reconstituted war aims majority crushingly ratified the draconian eastern peace, disguised as self-determination for Russia's subject peoples, that Hindenburg and Ludendorff had imposed at Brest-Litovsk. As the Reichstag voted, Ludendorff's assault divisions, exactingly retrained in *Stosstrupp* tactics and lavishly equipped with light machine guns, flamethrowers, trench mortars, small portable cannon, and other new support weapons, swept forward over the British lines on the Somme. A hitherto skeptical observer returned from battle to reassure the Foreign Office: Germany had "world mastery" in its grasp.[143]

The "Kaiser's battle" or *Kaiserschlacht* of March 1918 was the army's supreme effort. The troops climbed from their dugouts with a mixture of fatalism and savage elation, storming forward to end the war and seize the bacon,

---

his *The Old Huntsman and Other Poems* [London, 1918]). But only in Germany – and to a lesser extent in Italy – did such emotions acquire political force.

[142] Eric J. Leed, "Class and Disillusion in World War I," JMH 50:4 (1978), 680–99, and *No Man's Land*, overemphasizes upper-middle-class efforts to heal the "disillusionment" occasioned by the alleged pointlessness of trench warfare and by forced association with the brutish lower orders. The disillusionment model derives primarily from the memoirs of sheltered, highminded young Britons traumatized by battlefield squalor, by contact with the unwashed (see Corelli Barnett, "A Military Historian's View of the Great War," in Baroness Stocks, ed., *Essays by Divers Hands* [London, 1970]), 1–18, and by the tactical ineptitude of Sir Douglas Haig and his acolytes. Jünger, who loved this war precisely for its horrors ("Grauen" – a favorite word), does not fit the model at all. Nor does the "vehement grisly realism" found in so many German upper-middle-class letters from the front (see the comment on Philipp Witkop, ed., *Kriegsbriefe gefallener Studenten* [Munich, 1928] by Adolfo Omodeo, *Momenti della vita di guerra. Dai diari e dalle lettere dei caduti 1915–1918* [Turin, 1968 (1934)], 73). And if the source of the German front myth was upper-middle-class disillusionment, what explains its later mass appeal?

[143] "Ach, seien Sie ruhig! Wer das erlebt hat! . . . Die Weltherrschaft!" (Max von Baden, *Erinnerungen*, 268).

bully beef, and whisky of the British supply dumps. "The overpowering desire to kill gave my feet wings," wrote Jünger with relish a year or so later. At home the public took immense satisfaction that the blockading British were now at last tasting the "sharpness of the German sword." For an instant, victory and revenge raised emotions akin to those of August 1914. Salvation through Hindenburg and Ludendorff seemed at hand. The moneyed public raised its already enormous bet that indemnities from Germany's soon-to-be-defeated enemies would pay the Reich's debts. The war loan launched on 18 March raised an unprecedented 15 million marks from almost 7 million subscribers – more than 10 percent of Germany's population.[144] Ludendorff's strategic lunacy, the source of final defeat, was widely shared.

But after giving up almost fifty miles, the British grimly held. The German infantry knew before anyone else that the war was lost. From mid-April 1918 its performance in the attack fell off even more sharply than its numbers; the best of its platoon leaders and company commanders were dead; many assault divisions had lost a third of their strength. Replacements from Russia – the 80 percent who did not desert en route – often shrank from the rigors of the West. Men "combed out" from the army rear or sent to the front as punishment after the great strikes were even less inclined to spend the rest of their lives as dead heroes. Yet Ludendorff kept pounding at the British and French until troop exhaustion and Allied counteroffensives forced him to halt in mid-July. Thereafter the army slowly thinned and crumbled under repeated Allied blows backed by fresh American manpower, overwhelming superiority in artillery and aircraft, and ever-larger numbers of a machine, the tank, against which – when the as-yet-rudimentary machines worked – *Wille* alone was a foolish answer. Allied leaflets playing back USPD slogans about fighting for Germany's millionaires not Germany's honor, trumpeting the limitless resources of the Americans, and picturing jolly German prisoners peeling limitless mounds of potatoes in French prisoner-of-war camps may have helped.[145] But it was the failure of the great offensives that shattered the faith of the *Frontsoldat* even before the first mass surrenders to the British, and long before Germany's public armistice request in early October.[146]

[144] Jünger, *In Stahlgewittern* (1920 ed.), 146; the army's opinion reporting, summarized in Reichsarchiv, *Der Weltkrieg*, 14:506; Konrad Roesler, *Die Finanzpolitik des Deutschen Reiches im Ersten Weltkrieg* (Berlin, 1967), 206–07. Although inflation admittedly diminished the war loan's comparative performance, the prospect of victory nevertheless attracted over 4 million small subscribers (1–200 M.), and surpassed by a hair the previous peak in small subscriptions in spring 1917.

[145] "Wir kämpfen nicht für Deutschlands Ehre / Wir kämpfen nur für Millionäre"; for samples of Allied leaflets, see George G. Bruntz, *Allied Propaganda and the Collapse of the German Empire in 1918* (Stanford, CA, 1938), ch. 4; the best analysis remains Hans Thimme, *Weltkrieg ohne Waffen. Die Propaganda der Westmächte gegen Deutschland, ihre Wirkung und ihre Abwehr* (Stuttgart, 1932), chs. 5–6.

[146] See Benjamin Ziemann, "Enttäuschte Erwartung und kollektive Erschöpfung. Die deutschen Soldaten an den Westfront 1918 auf dem Weg zur Revolution," in Düppler and Gross, eds.,

Once Germany sued for armistice, only bitter obstinacy held the lonely infantrymen along its ever-thinner front in place. In the last months shirkers, malingerers, and deserters to the rear or the enemy may have numbered more than 750,000; the figures of missing – and the related Allied tally of German prisoners – on the Western front rose precipitously. A system that relied on individual initiative, loyalty, and sense of duty – and only executed forty-eight men in four years of war – was powerless once loyalty and duty seemed pointless. By October, the army rear seethed with incipient revolt. Some line units refused to fight. A regiment near Metz mutinied. The armistice that the Allies foolishly conceded saved the German army from ruin, from a collapse and rout at most a week or two away.[147]

Ludendorff's offensives destroyed the army. The armistice request destroyed the home front – with help from the naval high command. The urban public had suffered the "meatless weeks" decreed as an emergency measure in summer 1918 with the increasing conviction that an end – any end – must come soon. USPD and Spartacist appeals for "Peace and Bread" and Allied propaganda were of small importance compared to the message from the retreating front and the lengthening shop queues. The sense that further suffering served no useful purpose had begun to infect even the supporters of the *Vaterlandspartei*.[148]

The mass protests in the army and the streets that answered the sailors' rebellion and became the German revolution were simply a recognition of defeat, a bid for a peace that seemed unattainable while the now-despised "Firm of

Kriegsende 1918, 165–82, who demonstrates from the troops' letters home that decline of faith in victory was the decisive variable in German army collapse in the West. Niall Ferguson, "Prisoner Taking and Prisoner Killing in the Age of Total War: Towards a Political Economy of Military Defeat," WIH 11:2 (2004), 155–63, implies confusedly that a sudden (but undocumented) increase in the willingness of Allied infantry to take prisoners was also responsible for German collapse.

[147] For more on the army's crumbling from April on, UF, 2:276–77, 401–20 (including Ludendorff's wonderful remark about the "loneliness" of the infantry, 406), 441–46, 459–67; MIW, 2:1287–89 and note; Thaer, *Generalstabsdienst*, 170–259 passim, but especially 187–88; Eugen Neter, "Der seelische Zusammenbruch der deutschen Kampffront 1918. Betrachtungen eines Front-Arztes," *Süddeutsche Monatshefte* 22:2 (1925), 1–47; Volkmann, *Soziale Heeresmissstände*, especially 63 (forty-eight executions), 66 (750,000 to a million "who in the last months of the war evaded their obligation to fight"); Deist, "Dolchstosslegende," and "Auflösungserscheinungen in Armee und Marine als Voraussetzungen der deutschen Revolution," in Militärgeschichtliches Forschungsamt, *Vorträge zur Militärgeschichte*, vol. 2 (Herford, 1981); and Ziemann, "Enttäuschte Erwartung und kollektive Erschöpfung." For British miscalculations, David French, "'Had We Known How Bad Things Were in Germany, We Might Have Got Stiffer Terms': Great Britain and the German Armistice," in Manfred F. Boemeke, Gerald D. Feldman, and Elisabeth Glaser, eds., *The Treaty of Versailles: A Reassessment after 75 Years* (New York, 1998), especially 78–86. Pershing was one of the few who saw the situation clearly, and insubordinately demanded "unconditional surrender," lest the Allies "lose the chance actually to secure world peace on terms that would ensure its permanence" (Pershing to Supreme War Council [Paris], 30 October 1918, in Department of the Army, *The United States Army in the World War, 1917–1919*, vol. 10, *The Armistice* [Washington, D.C., 1948], 28).

[148] See for instance MIW, 2:1239–42, 1267–70, 961–66.

William & Sons" still ruled. Neither Ludendorff nor the political elites ultimately dared launch their preposterous appeal for a *levée en masse*. When in
early November the military command asked the good *Bürger* of Berlin to form
a home guard against threatening revolution, the citizenry reacted with studied indifference. Not social polarization but a surprising unanimity gripped the
German people; the old, defeated state was not worth dying – or even killing –
for.

When the fleet rebelled, the naval commanders on the spot were at first
unbelieving, then supine; only three officers died defending their flag or their
posts. The Empire's haphazard command structures and the navy's jealousy of
the senior service prevented the commitment of still-loyal army troops to Kiel
before the rebellion spread. Thereafter the army's leaders displayed a mixture
of ineptitude and lassitude unparalleled in Prussia-Germany since the catastrophic aftermath of Jena-Auerstädt in 1806. Disobedience from below was
so far outside the experience of senior commanders that many simply crumbled or fled. The uncanny passivity of the Prussian War Minister, *Generalmajor*
Heinrich Scheüch, and the weight of Prusso-German traditions of discipline
hobbled the few officers who at this point had a stomach for civil war. The
majority told themselves that their first duty was to avoid bloodshed and disorder – an odd notion indeed for a warrior elite. Then they meekly accepted or
actively assisted the new masters, Ebert and Scheidemann of the majority SPD,
in justified expectation of the army's institutional survival.[149]

Yet the manner in which defeat came inevitably fathered the second great
German myth of 1914–18. The *Dolchstosslegende* or myth of the dagger-stab-
in-the-back was implicit in the meaning that Germany's leaders and elites had
long since given this war. If *Geist* was supreme over matter and God was not
bound by the laws of arithmetic, then Germany could not have lost. Germany's
new leaders helped propagate the myth by duly proclaiming that it indeed had
not. The Baden revolutionary government announced to the troops in mid-
November 1918 that they returned "neither defeated nor beaten"; defeat was
the monarchy's. Friedrich Ebert of the SPD, acting as leader of the revolutionary
provisional government in Berlin, hailed the troops at the Brandenburg Gate
on 10 December 1918 with long-remembered words: "No enemy has subdued
you."[150]

But if the army had not suffered defeat, the disgraceful outcome could only
be the result of incompetence or treachery – that very treachery that the Right
and broad reaches of middle opinion already held responsible for the collapse
of the *Burgfrieden* and the splintering of Germany in 1917. General Hans von
Seeckt, organizer of the Gorlice-Tarnow breakthrough and the war's greatest

---

[149] On Kiel, see Herwig, *The German Naval Officer Corps. A Social and Political History, 1890–
    1918* (Oxford, 1973), 250–62; on the failure of the home army command structure, comman-
    ders, and officer corps, see the merciless analysis of Schmidt, *Heimatheer und Revolution*,
    above all 85–86, 294, 299–300, 331, 352 note 305.

[150] See Kaehler, "Quellenkritische Untersuchungen zum Kriegsende 1918," 303–05.

master of operational art, had formulated the legend clearly even then: "The home front has attacked us from behind [*ist uns in den Rücken gefallen*], and the war is therefore lost." Hindenburg apparently saw the January 1918 munitions strikes as a "dagger-blow from behind"; many in the weary infantry agreed: treachery by the "home-front idiots [*Heimidioten*]" would prolong the war.[151] Ludendorff aspired in October 1918 to brand responsibility for defeat upon the politicians. And the subordinate who saw him as Siegfried wounded by perfidy likewise had no doubt – on 7 November 1918 – of the meaning of the unrest spreading swiftly across Germany: "*Dolchstoss!*" Revolution had *caused* defeat, had planted Hagen's spear in the back of Germany's sacred band of Siegfried-*Frontkämpfer*.[152]

The myth reversed the actual sequence of events and the causal connections. It erased both the guilty secret of the naval high command – that its leadership failings and institutional autism had triggered revolution – and the culpable ineptitude and passivity in the face of mutiny of both naval and army officer corps.[153] It interlocked seamlessly with the envy and rage of the front against the rear echelons and home front. It also dovetailed neatly with Protestant war theology. God could not have failed the German people; defeat could only be a consequence of the German people – the German home front – failing God.[154] And the *Dolchstoss* myth was a wholly logical development of the claim that this war was a race-war. Only treachery could have blunted the edge of the German-Aryan superiority that had held the front so long against a world of enemies. Had not Germany's Jews been traitors from the beginning? For Class and Gebsattel, German collapse flowed naturally from the internationalist loyalties of the "Pan-Jewish" press and the "Jew-socialists." In mid-October 1918 they made their last stand against parliamentarization under Tirpitz's slogan: "Germany Awake!" At Class's urging the Pan-German League's leaders resolved on 19–20 October to make struggle against the Jews their central plank of their program for the threatening new era of democracy and defeat. The *Bildungsbürger* of the League could no longer hope to save Germany – as in the past – by bullying their peers in government. The masses, and slogans that moved the masses, were now the indispensable tools of politics. Class therefore proposed "to exploit the situation for fanfares against Jewry and the Jews as lightning-rods for all injustice."

[151] See Ziemann, "Enttäuschte Erwartung und kollektive Erschöpfung," 170–72.

[152] Seeckt (July 1917) in Deist, "Dolchstosslegende," 121; Thaer, *Generalstabsdienst*, 234, 254, 286.

[153] "[E]inem Fehlverhalten, der nach herkömmlichen berufsethischen Kategorien als moralisches Versagen zu bezeichnen ist." (Schmidt, *Heimatheer und Revolution*, 276, of the Berlin area commanders; see also 278.)

[154] Front and rear: Friedrich Hiller von Gaertringen, "'Dolchstoss'-Diskussion und 'Dolchstosslegende,'" in Waldemar Besson and idem, eds., *Geschichte und Gegenwartsbewusstsein. Festschrift für Hans Rothfels* (Göttingen, 1963), 125–26; war theology: Hoover, *God, Germany, and Britain in the Great War: A Study in Clerical Nationalism* (Westport, CT, 1989), 120–21.

Yet whatever the instrumental attraction of that "lightning rod" to those who had until now been reluctant to commit the League publicly to full-throated anti-Semitism, Class himself spoke from long-standing conviction. What was different, along with the final emancipation of German nationalism from monarchical restraint, was a new emphasis on violence. Class declared himself ready to "shrink from no method whatsoever" against the racial enemy, and took as his text the imprecation that the poet Kleist had hurled at the national enemy of the Napoleonic era: "Strike him dead: the Last Judgment will not ask your reasons!"[155] After four years of hunger, demoralization, and killing, amid defeat and the dissolution of political and social landmarks that had once seemed founded on rock, the anti-Semitism of the deed was coming to Germany.

II. Italy: "Enemies Without and Saboteurs Within"

Italy fought without a *Burgfrieden*, and even the dark days after Caporetto did not endow its peasant soldiers with the Germans' righteous glow of self-defense. Cleavages wider and deeper even than those in Germany swiftly opened further as the strains of war and privation mounted. The crisis of 1917–18 so rent Italian society and the Italian state that ambiguous victory failed to still the hate-filled struggle over the war's meaning.

At the front, artillery fire was normally thinner than in the West, thanks to the combatants' lesser industrial prowess. But hostile terrain and the *Regio Esercito*'s deficiencies in logistics, medical care, equipment, doctrine, training, and leadership nevertheless made the front lines a living hell for the Italian infantry. That infantry was far different in composition from its German counterpart. Italy's shortages in trained talent meant that those who could read and had technical skills could usually escape the trenches if they chose; industrial workers and artisans, drivers and clerks and technicians, and doctors and engineers were in desperate demand in the war economy and in service and support units. Of the 5 million men who ultimately served, more than half – 2.6 million – were *contadini*. Two-thirds of the infantry that suffered 94 percent of the casualties were rural – soldiers scarcely able to read danger warnings or road signs, much less equipment instruction manuals or maps.[156]

Perhaps at least partly in view of their provenance, the army hierarchy valued its troops less than its pack animals; dead mules, noted one junior officer, cost money and therefore required "forms on top of forms, committees of inquiry. When a soldier dies, it's much simpler: a stroke through his name on

---

[155] For all this, with quotations (including "Blitzableiter für alles Unrecht"), Lohalm, *Völkischer Radikalismus*, 52–53.

[156] Figures: Virgilio Ilari, *Storia del servizio militare in Italia*, 4 vols. (Rome, 1989–90), 2:437; Serpieri, *La guerra e le classi rurali*, 42 (64 percent of war orphans and children of war invalids were children of peasants); losses by combat arm calculated from Caporetto Inquiry, graph 30, 2:382–83; literacy estimates: Mario Silvestri, *Isonzo 1917* (Milan, 2nd ed., 1971), 126, and Melograni, *Storia politica*, 248.

the roster and a number on the morning report."[157] Even in quiet areas, typhus, cholera, malaria, dysentery, frostbite, and trench foot killed or disabled dispro-portionate numbers; almost 30 percent of the army's active service deaths came from illness, compared to the German army's 10 percent or less.[158] As late as 1917 the *Regio Esercito* did not issue rain gear, judged too expensive for the infantry – which fought, sickened, and died in soggy wool coats and boots that disintegrated unexpectedly. Long stays in the trenches turned the troops, in the words of one of Italy's most combative generals, into "walking gobs of mud." Army rations contained luxuries – meat, chocolate, tobacco, cognac or *grappa* – almost unknown to many *contadini*. But food often failed to reach forward units in the regulation quantities. And vital equipment and artillery support for the great offensives was initially almost absent; as an anonymous former corps commander put it, "The army's unpreparedness manifests itself in the absence of everything . . . the bravest officers break down and cry in the face of the futility of their efforts."[159]

In place of the German army's care after 1916 to keep its units fresh by short spells in the battle area, Cadorna and his subordinates favored or tolerated keeping units in the forward trenches for a month or more without relief.[160] Until 1918 the army was likewise parsimonious with individual leaves; Italy's soldiers often did not receive even their regulation fifteen days a year, which was only two-thirds of the French army's allotment before mid-1917, and half thereafter. Those not ground down through weariness and privation perished in Cadorna's eleven great offensives on the Isonzo, which produced daily averages of dead and wounded during campaigning season of 1220 in 1915, 1670 in 1916, and 2155 in 1917. The better the unit, the heavier its losses, for the reward of proven valor – in the *Regio Esercito* of 1915–18 even more than in most armies – was ever more dangerous and exhausting missions. Almost two-fifths of those in infantry units, on average, suffered death or serious wounds *annually* in the course of 1915–18, although as the field army's size more than doubled between 1915 and 1917 the incidence of battle casualties declined slightly.[161]

Cadorna's only concession to the stresses of endless war and the virtual cer-tainty of death or mutilation was the reintroduction of regimental and division chaplains after almost fifty years of anti-clerical banishment from the army. Nei-ther he nor the army hierarchy tolerated propaganda from any other quarter,

[157] Paolo Caccia-Dominioni, quoted in Melograni, *Storia politica*, 122 note 116.
[158] Italian casualty figures remain largely a matter of conjecture. One recent accounting gives 499,172 dead in the army's active units in 1915–18, of which 29.59 percent died of disease (Ilari, *Storia del servizio militare*, 2:444). For Germany's 1914–18 ratio of about ten combat deaths to one military death from illness, see F. Bumm, ed., *Deutschlands Gesundheitsverhältnisse unter dem Einfluss des Weltkrieges* (Stuttgart, 1928), 166.
[159] Melograni, *Storia politica*, 122, 65; similarly, Giuseppe Prezzolini, *Caporetto* (Rome, 1919), 12.
[160] See especially Silvestri, *Caporetto* (Milan, 1984), 50, 69–70.
[161] Table in Melograni, *Storia politica*, 238 note 77; Caporetto Inquiry, graphs 30, 32, 33, 2:362–63, 434–35, 348–39.

not even from the *interventisti*, many of whom (including corporal Mussolini of the *Bersaglieri*) the army with consummate spite excluded from officer candidate courses. True to its Piedmontese barrack-square roots, the army successfully held the enthusiastic and selfless *Risorgimento*-style volunteers that besieged it in May 1915 to a paltry 8,171 of the 5 million who passed through its wartime ranks.[162] Only the 304,000 emigrants who returned to fight – displaying a remarkable devotion to Italy – escaped the army's implacable distrust of spontaneity, and then only because they were technically conscripts.

Nor did the army's leaders use wisely the opportunity that war offered to improve unit cohesion and fighting power by recruiting regiments and divisions entirely from one region, as was standard practice in the German and British armies. Mobilization in 1915 partially suspended the army's dysfunctional system of "national" piecemeal recruitment: at least two-thirds of each unit that fought the first battles of the Isonzo came from a single district. But thereafter the army filled the huge gaps torn by battle with recruits from all over the peninsula, except in the case of the elite *Alpini*, who by tradition were encouraged to simply clothe in uniform the tightly woven social bonds of their native valleys. By 1917–18 common dialect and custom bound together only the *Alpini* and a few fortunate infantry units, Sardinian and Sicilian brigades among them.[163] The army's chronic tendency to shuffle brigades, regiments, and even battalions between divisions further compounded this lack of cohesion, and impaired the already tenuous cooperation between staffs, supporting arms, and infantry.

The army's aim was a passive faithfulness unto death, not ideological fervor or cohesion based on local or regional loyalties and shared experience. Cadorna's in-house expert on mass psychology, Father Agostino Gemelli, celebrated with singular obtuseness those peasant soldiers, "crude, ignorant, [and] passive, [who] have wholly succumbed... to the influence of military life without rebellion, without resistance." "Simplicity of soul" guaranteed obedience, the highest military virtue.[164] And for those who rebelled, death or imprisonment was the remedy. Thanks in large part to Cadorna's relentless prodding of his subordinates and the abdication of the civilian authorities, the *Regio Esercito* of 1915–18 tried by courts-martial some 350,000 of its officers and men – almost 7 percent of those who served.

That figure, naively celebrated from the 1960s onward as evidence of massive popular protest against the war, was above all testimony to the tactical-operational failings and punitive mentality of the officer corps. The army's blinkered professional culture, even more than that of other European armies, saw war as a moral rather than a military-technical test. Failure could only be the consequence of cowardice.[165] That mentality in turn invited further failure

---

[162] Figures: Ilari, *Storia del servizio militare*, 2:437, 453.

[163] See Massimo Mazzetti, "Note all'interpretazione interventista della grande guerra," in Stato Maggiore dell'Esercito, Ufficio Storico, *Memorie Storiche Militari 1979* (Rome, 1980), 118; for the prewar system, see Rochat and Massobrio, *Breve storia dell'esercito italiano*, 90–96.

[164] Gemelli, *Il nostro soldato. Saggi di psicologia militare* (Milan, 1917), 101.

[165] See – as well as Cadorna's communiqué blaming Caporetto on the troops, discussed in due course – the precedents mournfully cited in Albertini, *Venti anni di vita politica*, 5 vols.

by closing off dispassionate inquiry into the causes of disaster. Endless defeat in 1915–17, under leadership that largely failed to give its soldiers a minimum of rest and care and to distribute equitably the risks and hardships of the front, in turn inevitably impelled the troops to periodic despairing protest. Failure and protest in turn inspired Cadorna and his subordinates to hunt down the slightest sign of disaffection with ever-fiercer vengefulness. The "uneducated masses" that the country had foisted on him purportedly understood only severity; since severity was Cadorna's only leadership tool, his evidence could not prove him wrong. The army pursued not merely offenses such as murder, insubordination, and desertion, but also thought-crime. It prosecuted those who wrote "defeatist" or "denigratory" letters to relatives and friends; even private criticism of the failings of one's superiors warranted imprisonment. In forty-one months of war the army shot roughly 750 men after trial (15 per 100,000 men), and hundreds more on the simple order of an officer, compared to the 48 (0.4/100,000), 346 (5.4/100,000), and roughly 700 (8.9/100,000) executions over fifty-one months in the larger German, British, and French armies.[166]

Even in France, where the explosion of mutiny and desertion after General Robert Nivelle's catastrophic offensive of April 1917 generated an enduring legend of draconian *répression*, commanders and statesmen showed notable concern for the rights of the accused. France's civilian leaders kept firm control over the death sentence except during the 1914 invasion and the 1917 crisis. In smothering mass protest in 1917, France's high command inflicted fewer than seventy-five deaths by firing squad. Cadorna, by contrast, subverted from the outset the slender guarantees inherent in a code of military justice essentially unchanged since 1840. The near-collapse of the Tyrol-Trentino front in May–June 1916 and what the general described as the "morbid sentimentalism" of his own military courts impelled him to order executions without trial and the "decimation" of offending units – the execution of individuals selected by lot. His subordinates obliged; the army's summary executions also included civilians suspected of espionage or "hostility to the occupying forces," and resulted in at least another 350 dead.[167] But disciplinary terrorism alone could not make

(Bologna, 1950–53), 5:145; on the prewar army's tendency to value courage over intelligence, see Del Negro, "La professione militare nel Piemonte costituzionale e nell'Italia liberale," in Giuseppe Caforio and idem, eds., *Ufficiali e società. Interpretazioni e modelli* (Milan, 1988), 220–21.

[166] "Uneducated masses": Cadorna, *Pagine polemiche*, quoted in Melograni, *Storia politica*, 220; see also Cadorna in Malagodi, *Conversazioni*, 106. For the prosecution of thought-crime, see above all the sentences printed in Enzo Forcella and Monticone, *Plotone d'esecuzione. I processi della prima guerra mondiale* (Bari, 1968). For executions, and Cadorna's role, see Monticone in ibid., 433–512; Melograni, *Storia politica*, 124–30, 209–20; executions by month: Caporetto Inquiry, graph 29, 2:370–71 (a monthly average of seventeen executions after trial, compared to the French average of seven to eight for an army roughly twice the Italian size); executions by the other powers, David Englander, "Mutinies and Morale," in Hew Strachan, ed., *The Oxford Illustrated History of the First World War* (Oxford, 1998), 192; see also Volkmann, *Soziale Heeresmissstände*, 64–65.

[167] Marco Pluviano and Irene Guerrini, *Le fucilazioni sommarie nella prima guerra mondiale* (Udine, 2004), especially 72, 100, 269–82.

Italy's *contadini* – or any troops in the world – into the thinking warriors and skilled fanatics that the loneliness of the modern battlefield demands. Nor could fear guarantee fighting power if defeat and confusion precluded the application of terror.

Cadorna was almost as pitiless toward his commanders as toward the "uneducated masses." Failure to take objectives, in his view, was incontrovertible evidence of cowardice or weakness on high as well as below. He therefore relieved from command without warning or appeal some 807 senior officers. Their usual offense was a moral failing, although not necessarily an intellectual or military one: "absence of faith in the attack and consequent inability to instill [faith] in subordinates." Cadorna's relentless search for the guilty, along with wounds, illness, promotions, and transfers, meant that by May 1917 the army had gone through an average of two commanders for each field army, three to four for each corps, four each for divisions and brigades, and six for each regiment – some 1,500 colonels, or more than the army had possessed in 1915. In the first two years of war some regiments suffered as many as eighteen changes of command. The sole compensation – though of no small importance – was the insistence of Cadorna and of the officer caste as a whole that officers commanding line units be promoted to the permanent rank their command entailed. As a result, field-grade infantry officers of 1914 who survived their *generalissimo*, the enemy, and the hardships of war had become generals by 1918; company-grade officers became majors, lieutenant colonels, or colonels.[168]

Cadorna's rolling purge outdid in duration and consequences the precedent set by his French counterpart Marshal Joffre, who made the city of Limoges famous as a dumping-ground for failed generals. The results in Italy were profoundly damaging – even granted the jaundiced view of one insider that in the officer corps "imbecility... [was] proportional to age squared times rank cubed."[169] Cadorna's leadership technique convinced the *Regio Esercito*'s regular officers that their fate was entirely beyond their control. Only the bravest dared tell superiors the truth about the condition of their troops, or give unvarnished tactical or operational judgments. The worst facilely promised success in the hope of gaining a few more weeks or months of command time: "at the moment of action, if things go badly, some saint or other may help out."[170] Finally, although the army's manpower supply seemed limitless to Cadorna, its cadres lacked depth both for prewar budgetary reasons and for the cultural and social causes noted earlier; it had entered the war more than 5,000 regular

---

[168] 807 reliefs from command, including 217 generals and 255 colonels, to October 1917: *Caporetto Inquiry*, 2:325; changes of command figures – and consequences – in Gatti, *Caporetto*, 8, 15, 64, 73, 87, 94 (Gatti was Cadorna's staff historical officer, and greatly admired him); promotion policy: Rochat, *L'esercito italiano in pace e in guerra*, 121–25.

[169] The brilliant but erratic Giulio Douhet, quoted in Barbadoro, "La condotta della guerra," 45; see also Prezzolini, *Caporetto*, 12 ("L'eroismo dal basso si mescolava alla imbecillità dall'alto").

[170] General Roberto Bencivenga, chief of Cadorna's secretariat, in Gatti, *Caporetto*, 98, also 99.

and reserve officers short of authorized strength.[171] Many of those purged after May 1915 had gained precious experience; their indiscriminate removal helped further impair the army's already limited ability to learn from its mistakes.

At company level, leadership devolved almost entirely on the reserve junior officer corps, the young middle-class *ufficiali di complemento*. These brand-new lieutenants had rarely served the apprenticeship as one-year volunteer riflemen at the front that was obligatory for their German counterparts, and their sketchy officer training courses had in some cases lasted a mere sixty days. The *Regio Esercito* thus condemned its platoon leaders and company commanders to learn on the job or die in the attempt. They may well, as Cadorna's son later wrote in defense of his father, have come from a "playful, light-hearted, tumultuous undergraduate youth" that contrasted starkly with its Austrian opposite number, those "great solid young men of grave, sometimes positively sinister demeanor thanks to cheeks often deformed by the scars of student duels: men born to command." More than half of Italy's junior infantry officers, like the men they led, may likewise have originated in the South, among what one of Cadorna's staff despairingly described as "that pettiest of bourgeoisies which has no ideal beyond material satisfaction: sons of shoemakers, gatekeepers, and the like." By 1916–17 more and more of them were simply conscripts with secondary school degrees, selected without regard for aptitude in leading infantry.[172]

Their German and even Austrian counterparts joined armies that trained platoon leaders effectively and normally supported them with experienced NCOs. For despite the immense wartime expansion of the Central Powers' armies, the long-service German *Feldwebel*, like his career officer counterpart, continued to mold the ethos and battlefield performance of the war-service NCO corps. In Italy, virtually no professional combat-arms NCOs existed; the army's improvised reserve officers thus largely led Italy's platoons and companies in terrifying isolation.[173] The cultural gap between city and countryside and the passivity that the army's traditions demanded cut them off from their men. Nor did Italy's platoon leaders and company commanders receive much guidance from their regular army counterparts – whose absence from the battlefield registered in an overall death rate of 7.7 percent, barely more than half the death rate of the general run of Italians mobilized and less than a third that of German regular officers, of whom a staggering 24.8 percent died.[174]

[171] Calculated from figures in Ilari, *Storia del servizio militare*, 2:455–56; on the wartime officer corps see also Rochat, "Gli ufficiali italiani nella prima guerra mondiale," and Del Negro, "Ufficiali di carriera e ufficiali di complemento."

[172] General Raffaele Cadorna, introduction to Luigi Cadorna, *Lettere famigliari* (Milan, 1967), 38; Gatti, *Caporetto*, 376; recruitment from the South: Del Negro, "Ufficiali di carriera e ufficiali di complemento"; for the mutual recriminations between career officers and *ufficiali di complemento*, see Melograni, *Storia politica*, 227–33.

[173] See pp. 70 and 107.

[174] Figures: Ilari, *Storia del servizio militare*, 2:443, 446 and Constantin von Altrock, *Vom Sterben des deutschen Offizierkorps* (Berlin, 2nd rev. ed., 1922), 64, 69. Altrock's figures naturally cover

Cadorna's handling of men thus meshed with the army's preexisting deficiencies in culture, equipment, unit cohesion, and supply of skilled leaders at all levels. Yet what the army lacked above all else, as Cadorna's discerning historical officer, Angelo Gatti, conceded in early 1917, was effective doctrine and training. The decentralized German mission tactics system that demanded initiative and permitted swift adaptation to changing battle conditions was and remained unknown.[175] Reconnaissance and the conscious use of surprise were rare. Artillery fire control was preposterously overcentralized and counter-battery fire to suppress enemy artillery virtually unknown. Coordination between infantry and supporting arms before 1918 was far inferior to that of the Austro-Hungarians, whose hard-stretched defense depended on it. And Cadorna's "little red book," *Frontal Attack and Tactical Instruction*, written in 1905 and issued to the army in early 1915, displayed a proud obliviousness to the bloody lessons of the Russo-Japanese War, much less those of the western front. Its precepts condemned the infantry to mass forward under artillery fire from both sides, then rush strong-points in "successive and continuous waves," to the delight of concealed Austro-Hungarian machine-gunners. Defense under Cadorna required the massing of troops forward to hold every meter of ground, with consequent immense casualties from artillery fire and envelopment. Unit training was non-existent or eccentrically divorced from conditions at the front, and individual replacements frequently arrived in the trenches without knowing how to fire a rifle or throw a hand grenade.[176]

Above all, the *Regio Esercito* lacked either aptitude or mechanisms for learning from experience, for replacing massed frontal assaults on the enemy's strongest positions with something more subtle. Gatti concluded bitterly in June 1917 that the Austrians were "in [their] entire conception of war less rigid than are we . . . who constantly celebrate Latin geniality."[177] The bloody lessons in German defense-in-depth techniques that the Austro-Hungarians administered

a somewhat longer period (2 August 1914 to 10 January 1919) than Ilari's, but it is worth noting that German regular officers outdistanced in death not merely their Italian counterparts, but also their own troops, of whom only 15.4 percent died.

[175] For similar, if less severe, defects in the British army, Martin Samuels, *Command or Control? Command, Training and Tactics in the British and German Armies, 1888–1918* (London, 1995), and *Doctrine and Dogma: German and British Infantry Tactics in the First World War* (Westport, CT, 1992).

[176] Cadorna, "Attacco frontale e ammaestramento tattico," 25 February 1915, in Ministero della Guerra, *L'Esercito italiano nella Grande Guerra*, vol. 4, *Le istruzioni tattiche del Capo di Stato Maggiore dell'Esercito degli anni 1914–1915–1916* (Rome, 1932), 68–97 (especially 81–84), and Gatti, *Caporetto*, 154–55, whose admiration for Cadorna makes his testimony all the more telling. Gatti's efforts to help the high command learn by studying the errors of the 1917 offensives met with little support, and Cadorna's successors flatly vetoed his efforts to analyze the causes of Caporetto. For the German army's success – as an organization – in learning from experience in 1916–18, see especially Lupfer, "Dynamics of Doctrine" and the detailed comparison of German and Italian doctrine and training in Silvestri, *Caporetto*, 52–111; on Italian artillery doctrine, see also Silvestri, *Isonzo 1917*, 105–07.

[177] Gatti, *Caporetto*, 140, 154–56.

in spring–summer 1917 scarcely influenced Italian practice. Austria-Hungary's adoption of German *Stosstrupp* methods – with consequent humiliating local defeats for the *Regio Esercito* – did however have some effect. By 1917 a few subordinate commanders, under the aegis of Luigi Capello, commander of 2nd Italian Army along the Isonzo, had began to create small teams of infantry carrying their own fire support – the light machine gun – and able to penetrate enemy weak points. These *Arditi* explicitly rejected Father Gemelli's notion that ignorance and passivity were the chief ingredients of combat effectiveness.[178] They developed a doctrine: careful reconnaissance and selection of objectives, painstaking rehearsals, fire and movement, speed, and surprise. And of all the privileges that distinguished the *Arditi* from the infantry, the greatest by far was tactical training that included practice live-fire assaults.[179] The *Arditi* were nevertheless decisively different from the assault troops of the Central Powers. The Italian units were designed solely for swift raids, without the German emphasis on deep penetration. And the German and Austro-Hungarian assault units were either picked line platoons, companies, or battalions, or experimental temporary units formed to pioneer and teach the tactics that in fall–winter 1917–18 became standard throughout the German infantry. The *Arditi* by contrast were jealously separate from the line, distinguished by more leave, higher pay, better rations, better weapons, deliberately outlandish uniforms, and above all by their exemption from trench duty. As their expansion in 1918 into a corps-size formation suggested, their mission was above all to substitute for – rather than supplement and offer a tactical exemplar to – the flagging line infantry.[180] By summer–fall 1918, and thanks also to the example of the British and French divisions sent to the Italian front, Italy's line infantry did acquire some of the tools and techniques of the assault units. But the army's leadership distrusted the *Arditi* themselves as "a gang of brigands" who "did not know the value of human life" – a bizarre reproach indeed from Cadorna's staff.[181]

Despite its manifold weaknesses, the *Regio Esercito* nevertheless pounded at the Austrian defenses for almost two and a half years. When confident of victory, as in summer 1915, during the conquest of Gorizia in August 1916,

---

[178] See Salvatore Farina, *Le truppe d'assalto italiane* (Rome, 1938), 134, and Rochat, *Gli Arditi della Grande Guerra. Origini, battaglie e miti* (Gorizia, 2nd exp. ed., 1990), 37. Gemelli's eccentricities – mistaken for valid generalizations about modern warfare – have misled at least one practitioner of the literary-psychoanalytical-anthropological-social history of the war: see Antonio Gibelli, *L'officina della guerra. La Grande Guerra e le trasformazioni del mondo mentale* (Turin, 1991), 90–93.

[179] The presence of sizable numbers of *contadini* (as many as half in some units: Rochat, *Arditi*, 41–42, 45–46 note 18; but also 67 note 18) suggests that historians who see the root cause of the tactical rigidity of the Italian line infantry in 1915–18 in "the absence of popular support for the war" may be looking in the wrong place (see for instance the otherwise excellent Barbadoro, "La condotta della guerra," 44).

[180] See Gudmundsson, *Stormtroop Tactics*, especially chs. 3–6; Rochat, *Arditi*, chs. 1–7; and Alessandro Massignani, "La grande guerra al fronte italiano: Le truppe d'assalto austroungariche," IC 198 (1995), 37–62.

[181] Anonymous senior general, in Caporetto Inquiry, 2:186–87; Gatti, *Caporetto*, 229–30.

and in the headlong attack across the Bainsizza plateau in August–September 1917, Italy's infantry often advanced swiftly though at disproportionate cost. Even doomed offensives such as the tenth battle of the Isonzo in May 1917 went forward with what Austrian observers later described as "unparalleled tenacity."[182] But that tenacity coexisted with the all-pervasive sense that death was "both certain and useless"; "[t]hose who didn't fight on our front in 1915 have no idea of the meaning of the words *useless sacrifice*."[183]

The "uneducated masses" that Cadorna derided were perceptive enough to locate one major source of this war's seeming futility in the higher officer corps. The troops have left little written evidence, but the diaries and memoirs of junior officers occasionally report episodes such as the unhappy fate of an infantryman who stopped a balky mule from killing an erratic division commander. His squad fell upon him, shouting "Confess – you were bought by the Austrians!" and beat him bloody. Many junior officers took a similar view: "It appears that our generals have been sent us by the enemy, to destroy us."[184]

As in Germany and elsewhere in the Great War, those at the front viewed the rear with a hatred calibrated by risk. The infantry were – in their own words – *fessi*, poor benighted clods. Behind them stood a whole range of *imboscati*, those lying "in ambush" to the rear: the *fissi*, undying "immobile ones" on the staffs; then the *italiani*, happy denizens of the army rear; and finally the blessed *italianissimi* safe, warm, and dry at home.[185] The very notion of "Italian" thus came to represent not the national integration through bloodshed that the *interventisti* had celebrated, but the deepest cleavage of all. Thanks to the peasantry's preeminent share in death and mutilation, that cleavage took on a meaning entirely different from Germany's gulf between warriors and "rear-echelon swine." In Italy, the front-rear divide reinforced and deepened further

---

[182] Anton von Pitreich, in Max Schwarte, ed., *Der grosse Krieg 1914–1918*, vol. 5, *Der österreichische-ungarische Krieg* (Leipzig, 1922), 375.

[183] Prezzolini and Malaparte (respectively), quoted in Melograni, *Storia politica*, 72. Sacrifice did not become notably more functional as the army acquired better equipment in 1916–17: see the after-action report of a regimental commander on his unit's experience in the tenth battle of the Isonzo (May 1917), printed in Gatti, *Caporetto*, 89–91. After matter-of-factly describing misadventures and heavy losses due apparently to poor tactical and logistical planning by higher staffs, the author noted that "the bearing of officers and men was excellent; they jumped off in numerous assaults and held up well under bombardment, *although convinced of the uselessness of the effort*" (italics in original).

[184] For the impact of the army's doctrinal and leadership inadequacies on troop morale, see Silvestri, *Caporetto*, 202–03 and passim. Quotations: Emilio Lussu, *Un anno sull'altipiano* (Milan, 1970 [1938]), 80–81, 212, see also 114–16; the fury and despair of troops and junior officers at the higher leadership is the major theme of this masterpiece among combat memoirs. For pioneering efforts at using the troops' surviving memories, diaries, and letters, see Nuto Revelli, *Il mondo dei vinti. Testimonianze di vita contadina*, 2 vols. (Turin, 1977) and Gibelli, *L'officina della guerra* (whose interpretive framework unfortunately prevents him from exploring how the troops viewed the conduct of the war).

[185] For these categories, Arturo Marpicati, *La proletaria. Saggi sulla psicologia delle masse combattenti* (Florence, 1920), 68–69; *fesso* is notably ruder than "clod," but lacks a precise English equivalent.

Italian society's deepest fault line, the age-old subordination of the countryside to cities, of the *contadini* to the *signori*. And not only the *signori*; thanks to their decisive role in the war effort, urban workers inevitably enjoyed almost four times as many exemptions from conscription as peasants, although the peasantry still made up 55 percent of Italy's workforce.[186] Industrial workers earned up to fifteen times the half-*lira* a day that the *Regio Esercito* paid its riflemen. Worst of all in the infantry view, the urban *imboscati* of all classes were safe from a war that Italy's cities had made, and had sent the *contadini* – but rarely their own sons – to fight.

The gap between peasants and *signori* not only separated front from rear; it also helped divide the infantry itself. In Germany, the inherited *Stand* distinctions that divided officers from NCOs and men generated resentment as an assertion of privilege out of place in the *Volk*'s struggle for existence, unjustified by superior military efficiency now that the lower orders had proven themselves in battle, and dissolved in the brotherhood of *Frontsoldaten*. In Italy, officer status lacked the hard German caste edge, although like their German counterparts, Italian officers enjoyed separate messes and better rations. Yet because the divide between officers and men tended to run along the line between city and country, between literacy and semi-literacy or illiteracy, Italy's officers and men came – mentally as well as geographically – from worlds far more distant than those of their German counterparts.[187]

The Italian "front community" was thus fatally divided. The troops, with the exception of some alpine units from northeastern valleys where hatred of Austria and literacy were traditions, at best resigned themselves to the war as a natural catastrophe or divine judgment. At worst, the hopelessness induced by repeated bloody failure led them to damn it as the "war of the *signori*" and to curse the nation – "*el talian*" – held responsible.[188] Some sought escape through self-inflicted wounds, desertion, and mutiny. Courts-martial in 1915–18 condemned roughly 10,000 soldiers for shooting themselves in the hands or feet or provoking lesions, abscesses, and mutilations through a bizarre variety of techniques.[189] Desertions ran far ahead of German figures until 1918: a monthly average of 856 courts-martial sentences for desertion in 1915–16, 2,319 in 1916–17, and 4,586 in 1917–18. The 1917–18 rate was almost three times the French monthly figure at the height of the 1917 mutinies for a field army almost twice as large. Sicily had by far the highest total of deserters, followed by Tuscany,

---

[186] Workforce: SVIMEZ, *Nord e Sud*, 50 (1911); exemptions (1918): Serpieri, *La guerra e le classi rurali*, 67–68.

[187] See the convergent judgments ("due formazioni spirituali diverse") of Adolfo Omodeo and of the Austrian philologist and postal censor Leo Spitzer, whose published collection of Italian POW correspondence remains a vital source for popular attitudes: Omodeo, *Momenti della vita di guerra*, 9 note; Spitzer, *Italienische Kriegsgefangenenbriefe. Materialien zu einer Charakteristik der volkstümlichen italienischen Korrespondenz* (Bonn, 1921).

[188] Letter of Giacomo Morpurgo, July 1916, in Omodeo, *Momenti della vita di guerra*, 207.

[189] Melograni, *Storia politica*, 239–43, and the macabre catalog of methods in Attilio Frescura, *Diario di un imboscato* (Milan, 1981 [1919]), 194–201.

the region of central Italy most conspicuous for its lack of enthusiasm in 1915 and after.[190]

Yet the vast majority of the roughly 100,000 soldiers convicted of desertion were simply late returning from home, victims of the army's pitiless courts-martial and mean-spirited leave policies. Most of them ended back at the front, for Cadorna swiftly discerned that his trenches were more frightful punishment than his prisons. Sentences for battlefield desertion, desertion to the enemy, and unlawful surrender amounted to the relatively modest total of less than 14,000, not counting the many thousands who escaped prosecution in the Caporetto disaster for lack of witnesses.[191] "Acts of indiscipline" and collective revolts, the final recourse of the troops, began as early as winter 1915–16 among units shaken by heavy losses for meager gains and by inadequate rest and leaves. Units would insult or attack their officers, refuse to return to the front, and raise "seditious cries" such as "*viva Giolitti!*"[192] But sustained or politically inspired revolts remained conspicuously absent.

The junior officers and war volunteers who shared the dangers and hardships of the front with the peasant conscripts thus found themselves in a position of permanent tension and embarrassment. *Interventisti*, fighting exiles from Trento and Trieste, and war volunteers suffered from a lingering unease more painful even than the shock of battlefield reality. If they failed to hide their convictions or origins, they might seem "a nut-case or a nuisance." "They call me 'volunteer' in the same tone they would use to say crazy or leper or cuckold," one victim lamented. That universal sentiment among conscripts at war existed in the German infantry as well. But it had its sharpest edge in Italy, for the conscripts saw volunteers and *irredenti* as the preeminent *cause* of this war. One of Mussolini's fellow *Bersaglieri* took sadistic delight in informing him that the Austrians had killed Corridoni, syndicalist *interventista* and volunteer, and in wishing Mussolini himself an expeditious death.[193]

The *ufficiali di complemento*, especially if they had indeed supported war in 1915, thus bore a double burden. Tactically, they had to carry their units with little experience and only the sketchiest training. Politically, many of the most resolute increasingly felt the weight of the dead. "Some may die gladly for the history of Italy / And some perhaps to resolve somehow their lives / But I go as

---

[190] Figures: Guy Pedroncini, *Les mutineries de 1917* (Paris, 2nd ed., 1983), 4, 67–71 (112 divisions in early 1917, against Cadorna's 64-odd; 1,619 desertions in June 1917); Melograni, *Storia politica*, 305. See also the parallel Italian figures (compiled by Cadorna's staff) in the vital article of De Felice, "Ordine pubblico e orientamenti delle masse popolari italiane nella prima metà del 1919," RSS 6:20 (1963), 470.

[191] Figures: Forcella and Monticone, *Plotone d'esecuzione*, 437, 440.

[192] See Melograni, *Storia politica*, 125–26, 218–19; Lussu, *Un anno sull'altipiano*, 199–205, has a stunning description of one such occasion.

[193] "Un pazzo e un seccatore": Omodeo, *Momenti della vita di guerra*, 8 note; "Pazzo, o lebbroso, o cornuto": Frescura, *Diario di un imboscato*, 163; Jünger, *In Stahlgewittern* (1920 ed.), 5 ("To the common man the fact that we had volunteered was barely comprehensible"); Mussolini: Melograni, *Storia politica*, 71 and note; OO 38:94.

company for this unfed people / That knows not why it goes to die," wrote a former contributor to *Lacerba*.[194] The tactical burden proved heaviest of all. A doomed young Nationalist *interventista*, writing from the front in autumn 1915, summed up lucidly the consequences of the army's doctrinal vacuum: "In front of us stands an immense slippery wall without hand-holds; to climb it we must pile corpses at the bottom."[195] Climbing that wall nearly broke Cadorna's army.

It also unhinged the home front. There the war lacked the hard edge of daily hunger and social levelling that the blockade imposed on Germany. Overall per capita consumption throughout the war apparently increased slightly compared to 1914, and average per capita food consumption rose from an index number of 100 in 1914 to 113 in 1918.[196] But those increases were dearly bought. The cost of living in large cities such as Milan roughly tripled from July 1914 to 1918. Widespread stoppages in the distribution system and shortages of staples developed by winter–spring 1915–16. As in Germany, although less surprisingly given Italy's prewar record of popular tumult, disturbances throughout the peninsula followed. Price controls and then rationing became general from spring–summer 1916. That December even the army temporarily cut its daily bread allowance by a fifth. Winter 1916–17 was harsh and drew down almost to nothing Italy's coal stocks, as coal imports – industry's chief source of energy – descended to half or less of their monthly prewar tonnage. Then the German U-boat campaign cut Italy's total import tonnage for 1917 to roughly three-fifths of the 1913 level. Annual coal imports dropped to a bare 5 million tons, less than half the 11 million tons annually that had sustained industry in 1911–13. A poor harvest and massive sinkings of grain cargoes produced a series of food supply crises in the cities.[197]

Even before 1917, public health in parts of the South as well as in Venetia – invaded first by the Italian army, then by Germans and Austrians – had crumbled. In addition to the influenza pandemic of 1918–19 that attacked both belligerents and neutrals, wartime Italy suffered a major cholera outbreak in 1915–16 and marked increases in deaths from malaria, typhoid, typhus, diphtheria, smallpox, and other mortal diseases. The 325,000–350,000 deaths from influenza surpassed Germany's in absolute terms, with an incidence (8.8–9.5 per thousand) roughly double that of Germany and higher than that of any other European society. Italy's total civilian excess deaths thus exceeded 630,000,

---

[194] "Altri morirà per la Storia d'Italia volentieri / e forse qualcuno per risolvere in qualche modo la vita / Ma io per far compagnia a questo popolo digiuno / che non sa perché va a morire": Piero Jahier, *Opere di Piero Jahier*, vol. 3, *Ragazzo – Con me e con gli alpini* (Florence, 1967), 115.

[195] Letter of Napoleone Battaglia, September 1915, in Omodeo, *Momenti della vita di guerra*, 186.

[196] Index numbers calculated from Benedetto Barberi, *I consumi nel primo secolo dell'unità d'Italia (1861–1960)* (Milan, 1961), 62, by Melograni, *Storia politica*, 366–67.

[197] Import tonnage: C. Ernest Fayle, *Seaborne Trade*, vol. 3 (New York, 1924), 279; coal, 1913–20: Douglas J. Forsyth, *The Crisis of Liberal Italy: Monetary and Financial Policy, 1914–1922* (Cambridge, 1993), 323.

a figure that surpassed by more than 100,000 the most plausible estimate of Germany's, despite a population less than three-fifths the size of the Reich's. Italy's armies lost as many as 650,000 men, including just under half a million who died of wounds or illness with the units, and up to 100,000 in Austro-Hungarian prison camps, from the Italian government's vengefulness toward its own troops and from maltreatment by their captors.[198] Military dead amounted to 13 percent of those mobilized; dead and wounded together amounted to 34.3 percent, compared to 15.4 and 41 percent respectively for Germany. Military deaths and civilian excess deaths together amounted to a rough total of almost 1.3 million, or about 3.5 percent of Italy's 1914 population, only slightly lower than the corresponding German figure of 3.7 percent (see Figure 3.1).

As privation and disease, battlefield losses and civilian deaths mounted gradually but without apparent end in 1916–17, united Italy faced the greatest crisis in its fifty years as a nation-state. As elsewhere the demoralization of home front and army interacted reciprocally. From the "funereal autumn" of 1915 onward, the desperation of those facing the "immense slippery wall without hand-holds" began to leak homeward, despite the parsimony with leaves that was partly a product of Cadorna's embarrassment and control mania ("the Italians are hyper-critical, and don't know how to be silent").[199] News of want and overwork at home and of sumptuous high living by profiteering *imboscati* likewise enraged and demoralized the front.

Concurrently, the Liberal regime proved ever less equal to the task of war leadership. Salandra's fall in June 1916 was in retrospect almost as significant a moment in Italy's history as the subjugation of parliament in May 1915; it meant the end of government almost exclusively by liberals.[200] What followed, whether under Boselli or Orlando or his four postwar successors, were ill-assorted coalition cabinets that poorly concealed the power vacuum that had opened at the heart of the Liberal state. It was the *interventisti* who destroyed the government they had helped save in the "radiant days" of 1915. Along with eighty-seven Socialists and fifty Giolittians, they provided the decisive ninety votes that felled Salandra – amid recriminations over the Austrian "punitive expedition" from the Trentino – for insufficient ruthlessness in mobilizing the nation's resources and in throttling the "internal enemy." The *interventisti* failed to perceive that they had thus opened the road for the revival of the Giolittians – for the Catholics, fearful of isolation, resolved to enter the government in any numbers only with the Giolittians for cover.[201] But the token Giolittian and Catholic in Boselli's "national union" cabinet neither represented their respective forces nor could guarantee their support.

---

[198] Isnenghi and Rochat, *La Grande Guerra*, 228; Giorgio Mortara, *La salute pubblica in Italia durante e dopo la guerra* (Bari, 1925), 107; note 119 in this chapter (influenza, and German excess deaths); Kramer, "Italienische Kriegsgefangene," 248.

[199] Cadorna ("I was against these leaves") January 1916, in Malagodi, *Conversazioni*, 77.

[200] Melograni, *Storia politica*, 193, rightly emphasizes this point.

[201] On all this, see 127–28 of the brilliant analytical essay of De Caprariis, "Partiti politici e opinione pubblica," to which I and other students of Italy in the Great War owe a great deal.

The conquest of Gorizia in August 1916, along with widespread indignation over Austria-Hungary's bombing of churches in Venice and nearby cities, its first use on the Italian front of poison gas, its dispatching of gassed or wounded Italians with iron-spiked clubs, and its execution after capture of irredentist heroes such as Cesare Battisti, "martyrs" of Italy's "fourth war of independence," upheld Italian morale into the fall. Then three further Cadorna "pushes" from mid-September to November 1916 failed at a cost of 125,000 dead and wounded. That blow broke the home front loose. Rural Italy shared Cadorna's certainty that attrition would crack the Austrians even less than it shared the official rationale for war. From December 1916 on, as despair seeped homeward from the front, rural women in north and central Italy took to marching into the towns to incite munitions strikes and protest the state's meager family allowances: "we want our men back!" Filippo Turati of the PSI reformists privately summed up, with horror, the spreading movement: "[The disturbances] have a flavor of *jacquerie*, with the difference that [the demonstrators] are above all the women, who are genuine furies. They want to stop the war this instant; they want their men back; they're fed up with Milan, which willed the war and now despoils them of everything: grain, lard, rice . . . and they want to do in the *signori*, among whom – it's understood – we [Socialists] are also numbered."[202] The *classe proprietaria* both rural and urban trembled at the violent hostility with which "its" war had infused Italy's deepest social cleavage.

Conviction as well as fear of being counted among the *signori* had already impelled provincial Socialist cadres in the North to hold meetings and issue forbidden leaflets against the war in the summer and fall. A disingenuous Central Powers peace initiative in December 1916 acted as a spur to agitation; by January and February 1917 maximalist leaders were publicly denouncing the war "willed by the bourgeoisie for illicit gain" and offering the restless masses an arsenal of slogans. Then the February revolution in Russia, the peace proclamation of the Petrograd Soviet, and widespread spontaneous strikes across north Italy began to pry the PSI apart. The reformists around Turati, whose patriotic instincts had spurred him at the war's beginning to secretly promise Salandra to work to "defuse" PSI opposition, stood increasingly isolated. Tumult in the *piazza* and the example of Petrograd increasingly confirmed his maximalist adversaries in their course. But that course lacked a strategic compass, a notion of how to transmute popular fury into revolution. The PSI's majority leadership of verbal revolutionists found itself imprisoned by the very popular militance it celebrated, incapable equally of leading or of repudiating the masses.[203]

---

[202] De Stefano, "Moti popolari," 202–11 (211 for the influence of troops on leave and letters from the front); Turati to Anna Kuliscioff, 3 May 1917, in De Felice, "Ordine pubblico," 472; see also similar imprecations against Milan quoted in Isnenghi, *I vinti di Caporetto nella letteratura di guerra* (Padua, 1967), 65, and the frequent references to popular protests during these months in Martini, *Diario*.

[203] Turati and Salandra: De Caprariis, "Partiti politici e opinione pubblica," 119; "guerra voluta dalla borghesia a scopo di lucro": police opinion summary in De Felice, "Ordine pubblico," 479. Luigi Cortesi, "Il PSI dalla 'settimana rossa' al Congresso nazionale del 1918," RSS 32 (1967), offers useful analysis of the vacillations of the maximalist leaders in 1917–18.

Cadorna likewise held to his course. A long-prepared spring offensive on the Isonzo made May 1917, with 127,840 dead and wounded, Italy's bloodiest single month of war.[204] Then a deft Austrian counteroffensive against weak points in the shaky new Italian line instantly annulled most gains. A further Italian "push" toward the Trentino in June cost 12,000 more dead and broke against a seemingly impenetrable network of enemy machine guns dispersed in depth. In the bleak aftermath, the army's desertion rate more than doubled to a monthly average of 5,500. An entire brigade on the Isonzo front mutinied – and tried to storm a stately house where D'Annunzio was reputed to be a guest. Officers and military police backed by loyal units, armored cars, and artillery held the ring until the revolt collapsed. It cost eleven dead in fighting and at least twenty-eight executions, including twelve soldiers chosen by lot – in the words of their corps commander – "as a salutary example to the weak, inert, and pusillanimous elements that had aided, through their passivity, the activities of the mutineers." Cadorna then suggested in a circular that empathy (*"umana comprensione"*) toward the troops was now required. Later than the more perceptive of his staff officers and commanders, he had begun to recognize that his military instrument might be about to crack. Yet he and Capello, the most aggressive of his two army commanders on the Isonzo, remained confident that Austria-Hungary would crumble before Italy. It *must* crumble: the *Regio Esercito*'s weariness and Russian collapse together suggested that victory would come in 1917 or not at all.[205]

On the home front, the PSI reformists in parliament feared losing touch with the restive masses. In a warning that became a slogan, Claudio Treves, Turati's most important associate, told parliament on 12 July that Europe's peoples had issued "an ultimatum of life and death: out of the trenches by winter." Benedict XV, determined not to leave to the socialists of Europe a monopoly on calls for peace, urged negotiations in the diplomatic circular, describing the war as a "useless massacre" that had so outraged Protestant Prussia-Germany. That phrase, refashioned as a slogan, leaked to front and home front by mid-August despite all the efforts of Italy's censors. From the safety of Piedmont, a vengeful Giolitti outlined his postwar social program in a speech that the *interventisti* took as renewed evidence that his "impudence and maliciousness...pass[ed] all limits."[206] And on 22 August, four days after Cadorna had launched his

[204] Caporetto Inquiry, graph 33, 2:438–39.
[205] Desertion figures for June–September 1917: De Felice, "Ordine pubblico," 470. Catanzaro brigade revolt: Monticone, *Gli italiani in uniforme*, 227–28, and Pluviano and Guerrini, *Le fucilazioni sommarie*, 70–75; Salandra, *Diario*, 148 (Cadorna claimed thirty-six executions); survey of unrest and executions: Elio Giovannini, *L'Italia massimalista. Socialismo e lotta sociale e politica nel primo dopoguerra italiano* (Rome, 2001), 51–52; Cadorna circular, 20 July 1917, printed in Frescura, *Diario di un imboscato*, 294–95; on the high command's growing sensation that a crisis in morale was approaching, see Gatti, *Caporetto*, especially 61–62, 73, 154, 157.
[206] For Giolitti's continued "hatred and...contempt" for those who had willed the war, see the secondhand testimony in Gatti, *Caporetto*, 170; the *interventista* view: Martini, *Diario*, 969.

eleventh and last battle of the Isonzo, a temporary bread shortage in "red Turin," home of Italy's most concentrated and combative industrial workforce, ignited three days of leaderless insurrection and general strike. But despite the panegyrics of Antonio Gramsci, future founder and patron saint of the Communist Party of Italy, Turin was not "the Petrograd of the Italian revolution." Nor was it Kiel or Berlin. The *Regio Esercito*'s peasant infantry demonstrated that Italy was not Russia by shooting fifty-odd workers.[207]

Cadorna had long damned the Socialists as traitors whose continued liberty tainted the government that tolerated them. His clerical background likewise did not prevent him from considering the papal peace note a "dagger-stab in the army's back." His last offensive, backed by the heaviest weight of fire yet assembled on the Italian front, went forward. Like the German infantry the following March, the troops rushed the enemy wire in August 1917 in the conviction that this offensive would end the war. That faith sustained Capello's 2nd Italian Army as it scrambled upward onto the Bainsizza plateau and almost cracked open the Austro-Hungarian center. Yet in the end Cadorna's *Kaiserschlacht* stalled heartbreakingly short of its goal, thanks to doctrinal inadequacy, inexperience in open warfare, and the chronic difficulty of sustaining any advance with horse-drawn transport and the rickety trucks of 1917. The supreme effort of August–September left the army exhausted, demoralized by a further 165,000 dead and wounded, and ill-positioned for defense.[208]

Now the Pope's words seemed prophetic, and "out of the trenches by winter" the slogan of the hour. In Rome, the loose grouping of *interventisti* that had erected itself as guardians of the national cause sought to drive Orlando from the cabinet for what Bissolati described as his "never-ending grovelling toward the Socialists." They failed. With martial law clamped on Genoa, Alessandria, and Novara as well as on Turin, the government decreed imprisonment for up to ten years for instigating – much less committing – acts it might choose to define as sabotage of the war effort. On 18 October Socialist hecklers, with some Giolittian support, branded the government in parliament as assassins of the workers. Giolittians, Socialists, and *interventisti* exchanged accusations of buffoonery, treason, and murder. Bissolati summed up the interventionists' impotent fury with a shout: "To defend the army's back I would [gladly] shoot even you!" On 25 October, as Germans and Austro-Hungarians attacked yet before news of catastrophe reached Rome, Socialists, Giolittians, right-Liberals, and democrats combined to destroy the ministry by a vote of 314 to 96 after a disdainful Sonnino, speaking for the government, had discerned in the Pope's

---

[207] On the Turin episode, see especially Monticone, *Gli italiani in uniforme*, 89–144; Spriano, *Torino operaia nella Grande Guerra*, ch. 10 (Gramsci quotation, 110); Luigi Ambrosoli, *Né aderire né sabotare 1915–1918* (Milan, 1961), 229–37; and Bissolati, in Malagodi, *Conversazioni*, 165–66, on the infantry's hatred of the workers.

[208] Cadorna, the staffs, and the Pope: Rino Alessi, *Dall'Isonzo al Piave* (Milan, 1966), 95–97; Bissolati, quoting Cadorna, in Malagodi, *Conversazioni*, 165; Gallarati Scotti, "Idee e orientamenti politici e religiosi al Comando Supremo," 514. Losses: Caporetto Inquiry, graph 33, 2:438–39.

peace note "that same vagueness that characterizes communications from the enemy side." Orlando, to the stupor of many *interventisti*, emerged as prime minister in part because *interventista* attacks had endeared him to Giolittians and Socialists.[209]

Simultaneously, the Isonzo front collapsed. The Germans and Austrians, despite leakage of their intentions and dispositions, achieved strategic surprise, thanks to the refusal of Cadorna, Capello, and their staffs to take the threat seriously. Germany's newly developed tactical methods – a short but extraordinarily intense bombardment, infantry advancing in stealthy small groups with specialized weapons instead of the clumsy waves of Germany's adversaries, deep penetration and envelopment – came as an even greater shock, despite the foretaste administered in Austria-Hungary's June and September counterattacks. Gas, used massively on this front for the first time in conjunction with a major offensive, gave the Germans technological surprise as well. Gas and *Stosstrupp* tactics together punched holes in Capello's defense-without-depth at well-chosen points around Caporetto on the upper Isonzo, and opened the road far into the Italian rear.

The consequent collapse of the army's already shaky command structure, communications, and traffic control, along with the failure to redeploy in time the forces Capello and his subordinates had massed precariously forward, meant that Italian artillery fire was thin, reserves were lacking, and counterattacks uncoordinated or absent. Swift withdrawal to evade encirclement was the only recourse. But in seeking to fall back under pressure Capello's hardtried 2nd Italian Army disintegrated. Units worn down by attrition and in some cases abandoned by their officers melted away or surrendered. In a few cases, Italian troops cheered the Germans for having delivered them from the war. By the evening of 25 October a wave of 300,000-odd weaponless and surprisingly good-natured fugitives was flowing downward to the Venetian plain, greeting demoralized officers with shouts of "long live the Pope," "*viva Giolitti*," and "peace." Some rode the rails or walked homeward to Bologna or beyond; most meekly allowed the military police to herd them into encampments behind the Piave. Capello's army had suffered only 11,600 killed and 21,950 wounded, less than a tenth of the casualties of the Bainsizza offensive. In its retreat the *Regio Esercito* as a whole gave up a staggering 294,000 prisoners (of whom only 4,170 were wounded), almost 5,000 artillery pieces and heavy mortars, and immense mountains of supplies. Doctrinal vacuum, command failure at all levels, and enemy skill had briefly wrenched 2nd Italian Army apart along the country's deepest social and political fault line.[210]

---

209 Bissolati on Orlando ("una continua calata di brache ... ") in Malagodi, *Conversazioni*, 164–65; Bissolati ("Per difendere le spalle dell'esercito farei fuoco anche contro di voi!") and Sonnino in the Chamber: AP, Camera dei Deputati, 1917, 14648, 15019 (18, 25 October 1917).

210 Analysis and description of the collapse: Melograni, *Storia politica*, ch. 6; Silvestri, *Isonzo 1917*, ch. 7 and *Caporetto*, chs. 17–22; the best eyewitness account is probably Frescura ("Where, by God, are the generals?"), *Diario di un imboscato*, 247–79, but see also Curzio (Suckert)

The Germans and Austrians, understandably unprepared to exploit success on this scale and hampered by the same logistical constraints that had slowed Capello on the Bainsizza, moved too slowly and uncertainly to cut off 3rd Italian Army, to Capello's south; it fell back to the Piave along the coast. German sluggishness and unbroken units from the abandoned alpine perimeter east of the Trentino allowed the army to hold a new and far shorter front. Defeat, by loosening the grip of the high command, also allowed commanders in the decisive Mt. Grappa sector to experiment with an unplanned, almost instinctive version of defense-in-depth. By trading outlying mountains for time and Austro-German casualties, by counterattacking with a swiftness born of desperation and of involuntary decentralization of command, the army held. Even units hastily reconstituted from the wreckage of 2nd Italian Army acquitted themselves well in the mountains.[211] Sacrifice had acquired a purpose: the war now meant defense against further invasion, and some Italian commanders had begun to understand the enemy's tactics sufficiently to reply effectively. The battered *Regio Esercito* thus halted the enemy short of Venice and Milan. Italy remained in the war, despite a further crisis in front-line morale during the bleak months from December to March 1918 due to insistent Austro-Hungarian propaganda and a renewed sense of the futility of the struggle.[212]

On the home front, the invasion of Venetia emphatically failed to close the historic cleavages that had widened and deepened since May 1915. The northern rural population now in the front lines, wrote Cadorna's successor Armando Diaz, persisted in believing that "the war is willed by the *signori* and the generals [and] fought with the blood of the *contadini*, while the *signori* and staffs fatten and the contractors get rich...." A crowd in Parma apparently reviled newly arrived Allied troops for ostensibly prolonging the war at Italy's expense; Austrian propaganda on the same theme found a receptive audience at the front.[213] Nor did anything resembling the universal *union sacrée* celebrated in national-patriotic historiography emerge in Rome or in the northern cities after Caporetto. This first defensive war for an invaded *Patria* in united Italy's history did produce an unprecedented moment of unity among the urban upper and middle classes. But unity was also enforced, the product of a further bitter

---

Malaparte, "La rivolta dei santi maledetti," in idem, *L'Europa vivente e altri saggi politici (1921–1931)* (Florence, 1961), which perversely casts the rout as a revolt. The exclusively military-technical interpretation of Monticone, *La battaglia di Caporetto* (Rome, 1955) does not explain the widespread collapse of unit cohesion in the retreat; social factors were also in play. Figures: Melograni, ibid., 423; Caporetto Inquiry, 2:191, 217, 257–59, and 186–87 (graphs 25 and 26: POW losses by unit); see also the casualty estimates in Silvestri, *Caporetto,* 239–31.

[211] See the analysis of Silvestri, *Caporetto,* ch. 23.

[212] See Melograni, "Documenti sul 'morale delle truppe' dopo Caporetto e considerazioni sulla propaganda socialista," RSS 32 (1967), 217–63, and his *Storia politica,* 480–89.

[213] Diaz to Orlando, 16 December 1917, in Melograni, *Storia politica,* 474. On hostility to the French and British, and Austrian propaganda, see Malagodi, *Conversazioni,* 189, and Melograni, ibid., 485–86, 490–93.

campaign of propaganda and intimidation by *interventisti* seeking to defend their war – the war of 1915 – against masses that seemed to have abandoned it.

A parliamentary *"fascio* of national defense" under predominantly Nationalist leadership formed in Rome. Local committees representing urban *interventismo* and a broad spectrum of middle-class associations – from Nationalists and right-Liberals to republicans, syndicalists, and dissident Socialists; from masonic lodges to Catholic charities; from professional associations to the Red Cross – mobilized the home front for last-ditch resistance. A burst of Jacobin exasperation smothered open attacks on the war effort. The war against "enemies without and saboteurs within," the hunt for the traitors, defeatists, and "slaves of the foreigner" mandated by *Risorgimento* tradition, went forward in the spirit a young left-*interventista* had celebrated some months before: "History has reserved us the task, like the French *sans-culottes,* of bearing the ideas of liberty to triumph on the point of bayonets."[214]

Salvemini, the most democratic and humane of *interventisti* and later a celebrated anti-Fascist exile, proclaimed in January 1918 that opponents of the war had a right only to silence: "either silence in freedom, or silence in prison."[215] Arrest and imprisonment of civilians for the mere expression of discouragement or dissent became the order of the day; army and civilian authorities had long since applied enforced residence in the South and islands to "enemy aliens" and political suspects within Italy and the occupied border areas.[216] Nationalist enthusiasts in Rome attacked two deputies, a Catholic and a Socialist, with fists, boots, and clubs. Like the *Vaterlandspartei,* though with far less resonance, the "committees of internal resistance" temporarily gave organizational and mass propaganda shape to a nationalist culture that lacked the political cohesion and organization of the Socialist and Catholic subcultures. Like the *Vaterlandspartei,* this movement – outside and even against a parliament still dominated by Giolitti's 1913 majority – offered the hard-pressed supporters of the national cause a first chance at concerted political action.[217]

Caporetto likewise helped radicalize the "internal enemy." Political Catholicism either lay low or redoubled the bid for full membership in the political

---

[214] The young Pietro Nenni (sometime correspondent for *Il Popolo d'Italia* and after 1945 the most famous leader of a revived PSI), January 1917, quoted by Enzo Forcella, in Forcella and Monticone, *Plotone d'esecuzione,* lxi–lxii.

[215] *L'Unità,* 5 January 1918, quoted in Giovannini, *L'Italia massimalista,* 39.

[216] Carlo Spartaco Capogreco, *I campi del duce. L'internamento civile nell'Italia fascista (1940–1943)* (Turin, 2004), 36–40.

[217] For the 1917–18 war against the "internal enemy," see especially Giovanna Procacci, "Aspetti della mentalità collettiva durante la guerra: L'Italia dopo Caporetto," in Diego Leoni and Camillo Zadra, eds., *La Grande Guerra. Esperienza, memoria, immagini* (Bologna, 1986), 261–89; Franck Demers, "Caporetto e il sorgere del fascismo a Cremona," SC 8:3 (1977), 533–48; and Angelo Ventrone, *La seduzione totalitaria. Guerra, modernità, violenza politica (1914–1918)* (Rome, 2003), 211–70; for the attacks on Miglioli and Modigliani, Albertini, *Epistolario,* 2:838, 842, and Camera dei Deputati, *Comitati segreti sulla condotta della guerra* (Rome, 1967), 205.

nation it had made by accepting war in 1915.[218] The Socialists by contrast now split openly along the two branches of their equivocal slogan, "neither support nor sabotage." Turati, the PSI reformists who still dominated the party's parliamentary delegation, and some northern Socialist municipal officials courageously chose support – "On Mt. Grappa lies the *Patria*" – qualified by readiness for a peace negotiated from Italy's position of desperate weakness. But the majority of the party, wholly unlike its majority SPD counterpart north of the Alps, attacked with increasing fierceness a war that now figured as a war of national defense. For the Caporetto offensive, strategic first-fruit of Russia's military collapse, coincided with that collapse's most far-reaching political outcome: Lenin's seizure of power. Caporetto and the coup d'état of the "Russian maximalists" together made this the Italian extremists' hour. In mid-December, while the infantry died for Italy on Mt. Grappa, Socialist deputies provoked a quasi-riot at a secret session of the Chamber of Deputies with chants of "Down with the war! Up the revolution!" The *massimalisti*, faithful pupils of Mussolini and heirs to his seizure of the party leadership in 1912, cemented control over the party-affiliated national trade union confederation, the *Confederazione Generale del Lavoro*, in July 1918.[219] The PSI's first party congress since 1914 opened in Rome that September with thunderous acclamations to Lenin. And although the maximalists could not quite summon the dictatorial rigor to push the remaining reformists out, they backed their domination of the party machinery, press, and unions with a thumping 70 percent majority of the congress. That victory confirmed the estrangement of the PSI's remaining reformists from their own party and from the masses.[220]

The wars within and between the other political forces widened and intensified as the world conflict moved toward its culmination. The prospect of victory, distantly visible after Austria-Hungary's last failed offensive in June 1918 and Ludendorff's defeat in France, broke the always shaky unity of *interventismo*. Caporetto and the threat in early 1918 of a British-French compromise peace with Austria-Hungary at Italian expense had impelled even the Nationalists toward a brief tactical embrace of the Yugoslav exile movement. Promises of freedom for Austria-Hungary's oppressed peoples might yet break the enemy front where frontal assault had failed. The Wilsonian gospel of self-determination, tailored to cloak Italy's aims, might thwart the Entente's

---

[218] On the Catholic reaction to Caporetto, see especially Monticone, *Gli italiani in uniforme*, 179–84, and Danilo Veneruso, "I rapporti fra Stato e Chiesa durante la guerra nei giudizi dei maggiori organi della stampa italiana," in Rossini, ed., *Benedetto XV, i cattolici e la prima guerra mondiale*, 730–37.

[219] See especially the analysis of Vivarelli, *Origini*, 2:314–15.

[220] "Abbasso la guerra....Evviva la rivoluzione!": Albertini, *Epistolario*, 2:825–26 (see also the threat of revolution ascribed to Modigliani of the PSI, 828). The often sketchy official summary (Camera dei Deputati, *Comitati segreti*, 144–45) is silent on these disturbances, but Martini, *Diario*, 1075, registers "tumulti." For "Russian maximalists" and the splitting of the PSI, see especially Arfé, *Storia del socialismo italiano 1892–1926* (Turin, 1965), chs. 18–19 and 238; also Ambrosoli, *Né aderire né sabotare*, 249–305.

search for compromise with Vienna. But the Nationalists would not surrender their claim to Dalmatia, and were soon once more extolling Italy's historic mission to make the Adriatic a wholly Italian sea.

In August 1918 Albertini made a last attempt to unseat Sonnino, whose Adriatic fixation threatened isolation and disaster in the new Wilsonian age. But unlike 1914–15, Italy's elites deserted the *Corriere della Sera*. The Giolittians, whose hatred of Albertini was second to none and whose foreign policy inclinations were closer to Sonnino's territorial legalism than to the Mazzinian-Wilsonian enthusiasms of the democrats, backed the Treaty of London. Many democrats, reformists, and left-*interventisti* had already succumbed to the logic of the war they had hailed in 1915. The immensity of Italy's sacrifices cried out for recompense: Dalmatia, Balkan hegemony, and – from "the sense of justice and equity of France and England" – perhaps even Nice, Corsica, and Malta.[221] Orlando, upon whom Albertini and Bissolati had counted to unseat Sonnino, deftly pulled back. That left the democrats who opposed Sonnino to face a chorus of Nationalist and Dalmatian irredentist abuse that swelled steadily with victory and enjoyed the ever more passionate backing of non-Socialist Italian opinion.[222]

The twin crises of 1915 and 1917 had thus split virtually all Italy's political and social forces beyond repair. The masses, especially in the rural North and in cities such as Turin, harbored a fierce thirst for vengeance against all those connected with this war. War irreparably tore the Liberals. Giolitti and friends were slow to forgive those who had terrorized them in May 1915 and had damned them as traitors in 1917–18. Interventionist Liberals – and former natural allies of the Giolittians such as democrats and ex-PSI reformists – could not pardon Giolitti's 1915 contacts with the Germans or tolerate Giolittian hints that the war was a disaster and Caporetto a fit punishment for *interventista* presumption. The interventionist front, by autumn 1918, had itself shattered over Italy's claims to booty, the issue that superimposed on its tripartite division – democrats and ex-PSI reformists, left-interventionists, and nationalists – the new and deepening cleavage between Adriatic expansionists and "renouncers." The PSI had likewise fractured, thanks to Turin revolt, Caporetto, and Lenin's revolution, into a deranged majority and a reformist and trade union minority facing the same exile that had swallowed Bissolati and his associates in 1912. Only political Catholicism had retained its cohesion, but at the price of an ambiguity that increased the distrust of *interventisti* and PSI alike. The earthquake of 1915–18 had so shaken and fractured the political landscape that no force could heal its own internal divisions, or ally with other forces to govern through a parliamentary system further diminished in its already low prestige by its ineffectual conduct of the war.[223]

---

[221] The reformist socialist *Azione Socialista*, quoted in Vivarelli, *Origini*, 1:231 note 196; Colapietra, *Bissolati*, 247–48; De Caprariis, "Partiti politici e opinione pubblica," 143.

[222] See particularly Albertini, *Epistolario*, 2:946–47, 955–56, 958–59, 978–81, 986–88.

[223] On all this, see in particular the analysis of De Caprariis, "Partiti politici e opinione pubblica" and De Felice, 1, ch. 11.

As in Germany, war and disaster also generated powerful national myths that helped perpetuate war throughout the sham peace that followed. In the final year of the war, a new "discipline of conviction" that relied on nationalist fervor instilled in and by the army's junior officers supplemented the coercion of 1915–17. Urban intellectuals in uniform, enrolled in a newly founded "*Servizio P,*" plied the troops with patriotic slogans. Soldiers became *combattenti* – an exact linguistic parallel to Germany's *Kämpfer*.[224] The Italian myth of the "front community" nevertheless proved far weaker than its German counterpart, thanks to the deep cleavages between *interventisti* and the majority of those who fought, between the *contadini* and the cities, between spoken dialect and written Italian. The infatuation with truculent minorities that pervaded Italian elite culture nevertheless helped foster a partial surrogate: the legend of the *Arditi*, swaggering to the tune of their anthem "*Giovinezza*" or storming forward toward death "as if toward love" with daggers, grenades, and a brutal jest on their lips. It was no accident that the *Arditi* should by 1918 have invented a D'Annunzian ritual: a salute with daggers raised and the shout "Whose is the honor?," answered with the full-throated chorus "*A noi!*" Nor that Marinetti, whose Futurist war as an *Alpino* and armored car crewman had surpassed even his expectations of blood-drenched *festa*, should have sought and secured links to the *Arditi*. Nor, finally, that by 1918 Mussolini's bellicose *Il Popolo d'Italia* had became favored reading in assault units. The *Arditi* may not have begun as *interventisti*, but their appropriation by the most extreme elements of *interventismo* soon made them the foremost examples of the "discipline of conviction." In the eloquent words of an assault unit lieutenant, Giuseppe Bottai, future Fascist minister and anti-Semite, the *Arditi* were "the first prototype of a 'political' army, bearer and defender of an idea" in a "war on two fronts... against the enemies without and those within."[225] But unlike the myth of their Siegfried-helmeted German counterparts, the front myth of the Italian assault troops was less for the nation than for the supermen of urban, literate, literary Italy.

Other myths had more mass effect, although again primarily in the cities. Socialist, Giolittian, and Catholic resistance to war in 1914–15; popular protest and Socialist agitation after 1915; papal peace message, Turin rising, Russian-Bolshevik "betrayal" of the Entente's war effort, and Caporetto rout: all combined in the making of Italy's *Dolchstosslegende*. Long before Caporetto, Cadorna and the *interventisti* had fastened upon the "internal enemy" as the source of Italy's tribulations. Cadorna had repeatedly demanded from the government repressive measures against the PSI. Caporetto finished the process. For the *interventisti* and for broad segments of urban opinion, 2nd Italian Army's rout seemed a revelation of national inferiority – *les italiens ne se battent*

---

[224] Servizio P: O'Brien, *Mussolini*, 177–79; "Disciplina di convinzione": Marco Mondini, *La politica delle armi. Il ruolo dell'esercito nell'avvento del fascismo* (Rome, 2006), 43; "combattenti": Papafava, *Appunti*, 146–47.

[225] Rochat, *Arditi*, 22 ("la guerra in cui si va incontro alla morte come all'amore"), 80–88; 81 for Bottai on the "prototype of a 'political' army" (a retrospective – but in Rochat's view accurate – assessment).

pas – too painful to bear. Martini mourned privately over the "centuries of shame" now in store. Franchetti, Sonnino's long-standing associate, killed himself. Bissolati too contemplated suicide, and lamented that "[i]t's all over for us; we must disappear. We are those who dreamed of a greater Italy. We wanted to create a military Italy. We were wrong; we built on sand; the Italians were not ready." A new government, "the authentic representatives of those who prepared the spiritual collapse of our army," must now negotiate surrender – a nice Ludendorffian touch.[226]

But even before despair had given way to renewed hope, the inevitable search for the guilty had begun. Cadorna, with his communiqué of 28 October blaming disaster on "the absence of resistance by units of 2nd Italian Army which withdrew in cowardly fashion without fighting or ignominiously surrendered to the enemy," launched the myth. Privately he railed at the "internal enemy" – the "sedition of the Socialists and the Giolittians" and the "Russian-style Leninism" – that had allegedly destroyed his army.[227] Bissolati offered the legend's most durable formulation: a "military strike" had opened the road to Germans and Austrians. Although both Cadorna and Bissolati eventually disowned the more extreme versions of their thesis, the Caporetto legend was too natural an outgrowth of the interventionist war against the "internal enemy" not to prosper. Generals preferred it to military-technical explanations that might emphasize their own preeminent failings. *Interventisti*, steeped in *Risorgimento* tradition, chose to blame traitors rather than acknowledge the apparent ruin of their conception of Italy. By October 1918 Mussolini was damning in his newspaper the "evil brood of *caporettisti* . . . who had stabbed the nation in the back, [and] had expended every effort to make us lose the match." By 1919 the myth, held equally by Nationalists and democrats, left-interventionists and senior officers, was deeply entrenched. Catholics and Socialists – the "red and black defeatists" – wrote one of democratic *interventismo*'s sharpest pens, had shattered the army's morale in 1917 with their talk of "useless massacre" and "out of the trenches by winter." They were the representatives of "that cowardly, ignorant, and corrupt little Italy that stabbed us in the back as we fought."[228] That claim was but a short step from the call for vengeance.

---

[226] Martini, *Diario*, 1031; Bissolati, in Gatti, *Caporetto*, 285, 295 (1 November); Bissolati to Orlando, 2 November 1917, in Melograni, *Storia politica*, 454; Bissolati in Malagodi, *Conversazioni*, 191–94, but also 228–29. For a summary of the literature on Caporetto as an alleged revelation of Italy's historic failings, see Melograni, ibid., 467–69; Silvestri, *Caporetto*, is a thoughtful post-1945 example of the genre.

[227] Full text of communiqué in Caporetto Inquiry, 2:545; Cadorna, *Lettere Famigliari*, 231, 234, 236; also Malagodi, *Conversazioni*, 210; for some of the circumstances surrounding the communiqué see also Albertini, *Venti anni*, 5:144–45.

[228] OO, 11:402, and Piero Jahier, September 1919 ("quella Italiuccia vigliacca, ignorante e corrotta che ci pugnalava alle spalle mentre combattevamo"), in Isnenghi, *I vinti di Caporetto*, 258–59. In 1924 Jahier courageously took up the lost cause of anti-Fascism; his intemperance about Caporetto is therefore all the more noteworthy.

It was an equally short step to the charge that those same traitors, with the addition of the Giolittians and the democratic "renouncers" of Italy's Dalmatian heritage, were seeking to undo the victory they had failed to prevent. D'Annunzio, fresh from spectacular exploits as naval raider and aviator, and ever-sensitive to the "ghastly stench of peace," formulated the claim in late October 1918 in a way that guaranteed the perpetuation of the war: "Victory of ours, you shall not be mutilated." Without the imperial Dalmatia promised in the Treaty of London; without the "utterly Italian" city of Fiume (Rijeka); without Adriatic domination, the war would have lost its meaning. "Why then did we fight?" asked D'Annunzio in a letter to Corradini in December. The poet proclaimed himself "ready for any and all excesses to prevent my country from dishonoring itself in victory": "violence against violence."[229] Like the national cause from which it had sprung, the growing myth of the *vittoria mutilata* demanded blood sacrifice.

4. STRUCTURAL TRANSFORMATIONS AND THE END OF ALL LEGITIMACY

The Great War bequeathed to Germany and Italy not merely political fragmentation and rancorous struggles over its meaning. It also transformed the economic, social, and institutional landscape in ways that made peace elusive. The war's principal economic effects were two. First, it transmuted a sizable fraction of the national wealth – up to 35 percent in Germany and 26 percent in Italy – into steel, high explosive, and the sinews of war.[230] The destruction of savings through taxes and inflation imposed unprecedented strain on all classes. Moneyed Germans suffered a further staggering blow: defeat prevented the Reich from extracting the expected indemnities from its vanquished foes, and wartime and postwar inflation consequently devoured the value of war bonds to a far greater extent than in Italy. By 1920, by one count, German wholesale prices had multiplied by fourteen since 1913 whereas Italian prices had merely risen by a factor of six; those of France and Britain had merely quintupled and tripled respectively.[231] In both Italy and Germany the destruction of wealth slowed postwar recovery and exacted a stiff social and political price

---

[229] "Vittoria nostra, non sarai mutilata," *Corriere della Sera*, 24 October 1918, 1 (later re-titled "La preghiera di Sernaglia," after the site of the principal bridgehead across the Piave seized by Italian forces: D'Annunzio, *Versi d'amore e di gloria* [Milan, 1968], 2:1120); D'Annunzio to Albertini, 21 October 1918, in Albertini, *Epistolario*, 2:1014–15; D'Annunzio to Corradini, 27 December 1919, in Vivarelli, *Origini*, 1:607–08.

[230] Wolfgang J. Mommsen, "The Social Consequences of World War I: The Case of Germany," in Arthur Marwick, ed., *Total War and Social Change* (New York, 1988), 26; Castronovo, "La storia economica," in ESI 4/1:21 (France and Britain: 30 and 32 percent).

[231] 1920 wholesale price index figures (1913=100): Germany, 1,400; Italy, 591; France 509; Britain, 307, in Gianni Toniolo, "Alcune tendenze dello sviluppo economico italiano 1861–1940," in idem, ed., *Lo sviluppo economico italiano 1861–1940* (Bari, 1973), 32 note; Kocka, *Klassengesellschaft*, 17, gives an index figure for 1920 of 1,486 (1913=100).

from societies partially or entirely bereft of the psychological consolations of victory.

Second, war intensified the long-term shift of both economies' center of gravity toward industry and its workforce. And within the industrial sector, war disproportionately privileged heavy industry and drove forward its concentration in trusts and cartels, which in Germany more than tripled in number between 1906 and 1922. The German chemical industry increased its workforce by 170 percent, the machine and electrical industries by 49 percent, and metal smelting by 8 percent.[232] The branches that did prosper grew in unbalanced fashion, under conditions of autarchy and with total disregard for production costs; the laws of economics exacted their revenge after 1919. German agriculture also enjoyed a feverish prosperity thanks to its wartime indispensability. But the price was high: the exhaustion of soil and labor force, mass slaughter of livestock, and massive economic distortions from price controls, regulations, and the drive to maximize production regardless of costs. The wear and tear of war and the subsequent price collapse thanks to post-1918 imports made agriculture the most serious of the German economy's structural disasters.[233]

In Italy, industrial production swelled as a proportion of gross domestic product from 24 to 30 percent between 1914 and 1918. The war brought north Italy's second "big push," rivalling the swift growth of the Giolittian era, toward emergence as an industrial society. The steel, ship-building, and armaments combines of Ilva and Ansaldo jerry-built vast industrial empires on the insatiable demands of army and navy and the money of Italy's rentiers, taxpayers, and foreign lenders. Smaller, more specialized armament and steel firms such as Breda and Falck likewise grew several times over. FIAT multiplied vehicle production eightfold and its workforce tenfold. An aircraft industry sprang from nothing to produce 6,500 machines in 1918 alone. Hydroelectric power generation doubled. Yet the most striking feature of this feverish growth was its lack of economic and strategic self-sufficiency. Even the new full-cycle steel plants of the great armaments combines depended in many cases on imported fuel, and by 1917–18 almost two-fifths of the steel Italy consumed came from external sources. Without massive imports of coal, iron ore, scrap iron, pig-iron, copper, rubber, petroleum, cotton, and bulk chemicals, Italy's industries could not live. The war took an industrial base simultaneously dynamic and fragile, and forced it into a shape that only a continued high level of government demand and cheap and vulnerable imports could sustain.[234] Italian agriculture by contrast survived the war far better than its German counterpart; grain production

---

[232] See Kocka, *Klassengesellschaft*, 21–33.

[233] See Willy A. Boelcke, "Wandlungen in der deutschen Agrarwirtschaft in der Folge des Ersten Weltkriegs," *Francia* 3 (1975), 505–08; and Wolfgang J. Mommsen, "Social Consequences," 35–37.

[234] Industry as a proportion of GNP: Mitchell, *European Historical Statistics, 1750–1970* (New York, 1976), 802; on the effects of the war on industry, see particularly Castronovo, "La storia economica," ESI 4/1:206ff.; Caracciolo, "La crescita e la trasformazione della grande industria durante la prima guerra mondiale," in idem, ed., *La formazione dell'Italia industriale* (Bari,

rose, most other crops dropped only slightly, and only Italy's forests suffered permanent damage. The war's effects on rural Italy were above all social rather than economic.[235]

War unbalanced both societies, although in different ways. In Germany the further shifting of the economy's center of gravity toward heavy industry, its owners and its workforce, hit worst the two vital groups hitherto most loyal to the existing order. State employees, from railroad workers to government bureaucrats to schoolteachers and university professors, sold cherished possessions or went hungry: by 1917 the monthly real salaries of Reich civil servants had dropped to slightly more than two-fifths of 1913 levels. Only combat pay allowed the officer corps to retain its prewar purchasing power; officers stationed inside Germany fell behind.[236] Shopkeepers and artisans, the standard-bearers of the "old *Mittelstand*," also suffered disproportionately. In the medium term, their share of the workforce continued to diminish, although the war apparently did not accelerate the shrinkage that drove artisans down from 15.3 percent of the industrial and craft workforce in 1907 to 10.7 percent in 1925.[237] Call-ups often deprived their families of their craft skills, the collapse of foreign trade forced shops to close, and unlike the peasantry they lacked ready sources of food. Both groups increasingly looked with envy and hatred upon the munitions workers, whose indispensability guaranteed them wage increases that on average fell behind inflation until 1917, but thereafter recovered slightly. Finally, war bore heavily on Germany's peasants-in-arms, and on agriculture's *Junker* elite – which proportionate to its size paid the highest tribute in blood of any social group: between 4,500 and 4,800 men, roughly a quarter of all adult male nobles, died. The postwar collapse of prices inevitably combined with defeat and the Empire's ruin to brew an unholy mixture of rural resentments.[238]

Like their German counterparts, Italians on fixed incomes suffered disproportionately. Inflation ate steadily into the real incomes of state employees, rentiers, and the weaker members of the *classe proprietaria* with incomes crimped by wartime freezes on urban rents and tenant and sharecropper contracts. Industrial real wages, insofar as they kept pace, did so as a result of

1969), 163–219; Caizzi, *Storia dell'industria italiana*, 410–42; and Luigi Einaudi, *La condotta economica e gli effetti sociali della guerra italiana* (Bari, 1933), ch. 2/2.

[235] See Francesco Bogliari, "Le campagne nella prima guerra mondiale," in Alatri et al., *La disgregazione dello stato liberale*, 107–09.

[236] Andreas Kunz, *Civil Servants and the Politics of Inflation in Germany 1914–1924* (New York, 1986), 62; Schmidt, *Heimatheer und Revolution*, 271 note 694.

[237] SGAB, 2:69, 3:57: Self-employed in industry or industry and crafts: 1875, 41.7 percent; 1882, 34.4; 1895, 24.9; 1907, 15.3; 1925, 10.7; also Kocka, *Klassengesellschaft*, 87.

[238] Real wages: Kocka, *Klassengesellschaft*, 16–18. Dead nobles: Stephan Malinowski, *Vom König zum Führer: Sozialer Niedergang und politische Radikalisierung im deutschen Adel zwischen Kaiserreich und NS-Staat* (Berlin, 2003), 200; that a similar proportion (24.9 percent) of the Prussian regular officer corps died (calculated from Altrock, *Vom Sterben des Deutschen Offizierkorps*, 54, 61) also suggests the extent of *Junker* losses.

extensive compulsory overtime and the widened use of piecework.[239] Rural working families, deprived temporarily or permanently of more than half their men, upheld production by working longer hours. In this respect, if in no other, Italy's endemic prewar rural underemployment served it well. The sharecroppers of central Italy, especially if they paid cash rents, suffered less than other rural groups; they gained in war a new assertiveness against their landowners. The group that prospered most – in relative terms – and expanded thanks to the war was the landowning peasantry; owners who farmed their own land increased between 1911 and 1921 from 26.6 to 38.4 percent of the agricultural population of north Italy. Leaseholders received a windfall: the government froze their contract terms for the duration, inflation depreciated their rent obligations, and agricultural prices escalated, allowing many to buy the land they tilled. Sharecroppers became leaseholders. Those at the bottom prospered least: the *braccianti*, the agrarian wage-laborers associated with the PSI since the great Po Valley strikes of the Giolittian era. Their maximalist leaders answered "land to the *contadini*" by reiterating the prewar commitment of the *leghe* to "land to the collectivity" – a slogan for mortal conflict not only with rural and urban *signori*, but also with every peasant family with a stake, however meager, in the land.[240]

Accelerated economic change and the peculiar demands of war unsettled both societies; their wartime crises of government then unhinged them. Germany had launched its war in 1914 despite its vacuum at the center. But that vacuum had made the war hard to fight. The Reich's history had ordained its irresponsible monarchical executive, uncoordinated civil-military dualism, incoherent command structures, suspicion-laden quasi-federalism, and diffident pseudo-parliamentarism. Each authority with access to the Kaiser had the weight or prerogatives to thwart the others in some essential respect. Given the absence of a Bismarck or Frederick the Great, the Reich's political class of expert but narrow functionaries could only rule in time of crisis by a series of expedients.

The war accentuated all the imperial regime's manifold inadequacies of coordination. At the summit, the one entity with sufficient prerogatives to lead failed miserably. War loosened William II's never-too-firm grip on reality and intensified his incapacity for regular work. His moods swung perilously from manic verbal bloodlust – unheeded orders to give no quarter or to starve 90,000

---

[239] Retail staple food prices in Milan: Einaudi, *La condotta economica*, 305 (July 1915=100; December 1915=126; December 1916=138; December 1917=222; December 1918=305). For living standards, see the pessimistic assessment of Mariella Berra and Marco Revelli, "Salari," in Fabio Levi, Umberto Levra, and Nicola Tranfaglia, eds., *Storia d'Italia* (Florence, 1978), 3:1175, 1178, which uses too selectively the data of Stefano Somogyi, "Cento anni di bilanci familiari in Italia," *Istituto Giangiacomo Feltrinelli, Annali*, 2 (1959), 173–74; and the more optimistic Melograni, *Storia politica*, 360–66, which rests partly on the exhaustive consumption figures in Barberi, *I consumi nel primo secolo dell'unità d'Italia*.

[240] Figures (and some of the analysis), Serpieri, *La guerra e le classi rurali*, 368–69, 152–55; see also Antonio Papa, "Guerra e terra 1915–1918," SSt 1/1969, 3–45.

Russian prisoners to death – to black depression. Despite his inevitable pretensions to lead army and navy in person, he claimed dejectedly as early as November 1914 that his principal function was to "drink tea, saw wood, and go for walks." That was an exaggeration; the Kaiser sustained both Falkenhayn and Bethmann Hollweg against their rivals as long as he could. But with the advent of Hindenburg and Ludendorff, William's influence shrank. Dismissing the "victors of Tannenberg" would crush German morale, and William therefore quailed until October 1918 at the threat of resignation that Ludendorff wielded like a club in helping to force the removal of Bethmann Hollweg. In summer 1918 the Kaiser even acquiesced in a further diminution of his own authority, conceding to his navy a high command parallel to the army's supreme command. Yet almost to the end, William II obstinately resisted changes that diminished his formal constitutional position.[241]

War also intensified the Prusso-German state's civil-military dualism and ultimately led to total defeat of the civilians through Bethmann Hollweg's removal in 1917. But Hindenburg and Ludendorff did not thereby acquire full authority for their total war; the power of the supreme command extended only to military decisions and war aims, and fell short even of full mastery over what passed for German strategy.[242] Control of propaganda and of the allocation of scarcity in food, raw materials, and labor provoked fierce struggle between supreme command, military procurement offices, Reich civilian departments, Bavarian or lesser state bureaucracies, and the fifty-seven martial law commanders entrusted, under Bismarck's constitution and Prussian army regulations, with wartime civil authority at the local level except in Bavaria. Attempts at rationalization almost invariably failed, thanks to resistance from all authorities that might thereby lose; Ludendorff's futile effort to erect a Reich propaganda ministry in 1918 was a measure of his domestic impotence.[243] Terror, a possible solution, was simply not in the Second Reich's repertoire except as "military necessity" dictated, against enemy civilians and forced laborers. As Germany staggered toward defeat, the disorganization inherent in the structures Bismarck had created steadily intensified. By the end, the Reich had almost used up the fund, accumulated over many generations, of instinctive piety toward the state that Heinrich Mann, Thomas Mann's iconoclastic elder brother, had

---

[241] For the Kaiser at war, Holger Afflerbach, "Wilhelm II as Supreme Warlord in the First World War," WIH 5:4 (1998), 427–49, and Hull, *The Entourage of Kaiser Wilhelm II*, ch. 10; 267 for "take no prisoners" and the like, omitted from Walter Görlitz, ed., *Regierte der Kaiser? Kriegstagebücher, Aufzeichnungen und Briefe des Chefs des Marinekabinetts G. A. v. Müller 1914–1918* (Göttingen, 1959); ibid., 68, for the Kaiser on his wartime schedule; see also Fehrenbach, *Wandlungen*, 216–20.

[242] See above all Deist's criticism (MIW, 1:lxiv–vi) of the supreme command "dictatorship" thesis advanced by authors as widely separated in all else as Arthur Rosenberg and Gerhard Ritter.

[243] See Dirk Stegmann, "Die deutsche Inlandspropaganda 1917/18. Zum innenpolitischen Machtkampf zwischen OHL und ziviler Reichsleitung in der Endphase des Kaiserreichs," MGM 12 (1972), 92ff.

earnestly lampooned. And not only the Reich: to their increasingly hard-pressed populations and troops, the rulers of the lesser states appeared as the discredited creatures of an increasingly grasping, incompetent, and *foreign* Reich leadership.

By 1917, two alternative claims to fill Germany's leadership vacuum had emerged. Parliamentarization, by rooting the chancellor in a Reichstag majority, might in theory create both a German Clemenceau with the authority to run the war and the "identity of *Volk* and State" needed to fight it to the bitter end.[244] But that solution presupposed too much. It assumed that the emperor would consent to the open diminution of his inherited rights. It required that the Reichstag parties form a coherent majority that agreed on enough issues to govern. It also presupposed that the Reichstag had functioned in the previous decades as an incubator for political leadership – the one purpose that even relatively liberal German political theorists such as Max Weber were as yet prepared to concede it. Hard-working and intensely ambitious politicians of a new stripe such as Erzberger and Stresemann had indeed scrambled to the top of their parties. But in the process they had made many enemies among an older generation content with the existing domination of parliament by the monarchical executive. The parties thus lacked both the personnel and the will to power to challenge William II and Ludendorff for control of the war. The Reichstag helped topple Bethmann, but could offer no alternative.[245]

The aura of Hindenburg and Ludendorff and the instinctive deference of civilians to the "first *Stand*" thus ruled out parliamentarization unless the supreme command declared bankruptcy. Not until September 1918 did a Reichstag majority slowly form to press for a new chancellor and new policies, but Ludendorff's revolution from above struck first. And not until October did a politician – Friedrich von Payer of the Left-Liberals – dare to face down the general's invocation of military necessity and soldierly honor with a newfound civic pride: "I am a simple, modest *Bürger* and civilian. I see only the starving people."[246]

The alternative to leadership by parliament was the dictatorship prefigured in Class's 1912 call for a Führer to rescue the monarchy from its own incompetence.[247] Tirpitz, closer to the chaos of the inner circle than the pan-Germans and himself a potential candidate for the role, took the idea for his own in early 1915. He pressed it tirelessly thereafter, and even sought clandestinely to have the Kaiser removed for incapacity and ill-health. But William II's refusal to break the constitution or vacate the throne and Bethmann Hollweg's quasi-alliance with Hindenburg and Ludendorff against Falkenhayn from early 1915 onward

[244] For the phrase, Preuss, *Das deutsche Volk und die Politik*, especially 194–95.
[245] See Grosser, *Vom monarchischen Konstitutionalismus*, 129–35, and Epstein, "Der Interfraktionelle Ausschuss und das Problem der Parlamentarisierung 1917–1918," HZ 191 (1960), 575–76.
[246] Grosser, *Vom monarchischen Konstitutionalismus*, parts II.B and III.A; Payer: UF, 2:434.
[247] For what follows, I owe a great deal to Thoss, "Diktaturfrage."

blocked Tirpitz's path. When in due course Ludendorff and Hindenburg themselves turned on the chancellor, Tirpitz and Ludendorff's associate Bauer, along with a variety of other figures, pressed the twin titans of the supreme command to seize the chancellorship. Both repeatedly refused, while the Kaiser rejected other candidates such as Tirpitz or Bülow. Prussia before 1866 had shaped Hindenburg's mental world; he was unwilling to act against the monarch. Ludendorff was demonstrably willing to coerce the monarch, but for once recognized his own limitations and insisted that he must devote himself to running the war. Tirpitz created the *Vaterlandspartei* in part as a mass base for national dictatorship, but in vain. Only total victory – success in the Reich's final 1918 *va-banque* – could create a "military dictatorship joyfully born by the *Volk*," as Riezler aptly described it. Defeat had the inverse effect. From mid-summer 1918 the supreme command's aura and power dissolved; the late September 1918 call for the dictatorship of a general by the conservative leader, Count Cuno von Westarp, was delusion not politics. And in the longer term, defeat emancipated civilian radical nationalism from residual deference to armed forces and monarchy, while crippling army and navy as sources of national Führer-figures. That was a development of enormous if as yet unsuspected dynamic potential.

For defeat could not and did not abolish the role of Führer itself; it intensified its allure. What the moderate Center Party newspaper *Germania* had described in December 1916 as the "devotion of the masses to a genius" remained for many, many Germans the "true democracy of a *Volk* seasoned and made clear-sighted through hard necessity." The end of the Empire left an even greater vacuum and a deeper yearning for national unity through mythic leadership than before. On 11 November 1918, Germany's blackest day, a prominent Prussian pastor expressed to his son a widely felt sentiment: "we were without leadership, that was our cruel fate and in vain we stand here: God give us a man!"[248] War and revolution had created many of the preconditions for at last granting that wish.

The Italian Liberal regime, unlike Germany's military monarchy in so many respects, nevertheless resembled it in its failure in the conduct of war. Victor Emmanuel III helped steady high command and government after Caporetto, but otherwise spent the war as a peculiar military tourist, snapping photographs in the vicinity of the front. Foreign policy remained centralized and bitterly secretive. The perpetually divided cabinet neither debated whether or how to fight, nor represented the parliamentary majority of which it was ostensibly the expression. It distributed home-front scarcity and repressed dissent by emergency decree-laws enacted piecemeal and applied by an ever-swelling, ill-coordinated, inept, and sometimes corrupt bureaucracy. It had virtually no control over strategy or the leadership habits of the officer corps until after

---

[248] Riezler, *Tagebücher*, 460; Westarp and *Germania*: Grosser, *Vom monarchischen Konstitutionalismus*, 179, 140; Friedrich Lahusen of Berlin to his son, 11 November 1918, quoted in Hoover, *God, Germany, and Britain in the Great War*, 121.

Cadorna's fall, and little thereafter. Its chief as the climax of the war approached, the aged and voluble Boselli, offered a living symbol of drab inconclusiveness.[249] War and outcome – the immense and seemingly useless sacrifices of the first eleven battles of the Isonzo, catastrophe at Caporetto, and the inevitable "mutilation" of Italy's far-reaching war aims in 1919 – destroyed utterly the project of rejuvenating the Liberal regime with which Salandra had launched the war.

Parliament might have filled the vacuum at the top had it not been the vacuum's principal source. The congenital amorphousness of its groups and factions made it incapable of leading, even without the trampling the *interventisti* had administered in May 1915. Its only potential governing majority deferred to Giolitti. And Giolitti's "friends" in parliament, with an ambiguity that drove the *interventisti* to charges of treason that further poisoned the atmosphere, resolutely evaded sharing responsibility for the war. Although Giolitti himself publicly stood behind the government after Caporetto, that long-predicted disaster seemed to offer his friends both vindication and the prospect of revenge. A sardonic aside of Giolitti's from autumn 1915 summed up their attitude: "Who today would wish to relieve the present government of its responsibilities?"[250] In the end it was the army, by holding Germans and Austrians short of Venice and Milan, that blocked the Giolittians in Rome as well. Parliament ended the war as paralyzed as it had begun.

The remaining alternative was an anti-parliamentary dictatorship for which Italy lacked the traditions and mythology, and whose only possible claimant lacked the consecration of success. D'Annunzio extolled Cadorna as lord of the arc of fire that stretched from the Trentino to the mouths of the Isonzo, a *duce* "cut and sculpted in the hardest granite . . . by the hand of a master; and vigor overwhelmed art." But the Poet's exhortation to "nail in our breasts, O Lord, his certitude" was not likely to commend Cadorna to those who saw in that certitude the source of repeated bloody defeats. The Robespierres of *interventismo*, like the leaders of the *Vaterlandspartei*, nevertheless toyed with plans for a military regime in 1916–17. Democrats, Nationalists, and *Il Popolo d'Italia* repeatedly contrasted Cadorna's iron hand to the inept and flabby cabinet of Boselli and Orlando. Roman *interventisti* around a fiercely intolerant weekly entitled *Il Fronte Interno* publicly invoked a Cadorna dictatorship as early as January 1917. That summer one of the group's leaders, in league with *Il Popolo d'Italia* and probably with Mussolini himself, approached Cadorna's staff with proposals for a coup d'état. The general himself made a number of gestures of support toward the extremists, and maintained a lavish military intelligence branch office in Rome with mysterious political missions.[251] But as in Germany,

[249] For a more favorable view, Danilo Veneruso, *La grande guerra e l'unità nazionale. Il ministero Boselli, giugno 1916–ottobre 1917* (Turin, 1996).

[250] Giolitti in Malagodi, *Conversazioni*, 1:197–99, 71.

[251] D'Annunzio, "Pel generalissimo" (December 1915), in *Versi d'amore e di gloria*, 2:1065, 1070; De Felice, 1:338–39, 349–51; Melograni, *Storia politica*, 342–51.

military dictatorship required monarchical sanction, the consent of the putative dictator, and victories to give dictatorship a mass base. Cadorna, like Ludendorff, was too narrowly military to rise to the bait; like Ludendorff, he confined himself to bitter complaints about civilian feebleness and betrayal. And as with Ludendorff, although far more swiftly, defeat destroyed all basis for dictatorship by generals. Only the modest cult developing around D'Annunzio's own military exploits offered a possible Italian counterpart to Germany's unrequited yearning for a Führer.

The Great War left the civil societies of Italy and Germany, unlike that of Russia, battered but still in place. But the fates of their respective states – their executives, armies, and bureaucracies – and the ensuing relationships between states, political forces, and societies were far from identical. In Germany defeat and revolution decapitated the state, adding a further powerful element of disintegration to its already chaotic "polyarchy." Left standing amid the ruins of Germany's prewar establishment were defeated and mutinous armed forces, a tarnished and demoralized bureaucracy, and the ambiguous Reichstag coalition for constitutional monarchy that had formed with such trepidation in 1917–18. That balance of forces, and the commitment of the SPD to a parliamentary republic, made democracy possible once the Kaiser fled. But it scarcely guaranteed success amid the hatreds born of defeat and post-1918 left-extremist violence, and the persistence of the widely shared longing for national integration that had made August 1914 so different from Italy's "radiant May."

The Italian monarchy and state by contrast emerged superficially intact and temporarily swollen in prerogatives. Italy's destruction of Austria-Hungary's armies was definitive, unlike the armistice the Allies feebly conceded to Germany.[252] But Vittorio Veneto failed to end war against the "internal enemy." The bases of the Italian state remained far narrower than that of its German counterpart. The parliamentary underpinnings of the executive, already sapped in the 1913 elections, had crumbled invisibly but definitively in the shocks of 1915 and 1917–18 that split virtually all political forces both internally and from one another. The two mass political forces, the Socialists and Catholics, rejected the Liberal regime; unlike their German counterparts, they were also bitter rivals rather than distrustful parliamentary partners. Once the preexisting alienation of the rural and urban masses from the state, transmuted by war into a quest for vengeance, found means of expression through the universal suffrage instituted in 1912–13, parliamentary deadlock and social chaos were assured. External victory too dearly bought released at home the latent preponderance of forces opposed to the war, the Liberal regime, and the social order. It hurled power in Italy into the *piazza*, the preferred arena of those who had learned best from the Great War's synthesis of violence and politics.

[252] See especially French, "'Had We Known How Bad Things Were in Germany,'" 69–86.

4

Kampfzeit: The Road to Radical Nationalist Victory, 1918–1933

The Great War did not make nationalist dictatorship inevitable in Italy or Germany. It made it possible, within a range of outcomes stretching from parliamentary social democracy to military or nationalist dictatorship. Neither society, as 1918 ended, could regain the lost stability of 1914 without radically reshuffling its institutional arrangements and its distribution of political and social power. War – and in Germany revolution – had unleashed immense collective and individual expectations that neither system proved capable of containing. One possible governing formula, Lenin's "scientific concept of dictatorship" – "completely unlimited power, restrained by no laws or rules whatsoever, . . . relying directly on violence" – wielded by admirers of the Bolsheviks, loomed as an apparent threat in both countries.[1] A second, the democratic renewal of either or both polities and the final achievement of national integration through peaceful transformation appeared possible in 1919, and has enjoyed a wide and hopeful following among German historians ever since.[2] Yet in 1919 and after, a Bolshevik Revolution – consequence and reward of Russia's backwardness – was not even remotely within the political repertoire of Italy, of Germany, or of any Western society. And against democratic transformation in both Rome and Berlin stood all *three* extremes: the remains of the old order, the "light from the East" of Marxist utopianism, and the radical nationalism that had grown fat upon the war it had sought and found. The political forces and alignments of 1914–45 were taking leave of the naive left-right spectrum bequeathed by the French Revolution.

Despite the manifest social, political, and ideological divides between the two societies and the superficially different outcomes of their wars, the collapse of parliamentary government followed a common pattern, dictated largely by

---

[1] Lenin, "A Contribution to the History of the Question of Dictatorship" (1920), *Collected Works*, 31:353.

[2] See especially the summary of Wehler, DGG, 4:205–22 and 1025–28, of the debates of the 1960s and 1970s on possible alternatives to Weimar.

the preexisting tripartite division of Italian and German society into warring ideological camps, the unique degree of *innere Zerrissenheit* perfected in both countries through war and postwar upheaval, and the precarious postwar positions of their ruling elites, powerful enough to block change yet too hobbled by their own failures in war and by the advent of mass politics to rule without powerful allies.

In both countries, the descent into the pit – the progressive closing off of options other than the acceptance of Fascist and National Socialist claims to total power – divided neatly into three phases. First came postwar disorder, from 1918–19 in both countries to 1920–21 in Italy and 1923–24 in Germany. Second came a fleeting and largely apparent stabilization more marked in Germany than in Italy. Eight precarious German cabinets succeeded one another between November 1923 and March 1930 against the background of the economic growth that followed the catastrophic hyperinflation of 1923. Correspondingly, the valedictory government of Italy's uncontested parliamentary *maestro*, Giolitti (15 June 1920–4 July 1921) contended with an intractable postwar recession and seemingly irremediable economic-structural blockages (see Figure 4.1). Third came political paralysis and the disintegration of parliamentary government in 1921–22 and 1929–33, a terminal collapse assisted and in part provoked by the militant mass parties born from and dedicated to the perpetuation of the violence and hatreds of 1914–18.

Those seemingly parallel developments nevertheless raise many questions, of which the most salient are three. Why did Liberal Italy capitulate to Mussolini's "March on Rome" a mere forty-eight months from November 1918, whereas the German Republic endured for fourteen years? Why was militant nationalist dictatorship the outcome in both cases? And – given that societies receive only the dictatorships of which they are capable – what sort of dictatorships, and with what measure and depth of support from their societies, were these to be? Provisional answers to these and related questions require analysis of the structural constraints and forces acting upon and within the two political and social systems; of the war's enduring impact upon their political cultures; of the nature, dynamics, and *Kampfzeit* – "time of struggle" – of the two paramilitary nationalist-dictatorial movements; and of the chain of decisions and lapses that handed control of modern states to Benito Mussolini and Adolf Hitler.

I. POSTWAR ITALY AND WEIMAR GERMANY: STRUCTURES AND FORCES

External straitjacket and internal deadlock were the fate of both powers from 1919–20 onward. Yet the grip of outside forces was the less bearable for being largely unexpected. In spring–summer 1918 the German elites and people had anticipated final victory and world mastery, not a seemingly improbable, putatively unmerited, and largely unacknowledgeable defeat amid dismaying revolutionary disorder. Italian expectations of *vittoria romana* proved almost equally delusional and destructive.

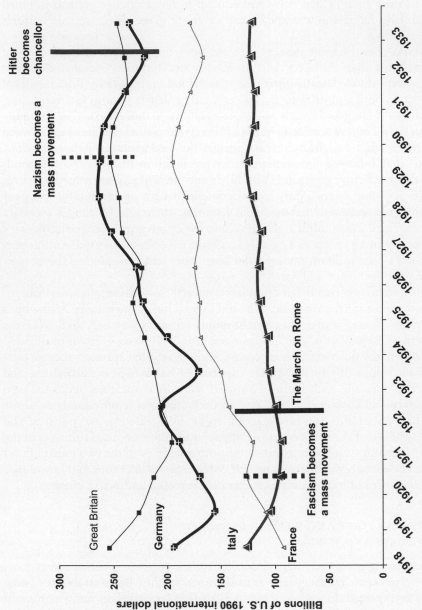

FIGURE 4.1. Economic and Political Trajectories: Italy and Germany from 1918 (GDP at purchasing-power parity)
Base data: Maddison, 48–51.

I. National Fantasies, Postwar Realities

Between the November armistice and the unveiling of the Allies' terms in April–May 1919, the German people took collective leave of reality, as in August 1914 and so often throughout the conflict – in favor of that same "dreamland" in which the German army had returned undefeated from the field.[3] Virtually all shades of German opinion harped passionately on Germany's inalienable right, now that it had overthrown the monarchy, to an essentially status-quo-ante peace, identified perversely or disingenuously with Wilson's Fourteen Points. The SPD-dominated provisional government and its successor, the first cabinet of the German Republic created in January–February 1919, failed to dampen these expectations, which it largely shared. Its negotiators, under the irascible leadership of the new foreign minister, Count Ulrich von Brockdorff-Rantzau, truculently denounced as an assertion of unilateral German "war guilt" an innocuous treaty clause – the famous Article 231 – drafted primarily to underpin Allied claims for expenses that included the enormous damage caused by Germany's invasion of Belgium and France, its calculated devastation of the occupied areas, and the depredations of its U-boats.

Brockdorff-Rantzau thus projected faithfully the wrathful delusions of his countrymen, and forced the Allies to spell out explicitly the self-evident truth that Imperial Germany had started the Great War. In the process, the Allies inevitably concluded that the revolution had changed little or nothing: the German people were incorrigible. The new Reich cabinet confirmed that view. In examining the collection of top secret 1914 foreign office documents that it had commissioned, many of its members concluded privately that Germany had indeed launched the war. But Ebert, now Reich president, and the Republic's first cabinet under Scheidemann as chancellor shrank from publication. That decision foreclosed the one course that might have partially assuaged the Western powers: open repudiation of Imperial Germany's actions, policies, and ethos. Middle-class opinion and the new government's grudging collaborators in army and civil service would never have tolerated such a step. But even the moderate Left, from the trade unions and majority SPD to the German Democratic Party (DDP), was fundamentally unwilling to concede publicly Germany's preeminent "war guilt." A DDP representative described the war of 1914 in cabinet discussion as a justified "preventive war," a claim identical to Bethmann Hollweg's own private self-justification. And within a few years

---

[3] For "dreamland" (the contemporary description of Ernst Troeltsch), and much of what follows, Sally Marks, "Smoke and Mirrors: In the Smoke-Filled Rooms and the Galérie des Glaces"; Fritz Klein, "Between Compiègne and Versailles: The Germans from a Misunderstood Defeat to an Unwanted Peace," both in Boemeke et al., *Versailles*, 203–20 and 337–70; and Peter Krüger, "German Disappointment and Anti-Western Resentment, 1918–19," in Hans-Jürgen Schröder, ed., *Confrontation and Cooperation: Germany and the United States in the Era of World War I, 1900–1924* (Oxford, 1993), especially 326–27. Ernst Fraenkel, "Das deutsche Wilsonbild," *Jahrbuch für Amerikastudien* 5 (1960), 66–120, remains informative.

Ebert himself could publicly proclaim that the German people had fought in 1914–18 to defend "Germany's freedom."[4]

The continuing blockage of seaborne food imports and consequent short- ages into spring 1919, which the German government publicly blamed on the Allied blockade, although scarcity actually stemmed from German hoarding of military rations and quibbling over payment terms and shipping, were a further galling reminder of the Reich's absolute dependence on its enemies and upon the world market – that same dependence it had gone to war to banish "for all imaginable time."[5] The approach of state bankruptcy in the absence of the lavish indemnities on which Germany had counted, and the pressing need to re-enter world trade or suffer economic and social collapse likewise enjoined German prudence. Nor was the Treaty itself particularly severe by comparison with Germany's most recent diplomatic efforts, the now annulled *Diktate* of Bucharest and Brest-Litovsk. The restrictions and exactions of Versailles were in any event insufficient to restrain Germany for long. For the new borders, despite the loss of 13 percent of the Reich's territory and 4.2 percent of its German-speaking population to France, Belgium, Denmark, Poland, Lithua- nia, and Czechoslovakia, preserved the territorial core of Bismarck's Reich, the most powerful industrial base in Europe, and an ethnically homogeneous and highly educated population that still contained three men of military age to France's two (see Map 2, pp. 238–39).[6]

No peace that the German elites and people would have willingly accepted in 1918–19 or later was within the power of Allied leaders to grant. The sup- posed iniquities of the Treaty that the Allies actually presented paled beside the intolerable fact that it was the consequence of German military defeat – a defeat that the German people increasingly refused to accept or admit. Ger- mans of all political stripes and social classes thus greeted the Allied terms with a passionate moralizing nationalist indignation that persisted long after the self-inflicted *finis Germaniae* of 1944–45 demonstrated to the meanest intel- lect how very civilized the 1919 outcome had been. Scheidemann, who had proclaimed the German Republic on 9 November, petulantly resigned as chan- cellor rather than sign the Treaty, after famously if confusedly announcing:

---

[4] See the overview of Ulrich Heinemann, *Die verdrängte Niederlage. Politische Öffentlichkeit und Kriegsschuldfrage in der Weimarer Republik* (Göttingen, 1983), 29–53; the discussions in AdR Scheidemann, 86–91, 146–47, 350–51 (Schiffer: "Preventive war no sin," 90); Heinrich August Winkler, *Weimar, 1918–1933: Die Geschichte der ersten deutschen Demokratie* (Munich, 1993), 88–89; Bethmann to Conrad Haussmann, 24 February 1918, quoted in Riezler, *Tagebücher*, 275 note 3; and Ebert's proclamation on the tenth anniversary of mobilization in 1914 (August 1924), in Reinhold Lütgemeier-Davin, "Basismobilisierung gegen den Krieg: Die Nie-wieder-Krieg-Bewegung in der Weimarer Republik," in Karl Holl and Wolfram Wette, eds., *Pazifismus in der Weimarer Republik* (Paderborn, 1981), 71.

[5] Food, shipping: Marks, "Smoke and Mirrors," 352 note 62; military food stockpiles: Offer, *First World War*, 387–89.

[6] Gerhard L. Weinberg, "The Defeat of Germany in 1918 and the European Balance of Power," CEH 2:3 (1969), 248–60; figures (percentages of Germany's 1910 values): SGAB, 3:23.

"What hand would not wither that laid these shackles upon itself, and upon us." Other supporters or soon-to-be supporters of the new German Republic ranted in a similar vein at the "political sadism" of this "greatest swindle in world history" (Thomas Mann) or insisted improbably that had the army and workers known in November 1918 what sort of peace it would be, they would have fought on (Conrad Haussmann, democratic liberal, vice-president of the national constituent assembly, and onetime enthusiast for *levée en masse* and suicidal *Endkampf*).[7]

Much of the *Bildungsbürgertum* and all of the traditional Right already regarded Wilson with hatred and distrust, as the leading representative of Anglo-American hypocrisy, spiritual emptiness, and mammonism. Wilson thus joined Germany's Jews, Socialists, and those same liberals who now also denounced him as a principal author of the mythical treachery that had felled the German *Volk*-in-arms. That Wilson had publicly promised to recreate a Polish state from "the territories inhabited by indisputably Polish populations" with "free and secure access to the sea" – the fundamental, and fundamentally intolerable feature of the Treaty's territorial terms – had seemingly escaped German readers of the Fourteen Points.

In the end Germany signed, although not before a last puerile gesture of revolt by the imperial naval officer corps, which on 21 June – in defiance of its own government as well as of the Allies – scuttled Tirpitz' creation, the interned High Seas Fleet, at Scapa Flow rather than surrender it. As the coolest heads in the cabinet had argued, only accepting Allied terms, however temporarily, would safeguard the unity of the Reich against further *Zersplitterung* in the form of French partition, west- and south-German separatism, strikes and uprisings by the industrial workers, the possible defection of the middle classes of western and central Germany in the face of renewed war and "hunger-blockade," and a predictably savage final campaign in the Prussian East that would pit civilian guerrillas and the German army's war-weary cornered remnants – a mere 389,000 men – against an estimated 1.25 million French, British, American, Polish, and Czech first-line troops. Groener, now the intellect behind Hindenburg, ignored his nominal superior's preference for an "honorable downfall over a disgraceful peace" and overrode with pitiless logic hotheaded commanders who preached military revolt in eastern Germany. Expectations that revolution would break out in the Allied homelands, that German obduracy would deter Allied use of force, or that Britain would restrain Foch were mere "German wish-fulfillment dreams [*deutsche Träumereien*]."[8]

[7] Scheidemann: UF, 3:350–53; Krüger, "Anti-Western Resentment," 328; Klein, "Between Compiègne and Versailles," 218 (further Mann effusions, including Clemenceau's alleged Mongol ancestry: 205–07).

[8] Groener record of discussions, 18–20 June 1919, AdR Scheidemann 476–92; "Untergang": Hindenburg to Noske, 17 June 1919, in AdR Bauer, 5; clear-eyed analysis of German "*Träumereien*" and the likely outcome should Germany resist: Groener appreciation of 17 June 1919, in Dorothea Groener-Geyer, *General Groener: Soldat und Staatsmann* (Frankfurt am Main, 1955), 379–85; context: AdR Scheidemann, 400–01, 500–07.

MAP 2. The German Reich, 1914–1933.

LITHUANIA
Memel territory
(to Lithuania)

Baltic Sea

Königsberg ●

East Prussia

Danzig ●

West Prussia

Masurian Lakes

Neudeck ●
✕ *Tannenberg*

Polish Corridor

Vistula

Posen

Warsaw ●

POLAND

Silesia

Breslau ●

Upper Silesia

✕ *Königgrätz (1866)*

Prague ●
EMIA

CZECHOSLOVAKIA

Territorial Losses and Treaty Restrictions
- Losses under the Versailles Treaty, 1919–20
- Upper Silesia plebiscite, 1921
- Left to Germany
- Under the League of Nations: Danzig
- Under the League of Nations: Saar
- Occupied Rhineland
- – – – Eastern border of the demilitarized zone
- —— Border of the German Reich, December 1921
- —·—· Border of the German Reich, August 1914

Danube

Vienna ● ● Pressburg

Danube

HUNGARY

AUSTRIA

| 0 | 50 | 100 | 150 | 200 | 250 km |
| 0 | 25 | 50 | 75 | 100 | 125 | 150 miles |

The Treaty merely sought to perpetuate the strategic vice in which the Allies briefly held Germany in 1918–19. In that aim it was more successful than often recognized, although France's effort to compel the Germans to pay reparations at bayonet point soon failed. The occupation of the Ruhr in 1923–24 demonstrated that against the opposition of Britain and the United States, France could not compel even a disarmed Germany to do its will. Stresemann's subsequent triumph, the Locarno western security treaty of October 1925, complemented Germany's financial stabilization and weakened French power over Germany, while largely precluding a new Franco-British coalition. The United States lent Germany the money needed for the reduced payments of the Dawes and Young Plan reparations settlements of 1924 and 1929 – the second with a payment schedule stretching absurdly to 1988. The stream of foreign credit, which survived the Wall Street crash and continued into 1931, likewise bound the German elites grudgingly to the internal and external status quo.[9]

The Treaty's disarmament provisions were even more effective: even after Germany haggled an end to interallied on-site inspections from January 1927, the army's Versailles limit of 96,000 long-service enlisted men and 4,000 officers and the concurrent ban on military training of the remaining male population were significant restraints on German power in the age of mass armies.[10] The German armed forces – the Reichswehr – experimented abroad with forbidden prototypes: tanks, aircraft, gas shells, and U-boats. At home the army maintained ties with a wide spectrum of paramilitary groups whose members it planned to incorporate as reserves in the event of renewed war. Yet large-scale rearmament would provoke major internal and international crises, threaten Germany's foreign trade and financial lifelines, and at the limit recreate the coalition that had brought Germany down in the Great War.

Strongest of all the "shackles" of Versailles were the French garrisons in the Rhineland until 1935, a seemingly far-distant date that assiduous diplomacy ultimately whittled down to 30 June 1930. France's "watch on the Rhine" had an effect that would have seemed paradoxical – had they understood it – to the many contemporary commentators and later historians who blamed the Versailles Treaty for the instability and ultimate collapse of German democracy.[11] The German people, for all their protestations about the Treaty's monstrous

---

[9] The necessity of foreign credit forces internal truce on the German elites after 1924: Geyer, "The State in National Socialist Germany," in Charles Bright and Susan Harding, eds., *Statemaking and Social Movements* (Ann Arbor, MI, 1984), 200.

[10] For the interallied confusion and conflicts surrounding the disarmament clauses, and Lloyd George's demagogic anti-French ploy of linking German limitations to putative future general disarmament, see David Stevenson, "Britain, France, and the Origins of German Disarmament, 1916–19," JSS 29:2 (2006), 195–224.

[11] The leading statesman of Weimar Prussia, Otto Braun of the SPD, memorably claimed that "*Versailles und Moskau*" destroyed the German Republic (Braun, *Von Weimar zu Hitler* [New York, 1940], 5). He was less than half right. It would be pointless to list even the salient works, British, American, and German, that have naively argued that Versailles destroyed or fatally damaged the Republic; Sally Marks has put the counter-argument most forcefully: "Not the treaty but Germany's burning resentment of it fostered Hitler's rise" (Marks, "Smoke and Mirrors," 367). The source of that resentment was refusal to accept defeat.

sadism and injustice, hated it above all because its exactions – and the undeniable fact that Germany could not avoid them – demonstrated that Germany had in fact lost the Great War. The physical presence of the loathed and despised French – and of their black troops – on the Rhine was thus a pressing and effective reminder of the continuing need for prudence. The Ruhr occupation, despite the German-nationalist paroxysms it provoked, had a similarly chastening effect. In the end it forced the creation of a superficially conciliatory government in Berlin under the reformed annexationist Gustav Stresemann. So long as the French army held its last Rhine bridgehead at Wiesbaden and Mainz, a government in Berlin that expressed the full depths of German hatred of the victors and of their Polish and Czech allies was an excessively hazardous luxury.[12] The democratic Republic, accepted in 1918–19 largely as a shield against Allied exactions, thus owed its survival in part to the relative effectiveness of the same "shackles" that its politicians – Communist, Socialist, democratic, Catholic, right-liberal, Conservative, and *völkisch* – fanatically and interminably denounced.

Italy's postwar plight was almost as galling as Germany's. The rude awakening that Italy's elites suffered after victory thus provoked resentments as savage and enduring, if less deeply rooted throughout the population, as German fury at unacknowledgeable defeat. Austria-Hungary's dissolution, Italy's victorious drive to the Brenner frontier, and the conquest of Trieste and Istria in no way diminished an almost complete dependence on foreign coal, oil, grain, meat, iron, and money. By January 1919 Italy was reduced to a ten-day supply of the Argentine frozen beef that had sustained its army and urban populations through the war. An impending strike in Wales threatened to interrupt its all-important coal imports, already running at less than half of 1913–14 levels. Emigration had provided a safety valve for social conflict and, through emigrant remittances, vital relief for Italy's balance of payments. But war, aftermath, and an increasingly rigid United States quota system after 1921 cut migration, while the agrarian overpopulation that drove migration persisted. Only additional U.S. and British loans would allow Italy to pay for further imports; but now that the Central Powers had collapsed, such credits made little strategic sense to Washington and London. Lifting this "economic yoke," as Badoglio, Diaz's deputy at the *Comando Supremo*, described it to Orlando and Colosimo in late November 1918, might require venturing far afield indeed; the general suggested coal concessions in China and grain-growing colonies in Asia Minor populated by Italian *contadini*.[13]

---

[12] The French for instance informed Berlin in November 1923 that they would not tolerate a German-nationalist military dictatorship; German reports noted their apparent unhappiness when the Hitler-Putsch failed, removing France's pretext for a march on Berlin (Harold J. Gordon, Jr., *Hitler and the Beer Hall Putsch* [Princeton, NJ, 1972], 453–54; also DDI 7/2/472). As late as 1929–30 French evacuation of the Rhineland appeared the essential precondition for nationalist experiments in government (see for instance Heinrich Brüning, *Memoiren 1918–1934* [Stuttgart, 1970], 145–46, 151–53).

[13] DDI/6/1/589, 735, 393; Forsyth, *Crisis of Liberal Italy*, 323 (October 1913–May 1914: 7,310,400 tons; October 1918–May 1919: 3,393,600 tons), 204–09.

Yet such dreams swiftly collapsed in the face of the palpable and increasing contempt for Italy that France and Britain displayed at Paris. Italian claims were neither proportionate to Italy's perceived contribution to victory, nor easily reconciled with Wilson's utopian principles, nor presented as a coherent package of objectives agreed between the Rome government and its Paris negotiators. Instead, Orlando, Sonnino, Colosimo, and the army and navy simply threw together a compendium of united Italy's great-power-fantasy perquisites: the Brenner frontier; *both* Dalmatia *and* Fiume; Colosimo's grand design for colonial "distributive justice," the throttling of Ethiopia through French and British cession of Djibouti and British Somaliland; a colony or mandate elsewhere in Africa; a protectorate over Albania with Valona and hinterland as a sovereign Italian naval base; Adriatic domination through the demilitarization of Yugoslavia's remaining coastline; mandate "administration" of wide areas in Asia Minor, with corresponding coal concessions; Italian coaling stations at Dar es Salaam, Lagos, and Kiaochow; and the cession of Austro-Hungarian and German concessions in China at Tientsin, Hankow, and Nanking.[14]

The Entente inevitably measured these claims against Italy's inability to make an impression on Austria-Hungary in 1915–16; its failure to declare war on Germany until August 1916; its absence from the fighting in the Near East and in Africa; its diminutive contribution – partially and foolishly withdrawn at a critical moment in July 1918 – to the war in France; and above all its débâcle at Caporetto and subsequent pleas for rescue, which had necessitated commitment at a critical moment of the war of eleven Anglo-French divisions.

Wilson, whose favor was infinitely more important to France and Britain than that of Italy, made a stand on the right to self-determination of the Yugoslavs, if not of German-Austrians south of the Brenner. France casually blocked Colosimo in Africa. Italian efforts to secure influence in Eastern Europe through intrigues in Hungary and Rumania failed in the face of France's superior ability to commit troops along the Danube, and the far greater prestige of its military advisors. France's imperative need to contain Germany guaranteed that Paris would make any effort required to secure and maintain preponderance in Eastern Europe – until Germany and Soviet Russia in the end retook that preponderance for themselves. Italian landings in Asia Minor in May 1919 proved equally abortive; Sonnino's unilateral initiatives and Orlando's claim to Fiume created an Anglo-French-American united front against Italy's Near Eastern ambitions. A harebrained British proposal that Italy send an expeditionary force to secure for itself and for the Entente the oil and minerals of the Caucasus – temporarily ownerless amid German collapse and Bolshevik chaos – fell through.[15] Even the occupation of Albania proved unsustainable once the Italian army belatedly demobilized between summer 1919 and mid-1920.

---

[14] DDI/6/1/398, 436, 475, 565, 853; DDI/6/2/63, 97, and, above all, the astonishing document 196.
[15] See especially Webster, "Una speranza rinviata: L'espansione industriale italiana e il problema del petrolio dopo la prima guerra mondiale," SC 11:2 (1980), 219–81.

In the end, after a theatrical withdrawal and sheepish return to the Paris peace conference, Orlando had to face parliament in June 1919 in the condition he and Salandra and all their predecessors had dreaded above all else: with largely empty hands. The French and British left Italy to haggle on alone over the Adriatic with the hated Yugoslavs.[16] Italy's dependence on imports and foreign credits endured, although demobilization and economic recovery gradually defused the immediate crisis. Orlando's only consolation was that the peace would not last: "more than two hundred and fifty million people will emerge from the conference disappointed and affronted and with the resolve to be revenged."[17] Italy, along with Germany and Russia, would be in the front rank.

D'Annunzio's "*Vittoria nostra, non sarai mutilata!*" thus proved negatively prophetic. The disjunction between the megalomania of the Italian cabinet, negotiators, and opinion and Italy's objective circumstances could scarcely have had any other result than deadlock and humiliation. When Wilson sought to prevail through an infantile message to the Italian people preaching a new world order that required surrender of both Dalmatia and Fiume, press and public throughout the peninsula, led by Orlando with ornate impassioned oratory, attacked Wilson in terms that paralleled Germany's simultaneous hysterical protests against the Versailles terms. In both cases, the rhetorical excesses of April–June 1919 gave the final shape to cults of national victimhood that endured for a quarter-century, before perishing in the catastrophe that they helped provoke, and that put all the wrongs and sufferings of 1914–19 in the shade.

II. From War to Civil War

The domestic counterpart to the external vise that gripped the two states and societies was civil war and political deadlock. The November revolution democratized Germany's constitution, but left largely intact Germany's far-from-democratic political culture and institutions.[18] In Italy the advent of universal suffrage and proportional representation produced a similarly precarious hybrid outcome. The German civil war began in December–January 1918, once

---

[16] For the conference, the outcome, and the domestic repercussions, see René Albrecht-Carrié, *Italy at the Paris Peace Conference* (New York, 1938), parts I and II; H. James Burgwyn, *The Legend of the Mutilated Victory: Italy, the Great War, and the Paris Peace Conference, 1915–1919* (Westport, CT, 1993), particularly 292–303; and the masterful survey in Vivarelli, *Origini*, vol. 1, ch. 4.

[17] Malagodi, *Conversazioni*, 669 (23 May 1919); see in general Vivarelli, *Origini*, vol. 1, ch. 4; and Maria Grazia Melchionni, *La vittoria mutilata* (Rome, 1981).

[18] For the persistence – and 1918–19 radicalization – of German political culture, see the exemplary sampler of Detlev Lehnert, "Propaganda des Bürgerkrieges? Politische Feindbilder in der Novemberrevolution als mentale Destabilisierung der Weimarer Demokratie," in idem and Klaus Megerle, eds., *Politische Teilkulturen zwischen Integration und Polarisierung* (Opladen, 1990), 61–101.

the 2.9 million troops from the western front had rolled back across the Rhine bridges into Germany. It subsided with the Republic's temporary consolidation in 1923–24, then revived in a new form during the final decline of 1930–33.

In its first phase, inchoate insurrections by Communists and USPD radicals in Berlin and across northern Germany and the seizure of power by the extreme Left in Munich compelled the majority SPD to defend the German Republic with the forces at hand. Ebert had inevitably accepted Groener's famous – or infamous – 10 November offer, on behalf of a suddenly deferential and compliant supreme command, to bring home and demobilize the army. The troops detrained in good order, then spontaneously demobilized themselves. By December, the forces remaining in Berlin proved useless against revolutionary sailors and armed Spartacists. From that point onward, with SPD authorization and under Groener's supervision, volunteer units – *Freikorps* – emerged, formed from officers, NCOs, and men who had enjoyed the war and were reluctant to give it up, and from those, especially university and *Gymnasium* students, who regretted being too young to have tasted it.[19] The returning troops also provided experienced cadres and recruits for an astonishing variety of nationalist ("*vaterländisch*") self-defense militias and paramilitary organizations across Germany and beyond its eastern borders, from the Baltic to Upper Silesia, from the anti-Socialist and anti-Danish peasant militias of Schleswig-Holstein to the armed student corps of the university towns and the Bavarian home guards.[20]

The leaders of the *Freikorps* were inevitably junior *Frontoffiziere* who incarnated the new type of brutal military Führer for whom "the will knows no impossibility." They wholly lacked respect for authority: a special case of the personal liberation that revolution had brought. Their aim was less to reestablish republican order than to revenge defeat upon the "internal enemy." Revenge they duly took, murdering Rosa Luxemburg and Karl Liebknecht in January 1919 and announcing that the latter had been "shot while attempting to escape" – a phrase with a long future. A second round of Communist insurrection in central Germany, the Ruhr, and Berlin in March–April 1919 prompted Gustav Noske, the resolute SPD defense minister, to order – in a manner befitting the Prussian NCO he had once been – that "any person found bearing arms against government troops... [be] immediately shot." By Noske's own estimate, the March fighting in Berlin alone cost 1,200 dead. In April, as

[19] For insight into this last category, prominent also in Italy, see especially the unrepentant testimony of a leader of the plot to murder Rathenau: Ernst von Salomon, *Die Geächteten* (Berlin, 1931).

[20] On Schleswig-Holstein's ideological climate and paramilitary leagues, estimated by the police to number 25,000–30,000 men in November 1920, see Kurlander, "The Rise of Völkisch-Nationalism and the Decline of German Liberalism: A Comparison of Liberal Political Cultures in Schleswig-Holstein and Silesia 1912–1924," *European Review of History* 9:1 (2002), 33–35; Gerhard Stoltenberg, *Politische Strömungen im schleswig-holsteinischen Landvolk 1918–1933* (Düsseldorf, 1962), 50; and Rudolf Rietzler, *"Kampf in der Nordmark." Das Aufkommen des Nationalsozialismus in Schleswig-Holstein (1919–1928)* (Neumünster, 1982), 135–39. Gordon, *Beer Hall Putsch*, ch. 4, offers a striking panorama of the Bavarian "patriotic movement."

Lenin telegraphed feverish exhortations to Munich to seize banks, "the houses of the rich," and "hostages from the bourgeoisie," and as *Freikorps* from across Germany closed in on the Bavarian capital, the last and most extreme of two ephemeral Munich Soviet republics shot ten *völkisch* hostages. The troops who reconquered the city for the Bavarian and Reich governments replied with indiscriminate executions; fighting and murder of those "attempting to escape" caused well over 600 deaths.[21]

Yet these bloodbaths bought the German Republic only temporary respite; what had evolved into a four-way struggle between the majority SPD government, Communists and USPD radicals, the army high command, and the reviving forces of the old Right erupted again in March 1920. Allied demands that the army – reformed in March 1919 by simply redesignating selected *Freikorps* as regular units of the new Reichswehr – must belatedly shrink from more than 200,000 men to the Treaty limit of 100,000 triggered a military revolt that seized Berlin for five days under the patronage of the old Right. Its leaders included transitional figures such as Wolfgang Kapp, co-founder with Tirpitz of the *Vaterlandspartei*; Ludendorff; and *General der Infanterie* Baron Walther von Lüttwitz, former commander of the army throughout eastern Germany. But the protagonist of the Kapp Putsch was above all the Ehrhardt Brigade – a 5,000-man naval *Freikorps* recruited in large part from the navy's elite, the U-boat crews, and distinguished even among its fellows by an insatiable thirst for blood. Noske's appeal to the army command, in which the formidable Hans von Seeckt now played a decisive role, met with a neutrality simultaneously embarrassed and sanctimonious. The Reichswehr would only fight the Left.

The government's only recourse was the perilous double-edged weapon of the general strike. Fence-sitting by much of the bureaucracy and the cut-off of transport, light, and heating by Berlin's workers forced "Reich Chancellor" Kapp out. Ehrhardt's men took revenge for their departure in style, turning their rifles and machine guns on an unfriendly crowd near the Brandenburg Gate.[22] The Kapp Putsch was the old Right's last frontal assault on the Republic. Yet Kapp's footsoldiers already bore the symbols of the new *völkisch*-nationalist radicalism: the marching song of Ehrhardt's men hailed the "hooked-cross" on their helmets and the black-white-red colors of the *Kaiserreich* that the Brigade had adopted as its symbol in January 1920.[23]

---

[21] Schulze, *Freikorps und Republik, 1918–1920* (Boppard, 1969), 54–100; Robert G. L. Waite, *Vanguard of Nazism. The Free Corps Movement in Postwar Germany, 1919–1923* (New York, 1968) (still noteworthy for astute use of *Freikorps* materials and memoirs), chs. 1, 4; Noske, *Von Kiel bis Kapp* (Berlin, 1920), 109–10; UF, 3:129 (Lenin to the Bavarian Soviet regime, 29 April 1919); Winkler, *Weimar*, 72–82.

[22] A vivid eyewitness account: John Hartman Morgan, *Assize of Arms* (London, 1945), 74–75; Gabriele Kruger, *Die Brigade Ehrhardt* (Hamburg, 1971), 62.

[23] "Hakenkreuz am Stahlhelm, / Schwarzweissrotes Band, / Die Brigade Ehrhardt / Werden wir genannt." For Ehrhardt's vague recollection ("Suddenly the swastika was *the* nationalist emblem"), Friedrich Freksa, ed., *Kapitän Ehrhardt: Abenteuer und Schicksale* (Berlin, 1924), 164–65; but see p. 285 in this volume.

Kapp's defeat in no way reestablished republican order. In the Ruhr, Communists, anarchists, and USPD militants exploited the government's general strike to arm 50,000 or more workers and mount a general insurrection throughout Germany's industrial heartland. *That* uprising the Reichswehr was delighted to crush, inflicting another thousand or more dead, many of them shot "attempting to escape." A further Communist hope, the Red Army's sweep westward in its 1920–21 war against Poland, failed at Warsaw in August 1920, much to the disappointment of surviving German Communists and of the Reichswehr, which had prepared to exploit Soviet success by attacking Poland from the west.[24] Yet the restructured Communist Party of Germany (KPD) that emerged from a fusion at the end of 1920 with the rebellious majority of the USPD base nevertheless tried for revolution twice more, under uncompromising orders from Moscow. In the "March action" of 1921 its supporters took on Republic and Reichswehr with strikes and uprisings in the Ruhr, central Germany, and the Hamburg area, and lost – at a cost of 180 dead. A final insurrectionary KPD push for a "German October" at the height of the Ruhr crisis and hyperinflation in 1923 similarly fizzled out, in part as a result of Reichswehr preemption.

The Republic likewise survived challenges from the *völkisch* combat leagues born of war and revolution. The army's enforced shrinkage to its Versailles limits – and bitterness on the Right after Kapp's failure – helped consolidate and strengthen a paramilitary underground whose principal targets were politicians associated with the acceptance of Allied terms. The clandestine "Consul Organization" (OC) that emerged from the debris of Ehrhardt's *Freikorps* proceeded to assassinate Matthias Erzberger – for his salient role in Reichstag peace resolution, Armistice, and Treaty – in August 1921. In June 1922 the OC killed the Republic's foreign minister – the Jewish aesthete, industrialist, and organizer of Germany's 1914–18 war economy, Walther Rathenau – in broad daylight on the streets of Berlin. The overtly anti-Semitic motivation of the murderers found expression in widely circulated doggerel predicting that Rathenau would not reach any great age, and urging the German public to "[g]un down Walther Rathenau, that god-damned *Judensau*."[25] The continued enthusiasm of the army – and of much of the male population of the nationalist majority culture – for the mass paramilitary organizations that had sprung up in 1918–19 guaranteed continued ferment, especially in Bavaria, which until 1923–24 asserted its independence from "red Berlin" by refusing to enforce Reich laws aimed at the radical Right.

Yet in its initial attempt to overthrow the Republic the new nationalism ultimately failed as miserably as Kapp. In autumn 1923, as the Reich moved against KPD subversion in central Germany, the Bavarian right-wing government put down the 8–9 November "Beer Hall Putsch" of a political upstart,

---

[24] Gaines Post, Jr., *The Civil-Military Fabric of Weimar Foreign Policy* (Princeton, NJ, 1973), 123.

[25] "Auch der Rathenau, der Walther, / Erreicht kein hohes Alter, / Knallt ab den Walther Rathenau, / Die gottverfluchte Judensau" (Winkler, *Weimar*, 173).

Adolf Hitler, Austrian emigré and wartime Bavarian army lance-corporal. By the end of 1923, the Republic had miraculously survived: the Communists vanquished, Hitler imprisoned, the currency stabilized, and a provisional settlement of the Ruhr and reparations crises possibly within reach. Dearly bought victory over its immediate opponents nevertheless failed to engage the German Republic's fundamental weaknesses.

Italy, even in normal times, enjoyed a per capita murder rate five to six times that of the German Reich, and no *Burgfrieden* had tempered the fractures opened or exacerbated in April–May 1915.[26] But the level and nature of Italian political and social violence from 1919 onward was wholly new, even if the Italian civil war initially proved far less bloody than its German counterpart because of the far slower pace of Italian demobilization and the insurrectional ineffectuality of the PSI. The army shrank slowly from around 4 million officers and men in November 1918 to just over 1.7 million in June 1919. Demobilization then accelerated, yet at the end of the year the army still retained 550,000 officers and men, and did not reach a provisional peacetime strength of around 300,000 men until summer.[27]

Italy's civil war developed not as a series of urban set-piece battles, but rather as a rural guerrilla war that corresponded to the far greater social weight of the Italian countryside compared to its German counterpart. The *massimalisti*, inflamed by the Russian example and by the rage against all authority of the masses that the state had mobilized for war and that the PSI now pretended to lead, took the initiative with relentless propaganda. The "war of the *signori*" must inevitably lead to the violent, total, and deserved destruction of the society that had engendered it. The extremists rammed through the October 1919 Socialist congress at Bologna a new party program committing Italian socialism to joining Lenin's Third International, and hailing the party's "violent struggle for liberation" and "violent conquest" of a political power to be exercised through "the dictatorship of the entire proletariat."[28] Into the winter of 1919–20 that "proletariat" gratuitously humiliated officers and soldiers in uniform by ripping off their badges of rank, and on occasion burned the national flag – while looting bakeries and food shops across Italy in archaic protest against

---

[26] See the official Italian and German murder and manslaughter statistics for 1902–36, in Sven Reichardt, *"Faschistische Kampfbünde." Gewalt und Gemeinschaft im italienischen Squadrismus und in der deutschen SA* (Cologne, 2002), 94–96; Reichardt apparently ignores the possibility that the criminal justice figures radically understated the actual levels of violence in both societies, by omission of cases in which the law played no role (including the massive casualties of German urban warfare in 1919–20; many other killings by *Freikorps*, Reichswehr, *Landespolizei, Carabinieri*, and *Guardia Regia*; and in many cases even political assassinations).

[27] The estimates of Rochat, *L'esercito italiano da Vittorio Veneto a Mussolini* (Bari, 1967), 25–27, 32, 35, 47–48, 50, 60, 170–72, remain the most credible, but see also Vincenzo Gallinari, *L'esercito italiano nel primo dopoguerra (1918–1920)* (Rome, 1980), 161 (380,000 conscripts under arms at the end of 1920); the documentation cited makes clear that the army had only the vaguest notions of its own strength.

[28] Partial text, with commentary, Vivarelli, *Origini*, 2:211–26.

inflation-driven price increases.[29] In redemption of the government's wartime motivational promises of "land to the *contadini*," the peasantry of the South and islands forcibly – if often only temporarily – occupied land held by absentee owners or lying fallow. The agricultural *leghe* of the Po Valley and Apulia swelled to encompass 1.8 million laborers, almost three-fifths of Italy's organized workers – a militant rural force, now trained in violence and stripped of inhibitions in war, and largely without a German counterpart.[30]

In June 1919 the national organization of the *braccianti*, the *Federterra*, formally adopted a program more Bolshevik than anything yet seen in Russia, reaffirming its long-standing final goal of the "socialization of the land."[31] Under that slogan the *leghe* launched a series of increasingly powerful strikes to seize total control of hiring and pay, and to dictate the numbers of *braccianti* to be imposed on each landowner or leaseholder – the "*imponibile della mano d'opera*" sought but only sporadically achieved before 1914. The *leghe* thus targeted not only landowning *signori*, their agents, and their strikebreakers, but also intermediate categories such as sharecroppers and permanent hired hands. They threatened and punished recalcitrant owners and dissenting laborers without mercy: fines and forced contributions; boycotts; arson; destruction of crops; abandonment, mutilation, or killing of livestock; beatings; and the occasional murder.[32] Small impromptu groups of "red guards" sprang up in major cities such as Milan; Socialist enforcers with rifles and shotguns patrolled Po Valley strike areas by bicycle. Landlords, especially in the South, replied in time-honored fashion with the shotguns and clubs of their retainers. The hard-pressed military police – the *Carabinieri* – and army units, with the addition of the *Guardia Regia*, a new national riot police that Nitti had created in September–October 1919, sought to contain disorder and defend property rights and their own lives. But although armed with pistols, rifles, and machine guns, Italy's police forces lacked motorized mobility and modern communications, intelligence, and administrative backup. Rifle butts, bayonets, and ball ammunition were their only crowd control tools.[33]

The mortal violence of 1919 peaked in July at forty-six dead, largely provoked by increases in food prices, snapped upward again during the

[29] For the furious resentment that the PSI stance toward veterans generated, see especially Ferruccio Parri, 1915–18 veteran, anti-Fascist exile, partisan leader, and first prime minister of liberated Italy in 1945, speaking in 1969: Stefano Folli, ed., "Prezzolini e Parri: Perché nacque il fascismo," NA 2198 (1996), 315.

[30] Zangheri, *Lotte agrarie*, xi, xiii.

[31] See p. 85; text: Zangheri, *Lotte agrarie*, 373 (see also 471–76); for comparison between the Federterra's agrarian program and that of the Bolsheviks, ibid., lxxxix–xc.

[32] See Vivarelli, *Origini*, 1:447–60 for the disorders of spring–summer 1919, and 2:303–06 for Socialist intimidation of opponents in the run-up to the November 1919 election; on *lega* tactics and the geography of protest, ibid., 2:743–47, 806–57; Luigi Preti, *Le lotte agrarie nella valle padana* (Turin, 1955), ch. 5; and Cardoza, *Bologna*, 274–89.

[33] Security forces, "Red Guards": Lorenzo Donati, "La Guardia Regia," SC 8:3 (1977), 441–87; Mondini, *Politica delle armi*, ch. 3; Vivarelli, *Origini*, 1:620–21; Giovannini, *L'Italia massimalista*, 193–95; and the panorama of 1919–20 mayhem in Mimmo Franzinelli, *Squadristi. Protagonisti e tecniche della violenza fascista 1919–1922* (Milan, 2003), 278–301.

parliamentary election campaign of October–November, then briefly subsided until spring 1920, when the army's belated final demobilization coincided with the incandescent rural struggles of the new growing season and with transport and industrial discontents (see Figure 4.2).

The *interventisti* at first answered primarily with words. Defeat of the "external enemy," D'Annunzio wrote in a January 1919 open letter to the Dalmatian irredentists that appeared in Mussolini's newspaper, "should have swept away the internal enemy or at least knocked the wind from him and broken his back. But instead he is more malignant, more loathsome, than before." Attempts to swindle Italy of its victory must meet the same response as earlier efforts to defraud it of its purifying war: "[i]f necessary, we will face this new conspiracy in the manner of the *Arditi*, with a grenade in each hand and a blade between our teeth."[34]

By January–February 1919, newly demobilized or active-duty *Arditi*, the Futurist-*interventista* lunatic fringe around Marinetti, and the following of Mussolini as the uncontested journalistic leader of *interventismo* had indeed begun to coalesce in Milan and elsewhere in defense of Italy's sacred war and "glorious martyrs" against "the reviving beast" of Socialist-Bolshevist agitation.[35] One consequence was the founding by Mussolini on 23 March 1919 of a new political movement, the *Fasci di combattimento* – the quintessential expression of that dynamic minority, the warrior *superuomini* of literate, urban Italy. A second result was the spectacular destruction on 15 April 1919 by *Arditi* and Futurists of the Milan headquarters and presses of the Socialist national newspaper, *Avanti!* Simultaneously, a broad spectrum of patriotic and thus vigorously anti-Socialist associations, some deriving from the 1917–18 *fascio* of national defense, some newly founded, arose across north and central Italy.

Yet despite the best efforts of the beleaguered remnants of *interventismo*, and occasional outrages by *Arditi* or Fascists, the masses, the strikers, and the *massimalisti* occupied center stage in the streets, fields, and factories of north Italy until autumn 1920. With one exception: as in Germany, demobilization and national humiliation provoked an explosion of military dissidence. The greatest of united Italy's wars had given to the army's once-derided and neglected officer corps power and self-respect. For all its intellectual limitations and cultural weaknesses, it had raised and led an army of 5 million men. It had directed the war economy and had ruled the war zone covering northeast Italy with a rod of iron, largely independent of civilian authority. Its ancestral enemy, Austria-Hungary, had in the end disintegrated utterly. Sacrifice, victory, and its taste of wartime power made it flatly unwilling to return to a prewar routine in which officers had allegedly enjoyed "pay and esteem less than those of a travelling salesman, surrounded by the condescension of workers and

[34] "Lettera ai Dalmati," in Alatri, ed., *Scritti Politici di Gabriele D'Annunzio*, 158, 162; see also Mussolini to D'Annunzio, 1 January 1919, OO, 12:331–32.

[35] OO, 12:76, 233; for the postwar role of Marinetti and friends, Gentile, "Il futurismo e la politica," 124–57.

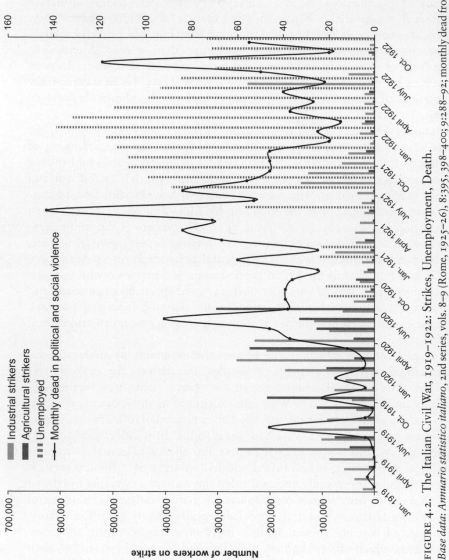

FIGURE 4.2. The Italian Civil War, 1919–1922: Strikes, Unemployment, Death.

Base data: Annuario statistico italiano, 2nd series, vols. 8–9 (Rome, 1925–26), 8:395, 398–400; 9:288–92; monthly dead from riots, assassinations, bombings, "punitive expeditions," overzealous crowd control, and other political and social violence derive from the detailed chronology, resting on prefect reports, police materials, and contemporary newspaper sources, of Franzinelli, *Squadristi,* 278–403 (accidents with firearms, explosives, and vehicles excluded; violence in and around Fiume included).

intellectuals alike."[36] A close if less than charitable observer from the warlike avant-garde, Giuseppe Prezzolini, lampooned the officer corps' 1919 attitudes toward Austria-Hungary's Yugoslav successor with only slight exaggeration:

> As the last cannon shot was fired at four in the afternoon on 4 November, toasts were already being raised at the various headquarters to the new war against France and Yugoslavia. To continue the good life, with a car, villas laid on, orderlies as servants, ladies for the evenings, fat pay and allowances, and swift promotion. . . . For all these people, Vittorio Veneto . . . could not be the end, but only the beginning.[37]

Such attitudes prepared the officer corps poorly for a reversal of expectations in spring–summer 1919 far worse than that of Italy's political elite, and almost as bitter as that visited upon the Germans. The crescendo of Socialist abuse directed at the army; the mutilation of Italy's war aims in Paris; the leakage and ultimate publication of an official inquiry into Caporetto that described in detail the pointless cruelty and ineptitude of Cadorna's conduct of the war; and the acceleration of demobilization, with its consequent need to downsize the officer corps, produced a crisis between government and armed forces unlike anything in united Italy's previous history.[38]

The high command of Diaz and Badoglio – who in effect replaced Diaz as chief of staff of the army at the end of 1919 – sought to preserve the army's influence by cooperation with Orlando's ambiguous successor, Francesco Saverio Nitti. But both in Rome and on the eastern border, army and navy authorities entertained contacts with dissident military figures, Nationalists, patriotic organizations, Italian activists from Dalmatia and Fiume, Mussolini and associates, and the inevitable D'Annunzio, who sought fervently if unsuccessfully to dissuade the king from appointing Nitti as Orlando's successor. The Italian military representative at Fiume, General Francesco Saverio Grazioli; the astute and highly political defender of the Grappa sector in 1918, General Gaetano Giardino; the king's ambitious cousin, Emanuele Filiberto of Savoia-Aosta, commanding 3rd Italian Army; Admiral Enrico Millo, governor of Dalmatia; the widely respected chief of the navy, Admiral Paolo Thaon di Revel; and a variety of lesser military figures formed a loose fraternity committed to ruthless assertion of Italy's Adriatic primacy. By June 1919, unprecedented rumors of a

---

[36] A long-serving infantry captain, summer 1915, quoted in the diary of Gino Frontali, *La prima estate di guerra* (Bologna, 1998), 58 (cited by Mondini, *Politica delle armi*, 12); see also Caciulli, "La paga di Marte."

[37] Prezzolini, *Vittorio Veneto* (Rome, 1920), 40, quoted in Mondini, *Politica delle armi*, 185 note 74.

[38] On the army's public humiliation, see the often reticent but nevertheless damning indictment of the Caporetto Inquiry, and the account of the ensuing polemics and further investigations of Andrea Ungari, "Le inchieste su Caporetto: uno scandalo italiano," *Nuova storia contemporanea* 2/1999, 37–80.

military coup aimed at seizing Dalmatia, northeast Italy from Venice to Trieste, and Fiume were proliferating in the press.[39]

By August, Nitti had abolished the military governorships – except, for the moment, Millo at Zara – and had reassigned the Duke of Aosta to inactive duty. A new wave of demobilization promised to reduce the army from more than 1.6 million officers and men to less than half that by December. Further delay would only weaken both military dissidence and Italy's hold on Fiume, which Nitti regarded as a diplomatic embarrassment. Plotters among the officers and men of the elite *Granatieri di Sardegna*, originally stationed at Fiume, then transferred because of too-close relationships to the Italian-speaking population of the "martyr city," finally triggered the explosion. On 12 September D'Annunzio, with least to lose of all the major figures and with clandestine assurances of support from local army commanders, placed himself at the head of the rebels and marched on the city.

Along the dusty roads across Istria he collected a motley force of 2,000 or so *Granatieri*, *Arditi*, and individual volunteers. Units half-heartedly sent to intercept him stood aside or deserted to the rebellion. His seizure of Fiume for Italy inaugurated fifteen months of sedition against the Italian state rather than for the city's cause. The poet assumed dictatorial status as *Il Comandante* by acclamation of troops and townspeople, proclaimed Fiume irrevocably annexed to Italy, and demanded the removal of "the slug" Nitti. The poet's harangues from the balcony of his headquarters perfected a new political style based on dialogue between demagogue and crowd and the slogans and symbols – daggers and death's heads – of the *Arditi*.

Like the early rightist and right-radical attacks on the German Republic from Kapp to Hitler, D'Annunzio nevertheless failed. Nitti shied away from confrontation even before his designated troubleshooter, Badoglio, reported that the army was so wholly in sympathy with the rebellion that government orders to retake Fiume would not be obeyed. Only logistical embarrassment prevented D'Annunzio from taking "as many [additional] troops as he wants"; in the end, up to 600 officers and 5,500 to 6,000 enlisted men deserted – with impunity – to serve at Fiume.[40] But the equivocal Badoglio, and still more his far firmer successor from December 1919, General Enrico Caviglia, gradually isolated Fiume with a cordon of increasingly reliable troops. Nitti secured the king's backing and publicly affirmed that he too sought Fiume for Italy, appropriating D'Annunzio's pretext for action and diminishing his respectability with the wider patriotic public. And the leftward drift after autumn 1919 of the Commander's experiment in government, which led him to contact a bizarre variety of groups and figures, from Russian Bolsheviks to Italian anarcho-syndicalists, also helped to isolate him from his original military and Nationalist

[39] See the lists of presumed plotters in Rochat, *Vittorio Veneto a Mussolini*, 53 note 68, and De Felice, 1:527–32.

[40] Longo, *L'esercito italiano e la questione fiumana* (Rome, 1996), 569.

constituency.[41] But D'Annunzio's success in harnessing both the fanaticism of *interventisti* and junior officers and the postwar dissidence of much of the senior officer corps set a powerful example of "Garibaldian" patriotic disobedience that might yet apply within Italy as well as at Fiume. Conversely, Nitti's spineless toleration of the breakdown of the state's monopoly of force set an equally perilous precedent.[42]

III. Advent, Fragility, and Decay of the Weimar Republic

The background of external impotence on the one hand, and on the other the incessant and sometimes massive internal violence driven by ideological fanaticism and urgent social pressures, markedly restricted the choices of those who framed or reframed German and Italian politics in 1918–20. The men of the majority SPD faced the necessity for action first and most pressingly. Ebert and his colleagues had aimed at a democratic constitutional monarchy, and had reluctantly accepted the receivership of Imperial Germany. Scheidemann had proclaimed the Republic – against the wishes of Ebert, who in his own words hated revolution "as he hated sin" – to avoid losing control of the masses.[43] And virtually every step Ebert took as head of the provisional government aimed at averting the explosion of revolutionary violence that the Spartacists suicidally provoked.

Suicide with massive collateral damage was indeed the only course of which the SPD's enemies on the Left were capable in 1918–19. They had no Lenin. They had no Leninist vanguard-party. Their noisy invocation of the Soviet example failed to command a mass following in the spontaneous "Soldiers' and Workers' Councils," or *Räte*, that had sprung up across Germany. The essential revolutionary precondition of "dual power" – Petrograd Soviet against Provisional Government – that Lenin had first analyzed clear-sightedly, then exploited to launch his coup d'état, failed to materialize.[44] Instead, the Spartacists – transmuted into the KPD on 30 December 1918 – succeeded in reinforcing a preexisting but wholly different sort of dual power: Reich Government and Reichswehr.

If the SPD leaders could scarcely have avoided the bloodshed their enemies on the left sought, their failure in restraining the countervailing and far greater excesses of *Freikorps* and Reichswehr was overdetermined by the nature of the army and navy officer corps and the absence in the first months after the

---

[41] On the Fiume episode as a whole, see above all the balanced analysis of Vivarelli, *Origini*, 1:538–87 (quotation, 577), and Alatri, *Questione adriatica*. D'Annunzio's famous epithet for Nitti, *Cagoia*, means "slug" in Trieste dialect.

[42] D'Annunzio, despite characteristic rhetorical inflation, was not wholly wrong about Nitti; see the verdict ("a man fearful beyond words") of the King, in Paolo Puntoni, *Parla Vittorio Emanuele III* (Milan, 1958), 7.

[43] Max von Baden, *Erinnerungen*, 567.

[44] Lenin, *Collected Works*, 24:38–41.

revolution of alternative means of self-defense. The SPD's feeble attempts to create reliably social-democratic or even republican volunteer forces failed. The social roots of the old army were too deep; the army high command too determined and expert both militarily and politically; the rivalry and revolutionary enthusiasms of the Spartacists and USPD radicals too dangerous; and the yearning for peace of the SPD base too strong. The only happy warriors on the German Left in 1919–20 fought for revolutionary dictatorship.[45]

Yet Ebert, his colleagues, and his party were remarkably successful in four respects. First, on 15 November 1918 the SPD's trade union leaders laid the groundwork for the postwar boom that helped stabilize the Republic by clinching a framework agreement with the industrialists that prolonged the wartime collaboration of industry and labor. Industry conceded to the SPD unions a monopoly over the representation of industrial workers and – if adopted internationally – the eight-hour day. In return the industrialists received protection against visionary demands for state confiscation of factories and mines.[46] Second, the national conference of delegates from the *Räte* all across Germany that convened in Berlin in mid-December 1918 willingly accepted SPD leadership and democratic not Bolshevik rules. It voted by the crushing majority of 400 to 50 for the immediate election of a national constituent assembly. Third, in the national election consequently held with astounding speed and efficiency in mid-January 1919, the SPD and its two partners in the "Weimar Coalition" for a democratic republic, the Center and the Left-Liberals reincarnated as the German Democratic Party (DDP), secured an almost equally crushing majority: 72.4 percent of votes cast by Germany's men and – for the first time – women. And fourth, when the constituent assembly convened in February 1919 at Weimar, Goethe's tranquil domain, under the benevolent guard of *Generalmajor* Georg Maercker's Volunteer Light Infantry, that same majority elected Friedrich Ebert as Reich president. In due course the new constitution gave him powerful emergency powers, the famous Article 48, and prerogatives that had belonged to the Kaiser: the exclusive right to appoint and dismiss chancellors, to dissolve the Reichstag and to call new elections in the event of political impasse, and supreme command of the armed forces. For the next six years

---

45 On the failure of efforts to recruit reliably republican forces in and around Berlin, see in general Schulze, *Freikorps und Republik*, 13–21, 53–54. The often-invoked example of Vienna, where the Austrian SPD succeeded in dominating postwar chaos by creating its own militia, is irrelevant. Allied pressure on Austria was far less than on Germany; no command structure resembling Groener's staff had survived; and above all, the absence of extremist rivals on the Left other than a ragtag "Red Guard" made the recruitment of a republican "*Volkswehr*" unproblematic; details: Karl Glabauf, *Die Volkswehr 1918–19 und die Gründung der Republik* (Vienna, 1993).

46 Some literature, especially in the 1960s and 1970s, suggested that "socialization" of at least some industries – coal in particular – and land reform east of the Elbe might have strengthened the Republic in the long term, in view of the congenital authoritarianism of the German industrial and agrarian elites. But it seems unlikely that the resulting confusion and economic dislocation would have won friends for the new regime in 1918–19, or that state-owned industries would have furthered long-term economic growth.

Ebert used those powers with skill and dedication – and the Republic miraculously survived civil war, French invasion, and the death and resurrection of its currency.

These constitutional arrangements nevertheless contained flaws that interlocked dangerously with the characteristics – inherited and recently acquired – of Germany's political forces, state institutions, and civil society. Germany's history and mythology had overdetermined a strong presidency. The central notion of nineteenth-century "German constitutionalism," a mighty executive above parliament ostensibly balancing popular passions expressed through the legislature, was wired into the thinking even of Left-Liberals such as Hugo Preuss, German-Jewish jurist and preeminent "founding father" of Germany's first democracy. Max Weber, who advised Preuss in the drafting of the constitution, had long prized parliamentarism primarily as a means of selecting and training great leaders; he too sought a popularly elected executive with powers sufficient to underpin the authority of a charismatic plebiscitary Führer.[47] The unreformed Foreign Office, acting from inborn reverence for the "German way," likewise urged a strong presidency on the transparent and ironic claim that seeming imitation of the United States would weigh in Germany's favor at the peace. And even without the chorus of jurists, savants, and bureaucrats of winter 1918–19, the men of the majority SPD saw a strong presidency as a guarantee against regional separatism and France's ambition to recreate a new version of the first Napoleon's Rhenish vassal states.[48]

The presidency nevertheless proved a threefold snare. Ebert used his powers forcefully to defend and preserve the Republic; in other hands, those same powers might subvert and destroy it. Worse still, a strong directly elected presidency inevitably undermined parliamentary government. The chancellor's dependence on the president as well as on a Reichstag majority created a dangerous zone of ambiguity, and sapped the authority of the chancellorship. Finally, the Weimar presidency interacted fatefully with Germany's preexisting "five-party system" – now seven parties after the three-way splintering of the Socialists in 1916–17 – and with the uncompromising style of proportional representation introduced in the Reich electoral laws of 1919–20.

The new system, applied in outline in January 1919 and perfected for the June 1920 Reichstag election, ensured that an absolute minimum of valid votes went to waste. Any shade of opinion that could attract 60,000 votes in a single one of the Reich's thirty-five election districts would receive a Reichstag seat; thereafter as few as 30,000 votes elsewhere might ensure an additional seat.[49]

[47] See the merciless analysis of Wolfgang J. Mommsen, *Max Weber*, chs. 9–10; Weber was in this regard hardly alone among German scholars: Klaus Schreiner, "Politischer Messianismus, Führergedanke und Führererwartung in der Weimarer Republik," in Manfred Hettling, ed., *Was ist Gesellschaftsgeschichte? Positionen, Themen, Analysen* (Munich, 1991), 237–47.

[48] Peter Grupp and Pierre Jardin, "Das Auswärtige Amt und die Entstehung der Weimarer Verfassung," *Francia* 9 (1981), 473–93.

[49] Mechanics: Alfred Milatz, *Wähler und Wahlen in die Weimarer Republik* (Bonn, 1968), 45, 47–48, and especially the clarifications of Falter, HW, 126–27.

Over time, given even minimal political conflict and electoral volatility, the system guaranteed the progressive fragmentation of Germany's already fractured party spectrum, by so easing access to the Reichstag that all but the most absurd single-issue or particularist protest groups could gain a seat or two. Even before it began to operate, Bavaria's Catholics declared independence from the Center Party in defense of Bavaria's peculiarities and from fierce hostility to the Center's Socialist allies. German democracy thus began with eight major political forces. KPD and USPD stood on the far anti-republican Left; the Weimar Coalition of majority SPD, Center, and DDP supported the Republic; and the Bavarian People's Party (BVP), right-liberal German People's Party (DVP), and Conservatives and *völkische* of the German-National People's Party (DNVP) constituted a potentially or actively anti-republican Right. Then the electoral shredding-machine – with a mighty assist in 1922–23 from hyperinflation, with its encouragement of interest-group proliferation – began its operation. The parliament that emerged in 1928 from the forty-three parties or groups that contested the fourth Reichstag election contained representatives of fifteen parties.[50]

The system, among its many negative effects, broke the *Kaiserreich*'s direct links between Reichstag deputies and constituents, and correspondingly increased the power of the party bureaucracies, which alone could bestow places on the party lists that proportional representation entailed. But the Weimar electoral system's chief defect was that by creating a Reichstag that reproduced so faithfully German society's mortal conflicts, it made government based on a stable majority difficult except in quiet times. And the presidency, as an authority of last resort elected by the whole people and equipped with emergency law-making powers, allowed the parties a welcome and much-used escape from political responsibility, a republican counterpart to the monarchical executive that had malformed and stunted Germany's parties from their infancy.

Prussia, which from 1918 lacked a president primarily because Ebert not unreasonably refused to tolerate a rival in Berlin, demonstrated the impact of this structural factor on the chances of democracy in post-1918 Germany. Prussia constituted three-fifths of Germany and was thus in most respects a faithful political and social replica of the Reich. Yet from 1920 until 1932 it enjoyed stable parliamentary government under the Weimar coalition parties, with the assistance of the right-liberal DVP – largely because the Prussian constitution of 1919 gave the parties a stark choice: coalition or anarchy. The absence from Prussia's responsibilities of many of the foreign policy and fiscal predicaments that generated instability at the Reich level; the grudging preference of the

---

[50] Falter, HW, 128–35, offers statistical models of the outcomes using two obvious alternatives to Weimar's "pure" proportionality. The exclusion from parliament of all parties polling under 5 percent of the vote (as practiced later, for cause, by the German Federal Republic) would have given the Weimar Coalition an absolute majority until July 1932 – although the "anti-system coalition" of KPD and NSDAP would nevertheless have enjoyed an absolute majority thereafter. The Anglo-American single-member constituency first-past-the-post system would have had similar effects, at least up to 1932.

Prussian Center Party (unlike its Bavarian counterpart) for the SPD as coalition partner over the DNVP (which had given moral support to Kapp and to the murderers of Erzberger and of Rathenau); and almost twelve years of firm leadership under Prussia's durable version of Friedrich Ebert, minister-president Otto Braun of the SPD, all helped. But Prussia's pure parliamentarism contributed decisively to forcing coherent government on a fiercely resisting society.[51]

If the German Republic's constitutional structures and electoral arrangements militated against stable democratic politics, the fundamental attitudes of the German people ultimately made such politics virtually impossible. The seemingly crushing majority for a democratic republic of January 1919 proved to be one of the many illusions of the revolutionary interlude. Military defeat and the monarchy's inglorious collapse had temporarily cowed much of the Right. The KPD for the moment preferred machine-gun fire to ballots. And large numbers of Germans had voted tactically. In particular, many of the 18.6 percent of the electorate that chose the DDP in January 1919 were far less interested in a democratic Germany than – as a DDP deputy put it – in an "insurance policy" against Leftist massacre.[52]

The election of June 1920, the first under the new constitution, dispelled most illusions. The Reichstag seats held by the Weimar Coalition parties shrank from 78 percent of the total to less than 44 percent. Correspondingly, the anti-system fanatics and revolutionary dissidents of DNVP, USPD, and KPD took more than a third of the seats in the legislature of the German Republic. The Reichstag elections of the decade that followed demonstrated the extent to which this was no passing electoral mood created by Versailles, reparations, Kapp Putsch, and Ruhr uprising, but rather a durable expression of the will of the German people (see Figure 4.3).

The Weimar Coalition never lastingly regained its lost majority. In the immediately following election of May 1924, anti-system forces pulled almost even with the Republic's defenders at 40 percent of Reichstag seats, making Germany largely ungovernable through parliament, and necessitating a new election seven months later. The December 1924 outcome allowed the formation of functioning if transitory coalitions, sometimes including resentful DNVP participation or support, and inaugurated Weimar's period of uneasy stabilization.[53]

The presidential election that followed Ebert's untimely death in February 1925 – from acute appendicitis left untended while defending against ludicrous

[51] See particularly the astute analysis of Horst Möller, "Les deux voies du parlamentarisme allemand. La Prusse et le Reich dans la République de Weimar," *Francia* 14 (1986), 461–73; context: Schulze, *Otto Braun: oder Preussens demokratische Sendung* (Frankfurt am Main, 1977); Dietrich Orlow, *Weimar Prussia, 1918–1925: The Unlikely Rock of Democracy* (Pittsburgh, 1985); idem, *Weimar Prussia, 1925–1933: The Illusion of Strength* (Pittsburgh, 1991); for society's resistance, see especially Detlev Lehnert, "Propaganda des Bürgerkrieges?"

[52] "Lebensversicherungspolice bei der befürchteten Bartholomäusnacht": Anton Erkelenz, in Winkler, *Weimar*, 139.

[53] Stürmer, *Coalition und Opposition in der Weimarer Republik 1924–1928* (Düsseldorf, 1967), offers a useful guide to Weimar's precarious interlude of quasi-stability.

FIGURE 4.3. Rise, Decline, and Triumph of the "Anti-System" Vote

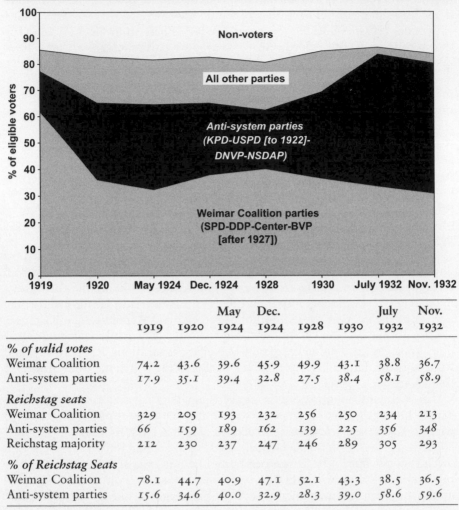

	1919	1920	May 1924	Dec. 1924	1928	1930	July 1932	Nov. 1932
% of valid votes								
Weimar Coalition	74.2	43.6	39.6	45.9	49.9	43.1	38.8	36.7
Anti-system parties	17.9	35.1	39.4	32.8	27.5	38.4	58.1	58.9
Reichstag seats								
Weimar Coalition	329	205	193	232	256	250	234	213
Anti-system parties	66	159	189	162	139	225	356	348
Reichstag majority	212	230	237	247	246	289	305	293
% of Reichstag Seats								
Weimar Coalition	78.1	44.7	40.9	47.1	52.1	43.3	38.5	36.5
Anti-system parties	15.6	34.6	40.0	32.9	28.3	39.0	58.6	59.6

Base data: Falter, WA, 44.

but wounding charges of high treason brought by his tireless anti-republican opponents – made clear how few Germans loved their Republic. It also delineated the background constraints on free expression of the population's ideological passions. The Center refused to support an SPD candidate.[54] The SPD, which in November 1923 had left the government of the Republic it had founded rather than share responsibility for disciplining leftist extremism in Saxony and Thuringia, and shunned the Reich cabinet until 1928, preempted

54 Hans Mommsen, *Aufstieg und Untergang der Republik von Weimar* (Munich, 2004), 292.

FIGURE 4.4. For or Against the Republic? The First Round, 29 March 1925

	% of Popular Vote	Marx +Braun	Marx +Braun +Hellpach	Jarres +Held +Ludendorff	Jarres +Held +Ludendorff +Thälmann
Braun (SPD)	29.0				
Marx (Center)	14.5				
Hellpach (DDP)	5.8				
Jarres (DVP-DNVP "Reichsblock")	38.8				
Held (BVP)	3.7				
Ludendorff (völkische)	1.0				
Thälmann (KPD)	7.0				
Others	0.1				
For Weimar		43.5	49.4		
Against Weimar				43.6	50.6

Note: Actual or potential anti-system candidates in italics.
Base data: Falter, WA, 46.

further efforts at a common Weimar Coalition candidate by announcing the candidacy of Otto Braun on 7 March 1925. Stresemann as leader of the DVP vetoed the possible center-Right unity candidacy of his cabinet colleague, *Reichswehrminister* Otto Gessler of the DDP, because Gessler's close ties to the armed forces and to their evasions of Versailles might provoke French and British antagonism. The major parties followed the SPD example (see Figure 4.4).[55]

The Weimar Coalition thus ran against itself as well as against the Right's worthy but colorless candidate, the DVP mayor of Duisburg, Karl Jarres: Braun for the SPD, the once-and-future chancellor Wilhelm Marx for the Center, and Willy Hellpach for the DDP. Yet the combined vote totals of the three Weimar Coalition candidates fell short of the absolute majority necessary for first-round victory, even without the likelihood that a republican unity candidate would have repelled toward Right or Left at least some of the three parties' voters. Conversely, the forces of the moderate to radical Right – BVP, DVP, DNVP, and *völkische* – when added to the KPD's 7 percent for the Communist Party leader, Ernst Thälmann, reached an absolute majority of 50.6 percent. The first-round result admirably represented Weimar's paralyzing crossfire of antagonisms, and demonstrated yet again the minority status of German democracy.

In the end a candidate commanding a decisive plurality emerged. The illogical and politically innocent presidential electoral law of 1924–25 allowed any candidate – even one who had not contested the first ballot – to run in the

---

[55] On Stresemann and Gessler – and the Right's 1925 search for a candidate capable of subverting the Republic from above, Noel D. Cary, "The Making of the Reich President, 1925: German Conservatism and the Nomination of Paul Von Hindenburg," CEH 23:2–3 (1990), 179–204.

FIGURE 4.5. Against the Republic: The Election of Paul Ludwig Hans
Anton von Beneckendorff und von Hindenburg, 26 April 1925

	% of Popular Vote	Hindenburg +Thälmann
Hindenburg ("Reichsblock": DNVP-DVP-BVP)	48.3	
Marx ("*Volksblock*": Center-SPD-DDP)	45.3	
Thälmann (KPD)	6.4	
Against Weimar		*54.7*

Note: Anti-system candidates in italics.
Base data: Falter, WA, 46.

second.[56] Deadlock in the first round and tireless lobbying by the wily Tirpitz
thus propelled the "old field marshal," Paul von Hindenburg, hesitantly forward into the vacuum the parties had created. Hindenburg's candidacy in place
of Jarres at last offered a charismatic symbol – if not the longed-for charismatic
Führer – to those hostile or skeptical toward the German Republic (see Figure 4.5). Nevertheless, as a DNVP house organ noted in reassurance of nervous voters, Hindenburg would bring no "imprudent change" to German foreign policy; fear of the Western powers was evidently an electoral factor for
others beside Stresemann.[57]

Hindenburg neither campaigned nor proclaimed a political program. He
was "*his own program*."[58] His "*Reichsblock*" constituted the largest group of
voters yet assembled behind a single candidate in the Republic's short history.
And his plurality was no sudden transitory statistical artifact. The geographic
distribution of Hindenburg's support, from the Bavarian Alpine foothills to the
windswept flatlands of the north and east, faithfully reproduced the rightist and
right-radical vote of the December 1924 Reichstag election, and offered a template for the day when the north-German Protestant nationalist majority culture
and its Bavarian Catholic-*völkisch* allies at last found the avenging Führer for
whom they hungered.[59] Even more ominous for the Republic than Hindenburg's
victory itself was the negative majority of almost 55 percent against the hated
"System" that Hindenburg and Thälmann together commanded.

Germany thus received its first head of state elected by the entire people: a
president of the Republic who for all his demonstrable inertia was no republican
at all. His inclinations could only become effective in a major crisis that would

[56] Text in Milatz, *Wähler und Wahlen*, 51–53.
[57] Cary, "The Making of the Reich President," 199.
[58] Oskar Hergt, a founder of the DNVP, in ibid., 201 (italics in original).
[59] See Milatz, *Wähler und Wahlen*, maps 2 (religion) and 7 (distribution of the 1925 Hindenburg vote); Jürgen W. Falter, "The Two Hindenburg Elections of 1925 and 1932: A Total
Reversal of Voter Coalitions," CEH 23:2–3 (1990), especially 229, 231–32; and Falter, HW,
357–61.

require the invocation of his emergency powers. Yet initially no crisis arose. The Weimar Coalition, thanks to a rapprochement between BVP and Center Party, secured a bare majority of Reichstag seats in the 1928 election, and the extremists correspondingly dipped briefly below 30 percent (see Figure 4.3). The resulting Grand Coalition from SPD to DVP under Hermann Müller of the SPD (June 1928–March 1930) appeared to minimize Hindenburg's opportunities for intervention. Yet appearances were deceptive. The long-established inflexibility of Germany's political forces; their often deep internal divisions; their perpetual exposure to flank attack from extremist competitors; and their reluctance to take responsibility for unpopular government measures made Müller's success predictably transitory.

The middle-class parties largely lacked the organizational frameworks required to aggregate the interests and ideologies of the population. Most parties had at least two dogmatically distinct and opposed wings, and harbored numerous interest-group lobbies whose intersecting demands produced or reinforced stalemate. Parliamentary groups quarreled with their party's ministers, while factions in the party base attacked one or both. Only Stresemann's indefatigable statesmanship and relative foreign policy success held the DVP's moderates and hard-line industrial interests together. The SPD, despite – or because of – Ebert's skill and resolve in defending the Republic, had lost contact with much of its base during the civil war of 1918–23. When the USPD collapsed in 1922 from its leaders' incompetence and the competition of the KPD, most USPD voters deserted to the Communists, whose hatred and contempt for the Republic was consistent and total from 1918 to 1990. The USPD's former leaders returned sheepishly to the majority SPD fold, where they served as a lobby for the leftist sentimentalism that defied Müller's statesmanship and – along with the ferocity of the Right – made Weimar's preservation increasingly difficult. The Center Party was infinitely more democratic than its spiritual guide in the Vatican, and attached to the power it shared with the SPD in Prussia. But it also possessed a powerful right wing perpetually pulling it toward DVP and DNVP at the national level. The only party that unconditionally supported German democracy was the DDP, which declined from a scant 8.28 percent of the popular vote in 1920 to 3.78 in 1930 before almost vanishing in the final elections: a sad career that testified to the numerical insignificance of non-Socialist, non-Catholic German democrats.

Along with "coalition fatigue" – the yearning for freedom to pander in opposition to favored constituencies and interest groups – three changes within the parties in 1928–29 rendered both the Grand Coalition and any conceivable replacement problematic. On the right, the egregious Alfred Hugenberg, lord of press and film and founding member of the Pan-Germans, secured control of the DNVP in October 1928. He committed the party to implacable enmity to the Republic, and ejected the DNVP's few moderates, ruling out the already improbable expedient of a future "bourgeois coalition" from Center to DNVP. That December, Prelate Ludwig Kaas, a priest who celebrated and shared the "call for Führerdom in the grand style" of the "German *Volk*-soul," replaced the

republican ex-chancellor Wilhelm Marx as leader of the Center Party.[60] Worst
of all, Stresemann died on 3 October 1929, a month before the Wall Street
crash. Like Ebert, he had held the Republic and his own party together; like
Ebert, he arguably died from the strain. His departure unleashed the DVP's right
wing against the SPD in cabinet, while rising unemployment and declining tax
receipts, as the Depression slowly deepened, made mortal conflict between the
parties of the Grand Coalition inevitable. That clash, when it occurred, would
hand to Paul Ludwig Hans Anton von Beneckendorff und von Hindenburg the
fate of parliamentary government in Germany.

Like the aged field marshal, the German state that his following had bestowed
upon him in 1925 was not republican either. Ebert and his colleagues of 1918–19
had ensured, not wholly intentionally, an astounding continuity. Under pressure
from the Allies; under attack by armed Spartacists and assorted revolutionaries
in Berlin; facing the imperative need to bring home and demobilize the army,
feed the population, and restart the economy, they had called upon the officer
corps and bureaucracy for support in the name of a shared German patriotism.
Perhaps that reluctance to improvise in the space of a few months a new army
and state on republican principles resulted – as the academic critics of the 1960s
often charged – from the innate timidity and state-piety of a cohort of stolid
trade unionists and parliamentarians who until October 1918 had aspired at
most to the role of loyal opposition.

Yet Communist violence and Kerensky's fate the previous year was enough
to foster caution in bolder men than Ebert. And on the positive side, the very
deliquescence of the old order, as dynasties that had ruled for up to a thousand
years vanished overnight, sapped the majority SPD's sense of urgency. Not
until Rathenau's murder in 1922 did a chancellor – Wirth of the Center – point
accusingly at the DNVP and *völkisch* benches, and proclaim that "[t]here is the
enemy; . . . this enemy stands on the Right."[61] Above all, Berlin 1918 was *not*
Petrograd 1917. Germany was an industrial giant and in most ways the most
advanced society in Europe. Within its highly articulated social structures, the
organized working classes scarcely constituted a minority; even in 1919 their
fiercely divided parties together commanded only 45.5 percent of the vote,
and declined sharply thereafter. No German revolution could survive without
"bourgeois" and aristocratic know-how, nor could it evade that expertise's
political price.

The permanent institutions of the German Reich – a proud name that the
national constituent assembly refused to relinquish – thus survived the collapse
of the *Kaiserreich*. The state bureaucracy fared best, achieving the astounding feat of persuading its new masters to write into the constitution itself its
"well-earned rights" to lifetime jobs and perquisites. Especially after the Kapp
Putsch had revealed wide disloyalty among the county administrators of eastern Germany, the Reich and Prussian governments reformed recruitment, and

---

[60] Kaas quotation: Winkler, *Weimar*, 343–44.
[61] Scheidemann had apparently devised the slogan in September 1919.

sought over the long term to remodel the administrative civil service as a republican or at least politically neutral force. But the Republic failed to break the quasi-monopoly in the administrative service of university-trained and thus almost invariably nationalist jurists, despite some reduction in the recruitment of duelling-fraternity "old boys."[62] The judges of the *Kaiserreich* retained their invulnerability to dismissal, and merrily freed the murderers of the Right while pursuing with pertinacity the misdeeds of the Left.[63] And even the bureaucracy's lower levels, after decades of recruitment from retired NCOs, retained a decidedly nationalist-military cast.

The armed forces themselves fared in a sense far worse: the collapse of the old army and the reduction of the career officer corps from the 34,000 active-duty survivors of 1914–18 to the treaty-authorized 4,000 was a break in tradition even more extreme than the sweeping purge carried out in 1806–08, after Napoleon's victory over Prussia at Jena-Auerstädt. The navy's passage to Weimar was even more traumatic than the army's. The mutiny of crews of the High Seas Fleet; the Fleet's internment and scuttling; the strictures of the Treaty; and the navy's open partisanship for Kapp's bungling left the junior service with a shattered reputation, its three senior commanders forcibly retired, a mere 1,500 officers and 13,500 men recruited in large part from the *Freikorps* of Ehrhardt and Löwenfeld, and no mission.

Yet all was very far from lost. Groener and Seeckt between them ensured that "young, energetic, and modern officers," seasoned in war, primarily from the general staff and thus already selected as the old army's best brains, furnished most of the chosen 4,000.[64] The 100,000-man army was thus no mere dwarf-copy of its monarchical progenitor, but something new and far more dangerous: the concentrated essence, unintentionally distilled by the restrictions of "shameful Treaty" itself, of the most innovative, craftsmanlike, narrow, reckless, willful, ruthless, independent, and implacably nationalist officer corps in Eurasia and the world. The navy similarly preserved sovereignty over its personnel decisions, and its calculated use of the naval *Freikorps* as its bloodstock guaranteed a force built on anti-republican hatreds and nationalist resentments even more pitiless than the army's.

Worse still, revolution had in effect emancipated the armed forces from all authority. Neither Ebert nor the aged Hindenburg could or did fill the shoes of the "All-Highest Warlord." Noske failed to tame Lüttwitz and Ehrhardt; his

---

[62] See Wehler, DGG, 4:361–63.

[63] See Emil Julius Gumbel, *Vier Jahre politischer Mord* (Berlin, 1922) and *Verräter verfallen der Feme: Opfer, Morder, Richter, 1919–1929* (Berlin, 1929); and the more nuanced Irmela Nagel, *Fememorde und Fememordprozesse in der Weimarer Republik* (Cologne, 1991).

[64] Groener to Noske, 14 August 1919, and Groener to Ebert, 17 September 1919, in Dieter Dreetz, "Denkschrift der deutschen Obersten Heeresleitung vom 17. September 1919 über die Reichswehr und deren Rolle bei Schaffung einer Imperialistischen deutschen Grossmacht," *Militärgeschichte* 21 (1982), 607–08, 603; Heinz Hürten, "Das Offizierkorps des Reichsheeres," in Hanns Hubert Hofmann, ed., *Das deutsche Offizierkorps 1860–1960* (Boppard, 1980), 232–34.

successor Gessler tacitly accepted Seeckt's boast that the army *was* the state, and covered the Reichswehr's clandestine doings without demur. Seeckt's sudden removal in October 1926 – ostensibly because he had allowed the son of the despised former crown prince to assist in uniform at field exercises, but actually because Hindenburg as well as Gessler resented his insufferable arrogance – made no difference to the army's independence from control.[65] Gessler was the Republic's last civilian *Reichswehrminister*; he departed in turn in early 1928, after the navy's misuse of secret rearmament funds embroiled him in scandal. His successor was Groener, masquerading as a civilian, yet as in 1918–19 giving substance through his organizational skills to Hindenburg's position as commander-in-chief, in pursuit of the army's vision of a new war in which it would command the entire resources of state and society.

Like the armed forces, Germany's elites – nobility, *Bildungsbürgertum* and professions, business magnates, technical experts, and managers – regarded the post-1918 order with emotions that ranged from distaste to vengeful hatred. With the fall of the monarchy and princely houses, Germany's 95,000 nobles lost their status as *Stände* enshrined in law; the Republic's willingness to tolerate the continued use of titles as part of family names gained it no thanks.[66] Even more vexing was the loss both of traditional noble predominance in the state administration and at least 9,000 of the 30,000 career army officer places abolished by the Treaty; the miniature Reichswehr officer corps accommodated only 900 nobles. Nevertheless, noble landownership showed remarkable persistence, despite the loss of the great estates of Posen and "Polish Corridor," and the Republic's belated abolition in 1927 of the *Rittergut*'s status as a unit of local government and legal jurisdiction. As of 1925, the nobility still controlled roughly 13 percent of Germany's arable land, with a regional concentration in the Prussian East that reached 27.8 percent in Pomerania and 30 percent in Silesia.[67]

The *Bildungsbürgertum*'s traditional closeness to the state did not extend to a state decapitated by revolution, recast in accordance with the "inauthentic" principles of Western liberalism, dominated by political parties that by their nature divided the *Volk*, in thrall to the SPD, and responsible for the destruction of the currency in which their savings, war bonds, annuities,

---

[65] Hans Meier-Welcker, *Seeckt* (Frankfurt am Main, 1967), 501–22. Post, *Civil-Military Fabric*, 93–97, argues that the limited cooperation between the services, foreign ministry, and cabinet on national defense from 1925 onward indicated Reichswehr acceptance of the Republic and of a measure of civilian control. Reichswehr cooperation with the Republic reflected budgetary necessity, the army's inescapable need for civilian help in the total mobilization of the nation's resources for future war, and the apparent absence of alternatives to Weimar; it did not alter the character of both army and navy as institutions independent of the transitory post-1918 form of the German state.

[66] Article 109 of the Weimar constitution: "All Germans are equal before the law. . . . Privileges or disabilities in public law due to birth or *Stand* are abolished. Titles of nobility henceforth serve merely as parts of names, and will no longer be conferred."

[67] Wehler, DGG, 4:323–31 and Malinowski, *Vom König zum Führer*, especially 200–01, 282–93.

and dividends were denominated. The learned professions were increasingly overcrowded; new arrivals from the universities, at 30,000 a year, outnumbered departures into retirement by up to three to one. The resulting academic proletariat was thrice-hostile to the Republic: through its largely middle-class German-national background; through its training in a university system in which faculties and student bodies burned with anti-Socialist, anti-Semitic, and anti-republican resentments; and through its subsequent inability to find positions appropriate to its own high – and not unreasonable – estimate of its talents.[68]

The business and industrial elites soon recovered from their 1918 fright, and increasingly denounced or challenged a political order that had forced on them compulsory arbitration of labor disputes, welfare state contributions far heavier than under the *Kaiserreich*, and numerous other restrictions on their untrammelled sovereignty over factories and mines. Ruhr crisis and hyperinflation erased the industrialists' debts and offered a welcome chance, swiftly exploited, to throw off the shackles of the eight-hour day. And the industrialists' underlying hostility to the post-1918 "trade-union state," although outwardly attenuated by the need to lobby bureaucracy and Reichstag, remained vigorous even during Weimar's four years of relative stability and prosperity from 1925 to 1928. In late 1928 the Ruhr steel barons, with backing from other branches of industry, declared independence from the Republic in definitive form by rebuffing wage demands with a lockout, then ignoring government-arbitrated settlements.

The working classes likewise found little to love in the new state. Germany's inflation-fuelled postwar boom lasted into 1922, and allowed industrial workers to recover some of the ground in real wages lost during the war, while lowering unemployment drastically. However, by summer 1923 hyperinflation had reduced industrial real wages to 48 percent of those of 1913. Currency stabilization, along with the Republic's brief midlife era of growth and the temporary recovery of real income to the 1913 level, brought structural unemployment that in 1926 reached as high as 13.4 of the insured labor force.[69] As for the peasantry, the Great War had left it savagely distrustful of both state and townsfolk. The Republic, to feed the cities, retained at least some of the *Kaiserreich*'s wartime price-control and requisitioning mechanisms until 1923–24, and thus damned itself irremediably in peasant eyes. The SPD, unlike its Italian counterpart, found the countryside inhospitable; membership in its agricultural unions peaked at around one million in 1921, and descended to a derisory 200,000 thereafter. Weimar's extension of social protection and collective bargaining rights to agricultural laborers nevertheless aroused the hostility

---

[68] Konrad H. Jarausch, "The Crisis of the German Professions 1918–1933," *JCH* 20:2 (1985), 379–98 offers a useful introduction.

[69] For the wide variety of ways of measuring unemployment, and comparison of Weimar Germany with Britain and the United States, see Theo Balderston, *The Origins and Course of the German Economic Crisis* (Berlin, 1993), 2–3, 9–13.

of the rural majority, from estate owners to smallholding families with a need for hired hands.[70] Nor did the erasure of mortgage debts by hyperinflation reconcile the peasantry to the new order. The Republic's subsequent inaction in the steadily worsening world agricultural slump after 1926/27 led to revolt in Schleswig-Holstein in 1927–29, complete with spectacular bombings of tax offices organized with technical assistance from Ehrhardt's terrorists.[71] Finally, demography and economics affected all social groups in ways that powerfully discouraged republican loyalty. Until 1924–25, the unusually large prewar birth-cohorts from 1890 to 1913 were startlingly mismatched with the shrunken and chaotic postwar job market. The eldest of those thus "dispossessed" had served in the Great War; the superimposition of the hatred of "front" for "rear" on top of the generational divide thus gave the contempt of German youth for their elders an additional – politically operative – sharpness. And after 1930 the Great Depression closed down opportunities even for members of wartime birth-cohorts that were less than half as large, by 1917, as those of years such as 1911.[72]

Despite all hardships, Germany's luxuriant organizational underbrush nevertheless enjoyed rapid growth after 1918. War, revolution, and violent aftermath had freed Germans to an unprecedented extent to express their views both individually and as organized groups.[73] Postwar inflation and the hyperinflation of 1922–23 encouraged the proliferation of noisy single-interest lobbies, on top of and intersecting with Germany's already highly organized interest groups. Few interest-group organizations supported the Republic from principle; hard times through 1924 and after 1929 ensured that fewer still did so from perceived self-interest. At the local level, networks of associations – hiking, cycling, singing, gymnastics, and shooting clubs, civic associations, and the inevitable *Kriegervereine* – enveloped small-town Germany. This warm organizational blanket could be as thick as one formally constituted club or association to every sixty-three inhabitants. Even the career criminals of Germany's great cities had their *Vereine*, with detailed regulations, meetings, dues, celebrations, beer evenings, and reserved group tables (*Stammtische*).[74] Yet for all Weimar's

---

[70] See Gregory M. Luebbert, "Social Foundations of Political Order in Interwar Europe," *World Politics* 39:4 (1987), 473–74.

[71] Wehler, DGG, 4:355–58; on the immediate postwar period, see especially Robert G. Moeller, *German Peasants and Agrarian Politics, 1914–1924: The Rhineland and Westphalia* (Chapel Hill, NC, 1986), and idem, "Winners as Losers in the German Inflation: Peasant Protest over the Controlled Economy, 1920–1923," in Feldman et al., eds., *Die deutsche Inflation: Eine Zwischenbilanz* (New York, 1982), 255–88.

[72] Generations: SGAB, 3:32; Wehler, DGG, 4:235–36; Peukert, *Weimar*, 15 (a vivid diagram), 87–88, 94.

[73] See especially Peter Fritzsche, *Rehearsals for Fascism: Populism and Political Mobilization in Weimar Germany* (New York, 1990), chs. 2–3, 5; and idem, *Germans into Nazis*, especially 107–36.

[74] Koshar, *Social Life, Local Politics, and Nazism*, 130; Patrick Wagner, "Feindbild 'Berufsverbrecher': Die Kriminalpolizei im Übergang von der Weimarer Republik zum Nationalsozialismus," in Frank Bajohr, Werner Johe, and Uwe Lohalm, eds., *Zivilisation und Barbarei*.

celebrated toleration of aesthetic, sexual, and political experimentation, its organizational subcultures remained almost uniformly German-national or even overtly *völkisch* in flavor, with the exception of organizations within the Socialist or Communist orbits and tiny minorities such as Weimar's forlorn and despised pacifist movement.

Among Germany's 110,000 university students, racist radicalism in the form of a newly founded general association of student clubs, the *Deutsche Hochschulring*, came by 1921–22 to dominate both university elections and the state-supported national *Deutsche Studentenschaft*. The *Hochschulring* embraced virtually all important fraternities, including Catholic ones, and explicitly excluded students of Jewish descent. That rule it imposed in principle on the *Studentenschaft* as well. When the Prussian Ministry of Culture threatened in 1926 to eliminate the national organization's state funding unless it rescinded the "Aryan clause," a student referendum throughout Prussia delivered – in heavy voting – a racist majority of 77 percent. The duelling fraternities, despite the republican authorities' anxious disapproval of their face-scarring rituals, gained in standing as the Republic's declined. After 1930 the student *"Corps"* embraced eight out of ten male students, and six of ten belonged to a "fighting fraternity." This was a generation of professionals and intelligentsia-to-be whose passionate "unconditional will to deeds," though as yet repressed by Weimar, was no sham.[75]

God likewise remained a German; roughly 80 percent of Germany's 18,000 pastors had belonged to the *Vaterlandspartei*; under Weimar 80 percent voted DNVP.[76] Protestantism's seamless identification since 1866 and before with the monarchy and the national cause ensured that in Protestant eyes armistice, revolution, and Republic were mere Bolshevist-Asiatic betrayal and usurpation. Cut loose, like the armed forces, from their organizational and emotional moorings to the sovereign, the Protestants sought a new focus for loyalty. They inevitably found it in even greater devotion to that preeminent "idea of God," the transcendent German *Volk*. The long-term erosion of pastoral influence through

---

Die widersprüchlichen Potentiale der Moderne, Detlev Peukert zum Gedenken (Hamburg, 1991), 236–38.

[75] It may seem gratuitously teleological to single out, from a wide literature, two especially fine discussions of 1920s student affairs during the "bright college years" of the future SD and RSHA leadership: Ulrich Herbert, *Best: Biographische Studien über Radikalismus, Weltanschauung und Vernunft 1903–1989* (Bonn, 1996), ch. 1, and Michael Wildt, *Generation des Unbedingten: Das Führungskorps des Reichssicherheitshauptamtes* (Hamburg, 2001), 72–142 (quotation, Heinz Gräfe, later a key RSHA Soviet expert, 1932: ibid., 128, 136). But perhaps not. The correspondence between student beliefs – *both* of the later SS elite *and* of the broader German university population of 1918–33 – and 1940s outcomes is merely *one* illustration of the sovereign force of ideology. For the *"schlagende Verbindungen"* under the Republic, see especially Frevert, *Ehrenmänner*, 247–52; for student anti-Semitism in the wider German universe of racist organizations and ideologies, Lohalm, *Völkischer Radikalismus*, 164–70, and Herbert, "'Generation der Sachlichkeit': Die völkische Studentenbewegung der frühen zwanziger Jahre in Deutschland," in Bajohr et al., eds., *Zivilisation und Barbarei*, 115–44.

[76] Estimates cited as reliable by Wehler, DGG, 4:438.

urbanization and the break-up or weakening of traditional communities left the Protestant hierarchy predisposed to engage its constituency through nationalist fervor, in the widely shared hope of a new Führer to assume the mantle of the failed monarchy and at last heal the spiritual and political fragmentation of the German *Volk*. The more extreme took to speculating, following precedents set by anti-Semites throughout the previous century, that Christ simply could not have been Jewish. The mainstream irrevocably damned the Republic and all its works.[77]

The Catholic Church's organizational independence protected it and its sub-culture from much of the disorientation found in the Protestant *Lager*. The Church's millennial doctrine of rendering "unto Caesar that which is Caesar's" had from the 1890s applied to the Prusso-German monarchy if not yet to the Piedmontese-Italian one. But it offered the German Republic small com-fort. Catholic politicians might cooperate with Ebert and Otto Braun. Yet the Church, in the person of Cardinal Archbishop Michael von Faulhaber of Munich, onetime reserve officer, wartime chaplain-general of the Bavarian army, and one of Germany's two highest prelates, famously damned the revolu-tion as "perjury and high treason" and reviled a Republic thus "branded with the mark of Cain." Only a national Concordat that pledged the state in perpetu-ity to respect Church autonomy and perquisites might perhaps secure a belated absolution. But Weimar proved unwilling to grant satisfactory terms. The Cen-ter Party's already feeble democratic beliefs eroded as the Republic's position deteriorated after 1928. And the Munich Soviet interlude of 1919 had given south German Catholicism a lasting and bitter anti-Bolshevik, anti-Semitic, and anti-Republican edge.[78]

IV. The Dissolution of Liberal Italy, 1919–1921

Italy's postwar crisis began without revolutionary fireworks, despite the grad-ual increase in background intensity of its civil war. Victory, however mutilated, ensured the continuity of the state in even greater measure than in Germany. The thirst for a new democratic beginning, a constituent assembly to revise the out-worn quasi-autocratic *Statuto* of 1848, was widespread among left-*interventisti* and democratic elements within political Catholicism – but virtually nowhere else. Against the hostility of king, Senate, Liberal governing class, and armed forces, proposals for a *costituente* to recast Italy stood no chance.

Yet Italy nevertheless suffered in 1919 a discontinuity as severe as Germany's 1918 revolution and 1920 election rolled into one: the faithful if belated imposi-tion on parliament of Italian society's irreconcilable divisions between Liberals, Catholics, and Socialists.[79] That break with the past was if anything sharper

---

77 Elegant summary: Wehler, DGG, 4:436–45 ("Das deutsche Volk ist...eine Idee Gottes," 440).

78 Wehler, DGG, 4:445–50; quotation, Ludwig Volk S.J., "Kardinal Faulhaber's Stellung zur Weimarer Republik und zum NS-Staat," *Stimmen der Zeit* 177 (1966), 177.

79 "Terremoto": Giovanni Sabbatucci, in Sabbatucci and Vittorio Vidotto, eds., *Storia d'Italia. Guerre e fascismo 1914–1943* (Rome, 1998), 116.

than the collapse of the German ruling houses; the Reich's new republican order, for all the revolutionary drama of its origins, merely imposed on parties and tendencies already seasoned by universal suffrage the impossible requirement that they govern. In Italy by contrast the belated coupling of unrestricted universal suffrage to a system that was *parliamentary* but had never been *representative* produced instantaneous and abiding deadlock. The Liberal executive – partially disconnected in 1915 from a cowed parliament by the mobs of "radiant May"; the high-handedness of Salandra, Sonnino, and Victor Emmanuel III; and the unending emergency of the Great War – failed to reconnect.

Giolitti had sought to harness the masses in 1912–13 by enfranchising illiterate males at age thirty. In 1918 Orlando eliminated that age restriction, expanding the electorate to 31 percent of the population: no literacy test had denied the *contadini* the privilege of dying for Italy. In summer 1919 Orlando's successor, Nitti, in turn accepted as inevitable the proportional representation that the mass parties demanded. It might preserve Liberal bastions in the North and Center that would otherwise succumb to the onslaught of the Socialists and of the Catholic *Partito popolare italiano* (PPI or *"popolari"*) founded in January 1919. Nitti and his colleagues nevertheless sought to temper the impact of proportionality, especially on their traditional fiefs in the South and islands, with a variety of ingenious mechanisms designed to give voters choices other than the straight party lists favored by the two mass parties. The law also consciously penalized splinter parties, rather than following its German counterpart's merciless precision in registering political and social fragmentation.[80] And in any event, Nitti's law only governed the elections of November 1919 and May 1921; its long-term effects, unlike those of its Weimar counterpart, remain conjectural.

Liberal Italy's postwar crisis was thus above all the product of the ideological fixations and political peculiarities of the Liberal majority culture and of the Socialist and Catholic subcultures themselves. When the inflated expectations of "Roman victory" that Orlando had frivolously cultivated to stabilize his cabinet

---

[80] See Serge Noiret, *La nascita del sistema dei partiti nell'Italia contemporanea: La proporzionale del 1919* (Bari, 1994), ch. 1, and Sabbatucci, "La crisi del sistema politico liberale," in Fabio Grassi Orsini and Gaetano Quagliariello, eds., *Il partito politico dalla grande guerra al fascismo* (Bologna, 1996), 255–58, for the debate over the law's effect; Maranini, *Storia del Potere*, 283–84, and Ghisalberti, *Storia costituzionale*, 331–34, for the claim that proportional representation was a decisive factor in Liberal defeat. Conversely, Giusti, *Le correnti politiche*, 37–43, and Noiret, *La proporzionale del 1919*, 195–209, and idem, "Riforme elettorali e crisi dello Stato liberale. La 'proporzionale' 1918–1919," IC 174 (1989), 29–51, offer persuasive simulations that suggest that the culprit was universal suffrage, and that proportional representation actually limited the Liberal débâcle of November 1919. For the major departures of the Italian law from "pure" proportionality, see Noiret, *La proporzionale del 1919*, ch. 4, and 74–75: (i) a simplified version of the d'Hondt system (a Belgian contrivance that eliminates lists with vote totals below an arithmetically determined threshold, or "quotient," of votes in a given district); (ii) write-in changes to party lists; (iii) an "additional vote," for each voter bestowable upon a single individual candidate; and (iv) preference votes for individuals within a given list. In addition, Italy's fifty-four electoral districts (1919) were smaller than their thirty-seven (1919; thirty-five thereafter) German counterparts, to the slight disadvantage of the Italian mass parties.

FIGURE 4.6. The Caporetto of Liberalism: 16 November 1919

The Chamber of Deputies, 1913–21	1913	% of Seats 1913	1919	% of Seats 1919
Liberals ("*partito liberale*")	270	53.1	41	8.1
Democratic Liberals ("*partito democratico*")	40	7.9	60	11.8
Democratic Radicals ("*partito radicale*")	73	14.4	12	2.4
Mixed lists of Liberals, Democratic Liberals, and Radicals			96	18.9
Liberals, Democrats, Radicals: total	383	75.4	209	41.1
"*Partito economico*"			7	1.4
Veterans ("*Combattenti*")			20	3.9
Reformist socialists	19	3.7	6	1.2
Mixed lists of radicals, republicans, and veterans			5	1.0
Republicans	17	3.3	4	0.8
Independent Socialists	8	1.6	1	0.2
Catholics/*Partito Popolare Italiano* (PPI)	29	5.7	100	19.7
Partito Socialista Italiano (PSI)	52	10.2	156	30.7
All deputies except PSI and PPI	427	84.1	252	49.6
Mass parties (PSI plus PPI)	81	15.9	256	50.4
Total seats	508		508	
Absolute majority	255		255	

Base data: (1913) adapted, with adjustments, from Paolo Farneti, "La crisi della democrazia italiana e l'avvento del fascismo: 1919–1922," *Rivista italiana di scienze politiche* 5:1 (1975), 57; (1919) government figures (1920), in Noiret, *La proporzionale del 1919*, 171.

recoiled upon him in April–May 1919, the struggle over the war's meaning that had torn Italy since 1914–15 resumed with unparalleled ferocity. The election of 16 November 1919 became less an occasion for democratic renewal than a referendum for or against the war of the *signori*. The predictable result was the "electoral Caporetto" of Italian Liberalism: 156 Socialists, 100 Catholics, and a mere 200-odd "constitutional" deputies (see Figure 4.6). Of the 168 deputies of the 1917 "*fascio* of national defense," only 15 returned to office. Even more damning – and ironic – than the parliamentary outcome was the regional distribution of this massive repudiation of the Italy born in the *Risorgimento* within a year of its crowning victory in November 1918. North and Center had voted overwhelmingly for Socialists and Catholics. The Socialists secured 60.1 percent of the vote in Emilia and 50.2 in Piedmont; the *popolari* gained a plurality in Venetia. And the Liberals, who had claimed to bring order and progress to united Italy, gained absolute majorities only from the backward Abruzzi southward.[81]

---

[81] "Caporetto": *La Perseveranza*, 19 November 1919, in Vivarelli, *Origini*, 2:162, note 341; for the campaign and results, ibid., 2:13–32, 160–92, 911–17 (the deputies, by name, divided into a "democratic area" of 85 deputies and a "liberal area" of 167); Noiret, *La proporzionale del 1919*, ch. 5; and for breakdowns by region and district: Giusti, *Le correnti politiche*, 22 and map, 28, 93–98; and De Caprariis, "Partiti politici e opinione pubblica," 144: "resterà un sordo rancore, una chiusa avversione, quasi un segreto desiderio di vendetta . . ."

The mutual loathing and rivalry of Socialists and Catholics was sufficiently intense that their parliamentary majority of two votes remained purely negative; only the Liberal plurality had freedom of maneuver. The domination of Italy's parliament from November 1919 onward by forces totally or partially opposed to the Liberal state itself nevertheless contrasted starkly and ominously with the German Republic, where despite the Weimar coalition's weakness after June 1920, a Reichstag anti-system majority did not emerge until July 1932. Worse still, Italy's Liberals themselves lacked the coherence required to govern. The manifold cleavages dividing the lay non-Socialist forces by 1919 were indeed so complex as to defy graphic representation. Figures 4.6 and 4.7 depict only part of the *innere Zerrissenheit* determined by personal hatreds and rivalries, and omit both the 1918–19 division of the *interventisti* between supporters and "renouncers" of Italy's Adriatic claims, and the fiery border between clerical and anti-clerical, Catholic and Freemason, that coincided only imperfectly with the boundary between "Left" and "Right."

The manifold self-described parties, "*correnti*," interests, leaders, and personal followings or "*amici*" within the 252 deputies stretching from the Nationalists and Salandra on the right to the democrats, *Radicali*, veterans, and Reformists on the Left had resisted electoral coordination.[82] Nitti deliberately refrained from announcing a government program, merely urging the voters to trust him. Giolitti set forth a reform agenda, but was insufficiently credible to attract votes from the Left, and remained anathema to the Right and the *interventisti*. As he himself argued privately, any Liberal attempt to emulate the mass parties by running a single list in each election district would repel both neutralists and *interventisti*.[83] A notable proportion of the Liberal deputies elected in 1913, Sonnino at their head, retired from active politics or accepted appointment to the Senate in the face of the hateful novelty of the new electoral system. But the advent of a massive cohort of new men made no difference to Liberal fragmentation.[84]

The *massimalisti*, under the frenetic leadership of a Bolshevik adept and former pupil of Mussolini, Nicola Bombacci, now at last dominated the much-reinforced Socialist parliamentary delegation, and entered the Chamber of Deputies noisily proclaiming their intention of erecting proletarian dictatorship on its ruins. Turati, the historic reformist leader who had briefly defied the party base and central organization after Caporetto, was now wholly isolated, and had in any event never dared challenge the *massimalisti* with more than words. No rightward split of the PSI, in support of contemptible "bourgeois"

---

[82] See especially the detailed analysis of Charles S. Maier, *Recasting Bourgeois Europe: Stabilization in France, Germany, and Italy in the Decade after World War I* (Princeton, NJ, 1975), 123–28.

[83] Vivarelli, *Origini*, 2:199–206, and Giolitti's reported remarks to Frassati, September 1919, in Noiret, *La proporzionale del 1919*, 73–74, which establishes Giolitti's complete incomprehension of the extent to which the new electoral mechanism rewarded coherent party organization.

[84] For analysis of the turnover (65.3 percent of the deputies elected in 1919 were new to the Chamber) see Piretti, *Elezioni politiche*, 218–19; Vivarelli, *Origini*, 2:164–68; and Maier, *Bourgeois Europe*, 128–34.

FIGURE 4.7. Fragmentation in Two Dimensions: The Chamber of Deputies, 1913–1921

	Left	Seats	Right	Seats	Totals
The Last Liberal-Dominated Chamber, 1913–1919					
Interventisti	Radicals ("*radicali*")	73	Democratic liberals ("*democratico-costituzionali*")	29	
	Republicans ("*repubblicani*")	17	Democrats ("*democratici*")	11	
	Independent socialists ("*socialisti indipendenti*")	8	Non-Giolittian liberals	70	
	Reformist Socialists ("*Socialriformisti*")	19	Catholics	20	
			Conservative Catholics	9	
	Total Left-*interventisti*	117	Total Right-*interventisti*	139	256
			508 total seats; absolute majority:		255
Neutralisti	Socialists	52	Giolittian liberals ("*democrazia liberale*")	200	
	Total Left-*neutralisti*	52	Total Right-*neutralisti*	200	252
Totals	Left	169	Right	339	

Deadlock, 1919–1921

Group	Category	Seats		Category	Seats	Total
Interventisti	Radicals ("*radicali*")	57		Salandra liberals	23	
	Republicans ("*repubblicani*")	9		*Partito Economico, Partito Agrario,* and others	15	
	Independent and reformist socialists	22				
	"*Rinnovamento*" (veterans' movement)	33				
	Total Left-*interventisti*	121		Total Right-*interventisti*	38	159
				508 total seats; absolute majority:		255
Neutralisti	Socialists (PSI)	156		Giolittian liberals ("*Democrazia Liberale*")	91	
	Total Left-*neutralisti*	156		Total Right-*neutralisti*	91	247
Totals	Left	277		Right	129	
Uncommitted				*Partito popolare italiano* (Catholics)	100	

Adapted, with adjustments, from Farneti, "La crisi della democrazia italiana," 57 and Giusti, *Le correnti politiche*, 28. The lack of congruence between Farneti's figures and categories for 1919 and those of Figure 4.6 is symptomatic of the difficulties of discerning and disentangling the affiliations, loyalties, and ideological camps of the 252 deputies not belonging to the two mass parties.

democratic reforms, was conceivable. The party's loudly trumpeted decision to join Lenin's Third International promised still further radicalization. And mere election victories left the Socialist masses – which the *massimalisti*, as their leaders, were obliged to follow – wholly unsatiated.[85]

The Catholics were seemingly more amenable to cooperation with Nitti. Their preeminent founder, the Sicilian priest Don Luigi Sturzo, proclaimed the new *Partito popolare*'s commitment to a democratic renewal of Italian politics. Yet the PPI's actual course was the resultant of acute tensions between its disparate components, the demands of Vatican and Church hierarchy, and the irreducible illiberalism of a religious tradition bound letter and spirit by the violent hostility toward modernity expressed in the *Syllabus Errorum* of 1864.[86] The party's ostensible independence of the Vatican preserved the freedom of the hierarchy, not that of the *popolari*. Only an explicit papal blessing had freed Sturzo to enter politics; its withdrawal would dictate his exit. Preserving the party's peasant base in North and Center demanded that the Catholic "white *leghe*" compete in radicalism with their "red" counterparts in the *Federterra*, while Catholic rural magnates and traditional "clerico-moderate" notables stood foursquare for landowners' rights and public order. And for all its assertions of democratic principle, the *Partito popolare* – and even Sturzo himself – ultimately sought the theocratic reconquest of Italian society. That utopian aspiration, and political Catholicism's vehement if more practical refusal to serve any longer as a mere appendage to Liberal rule, clashed frontally with the Liberals' often visceral anti-clericalism and their instinctive assumption that effortless domination of parliament and state was theirs by right.

The freest election in united Italy's history thus produced a parliament in which genuine democrats were almost as rare as in the German Reichstag after the 1920 election. Liberals who called themselves "*democratici*" were predominantly the products of the clienteles of the South. The *popolari*, with a totalizing zeal denied to their German counterparts by German Catholicism's minority status, demanded literal and all-embracing application of Article 1 of the *Statuto* ("The Roman, Apostolic, and Catholic religion is the sole religion of the State"). And the Socialist delegation marked its parliamentary debut by noisily and abusively walking out rather than hear the king's speech.[87]

Nitti, insofar as he pursued a coherent strategy at all, had even before the election aimed to maintain Italy's lifeline to American and British finance in order to defend the *lira*'s exchange rate; to improve Italy's catastrophic balance

---

[85] See the biting and persuasive analysis of Vivarelli, *Origini*, 2:211–85, 328–44, 484–92, 616–34, 640–42; also Noiret, "Il partito di massa massimalista dal PSI and PCd'I, 1917–1924: La scalata alle istituzioni democratiche," in Grassi Orsini and Quagliariello, eds., *Il partito politico*, 909–65, and, for Bombacci's catastrophic leadership, Noiret, *Massimalismo e crisi dello stato liberale: Nicola Bombacci (1879–1924)* (Milan, 1992).

[86] Vivarelli, *Origini*, 2:440–44, persuasively takes issue on this point with much apologetic literature on the PPI.

[87] See, among other sources, Noiret, *Bombacci*, 331–32.

of payments and balance the state budget by demobilizing more rapidly, exporting more goods, and collecting more taxes than before; to restructure Italian industry yet preserve its precarious wartime growth; and to defuse discontent by retaining the wartime price-support for bread, by conciliatory gestures toward the Socialists, and by enforcing public order with a light touch. These aims were for the most part mutually irreconcilable. The bread subsidy was the most prominent source of government deficits, continued inflation, and consequent exchange-rate pressure on the *lira*. Higher taxes were scarcely the indicated remedy for Italy's overextended, capital-starved, and state-dependent wartime conglomerates. Increased production presupposed an end to the free exercise of the "moral economy of the crowd" and to political killings. And the Socialists, whom Nitti persistently wooed with unparalleled fatuousness, were neither willing to support the "bourgeois" state in parliament nor capable of calming the masses they claimed to lead.

From January through April 1920 the lira plunged from 13.99 to 22.94 to the U.S. dollar. Entreaties to the United States and repeated pilgrimages by Nitti to London in search of further loans led only to humiliation. But ultimately more destructive than the financial crisis was the intensifying erosion of the state's always imperfect monopoly of force. That spring, Italy's postwar strike wave reached maximum intensity. Widespread agitation by Socialist *leghe* and industrial, railroad, and postal workers and D'Annunzio's continuing sedition at Fiume all challenged Nitti's already tenuous authority. Deaths from political violence mounted from five in February 1920 to a staggering ninety-two in June. Mobs attacked public buildings, police barracks, shops, farmsteads, and one another over the most varied discontents and causes, from "rotten bread" to labor disputes to solidarity with Soviet Russia. Socialist *braccianti* attacked strikebreakers, Catholic labor organizations, landlords, and police. Anarchists seized weapons from army barracks, and fired on the police from the cover provided by Socialist protest marches. Beleaguered detachments of *Carabinieri* and *Guardie Regie* repeatedly dispersed rioters, demonstrators, and peaceful crowds with rifle and machine-gun fire.[88]

Neither the police forces nor the army units detailed for riot duty possessed the attitudes, leadership, numbers, communications, and mobility required to tame unrest on such a scale. Their efforts to maintain even a minimal degree of order produced large numbers of civilian dead and wounded, and compounded the perennial popular hatred of the Italian state. To preserve his delusional project of a bargain with at least some Socialist deputies, Nitti compensated by supinely accepting all manner of humiliations imposed upon the state by strikers, rioters, and Socialist leaders.[89] He survived through the spring of 1920

---

[88] Franzinelli, *Squadristi*, 285–92; Vivarelli, *Origini*, 2:502–20; and the chronological-descriptive passages in Giovannini, *L'Italia massimalista*, especially 101–03, 120–21, 146–49, 152–53, 160–62, 165–68, 174–82, 198–200.

[89] Vivarelli, *Origini*, 2:533–36 (also 1:465–70 for Nitti's fundamentally evasive and improvisational approach to "ordine pubblico").

only thanks to grudging support from the *popolari*, whom he characteristically treated with sovereign arrogance.

Nitti's greatest parliamentary advantage had been that he was not Giolitti. But by late spring 1920 the aged grandmaster had come to appear the lesser evil even to many *interventisti*.[90] Nitti's cowardice in the face of popular disorder and Socialist pretensions demoralized police, army, and administrative bureaucracy. Much of the parliamentary Right came to damn the prime minister as the "Italian Kerensky," and excoriate his conspicuous compensatory harshness toward patriotic demonstrators. In early June, with supremely poor timing, Nitti introduced legislation to eliminate the bread subsidy, a step the Socialists fiercely opposed, and that the all-important *popolari* – to Nitti's dismay – also resisted. He hastily resigned.

The successive humiliations of Orlando and of Nitti, the continuing fragmentation of the Liberals, and the pressure of the two mass parties had radically diminished whatever chances had existed in 1918 of stabilizing the Liberal regime. Only Giolitti now commanded the necessary authority, and he duly returned with broad if momentary parliamentary support. The *maestro*'s final year in power was initially everything his parliamentary friends had promised; age had not blunted his decisiveness. He evacuated Albania – after reinforcements embarking at Ancona in late June had mutinied, and the city and surrounding areas had risen, at a cost of thirty-three dead, in a revolt reminiscent of Red Week 1914. He reached a border agreement with Yugoslavia, the treaty of Rapallo of November 1920, that secured all of Istria, an assortment of Dalmatian islands, and an enclave at Zara for Italy. At the end of 1920 he drove D'Annunzio from Fiume, which the treaty had designated as a free city, with naval gunfire and loyal troops – an event the Poet, with characteristic melodrama, denounced as the "Christmas of Blood." And in early 1921 Giolitti at last ended the bread subsidy by stages, after seeking to compensate the poorer classes with parliamentary approval for new taxes and for the registration – and thus taxation – of stocks and bonds.

But contrary to widespread expectation, Giolitti failed to dominate the *piazza*. Like Nitti, who had imitated Giolitti's own prewar efforts to reduce at least some Socialists to junior partnership, he wooed the PSI. But the Socialist leaders and masses had other ideas. In February 1920 the Socialist *leghe* of Bologna – with characteristic lack of coordination with the industrial workers – launched a nine-month agricultural strike fought with unparalleled ferocity. Similar struggles raged across Venetia, the lower Po Valley, and Tuscany, where – uniquely – militant *mezzadri*, a category that made up almost three-fifths of the region's agricultural population, gave the Socialist movement its power.[91] The metal-workers of Turin and much of Piedmont struck in

---

[90] As Mussolini archly noted: OO, 15:8 (28 May 1920).

[91] For the role of the *mezzadri*, the consequent limits on Fascist recruitment in the countryside, and the related extreme violence of Tuscan *squadrismo*, see especially Frank M. Snowden, *The*

March–April 1920 against the reimposition of daylight saving time – a preposterous pretext for a trial of strength with FIAT over mastery of the shop floor.[92]
And in August–September the metal-workers throughout north Italy, half a million strong, countered a lockout by the industrialists by seizing factories and
hoisting the red flag.

Giolitti's response to this surge of unrest was wholly consistent with his
past. As before 1914, he held the ring for the contenders until deadlock super-
vened, then brokered or imposed a compromise. But by summer 1920, the
Great War and Lenin's seizure of power had made that casual posture seem
painfully anachronistic. PSI orators ranted of revolution, the Red Army briefly
drove westward toward Warsaw in mid-August, and Italian patriotic opinion
inevitably came to see Giolitti as yet another Nitti or Kerensky. Industrialists
and landowners, great and small, forced to settle on terms that established
Socialist "dual power" on the shop floor and in the fields, emerged from the
second of Italy's "two red years" vengefully unreconciled to their promised end
on the rubbish heap of history. Meanwhile, the failure of the occupation of the
factories and the onset of the worldwide postwar slump of 1920–21 (see Figure 4.2) sapped the militancy of the Socialist base.

The municipal elections throughout Italy from September to early November
1920 proved a turning point far more decisive than the occupation of the factories.[93] In the North they confirmed at the local level the 1919 majorities achieved
by Socialists and Catholics (see Figure 4.8, p. 312). The mass parties suffered
significant defeats, as the "constitutional" forces combined against the threat
to a greater extent than in 1919 by forming "national" voting blocs. In Italy's
major cities, the PSI won absolute majorities only in Milan and Bologna. Yet at
local and provincial level throughout the Po Valley and Tuscan "red belt," the
PSI had nevertheless conquered taxing, spending, and hiring powers in addition
to the local monopolies of its consumer cooperatives and the coercive armory of
its *leghe* committed to the "socialization of the land."[94] That left non-Socialists
two apparent options: extinction, or the appeal to arms that *Freikorps*, *Arditi*,
and Fascists had pioneered. And at the national level the slight apparent retreat

---

Fascist Revolution in Tuscany, 1919–1922 (Cambridge, 1989), chs. 1–2; Marco Palla, "I fascisti
toscani," in Giorgio Mori, ed., *La Toscana* (Turin, 1986), 456–78, is exemplary on the violence
itself.

[92] See the 1970s period piece of Giuseppe Maione, "Il biennio rosso: lo sciopero delle lancette,"
SC 3:2 (1972), 239–304; Angelo Tasca, *Nascita e avvento del fascismo* (Florence, 2nd ed.,
2002), 173–75 note 5; and the 1930s comments of the moderate and respected leader of the
metal-workers' union, Bruno Buozzi, on "strike-for-strike's-sake mania," in Tasca's notes, now
published as *Interviste sul fascismo* (Milan, 2002), 24 (http://www.feltrinelli.it/Fondazione/testo-
ritrovato-tasca-fascismo.htm).

[93] Lawrence Squeri, "The Italian Local Elections of 1920 and the Outbreak of Fascism," *Historian*,
3 (1983), 324–36; among the local studies, see especially Corner, *Fascism in Ferrara*, 107–08;
and Snowden, *Tuscany*, 54–55.

[94] Squeri, "The Italian Local Elections of 1920," 330–32; Tasca, *Avvento*, 194.

of the red tide, and the leftward split of the PSI at the congress of Livorno in January 1921 through the foundation of the Communist Party of Italy (PCI), tempted Giolitti to try his hand that spring at creating a new Chamber of Deputies that he could once more dominate. It was the master's last and greatest political misjudgment, and one from which Liberal Italy never recovered.

State and society likewise took leave of the Liberal era in the course of the "two red years." The administrative bureaucracy that reached downward and outward from the interior ministry in Rome to Italy's seventy-odd provincial capitals had, like parliament, become disconnected in the course of 1915–18 from an executive ever less able to control an unwieldy and often corrupt instrument. Nitti's repeated punitive transfers of the few prefects, police chiefs, and functionaries who acted decisively against the disorders of 1919–20, and the incorrigible ambiguity of his instructions – even when he sought to project legalitarian resolve – completed the process.[95] By Giolitti's advent in June 1920, only immediate, ruthless, and lasting pressure from a forceful prime minister or minister of the interior with a stable parliamentary majority behind him might have restored some degree of control.[96] But Giolitti, formerly the inimitable master of the central bureaucracy, now delegated to assistants the critical task of monitoring and maintaining public order at the periphery. The administration's capacity and willingness to execute instructions from the center consequently declined further. Giolitti himself concentrated on dominating parliament, and failed to acquire the indispensable close acquaintance with the chaotic and swiftly evolving struggles across north Italy – where Socialist preponderance, by the end of 1920, was triggering violence of a new type on a scale that soon dwarfed the amateur efforts of the Socialist masses.

The army, partially unhinged by the Fiume sedition, if grudgingly brought to heel by mid-1920, likewise went its own way. Nitti's temporizing evasion in the face of mutiny and desertion by members of the officer corps made patriotic disobedience seem both legitimate and effortless. But equally vital in further undermining the army's reliability as an instrument of Italy's executive were Nitti's alleged or actual pandering to the Left and his muddled efforts to create a peacetime army that Italy could afford. Four powerful symbols dramatized the first complaint: Nitti's publication of the Caporetto Inquiry; the September 1919 amnesty that largely eliminated the military justice legacy of Cadorna and Diaz; Nitti's alleged pressure on officers to refrain from wearing uniform in public in order to avoid incidents; and Nitti's refusal to celebrate the first anniversary of Italy's historic victory over Austria-Hungary.

The "amnesty of the deserters" that freed 40,000 military prisoners and purged the books of 600,000-odd cases was as overdue as it was open to

---

[95] See especially Vivarelli, *Origini*, 2:532–36, 562–63: the symptomatic removal of the energetic and highly professional police chief (*questore*) of Rome, Cesare Mori, as scapegoat for the outcome of Nitti's own instructions to bear down hard on nationalist demonstrations on 24 May 1920, fifth anniversary of Italy's declaration of war.

[96] See Vivarelli, *Origini*, 2:71–74, 501–36.

defamation from *interventisti* and the Right. It henceforth figured in the lengthening catalog of Nitti's purported crimes. The uniform advisory was soon known widely as his order to "avoid provoking the deserters."[97] But perhaps most offensive of all to the officer corps' post-1918 self-esteem was Nitti's refusal to celebrate the anniversary of victory, lest parades and ceremonies lead to bloodshed during the run-up to the November 1919 elections. The minister of war noted ominously to Nitti in late December the consequence of these affronts and of Socialist propaganda aimed at undermining the loyalty of the troops: "officers, in particular, are beginning to think that the government does not sufficiently support them in the face of the relentless increase [*l'incalzare*] of threats and insults for which they are targets on an everyday basis."[98]

Nitti's departure scarcely altered a situation that moved the officer corps to abiding fury. Giolitti proved little better than Nitti in controlling the streets. But in army eyes the Italian state's most serious offence of all was its continuing inability to replace the war army with a peacetime force structure that gave the officer corps the recognition and perquisites for which it had fought, and – in its own view – richly deserved. The hierarchy managed to prolong demobilization into mid-1920, with some cooperation from Yugoslav irredentist agitators, D'Annunzio's posturing, and the Nationalist press. Then repeated prodding by Nitti and Giolitti ultimately forced consideration of how to accommodate within the crisis-ridden finances of the Italian state an army that had accumulated 400 more generals, 4,200 more field-grade regular officers, and 3,000 more regular captains than in 1914.[99] The inevitable reductions in force, accompanied by inflation-driven increases in officer pay and allowances that the hierarchy judged lamentably insufficient, nurtured the latent military disaffection present since 1919. The navy, although unlike its German counterpart largely absent from the internal battlefield, likewise found small reason to love the Liberal state. Its war leader, Admiral Thaon di Revel, resigned in November 1919 as chief of the navy rather than cover with his prestige what he regarded as Italy's Adriatic surrender. With tacit support from the naval staff, he subsequently exploited his seat in the Senate to demand the retention of both Dalmatia and Fiume, to vote against Giolitti's November 1920 settlement with the Yugoslavs, and to attack the postwar governments for failing to secure "a strategically Italian outcome [*assetto*]" in the Adriatic.[100]

---

97 "Amnistia ai disertori": analysis and statistics in Rochat, *Vittorio Veneto a Mussolini*, 120–28, and Mondini, *Politica delle armi*, 22; Uniform order: Giardino denounced it in parliament, and other contemporary sources mention it, but documentation has not yet surfaced: ibid., 25, 188 note 111, and especially "[V]enne dato l'ordine di girare in borghese per non provocare i disertori": Mario Piazzesi, *Diario di uno squadrista toscano* (Rome, 1980), 232.

98 Albricci to Nitti, 24 December 1919, in Vivarelli, *Origini*, 2:533 note 150.

99 Figures: Rochat, *Vittorio Veneto a Mussolini*, 139, on whose incisive and durable analysis of both political and military aspects of the army's postwar force structure (ibid., ch. 3, 184–87, 224–31, 260–325, and ch. 6) this and following paragraphs are based.

100 AP, Senato, 1919, 754, 1 April 1920; ibid., 1919–20, 2287–88, 15 December 1920; ibid., 1921–22, vol. 3, 3833, 14 August 1922; for the support of the chief of naval staff, Admiral Alfredo

The wider society showed equally small affection for the Liberal regime. The cutoff of trans-Atlantic emigration from 1914 onward had placed Italy in a gradually heating demographic pressure cooker. As in Germany, the war had created a generation of displaced and discontented individuals, from landless peasants to unemployed junior officers. Even before 1914, habit, not affection, on balance bound the elites of Italy's majority culture to the Liberal state; few indeed loved it for itself. And as the ferment in avant-garde periodicals and the convulsions of winter–spring 1914–15 demonstrated, most intellectuals had long since declared their hatred for Giolitti – symbol of the Liberal regime – and all his works. The recession of 1920–22, which peaked at an official – if understated – figure of 606,819 unemployed in February 1922 (Figure 4.2), dampened agitation among the industrial and agricultural working classes, but further accentuated their long-standing disaffection. The landlords who wielded social power in the South asked of Rome only that its police and army defend their property. By 1920–21, in areas of maximum unrest, from Bologna and Ferrara to Apulia, the parliamentary regime was failing that simple test. For the industrialists, the "abdication" of Giolitti's state in September 1920 was decisive; that the workers had nevertheless lost the battle irrelevant. All across the North, those who were not Socialists felt increasingly threatened by the violent coercion of the *leghe* and the periodic mutinies of transport, postal, and industrial workers, justified or encouraged by PSI authorities throughout the "red belt" stretching from Tuscany to the mouths of the Po.

Italy lacked Germany's luxuriant networks of voluntary organizations. But it had Freemasonry, which Gramsci once memorably described as the "sole genuine and effective political party" of the Italian bourgeoisie.[101] Yet the Masons, long divided into two fiercely hostile sects, also replicated all the manifold divisions of the Liberal governing class. An ostensible commitment to democratic values did not prevent key segments of Freemasonry from aiding and supporting "brother" D'Annunzio's march on Fiume. Mussolini likewise enjoyed the early favor of one sect, as ostensible savior of Italy from chaos; the other found itself compelled to compete.[102] Even more symptomatically, a broad spectrum of patriotic and vigorously anti-Socialist associations, some deriving from the 1917–18 *fascio* of national defense, some newly founded, emerged across north and central Italy from spring 1919 onward. All regarded the failed Liberal state of Orlando, Nitti, and Giolitti with increasing contempt. The "New Pact" and "The Italian League for the Protection of the National Interest" were brain-children of Giuriati, veteran of the "Trento and Trieste," *interventismo*, and

Acton, see Ezio Ferrante, *Il Grande Ammiraglio Paolo Thaon di Revel* (Rome, 1989), 157 note 90.

[101] "[L]a massoneria è stata l'unico partito reale ed efficiente che la classe borghese ha avuto per lungo tempo": parliamentary speech of 16 May 1924, in Gramsci, *Sul fascismo*, ed. Enzo Santarelli (Rome, 1973), 280.

[102] See Aldo Alessandro Mola, *Storia della Massoneria italiana dalle origini ai giorni nostri* (Milan, 2001), chs. 14–15.

the Isonzo fighting – and future secretary (1930–31) of the Fascist Party. The November 1919 elections prompted the formation of "anti-Bolshevik *fasci*" and a "patriotic league" (Cremona), a "union of national renewal" (Venice), an association for "order and liberty" (Modena); a "municipal defense alliance" (Florence), an "association for social renewal and defense" (Mantua), as well as local partnerships between preexisting associations, including small groups of Nationalist paramilitary "blue shirts" and the embryonic *Fasci di combattimento*, aimed at replacing striking public service workers with their own members.[103] Finally, the Vatican and the Italian hierarchy, committed to the reconquest of Italian society from the "Masonic" state of the *Risorgimento*, saw the *popolari* from the beginning as a mere expedient. Other forces and institutions might better serve the Church's purposes. As Giolitti resigned for the last time in June 1921, whatever authority liberal parliamentarism had once enjoyed in Italy had vanished.[104]

2. THE PERPETUATION OF THE WAR: IDEAS AND INSTITUTIONS

Not least of the forces that undermined the Liberal regime and the German Republic was the abiding conviction of individuals and of institutions that the war had not ended. Italy's great-power aspirations and Germany's hegemonic claims remained unfulfilled. The war's promise of individual distinction and social elevation had tantalized its adepts, then vanished with the armistices. Vast numbers of combative young men saw the peace settlements as national humiliations and burning personal affronts. The disappointment of educated males just too young to fight proved especially explosive, to the benefit of *Freikorps* and Fascist gangs in the immediate present, and with powerful long-term effects.

I. Germany: Hatred, Ambition, Eugenics

The Germans had inaugurated the Great War, and inevitably took the lead in its perpetuation. With equal inevitability, the officer corps took the lead within Germany. The war had ended in defeat. But defeat was not an outcome that German military culture could envisage or tolerate. With its reputation and future at stake, the army bent immediately to the task of erasing its own preeminent part in Germany's strategic misadventures. That effort did not preclude

---

[103] See the excellent survey in Gentile, *Storia del partito fascista 1919–1922. Movimento e milizia* (Bari, 1989), 71–77, and – for the case of Florence – the vivid account of Piazzesi, *Diario*, 55–56, 59–60, 63–68.

[104] For the subversive nationalism and anti-governmental plotting of the leadership of the "Trento and Trieste" (which mutated in August 1920 into the "Italian League for the Protection of the National Interests"), see Alessandra Staderini, "Rivendicazioni territoriali e mobilitazione nazionale nei documenti del 1919 di Giovanni Giuriati e Oscar Sinigaglia," SC 14:1 (1983), 81–140, and Domenico Fabiano, "La lega Italiana per la tutela degli interessi nazionali e le origini dei fasci italiani all'estero, 1920–1923," SC 16:2 (1985), 206–11.

occasional indecorous public wrangles between generals; Groener in particular suffered throughout his postwar career for having saved the army from disintegration by advising William II to abdicate. But even Groener firmly believed, as he wrote on 17 November 1918, that the German people's heroic "unbroken [resistance] for four years against a world of enemies" had fallen victim to Jewish "wire-pullers."[105] When agitation by the right-wing press and by Ludendorff in spring 1919 intersected with efforts by the Scheidemann government to shed light on the launching, conduct, and loss of the war, the officer corps closed ranks. In a solemn and carefully staged appearance in November 1919 before the Reichstag committee of inquiry that the government had instituted, Hindenburg read a cleverly prepared statement that ascribed to a (drastically misquoted) "English general" the claim that the German army had been stabbed in the back. Home-front treason was the only explanation for defeat compatible with the mental world of the officer corps, and of much of the German nation. And the stab-in-the-back myth conveniently eliminated any need to brood on Germany's strategic blunders, from Schlieffen's lunacy to the navy's submarine folly to Ludendorff's maniacal offensives and panicked bid for an armistice. It offered an ideal platform upon which to unite the armed forces and all shades of German opinion, from racist fanatics to German democrats – whose press attacked the committee of inquiry not for supinely providing a forum for nationalist propaganda, but for offering aid and comfort to Germany's enemies through its feeble efforts to cross-examine the generals. The racists offered a more memorable version of that same charge: the committee was a "Jewish inquisition."[106]

The lost war's other great myth, of the Siegfried-helmeted aristocracy of *Frontkämpfer*, likewise prospered mightily under the hated Republic. Ernst Jünger was not alone in invoking Heraclitus: war, "father of all things, is also our father; it has hammered, hewn, and tempered us into what we are." War was all-pervasive and permanent, as an accomplice of the Rathenau murder plot wrote: "They told us the war was now over. We laughed. For we ourselves were the war."[107] The stern helmet-shadowed face of the front-fighter graced the election placards of the nationalist parties to Weimar's very end. And Jünger and a legion of like-minded warriors celebrated in print the birth of a new ideology, a cold and steely "soldierly nationalism" a world war away from the shallow "hurrah-patriotism" of Wilhelmine Germany's middle classes and of the aged notables who had presided over defeat.[108] The war's meaning was

---

[105] "Und wer sind die Drahtzieher? Juden hier wie dort.": Letter of 17 November 1918, in Groener, *Lebenserinnerungen*, 472.

[106] See Boris Barth, *Dolchstosslegenden und politische Desintegration. Die Trauma der deutschen Niederlage im ersten Weltkrieg 1914–1933* (Düsseldorf, 2003), 324–25, for what Sir Frederick Maurice, a former acolyte of Haig's, actually said; Heinemann, *Verdrängte Niederlage*, 163–64; Lohalm, *Völkischer Radikalismus*, 187.

[107] Jünger, *Der Kampf als inneres Erlebnis*, 11–12; Friedrich Wilhelm Heinz, *Sprengstoff* (Berlin, 1930), 7.

[108] Useful surveys: DRZW, 1:46–52; Kurt Sontheimer, *Antidemokratisches Denken in der Weimarer Republik* (Munich, 1962), ch. 5.

bound up with the belated achievement of national integration: the creation in 1914–18 of the perfect classless national community, the *Kameradschaft* of the front celebrated in a "national wave" of popular literature inspired by Jünger's *Storm of Steel* (1920) that swept across Germany with particular force from 1929 onward.[109] The imagined community of *Frontkämpfer* defined itself through a hatred of the rear not in the least imagined, but born of the universal division between the combat soldier and all other forms of life, multiplied by the extraordinary lethality and spatial constriction of the Great War's battlefields, by Germany's political peculiarities, and by the trauma of unacknowledgeable defeat. Hatred of the rear, translated into politics throughout the German-national majority culture, meant death to "November-traitors." It also meant yearning for an authentic – German not "Jewish" – revolution to sweep the Republic away, and replace it with a dictatorship that replicated in everyday life the perfect communion between military Führer and battlefield following.

The preeminent goal of such a state would inevitably be the violent reversal of the "political, economic, and military castration" of Germany by the Republic and the Western powers, and the destruction of the post-1918 world order.[110] The *Stahlhelm* ("League of Front-Soldiers"), largest of the militant veterans' movements, was for a time the political home of Jünger and other like-minded intellectuals, while enjoying the high patronage of Hindenburg as its most illustrious honorary member. It freely expressed its views of the Republic over which Hindenburg presided in the widely applauded 1928 "declaration of hate [*Hassbotschaft*]" of its Brandenburg branch:

> We hate the present momentary form of the German state with our entire souls, . . . because it denies us the prospect of liberating our enslaved Fatherland, of purifying the German people of the lying accusation of war-guilt, of securing the necessary German living space [*Lebensraum*] in the East, [and] of once more making the German people eager to bear arms.[111]

The delicious irony of denying "war-guilt" while calling for the destruction of the eastern neighbors apparently escaped the *Stahlhelm*. But resuming "the struggle over who is to rule the earth," in the 1926 words of Jünger's equally ferocious younger brother, was from the beginning the central aspiration of "soldierly nationalism."[112]

That aspiration, with varying degrees of vehemence, also pervaded the vast movement of nationalist [*vaterländisch*] organizations that had survived the war or sprung up in its aftermath: veterans' leagues, local militias, paramilitary bands, *Freikorps*, clandestine murder networks, racist sects, student corps, and nationalist parties. The *Kriegervereine*, like the army, survived the war and in

---

[109] Jünger, *In Stahlgewittern*; and the comprehensive war-book survey of Wolfram Wette, DRZW, 1, part I, I.10.

[110] Quotation: declaration of the Harzburg Front, 11 October 1931, in Erich Eyck, *A History of the Weimar Republic*, 2 vols. (Cambridge, MA, 1963), 2:332.

[111] Printed in Wilhelm Kleinau, *Soldaten der Nation. Die geschichtliche Sendung des Stahlhelm* (Berlin, 1933), 56–61; numbers, Wehler, DGG, 4:391.

[112] DRZW, 1:51 (Friedrich Georg Jünger, 1898–1977).

1920 acquired Hindenburg as honorary president. Unlike the army, they shrank only marginally in the war's aftermath, and thereafter maintained some 30,000 local groups with 2.2 (1922) to 2.8 million members (1928), far dwarfing the 800,000 members of the SPD (1928). An estimated 10 percent of these "warriors" practiced riflery regularly, mostly using the weapon of the Great War, the accurate and highly reliable 1898 Mauser. And although the *Kriegervereine* were ostensibly apolitical, their national organization campaigned actively against the "war-guilt lie," and their inescapable presence in uniformed splendor at civic and patriotic occasions was a constant reminder of pre-1914 glories and present wretchedness.[113]

If the *Kriegervereine* preserved an ambiguous political neutrality, all other elements within the broad spectrum of the postwar nationalist movement were unabashedly hostile to the Republic. In the first phase of the German civil war, up to 1924, the *Stahlhelm*'s numbers swelled to 100,000 and its militance increased as the Republic gradually demobilized the *Freikorps* and dismantled the paramilitary undergrounds. Thereafter, as its numbers rose toward the 750,000 mark (1933), it inclined increasingly toward a DNVP that itself, from 1928 onward, moved into the radical Right. The *Stahlhelm* banned Jews from membership in 1924, and increasingly cultivated "military sport." But a wide range of explicitly military organizations outbid it in bloodthirsty radicalism. The fluctuating tripartite division of 1918–20 – *Freikorps* that were or aspired to be army or navy units, "temporary volunteers" with regional responsibilities, and "home guards" for local defense against "Bolshevism" – mutated into a bewildering underbrush of open and clandestine nationalist militance divided both regionally and by political tendency. Bavaria, by far the largest German state other than Prussia, proclaimed its distinctiveness from "red Berlin" – from the bloody end of the Munich Soviet to the suppression of the Beer Hall Putsch – by extending a tolerant hospitality to political murderers, paramilitary gangs, and *völkisch* sects.

That last category played a role both in Bavaria and throughout the Reich out of all proportion to its organizational coherence. It also demonstrated, in its continuity with pre-1914 anti-Semitic agitation by groups such as the *Reichshammerbund*, the *Germanen Orden*, and the Pan-Germans under Class's determinedly racist leadership, that war, defeat, and aftermath had at best a catalytic effect on Germany's peculiarities. On 16 February 1919, as the national constituent assembly met at Weimar, the leaders of the Pan-German League solemnly and publicly damned the newborn Republic as "a form of government [in]appropriate to the German people," under the leadership of the same "unscrupulous traitors" responsible for defeat. From the picturesque town of Bamberg in Upper Franconia, Class and associates announced their aspiration to serve as the "*Stosstrupp* of the *völkisch* philosophy." They called for

---

[113] C. J. Elliott, "The Kriegervereine and the Weimar Republic," JCH 10:1 (1975), 118, 114, 124; Winkler, *Der Schein der Normalität: Arbeiter und Arbeiterbewegung in der Weimarer Republik 1924 bis 1930* (Berlin, 1988), 347.

a German "racial rebirth" that would put the "ethnically foreign component of the Reich population," Jewry, in its rightful place. Germany "belonged to the Germans." The Bamberg proclamation inevitably demanded the preservation of the Reich's existing eastern territories, but also claimed Austria, western Hungary, the "primeval-German Baltic colonization lands," and "the primeval-German ethnic soil" of Alsace-Lorraine. It scoffed mightily at the "so-called League of Nations" and "eternal peace" that Germany's foes had promised. Three hundred thousand copies went out as supplements to major German newspapers.[114]

The Pan-Germans did not limit themselves to words. At Bamberg they also launched the new enterprise foreshadowed in their autumn 1918 deliberations.[115] The "German-Racist Defense and Defiance League [*Deutschvölkischer Schutz- und Trutz-Bund*]" was a front organization that aimed to unite at last Germany's fissiparous anti-Semitic splinter parties, sects, clubs, and associations into a mass movement to smash the "Jew-republic" and inaugurate national-racial rebirth. In the spring of Spartacist insurrections and Munich Soviets, that message proved highly contagious, and even more so in 1920, the year of the Kapp Putsch. The *Schutz- und Trutz-Bund* expanded swiftly to encompass 110,000 members throughout Germany by the end of 1921, and reached 160,000–180,000 immediately before the Republic ended its brief career by banning it after Rathenau's murder in 1922. Perhaps 200,000 Germans in all at some point belonged to the *Bund*.[116]

Its message – the "*völkische Weltanschauung*" – was a concentrated distillate of nineteenth-century pseudo-biological wisdom. The concept of race was "the key to world history." The "struggle for survival" was the foundation of existence. Humanity was hierarchically structured in accordance with biological law. And with implacable illogic, given Judaism's unique record of survival, the *Bund* proclaimed the Jews the lowest of "races": a "ferment of decomposition," "fungus of putrefaction," and "parasite of the peoples of the Aryan race." The resulting conflict was a cosmic "*Kampf* between good and evil": "for the survival of humanity Jewry must perish." That message the *Bund* propagated indefatigably through newspapers, pamphlets, books, and itinerant speakers linked to its national organization, its regional *Gaue*, and its local groups. Millions of the *Bund*'s swastika-adorned leaflets, stickers, and placards – as well as swastika graffiti – blanketed Germany.[117] The *Bund* failed organizationally and politically. Not all racist groups adhered. No mainstream political party explicitly adopted its views. No charismatic Führer emerged to weld its disparate components together and hurl them against the Republic. Nor did the

---

[114] Werner Jochmann, *Nationalsozialismus und Revolution. Ursprung und Geschichte der NSDAP in Hamburg 1922–1933: Dokumente* (Frankfurt am Main, 1963), 10–24; Lohalm, *Völkischer Radikalismus*, 15–19.

[115] See p. 199.

[116] Lohalm, *Völkischer Radikalismus*, 15–19, 89–90.

[117] Quotations, and following remarks, ibid., 136–38, 123, and part 5.

Bund possess a paramilitary wing capable of taking its message to the streets with the violence that its beliefs demanded. But its worldview nevertheless pervaded the German nationalist majority culture and that culture's organizations, from the parties of the Right to the *Stahlhelm*, the Ehrhardt Brigade and its fellows, and the student associations and corps in which "Aryan" blood was or soon became a condition of membership. And the *Bund*'s Jew-free vision of the imperial future of the German *Volk* demanded the Great War's perpetuation.

That mission belonged above all to Germany's mightiest institution, the Reichswehr. And to the army in particular, which in its 1920s fantasies and force structure plans aimed from the beginning to shake the post-1918 order to its foundations. As it angrily assumed its Treaty-prescribed shape in 1920–21, the army of the Reichswehr bent with one mind to the resumption of continental hegemonic conflict against the French "ancestral enemy": a "war of liberation" like that of 1807–13, as prelude to final global confrontation with Anglo-America "over raw materials and markets." Groener had pointed the way, invoking the military reformers of 1807–13 in his farewell address to the general staff in August 1919. Seeckt later summed up: Germany would rearm and "take back everything that we have lost." In the process, Poland "must and will disappear, through its own inner weakness and through Russia, with our help."[118] The army reshaped its image of war and resulting doctrine, sought backing for the nation's military resurgence across the political elites and throughout German society, and courted foreign allies. At the root of all its efforts was the recognition, born in the trauma of 1914–18, that war in the industrial age was a total social process. That insight impelled the army's planners and experts into ever-wider endeavors. These included a concerted if blinkered effort to learn from the lost war; the conception and implementation of a series of multi-year rearmament plans; camouflaged industrial mobilization preparations involving most German firms with military-industrial potential; a clandestine parallel foreign policy and military-industrial quasi-alliance with Germany's fellow pariah-state, Soviet Russia; surreptitious army and navy ties to Dutch, Spanish, Italian, Swiss, Danish, and Swedish subsidiaries, shell corporations, industrial concerns, and armed forces; an officer exchange program with the U.S. Army focused on a common deep interest in industrial mobilization planning; major roles in the Reich's police affairs, transport policy, and public works; and a country-wide program from 1932 to indoctrinate and physically harden German youth for service in the coming mass army.[119]

---

[118] Hürten, ed., *Zwischen Revolution und Kapp-Putsch*, 196; Stülpnagel memorandum, 6 March 1926, ADAP B/1/1/144 (343, 345) for world power by stages; Meier-Welcker, *Seeckt*, 294–96, 341 (Wirth entirely agrees that "Polen muss erledigt werden"), 343, 460; and the Truppenamt position (1920) in Post, *Civil-Military Fabric*, 98. For the centrality of Russia in German interwar strategic thinking and military-economic planning, see above all Rolf-Dieter Müller, *Das Tor zur Weltmacht. Die Bedeutung der Sowjetunion für die deutsche Wirtschafts- und Rüstungspolitik zwischen den Weltkriegen* (Boppard am Rhein, 1984).

[119] Ibid., chs. 1–2; Hans W. Gatzke, "Russo-German Military Collaboration During the Weimar Republic," AHR 63:3 (1958), 565–97; Sergej A. Gorlow, "Geheimsache Moskau-Berlin: Die

Seeckt's initial doctrinal efforts continued to bear fruit long after his abrupt departure in 1926. In December 1919, "while the impressions won on the battlefield are still fresh," he ordered a massive effort to study the tactical, operational, logistical, administrative, and leadership lessons of the Great War. The resulting committees and consultative groups embraced air as well as ground warfare, and ultimately involved some 500 senior and mid-ranking officers. Only the British attempted a "lessons learned" exercise on that scale or so swiftly, although like the *Regio Esercito* they rejected the German insight that battle was chaotic and initiative from below consequently indispensable.[120] The resulting Reichswehr field service regulations, *Leadership and Combat with Combined Arms* (1921–24), were a striking summation of the army's collective wisdom, a group effort on the part of its best minds to escape the flypaper battlefield of 1914–18, implementing and perfecting through "modern" machinery the army's traditional offensive fanaticism and tactical freedom.

Führung und Gefecht, as Seeckt stated uncompromisingly in his preface, cast aside the Versailles dwarf-army and assumed "the strength, weaponry, and equipment of a modern military great power." It was relentlessly offensive, and sought not "ordinary victory" but "annihilational decision [*vernichtende Entscheidung*]." It demanded that even senior commanders lead from the front. It reaffirmed and amplified the army's mission tactics tradition: junior leaders must act "daringly and independently," exploiting the slightest enemy weakness with frenetic aggressiveness and – above all – "*without waiting for orders.*"[121] *Führung und Gefecht* innovated primarily in its detailed codification of the tactical and technological experience of the Great War, from Seeckt's great eastern breakthrough in 1915 to the new war tools of 1917–18, above all tanks and ground-attack aircraft. Jünger, before he left the Reichswehr from boredom to follow a writing career, happily anticipated later developments. Cannae and Tannenberg could remain shining examples for the future: "a war of position cannot occur, once you can crush the enemy with armored troops in motor vehicles."[122]

For the moment, as France's unpunished incursion into western Germany in 1923–24 demonstrated, the army could not fight at all. Or at least not a conventional war: its seven infantry divisions had munitions for a single hour

---

militärpolitische Zusammenarbeit zwischen der Sowjetunion und dem Deutschen Reich 1920–1933," VfZ 44:1 (1996), 133–65; Carsten, *The Reichswehr and Politics, 1918 to 1933* (Berkeley, CA, 1973), 135–47, 232–45; ADAP B/4/132, 134; Geyer, *Aufrüstung oder Sicherheit: Die Reichswehr in der Krise der Machtpolitik 1924–1936* (Wiesbaden, 1980), 97–112, 149–65, 295–96.

[120] See David French, "Doctrine and Organization in the British Army, 1919–1932," HJ 44:2 (2001), 497–515; antecedents: Samuels, *Command or Control*.

[121] H. Dv. 487, *Führung und Gefecht der verbundenen Waffen*, 3 vols. (Berlin, 1921–24), 1:3; 3:31 ("Der Führer . . . kann . . . aus einen 'ordinären Sieg' eine vernichtende Entscheidung gestalten"); 1:9–10, 35, 37, 156; 3:17–18 (my emphasis). For context, see particularly James S. Corum, *The Roots of Blitzkrieg. Hans von Seeckt and German Military Reform* (Lawrence, KA, 1992).

[122] Jünger, "Die Technik in der Zukunftsschlacht," *Militär-Wochenblatt* 106:14, 1 October 1921, 2.

of combat. That lamentable fact was the starting point of a famous lecture to the assembled officers of the Reichswehr Ministry in February 1924 by Lieutenant Colonel Joachim von Stülpnagel, leading member of an increasingly powerful group of mid-level total war enthusiasts within the camouflaged general staff.[123] Stülpnagel inevitably invoked 1807–14. Germany was "powerless under the fist of the ancestral enemy"; the time would nevertheless come to "decide by force of arms whether a hundred million [sic] Germans must become the slaves of forty million Frenchmen."[124] Yet Stülpnagel's conclusions were wholly modern in their radicalism: Germany's only present recourse was a "people's war" to exhaust and demoralize the French and Polish invaders in unremitting combat throughout the full depth of the German Reich. Stülpnagel ascribed to the French "half-breed *Volk*" a long-harbored "sadistic plan" of hostage-murder, reprisals, and gas-bombing of German civilians, and accepted all such collateral damage with equanimity.[125] Regardless of French actions, Germany's response to invasion must be scorched-earth withdrawal deep into the interior, while stay-behind guerrilla bands inspired by "national hatred raised to the furthest extreme" tormented the enemy through "sabotage, murder, and chemical and biological attack [*Verseuchung*]."[126]

Stülpnagel's advocacy of a "massively implemented *Volk*-uprising" tacitly and ironically repressed the traditional self-righteous hatred and ferocity with which the army regarded *franc-tireurs*. The prerequisites for success in a German "people's war" were above all political, and were the same as for any other form of modern, and – in the planners' eyes – thus necessarily total, war. They included the end of parliamentarism and the creation of a "strong central Reich authority [*Reichsgewalt*]"; the harnessing of all organs of the state to national defense; and the "national and military indoctrination [*wehrhafte Erziehung*] of our youth," branding upon them "the categorical imperative of fighting and dying for the Fatherland."[127] Yet the legacy of Moltke and Schlieffen was wholly safe in Stülpnagel's revolutionary hands. He was faithful to their fatalistic dedication to extreme risk: "We [must] always fight [facing the alternative of] victory or annihilation."[128] And in the second phase of

---

123 Partial texts: Carl Dirks and Karl-Heinz Janssen, *Der Krieg der Generäle* (Munich, 2001), 193–209; Heinz Hürten, ed., *Das Krisenjahr 1923. Militär und Innenpolitik 1922–1924* (Düsseldorf, 1980), 266–72; incisive commentary: Geyer, *Aufrüstung*, especially 85–89; also 42, 65, 81–84, 93 note 74 for the salient role of Stülpnagel, Kurt von Schleicher, and associates.

124 Stülpnagel, in Hürten, ed., *Krisenjahr 1923*, 272, 236, 268.

125 See also the bloodthirsty remarks quoted in Geyer, *Aufrüstung*, 99; "Mestizenvolk": Stülpnagel to Truppenamt, 270/24 T.1 I B geh., 18 March 1924, p. 6, BA-MA N5/20 (warm thanks to Gil-li Vardi for this document).

126 Stülpnagel, in Hürten, ed., *Krisenjahr 1923*, 270–71; Geyer, *Aufrüstung*, 86–87 and notes; Stülpnagel, in Dirks and Janssen, *Krieg*, 199, 208; and the later pithy outline in Stülpnagel to Truppenamt, 18 March 1924, BA-MA N5/20.

127 See also "Denkschrift über die geistige Kriegsvorbereitung des Volkes," March 1924, in Hürten, ed., *Krisenjahr 1923*, 308–14.

128 "Wir kämpfen immer um Sieg oder Vernichtung": Stülpnagel, ibid., 268, quoting Oswald Spengler with fierce approval.

Stülpnagel's plan of campaign, "the struggle to gain time" gave way to "the struggle for the annihilation of the enemy": the time-hallowed "strategic offensive" enshrined in *Führung und Gefecht*.[129] The putatively moderate Groener, in his second coming as *Reichswehrminister* from 1928 to 1932, offered a seeming dissent. He rejected the increasingly despairing efforts of the total war faction to preserve war as an option for the present or medium-term future, and in fall 1929 he and his associate, Kurf von Schleicher, removed as army chief of staff the group's most senior member, General Werner von Blomberg, and exiled him to the East Prussian command. In an authoritative 1930 directive setting forth "the tasks of the armed forces," Groener unlike Blomberg refused to commit the Reichswehr to battle in the many foreseeable conflict situations with Poland and/or France in which "*definite* prospects of success" were absent. But even Groener conceded that commitment to combat could result from a "freely taken decision of our own, when a favorable international configuration permits us [to take] the risk."[130]

The Reichswehr's *Kampf* to perpetuate the Great War also put into practice Groener's May 1919 admonition that "to *fight* for world mastery you must prepare long beforehand with foresight and ruthless consistency."[131] In January 1921 Seeckt projected a revived wartime force that would multiply the Treaty dwarf-army by nine to produce sixty-three first-line infantry divisions.[132] That utopian aspiration, with the addition of a further thirty-nine militia divisions, remained the planners' ultimate goal throughout.[133] But international, political, and budgetary reality imposed narrow limits. The camouflaged general staff and the Reichswehr ministry's organization and ordnance departments nevertheless developed a phased military-industrial build-up plan, a revolutionary concept otherwise found in this period only in Soviet Russia.[134] A "first rearmament plan" (1928/29–1932/33) went into effect following the end of Allied on-site inspections in January 1927. Its purpose was to provide the equipment for mobilizing the shadow and forerunner of the future mass army, a planned "emergency army" of sixteen divisions, with trained men for five more. The

---

[129] Stülpnagel, in Dirks and Janssen, *Krieg*, 207; Geyer, *Aufrüstung*, 99–100 note 6; Stülpnagel to Truppenamt, 18 March 1924, p. 5, BA-MA N5/20.

[130] Post, *Civil-Military Fabric*, 154–57; DRZW, 1:384.

[131] "[V]on langer Hand her vorausschauend mit rücksichtsloser Konsequenz vorbereiten": Groener situation briefing, 19–20 May 1919, in Hürten, ed., *Zwischen Revolution und Kapp-Putsch*, 121 (emphasis in original).

[132] Friedrich von Rabenau, *Seeckt. Aus seinem Leben 1918–1936* (Leipzig, 1941), 474–75; Seeckt's reputation as an opponent of the mass army lives on in the literature, but rests on serious misapprehensions.

[133] For the persistence of the target of sixty-three line divisions, along with five cavalry divisions and between thirty and thirty-nine border defense militia divisions, see army ordnance office conference minutes, 24 November 1924; memorandum by "Pfennig," 22/25, 20 May 1925 (post-1945 Allied transcripts), IWM AL695; "Pfennig" to "Fernrohr," 363/25 and "Pfennig" memorandum, 407/25, 24 September 1925, IWM AL1774.

[134] Details: Lennart Samuelson, *Plans for Stalin's War Machine: Tukachevskii and Military-Economic Planning, 1925–1941* (New York, 1999).

"second rearmament plan," drafted in 1930–31 and covering the years 1933–38, was to provide that army with munitions and supplies for six weeks of combat, while making a start on motorization.

Yet the planners' mid-range target of a twenty-one-division army "of assured fighting power and operational capabilities with modern equipment and adequate logistical support" receded rapidly into the far future. For even that modest force was incompatible both with the restrictions of Versailles and with Weimar politics, despite the Reich cabinet's 1927 agreement to fund – behind the back of the Reichstag, the public, and the foreign powers – the clandestine programs for heavy artillery, tanks, aircraft, and gas warfare that were already under way with Soviet help.[135] After 1931, the planners incessantly warned, Germany's residue of war-trained ex-soldiers would be too old to serve in first-line units; only conscription could provide the hundreds of thousands of youthful warriors that an expanded army would require. The Reichswehr needed to train with and deploy its forbidden weapons. And the roughly 7 percent of the Reich budget spent on army, navy, and the multi-year rearmament plan from October 1928 inevitably became a battleground in both cabinet and Reichstag as the Great Depression drew on.[136]

Last but not least in importance among the Reichswehr's ruminations was its effort to understand and create the conditions in which, as Stülpnagel put it, "sacrifices [could] be demanded of every *Volk*-comrade [*Volksgenosse*]." Only a national leadership simultaneously stern and charismatic – so conspicuously absent in 1914–18 – could make such demands with prospects of success. The most striking proposal derived from a Reichswehr first lieutenant and author, Kurt Hesse, who celebrated in liturgical tones Germany's coming "psychologist warlord" and Führer, *"ruler of souls,"* a "brutal and yet a benevolent one":[137]

> All of his same *Volk* who encounter him place their trust in him, for his eyes are clear and deep, and the pressure of his hand imparts strength and life. But his speech is his most beautiful aspect: for it resonates as rich and pure as a bell, and penetrates every human heart.

That fantasy was no isolated aberration. The Reichswehr both shared the collective German-national yearning for a "Führer" and possessed a burning instrumental need for such a figure. As Stülpnagel wrote to a colleague in January 1924: "It is our misfortune to lack in Germany a man of remarkable qualities who can and will rule as a dictator. *We* would support such a man,

---

[135] Geyer, "Das zweite Rüstungsprogramm (1930–34)," MGM 17 (1975), 128–29, 149; idem, *Aufrüstung*, 297; Post, *Civil-Military Fabric*, 194–95; legitimization of secret rearmament, budgetary struggles: Geyer, *Aufrüstung*, 197–98, 199–207; Post, *Civil-Military Fabric*, 197–202; Johannes Hürter, *Wilhelm Groener: Reichswehrminister am Ende der Weimarer Republik (1928–1932)* (Munich, 1993), chs. 3.2, 4.5; DRZW, 1:382–99.

[136] Figures: Ernst Willi Hansen, "Zum 'Militärisch-Industriellen-Komplex' in der Weimarer Republik," in Klaus-Jürgen Müller and Eckhardt Opitz, eds., *Militär und Militarismus in der Weimarer Republik* (Düsseldorf, 1978), 137.

[137] Kurt Hesse, *Der Feldherr Psychologos* (Berlin, 1922), 206–07.

but *we* neither wish to nor can play the role ourselves."[138] This self-confessed political-ideological barrenness intersected with the rearmament imperative to create a permanent and ultimately irresistible structural pressure within the army hierarchy against the Republic that it ostensibly served. Yet if the army lacked a political Führer, it did not lack political operators. Groener's longtime associate Schleicher had helped to raise the *Freikorps*, and had acquired remarkable influence as Seeckt's liaison to Germany's parties and pressure groups. When Gessler fell, it was Schleicher who "invented" Groener's reincarnation as *Reichswehrminister*. He thereby secured for himself early promotion to *Generalmajor* and unparalleled opportunities, as Groener's indispensable advisor, to advance the Reichswehr's institutional agenda regardless of consequences for the German Republic.

The navy too, despite its desperate condition throughout the 1920s, harbored aspirations inherited from Tirpitz and from the maniacal war-aims planners of 1914–18, whose lists of coveted French, Belgian, Scandinavian, Balkan, and Black Sea ports, and of bases and colonies throughout the wider world, lived on in the navy's files and in the hearts of its leaders.[139] The navy's 1918 collapse and subsequent disgrace in the Kapp Putsch limited forward planning for several years. But by 1925–27 the navy's leaders, like those of the army, had begun to acquire the rudiments of a grand design. The legacy of Tirpitz remained at least formally unassailable, despite the Great War's stinging demonstration of the futility of his fleet. The navy's first postwar chief, Admiral Adolf von Trotha, had for a time been Tirpitz's right hand – and chief proponent of the death ride of October 1918. Trotha's own right hand, until the admiral's removal after the Kapp Putsch, was Erich Raeder, who became the navy's chief in 1928 and served with remarkable longevity and adroitness until 1943. Yet even *Tirpitzianer* of strict observance recognized that the master's strategic concept – decisive fleet action against "England" in the North Sea – had been deluded, and not merely because the German fleet had failed to achieve the numerical parity with the Royal Navy required for Tirpitz's "authentic chance of victory."[140]

An officer whose forcefully expressed heresies dated from 1915, Admiral Wolfgang Wegener, lobbied his fellows in 1925–26 with a privately printed indictment of Germany's 1914–18 naval strategy that proposed alternatives for the future. Wegener was an original thinker only within the blinkered German naval context; he borrowed his chief insight, that the purpose of war at sea was the control of maritime communications, from Britain's foremost pre-1914 naval theorist, Sir Julian Corbett.[141] Victory in Tirpitz's single cataclysmic battle

[138] Stülpnagel, in Hürten, ed., *Krisenjahr 1923*, 243.
[139] See Herwig, "War Aims of the Imperial German Navy."
[140] On this and what follows, see Jost Dülffer, *Weimar, Hitler und die Marine. Reichspolitik und Flottenbau 1920–1939* (Düsseldorf, 1972); Carl-Axel Gemzell, *Raeder, Hitler und Skandinavien. Der Kampf für einen maritimen Operationsplan* (Lund, 1965); and idem, *Organization, Conflict, and Innovation: A Study of German Naval Strategic Planning, 1888–1940* (Stockholm, 1973), ch. 4.
[141] Julian S. Corbett, *Some Principles of Maritime Strategy* (London, 1911), 80: "The object of naval warfare is the control of communications."

was consequently merely one path to "command of the sea," and scarcely the most promising. Wegener's second insight, born of Germany's traumatic 1914–18 blockade experience and of the earlier musings of figures such as Ratzel, was that geographic position was a component of naval power co-equal with naval forces themselves. Britain, by location and topography, penned the German navy in the narrow waters of the North Sea. Wegener's answer was to seize distant bases that would place the German fleet athwart Britain's commerce routes. Failure on the Marne in 1914 had deprived the High Seas Fleet of the Atlantic stronghold at Brest that Wegener coveted. But "if the road to Brest remains closed, then we must take up the march to the north." Conquest of Denmark and Norway would open the road to the Shetlands, "door to the Atlantic," and to decisive attack on Britain's lifelines.[142]

Wegener shared with fanatical *Tirpitzianer* such as Trotha the presumption that "poisonous English hatred [and]...ruthless English inhumanity" made German great-power status inseparable from possession of a great fleet. Such a fleet, regardless of short-term strategic rationales – defense against Poland and France – would inevitably take final form as an offensive instrument against Britain. In perfect synchronicity with army figures such as Stülpnagel, Captain Magnus von Levetzow, one of the navy's leading lights, affirmed that "in the end only the sword will set us free."[143] But for the present, "the dwarf-navy... left us by the shame-treaty" was useless except for coastal defense. And the Treaty limitation of new ships to a maximum displacement of 10,000 tons threatened to throttle Germany's naval resurgence. After much hesitation and internal debate, the navy in 1927–28 nevertheless chose the most offensive design possible within that tonnage limit, at the proposal of the former naval *Freikorps* leader, Admiral Wilfried von Löwenfeld. The resulting super-cruiser – "pocket-battleship" to Germany's once and future adversaries – had six eleven-inch main guns, advanced diesel propulsion, a high top-speed, and a staggering range of up to 20,000 sea-miles.[144] The design was singularly ill-suited to war in the Baltic or North Sea; its designers' ruthless trade-off of armor for speed, gunpower, and range would only come into its own far beyond the Shetlands and Faeroes. Yet the naval high command and a surprisingly supportive Groener extracted funding for three ships from cabinet and Reichstag from 1928 onward

---

[142] Summary and Wegener quotation: Gemzell, *Skandinavien*, 16–24; for the expurgated version published in 1929, Wegener, *The Naval Strategy of the World War* (Annapolis, MD, 1989).

[143] "Frei werden wir schliesslich nur durch das Schwert": Dülffer, *Marine*, 48; "dwarf-navy," 51; similarly, captain, later admiral, Hermann Boehm, in Gerhard Schreiber, *Revisionismus und Weltmachtstreben. Marineführung und deutsch-italienische Beziehungen 1919/1944* (Stuttgart, 1978), 54–55.

[144] Gert Sandhofer, "Das Panzerschiff 'A' und die Vorentwürfe von 1920 bis 1928," MGM 3/1968, 35–62; Sandhofer takes too literally Löwenfeld's transparent political rationale – that the ship's superiority to the Washington Treaty–mandated 8″gun, 10,000-ton cruisers would force the maritime powers to concede a place to Germany in the treaty structure, and thus undermine Versailles. The ship's design was a mission statement.

without arousing excessive scrutiny of their design and purposes: all major parties except SPD and KPD supported the rebirth of the German fleet.

Yet Atlantic commerce raiding by a few fast ships, or the naval planners' fantasies of attack on France's supply lines to North Africa, was not a strategy. As with the navy's 1914–18 experiment in U-boat warfare, over which the post-1918 official historians puzzled mightily without discerning strategic lessons, the naval leadership never enunciated a plausible strategic purpose and operational mission for a German oceangoing fleet.[145] Tonnage warfare, whether by U-boats or by fast surface units, was an attritional struggle that would ultimately pit a resource-poor Germany against both Britain and the United States, and inescapably replicate the verdict of 1917–18. Even surface breakout onto the world's oceans required the defeat of the numerically superior Royal Navy, a task already beyond German strength in 1914–18. The *Reichsmarine* of the 1920s nevertheless shared the army's preoccupation with its immediate enemies, the despised Poles and hated French. Some of its leaders speculated that Anglo-American global conflict would unhinge the post-1918 order. Others found a temporary alliance of convenience with Britain itself against Soviet Russia or even France alluring. Mussolini's Italy – which figures such as Löwenfeld esteemed for its dictatorial form and zeal against socialism and "Jewish Freemasonry" – might also serve as a natural ally against France, diverting enemy forces from the navy's Atlantic struggle.[146]

For the present, any such struggle took second place to the domestic funding contest, in competition with Germany's senior service. The army of the Reichswehr proved accommodating, largely because only naval forces could assure its communications with East Prussia; Groener tirelessly promoted the pocket-battleship program. But the 1928–30 Grand Coalition cabinet and the Reichstag majority on which it rested proved less complaisant. The SPD had furnished the chancellor, Hermann Müller, and three other ministers after an election campaign focused gleefully on the slogan "Not armored cruisers, but food for kids." Raeder had long since accepted that naval funding depended for the moment on formal obeisance to the Republic. As he had remarked to Levetzow in 1924, "a dictatorship in itself [*an sich*] would not *currently* advance our cause . . . , so long as the *economic* foundations of a renewed build-up have not been laid."[147] The SPD was unwilling to smash its precarious government – stretching from DVP to SPD – over navy or army ambitions. At least some Socialist leaders were remarkably supportive of the Reichswehr, in defiance of their party's vociferous Left. But should the Republic fail to sustain the navy's wider ambitions, dictatorship would scarcely meet with objections from Raeder or his impatient subordinates.

[145] For the navy's inability to conceptualize, much less draw lessons from, the defeat of its U-boats, see Lundeberg, "German Naval Critique" and Dülffer, *Marine*, 188.

[146] Schreiber, *Revisionismus und Weltmachtstreben*, 39–61; Löwenfeld on Italy: 43.

[147] Dülffer, *Marine*, 103 ("currently": my emphasis), 105; see also Levetzow to Ludendorff, 29 July 1923, in Granier, *Levetzow*, 239–42.

One further foundation of the renewal of German power attracted uncommon attention during Germany's brief democratic interlude: the strengthening of the German "*Volk*-body." The preservation of "German blood" both within Germany and outside its post-1919 borders enjoyed a high priority even for educated Germans who regarded nation and race as spiritual rather than biological realities. Care of "Germans abroad" had long been fundamental to German middle-class associational life; the flagship *Verein für das Deutschtum im Ausland* and its associated organization for German-language schools outside Germany dated from 1881. The Pan-Germans had assiduously cultivated German-speakers beyond the Reich's borders. But in the aftermath of Versailles and of the collapse of Austria-Hungary, the issue acquired a burning urgency for far wider circles. By German estimates, roughly 3 million "Reich Germans" lay marooned outside the new borders: 1.8 million in Alsace-Lorraine; 600,000 in Posen, West Prussia, and other areas lost to Poland; and 400,000 in the League of Nations "free city" of Danzig. Beyond them lay a further 128,000 ethnic Germans in the newly independent Baltic States, and more than 6 million in the non-German successor states of Austria-Hungary, including 3.5 million Sudeten Germans on the mountainous fringes of Bohemia. Last but not least, a further 6 million German-speakers inhabited the truncated Austrian state created, in defiance of both German and Austrian opinion, by the victors.[148] For the propagation of the German language and of German nationalism throughout this diaspora of 16.5 million souls, the foreign office and a bewildering variety of voluntary organizations spent considerable sums throughout the 1920s. Organizations linking the Reich with Austria, with the Sudeten Germans, and with the ostensibly beleaguered German "*Volk*-groups" from Denmark to Hungary sprang up. One of Admiral von Trotha's retirement projects was leadership of the "German Protective League [*Schutzbund*]" formed in 1919 as a militant central organization for Reich-German propaganda among Germans in Poland and beyond.[149] Underlying virtually all such organizational work was the aim of preserving Germany's irredenta until Germany was strong enough to reconquer them, and to husband "German blood" as a resource for the Reich's renewed expansion.[150]

Domestically, similar concerns increasingly impassioned the public and Germany's numerous specialists in demography, medicine, public health, and social welfare. As "Germandom" acquired increasingly racial connotations, especially within the universities and learned professions, the lamentable conditions of the "race" appeared to demand ruthless action. Demographers had already

---

[148] Figures: Hans-Adolf Jacobsen, *Nationalsozialistische Aussenpolitik 1933–1938* (Frankfurt am Main, 1968), 161.

[149] Jacobsen, *Aussenpolitik*, 163–67.

[150] For the excessively literal-minded debate over the ultimate purposes of this effort, see R. Carey Goodman III, "Did Weimar have a National Ethnic Policy?," *Essays in History* 31 (1988), 31–51; no German policy-maker or significant segment of Weimar opinion accepted Versailles, and support of "Germans abroad," whatever its contingent justifications, was one of many policies aimed at destroying the 1919 settlement.

deplored the "blood loss" of emigration and the gradual decline of the birthrate as Germany passed through the perceived decadence of demographic transition. The war, with its 4 million "lost births," 2 million battlefield dead, hundreds of thousands of crippling wounds, and vastly increased mortality from cold, malnutrition, infectious diseases, and the influenza pandemic, appeared to legitimate drastic measures in this as in other areas.[151] The inmates of Germany's asylums and hospitals for long-term invalids had already paid: perhaps 30 percent of the prewar psychiatric asylum population died from overcrowding, hunger, disease, and neglect in 1914–18.[152] In the postwar atmosphere of existential national and "racial" crisis, positive eugenic measures, from preventing the spread of tuberculosis and venereal disease to raising Germany's flagging birthrate, occupied government bureaucrats, an army of medical and racial experts, and agitational groups such as the "Reich League for Child-Rich Families."

But war and civil war also legitimated more total and incisive approaches to the "preservation of the race." Increasing numbers of experts, while approving positive eugenic measures, took Haeckel's view that preventing the "less valuable" from breeding was a minimum requirement for sound social policy. The morality and technical feasibility of mass sterilization of the "degenerate" and criminal aroused passionate long-running debate. A German Psychiatric Institute, founded in 1918, compiled "criminal-biological" data on thousands of individuals; in 1926 the Reich Ministry of the Interior gave the Institute's Genealogical Department the right to consult official records freely. In due course the Institute also absorbed the files of the "Criminal Biological Record Office" that Bavaria's justice ministry – in full accordance with the spirit of the age – had established in 1924.[153] Yet sterilization was clearly insufficiently total. For many experts and political agitators, the racial hazard and economic burden of the "less valuable," the potential resurgence of the "fanatic psychopaths" held responsible for the 1918 revolution, and the mere existence of the "Rhineland bastards" – the 500 to 800 children of unions between German women and African, Asian, or Afro-Caribbean French occupation troops – were intolerable affronts.[154] An influential 1920 pamphlet by two "racial hygiene" experts, Karl Binding and Alfred Hoche, offered a definitive solution: the "destruction [*Vernichtung*] of life unworthy of life" by doctors acting for the *Volk* as a collective biological entity.

Yet despite increasing pressure on asylum budgets, the partisans of killing Germany's putative half-million "idiots" as an act of mercy, "eugenic

---

[151] For this and what follows, see especially Paul Weindling, *Health, Race and German Politics between National Unification and Nazism, 1870–1945* (Cambridge, 1989), chs. 5–7, and Michael Burleigh, *Death and Deliverance: "Euthanasia" in Germany, 1900–1945* (Cambridge, 1994), ch. 1. "Lost births": Weindling, *Race*, 339.

[152] Burleigh, *Death*, 11; see also Heinz Faulstich, *Hungersterben in der Psychiatrie 1914–1949* (Freiburg im Breisgau, 1998), ch. 1.

[153] Weindling, *Race*, 384–85.

[154] Ibid., 385–93, 383; Burleigh, *Death*, 26.

prophylaxis," and economic good sense nevertheless failed for the time being to overcome the moral, religious, and legal scruples of the public and the political elites. The advocates of compulsory sterilization included even Roman Catholic experts, and drew on precedents from Scandinavia to the United States.[155] By 1932 they had placed the issue firmly on the Prussian and Reich government agenda. As Weimar collapsed, a disparate community of savants – some of them steeled in war and *Freikorps* – was proclaiming its vocation as "executors of the eugenic will of the nation." A new regime that dared to found social policy on "race" would find eager and highly professional helpers in the perpetuation of the Great War, and in its renewal as a race-war both internal and external.[156]

II. Italy: Violence, State-Worship, Geopolitics

Italy's elites and institutions had only four years, not fourteen, to meditate on the legacy of 1915–18. In most cases that time was too short to produce the fanatical dreams and violent institutional agendas characteristic of Germany. Italy's version of "soldierly nationalism" was thin on the ground: no equivalents to the *Kriegervereine*, the popular militias, or *Freikorps* incubated violent dissatisfaction with the postwar order. The principal veterans' movement, the National Association of *Combattenti* of 1919, was pacific and democratic in its convictions, and reflected the claims for social justice of the peasant masses that had fought the war. Despite D'Annunzio's ravings about national mutilation, 1918 could symbolize not defeat and revolution but a historic victory, especially if measured against united Italy's previous career. And given the incomplete nationalization of the masses, the impulse to future external violence was less widespread than in Germany.

But four political forces or organizations were nevertheless preeminent in keeping the war alive: the Jacobin patriots of *interventismo*, the Nationalists, the army, and the Italian navy. The patriots agitated for D'Annunzio against Nitti, joined or led the municipal or regional anti-Socialist organizations already described, or found their way to the *Fasci di combattimento*. The *nazionalisti* retained much of their prewar character as journalistic agitators. Their postwar leaders – above all Rocco and Coppola, editors of the movement's flagship journal, *Politica*, from its founding in November–December 1918 – never quite evolved into totalitarians. Rocco's curiously static reverence for the state, "the necessary and historical form of social existence," led him to envisage an unyielding framework of draconian laws rather than a dynamic system of belief. His demand for "the government of the most able, that is, those who by

[155] For pre-1933 Catholic advocacy of sterilization, see especially Ernst Klee, *Dokumente zur "Euthanasie"* (Frankfurt am Main, 1985), 38–39, 40–46, 49–50.

[156] Karl Binding and Alfred Hoche, *Die Freigabe der Vernichtung lebensunwerten Lebens: ihr Mass und ihre Form* (Leipzig, 1920); Weindling, *Race*, 393–97, 307–10 (*Freikorps* days), 444–45, 450–57; Burleigh, *Death*, 15–24 ("prophylaxis": 21), 36–44 ("will": 41).

traditions, culture, and social position, are capable of raising themselves above immediate interests...and of discerning and realizing the foremost historical interests of the state" was only credible to narrow elites.[157] For Rocco and associates lacked the personal charisma needed to lead the masses that the Great War had mobilized.

Yet in the realm of ideas they did offer a twofold contribution to the future, both domestic and foreign. As before 1915, their enthusiastic and widely imitated vilification of parliamentarism and democracy from the right achieved almost perfect symmetry with the concurrent attack from the left. The mission of the dictatorship of the bourgeoisie – should the bourgeoisie, under Nationalist prodding, summon the guts to erect it – was to smash that of the proletariat. The resulting "military and imperial dictatorship," a prominent Nationalist insisted after the occupation of the factories in September 1920, might find inspiration in "the Russian example." But its aim would merely be the restoration of "the rule of some sort of law."[158] The nationalists' domestic vision thus lacked a center; they neither yearned for a Führer nor possessed one.

"Discipline, order, hierarchy" at home nevertheless had a foreign policy purpose. The Great War was merely one "conflict of nations, races, and empires," a passing episode in an "eternal struggle of the peoples for domination and existence." The ideological cast given it by the contenders, and especially by Woodrow Wilson, was mere window dressing. Italy's goal, if it could throw off the debilitating effects of "democratic ideology, by definition the ideology of defeat," must be to secure the preconditions for "worldwide expansion." That meant the full incorporation of all irredenta to the east, "absolute strategic security" by land and sea, economic security through industrial and naval might, and control of essential raw materials.[159] Demography consecrated Italy's right to expansion, along with that of other "prolific peoples." And geography, which the Nationalists had already identified in their prewar musings as a key to Italy's destiny, again reared its head. Coppola lamented the seapowers' domination of the world's maritime choke-points, and in particular of the "gates of the Mediterranean." Attilio Tamaro, another eminent Nationalist, denounced Malta, Biserte, and Toulon as "a chain of formidable strongholds that surround and can blockade Italy."[160] Finally, despite vacillations – for many Nationalists hoped for collaboration with a weakened France – Coppola and others identified German resurgence as a prerequisite for Italian

---

[157] Quotations: Rocco and Coppola, "Manifesto," *Politica* 1:1 (December 1918), 10–11.

[158] Attilio Tamaro, "La necessità della dittatura," ibid. 2:16–17 (30 September 1920), 82, 75, 77–78.

[159] Coppola and Rocco, "Manifesto," 1–4, and Coppola, "La pace italiana," *Politica* 1:1 (1918), 66–67, 72, 75–76.

[160] Demography: Orazio Pedrazzi, "Politica coloniale," *Politica* 2:1 (1919), 154; Coppola, "Nuova fase," ibid. 2:3 (1919), 383. Geography: Coppola, "Accademia sinistra," "L'intesa è finita," "La 'pace' adriatica," and "La paralisi della storia," *Politica* 2:2 (1919), 239; 4:2 (1920), 163; 6:3 (1920), 235–36; 3:29 (1921), 187; Tamaro, "L'Italia tradita nell'Adriatico," ibid. 3:3 (1920), 339. For prewar notions of geopolitical encirclement by France, see p. 117.

"freedom."[161] But the *nazionalisti* failed to enunciate a program that reached beyond vague threats against the Western powers.

The army's leaders were even less ambitious than the Nationalists. Their reputed November 1918 toasts to war against France and Yugoslavia were not a prelude to swift action, although both Badoglio's participation in designs for the destruction of Yugoslavia in 1920 and surviving studies for an offensive war against Yugoslavia by Badoglio and others dating from 1923 suggest the existence of earlier planning; the army staffs were also deeply involved in 1919–20 in extensive plotting for a Croat uprising to demolish Yugoslavia with Italian help.[162] Yet the army's corporate answer to the "ghastly stench of peace" was a stunning illustration both of the enduring characteristics of Italy's military culture and institutions, and of the massive favor the Allies had involuntarily done the Reichswehr. The *Regio Esercito* scorned the obvious solution to its imposing surplus of senior officers: the option of continued service at a lower rank or early retirement. Instead, it resolved its difficulties by dismissing virtually all reserve officers, cutting back drastically on recruitment of junior career officers, pensioning off with advantageous financial settlements a mere 2,700 senior officers, and finding jobs for as many active-duty career officers as possible. To accomplish that last and paramount objective, it restored much of the structure of the prewar "barracks army," reestablished its bloated ancillary organizations, lovingly preserved numerous wartime bureaucratic and logistical innovations, and created new and largely superfluous inspectorates and other entities.[163] A measure by the Giolitti government ostensibly aimed at eliminating duplication, the drastic reduction in late 1920 of the army staff's powers and personnel, had effects the civilians neither intended nor understood. In place of the wartime and postwar high command, an army council composed of intellectual dinosaurs, the "generals of victory," henceforth blocked innovation and prevented the reemergence of a single authoritative figure charged with the preparation and conduct of war. Worse still, the corps commanders across Italy responsible for backing police and prefects with troops henceforth lacked a military superior capable of enforcing obedience.[164]

---

[161] Coppola, "Accademia sinistra," 225, 254; Pedrazzi, "Politica coloniale," *Politica* 2:2 (1919), 319.

[162] "Studi sulla radunata delle L. L. E. E. Caviglia, Badoglio, e Tassoni," September 1923, Stato Maggiore dell'Esercito, Ufficio Storico, Rome, L10/82; given the detailed nature of these "*studi*" and the continued existence after 1918 of the army general staff, the claim of Fortunato Minniti, *Fino alla guerra* (Naples, 2000), 39–42, that they constituted the *Regio Esercito*'s first operational planning after 1918 seems wholly implausible. See also the evidence of army complicity, and particularly of Badoglio's involvement, in Guglielmo Salotti, "Gli intrighi balcanici del 1919–'20 in un memorandum a Mussolini del 1932 di Vladimiro Petrovich-Saxe," SC 20:4 (1989), 699–701 ("ad exclusivum usum Ducis"), and in Massimo Bucarelli, "'Delenda Jugoslavia.' D'Annunzio, Sforza, e gli intrighi balcanici del '19–20," *Nuova Storia Contemporanea* 6:6 (2002), 19–34.

[163] Rochat, *Vittorio Veneto a Mussolini*, 260–82, 312–25; for the foundations of Italian military culture, see pp. 25, 37, 45, 72, and 106–09.

[164] Mondini, *Politica delle armi*, 88–94.

The outcome of the army's postwar turmoil was a peacetime force of twenty-seven to thirty reduced-strength divisions, compared to twenty-five in 1914. At mobilization, the divisions were to double, producing a war army of sixty divisions. Within this megalomaniacal creation, the 200,000-odd conscripts that were all Italy could afford to pay and house at any one time rattled about disconsolately. The hierarchy's priorities dictated the troops' distribution across so many units and bureaucracies that mustering infantry companies for crowd control was difficult and unit combat training virtually impossible. Economy and hostility to innovation also enforced the removal of virtually all the desperately needed additional infantry firepower – machine pistols, light machine guns, mortars, light cannon – added in the course of the war, and the abolition, along with the *Arditi* and their indiscipline, of their tactical innovations. Some contemporary military critics did suggest a practical alternative that promised an effective and innovative force within Italy's narrow budgetary constraints: a standing army of fifteen full-strength divisions equipped for modern mobile warfare; capable of extended training; located not in barracks but along rail lines outside the great cities; ready for combat at short notice; and backed up as needed by a militia. But such proposals were as unthinkable to the hierarchy as the notion that machinery might prove decisive in war. As of spring 1920, the upkeep of the army's 85,000 horses and mules drew down the budget almost as much as motor transport and the air force combined.[165] Nor did success in war lead to rethinking the army's dysfunctional recruitment system, which continued to mix soldiers from several regions and station them in a third. Finally, demobilization and repeated reshuffling of the army's force structure between 1919 and 1926 further intensified the institution's bureaucratic hypertrophy, as well as its perennial budgetary and organizational chaos. An Italian government that might wish to use its post-1918 military instrument would have much work ahead.

The navy's strategic irrelevance in 1914–18, except in helping defend Italy's vital maritime supply lines against U-boat attack, perhaps disposed it to greater ambition than the army. Victory provided enough landward security in the east and at the Brenner so that Italy could at last wholeheartedly contemplate Mediterranean expansion. And Italy's victory placed it within the charmed circle of maritime world powers codified in the 1922 Washington naval treaty; the parity in battleship tonnage with France that Italy's astute negotiators secured was the most conspicuous symbol of Italy's great-power status. In making its claims against France and on the national budget, the navy itself developed from its wartime experience a geopolitical theory that resembled Wegener's, although as yet without a prescription for action. Italy, the naval staff insisted in October 1921, required superior naval power by virtue of its "geographical position in a

---

[165] The originator of this "lance and shield" proposal was General Roberto Bencivenga, one of the army's few prominent original thinkers; he had served as Cadorna's right hand from 1914 to 1917, then brilliantly commanded a brigade on Grappa and Piave in 1918 (Rochat, *Vittorio Veneto a Mussolini*, 224–31; expenses: ibid., 178).

closed sea" and its dependence on 12 million tons of seaborne coal and 5 million tons of other imports annually. From the Senate, Thaon di Revel, in attacking Giolitti's Adriatic settlement, also insisted that the four-fifths of Italy's imports that came by sea were perpetually at risk: "with Gibraltar and Suez barred, Italy would swiftly be at the mercy of [its] adversary" without a shot fired.[166] The navy did not suggest how it proposed to secure Italy's freedom. But its geopolitics, even more than that of the Nationalists, embodied an imperative that ultimately threatened Mediterranean war against Britain and France.

3. "WITHOUT ARMISTICE OR QUARTER": FASCISM AND NATIONAL SOCIALISM

The many forces in Italian and German society and politics that proclaimed the Great War's immanence and permanence, however fervent their beliefs or ambitious their forecasts of the "war of the future," could not translate hatred into policy unaided. In both countries, the prerequisite for action was the creation of mass movements dedicated to the war's continuation, capable of uniting the fragmented constituencies of the nationalist majority culture, and intent on seizing power in the name of nation and *Volk*. The discrediting or decapitating of the two states in war and aftermath, the shock of the advent of mass politics, and the postwar threats from the Left were necessary conditions for their rise. But they were not sufficient. The actions, beliefs, and charismatic force of two individuals were indispensable to the outcome. The biographies of Benito Mussolini (1883–1945) and Adolf Hitler (1889–1945) often figure as surrogates for the histories of their movements, regimes, and peoples in the "Fascist era."[167] Yet their personal histories are perhaps less central to understanding the rise and affirmation of the two movements than many biographical treatments imply. The genuinely vital biographical questions in that connection are three, and are closely interrelated. First, what personal qualities made these particular individuals indispensable? Second, where did the "dictators" come from – that is, how did Mussolini and Hitler come to believe that they were "chosen," and when, precisely did they acquire full cognizance of their respective "missions"? And, finally, how and why did they acquire mass followings?

Charismatic domination, in Max Weber's fundamental contemporary analysis, the posthumously published *Economy and Society* (1922), was "by no means limited to primitive stages of development."[168] It applied equally to

---

[166] Chief of naval staff memorandum, 23 October 1921, in Giovanni Bernardi, *Il disarmo navale fra le due guerre mondiali (1919–1939)* (Rome, 1975), 46; AP, Senato, 1921–22, 3:3833 (14 August 1922).

[167] See above all De Felice's sometimes naive *Mussolini* (1883–1945 in eight volumes and 6,416 pages) and Kershaw's frequently insightful *Hitler, 1889–1936: Hubris*, and *Hitler, 1936–1945: Nemesis* (London, 1998–2000) (1,960 pages).

[168] Carping by Weber's post-1945 exegetes about the concept's alleged weaknesses reflects its debasement into an all-purpose catchphrase for effective political leadership, as well as pious horror at Weber's value-neutral lumping of figures such as the Buddha and Jesus Christ with

"purely plebiscitary rulers (Napoleon's 'rule of genius' elevated people of humble origins to thrones and high military commands) just as much as it applie[d] to religious prophets or to war heroes." Weber defined it as the "quality of an individual personality by which he is considered extraordinary and treated as endowed with supernatural, superhuman, or...exceptional powers or qualities." The master (*"der Führer"*) affirmed himself through "magical capabilities, revelations or heroism, power of the spirit and of the spoken word [*Macht des Geistes und der Rede*]." Charisma is thus relational and personal: the charismatic following or community (*Gefolgschaft*) is directly linked – or feels directly linked – to the leader and in turn partakes of and extends his charismatic aura. Charisma is the "specifically revolutionary force in history" that in its most compelling forms has "inverted all value hierarchies and overthrown custom, law, and tradition": "charismatic belief revolutionizes men 'from within' and seeks to shape material and social conditions according to its revolutionary will." In the community it creates, "there is no system of formal rules, of abstract legal principles...concrete judgments are newly created from case to case and are...regarded as divine judgments and revelations." Above all, charisma depends on success: its possessor

> must work miracles, if he wants to be a prophet; he must perform heroic deeds, if he wants to be a warlord [*Kriegsführer*]. Most of all, he must prove [*bewähren*] his divine mission by *bringing well-being* to his faithful followers; if they do not fare well, he obviously is not the god-sent master.

And charisma can thus neither "be 'learned' [n]or 'taught,'" but only "'awakened' and 'tested.'" [169]

I. The *Fasci* from Truculent Sect to Merciless Mass Movement, 1919–1921

The awakening and testing of Mussolini as the historic leader of Italian radical nationalism proved a slow and arduous process. His humble origins in the Romagna, his hand-to-mouth wandering existence as schoolteacher and journalist scarcely suggested a future as a man of destiny. [170] Politics rescued him. His astonishing rise in 1910–14 from Socialist leader of the small Emilia-Romagna city of Forlì and editor of its party weekly, *The Class Struggle*, to a triumphantly successful editorship of the party's national daily, *Avanti!*, established him as

the "war heroes" and "great demagogues" of the modern era (see for instance Carl J. Friedrich, "Political Leadership and the Problem of Charismatic Power," *Journal of Politics* 23:1 [1961], 3–23; Martin E. Spencer, "What is Charisma?," *British Journal of Sociology* 24:3 [1973], 341–54, offers a thoughtful reply). Readers can assess for themselves the notion's usefulness in understanding the dynamics of the Fascist and National Socialist movements.

[169] Weber, *Economy and Society: An Outline of Interpretive Sociology*, ed. Guenther Roth and Claus Wittich, 2 vols. (Berkeley, CA, 1978), 2:1133, 1:241, 1:244, 2:1115–17, 1:243, 2:1114, 1:249; idem, *Wirtschaft und Gesellschaft*, vol. 4, *Herrschaft*, ed. Edith Hanke and Thomas Kroll (Tübingen, 2005) (*Max Weber Gesamtausgabe*, vol. 22/1), 481–83, 466, 734 (quotation marks and italics in original).

[170] See (but with caution), De Felice, 1.

the most ferocious, irresponsible, and resonant voice of *massimalismo*. Yet as one shrewd ex-syndicalist devotee later observed, the future Duce had become a Socialist because he was a revolutionary – not vice versa.[171] From 1908 onward Mussolini reveled in what he described as his "barbarous notion of socialism" – not the prosaic anti-capitalist utopia of the Marxists, but a violent neo-pagan upheaval by an elite of happy savages. His public anti-militarist outbursts ("for us the national flag is a rag to be planted on a dunghill") coexisted uneasily with covert flirtation with the literary nationalists of *Leonardo* and *La Voce*, complaints that Trieste was "about to be *swallowed* by the Slavs," insistence that "we must fashion the spiritual unity of the Italians," and surreptitious confession that he was an "assiduous and devoted reader" of Oriani, the bloodthirsty seer of his native region.[172]

Mussolini's swift conversion in summer–autumn 1914 to "that fearful and enthralling word: war" was thus wholly consistent with his innermost beliefs. Italy's entry into the Great War would dash "the archaic forces of Italy's political and social life... into fragments."[173] His mortifying expulsion from the Socialist party and reemergence as the foremost prophet of left-*interventismo* gave him a following far smaller than he had enjoyed as a Socialist, but perhaps even more devoted. His rapidly improvised Milan newspaper, the supremely bellicose *Il Popolo d'Italia*, took as its title a transparent allusion to Mazzini's "Italy of the Italian People." Its founding testified to Mussolini's reputation as an agitator – for its covert sponsors and bankers included the French embassy, Italian industrialists, the French Socialist party, and perhaps even the Tsarist secret service, all intent on provoking Italy's intervention alongside the Entente.[174] It trumpeted war from mid-November 1915, abused the PSI for its "propaganda of cowardice" and "hermaphroditism," and hailed Italy's imperial destinies: Trento, Trieste, Fiume, Dalmatia, Adriatic domination ("*mare nostro*"), and Balkan and Mediterranean expansion.[175] From the beginning, Mussolini also sternly demanded that Italy foreclose all prospects of compromise or mediation: it must fight Imperial Germany as well as Austria-Hungary, a wise strategic counsel the government foolishly ignored until mid-1916.

[171] The Socialist, syndicalist, *interventista*, and "Fascist of the first hour" Sergio Panunzio (1942), cited with qualified approval in Vivarelli, *Origini*, 1:260–61 note.

[172] OO, 38:5 (and subsequent extensive correspondence with Prezzolini), 9–10 (emphasis in original), 11, 45, 104–05; 2:53–56, 127, 128, 165–66 (approvingly summarizing Sorel: "Socialism... must have the courage to be barbarous"); 3:26, 66, 86–87, 137 ("dunghill"); 4:183 ("I am a primitive").

[173] OO, 7:7, 148. On Mussolini's "socialism for supermen" and choice for war, see also pp. 86, 116, 178–179 and Chapter 3, note 101; Gentile, *Ideologia fascista*, 6–16, 26; and Vivarelli, *Origini*, 1:265, 307 note.

[174] The PSI, anticipating by half a decade the agent theory of fascism, immediately asked "Who's paying?"; for the current range of answers, see De Felice, 1:273–77, 285–87; William A. Renzi, "Mussolini's Sources of Financial Support, 1914–1915," *History* 56:187 (1971), 189–206; and Luc Nemeth, "Dolci corrispondenze. La Francia e i finanziamenti a 'Il Popolo d'Italia' 1914–1917," IC 212 (1998), 605–15.

[175] OO, 7:6, 182; war aims, spring 1915: OO, 7:140, 233, 253–55, 310.

But alongside these external goals, Mussolini triumphantly invoked the subversive tradition of the *Risorgimento* and post-*Risorgimento*: Mazzini, Garibaldi, and Oriani. "War must reveal Italy to the Italians"; this would be "Italy's first war; of Italy the nation, of Italy, the people, united at last." Not the Liberal regime, object of Salandra's "absurd state idolatry [*statolatria*]," but the Italian *nation* must make this war.[176] That was the revolution that Mussolini and his winter 1914–15 "fascist movement" proposed to lead – the national integration through slaughter that the *Risorgimento* had failed to deliver and for which the *literati* had pined. To achieve that end, no violence against the "internal enemies" was too extreme: in mid-May 1915 Mussolini demanded with sadistic relish that the "few dozen deputies" of Giolitti's "criminal gang" who still barred Italy's path to war should be "executed by firing squad [*fucilati*]; I repeat, *shot* in the back."[177]

Mussolini's war lived up to expectations. His own military service to the rank of sergeant, truncated in February 1917 by fragmentation wounds received in a training accident and by the effects of syphilis, decorously covered up by patriotic army doctors, was scarcely heroic. But it sufficed for admission to Italy's *Frontgemeinschaft*, the company of those "who [had] been there." Well before Caporetto he returned gleefully to the limelight in Milan as "a sword for Italy...against [its] internal enemies," in the naive words of his wartime ally Bissolati.[178] The *"DUCE"* – for so his newspaper prematurely hailed him in February 1917 – defied the hostility of the "masses." His following was youthful, a new generation, an "elite public; the public of the cities," the true Italians, who "went to die with a song on their lips."[179] He tenaciously championed Italy's national and imperial claims, from South Tyrol to Zara in Dalmatia, even when the new age of Wilson and Lenin required tactical adjustment.[180] He had urged in his 1916–17 letters from the front the mounting of "search-and-destroy" operations against "saboteurs of the war." The "three hundred Austrians of the Italian parliament" must die, their skulls shattered by the same

---

[176] Necessity of war against Germany: OO, 38:72; 7:138, 140, 146, 197, 247, 250, 316; Mazzini, Garibaldi, Oriani: 7:196–97, 102, 109–10, 253–55, 295, 379.

[177] "[M]ovimento 'fascista'": OO, 7:317; enemies: 251, 341–43, 376, 379–81; 38:85 ("five revolver bullets in the stomach" for Giolitti). O'Brien, *Mussolini*, 52, 53–56 and throughout, implausibly interprets Mussolini as "social conservative" and "defender of State authority," because his expansionist aims and visceral enmity toward the PSI were allegedly indistinguishable from those of the Nationalists and of the Italian establishment.

[178] See the delectable revelations of O'Brien, "Al capezzale di Mussolini: ferite e malattia 1917–1945," IC 226 (2002), 5–29 (also mentioned in a 1919 police report, printed in De Felice, 1:463); OO, 10:140–41: "L'Italia va verso due grandi partiti: quelli che ci sono stati, e quelli che non ci sono stati."

[179] "IL DUCE": OO, 8:354–56 and facsimile (26 February 1917); masses and élite: OO, 9:247 (9 October 1917).

[180] OO, 8:250–52, 263–64, 268–69; 9:49–51, 60–61, 116; 10:180, 205, 228–29, 262–63, 268, 279, 327–29, 339–41, 434–35 ("imperial" Italy); 11:91–92, 299, 326–26, 376; and, despite outspoken skepticism about Mussolini's capacity to entertain political convictions, Vivarelli, *Origini*, 1:267–89.

iron-spiked maces the Austrians had devised for trench fighting. His 1917–18 agitation hammered relentlessly at the need to "impose victory" as the *interventisti* had imposed war. He sought a man of "ferocity and energy, the energy to smash [and] the inflexibility to punish, to strike without hesitation" at the internal enemy.[181] He incessantly demanded the imprisonment on a remote and desolate Tyrrhenian island or in "concentration camps" behind barbed wire of enemy aliens "without regard for status, sex, or age," and ruthless confiscation of their assets.[182] By mid-1918 he had appropriated a central Nationalist theme, the celebration of "producers" rather than workers; class conflict was treason toward the nation's struggle for life.[183] His post-Caporetto recipe for victory was a prototype for the Fascist movement and regime: "*the entire nation must be militarized.*"[184]

War's end, the rising popular clamor against those who had made it, and the inexorable advance of the insufferable Socialist and Catholic mass parties threatened to deprive Mussolini of whatever influence he possessed. His political resurrection in 1919–20 thus taxed his considerable powers to the utmost. The personal qualities on which he relied had nevertheless long since emerged during his Socialist apprenticeship: an astonishing ability to articulate in the most extreme and attractive form what his chosen constituency wanted to hear, indefatigable zeal as journalist and orator, and perhaps most of all – given the openings offered in war and aftermath – a delight in redemptive violence.

Criticism or celebration throughout his career of his purported opportunism and lack of convictions merely reflects his tactical flexibility and the authors' lack of discernment. For many observers have simply missed his underlying consistency and disruptive purpose, have presumed that Mussolini's migration from Socialism to war and ultimately to Fascism robbed him of all claim to be a revolutionary, and have believed that the absence from his rantings of anything resembling Marxist or post-Marxist social thought, or a conventional "analysis of Italian society … and its fundamental problems," irrevocably disqualified him as a creative political leader.[185]

The future Duce's defects in that regard were entirely different ones: an almost pathological suspicion of the motives and competence of his followers and consequent control-mania, and a singular lack of understanding of the very

---

[181] OO, 38:96 ("bisogna 'rastrellare' l'*interno* da tutti i sabotatori della guerra") (emphasis in original), 100, 101; 9:251, 275; 10:37–38, 54, 81–82, 123, 193; 10:347; 11:402 ("caporettisti").

[182] OO, 9:7, 300; 10:105–06, 123, 158–60, 167, 178, 191–93, 210–11, 252–54; 38:103; 11:214–16, 253–54 ("campi di concentramento"), 306–08.

[183] OO, 11:257; Corradini, *La marcia dei produttori* (Rome, 1916).

[184] "Diciamo la parola: *tutta la Nazione deve essere militarizzata*" (italics in original: OO, 10:38).

[185] Among numerous comments on these issues, see particularly Vivarelli, *Origini*, 1:259–336 (quotation, 1:333). O'Brien, *Mussolini*, persuasively documents Mussolini's essential "Fascism" virtually from the beginning of his career; Giorgio Rumi, *Alle origini della politica estera fascista (1918–1923)* (Bari, 1968), and idem, "Il Popolo d'Italia (1918–1925)," in Vigezzi, ed., *1919–1925. Dopoguerra e fascismo. Politica e stampa in Italia* (Bari, 1965), 423–491, offers brilliant demonstration of the extent to which, throughout 1919–22, "Mussolini's contradictions [were] more apparent than real" (ibid., 468).

force that he most prized, the coordinated employment of mass violence. As a close subordinate, General Emilio De Bono, commented in 1934 after more than a decade of loyalty, "this mistrust of his faithful followers [*dei suoi fedeli*] is the greatest of his defects." Mussolini himself was sufficiently conscious of his stance by 1924 to rationalize it, modestly comparing his own distrust of humanity to that of Machiavelli.[186] But he remained unaware of the extent to which his intolerance of initiative from below and his periodic summary dismissal of subordinates sapped the dynamism of his party and regime.[187] Worse still, a peculiar compound of the agitational techniques learned as a Socialist and the supremely dysfunctional features of Italian military culture distinguished Mussolini's warrior vocation. German soldiers and ideologues also proclaimed the sovereignty of *Geist* over matter. But they tended to have a noteworthy grasp of tactics, and some conception of operations, training, logistics, and machines – if never of strategy. Mussolini's understanding of warfare remained that of a journalist and connoisseur of mass psychology: "if morale is low, machines are useless."[188]

In the conquest of power in 1919–22, these defects proved of small importance. Ceaseless war against the "internal enemy," the *caporettisti* who "had stabbed the nation in the back," the "renouncers" of Italy's Adriatic conquests, and the "reviving beast" of Socialism was inherent in the meaning that Mussolini, D'Annunzio, and so many others had given to the Great War itself. And Mussolini grasped immediately that only war's prolongation promised political survival. His course after November 1918 was remarkably straightforward, despite occasional demagogic and "national-syndicalist" gestures aimed at stealing supporters from the Socialists. Mussolini, in spite of his origins, was neither "Left" nor "Right," but a radical nationalist.[189] Italy had fought for Adriatic domination, and must have it. Imperialism was "the eternal and immutable law of life." And he and his followers proposed to "defend...all [our] dead, even at the cost of digging trenches in the squares and streets of our cities."[190] At a tumultuous mass meeting at La Scala opera house in mid-January 1919, Mussolini personally savaged his former comrade Bissolati for

[186] De Bono diary, 16 January 1934, Carte De Bono, Archivio Centrale dello Stato, Rome; OO, 20:253.

[187] Stalin was spectacularly guilty of the same vice, but mitigated its consequences by the manner of removal: mortal fear was his preferred motivation for subordinates. Mussolini's regime, for reasons that will emerge, and contrary to the Duce's intentions, failed to add mass terror to its arsenal.

[188] OO, 11:160 (*Il Popolo d'Italia*, 29 June 1918, 1), and the analysis of Antonio Sema, "1914–1934: guerra e politica militare secondo Mussolini," in Virgilio Ilari and Antonio Sema, *Marte in orbace. Guerra, esercito e milizia nella concezione fascista della nazione* (Ancona, 1988), 15–118. Sema's remarks on method, and on the evidence-value of Mussolini's journalism and speeches (16–17) are particularly acute, but see also the detailed exegesis of the wartime and immediate postwar writings in O'Brien, *Mussolini*.

[189] The famous and much-disputed claim of De Felice, 1:460–62 (repeated at intervals throughout his many works) that Mussolini was a man of the "Left" until late 1920 misstates Mussolini's position even before 1914 (see note 193).

[190] OO, 11:402; 12:46, 72, 84, 101–03, 233, 332.

his relative moderation in the Adriatic, then denounced him in *Il Popolo d'Italia* as "leader of the Germans" responsible for a "dagger-blow against Italy." He swiftly positioned himself in both Milanese and national politics as the only major figure with left-wing credentials, however suspect, who could occupy alongside D'Annunzio and the Nationalists "the terrain of the nation, of the war, of [our] victory."[191]

The early Fascist movement was thus Mussolini's personal creation. The founding rally of the *Fasci di combattimento* on 23 March 1919 at Piazza San Sepolcro in Milan was sparsely attended, with an audience of perhaps 300 including journalists and curiosity-seekers.[192] In summoning the faithful, Mussolini had insisted on the iron continuity between *interventismo*, "first episode of the revolution," and postwar conflict: "the revolution continued for forty months under the name of war; *it has not ended*." The conference proceedings were vapid in virtually all respects except an insistence on "declaring war on Socialism, not because it is Socialist, but because it has been hostile to the nation," the celebration of Italy's victory, and the reiteration – in Mussolini's words – that "imperialism is the foundation of life for any people that aims to expand itself economically and spiritually."[193] But the *Fasci*'s lack of a formal program was largely irrelevant to their appeal. The new movement sought to collect veterans of the war, of Mussolini's "Fascist movement" of 1914–15, of the death-struggle against the "internal enemy" in 1917–18, and of the patriotic self-defense organizations of 1919–20 into an "anti-party" of nationalist revolution. Hostility to the notion of party stemmed in part from Mussolini's detestation of the Socialists, whose sheeplike conformism – in his view – had led them to oppose both Italy and his own person in winter–spring 1914–15. It also spoke to the widespread loathing of party organization derived from *Risorgimento* and Liberal tradition, and to the anti-parliamentary and anti-Giolittian passions of the intelligentsia. Finally, like the *interventismo* from which it derived, Fascism appealed to youth: a political movement without a past, led by young men, and devoted to violence.

Mussolini's movement initially drew its sparse support in Milan and across north Italy from five groups: syndicalist and Socialist "heretics," as Mussolini repeatedly styled himself; Marinetti and the surviving Futurists; veterans of the *Arditi*; young ex-officers and NCOs nostalgic for the war and displaced

[191] OO, 12:142–43, 309.

[192] OO, 12:338–40 provides a partial list of ninety-seven attendees, many of them subsequently obscure; for the group's composition, O'Brien, *Mussolini*, 19–20 and De Felice, 1:504–06.

[193] OO, 12:310 (emphasis in original), 325, 323; Rumi, "Mussolini e il 'programma' di San Sepolcro," *Il Movimento di Liberazione in Italia*, 71 (1963), 21–26, and idem, "*Il Popolo d'Italia* (1918–1925)," 439–44. For disagreement over whether Mussolini's 23 March celebration of Italian imperialism constituted a "program," and if so, whether it (or its June 1919 sequels, De Felice 1:742–45) placed Fascism on the left or the right, see De Felice 1:513 and O'Brien, *Mussolini*, 29. The nineteenth-century concepts of Left and Right are actively misleading when applied to twentieth-century radical nationalist totalitarianism, of which Fascism was the prototype; Lenin and his successor are likewise best understood as totalitarians rather than as "men of the Left."

in its aftermath; and university and high school students distressed at having missed the great slaughter. Italy's paramilitary subculture was thus a specifically Fascist creation. The Futurists, although filled with hatred for Italy's past – of which the monuments of Roman antiquity, the Vatican, and Giolitti were foremost symbols – and happy to parade and fight in the *piazza*, were allergic to organization, and ultimately privileged aesthetics over politics. The *Arditi*, as Italy's self-proclaimed warrior elite, organized small paramilitary bands in Milan and other northern cities, and rallied to Mussolini and to their wartime house organ, *Il Popolo d'Italia*. The military desperadoes lacked an ideology other than rage against "Bolsheviks" and other denigrators of war and victory. But they brought Mussolini the indispensable and unique gift of military force. In the months before the founding of the *Fasci*, the offices of *Il Popolo d'Italia* mutated into a fortified camp. Never before in the history of united Italy had a newspaper editor commanded a private army.[194]

A Socialist-led Milan general strike and mass meeting on 15 April 1919 occasioned the highpoint of *Arditi* and Futurist violence. Crowds of *Arditi*, Marinetti and his Futurists, army officers, veterans, and students of the Milan *Politecnico*, many of them in uniform, attacked and dispersed columns of Socialist demonstrators with hand grenades and pistol fire, took possession of Milan's cathedral square, assaulted the nearby offices of the *Avanti!*, broke the protective cordon of army troops, easily suppressed the return fire of the editorial staff, smashed the presses and devastated the newspaper's offices, and set the building on fire. Finally, the merry band marched on the offices of *Il Popolo d'Italia*, where they hailed Mussolini as their inspiration. He in turn celebrated their attack on the "Leninist horde" intent on "sabotaging and mutilating [our] victory." The outcome of this recrudescence of "the good old *interventismo*" of 1915 was four dead – including a soldier – and thirty-nine wounded.[195]

Thereafter, the organized *Arditi* receded in importance, as local *Fasci di combattimento* across north Italy gradually took over their role as the preeminent armed force facing socialism in the *piazza*.[196] Yet throughout 1919 and much of 1920 the *massimalisti* retained the upper hand. Their mass support allowed them to dominate most northern cities and the surrounding countryside, and paralyze transport and industry at will. D'Annunzio's Fiume enterprise drained off nationalist activists and veterans, cutting across the efforts of Mussolini and of others to form "squads of twenty men with a kind of uniform, and with weapons."[197]

The triumph of the PSI in the November 1919 elections provisionally destroyed the pretensions of Mussolini and his movement to mass support:

[194] Vivarelli, *Origini*, 1:326; Lyttelton, *The Seizure of Power. Fascism in Italy, 1919–1929* (New York, 1973), 52; and the detailed analysis by the Milan police, printed in Franzinelli, *Squadristi*, 30–31.
[195] Quotations: OO, 13:60, 65; see also Vivarelli, *Origini*, 1:367–73; and De Felice, 1:320–21.
[196] Rochat, *Arditi*, 124 (and, in general, chs. 8–9); for the extent of the "anti-Bolshevist guerrilla war" of *Arditi* and *Fasci* in summer–autumn 1919, see especially Franzinelli, *Squadristi*, 22–34.
[197] Mussolini to D'Annunzio, 30 October 1919, in Gentile, *Storia*, 54; see also Reichardt, *Kampfbünde*, 393–94.

MAP 3. Italy: War and Civil War, 1915–1922.

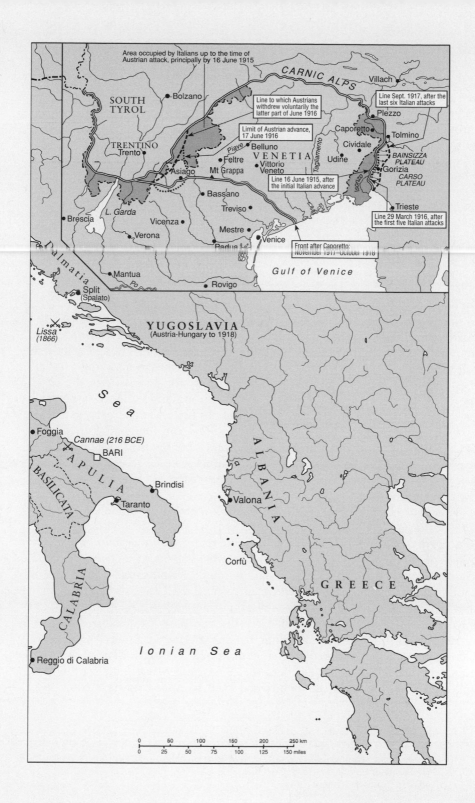

Area occupied by Italians up to the time of
Austrian attack, principally by 16 June 1915

CARNIC ALPS

Villach

SOUTH
TYROL

Bolzano

Line to which Austrians
withdrew voluntarily the
latter part of June 1916

Line Sept. 1917, after the
last six Italian attacks

Plezzo

Caporetto

TRENTINO

Limit of Austrian advance,
17 June 1916

Trento

Piave

Belluno

Tolmino

Cividale

BAINSIZZA
PLATEAU

Feltre

VENETIA

Udine

Asiago

Mt Grappa

Vittorio
Veneto

Tagliamento

Gorizia

CARSO
PLATEAU

Bassano

Line 16 June 1915, after
the initial Italian advance

L. Garda

Treviso

Brescia

Vicenza

Mestre

Line 29 March 1916, after
the first five Italian attacks

Trieste

Verona

Venice

Padua

Mantua

Po

Front after Caporetto:
November 1917–October 1918

Gulf of Venice

Rovigo

Dalmatia

Split
(Spalato)

YUGOSLAVIA
(Austria-Hungary to 1918)

Lissa
(1866)

Adriatic Sea

Foggia

Cannae (216 BCE)

BARI

APULIA

ALBANIA

Brindisi

BASILICATA

Taranto

Valona

CALABRIA

Corfù

GREECE

Reggio di Calabria

Ionian Sea

| 0 | 50 | 100 | 150 | 200 | 250 km |
| 0 | 25 | 50 | 75 | 100 | 125 | 150 miles |

4,796 votes in Milan against 170,315 for the Socialists, 73,951 for the *popolari*, and 44,284 for a middle-class nationalist *"fascio patriottico."* At year's end the Fascist movement had a mere 37 local groups and 800-odd members throughout Italy. Yet the movement and Mussolini himself survived, despite a belated and sheepish post-election gesture by the government. After the *Arditi* avenged election defeat and Socialist mockery of Mussolini with hand grenades, wounding eight, the police arrested Mussolini overnight and confiscated thirteen revolvers and a flare pistol from his office safe. Nitti immediately ordered the Duce released, rather than appearing to pander yet again to the PSI, which had demanded the banishment of the *Arditi* from Milan and the dissolution of the *Fasci.*[198]

Electoral débâcle could scarcely finish off a movement that took pride in its isolation, and could invoke force in place of votes. The *Popolo d'Italia's* violent agitation continued tirelessly, against the *"Pus,"* Mussolini's mocking term for the Socialists; against Nitti "the slug"; and for D'Annunzio and the sacred cause of Fiume, despite private reservations about the political competition that the Poet represented. Circumstances were working for the *Fasci* and their leader: above all the paroxysmal unrest in Italy's public services, streets, and fields that followed the election, and the state's continuing inability to master chaos. The hard-pressed police and army looked increasingly for assistance to the *Fasci*, most combative of the "healthy forces of the nation." Indeed Nitti – among his many sins against the Italian state's monopoly of force – had as early as in July 1919 exhorted prefects to seek out help from "*Fasci* and veterans' associations" in the "repression of violence and revolutionary endeavors."[199] The result of these convergent forces was a slow expansion between December 1919 and May 1920 to perhaps 3,000 members of the *Fasci* and of "Student Vanguard," the movement's youth organization.[200]

Then the "hour of Fascism," which Mussolini hailed as "imminent" in April 1920, came at last.[201] Early in the year, Mussolini and the Milan leadership had sent Francesco Giunta, a Tuscan lawyer, *interventista*, ex-captain of infantry, and former Fiume volunteer to take the languishing *Fascio* of Trieste in hand. Giunta organized its members into paramilitary "action squads" in May, and took the offensive both against the local PSI and the Croat and Slovene communities whose very presence was a mortal offense against the redeemed city's purported *italianità*. On 13 July, in ostensible reprisal for the killing by Croats of two Italian navy men in an ethnic dispute at Spalato (Split) in Dalmatia, Giunta and his men attacked the Trieste headquarters of the Slav labor movement, the Narodni Dom. Police and troops also opened fire on the building, and the gasoline the Fascists used to reduce it to ruins may have come from

---

[198] Gentile, *Storia*, 57–59; Franzinelli, *Squadristi*, 28–29.
[199] Nitti to prefects, 14 July 1919, in Vivarelli, *Origini*, 1:623; for the army's tilt toward Fascism, see the pioneering account of Mondini, *Politica delle armi*, ch. 3.
[200] See the estimate of Gentile, *Storia*, 115–16.
[201] OO, 38:122, 15:152 (21 August 1920).

a nearby army barracks. Mussolini hailed this "masterpiece of Trieste Fascism," and likewise applauded the contemporaneous "legitimate reprisal" that destroyed the presses of the Rome edition of *Avanti!* By late September, after the army and Giunta's men had suppressed a general strike and reconquered a working-class quarter with artillery fire, Mussolini visited Trieste and the neighboring port of Pola, and hailed the *Fascio* as "the preponderant and dominant element on the local political scene." That was premature: but further atrocities by Giunta and his followers, under a slogan ("ready to kill, ready to die") that Mussolini adopted as a *Popolo d'Italia* headline, made it so throughout Trieste's surrounding region, newly annexed Venezia Giulia, by summer 1921.[202]

Trieste and Venezia Giulia were anomalies. The precocity of their Fascism derived from the strength in Trieste and environs of *both* perceived enemies of Italy: the Socialists and the 350,000 Slovenes and Croats who made up more than 40 percent of the new region's population.[203] Giunta's *Fascio* appealed to the long-standing ethnic intolerance and sense of existential threat in the face of "Slav encroachment" of the Italian border communities – Austria-Hungary's poisonous legacy. D'Annunzio's defiant example across the Istrian peninsula at Fiume, the extravagant irredentist claims of the new Yugoslav state, and the mixed settlement pattern – largely absent in annexed South Tyrol – that placed Italians and their perceived enemies in close contact throughout the area did the rest.

A different alchemy transmuted the *Fasci* of northern Italy into powerful military-political organizations, and gave Fascism 200,000 adherents by June 1921. A common element nevertheless existed: a sense of existential threat. The seeming demonstration of the complete and final abdication of Giolitti and of the Italian state in the factory occupations in September, and above all the PSI's victories all across the northern flatlands and Tuscany in the local elections from September through November 1920, made Fascism a mass movement (see Figure 4.8).[204]

The local elections brought not the revolution that the PSI invoked with fervor proportionate to its inability to deliver, but rather the consolidation of Socialist local domination across the Po Valley and Tuscany. "Dictatorship" and "red tyranny [*sopraffazione rossa*]," as even reformist Socialists described it, now faced non-Socialists, of whatever persuasion or class, with political impotence and economic ruin.[205] In Emilia, in particular, 215 of the region's

---

[202] OO, 15:153–54, 157 ("capolavoro"), 184, 226; Rusinow, *Austrian Heritage*, 101–08; Franzinelli, *Squadristi*, 32–34, 292–99; Tasca, *Avvento*, 203–05; the army role: Mondini, *Politica delle armi*, 74–78.

[203] The 1921 census, conducted by Italy and probably underestimating the non-Italian population: 516,690 Italians, 257,038 Slovenes, 90,262 Croats (Ernesto Sestan, *Venezia Giulia: lineamenti di una storia etnica e culturale* [Bari, 1965], 121; also the ethnographic map facing 118).

[204] See in particular the neglected but persuasive analysis of Squeri, "The Italian Local Elections of 1920."

[205] Kuliscioff to Turati, 20 December 1920 and 1 February 1921, describing PSI domination in the Bologna area, in Filippo Turati and Anna Kuliscioff, *Carteggio*, vol. 5, *Dopoguerra e fascismo*

FIGURE 4.8. From PSI Local Power to Fascist Mass Movement, 1920–1921

Note: Rows in boldface represent the five leading regions.

	% of comuni with a PSI Majority	% of comuni with a "Constitutional" Majority	% of comuni with a PPI Majority	Federterra Members Aug. 1920	Fasci Members March 1921	Fasci Members June 1921	Braccianti (% of rural labor [1921])
		Fall 1920 Elections					
Emilia	65.2	17.0	14.8	284,831	17,652	33,024	32.0
Tuscany	52.1	27.6	18.7	55,574	2,600	14,840	16.8
Lombardy	32.4	37.0	30.6	175,620	13,968	35,769	37.5
Umbria	30.3	65.8	3.3	18,000	485	4,000	17.7
Piedmont	28.6	57.5	13.9	65,504	2,411	8,647	20.9
Venetia	26.5	31.6	41.8	150,093	8,238	25,612	35.8
Lazio	24.6	53.9	20.6	18,050	1,480	4,163	35.4
Marche	24.4	48.5	24.7	13,485	814	1,984	21.5
Apulia	17.4	80.1	2.5	30,450	3,711	18,265	52.7
Liguria	16.0	61.0	23.0	4,300	2,749	7,405	19.8
Abruzzi	9.8	88.3	1.9	9,282	1,626	5,596	28.9
Sicily	8.7	78.4	12.9	7,884	3,569	9,806	49.3
Calabria	8.6	83.9	7.5	2,700	712	2,236	55.8
Basilicata	7.1	91.3	1.6	25	500	610	49.7
Campania	2.9	86.2	10.9	3,161	3,550	11,483	42.7
Sardinia	2.7	85.4	11.9	802	1,100	3,372	39.0

Base data: Giusti, Le correnti politiche, 32; Gentile, Storia, 154–57; Zangheri, ed., Lotte agrarie, 403–04; Serpieri, La guerra e le classi rurali, 369 (adjusted 1921 census data).

329 municipalities (*comuni*) were now in Socialist hands, and the PSI enjoyed a similar preponderance at the provincial level.

The spring–summer 1920 adjustments of the Fascist message by Mussolini and his associates to make it friendlier to a variety of material interests have led some historians to postulate a "conversion" of early Fascism from "left" to "right."[206] But the causal value of Mussolini's verbal concessions to Italy's "producers" – a notion borrowed from Corradini and emblazoned on *Il Popolo d'Italia*'s masthead from August 1918 – is as limited as the early Fascist movement's occasional espousal of the "expropriation of capital" and other postwar fads. Mussolini's core beliefs centered on the radical nationalist fanaticism and vocation for violence already described. The foremost Fascist appeals, from the movement's beginnings in 1919, were the unconditional defense of Italy's victory and imperial claims, and the continuation of the war of 1915–18 against the "internal enemy." Those appeals had in 1919–20 merely inspired small savage bands of enthusiasts; Mussolini had repeatedly hailed his 1919 creation as a "movement of minorities," that "could not spread outside the cities."[207] What happened from fall–winter 1920 onward was that ever-larger groups of Italians, in the areas where local government had just fallen to the PSI, realized that violence was both feasible and their last best hope of individual and collective survival. Trieste had shown the way.

Bologna and Ferrara provinces detonated the explosion. With 73,000 and 74,720 *Federterra* members respectively, they already possessed the largest and most militant armies of organized *braccianti* in all Italy. They now received town and provincial councils wholly dominated by the *massimalisti*; the PSI gained absolute majorities in fifty-four of Bologna province's sixty-one *comuni*, and in fifteen of twenty-one in Ferrara.[208] In Bologna a Socialist-anarchist mob had assaulted a *Guardia Regia* barracks and killed two police officials on 14 October. On 25 October the *Federterra* won total victory over the province's landowners in the nine-month strike that the *leghe* had fought with unparalleled violence and loudly proclaimed expropriational intent.[209] The installation on 21 November of the new *massimalista* city council, and red flags flying from Bologna's highest tower – a twelfth-century monument to another era of civil war – gave the local Fascists their long-sought opening to challenge the "Bolsheviks" publicly to "a great trial of strength in the name of Italy."

(1919–22), ed. Alessandro Schiavi (Turin, 1953), 412–13, 428–29; Cardoza, *Bologna*, 274–89; and the detailed description, from a PCI perspective, of PSI punitive measures in Luigi Arbizzani, "Lotte agrarie in provincia di Bologna nel primo dopoguerra," in Renato Zangheri, ed., *Le campagne emiliane nell'età moderna* (Milan, 1957), 283–332.

[206] Above all De Felice, 1:589–98, 617–18, 2:3–5; Gentile, *Ideologia fascista*, 191–209, and idem, *Storia*, 92–105, are far more nuanced.

[207] OO, 13:220 (July 1919).

[208] Istituto Centrale di Statistica, *Compendio delle statistiche elettorali italiane dal 1848 al 1934*, 2 vols. (Rome, 1946–47), tables, 2:162.

[209] See (from very different viewpoints), Arbizzani, "Lotte agrarie," 307–27, and Vivarelli, *Origini*, 2:883–907.

When the newly elected Socialist mayor attempted to speak from the *palazzo* balcony, the leader of the Bologna *Fascio*, Leandro Arpinati, and his 300-odd armed followers swept away the cordon of police, *Carabinieri*, and troops. The ensuing firefight, grenades thrown into the crowd by the Red Guards, and shooting inside the building left ten dead, including the lone Nationalist town counselor, and fifty-odd wounded. "Bolshevist" savagery thus ostensibly justified the Bologna *Fascio*'s solemn "second declaration of war: without armistice or quarter," and a relentless and highly effective military campaign that destroyed the PSI's organizations throughout the city before proceeding, from March onward, against the *leghe* of the flatlands.[210] Motorized *squadre*, usually led by former infantry officers and manned by combat veterans and student enthusiasts, clothed themselves in black and carried brass knuckles, knives, knotty clubs, iron bars, pistols, shotguns, rifles, machine guns, cans of gasoline, and the ubiquitous army surplus fragmentation and concussion grenades. *Squadrista* tactics were highly effective against the PSI's sedentary rural organizations. Mobility ensured surprise. The *squadre* drove in unexpectedly, usually after dark, and destroyed local PSI and *lega* headquarters, labor exchanges, press, and consumer cooperatives, and killed, or beat and banished upon pain of death, all Socialist leaders caught in the net. "The Communist meeting-hall of Broni is set alight, and the holy flames purify the surroundings," as a Fascist leader in the Lomellina, the fertile rice fields of western Pavia province, described one of many such exploits.[211] A shooting incident on 20 December similar to the Palazzo d'Accursio "massacre" gave the *Fascio* of Ferrara its own pretext to unleash a crescendo of "punitive expeditions" across the province from January through April 1921. The *Fasci* of Modena, Mantua, Pavia, and Cremona followed suit. And the Florentine *Fascio*, with strong support from a regional *classe proprietaria* and industrial interests noteworthy for their concentration of ownership and power, created by mid-1921 the most savage and venturesome bands of the entire peninsula.

The nature and social composition of the new mass movement of 1920–21 has inevitably aroused endless debate. The Fascists themselves proclaimed – if sometimes uneasily – the highest of patriotic motives, and insisted that their violence was invariably a sacred patriotic response to Bolshevik barbarism.[212]

---

[210] Quotation: Dino Grandi, in *L'Assalto* (the Fascio's newly founded newspaper), 1 December 1920, quoted in Luigi Salvatorelli, *Storia d'Italia nel periodo fascista*, 2 vols. (Milan, 1969), 2:169; similarly, "without quarter and without mercy" (29 January 1921), in De Felice, 2:43; Cardoza, *Bologna*, 306–08, and the exemplary maps and analysis of the movement's oil-blot spread across the province, 325–27.

[211] Franzinelli, *Squadristi*, 34–57, 336; Tasca, *Avvento*, 201–17; Corner, *Fascism in Ferrara*, 139–40; Gentile, *Storia*, 482–94; Arturo Bianchi, *A Noi! Storia del fascismo pavese* (Pavia, 1929), 127.

[212] See the unique and vivid diary of a high school recruit, Piazzesi, *Diario*, and the comments of Lucio Ceva, "L'organizzazione culturale di uno squadrista toscano," NA 2141 (1982), 368–69.

Marxists and non-Marxists have echoed the PSI's denunciations of the *squadre* as the "white guards" of "reaction" or "counter-revolution," agents or puppets of north Italy's vengeful landowners and industrialists.[213] The sociologically inclined have seen the movement as a "*massimalismo* of the middle classes," the cutting edge of a "secondary mobilization" by Italy's *ceti medi* or "petty bourgeoisie" in response to the "primary mobilization" in 1919–20 of the urban and rural working classes.[214] Finally, commentators have discerned at least three principal categories, each with its own characteristics and origins, within the wide range of local realities typical of early Fascism: the original "urban" Fascism of 1919–20 and after; the "agrarian" Fascism especially prominent from 1921 onward in the southern Po Valley, from Bologna to Ferrara; and an "industrial" Fascism characteristic of smaller northern cities dominated by a few local firms and of Tuscan areas such the marble-quarrying district of Massa-Carrara.[215]

None of these causational schemes or taxonomies captures the complexity of the nature and spread of the early Fascist movement particularly well. Italy was and remains a nation of city-states, each dominating its *contado* through land ownership and immemorial tradition. A Fascism appropriate to each local reality inevitably emerged; the Fascist movement was first of all a *provincial* and regional phenomenon seemingly created to puncture generalizations.[216] Interpretations that categorize Fascism before 1922 ideologically as radical nationalism often fail to address sufficiently the obvious role of material interests in the birth of the mass movement.[217] Interpretations that place the "class character" of the movement's recruitment, funding, and support in the foreground normally evidence a naive reductionist belief that social origins and material interests are the characteristics most relevant to historical understanding, and direct and sufficient explanations of social and political action. And

---

[213] See for instance – ironically in view of his later denunciations of a purported Italian Marxist "vulgate" on Fascism – De Felice, 2:4 ("Historically there is no doubt – today – that Fascism was above all a capitalist-bourgeois reaction against the working class"). The most sophisticated analyses along these lines are Frank Snowden, "On the Social Origins of Agrarian Fascism in Italy," *Archives europeénnes de sociologie* 13 (1972), 268–95; idem, *Tuscany*; and Corner, *Fascism in Ferrara*.

[214] Gentile, *Storia*, 78, 556–66; idem, "La crisi del socialismo e la nascita del fascismo nel mantovano," SC 10:4–5 (1979), 691, 696; Gino Germani, "Fascism and Class," in Stuart J. Woolf, ed., *The Nature of Fascism* (New York, 1969), 86–90.

[215] See Lyttelton, *Seizure*, especially 55–56, on the "industrial" Fascisms of Liguria; also the exemplary local study of Roger Engelmann, *Provinzfaschismus in Italien. Politische Gewalt und Herrschaftsbildung in der Marmorregion von Carrara 1921–1924* (Munich, 1992).

[216] A point emphasized by Lyttelton, *Seizure*, 54; Roberta Suzzi Valli, *Le origini del fascismo* (Rome, 2003), 65; De Felice, 2:115–16; Gentile, *Storia*, 160–62; and Ivano Granata's discerning "Storia nazionale e storia locale: alcune considerazioni sulla problematica del fascismo delle origini, 1919–1922," SC 11:3 (1980), 503–44.

[217] See for instance the largely plausible ideological analysis of Paolo Nello, "La violenza fascista ovvero dello squadrismo nazionalrivoluzionario," SC 13:6 (1982), 1009–25, and idem, *L'avanguardismo giovanile alle origini del fascismo* (Bari, 1978).

the widespread notion that local Fascism's putative "original" characteristics as "class reaction" explain its subsequent policies and trajectory at the national level is equally implausible.

The factors that determined the timing of Fascism's emergence as a mass movement and the nature of its following are nevertheless susceptible of description. In the background, the long-delayed completion of demobilization released a million men into the peninsula's overpopulated rural areas and their overcrowded labor markets between mid-1919 and mid-1920. Italy's customary emigration outlets reopened briefly in 1919–20, but thereafter U.S. restrictions and the recession helped limit the exodus to less than half of prewar levels, intensifying the squeeze on wages and employment.[218] The worldwide postwar recession (Figures 4.1 and 4.2) did not bottom out until early 1922. Along with the concurrent and related collapse of Italy's overextended wartime industrial combines, it further restricted employment, made landowners and industrialists increasingly fretful about costs, and sapped the militancy of labor. The Red Army's sweep westward and ultimate battlefield failure at Warsaw in August 1920 dramatized both the Bolshevist threat and the sovereign efficacy of countervailing force. And Lenin's "twenty-one demands" upon the world's socialist parties split the Italian working-class movement at the worst possible moment into what one Socialist leader later described as "*two* communist parties in ferocious and merciless mutual combat, within one of which reformists and centrists were incarcerated."[219] At the Livorno congress of January 1921, the new *Partito Comunista d'Italia* (PCI) emerged to divide the PSI's regional and local organizations with the rump-PSI – just as the Fascist offensive hit its stride. Simultaneously, D'Annunzio's December 1920 eviction from Fiume released his military desperadoes to avenge defeat closer to home. But at the origin of the Fascist offensive lay the PSI's successes in the fall 1920 local elections, in the Po Valley and Tuscan areas most affected by seemingly ever-increasing PSI and *lega* militance.

The resulting mass movement was above all a consequence of the weight of agriculture on the history of united Italy, of north and central Italy's bifurcated socioeconomic structure and forty-year lag behind Germany. The Po Valley's motor of economic growth had not merely been the great industrial center of Milan. By 1921, despite the wartime spurt of industry, and a per capita GDP that rivalled or surpassed that of Germany as a whole, 52 percent of north Italy's workforce remained in agriculture, and industry's share had actually declined from 29.6 percent (1911) to 27.0 percent – compared to the 41.4 percent of the German workforce in industry and 31.1 percent in agriculture (1925) (see also Figures 2.5 and 2.4).

---

[218] Postwar emigration: 1919: 253,224; 1920: 614,611; 1921: 201,291; 1922: 281,270; 1923: 389,957 (Commissariato Generale dell'Emigrazione, *L'emigrazione italiana dal 1910 al 1923*, 1:4).

[219] Pietro Nenni (1945), in De Felice, 2:49 (my emphasis).

Wars between and within agricultural societies are about land; in Emilia, epicenter of the Italian civil war, the working agricultural population in 1920–21 fell into five groups: 33.1 percent owner-cultivators and leaseholders; 32.9 percent *mezzadri*, 2.0 percent resident laborers, and 32.0 percent *braccianti*. The owner-cultivators and leaseholders were in many cases new men: they had made up only 26.6 percent of Emilia's agricultural population in 1911. War had markedly improved their fortunes, and postwar unrest had further increased opportunities by panicking absentee landlords into selling.[220] Emilia's *mezzadri* had on balance likewise done well in 1915–20; until the *lega* labor monopoly had descended, many had taken on hired hands or permanent laborers, and most had traded their labor in customary fashion with neighboring *mezzadri*. Permanent hired hands likewise aspired to retain a status, however lowly, that the *leghe* despised as "privilege" and sought to abolish with egalitarian zeal. The *leghe* of the day-laborers had thus insulted, threatened, and indiscriminately coerced from spring 1919 onward the other four classes (as defined by their relationships to the means of production) of the northern countryside.[221] The PSI's endlessly reiterated delusional demand for the "socialization of the land," an outcome seemingly imminent across the Po Valley by fall 1920, was a remarkable demonstration of ineptitude, equally innocent of Marxist analysis and political arithmetic. Had Italy's Socialists set out to arouse the united violent hostility of the half to three-fifths of the rural inhabitants of the key Po Valley provinces who were not *braccianti*, they could scarcely have chosen a more effective strategy than the "abuse of violence" and "stupid and ruinous ranting" that Ferrara's belatedly penitent Socialist newspaper condemned in March 1921.[222]

At the end of 1920 Mussolini's summons to perpetuate the Great War thus intersected with the wrath and fear of the Po Valley's elites and rural majority (see Figure 4.9). The cadres of "urban Fascism" remained vital. In Bologna the two "historic leaders" were both expressions, in very different ways, of city domination over the countryside: Arpinati, autodidact, former railroad worker, Socialist and anarcho-syndicalist organizer, personal friend of Mussolini from 1918, and revolutionary man of blood; and Dino Grandi, *interventista*, former captain of *Alpini*, youthful law graduate of Bologna University, and the

---

[220] Serpieri, *La guerra e le classi rurali*, 368–69 (1921 adjusted census figures); Cardoza, *Bologna*, 321–22.

[221] By the end of the nineteenth century Marx's notion of class had lost what little relevance to industrial society it might once have possessed. But it paradoxically offers useful insights into the dynamics of the PSI's rural débâcle.

[222] Quotations: *La Scintilla*, 5 March 1921, in Corner, *Fascism in Ferrara*, 143. For a master-class in the revolutionary social analysis of peasant society, see the Vietnamese Communist materials printed, excerpted, and analyzed in Jeffrey Race's classic, *War Comes to Long An: Revolutionary Conflict in a Vietnamese Province* (Berkeley, CA, 1972), particularly 92 note 39, 121 ("Turn the landless, poor, and middle peasants into one bloc, allied with the rich peasants; fragment or win over the landlords"), 125–30, 141–51, 204–05.

FIGURE 4.9. At the Epicenter: Agricultural Strikes, PSI-PPI Political Control, and Fascist Civil War in Emilia-Romagna, 1920–21

Province	Total Agricultural Workforce	Braccianti	Braccianti (% of the Agricultural Workforce)	Federterra Members Aug. 1920	Number of Strikers 1920	% of comuni with a PSI Majority (1920)	% of comuni with a PPI Majority (1920)	% of comuni not under Liberal Control (1920)	Fasci Members 31 March 1921	Fasci Members 31 May 1921
Bologna	158,092	56,974	36.0	73,000	80,000	88.5	9.8	98.4	5,130	10,280
Ferrara	106,028	70,981	66.9	74,720	69,600	71.4	0.0	71.4	7,000	7,880
Forlì	105,030	31,718	30.2		9,400	73.2	2.4	97.6	300	215
Modena	128,985	40,133	31.1	45,060	12,050	60.0	24.4	84.4	2,510	4,400
Parma	116,376	35,054	30.1		31,700	27.5	35.3	62.7	770	1,985
Piacenza	92,894	31,889	34.3		20,000	53.2	10.6	63.8	1,040	1,280
Ravenna	89,823	35,869	39.9	19,403	3,850	66.7	11.1	88.9	70	1,120
Reggio Emilia										
Emilia	116,774	40,797	34.9	24,400	41,800	84.4	11.1	95.6	832	3,296

Base data: Censimento 1921, 8:308, 334, 360, 361, 386–87, 412, 413; Zangheri, ed., Lotte agrarie, 403–04; Ministero dell'Economia Nazionale, I conflitti del lavoro in Italia nel decennio 1914–1923 (Rome, 1924), 295; idem, Statistica delle Elezioni generali politiche per la XXVI Legislatura (15 maggio 1921) (Rome, 1924), LVII; Gentile, Storia, 155.

smoothest of drawing-room Fascists, with close connections to the local moneyed and landed elite. In Ferrara the transition from radical nationalist sect to agrarian mass movement was even more swift and total than in Bologna. Its foremost leader was a highly decorated *interventista* and ex-lieutenant – like Grandi – of *Alpini*, Italo Balbo, who had recently earned a degree in political science from the University of Florence with a thesis on Giuseppe Mazzini. Even before reaching the age of twenty-five in June 1921, Balbo had distinguished himself as Fascism's single most powerful and enterprising regional chieftain. Rural recruits swelled the followings of these provincial *ras* – an Amharic word for feudal lord, acquired during Italy's unhappy colonial apprenticeship – as the Fascist appeal to arms found its mass audience among all those reluctant to surrender their hard-won stakes in the land.

By spring 1921 the Fascist movement was also developing mechanisms for consolidating victory. The excursions of the *squadre* left behind *Fasci* as well as burnt-out buildings and corpses. Helping neighboring Fascists to achieve domination or repel Socialist counterattack was the primary means by which the movement spread: the turbulent frontier of the next *comune*, the next province, the next region, lured the *squadre* ever-farther afield in ever-larger numbers. Wherever powerful Socialist organizations existed, Fascism took root. By summer 1921, concentrations of *squadristi* from several provinces were descending upon inoffensive towns and cities throughout the lower Po Valley and imposing their will on inhabitants and state authorities alike. The Ferrara *Fascio*, following yet another precedent set in Trieste, exploited the experience, the local knowledge, and the thirst for revenge on the PSI of syndicalists and ex-Socialists among its cadres, and from early 1921 created its own agricultural unions. These *sindacati* – lavishly subsidized, like the Fasci themselves, by landowners and their organizations through individual contributions and the organized taxation of members, took over the followers of the *leghe* by offering the employment upon which life depended.[223] The Fascist movement also organized *mezzadri* and hired hands with all too credible promises of immunity from further "red" vexations. Bologna followed suit, if more slowly, due to the more variegated structure of land ownership, the less complete domination of the *leghe* across the province, and the lesser influence of Fascist ex-syndicalists compared to Ferrara. At the end of January 1921 the Milan leadership launched a sketchy but enticing agrarian program: "To every *contadino* his own land." Mussolini himself publicly blessed the pioneering role of the Ferrara *Fasci* in February; the two foremost members of his entourage had both played leading roles in Ferrara's pre-1914 labor struggles: Michele Bianchi, editor of *Il Popolo d'Italia* and future secretary of the Fascist Party, and Umberto Pasella, architect of the national organization of the *Fasci* from 1919 to late 1921.[224]

---

[223] See especially Ferdinando Cordova, "Le origini dei sindacati fascisti," SC 1:4 (1970), 973–74.
[224] Cordova, "Origini dei sindacati fascisti," 974; OO, 16:170–73. Bianchi: Gentile, *Storia*, 333–34 note 24, and Snowden, in Victoria de Grazia and Sergio Luzzatto, eds., *Dizionario del fascismo*, 2 vols. (Turin, 2002–03), 1:159–62; Pasella: Gentile, *Storia*, 37–38 note 71.

The revived and expanding Fascist movement of 1921 was indeed deeply indebted to the local landowning elites. But the explanatory power of that connection is weak. The *agrari* themselves, even those disposed to violence since the great strikes of the decade before 1914, had failed to create a mass movement; Italy's fragmented landed interests never developed a *Bund der Landwirte*, an interest bloc of great landowners and loyal peasants.[225] And for violent self-help under the conditions of 1919–21 the *agrari* lacked the necessary skills, and for the most part – as the *squadristi* and their leaders periodically reminded their sponsors – even the guts. The belated patronage of local elites throughout north Italy helps explain the timing and speed of the movement's spread, but contributes little to an understanding of its specific nature; the *Fasci* had already been fighting the "internal enemy" in the *piazza* since spring 1919.

The sociological interpretation – Fascism as "secondary mobilization" of the *ceti medi* squeezed between the Socialist masses and upper bourgeoisie – is equally generic, quasi-tautological, and above all confuses provenance and status with political action. Tabulating by social category the heterogeneous jumble of small-town lawyers, schoolteachers, lower bureaucrats, and secondary school and university students found in the surviving membership lists of the *Fasci* scarcely validates a class explanation of Fascism's rise and triumph. Given the structure of Italian society and politics, *any* non-Socialist and non-Catholic mass movement in postwar Italy would necessarily have drawn its members predominantly from the *ceti medi*.[226] But the conclusion that Fascism was in some sense the political *expression* or *embodiment* of that "class" does not follow at all. And why should the action of that "class," even if – entirely hypothetically – classes *can* act politically in a discernibly unitary way, express itself through *this* particular movement, through Fascism's "pagan style" and "cult of force and audacity"?[227] Why an organization merging war and politics, fanatically devoted to violence in the name of the nation, and in which virtually all significant political leaders except the group around *Il Popolo d'Italia* personally commanded armed bands seemingly intent on the military conquest of Italian society?

At the core of the 1921 mass followings of the Po Valley and Tuscan *ras* stood the same people – and the same categories – as in 1919–20: the difference was above all in the mass recruitment that the apparent consolidation of PSI

---

[225] For the sad tale of agrarian efforts to organize nationally, see Pier Paolo D'Attorre, "Conservatorismo agrario e fascismo negli anni venti: linee di ricerca sull'area padana," IC 151/152 (1983), 41–63.

[226] For the distinction (social situation/cultural formation) in relation to Fascism's rise and career, see the wise analysis of Mariuccia Salvati, "Da piccola borghesia a ceti medi," in Angelo Del Boca, Massimo Legnani, and Mario G. Rossi, eds, *Il regime fascista. Storia e storiografia* (Rome, 1995), 446–74. Salvatorelli, *Nazionalfascismo* (Turin, 1977 [1923]), 12–16, pioneered in 1922–23 – without a scrap of evidence – the influential interpretation of Fascism as a revolt against both labor and capital by the "piccola borghesia umanistica," a class defined by "rhetoric"; see also the endorsement of De Felice, 2:117–19, 3:5.

[227] OO, 14:193.

local power made possible. Three characteristics stand out: trade union pasts, military experience, and youth. The syndicalist organizers and ex-Socialists were numerically insignificant, but their expertise at mass organization was an essential ingredient in Fascist success. Those who had enjoyed the Great War – *Arditi*, *Alpini*, and junior officers – were even more vital. Without their military skill, no *squadre d'azione*, no relentless, expert, and joyous pursuit of the beaten enemy. This greatest of wars before 1941–45 had made combat service into a *social* category, a tie that bound together those who had fought – against those who had not – and above all against those who mocked sacrifice for the cause of Italy.[228] In apparently representative samples of Florence and Bologna *squadristi* from late 1921, almost half had war service, whereas 57.4 percent of the movement's national membership in November 1921 at least claimed it.[229] Finally, youth was the other decisive marker of membership in the movement's core, the *squadre d'azione*. The power of life and death intoxicated the adepts of patriotic juvenile delinquency throughout this "romantic era of violence" – a phrase of Renato Ricci, ex-lieutenant of *Bersaglieri* and chieftain at twenty-five of the notably savage *Fascio* of Carrara. A high school boy of good family could later preface his "diary of a Tuscan *squadrista*" with the claim that "most of those who fell in the Florentine *Fascio di combattimento* along the bleached dusty roads of the Arno valley, or stained with their blood the peaceful stones of the streets of Florence, were no more than twenty years of age."[230] The available membership statistics scarcely disconfirm that claim: 46.7 percent of Florence *squadristi* sampled were born after 1900, the average age of the sample was 22.9 years, and 83.5 percent were aged between sixteen and twenty-seven; similar samples for Bologna, Reggio Emilia, and Carrara give only slightly higher averages.[231]

War, youth, . . . and ideology: the paramilitary character of the *squadre* was without Italian precedent, but their ideology and associated ceremonial were not. The rituals, as essential a feature of *squadrismo* as combat against the internal enemies of the Italian nation, revolved around the solidarity of *squadra* and movement, the bond between leader and followers, and the celebration of

---

[228] The ironic observation of Wolfgang Sauer, "National Socialism: Totalitarianism or Fascism?," AHR 73:2 (1967), 411, that "the military is apparently still not a category for social analysts," remains all too true.

[229] Suzzi Valli, "The Myth of Squadrismo in the Fascist Regime," JCH 35:2 (2000), 135–36; similarly, for Carrara, Engelmann, *Provinzfaschismus*, 172–73 (if ex-officers are included, 60 percent of Engelmann's sample of 130 *squadristi* had served in the war, most of them at the front).

[230] "L'epoca romantica della violenza": quoted in Sandro Setta, *Renato Ricci. Dallo squadrismo alla Repubblica Sociale Italiana* (Bologna, 1986), 31; Florence: Piazzesi, *Diario*, 47; Franzinelli, *Squadristi*, 39, estimates that 40 percent of *squadristi* were students; for their enthusiastic acceptance of the Fascist "adventure," see Cristina Baldassini, "Fascismo e memoria. L'autorappresentazione dello squadrismo," *Contemporanea* 5:3 (2002), 494–98.

[231] Suzzi Valli, "Myth of Squadrismo," 135–36; Engelmann, *Provinzfaschismus*, 170–71; 284 for Engelmann's dismissal of the lower-middle-class thesis in favor of youth and ideology ("the primacy of politics"); also Reichardt, *Kampfbünde*, 366–69: a sample of 192 Fascist "martyrs" with a similar age profile.

the honored dead, "martyrs of the Fascist Revolution." Each *Fascio* and *squadra* possessed a symbolic black guidon (*gagliardetto*), often adorned with a death's head, presented on inauguration, witness to solemn oaths and dedications, paraded in the face of the enemy, and – at least theoretically – guarded faithfully unto death; conversely, attacks on the Socialists often resembled a murderous game of capture-the-flag, with the enemy's "red rag" as trophy.

To that military symbolism, Poet and *Arditi* had contributed further refinements, above all the choreographed dialogue of leader and followers, with black-shirted crowds brandishing weapons and roaring at the orator's cue "*A noi!*" or the nonsensical D'Annunzian war-cry "*Eia eia eia alalà!*"[232] Finally, the cult of martyrs, a notion deeply embedded in Italian nationalism from the earliest years of the *Risorgimento*, was of central importance to Fascist political tactics, ritual, and ideology. The blood of martyrs – from the Isonzo and Piave fronts of 1915–18 to the Po Valley flatlands of 1920–22 – sanctified both the "reprisals" and "punitive expeditions" of the *squadre* and Fascism's emerging claim to rule Italy. The funerals of the fallen, as at Bologna and Ferrara in November–December 1920, offered immense propaganda opportunities. Nor did the *Fasci* neglect the many dramatic ritual possibilities: the candle-lit lying in state; the motionless honor-guard of close comrades; the local *Fascio* and contingents from province and region on parade; the grieving mother of the fallen dressed in black surrounded and comforted by the movement's leaders; and the awed citizenry lining the streets or accompanying the cortège. The movement had by 1921 successfully identified Mazzini's celebration of martyrdom for the cause of Italy with its own street-fighting dead.

Ideology, insofar as provincial Fascism had time and inclination to express one – or several – was in line with ritual. The *ras* and their followers, however deeply enmeshed with local landowners or industrialists, enunciated with frequency and vehemence a vision of Italy extending far beyond hatred of the "internal enemy." That vision embraced domestic policy: Fascism was and remained a revolt against the liberal state, imbued with all the scorn of the pre-war anti-Giolittian avant-garde and the Jacobin intolerance of *interventismo* toward the old Italy, "sickened by the demagogic syphilis injected over long years of the sorriest democracy." The nature of the new order remained hazy indeed, but the Fascist bond between leader and followers and the anti-Socialist appeal of the Fascist labor unions offered obvious clues. And in foreign policy the provincial Fascist press was as passionately committed to Fascist empire as the Nationalists or the *Popolo d'Italia*. Grandi's Bologna paper, *L'Assalto*, was not alone in assuming that a reborn – Fascist – Italy "would soon dominate over the feebleness and decadence of the others." The nation's claim to be a great power and its consequent imperial destinies – the central political myth of united Italy – were a vital element in the glue that bound together "urban" and

---

[232] D'Annunzio: p. 252, and Vivarelli, *Origini*, 1:574; *squadrista* ideology and ritual: see especially Gentile, *Storia*, 494–534.

"agrarian" Fascists, border xenophobes and Milanese newspapermen, thugs and politicians. Italy's "expansionist" mission was to once more emerge as the leading nation of the Mediterranean basin. That exalted status, as Giunta claimed from Trieste in February 1921, with all the strategic myopia characteristic of the coming Fascist regime, would enable Italy to "dominate the world."[233] The violent means required to secure that domination were equally congenial; despite almost invariable insistence in the face of genteel middle-class opinion in the present – and foreign opinion in the future – that Fascist violence was retributive and just, its centrality betrayed its true nature. It was the most expeditious and forthright means of destroying Italy's degenerate liberal-democratic past. It was a *value*, not a mere means to an end. And as well as a positive good, a "natural and gratifying continuation of the lived experience of the trenches," violence was a career.[234] By late 1921 the leaders of provincial Fascism dominated their provinces or districts. Theirs was the power and patronage of the red baronies they had laid waste. But power achieved by Fascist violence was by its nature unstable. *Ras* and followers thus had the most powerful and tangible motivation for continuing the struggle on a scale, extent, and duration entirely incommensurate with the requirements of agrarian or industrial "class reaction."

That dynamic – the impossibility of rest and the precariousness even of regional domination – drew the tumultuous *ras* and their followers inexorably toward the "retarded jerks [*bischeracci*] in Milan" whom the *squadristi*, as befitted the *Frontkämpfer* so many had been, cordially despised. "The guy at *Il Popolo d'Italia*" was initially a figure almost of fun – and remained enduringly suspect for his personal remoteness from the risks and joys of *squadrismo*; if anyone excited the *squadre* of 1920–21 to "messianic expectations" it was D'Annunzio.[235] But while conciliating the Poet until late 1920 with desultory plotting for a march on Rome from Fiume, Mussolini nevertheless sought fiercely to assert command over his growing mass movement. As early as September 1920 his inspection tours of Fascist provincial conquests, from Cremona on the Po southeast of Milan to Trieste and Pola, culminated in speeches to large crowds moved to "stormy enthusiasm."[236]

D'Annunzio's eviction from Fiume in December 1920 provoked repeated protests from *Il Popolo d'Italia*, but the Poet's eclipse was highly convenient. Mussolini had been signalling since May–June 1920 his readiness for tactical accommodation with the parliamentary *maestro*, and soon established a back-channel to Rome through the prefect of Milan and Giolitti stalwart Alfredo

[233] Rumi, *Alle origini della politica estera fascista*, 113, 119, 126–28; also 196 for Giunta's memorable "Mediterranean Italy will be imperial, or will not be" (quotations from *L'Assalto*, 30 and 2 April 1921, and *Il Popolo di Trieste*, 28 February 1921, 15 September 1922).

[234] Baldassini, "Fascismo e memoria," 488–90 (quotation, 489).

[235] "Quello del popolo d'Italia"; "quel Mussolini"; "questi bischeracci di Milano": Piazzesi, Diario, 168, 197, 198, 162; and the analysis of Baldassini, "Fascismo e memoria," 498–505 (quoting the memoir of Alfredo Signoretti of the Rome *Fascio*).

[236] OO, 15:313–18; De Felice, 1:638–43; OO, 15:182–89, 214–23, 322–30.

Lusignoli.[237] Giolitti himself was well aware from prefect and police reports of the murderous excursions of the *squadre* and of their ceaseless and successful defiance of the Italian state. He had even sought repeatedly to compel prefects, police chiefs, *Carabinieri*, and army commanders across northern Italy to crack down – although with minimal results, given the already noted inadequacies of Italy's "public order" forces; the shared perception of prefects, judiciary, police, army, and *Fasci* that the PSI was as much an enemy as the Austrians had been; and the resulting ongoing complicity of most peripheral authorities with the *squadre*.[238] Giolitti's minister of war, the ex-Socialist reformist and *interventista* Ivanoe Bonomi, actively encouraged army cooperation with the *Fasci*; an army staff circular of September 1920 hailed the new movement as "vigorous forces that may possibly [*eventualmente*] be deployed against subversive and anti-national elements."[239]

Giolitti's enduring tone-deafness to ideology and pacific temperament had led him to conclude ingenuously in autumn 1918 that German and Austro-Hungarian defeat had forever banished "militarism." His corresponding inability to comprehend the war's savage consequences for Italian political culture thus led him to assume that he could tame and coopt Mussolini's new and eccentric movement simply by inviting it into parliament.[240] The rump-PSI that emerged from the Livorno split had remained adamantly *massimalista*, denying him once more the alliance with the reformists he had sought since the first years of the century. Instead, Giolitti turned to the Fascists as make-weight for the "national bloc" electoral coalitions formed, following the precedent of the previous fall, for the May 1921 national elections. Fascism's cowing of Socialists and *popolari* through violence – however deplorable – was in political terms not unwelcome, and Mussolini's movement had undeniably attracted the support of large segments of patriotic and Liberal opinion.

Even before securing Giolitti's blessing, Mussolini had embarked on a further round of speeches – Bologna, Ferrara, Fiume, Milan, Verona, and the *squadrista* stronghold of Mortara in the Lomellina. The *Popolo d'Italia* doubtless exaggerated the "indescribable" passion of the crowds, and its claimed turnout of 50,000 citizens and 20,000 Fascists to greet Mussolini at Ferrara on 4 April 1921 constituted an improbable 20 percent of the province's population. But Mussolini's presence and oratory undeniably made a noteworthy impression. The regional chieftains duly assisted his "apotheosis" as "man of iron" and

---

[237] OO, 15:8, 9–10, 30–32; De Felice, 1:650, 653–55, 2:42–43.

[238] On these issues, central to Liberal Italy's collapse, see especially Mondini, *Politica delle armi*, chs. 3–4; Gentile, *Storia*, 203, 210; De Felice, 1:602–07, 2:27–42; and Danilo Veneruso, *La vigilia del fascismo: Il primo ministero Facta nella crisi dello stato liberale in Italia* (Bologna, 1968), 319–73.

[239] Army staff to corps commands, 24 October 1920, in Vivarelli, "Bonomi e il fascismo in alcuni documenti inediti," *Rivista storica italiana*, 72:1 (1960), 152–53; Mondini, *Politica delle armi*, 71.

[240] Malagodi, *Conversazioni*, 1:86, 2:409–10, 455, and Edgar R. Rosen, "Giovanni Giolitti und die italienische Politik im Ersten Weltkriege," HZ 194 (1962), 339–40; on Giolitti and Fascism in 1920–21, see especially De Felice, 1:607.

"*duce trionfatore*" – in the words of the *Popolo d'Italia* and of Dino Grandi; the crowds likewise "saluted [Mussolini] as duce."[241] And Mussolini's speeches themselves demonstrated not only the nature of Fascism's appeal but also, and more significantly, what Mussolini sought to make of Fascism.

Most heavily emphasized foreign policy, an area in which Mussolini had since December 1918 carved out a unique position as the most fanatical prophet, far beyond the feeble scheming of the nationalists, of Italy's self-evident claim to empire: "the Mediterranean shall once again be ours."[242] He had railed repeatedly at the "plutocratic West" for mutilating Italy's victory and seeking to "strangle it with the blackmail of grain and coal." From April 1919 he had intermittently wielded the ultimate threat: to "unhinge the English [sic] Asiatic and African empire," perhaps by joining the otherwise repellent Germans in a "bloc of anti-British forces." The demographic pressure of Italy's "prolific and industrious" 40 millions, the demands of its Roman heritage, and the self-evident superiority of its "Aryan and Mediterranean race" demanded empire. Autarchy – the "gradual disengagement [*svincolamento*] from the group of Western plutocratic powers and the development of our [own] internal productive forces" – was a further point of emphasis, as were the geopolitics of national independence already set forth by the Nationalists: Italy's sovereign right not to be "encircled" by the "chain of hostility" that allegedly surrounded the nation "in its own sea."[243]

On occasion Mussolini let slip asides about the "great Jewish bankers of London and New York, linked by racial ties [*vincoli di razza*] with the Jews who in Moscow as in Budapest are taking revenge on the Aryan race," the advent of "new oriental-Semitic myths," or the Jewish descent of leaders of the PSI. Such notions dated from his Socialist years and remained mere background music in a minor key, but were nevertheless significant for the future.[244] In his April–May 1921 round of pre-election speeches he made a further show of ethnic

---

[241] OO, 16:467–76; Gentile, *Storia*, 188–89; *Censimento 1921*, 19:25. For Mussolini's skill and technique, see especially Prezzolini, "Mussolini oratore, ovvero eloquenza e carisma," in Gentile, ed., *Mussolini e "La Voce"* (Florence, 1976), 213–26.

[242] Compare the remarks of postwar Nationalist foreign policy spokesmen such as Tamaro and Coppola (notes 159–61) with the utterances documented in the next footnote.

[243] OO, 12:77, 101, 323; 13:71–72 ("far saltare l'Impero inglese asiatico-africano"), 75–76, 108–09, 126–27, 142–46 (not published until 1937, and thus perhaps excessively reflective of Mussolini's later course), 147–49; 14:5, 202, 217–20, 222–23, 227, 469, 471; 15:29, 37 (encirclement; see also the Nationalist contribution, note 160) 122, 184–85, 214; 16:6, 68, 89, 102–03, 104–06, 128, 131, 158–59, 239, 241, 244, 265, 300–01, 335–36, 347; 17:178, 218–19; 18:77–78, 144, 160–61, 180, 331, 412, 432 ("Non è interesse italiano contribuire al mantenimento dell'impero inglese [sic]: interesse italiano è collaborare a demolirlo"), 439, 459. Context for these programmatic statements: Knox, *Common Destiny*, 61–63, 117–19; but see also the unsupported claim of De Felice, 2:229–30, that "there is no doubt that Mussolini's 'Mediterranean' anti-British line was determined by a series of tactical and demagogic considerations" (which De Felice does not specify).

[244] OO, 13:168–70 ("I complici"); 14:135; Ventura, "La svolta antiebraica," 49–52; Giorgio Fabre, *Mussolini razzista* (Milan, 2005), chs. 1, 6, and especially 8; for a snapshot of later events, Knox, "Das faschistische Italien und die 'Endlösung' 1942/43," VfZ 55 (2007), 53–92.

intolerance, demanding the Italianization of the German-inhabited South Tyrol and deriding the "accursedly Croat" populations in Italy's eastern borderlands. He repeatedly invoked Mazzini, and Fascism's "martyrs who are counted by the tens and hundreds." And on 23 March 1921, second anniversary of the founding of the *Fasci*, he took up a theme already sketched in summer–fall 1920, and proclaimed – undeniably "without false modesty" – that Fascism's aim was "to govern the nation"; soon Fascism and Italy "would be identical."[245] A clearer statement of totalitarian intent was scarcely conceivable.

Mussolini's good relations with the provincial chieftains suffered a brusque deterioration after the election, which destroyed Giolitti's hopes of securing a stable majority (see Figure 4.10). Thirty-six newly minted Fascist deputies emerged, most of them as top vote-winners or runners-up on their lists. Fascism secured a majority of "national bloc" seats from Venezia Giulia and Emilia, a third or more of those from Lombardy and Liguria, 29 percent in Tuscany, and 25 percent in Piedmont. Mussolini himself won in Milan (56 percent of additional and preference votes) and Bologna (79 percent), with a grand total of almost 370,000 votes.[246]

But that demonstration of charismatic appeal served little in the movement's ensuing internal wrangling. In June–July 1921 Mussolini deliberately provoked two major quarrels in order to impose discipline both on Fascism's parliamentary delegation and on the movement as a whole. The first revolved around the long-standing and frequently proclaimed "republican inclination [*tendenzionalità*]" of the *Fasci*, which reflected both Mussolini's revolutionary aspirations and the attitudes of most "urban" Fascists; the monarchy, with the army behind it, remained the most serious obstacle to the movement's claim to total power. But after long argument between the Milan leadership and the small number of newly elected deputies who deigned to appear at Mussolini's summons, he rancorously accepted a compromise that left deputies free to attend the king's speech and thus parade their monarchical loyalty.[247]

Worse followed. Mussolini challenged the power of the *ras* in the most decisive way possible, by concluding at the beginning of August 1921 a "pact of pacification" with the PSI aimed at bringing Italy's civil war to a provisional end. He had sensed early in the year that the intensity and unpredictability of Fascist violence risked alienating patriotic opinion, which was beginning to perceive the retreat of the "Bolshevist" threat. After almost three hundred dead from March through May (twenty-two on election day alone), continuing Po Valley and Tuscan violence would now complicate rather than further Mussolini's efforts to secure power in Rome – where he had already announced that he

---

[245] OO, 15:152, 259; 16:31, 57, 65, 68, 176, 192, 211, 313.

[246] Figures and analysis: Jens Petersen, "Elettorato e base sociale del fascismo italiano negli anni venti," SSt 16:3 (1975), 641–43; for the mechanics of preference and additional votes, note 80.

[247] On the summer 1921 "revolt against the Duce," see especially the exemplary account of Gentile, *Storia*, ch. 4.

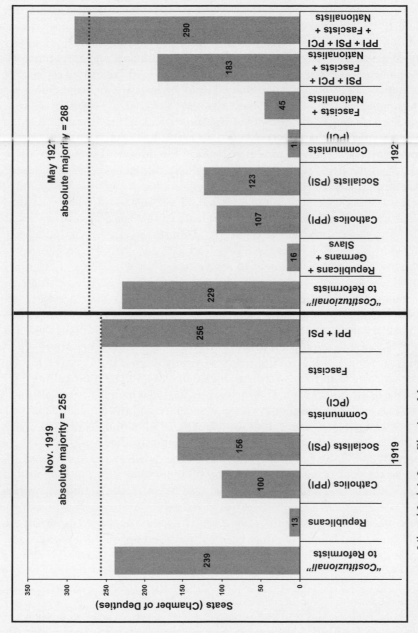

FIGURE 4.10. Liberal Italy's Last Election, May 1921.
Base data: Giusti, *Le correnti politiche*, 28, 29 (with adjustments).

would oppose Giolitti.[248] Mussolini had therefore admonished his movement with increasing if disingenuous vehemence: Fascist violence must be "chivalric"; "intelligent, not animal [*bruta*]"; "violence of warriors, not of thugs"; "a tactic adopted out of necessity, not a system"; "not an aesthetic experience, and still less a sport."[249] This was hardly a line calculated to appeal even to Fascist parliamentarians, who inaugurated the movement's legislative career by severely beating and dragging from the Chamber the Communist deputy Francesco Misiano, a deserter in the Great War and in Fascist eyes "the most repugnant representative of national pusillanimity." And Mussolini's message coincided with a stinging Fascist defeat at Sarzana, north of Carrara on the Liguria-Tuscany border. On 21 July 1921 the *Carabinieri*, for once in line with Rome's demands that the law be enforced, replied with lethal effectiveness to Fascist fire, and dispersed some 500 *squadristi*, whom the infuriated population then hunted across the fields with shotguns, axes, and pitchforks.[250] The blood of eighteen fresh "martyrs" thus cried out for vengeance.

The result was the open revolt of provincial Fascism against what Farinacci, lord of Cremona, denounced as the Milan leadership's "pacifist attitude" that "devalues our power, debases our dignity, and abuses our dead." Grandi openly challenged Mussolini's claims to be recognized as "*padrone*" of "this our movement." Mussolini, who had sought to assert "the clear and decisive hegemony of the political element ... over the – as it were – 'military' element" within Fascism, retaliated by resigning all his offices: "Fascism can do without me? Certainly – but I can also do without Fascism."[251] In mid-August 1921 the *ras* met at Bologna in solemn conclave, without inviting Mussolini, and flatly refused to demobilize. Grandi and Balbo, authorized by their comrades, approached D'Annunzio at his Lake Garda retreat and vainly offered the Poet the leadership of Fascism. But in the end, Mussolini's defiance and D'Annunzio's refusal brought the dissidents to heel. They neither possessed nor could create a substitute national leader to conquer power at the center and thus consolidate their mastery of northern and central Italy. By late August Mussolini had tacitly abandoned his pact with the PSI, while the *squadre* intensified and expanded their murderous work. On 12 September Balbo and Grandi led "march on Ravenna," an anniversary pilgrimage to Dante's tomb by more than 2,000 heavily armed Fascists. And the *ras* publicly acknowledged their leader's authority once more.

To consolidate that precarious advantage Mussolini sought to transform the *Fasci* gradually and belatedly into a political party, equipped with regulations, a program, party discipline, and a strengthened central bureaucracy befitting

---

[248] Numbers: Franzinelli, *Squadristi*, 307–36.
[249] OO, 16:181–82, 323, 445 (this last in Mussolini's maiden Chamber of Deputies speech).
[250] Misiano: Gentile, *Storia*, 245 (quoting *Il Popolo d'Italia*, 14 June 1921); Sarzana: ibid., 268, and Franzinelli, *Squadristi*, 120–29, 344–45.
[251] Gentile, *Storia*, 271, 282–83 and notes; OO, 17:84–86, 91; for the abortive contact with D'Annunzio, De Felice 2:151–52 and note 3.

a movement of 200,000 members that was now Italy's most powerful political force. Brusque assertions in the manner of Cadorna ("We are an army. I command that army.") gave way to patient organizational work, building on the efforts of Pasella and others to centralize the growing movement over the previous year.[252] Bianchi, soon to be the first secretary of the *Partito Nazionale Fascista* (PNF), received the unenviable task of codifying Fascist ideology and disseminating it throughout the movement. Mussolini's relative lack of interest in that enterprise suggested his distaste for the tedious and potentially divisive domestic issues involved. The party-to-be acquired in September–October a program infinitely less relevant to its future course than Mussolini's continuing foreign policy rantings.[253] And on 7–10 November it convened – 10,000 Fascists and 2,000 delegates – in the theater at the mausoleum of Augustus in Rome to solemnize the movement's transformation and Mussolini's "apotheosis." Despite initial acrimony, Mussolini achieved his objective: at the climactic moment, Dino Grandi ascended the stage as the representative of provincial Fascism, and theatrically embraced Mussolini. The Duce of Fascism, as he now became by acclamation, had secured both the organizational consolidation of his movement and – at least provisionally – of his own authority. In his keynote speech, he insisted that "we, on behalf of the nation, accept dictatorship"; "we are the state." Two weeks later, he theorized in *Il Popolo d'Italia* that "people may perhaps desire a dictator." To achieve that exalted status, of which only Garibaldi's brief 1860 command over Sicily and the South offered a modern Italian precedent, Mussolini would nevertheless have to "work miracles," "perform heroic deeds," and "prove his mission by *bringing well-being* to his faithful followers." As 1921 waned and power slipped away from Giolitti's hapless successor, the reformist Bonomi, the chances of accomplishing all those things, and more, were rapidly increasing. Had the Duce not suggested as long ago as October 1919 that yearning to join D'Annunzio at Fiume was misplaced: "Does no one remain who knows the road to Rome?"[254]

II. The National Socialist Capture of the "National Idea," 1919–1930

Hitler's progress toward uncontested mastery of a militant mass movement that knew the road to Berlin was almost as short as Mussolini's. But the road itself proved far longer than the Duce's. Structural factors already described, above all the unacknowledged and unavenged lost war and the existence, long before Hitler's advent, of a widespread and desperate yearning for a national Führer "for whom we can march through fire," made his ascent possible. But

---

[252] Gentile, *Storia*, 272–73, 37–42.

[253] Numbers: Gentile, *Storia*, 157; OO, 17:175–78.

[254] OO, 17:217, 219, 268; 14:36; and note 169. See also Balbo's emphatic endorsement of Mussolini as "il Duce del fascismo" at the Ferrara provincial congress, 29 November 1921, in Alessandro Roveri, *L'affermazione dello squadrismo fascista nelle campagne ferraresi 1921–1922* (Ferrara, 1979), 93.

Weimar's resilience – so long as Fritz Ebert and Otto Braun ruled in Berlin – and the French threat, ever-present until the final Rhineland evacuation of June 1930, then blocked his path.

His initial trajectory from Linz, to Vienna (1908–13), to Munich (1913–14), and onward through four and a half years of war with the Bavarian infantry remains poorly documented. The former lance-corporal (*Gefreiter*), once in power, displayed notable interest in covering his tracks. The post-1933 memoirs of those who knew him before his political career tend to lack corroboration and credibility. And unlike Mussolini, whose leadership style derived in part from his long journalistic apprenticeship, Hitler was and remained to the end the foremost apostle of the "spoken word"; much of the contemporary evidence of his views thus stems from others.[255] His prewar career as failed art student, drifter, and painter of Munich architectural scenes scarcely suggested a bright future. Nor does much evidence exist that Vienna – as Hitler invariably claimed later – decisively shaped his worldview, beyond instilling a fanatical devotion to Wagner's "*Weltanschauung*-operas." One credible witness attests to an early and passionate German-national politics, and a detestation of "reds" and Jesuits. But credibly documented anti-Semitic utterances before 1919 are lacking.[256]

The Great War – "greatest and most unforgettable phase of my earthly existence" – gave Hitler both a home and a vocation. Comrades and superiors seem to have considered him somewhat odd. Yet Lance-Corporal Hitler emerged with the iron cross first class – a decoration not given idly to enlisted men. He inexplicably survived Falkenhayn's great slaughter at Ypres in November 1914 as a rifleman, then graduated to regimental messenger – carrying orders above ground to the forward units, often in daylight, during the heavy bombardments that routinely cut even deep-buried field telephone wires. His new duty meant better food, dryer dugouts, and a less exhausting daily routine, in exchange for even greater danger than the men of the rifle companies. It suited him; he appears to have declined further promotion, perhaps because it would have meant a return to a line company and the combat leadership responsibility for which his superiors appear to have judged him unsuited. The armistice caught Hitler in hospital recovering from poison gas, his second major wound. On his return to Munich he sought desperately to remain in the rapidly disintegrating army. He served briefly – and ironically – as a company "spokesman [*Vertrauensmann*]" tasked by the new SPD-USPD Bavarian government with ensuring the republican loyalty of the troops, and seemingly sat prudently in

---

[255] For the crucial political significance of "the magic power [Zauberkraft] of the spoken word" (MK, 106–07 and book 2, ch. 6), see Volkov, "The Written Matter and the Spoken Word."

[256] Anton Joachimsthaler, *Hitlers Weg begann in München 1913–1923* (Munich, 2000) provides the least tendentious overview of the evidence and of its limitations (50 for Wagner; 57 for "reds" and Jesuits; 130 [HSA, 69] for Hitler's one surviving wartime denunciation, in a letter of February 1915, of "foreign influences [Fremdländerei]" and "internationalism" on the home front); Hitler's own often fanciful version of his origins and ideological development: MK, book 1, chs. 1–7.

barracks during Munich's brief and bloody Soviet interlude in April 1919. But once the *Freikorps* had reconquered the city, he reemerged as enlisted representative on an investigatory committee charged with detecting soldiers guilty of "Spartacist, Bolshevist, or Communist agitation" in the previous weeks.[257]

The intelligence branch of the Reichswehr's Bavarian headquarters, led by a fiercely anti-Semitic contact of Wolfgang Kapp's, Captain Karl Mayr, found Hitler sufficiently reliable and useful to assign him in June 1919 to a newly established training course in political "enlightenment" techniques for soldiers and NCOs. The Reichswehr's aim was to immunize both troops and population against any repetition of the Soviet experiment. The course organizers naturally provided all necessary indoctrination material from the armory of the Pan-Germans and of the local branch of the *Schutz- und Trutz-Bund*; one key anti-Semite associated with the local *Bund* – the economic crank Gottfried Feder – acted as a course instructor.[258]

Mayr and the Munich anti-Semites thus introduced *Gefreiter* Hitler to his true calling. Hitler remained a soldier, a condition that remained central to his notion of himself to the bitter end. But the course also encouraged him to address sizable audiences, and he discovered, as he later put it, "that I could 'speak.'"[259] His evident talent earned assignment in August 1919 to a trial run in "enlightenment" at a camp for returned prisoners-of-war suspected of exposure to Bolshevism in Russia. There he immediately distinguished himself, in the words of a witness, as a "born agitator [*Volksredner*], whose fanaticism and folksy manner...indisputably compel the attention and assent of his audience." The camp's commanding officer reported "a very fine, clear, and fiery [*temperamentvollen*] lecture by Corp[oral] Hitler on capitalism, in the course of which he sketched in the Jewish question." And on 19 September 1919, Hitler, in response to a request of Mayr's, set forth in some detail for the first time his views on that "question." Jews were the "race-tuberculosis of peoples." "Anti-Semitism on purely emotional grounds" produced only pogroms; "the anti-Semitism of reason," by contrast, "must have as its irrevocable final goal the total removal of the Jews [*sein letztes Ziel aber muss unverrückbar die Entfernung der Juden überhaupt sein*]."[260]

---

[257] MK, 163; Hitler, the SPD, and the Munich Soviets: the archivally documented account in Joachimsthaler, *Hitlers Weg*, 198–218; also HSA, 851–53.

[258] For Feder, Eckart, the *Schutz- und Trutz-Bund*, and the DAP/NSDAP, see Lohalm, *Völkischer Radikalismus*, 141, 168, and part 6.

[259] MK, 215–16, 355.

[260] Joachimsthaler, *Hitlers Weg*, 223–56 (including course lesson plans); Ernst Deuerlein, "Hitlers Eintritt in die Politik und der Reichswehr," VfZ 7 (1959), 200, 199, 204 (Bavarian Reichswehr files); HSA, 88–89. Hitler's genocidal focus on "the Jew" from the very beginning demonstrates the full inadequacy, if applied to National Socialism, of Ernst Nolte's famous definition of "fascism" as "an anti-Marxism" (*Three Faces of Fascism* [New York, 1966], 20–21), and suggests the absurdity of Nolte's later and related insistence that Auschwitz "was above all a reaction, born of fear, to the genocidal processes of the Russian Revolution" (Nolte, "Zwischen Geschichtslegende und Revisionismus? Das Dritte Reich im Blickwinkel des Jahres 1980," in

A week earlier, as an "education officer" in Mayr's service, Hitler had attended a small beer-hall meeting of an obscure sect of *völkisch* workers with about forty members, the "German Workers' Party" (DAP). The DAP was a creation of the turn of the year 1918–19, but rooted in the *Vaterlandspartei* and the prewar and wartime anti-Semitic agitational and conspiratorial groups such as the *Germanen Orden* and its Munich offshoot, the Thule Society – seven of whose members had figured among the hostages the Communists had shot on 30 April.[261] Hitler found the group's politics congenial, and distinguished himself by scornfully beating down the claims of a Bavarian separatist professor. Perhaps in view of the impending shrinkage of the army, at the next meeting he agreed to join. As he later wrote, unlike the established parties, the DAP's "substance, aim, and course could still be determined."[262]

He proceeded to do just that. Hitler's emergence as unchallenged Führer of the Party, accompanied by ever more insistent claims that the Party would conquer and "heal" Germany, was far swifter than often assumed. The excorporal's well-attested oddness and extreme social awkwardness, only gradually attenuated by the patronage of conspicuous members of the Munich elite such as the piano heiress Helene Bechstein, may be partially responsible for this misconception.[263] Post-1945 revulsion and a predisposition to structural explanations that implicate the German elites and people as well as the later dictator have also played a role. Even Hitler's charisma has been subject to a peculiar depersonalization, as if it were a mere structural condition generated primarily by the predispositions of Hitler's audiences, and largely independent of his views, acts, and decisions.[264]

Charisma, actions, and decisions manifested themselves immediately – but in miniature, compared to the early Fascist career of Benito Mussolini, who by 1919 had been a national figure for almost a decade, and whose vocation as newspaperman had long given him resonance far beyond Milan. Hitler nevertheless employed with increasing zeal and frequency his newly discovered talent. By November–December 1919, the DAP's audiences had swelled to several hundred and were beginning to revolve around him as foremost speaker

---

"*Historikerstreit*" [Munich, 1987], 32–33). Compare Nolte's definition with the page and a quarter of HSA index entries for Jews and Judaism, and the two column-inches each for "Marxismus" and "Russland." The texts themselves make amply clear that Marxism and Soviet Russia were for Hitler merely two subordinate manifestations, among many, of the Jewish "world-enemy"; see also Rainer Zitelmann, "Nationalsozialismus und Antikommunismus. Aus Anlass der Thesen von Ernst Nolte," in Uwe Backes, Eckhard Jesse, and idem, eds., *Die Schatten der Vergangenheit* (Frankfurt am Main, 1990), 218–42.

[261] See especially Joe Hatheway, "The Pre-1920 Origins of the National Socialist German Workers' Party," JCH 29:3 (1994), 443–62; Phelps, "Before Hitler Came"; and idem, "Hitler and the *Deutsche Arbeiterpartei*," AHR 68:4 (1963), 974–86.

[262] MK, 223.

[263] Hitler's early society patrons: Hellmuth Auerbach, "Hitlers politische Lehrjahre und die Münchener Gesellschaft 1919–1923," VfZ 25 (1977), 1–45.

[264] See Michel Dobry, "Hitler, Charisma and Structure: Reflections on Historical Methodology," TMPR 7:2 (2006), 157–71.

and, from early January, Party propaganda chief [*Werbeobmann*]. In the following year he gave thirty-one speeches in Munich alone.[265] Along with the more forward-looking of the DAP's two original founders, a machinist from the Munich railway yards, Anton Drexler, Hitler proceeded in December–January 1920 to draft a twenty-five-point program for what now – at his urging – became the National Socialist German Workers' Party (NSDAP). After intervening heatedly on 7 January 1920 in discussion at a *Schutz- und Trutz-Bund* rally on the "Jewish Question" that had drawn an audience of 7,000, Hitler promulgated the program at a DAP/NSDAP mass meeting on 24 February 1920 before 2,000 enthusiastic listeners.[266]

The program, like its Fascist counterparts of 1919–20, was a collection of commonplaces – including the abolition of department stores and Gottfried Feder's "breaking of interest slavery" – calculated to appeal to an immediate audience unnerved by postwar humiliation, inflation and scarcity, and – unique to Munich – the traumatic experience of "Jewish dictatorship" in April–May 1919. Hitler summed up the Party's message far more trenchantly than the program itself: "Our only slogan is battle [*Kampf*]; we shall proceed directly and implacably on our path to our goal (long-lasting stormy applause)." Only a few of the program points – unification of German-speakers throughout Europe in a single state, destruction of Versailles, "land and soil (colonies)," the incompatibility of Jewish blood with German citizenship, and a new mass army – bore much relevance to the Party's future, even before Hitler cut off debate over sectarian-*völkisch* minutiae by decreeing in July 1921 that the Party's "name, program, and political line [were] immutable."[267]

Hitler's capacity to stir audiences intensified as he acquired experience, and lifted the DAP/NSDAP from its previous obscurity; by January 1921 paid membership had reached 3,000. Postwar Munich was uniquely provided with racist agitators, and Hitler's many competitors addressed the same public on much the same themes. But none approached his power over his audiences. His rhetorical armory combined colorful sarcasm with an implacable anti-Semitic fury fully in line with Heinrich Class's October 1918 formula, duly if ploddingly applied by the *Schutz- und Trutz-Bund*, of "fanfares against Jewry and the Jews as lightning rods for all injustice." Hitler denounced Germany's fall from past greatness to present humiliation ("swindled, betrayed, and sold down the river"). He railed at the Jewish "oriental syphilitic guests" allegedly responsible for the war and the 1918 "Jew-revolution" – a favorite *Schutz- und Trutz-Bund* slogan. The Jew had caused the fragmentation, the "*Zerplitterung*," of the German people: the class struggle was an invention of Marx the Jew, explicitly designed to tear the *Volk* apart and perpetuate Jewish domination. Correspondingly, the

---

[265] HSA, 92–93, 96–99, 100; detailed speech listing: Deuerlein, "Hitler's Eintritt in die Politik," 188–89.
[266] HSA, 101, 109–11.
[267] HSA, 110; NSDAP program: Jeremy Noakes and Geoffrey Pridham, eds., *Nazism, 1919–45: A Documentary Reader*, 4 vols. (Exeter, 1988–98), 1:14–16.

NSDAP itself was "*no class organization, but a Volk-movement*" that rejected all "class and *Stand* snobbery [*Klassen- und Standesdünkel*]": "We know no classes, [but] only *Volk*-comrades."[268]

The Party's mission was simple: insurrection against the "dictatorship of th[e] race that has brought us all this misery": "We shall fight on until the last Jew has been removed from the German Reich, even if it comes to a Putsch and, far more, even if it comes once more *to a revolution.*" The Party's immediate task as "the only Party of Germans" was to organize "a single ever-intensifying mass demonstration, consisting of protest upon protest, in halls and in the streets...a firestorm [*Glutwelle*] of defiance, rage, and embittered scorn," a "revolution in consciousness [*Gesinnung*]" that would sweep away both Weimar and Versailles.[269] In February 1921 Hitler correspondingly proclaimed that the NSDAP's swastika banner in the colors of the *Kaiserreich* ("black hooked-cross on a white disk on a red ground") was the only flag appropriate to the coming "Germanic state of the German nation."[270] By spring 1921 the Party's future, as protagonist in the German people's cosmic struggle against Judaism, stretched far beyond Germany itself. Like early Christianity, National Socialism was bound for global power: "We are indeed small [in numbers], *but a man once stood in Galilee, and today his teachings rule the entire world.*"[271]

Hitler – on the day after his thirty-second birthday in April 1921 – may not yet have intended to compare his own person explicitly to Jesus Christ. But from September 1919 onward he had been keenly aware that national and racial salvation required "the ruthless commitment of nationally inclined leader-personalities."[272] Perhaps, as often suggested, he came only hesitantly in 1919–23 to the realization that he himself was or might become such a *Führerpersönlichkeit*. His devotion to high living and Bohemian disorder after his discharge from the army at the end of March 1920 might suggest a lack of interest in Party leadership, and even a "maladjustment and indecisiveness" appropriate to the mere nationalist "drummer" he allegedly was and the "weak dictator" he purportedly became.[273] But an equally plausible cause of his early

---

[268] HSA, 220, 138, 156 (emphasis in original), 146, 174–75, 254–55, 262, 276, 279, 281, 215.

[269] HSA, 221 ("Betrogen, verraten und verkauft"), 144, 323, 115, 128–29 (27 April 1920; emphasis in original) 134, 314, 239; similarly, 179, 199, 203, 247–48, 255, 448 (Hitler citations, as in this case, often include an unspoken "and passim"; repetition was central to Hitler's style, theory, and practice).

[270] HSA, 323.

[271] HSA, 134, 179, 239, 367 (21 April 1921; my emphasis); further comparisons of Nazism to Christianity (as a doctrine of intolerance and "Kampf"): HSA, 221, 623–24 (Jesus as "agitator"), 636, 756, 769, 770, 867, 877, 879, 947.

[272] HSA, 90 ("rücksichtslosen Einsatz nationalgesinnter Führerpersönlichkeiten").

[273] "Unausgeglichenheit und Entscheidungsschwäche": the words of the very influential Albrecht Tyrell, *Vom "Trommler" zum "Führer." Der Wandel von Hitlers Selbstverständnis zwischen 1919 und 1924 und die Entwicklung der NSDAP* (Munich, 1975), 108–09; for the "drummer" thesis, passim, and Kershaw, *Hitler, 1889–1936*, ch. 6; "weak dictator": the classic formulation of Hans Mommsen, "National Socialism," in *Marxism, Communism, and Western*

reticence in internal Party matters was a demonstrable aversion to compromise and an instinctual hatred of programmatic quibbling. He as yet lacked the backing within the NSDAP to impose directly his conception of its nature and of his own role. But he could afford to wait: *his* de facto leadership was the source of the Party's growth. His ever-more-grandiose descriptions in 1919–21 of the global struggle in which the Party's *Kampf* allegedly played a leading part, and his increasingly explicit insistence on dictatorial leadership in that struggle, prefigured the role he assumed within the NSDAP in July–August 1921 and sought throughout Germany thereafter.

The struggle was absolute and admitted no compromise. "Scientific understanding [*wissenschaftliche Erkenntnis*]" dictated the eradication of "race-tuberculosis". "We are possessed by the inexorable resolve to strike the evil at its root and exterminate it root and branch."[274] The struggle was cosmic: only "a national force as strong as itself, and that would be the German *Volk*" could thwart the Jewish robber-nomads in their quest for the "eternal Jewish goal – world domination."[275] And as early as April 1920 the corresponding and necessary leadership style had a name: "we need a dictator who is a genius, if we wish to rise again." Either parliamentarism would destroy Germany, or "one day a [man with an] iron skull shall come, with muddy boots, perhaps, but with a clear conscience and a steel fist, who will end the blathering of these [Reichstag] drawing-room heroes, and give the nation a deed."[276]

The growth of the muddy-booted *Gefreiter* of the western front into the role that the German past had created and the lost war had opened to commoners accelerated in spring–summer 1921. Hitler was now drawing Munich audiences of up to 5,000.[277] He had acquired an entourage, a small group of close followers bound personally to him by his unique gifts: Dietrich Eckart, drunkard, poet, and Catholic-*völkisch* journalist; a group of younger men, the dog-faithful Rudolf Hess, the German-Balt neo-pagan ideologue Alfred Rosenberg, and the disreputable agitator Hermann Esser; a coterie of chauffeurs and hangers-on; and bodyguards from the Party "gymnastics and sports branch" charged with beating up opponents and Jews who dared frequent NSDAP functions. Eckart's anti-Semitic lore and slogans – including "Germany Awake!," a staple of *Vaterlandspartei* and *Schutz- und Trutz-Bund* propaganda – provided Hitler with at least some of his material.[278] Through Eckhart's extensive

Society, 6:68. High living (a gleeful and perhaps embellished SPD account): Tyrell, ed., *Führer befiehl... Selbstzeugnisse aus der 'Kampfzeit' der NSDAP* (Düsseldorf, 1969), 58–60.

[274] HSA, 119–20 (6 April 1920; my emphasis): "[E]s beseelt uns die unerbittliche Entschlossenheit, das Übel an die Wurzel zu packen und mit Stumpf und Stiel auszurotten (lebhafter Beifall)."

[275] "Scientific understanding" / "the anti-Semitism of reason": HSA, 89–90, 119–20, 128, 175, 199, 201; "Race-tuberculosis": HSA, 89, 156, 176, 386; Jewish world domination: HSA, 137–38, 145–46, 195, 220, 254, 273, 464, 644, 714.

[276] HSA, 127, 333 (6 March 1921).

[277] HSA, 337 note 9, 353 note 3.

[278] Orlow, *The History of the Nazi Party, 1919–1933* (London, 1971), 22–23, 31; Peter Longerich, *Geschichte der SA* (Munich, 2nd rev. ed., 2003), 22–23; on Eckart, "*völkisch* poet and martyr"

contacts, and in part with Reichswehr secret funds, the Party acquired at the end of 1920 a Munich anti-Semitic newspaper, the *Völkischer Beobachter* ("racist observer"). Hitler as propaganda chief controlled both editorial policy and content, and henceforth possessed the means to communicate in uniform fashion with the local groups across Bavaria that had sprung up in the course of 1920, and of attracting those not initially drawn to NSDAP meetings.[279]

Hitler had won a first trial of strength within the DAP leadership at the turn of the year 1919–20, ejecting the Party's other co-founder, the sports journalist and *völkisch* pedant Karl Harrer, who had sought to preserve the group's original character as an abstruse discussion circle. In draft bylaws aimed at Harrer, Hitler disclosed – as in his beer-hall rhetoric – notions that anticipated later events: "the goals of the Party are so far-reaching that they are only to be assured by an organization as tight as it is suitably flexible," and possessing a clear center of "authority."[280] Drexler had concurred; he had long favored the mass agitation that Hitler alone had made possible. In winter–spring 1920–21 Hitler nevertheless also came into conflict with Drexler and with the majority of the NSDAP's steering committee – which he had haughtily declined to join – over negotiations for cooperation and eventual merger with another anti-Semitic group with both Bavarian and north-German ramifications, the *Deutsch-Sozialistische Partei* (DSP). Hitler as NSDAP propaganda chief had laid down the condition that mergers must not involve "watering-down our manner of struggle," the movement's frenetic extra- and anti-parliamentary insurrectional agitation. Not "majority decisions," but "machine guns and hand grenades in the streets" would determine Germany's fate.[281] DSP interest in elections and relaxed sect-like character disqualified it in Hitler's eyes, and its demand that the combined movement's headquarters move to Berlin threatened his power, which as yet resided primarily in his Munich following.

Hitler fought a delaying action throughout spring 1921, but failed to convince Drexler and others of the unwisdom of the merger – which Drexler then sought to implement in June–July 1921 during one of Hitler's unpredictable absences. Hitler's seeming inactivity, as demonstrably on later occasions, was

---

(MK, German editions, index) see his *Der Bolschewismus von Moses bis Lenin: Zwiegespräch zwischen Adolf Hitler und mir* (Munich, 1924); Ernst Nolte, "Ein frühe Quelle zu Hitlers Antisemitismus," HZ 192 (1961), 584–606; and Margarete Plewnia, *Auf dem Weg zu Hitler. Der "völkische" Publizist Dietrich Eckart* (Bremen, 1970), especially 85–87 (Eckart's "Sturmlied der SA," illustrated, from the guest book of the Munich "Bratwurstglöckl").

[279] For the paper's initial vicissitudes and rise to a daily circulation of 25,000 by July 1923, see Charles F. Sidman, "Die Auflagen-Kurve des Völkischen Beobachters und die Entwicklung des Nationalsozialismus Dezember 1920–November 1923," VfZ 13 (1965), 112–18.

[280] HSA, 95.

[281] Drexler (but largely in Hitler's unique style) to Riehl, 19 January 1921, in Alexander Schilling, *Dr. Walter Riehl und die Geschichte des Nationalsozialismus* (Leipzig, 1933), 268, 265; Tyrell, *Trommler*, 92–94; Tyrell's correct analysis of the "claim to absolute power" of the NSDAP of early 1921 – a characteristic introduced *by* and inextricably intertwined *with* Hitler's de facto leadership of the Party from winter 1919–20 onward – directly contradicts his concurrent insistence that Hitler "did not intend to shape the instrument himself."

perhaps calculated to draw his adversaries into exposing themselves. It certainly had that effect. His reply to the merger was the same as Mussolini's the following month: a theatrical resignation. But the result was very different from the awkward compromises through which Mussolini clambered upward toward recognition in November 1921 as Duce of Fascism's far-flung and heavily armed 217,000 members. Hitler's self-evident indispensability to the far smaller NSDAP, the likelihood that unless appeased he would simply build a rival party around his youthful and dynamic faithful followers, and the very great differences in character and power between the *Stammtisch* stalwarts of the NSDAP steering committee and youthful lords of the *squadre* such as Balbo and Grandi dictated swift capitulation. So swift, indeed, that the committee interpreted Hitler's ostensibly temporary demand for "dictatorial prerogatives [*diktatorische Machtbefugnisse*]" as it was meant, and offered him "dictatorship over the movement" without qualification or limitation.[282]

Hitler celebrated victory on 20 July 1921 with a speech before his now customary large crowd; his rough notes contain the lines "Not Jew dictatorship / But rather dictatorship of a genius." On 29 July 554 Munich Party members unanimously confirmed him as "first chairman" of the NSDAP, and accepted by a vote of 553 to 1 the lengthy and detailed party statute – clearly not drafted on the spur of the moment – through which Hitler implemented the prerogatives he claimed. Only the full Party membership, to which – alone – he was now theoretically responsible and that met only at the annual Party meeting instituted in January 1921, could revoke his mandate. As he remarked a few months later, in an "authentically *Germanic* democracy" decisions belonged not to "the feebleness of the majority, but to the most capable brain (lively applause)." Drexler's reward for capitulation was the exalted but irrelevant position of "founding honorary chairman." Eckart and Rosenberg took charge of the *Völkischer Beobachter*, which in an article by Hess hailed Hitler as "the Führer-personality who alone is capable of carrying through this *Kampf.*"[283] Max Amann, a former sergeant in Hitler's regiment and an expert and tireless organizer who proved devoted to his former subordinate, became Party business manager with far-reaching powers; by April 1922 he was publisher of the *Völkischer Beobachter* as well. Other individuals loyal to and dependent upon Hitler occupied key positions throughout a growing Party bureaucracy, now subdivided into sectoral subcommittees directly subordinate to the leader, with chairmen whom he could for the most part remove at will. He moved to subjugate to the Munich Party leadership all outlying NSDAP locals, issuing

[282] "Diktatorische Machtbefugnisse": HSA, 438; Georg Franz-Willing, *Ursprung der Hitlerbewegung 1919–1922* (Preussisch Oldendorf, 1974), 168, for the committee's reply. Tyrell's theory that Hitler's acquisition of permanent command of the movement was accidental rather than intended lacks documentary foundation, and ignores both Hitler's prior invocations of dictatorship as an ideal, and his instantaneous methodical exploitation of his new powers.

[283] HSA, 443, 447–50, 461, 622 (emphasis in original); Tyrell, *Trommler*, 134–36, 124; statute text: idem, ed., *Führer befiehl*, 31–36.

circulars in a tone and language borrowed directly from the army in which he had served.[284] He decreed precise specifications for the Party flag ("the red is social, the white is national, and the [black] hooked-cross is anti-Semitic"), armbands and party insignia. And he fostered the rapid growth under his personal patronage of the "gymnastics and sports branch," re-christened "storm detachments [*Sturmabteilungen*]" (SA) in August 1921. In that endeavor he had the assistance of Ehrhardt and associates; of Hermann Göring, an ex–fighter pilot and *Pour le mérite* holder of noteworthy brutality and bonhomie; and – most significantly – of Captain Ernst Röhm, chief of staff of the Bavarian Reichswehr division and Mayr's successor as Hitler's Reichswehr patron and protector.[285]

The sources of the speed and radicalism with which Hitler restructured the NSDAP to fit his plebiscitarily confirmed role as "Führer of the movement" are no mystery. The principles he applied did not derive fortuitously from recent unpleasant experiences of internal Party conflict, nor did they necessarily correspond to whatever change in Hitler's putatively diffident "self-understanding" may have resulted from victory over his puny Party adversaries in July 1921. In reality, his first apprenticeship – as warrior – had provided the two key concepts required to organize and lead the revolutionary paramilitary "party of a new type" that his rhetorical gifts had now made possible.

The first was the hierarchical structure common to all Western armies – but in its specifically Prusso-German form, as tempered in the fires of 1914–18. By mid-war at the latest, the decentralization imposed by industrial firepower and rudimentary battlefield communications had loosened further a system that had already privileged effectiveness over formal rank, and promoted rather than reproved men whose "self-will at times overstepp[ed] the normal bounds of leadership and initiative."[286] German conceptions of military hierarchy thus already contained a charismatic element, which the *Freikorps* interlude reinforced. Hitler's charisma and Hitler's policies – set forth in his July 1921 Party statute – transformed that inheritance into a political concept, the "Führer principle": individual rather than collective leadership responsibility at every level, and strict subordination to higher authority. The result scarcely replicated the army's orderly pyramidal structures, although the Prussian army, like the Catholic Church and Germany's preeminent mass party, the SPD, was indeed a source of organizational lessons that Hitler on occasion publicly hailed.[287] The NSDAP and its offshoots emerged from Hitler's mid-1921 reforms as parallel and conflicting hierarchies of subordinate Führer, each looking upward toward Hitler. But henceforth the military ethos and practices that pervaded

---

[284] See especially HSA, 480–82, 483–84.

[285] HSA, 483–84, 499; antecedents: HSA, 183, 323 and Tyrell, ed., *Führer befiehl*, 46–47; Franz-Willing, *Ursprung der Hitlerbewegung*, 123–26, for the wider context; MK, 494–97, also documents Hitler's deep personal interest in the movement's symbols. Röhm, Hitler, SA: Longerich, *Geschichte der SA*, 21–25.

[286] Ludwig von Gebsattel (1905) on Prussian military culture, p. 38.

[287] HRSA, 1:91–92; MK, 249–50.

German nationalism reinforced an ascendancy already legitimated by a century of schoolbook ancestor-worship – Arminius, Luther, Frederick the Great, Bismarck. Of all the *völkisch* leaders, only Hitler possessed the "unique gifts" required to harness *both* "great men" and military-organizational technique to his political aims.

The essential corollary to the post-1921 *Führerprinzip* of the NSDAP derived from a wholly unique element of Prusso-German military culture: mission tactics, the demand that subordinates neither require nor await detailed orders, but rather exercise initiative to the fullest in carrying out *tasks* (*Aufträge*) in accordance with their superiors' *intent* (*Absichten*). Hitler's predilection from the beginning for parallel hierarchies may have derived both from social Darwinist faith in the virtues of *Kampf*, and from an instinctual distrust of the power that principal subordinates might enjoy within a rationalized and strictly pyramidal structure. Yet internal competition alone would not necessarily secure the movement's expansion. The Prusso-German tradition of decentralized decision-making complemented and reinforced Hitler's position as motive force at the movement's center. At the periphery, subordinates "working toward the Führer," as Werner Willikens, a Nazi Reichstag member from 1928, agricultural bureaucrat, and *SS-Gruppenführer*, remarked in 1934, made it unnecessary for Hitler, especially in routine matters, to do more than express intent – such as his characteristic April 1922 remark that NSDAP local groups must "grasp political power in our movement's fist."[288] Such a dynamic required, for its smooth operation, cadres imbued with the qualities that German military culture uniquely fostered: implacable boldness and predilection for extreme risks, "joy in responsibility," organizational skill, indefatigability, and the ability to inspire subordinates. Those cadres – Germany's military desperadoes – the lost war and the Versailles Treaty had provided in abundance. The Imperial German Army's shrinkage to the dwarf-Reichswehr, followed in 1920–21 by the dissolution of the *Freikorps*, deprived 30,000 career officers and hundreds of thousands of reserve officers and NCOs of the careers and status that had given their lives meaning.[289] The NSDAP, more vehemently and credibly than any other postwar movement, promised to restore that meaning through bloody revenge at home and expansion abroad. It was no accident that most significant National Socialist leaders of the *Kampfzeit* had served in 1914–18, and that many had experience of wartime command – an advantage denied to Germany's traditional parties, whose leaders at all levels tended to be settled civilians in late middle age.[290]

[288] Willikens: Noakes and Pridham, *Nazism*, 2:207 and Kershaw, *Hitler, 1889–1936*, 530; HSA, 634 (inimitably: "in ihrem Ort die politische Macht in die Faust unserer Bewegung zu bringen").

[289] Background: Knox, "The 'Prussian Idea of Freedom' and the Career Open to Talent: Battlefield Initiative and Social Ascent from Prussian Reform to Nazi Revolution, 1807–1944," in idem, *Common Destiny*, 186–226.

[290] For the indispensable role of ex-military cadres in the National Socialist electoral machine, see especially Richard F. Hamilton, "Hitler's Electoral Support: Recent Findings and Theoretical

A final element of Hitler's leadership style was his offer, from the beginning, of the career open to talent: *"Freie Bahn dem Tüchtigen!"*[291] Those who aspired to join the Party "must learn above all else to judge a man by achievement [*Leistung*] and not by his birth certificate or the clothes on his back." And from July 1921 Hitler could point to himself as the foremost exemplar of National Socialism's social promise: he had risen from obscure beginnings to leadership as the movement's "most capable brain, *judged only according to [his] Leistung.*"[292] His movement, then and later, proved uniquely adept at exploiting the inherited barriers of *Stand* for its own dynamic purposes. The parties of both Left and Right, as Hitler never tired of pointing out, were in their very different ways committed to the maintenance or exacerbation of Germany's many social distinctions. National Socialism by contrast was the only major political movement across the Weimar spectrum that emphatically denied class and *Stand*, and appeared to offer the careers transcending social barriers that corresponded to the individual aspirations raised by industrialization, education, and the failure of the old order in 1914–18.[293] For the military desperadoes, the expanding Nazi movement thus offered a welcome change from the Imperial German Army, with its slow promotions and jealous guardianship of officer status even in wartime. As the volume and intensity of the message emanating from Munich swelled in 1922–23 – and in 1925–33 – it spoke to increasing numbers of Germans.

That message was compelling in its own right; the widespread assumption that National Socialist ideology lacked coherence or content is only sustainable by ignoring its basic texts – Hitler's speeches and writings. Far more effectively than Mussolini and his associates, Hitler as early as 1921–22 succeeded in constructing an internally coherent self-referential universe that scarcely changed thereafter. None of its building blocks were at all original; many of Hitler's slogans derived word for word from the propaganda of the *Schutz- und Trutz-Bund.*[294] But Hitler's synthesis was uniquely compelling and consistent: an all-embracing all-explanatory system of belief.[295]

Implications," *Canadian Journal of Sociology* 11 (1986), 11–14; also the biographical data in Peter Hüttenberger, *Die Gauleiter. Studie zum Wandel des Machtgefüges in der NSDAP* (Stuttgart, 1969), 213–20.

[291] Roughly, "Make way for talent!": HSA, 296 (12 January 1921).

[292] HSA, 149, 461 (8 September 1921; emphasis in original).

[293] For Nazism as product and vehicle of the German people's revolution of rising expectations, see especially Fritzsche, *Germans into Nazis*.

[294] Compare HSA (1919–21) with the slogans and material in Lohalm, *Völkischer Radicalismus*, 136–52.

[295] "Ideology denial" is a central feature of the historiography of National Socialism, in two senses: denial that Nazism had an ideology, and denial that the ideology, if it existed, could have had much bearing on Nazi practice. Such claims normally derive from: (i) the unspoken assumption that the ideal-type "ideology" is Marxism, from which Nazism ostensibly differs radically in structure, coherence, intellectual elegance, and moral stature (for the parallels, see however p. 347 and note 323; (ii) the belief that Hitler's utterances do not add up to a coherent ideology (a position most easily sustainable in the absence of familiarity with his speeches and writings); and (iii) the faith, widespread from the 1960s onward, that "rhetoric" or "discourse"

Race was the foundation. Politics, as Haeckel, Ratzel, and others had long since taught, was biology: "The racial question is the driving force of world history."[296] The resulting *Kampf* was the all-or-nothing struggle ingrained in the intellectual DNA of *Bildungsbürgertum* and officer corps, but in an especially global, pitiless, and pseudo-scientific form: "either victory of the Aryan side or its annihilation [*Vernichtung*] and victory of the Jews." The "gigantic world struggle of the Aryan against the Jew in Germany" had cosmic implications: "The greatest deed of our *Volk* is as yet ahead of it: to act as Führer in the coming struggle of the Aryans against the Jewish world peril." It was Germany's "historic mission" to "heal an ailing world."[297]

Victory must first of all be internal – to create a mass movement that would encompass the entire nation, overthrow the "Jew-republic" of the "November criminals" and lay the foundations for German resurgence. By late 1922 Hitler had added the next step, a foreign policy concept that remained largely unchanged thereafter. His ruminations had begun in 1919–20 conventionally enough: the obliteration of the Versailles order and "a Germanic Reich of the German nation" that stretched "from Memel to Pressburg and from Königsberg to Strassburg," or even – Arndt's extravagant 1813 formula – "as far as the German tongue resounds."[298] As late as December 1920 Hitler argued in impeccably Wilhelmine fashion that national survival required reasserting Germany's position in the world market through the reestablishment of German military power.

Not until May 1921 did he gradually formulate a first indistinct version of the racialist geopolitics that henceforth constituted the foundation of his policies both foreign and domestic. Demographic growth had left Germans a mere eighteenth of the per capita land area available to Russians, and posed harsh choices: birth control, which reduced nations to the "plaything [*Fangball*] of others"; colonies, but Germany had come too late; emigration, which made German blood mere "cultural fertilizer [*Kulturdünger*]" for others; and industrial export to underwrite food imports. Prewar Germany had taken the last course, but had failed because of England's envy, "the innermost root cause of the outbreak of war." Yet Brest-Litovsk had offered – however briefly – a German road to world power: unlimited raw materials and the "land and soil"

is irrelevant to political action: life is all TV. To outline the convolutions of the resulting absurd debates is pointless; a potentially valid objection to any claims made for the Hitler utterances deployed here is circularity: their selection, insofar as it is not potentially arbitrary, is inevitably a product of later events – *historians do it with hindsight*. But utterances selected on that basis also correspond in large part to the results of a recent self-contained hermeneutic analysis of the major text in which Hitler *himself* structured and expounded the "National Socialist idea": Barbara Zehnpfennig, *Hitlers Mein Kampf: Eine Interpretation* (Munich, 2nd rev. ed., 2002).

[296] HSA, 301 (27 January 1920); compare MK, 339: "The racial question gives the key not only to world history, but to all human culture"; useful analysis of the implications: Frank-Lothar Kroll, "Geschichte und Politik im Weltbild Hitlers," VfZ 44 (1996), 336–38.

[297] HSA, 620, 636, 631 (emphasis in original), 779, 354, 693–94, 738 (references to Geibel's nineteenth-century doggerel, p. 55 in this volume).

[298] HSA, 92–93, 112, 180, 115, 242, 282, 128.

of the party program.[299] By December 1922 these convictions had hardened sufficiently so that Hitler, in a remarkable indiscretion, could present a sympathetic Munich newspaper proprietor with ties to the Cuno government with the finished concept:

> In foreign policy Germany must adjust itself to a purely continental policy, while avoiding the harming of English interests. We should attempt the carving up [*Zertrümmerung*] of Russia with English help. Russia would provide soil enough for German settlers, and a broad field of action for German industry. Then, when [we] settle accounts with France, England would not get in the way.

Hitler had from the beginning appreciated the interdependence of foreign and domestic policy; the domestic corollary to this program, as he informed Cuno's correspondent with remarkable impudence, would be a "man who if necessary would march through blood and fields of corpses," and a "dictatorship with an iron fist." He preserved a decent modesty about who that man should be; after harsh necessity was past, the monarchy – upon which Hitler had repeatedly poured scorn in public – might even reappear.[300]

Yet by December 1922 Hitler had long since voiced the claim of his movement – and on occasion a personal claim – to rule Germany "when the rotten edifice [of the Republic] finally collapse[d]." He had hailed the swastika flag, virtually from its origins, as the national flag of the future, and in 1922–23 repeatedly predicted that it would fly in due course from the Reichstag or the former royal castle in Berlin; the NSDAP was the "future of the German people."[301] His own role he often left vague, as in his talk with Cuno's informant. And on one occasion, in May 1922, he described himself to the dignitaries of the National Club of 1919 in Berlin as the mere "drummer of the national liberation movement." But this was the tactical false humility appropriate to that exalted audience; the coincidence of his seizure of power within the Party in July 1921 with his call for a "dictator who is a genius" was no coincidence. Yet Mussolini's ascent to power in Rome at the end of October 1922 nevertheless proved powerful encouragement with regard to both method and outcome; several weeks before his talk with Cuno's informant that December, Hitler had insisted that "we need a *strong man*, and the *National Socialists* shall provide him."[302] Thenceforth he reverted to tactical modesty: "our task is not to seek for the individual... our task is to forge the sword... to give the dictator, when

---

[299] HSA, 96, 103, 113, 207–08, 218, 384, 421, 423, 426–27 (31 May 1921: the four alternatives, and the ideal of eastern empire as delineated at Brest-Litovsk – of which Hitler's view was hardly unique); for Hitler's increasingly radical critique of Wilhelmine policy, HSA, 505, 511. See also p. 114 for parallel prewar musings by Corradini.

[300] HSA, 773 (Eduard August Scharrer, report of a conversation with Hitler, end December 1922, 770–75); see also HSA, 869–70, 874, 901, 1023.

[301] HSA, 565 (2 February 1922); Flag: HSA, 323, 780, 819, 873, 920, 950, 989, 1043, 1051; the NSDAP as Germany's savior, liberator, ruler, and/or fate: HSA, 646, 688, 695, 711, 723, 754, 796, 801, 809, 909, 918, 951, 952, 1042.

[302] HSA, 754 (emphasis in original).

he comes, a *Volk* that is ripe for him."[303] Yet the logic of insurrection, of the "march on Berlin" by the Bavarian paramilitary Right under National Socialist leadership that gradually took shape amid Ruhr occupation, hyperinflation, and Communist agitation in 1923, demanded Hitler the individual. As he was well aware.

Forging the sword proved arduous indeed, for the NSDAP, despite a membership that soared from 2,000 at the end of 1920 to 20,000 by the end of 1922 to around 50,000 by November 1923, was by 1922–23 merely the most dynamic force among the many *völkisch* sects and paramilitary bands that made up the postwar Bavarian "patriotic" movement.[304] Its SA, with units encompassing perhaps 4,000 trained if under-equipped men by mid-1923, was merely one – and not the largest – of three principal components of the radical paramilitary *Kampfbund* formed for insurrection by Ernst Röhm, in cooperation with Hitler, at the beginning of September 1923. The *Kampfbund* in turn was informally subordinate to the retired but conspiratorially active Ludendorff, and formally so to the Bavarian Reichswehr command's mobilization preparations either to fight the French or to launch its own "march on Berlin" to depose the Reich government of Stresemann and Ebert.

Hitler's position throughout 1922–23, as his insurrectionary propaganda against the "Jew-republic" gained an increasing following, was and remained precarious.[305] Recurrent quarrels with the Bavarian governments of the moderate Right imperfectly masked his reliance on their protection. His Austrian citizenship exposed him to possible deportation, and the Reich "Law for the Protection of the Republic" following Rathenau's murder in July 1922 and Prussia's November 1922 ban on the NSDAP largely confined Nazi propaganda and growth to Bavaria, although all across central, northern, and western Germany orphaned groups from the outlawed *Schutz- und Trutz-Bund* hastened to pledge fealty.[306] The Party's unique status as the only force that combined incessant agitation with paramilitary force brought both a galling dependence on Ludendorff, Röhm, and the Munich Reichswehr command, and constant distasteful haggling with the fractious leaders of Bavaria's numerous armed bands. Hitler's continuing need for a force under his sole control and his love of parallel hierarchies led, logically enough, to the founding of a *Stosstrupp Hitler* in spring–summer 1923 as his personal guard, a prototype

303 HSA, 924; similarly HSA, 966, and 1037 (interview with the *Corriere Italiano*, Rome: "the dictator is designated by the will [*coscienza*] of the nation").

304 Numbers, based on surviving membership lists (which do not reflect departures from the Party): Detlev Mühlberger, *The Social Bases of Nazism* (Cambridge, 2003), 38–39; for a much higher contemporary estimate by the Munich police (150,000 members across Bavaria, summer 1923), Gordon, *Beer Hall Putsch*, 64–65.

305 For useful analysis of Hitler's role in 1923, see particularly Longerich, *Geschichte der SA*, 22–44; Wolfgang Horn, *Führerideologie und Parteiorganization in der NSDAP (1919–1933)* (Düsseldorf, 1972), ch. 2; and Gordon, *Beer Hall Putsch*, which offers the most analytically balanced and carefully documented account.

306 Lohalm, *Völkischer Radikalismus*, 304–26.

for the later *Schutzstaffel* (SS). The rising status of SA and NSDAP within the broader Bavarian anti-republican front increased Hitler's own prestige, and attracted the interest of notables such as Heinrich Class and Tirpitz, who both contacted or met inconclusively with Hitler; Class innocently suggested that the NSDAP "share in a dictatorship to be erected by him."[307]

Yet despite a disagreeable dependence on others that replicated on a larger scale his situation within the Party before July 1921, Hitler nevertheless maintained the initiative throughout 1923. He achieved unique notoriety among nationalists by gleefully rejecting Berlin's call for unity against the French invaders: "*Not down with France, but down with the November criminals*"; "*the national unity front is stinking manure.*"[308] Incessant mass meetings and paramilitary demonstrations, assisted by hyperinflation and the French, who obligingly made a "martyr" of Leo Schlageter, a National Socialist terrorist in the Ruhr, created a momentum evidenced by accelerating recruitment – 10,000 new members from 25 September to 9 November 1923 alone – and by Hitler's recurring prophetic utterances ("*We are coming* [frenetic applause]") and reiterated demands for "pride, *Wille*, defiance, hate, hate, and yet again hate."[309]

Hitler's appointment as political leader of the *Kampfbund* on 25 September, NSDAP plans for yet more mass rallies, the inevitable rumors of a coming Putsch, and the Stresemann government's abandonment of the ruinous policy of passive resistance in the Ruhr terrified the Bavarian government, which thereupon appointed a dictator of its own with full although temporary powers: *Generalstaatskommissar* Gustav von Kahr. Hitler disparaged Kahr as an honest bureaucrat lacking in "heroic qualities" – a wholly accurate assessment.[310] But Kahr had the overwhelming force of the Bavarian Reichswehr and militarized police (*Landespolizei*) in his corner, and plans of his own for a march on Berlin far more sedate and conservative than Hitler's radical nationalist crusade to plant the hooked cross atop the Reichstag and "cleanse Germany of the November criminals." By late October, Hitler found himself squeezed between Kahr's foot-dragging, the millenarian expectations he had aroused among his followers since spring, and the passing of Bavaria's opportunity to act, as Ebert, Stresemann, and Seeckt forcibly deposed the SPD-KPD coalition governments in Saxony and Thuringia that served as pretext for a march on Berlin, and Stresemann moved to tame the inflation and achieve a modus vivendi with France.[311]

---

[307] HSA, 1195 (see also 530); Raffael Scheck, "Politics of Illusion: Tirpitz and Right-Wing Putschism, 1922–24," GSR 18:1 (1995), 33; context: Thoss, "Diktaturfrage," 62–68.

[308] HSA, 786, 830 ("stinkende Jauche"; emphasis in original).

[309] HSA, 813, 918, 1013. For the NSDAP's exploitation of Schlageter, see especially Derek Hastings, "How 'Catholic' Was the Early Nazi Movement? Religion, Race, and Culture in Munich, 1919–1924," CEH 36:3 (2003), 405–09; Reichardt, "'Martyrer' der Nation. Überlegungen zum Nationalismus in der Weimarer Republik," in Jörg Echternkamp and Sven Oliver Müller, eds., *Die Politik der Nation* (Munich, 2002), 173–202, offers useful comparative insights.

[310] HSA, 1032–33.

[311] HSA, 950, 998, 1004, 1013, 1022, 1037, 1039 (emphasis in original), 1043, 1050, 1051; Scheck, "Politics of Illusion," 34–37; Gordon, *Beer Hall Putsch*, ch. 10 and 389–92.

Hitler's response was characteristic of later occasions, and wholly in keeping with Prusso-German military tradition: a *ganzer Entschluss* – for insurrection: "I shall pursue the road on which I have entered alone, [even if] and abandoned [by all] (thunderous *Heil!*)."[312] The resulting "Beer Hall Putsch" of 8/9 November 1923 – a tale often told – was Hitler's personal initiative; the multifarious overlapping conspiracies of the Bavarian Right were running down. At the head of the heavily armed *Stosstrupp Hitler*, he hijacked a sedate gathering of Kahr's and the Bavarian elite at the *Bürgerbraukeller* by firing into the ceiling to gain the attention of a somewhat jaded crowd and threatening to emplace a machine gun to cover the hall. He then coerced and wheedled Kahr, the commander of the Bavarian Reichswehr, Otto Hermann von Lossow, and the commandant of the *Landespolizei* at gunpoint into proclaiming him Reich chancellor and Ludendorff – who appeared on cue – as "Reich Regent" and military commander of the insurrection. But once Hitler and Ludendorff amateurishly released Kahr and associates on their words of honor to prepare Bavaria's march northward, the authorities took immediate and effective countermeasures against the Putsch, which had mobilized only 4,000 *Kampfbund* troops, of which 1,500 were SA. Hitler – so often comfortingly depicted as indecisive – chose one more throw of the dice, the despairing march next morning that ended under a hail of *Landespolizei* rifle fire with the death of fourteen of the movement's historic "martyrs," and Hitler's flight, arrest, trial, and imprisonment.[313]

Despite verbal concessions to Ludendorff's military aura, Hitler had laid claim to the chancellorship – and dictatorship – of Germany in a fashion wholly consistent with his later course. He had recognized as early as spring 1920 that soldiers could never be "bearers of the movement" of national liberation, but only play supporting roles. Despite flattering public references to Ludendorff both before and after the Putsch, he took the decided view that "policy would be set exclusively by himself." Ludendorff's role was simply "to win over the rest of the Reichswehr" outside Bavaria; in other respects the victor of Tannenberg and wounded Siegfried of 1918 would "not have the slightest influence." Lossow, who had dealt extensively with Hitler since January 1923, described Hitler's self-conception accurately: the ex-corporal "considered himself the German Mussolini," and Hitler's entourage hailed him as "the German Messiah . . . the Chosen One."[314]

At the resulting treason trial in February–April 1924, Hitler made the most of the national publicity offered him by complaisant judges. In contrast to the shabby evasions of the other defendants, he took full personal responsibility for

---

[312] HSA, 1050 (30 October 1923, as reported in the *Völkischer Beobachter*). The style did not change; see for instance "I must choose between victory and annihilation. I choose victory" (23 November 1939, ADAP D/8/384 (349), demanding that the Wehrmacht attack France).

[313] For Hitler's role, Gordon, *Beer Hall Putsch*, 329, 331, 351–52, 401–02.

[314] HSA, 118; interrogation testimony of Berchem (chief of staff, Bavarian Reichswehr division), in Horn, *Führerideologie*, 120 note 62; "Der Berufene": Lossow in HRSA, *Der Hitler-Prozess*, 2:737–38; see also HSA, 1027 (Hitler to *The Daily Mail*, 2 October 1923: "If a German Mussolini is given to Germany . . . people would fall down on their knees and worship him more than Mussolini has ever been worshipped").

the Putsch as a supremely noble effort that had not failed, but had borne witness against Germany's enslavement. He impudently denied that seizing power in Berlin would have brought French and possibly Czech retribution. And he promised that he would be back, his army growing "from rowdy bands to battalions, from battalions to regiments, regiments to divisions, and the old insignia shall be lifted from the muck and the old flags shall wave again. . . ." The court might condemn; history would acquit.[315]

The resulting vacation was brief. Despite a nominal sentence of five years, Hitler gave the necessary insincere promises of good behavior, and left Landsberg fortress just before Christmas 1924. The respite from agitation and plotting was nevertheless fundamental for the development of the Führer and of his movement. His absence, and subsequent astute refusal to play any part in the squabbles within the banned and truncated fragments of the NSDAP demonstrated yet again his utter indispensability. Without him the Party and its constituency were likely to remain forever on the fringes of German politics to which the December 1924 election consigned them (see Figure 4.3). Hitler himself profited mightily from an exceedingly comfortable imprisonment, surrounded by cronies, members of *Stosstrupp Hitler*, and solicitous warders. The enforced time for reading and reflection allowed him, as he later put it, a chance to "confirm his ideological construct by the study of natural history [*den Gedankenbau naturgeschichtlich zu begründen*]."[316] That construct took the form of a memoir, dictated to his entourage at Landsberg and over the year following his release, and published in 1925–26. Its working title was "Four and One-Half Years' Struggle Against Lies, Stupidity, and Cowardice: A Settling of Accounts with the Destroyers of the National Socialist Movement," later mercifully shortened, apparently on Amann's sage advice, to *Mein Kampf*.

The book, despite its prolixity, stylistic eccentricities, and durable reputation for turgid incoherence, presented the ideology assembled between 1919 and 1922–23 in lucid and consistent form.[317] Merciless conclusions derived logically and inexorably from a single irrational premise about the structure of past and future. The axis of world history was the cosmic Darwinian-biological struggle between the Aryans – the one "race" qualified as "bearers" and "founders" of culture – and the Jewish "world-pestilence." The radically unsatisfactory present – defeat, demoralization, inflation, French invasion, and alleged Jewish rule – was merely a surface manifestation of that underlying conflict. Disaster had overtaken the "Aryan-Nordic race" through "race-shame [*Rassenschande*], the original sin of mankind": miscegenation with Jews and

---

[315] French intervention: HSA, 1146, 1167, 1169–70, 1193–94; closing harangue: HSA, 1215–16.

[316] Hitler, *Monologe*, 49 (July 1941); see also 262.

[317] For this and what follows, see MK, and the exhaustive analysis of Zehnpfennig, *Mein Kampf*. Among the innumerable comments on Hitler's literary talents, see particularly Ralph Manheim, "Translator's Note," MK, xi–xiv, and the numerous stylistic changes imposed over the years on Hitler's dictated text: Hermann Hammer, "Die deutschen Ausgaben von Hitlers 'Mein Kampf,'" VfZ 4 (1956), 161–78.

other lesser breeds.[318] Germany had failed to achieve the "world domination" that was its due because of that interbreeding, and consequent loss of the necessary "herd-like unity."[319]

Revival and the assurance of ultimate victory demanded the "nationalization of the masses" through the expunging of Jewish influences and racist revolution: the violent ejection of the Jews from the German "*Volk*-body" they had allegedly corrupted. Bloodshed and eugenics – "the racist state must ensure that only the healthy beget children" – would restore the inherent qualitative advantage of pure Aryan blood, and allow fulfillment of Germany's global mission, the conquest of living space in Russia, and the achievement of the Aryan world domination due to any state "that dedicate[d] itself to the care of its best racial elements."[320] Italy and Britain were Germany's foreordained allies. And as Hitler noted in a slightly later literary effort, the unpublished "second book" of 1928, domestic and foreign policy were closely interdependent and must "reciprocally enhance one another," the one securing the racial quality ("*Rassenwert*") and military power for expansion, the other providing the *Lebensraum* for further "internal development."[321] The global scale both of the Jewish challenge and of the necessary German-Aryan response also made the total genocidal elimination of the Jewish "bacillus" a central and inescapable part of the project. Nor did Hitler shy away from more immediate measures, as he suggested in an eerie retrospective prophecy: "If at the beginning of the war and during the war twelve or fifteen thousand of these Hebrew corrupters of the people had been held under poison gas [*unter Giftgas gehalten*], ... then the sacrifices of millions at the front would not have been in vain."[322]

Marxism's structural similarities are obvious: a present rendered intolerable by humanity's alienation from its very nature; a cosmic villain, the capitalist; a chosen people, the industrial proletariat; a teleological global process, the development of the means of production, as monocausal prime mover; and an outcome that would bring that process to completion – bloody revolution to destroy the class enemy and heal the human race.[323] Yet both Marxism and National Socialism derived their structure and some of their resonance from

---

[318] MK, 624 ("Erbsünde der Menschen").

[319] MK, 396 ("es hat uns um die Weltherrschaft gebracht").

[320] Eugenics: MK, 396–406, anticipated in HSA, 1025–26; world domination: HSA, 383–84, 688 ("must some day become lord of the earth"); also pp. 335 and 360 in this volume.

[321] MK, book II, chs. 13–14; Gerhard Weinberg, ed., *Hitlers Zweites Buch* (Stuttgart, 1961), 70, 65–66, 62; Martin Broszat, "Betrachtungen zu 'Hitlers Zweitem Buch,'" VfZ 9 (1961), 422.

[322] MK, 679.

[323] For a cogent statement of this minority viewpoint, see the detailed comparison of the systems of Hitler and Marx by Zehnpfennig, *Mein Kampf*, especially 277–80. For a different but even more embarrassing parallel, Robert C. Tucker, *Philosophy and Myth in Karl Marx* (London, 1961), 111–13; also compare Marx's quasi-*völkisch* description of "the Jew" ("What is the earthly religion of the Jew? *Usury*. What is his earthly god? *Money*") in "On the Jewish Question" (1844) with the language of *Das Kapital*, part III, ch. 8.1, on the "vampire-like" character of capital, and the capitalist as "capital personified." Leszek Kolakowski, *Main Currents of*

something far older: the biblical cycle of humanity's primordial innocence, fall, and redemption. Marx borrowed the mechanism from Hegel's variation on Joachim of Fiore's stage-theory of history; Hitler had imbibed it from his Austrian Catholic origins. Yet Nazi comparisons of Hitler to Christ and of the movement to the early Church were just that: comparisons. Hitler himself fiercely rejected the notion that National Socialism was or should become a religion: "A movement such as ours...must remain in the realm of the exact sciences. The Party must not be a substitute for the Church; its task is of a scientific-methodological nature." He himself was "only and exclusively a politician," and he feared that posterity would transmute him into a Buddha or "SS-saint."[324] National Socialism enthusiastically and effectively deployed the Christian images that pervaded its constituencies for its own this-worldly purposes.[325] Like Mazzini and Fascism, it appropriated Christian martyrdom for its hallowed dead. But its ideology, although structured in a way that maximized Christian resonances, was relentlessly this-worldly. It derived much of its power from an entirely different claim of connection to the structure of the universe: the claim to be science, a claim Fascism could not wield effectively, and that, in a half-peasant society, did not arouse the reverence attending *Wissenschaft* in Germany.

Hitler also reserved in his memoir a place for himself far more central than protagonist of a racist *Bildungsroman* situated in prewar Vienna and Munich. Great upheavals required and generated great men – of two types: the theoretician – *Programmatiker* or *Theoretiker* – and the political leader. And the "combination of theoretician, organizer, and Führer in one individual is the rarest thing on this earth; this combination makes the great man."[326] Rallying the disparate and discouraged fragments of the movement after the great man's release nevertheless proved arduous. But the result was the completion of the structure sketched in outline before November 1923: a movement in which program and leader were identical. Shrill NSDAP support of Ludendorff's candidacy in the first round of the 1925 presidential election fulfilled two vital purposes. It once again sharply delimited the refounded Party from *völkisch* and conservative rivals, which in general supported the Right's unity candidate,

　　　Marxism, 3 vols. (Oxford, 1978), especially 1:466–70, persuasively outlines the intrinsically totalitarian nature of Marx's project.

324　Goebbels, 7:248 (December 1939); Hitler, *Monologe*, 84–85 (October 1941; special guest: Heinrich Himmler); similarly, Albert Speer, *Inside the Third Reich* (New York, 1970), 141.

325　The revival in recent decades of the suggestion of Erich Vögelin (*Die politischen Religionen* [Vienna, 1938]) that totalitarianism was a religious phenomenon (for Vögelin, Gnostic rather than Christian) has created additional areas of confusion in the understanding of Nazism, Fascism, generic fascism, and totalitarian movements. Richard Steigmann-Gall, "Nazism and the Revival of Political Religion Theory," TMPR 5:3 (2004), 376–96, offers pointed analysis of the empirical failings of the theory as a guide to the Nazi movement and regime; Hans Maier, ed., *"Totalitarismus" und "Politische Religionen." Konzepte des Diktaturvergleichs*, 2 vols. (Paderborn, 1996–97) provides a useful sampling of the debates.

326　MK, 580–81; also 212. For the accuracy of Hitler's printed recollections of the pre-1914 period, see note 256.

Jarres. And Ludendorff's derisory 1 percent of the vote (Figure 4.4) liquidated him as a potential rival. Weimar's return to apparent stability then loosened the Prussian and Reich restrictions that had inhibited the spread of the NSDAP outside Bavaria up to 1924. The result was the absorption by the Party of a variety of groups and leaders across northern Germany and the Ruhr. Expansion in turn led inescapably to programmatic dispute between the Munich wing of the Party, where primordial anti-Semitism and personal loyalty to Hitler was the norm, and the more self-consciously "socialist," less personally devoted, and often younger groups and leaders of Germany's industrial cities. Hitler resolved the internal dispute through a carefully choreographed showdown with the northern wing at Bamberg in February 1926. The subsequent conversion and cooption of a key northerner, the young Joseph Goebbels, registered a general if often grudging acceptance of Hitler's claim to total domination of the movement.[327]

That outcome did not as yet provide the NSDAP with a strategy or a road, however long, back toward the mastery over Germany that it continued to claim. Hitler and his Munich cronies failed to enunciate a plan, other than the prospect of slowly building up a mass of supporters sufficient to paralyze Germany: "580,000 Fascists rule the Italian State.... If we had 600,000 men ... we would be a power [in the land]."[328] Oratory alone was of doubtful use: after a first tolerated public speech proved too inflammatory for the post-Putsch BVP Munich government, Hitler found himself banned from speaking except to closed Party or group audiences in Bavaria until March 1927, and in Prussia from September 1925 to September 1928. Most other states followed suit.[329] Electoral agitation and parliamentary activity was ideologically repugnant, and unpromising in view of Weimar's stabilization – even if a few Reichstag and Landtag seats, acquired in 1924 by *völkisch* splinter groups and bequeathed to the NSDAP, offered salaries and rail passes for agitation against the Republic. The northerners had a concept: systematic agitation to convert the urban working classes of Germany's great cities to *national* socialism. But full commitment clearly required the creation of NSDAP trade unions, a step Hitler successfully resisted. Class representation was inappropriate if the class struggle was a Jewish conspiracy, and trade unions might easily acquire a life of their own, detract from his charisma, and split the movement. Until 1928 the Party indeed concentrated its efforts on the larger cities; Hitler himself spoke in the Ruhr to Party gatherings or invitation-only groups no less than eleven times in 1926.[330] But the results, as revealed in the May 1928 Reichstag election in which the NSDAP polled a mere 2.6 percent of the popular vote and received 12 seats, were notably disheartening.

---

[327] See Goebbels, 1/2:71–74, for the conversion experience of the future "Reich Minister for Propaganda and *Volk*-Enlightenment."

[328] HRSA, 1:97.

[329] Table in Tyrell, ed., *Führer befiehl*, 107–08.

[330] Base data for Hitler's 1925–33 travels and appearances: the maps in HRSA, 6:301–09.

The Party and Hitler had nevertheless achieved much in the interim. Membership by spring 1928 was around 80,000 throughout the Reich. The SA had reemerged as a putatively legal brass-knuckles street-fighting force very different from the combat infantry of November 1923. The *Schutzstaffel* (SS), although formally a subordinate branch of the SA, succeeded *Stosstrupp Hitler* as the movement's elite guard; in 1929 it acquired a new and dynamic leader, the youthful Heinrich Himmler, standard-bearer for Röhm's paramilitaries in the Putsch and NSDAP deputy Reich propaganda leader from 1926 onward. A series of supporting organizations, from *Hitler Jugend* and "National Socialist German Student League" to a women's auxiliary sprang up. Above all, the NSDAP was now a centralized Führer-party of a kind never before seen; although still exiled to the fringes of German politics, it already possessed greater cohesion, endurance, and devotion to its leader than its Fascist counterpart ever achieved.

Hitler, perhaps in part because he valued his own leisure so much, had displayed from 1919 a keen and distinctly modern sense of organization and logistics. Card indexes, typewriters, printing presses, uniforms, vehicles, and bureaucrats were necessary tools of political as well as military conquest.[331] The long-serving managers whom Hitler appointed or reappointed, from Max Amann as chief of the Party press (1925–45), to Philipp Bouhler as "Reich business manager" (1925–34), to Franz Xaver Schwarz as Reich treasurer and comptroller of accounts (1925–45), to the "socialist" Gregor Strasser as "Reich organization leader" (1928–32) constituted, along with a variety of other long-serving cadres, a highly effective "institutional Hitler."[332] The *Reichsleitung* created the Party's extraordinarily successful system of self-financing, based above all on dues, admission charges to political meetings, and small contributors.[333] It organized the Party's propaganda on a national basis and with increasing professionalism after 1926.[334] And it freed the physical Hitler to give 144 speeches outside Munich from 1925 though 1928, to renew or establish personal contact with key regional subordinates and with the growing masses of NSDAP members, and to withdraw periodically to ponder the movement's future or gather strength for the next frenzied round of agitation.

At the periphery, the Party constituted itself after 1925 into thirty-odd regional units, or *Gaue*, each under a *Gauleiter* directly subordinate to Hitler, acting as his agent, and partaking of his charisma. In practice, and especially until the Party developed a sufficient supply of eligible cadres, at least some of

---

[331] For an early example of Hitler's deep interest in the practical aspects of organizing the national will, see his very detailed October 1922 memorandum on party organization, HSA, 702–08.

[332] Orlow, *Nazi Party*, 150; Orlow offers a still exemplary analysis of the NSDAP's organizational development.

[333] Horst Matzerath and Turner, "Die Selbstfinanzierung der NSDAP 1930–32," GG 3:1 (1977), 59–92, effectively destroy the "agent theory" of Nazism, the enduring myth that "big business" bankrolled Hitler's triumph.

[334] Gerhard Paul, *Aufstand der Bilder. Die NS-Propaganda vor 1933* (Bonn, 1990), 64–69.

these figures enjoyed an independence approaching that of Mussolini's unruly *ras*. But by 1928 Hitler's exercise of his unique gifts and the inexorable bureau-cratic mills of the *Reichsleitung* had nevertheless reduced the provinces to fealty. Hitler in his travels wielded the reward of his presence – and the punishment of his absence – with skill. The bureaucrats applied stringent financial controls, issued uniform organizational and propaganda directives, and demanded peri-odic political progress reports – a highly effective feedback mechanism. The *Gauleiter*, in return for submission, received a relatively free hand, within the framework of the center's directives, in both personnel decisions and political action throughout their *Gaue*.

Further organizational change accompanied the gradual emergence of a national strategy for the conquest of power. Hitler lost interest in the Ruhr after spring 1927; in November 1927 he designated the peasantry as a prior-ity target. And the May 1928 election, despite the depressing overall picture, duly provided surprising gains – up to 18.1 percent of the vote in one county – in the poorer agricultural areas of Schleswig-Holstein hit hard by the agricul-tural depression and convulsed by the resulting violent tax revolt.[335] The 1928 outcome encouraged the Party to redraw its *Gau* boundaries to coincide with the Republic's electoral districts, and to tailor the Party and its affiliated orga-nizations exclusively for the mobilization of the population and the conquest of votes. Munich instituted a crash training course for agitators and created a travelling cinema program that proved particularly effective in rural Germany, where Nazi films might well be the only films for miles.[336] The Reich Party Day of August 1929, held like its 1927 predecessor at Nuremberg, provided an impressive spectacle of unity and mass support, and duly rewarded the local *Gauleiter*, the gutter anti-Semite Julius Streicher, a close Hitler associate since 1921.

The new emphasis on electoral success also affected the Party's propaganda themes, although not sufficiently to justify the widespread assumption, then and later, that Hitler opted after 1928 for the creation of a middle-class movement, abandoning "socialism" for the delights of associating with Ruhr magnates and retired generals. The socialism of the "Nazi Left," most notably that of the Strasser brothers, Gregor and Otto, was in any case an emotional commitment to building a shopkeepers' paradise, a resurrection of the guild-ridden German home town; Gregor was an apothecary by trade.[337] The Party had failed to conquer the Ruhr or "red Berlin," but "socialism" – the claim to be a more sincerely socialist as well as a more nationalist SPD – remained a major NSDAP

---

[335] Hitler's travels, 1926–29: HRSA, 6:302–05; rural emphasis: Paul, *Aufstand*, 85; Schleswig-Holstein: Stoltenberg, *Landvolk*, chs. 6–7; Rietzler, *"Kampf in der Nordmark,"* 399–432.

[336] Propaganda organization and technique from 1928 onward: Paul, *Aufstand*, 64–79; film as medium: ibid., 187–94.

[337] See the excerpt from Strasser's 1925 program in Tyrell, ed., *Führer befiehl*, 119, and the con-temptuous judgment of Reinhard Kühnl, *Die nationalsozialistische Linke 1925–1930* (Meisen-heim am Glan, 1966), especially 86–98.

theme, along with a fanfare of appeals to special interests and the basso continuo of national fanaticism.[338]

What determined the Party's seeming rapprochement with its middle-class nationalist rivals was less a change in agitational targets than increasing strength and self-confidence; the rivals, not the NSDAP, would soon have reason to fear vassalage. Hitler thus abandoned his movement's hostility to political alliances in mid-1929. He joined the "old gang" – the *Stahlhelm*, the durable Heinrich Class of the Pan-Germans, and Hugenberg of the DNVP – in a referendum campaign against the "enslavement of the German people" and the "war-guilt lie" allegedly embodied in the recently negotiated Young Plan reparations settlement. Only 13.8 percent of eligible voters turned out to damn the Young Plan in the December 1929 plebiscite, but NSDAP participation in the campaign increased the movement's national presence. The local and regional arena proved far more important than the Young Plan campaign: throughout the extraordinarily cold winter of 1929–30, as the Müller cabinet crumbled and recession deepened, the NSDAP vote in *Land* and municipal elections crept above 10 percent.[339] By summer 1930 the Party, apparently on the initiative of the young Himmler, had developed an electoral counterpart of the methods of the Fascist *squadre*: regional and local concentrations, through modern transport, communications, and military organizational techniques, of Party workers, speakers, SA, posters, and leaflets on areas that the *Reichsleitung*'s card databases or the local knowledge of the *Gauleiter* suggested were particularly vulnerable to the "National Socialist Idea," or especially vital conquests.[340] Saxony's Landtag election on 22 June 1930 gave a foretaste: 357,788 National Socialist votes, or 14.4 percent.

At that point, high politics in Berlin intersected fatally with the rise of the Nazi Party machine. By autumn 1929 the collapse of the Grand Coalition from internal enmities and external strains was foreseeable. But forces other than the irreconcilable SPD Left and DVP Right, and the resulting quarrel over the level of support for the unemployed that led to the final breach in March 1930, determined the outcome of the crisis. The Reichswehr had since 1925 secured between 6.8 and 8.3 percent of the Reich budget, and required more – as Groener told the cabinet in January 1929, "unless we plan to render eternal our defenselessness." Yet the Reich's deteriorating financial position after mid-1928 had forced the Reichswehr minister to accept a funding cut for 1929 on a one-time basis – just as the enormous expenditures for the "second rearmament

---

[338] On the persistence of the socialist theme and symbolism, and its apparent effectiveness, see Paul, *Aufstand*, 85, 88 (1928), 92–93 (1930), 105, 107 (1932), and Falter, HW, 226–28.

[339] See especially Othmar Jung, "Plebiszitärer Durchbruch 1929? Zur Bedeutung von Volksbegehren und Volksentscheid gegen den Youngplan für die NSDAP," GG 15 (1989), 489–510, which corrects the customary view that Hugenberg and industry underwrote Nazism's rise to national prominence during the Young Plan campaign; for the 1928–30 regional and city elections through which the Nazis actually established themselves as the leading force of the "national opposition," Falter, WA, 90, 91, 96, 97, 107, 108, 111.

[340] Technique: Paul, *Aufstand*, chs. 3–4.

plan" approached. Only threats of a resignation that would bring the coalition down and repeated invocation of Hindenburg secured most of the funds sought for 1930.[341] The continuing crusade of the SPD Left against great armaments and the further deterioration of the Reich's finances inevitably revived a thought never far from the army's collective mind: to expel the SPD from government. By late 1929, Schleicher had begun to explore drastic remedies with Hindenburg and the field marshal's entourage. The newly minted *Generalmajor* appears to have been increasingly sensitive to the hostility of much of the officer corps to desk generals who seemingly pandered to the "party of traitors and deserters." But the pressure from the planners for massive guaranteed appropriations stretching far into the future was the decisive force that propelled the most fateful Reichswehr intervention in Weimar politics.[342] Schleicher's solution was a cabinet extending rightward from the Center Party, equipped with the president's Article 48 decree powers against a potentially recalcitrant Reichstag, and provided in advance with the ultimate threat: the power to dissolve the Reichstag and elect a new and more cooperative one. The army thus proposed the end of parliamentary government. Hindenburg had as early as March 1929 indicated eagerness to replace the Grand Coalition with a non-party cabinet supported by the Right; he readily assented. From early 1929 onward Schleicher's choice as Führer for the experiment was Heinrich Brüning, leader of the Center Party's Reichstag delegation, a self-consciously nationalist member of the "front generation," former machine-gun company commander, and proud holder of the iron cross first class.[343]

The necessity of blaming the Left for reparations required that Müller remain in office until the laws implementing the Young Plan – against which the Right had so fervently campaigned – passed the Reichstag. Müller's successor could then collect the quid pro quo the Allies had offered: France's early evacuation of its last Rhineland zone that summer. On 12 March the Young Plan passed; by month's end the Grand Coalition had collapsed and Brüning was in office. No durable majority dutifully assembled. The slump deepened and the resulting outlays for unemployment support continued to rise. The Reichstag rejected Brüning's emergency budgetary programs. He issued them by decree. SPD, KPD, NSDAP, and the Hugenberg wing of the DNVP duly overturned Brüning's decrees, as the constitution provided. Brüning in turn read out Hindenburg's order dissolving the Reichstag.

That catastrophic misjudgment offered the NSDAP's smoothly running electoral machine a unique opportunity. Germany was free of foreign occupation and could choose its government without fear. The expulsion of the SPD from the cabinet and the option of rule by presidential decree was the anticipatory

[341] Figures: Hansen, "Militärisch-Industriellen-Komplex," 127 note and idem, *Reichswehr und Industrie* (Boppard am Rhein, 1978), 201; Hürter, *Groener*, 151–56; Geyer, *Deutsche Rüstungspolitik*, 132–35.

[342] For the extent of Reichswehr ambitions, see especially Geyer, "Zweite Rüstungsprogramm."

[343] Brüning, *Memoiren*, 140, 145–47; Winkler, *Weimar*, 363.

response of the armed forces and of Hindenburg: a revolution from above. Brüning now gave the German people the chance, after France's last soldier had departed, to mount their own revolution from below. Hitler from the outset triumphantly designated election day, 14 September 1930, as a turning point in Germany's long history: democracy must and would "be defeated with the weapon of democracy."[344] After a frenetic and thoroughly modern electoral campaign in which the Party's cadres far outdid all rivals in organization, dedication, and intensity of effort, the NSDAP duly received 6.3 million votes, or 18.3 percent of the popular vote.[345] It was suddenly the second-largest party in Germany, after the SPD and ahead of the Communists and the Center (see Figure 4.11).

The German people had spoken. But what had the German people said? And why had they said it? The conventional wisdom for many years directly paralleled the "*ceti medi*" model of Fascism, and derived from the same intellectual traditions. Nazism, Fascism, and "fascism" allegedly had indisputable socioeconomic coordinates as the "extremism of the middle." Analysis of NSDAP membership likewise appeared to confirm the lower-middle-class thesis.[346] The notion of Nazism as a revolt of demented pub-keepers, bakers, and white-collar workers fitted neatly with the condescension toward the "petty bourgeoisie" shared by Marxist and non-Marxist intellectuals alike, and with the almost universal unspoken assumption that socioeconomic categories are invariably the most significant or even the *only* significant determinants of political behavior.[347]

Yet increasing distance from the events, a much-improved understanding of German social stratification, a flood of new archival evidence that included roughly 12 million NSDAP membership cards, and the advent of electronic data processing gradually produced a picture that largely confirmed Nazism's incessantly proclaimed view of itself as forerunner of a seamless *Volk*-community beyond class and *Stand*.[348] Party membership, especially in the pre-1923 Bavarian period, did display a "middle-class paunch." But the NSDAP from its beginning also recruited working-class members in numbers only slightly below their proportion throughout the German population.[349] The SA, which had 60,000 members by November 1930 to the NSDAP's 350,000, was notably more working-class than the Party. The NSDAP leadership corps, the *Gauleiter*

---

344 HRSA, 3/3:281, 279, 341, 390.

345 NSDAP themes and technique: Paul, *Aufstand*, 90–94.

346 Seymour Martin Lipset, *Political Man* (New York, 1963), 135 and ch. 5; Michael H. Kater, *The Nazi Party: A Social Profile of Members and Leaders, 1919–1945* (Cambridge, 1983).

347 For a recent extreme example of economic determinism, see the "rational-choice theory" approach of William Brustein, *The Logic of Evil: The Social Origins of the Nazi Party, 1925–1933* (New Haven, CT, 1996).

348 For able summary of the issues and debates, Mühlberger, *Social Bases*, chs. 1–2, and – for unrivalled exposition of the new wisdom – Falter, HW.

349 Mühlberger, *Social Bases*, 41–43, 48–51 ("On the eve of its acquisition of power, the Nazi Party represented a microcosm of German society in terms of the social makeup of its membership").

FIGURE 4.11. The Final Elections, 1928–1932

	1928		1930		July 1932		Oct. 1932	
	Votes	% of Vote	Votes	% of Vote	Votes	% of Vote	Votes	% of Vote
KPD	3,264,793	10.6	4,592,090	13.1	5,369,708	14.6	5,980,614	16.9
SPD	9,152,979	29.8	8,577,738	24.5	7,959,712	21.6	7,251,690	20.4
DDP	1,505,664	4.9	1,322,385	3.8	373,339	1.0	338,609	1.0
Center	3,712,152	12.1	4,127,910	11.8	4,589,430	12.4	4,230,545	11.9
BVP	945,644	3.1	1,059,141	3.0	1,350,047	3.7	1,206,247	3.4
DVP	2,679,703	8.7	1,659,774	4.7	436,002	1.2	660,889	1.9
DNVP	4,381,563	14.2	2,458,246	7.0	2,277,215	6.2	3,131,674	8.8
NSDAP	810,127	2.6	6,409,610	18.3	13,779,017	37.4	11,737,395	33.1
Others	4,300,622	14.0	4,763,963	13.6	747,884	2.0	933,125	2.6
Nonvoters	10,058,889		7,731,917		7,049,135		8,615,826	

Data: Falter, WA, 41.

and Reichstag deputies, inevitably reflected the managerial skills of the middle classes; recent estimates assign only 14.4 percent of *Gauleiter* and 13.4 percent of NSDAP Reichstag deputies in 1932–33 to the "lower class."[350] Yet no other major non-Socialist party in Weimar Germany could boast similar figures, which testify to the NSDAP's devotion to *Leistung* as the chief criterion for advancement. The youth of both rank and file and senior cadres – a *Gauleiter* corps and Reichstag deputies with an average age of 40 in 1933 – embodied and symbolized the career open to talent.[351] The class profile of the Party's vote after 1928, as revealed in exhaustive multiple-regression analysis of precinct-level voting and census data across Germany, has likewise confirmed the Nazi claim to be Germany's first *Volkspartei* – a movement that recruited adherents from all classes, and drew approximately 40 percent of its voters from working-class households in the 1928, 1930, and 1932 Reichstag elections.[352]

Yet the most startling new finding was wholly different. The Party and its affiliates had indeed appealed vigorously and incessantly to groups dissatisfied with their fate or prospects under Weimar, from peasants facing foreclosure to university students contemplating a future in the "intellectual proletariat." But material interests fail to account for the pattern of the Nazi vote. The peasantry of northern Europe in its entirety faced economic disaster from 1927 onward, but only German Protestant peasants blew up tax offices, then voted overwhelmingly for a militant totalitarian Führer-party.[353] The geographic footprint of Nazism in and after September 1930 had two salient features. The first and most powerful factor was religion. Despite the movement's origins in Catholic Bavaria, the pattern of its distribution in 1930 confirmed an affinity to German Protestantism already prominent in Streicher's north Bavarian domain, the Protestant enclave of Franconia.[354] In 1930, Protestants were on average twice as likely to vote NSDAP as Catholics. But a second – probably related – pattern also emerged: the distribution of the Nazi vote from 1930 onward also correlated closely with Hindenburg's 1925 presidential election plurality and with the 1929 vote against the Young Plan.[355]

Analysis of the implications of these discoveries has lagged far behind the data-processing techniques that made them possible. No Weimar-era opinion data exist; the Frankfurt Institute for Social Research was too engaged with Marxist-Freudian rumination to stoop to voter questionnaires. The census and vote data itself has severe limitations: demographic variables – such as age and

---

350 Ibid., 52–56.

351 Kater, *Nazi Party*, 256–57.

352 Including working-class housewives and pensioners: Mühlberger, *Social Bases*, 76; Falter, "Warum die deutschen Arbeiter während des 'Dritten Reiches' zu Hitler standen," GG 13 (1987), 229–30.

353 Timothy A. Tilton, *Nazism, Neo-Nazism, and the Peasantry* (Bloomington, IN, 1975), ch. 2.

354 Falter, "Der Aufstieg der NSDAP in Franken bei den Reichstagswahlen 1924–1933," GSR 9:2 (1986), 323.

355 Falter, HW, 123–25, 177–78, 355–63, 374, and ch. 6.5; also compare maps 2 (confessional distribution, 1925 census) and 10 (1930 vote) in Milatz, *Wähler und Wahlen*.

sex – relatively constant throughout Germany cannot be sorted meaningfully against precinct voting figures.[356] Nor does any large "dataset" capture war, *Freikorps* service, and military enthusiasm. Other non-socioeconomic characteristics of the German population relevant to political behavior may simply have escaped the analysts. Even the causes of the Protestant-Catholic divide are far from clear. One obvious source is the relative immunity or imperviousness – for which scholars later coined the term *Resistenz* – to the Nazi appeal, both before and after 1933, of both Catholic and Socialist-industrial-worker subcultures. Both milieux already had political parties with long-established traditions, even if by 1932–33 both had begun to lose voters to the Nazis. From 1924 the Catholic episcopate publicly damned the *völkisch* neo-paganism of Ludendorff and of prominent NSDAP figures such as Rosenberg, reinforcing the Center and BVP loyalties of the devout.[357] The KPD likewise drew on part of the Socialist subculture, and – especially in 1932–33 – on the growing legions of the unemployed.[358]

Protestant reasons for voting *for* Hitler are less immediately obvious. The usual implicit verdict is that little explanation is needed. Given Catholic commitment to the Center Party, the NSDAP's potential primary constituency was the Protestant majority of the German population. The NSDAP, in its leap to mass party status, thus became a "*Volkspartei* of protest" against Weimar by Protestants presumably moved by economic fear or distress. That suggestion, which recalls earlier formulations ("catchall party of protest") by adepts of class analysis, nevertheless fails to capture the specific character of the mass electorate that the NSDAP had now assembled.[359] The peasants of Schleswig-Holstein – forerunners of rural Nazi majorities all across the north-German flatlands – did not vote for Hitler simply from fury over the Republic's failure to offer timely price supports and foreclosure protection. They discovered and chose Nazism because they were already, by border tradition, intensely and militantly nationalist.[360] Nor had the German economy as yet suffered notably; 1930 GDP only fell to an index of 94 (1928 = 100). Unemployment in September 1930, at 3 million (or roughly 14 percent of the labor force) was only one million higher than the previous year's peak, and in any case at precinct level

---

[356] The Weimar authorities did however take enough local voting samples sorted by sex to allow Falter (HW, 139–46) and others to dispel the durable myth of a disproportionate female vote for the NSDAP; for age, see ibid., 147; data: Falter, WA, 81–85.

[357] For the NSDAP's 1923–24 estrangement from Catholicism (and vice versa), see especially Hastings, "How 'Catholic' was the Early Nazi Movement?," 421–33; electoral effects: Falter, HW, 186–90, and Walter Dean Burnham, "Political Immunization and Political Confessionalism: The United States and Germany," *Journal of Interdisciplinary History* 3 (1972) 4–15.

[358] Falter, HW, 310–14; for the concept of *Resistenz*, see Martin Broszat, "Resistenz und Widerstand," in Broszat, Elke Frölich, and Anton Grossmann, eds., *Bayern im NS-Zeit*, 4 vols. (Munich, 1979–81), 4:697.

[359] Thomas Childers, *The Nazi Voter: The Social Foundations of Fascism in Germany, 1919–1933* (Chapel Hill, NC, 1983), 268.

[360] See Stoltenberg, *Landvolk*, 48–56; Rietzler, "*Kampf in der Nordmark,*" passim.

the Nazi vote from 1930 onward was inversely proportional to the number of unemployed.[361]

The other major finding – that Nazism was heir to the traditions and milieux reflected in Hindenburg's 1925 electoral following – is more helpful.[362] What it suggests is that Nazism was the party that best expressed the yearnings of that majority of non-Socialist and non-Communist German voters that hated the Republic on political-ideological grounds. Germany's Protestants had been in the forefront of that potential mass *Gefolgschaft* from 1918–20 onward; German Protestantism and Prusso-German nationalism had since 1866–71 been sufficiently intertwined as to be almost indistinguishable. Now that following was groping its way toward a leader increasingly perceived as the man yearned for since 1918 and before, and toward a movement dedicated to the destruction of the 1918–19 order at home, and far beyond the borders forced upon Germany by the 1919 "shame-treaty."

The ultimate frailty of regression analysis, especially in the absence of opinion data, for the understanding of individual motivation suggests the necessity of interpretive risks.[363] Content analysis of the enormous volume of NSDAP propaganda spread across the Reich in 1929–30 might well tax even the capacity of a large research team, nor does any means of measuring audience response exist.[364] But given the NSDAP's insistence that its program was Adolf Hitler, the Führer's words might perhaps offer a clue to the Nazi appeal. Those words were as always remarkably consistent. In refounding the movement in February 1925 Hitler promised the German people that National Socialism would recreate Germany as a "cohesive *Volk*-community." That promise was part of virtually every subsequent speech, and in summer 1930 Hitler fondly recalled the "authentic *Volksgemeinschaft*" of 1914 and repeatedly proclaimed "liberation from German discord and fragmentation [*Zerrissenheit*]" as the movement's first mission. Of the "thirty parties" that now claimed to represent the *Volk*, only National Socialism consisted "only of Germans" rather than of classes and interest groups.[365] Hitler's public emphasis on "the Jew" diminished as the NSDAP spread beyond Bavaria, and electoral feedback suggested its lesser appeal in northern and western Germany.[366] But other aspects of his ideological

[361] Wehler, DGG, 4:260; SGAB, 3:119; Falter, HW, 296–300.

[362] Falter, HW, 357–63, 374.

[363] W. S. Robinson, "Ecological Correlations and the Behavior of Individuals," *American Journal of Sociology* 15:3 (1950), offers the classic description of the "ecological fallacy" – the indiscriminate ascription of causal value for *individual* motivation to correlations between variables within a sample; see also Falter, HW, 55–57, 61, 442–43.

[364] Paul, *Aufstand*, offers the best analysis of propaganda organization, themes, and effects.

[365] HRSA, 1:16; it would be pointless to trace the ceaseless recurrence of this theme throughout the 4,800 pages of Hitler's 1925–33 speeches and writings; for the 1930 campaigns, HRSA, 3/3:231–32, 235, 280, 317, 337–38 ("30 Parteien"), 385 (1914); likewise, 3/2:213, 346–47, 385–86, 409, 413.

[366] Paul, *Aufstand*, 87–88, documents the consciously tactical character of NSDAP reticence; in the 1930 campaign Hitler attacked "the Jew" only when speaking in Bavaria: HRSA, 3/3:276–77, 285, 788–89, 392.

system remained in full public view. The "socialist" appeal that supposedly vanished in 1929–30 as Nazism purportedly sought bourgeois respectability persisted, alongside Hitler's proclamation of the career open to *Leistung* as National Socialism's preeminent social promise.[367] The German racial superiority that – if brutally restored – would overcome all obstacles, and its corollary, the central historical importance of Führer-personalities, made repeated appearances. Eugenics, both positive and negative, was unusually prominent at the widely publicized 1929 Nuremberg Party rally, where Hitler proudly invoked the example of Sparta, "the most explicit race-state in history": "If Germany were to get a million children a year, and could eliminate [*beseitigen*] 700,000–800,000 of its weakest [inhabitants], then the ultimate result might even be an increase in strength."[368]

Yet foreign policy was Hitler's most persistent theme – which suggests that his boundless radicalism in that area was a major source of the enthusiasm of his audiences. Germany's possession of one-eighteenth the per capita "living space" of the Russians defined its biogeographic plight. The alternatives it faced were those Hitler had outlined since spring 1921: "Marxist" birth control and *Volk*-death; the ethnic calamity of emigration; the dependence on the world market that had allegedly led to "English" preventive war in 1914; and the biogeographical solution that Ratzel had proposed at the turn of the century: the "adjustment of soil [area] to population size, the most natural, healthy, and enduring [solution]." That final option Hitler sometimes decently veiled. But on occasion he also indicated a willingness to take "upon myself the responsibility for bloodshed" to secure a favorable biogeographic outcome. And he predicted that the Darwinian "free play of forces" would ensure that "in the end the bravest and most capable *Volk* would rule the earth."[369]

The movement's sudden emergence as a protagonist in national politics in summer 1930 seems to have encouraged Hitler to even greater explicitness than hitherto. In mid-August, after France's final withdrawal from the Rhineland, he tauntingly emphasized both Germany's freedom to vote for him, and France's impotence: "We have a watchword . . . for the electoral battle that is more than worth its weight in gold: *France believes that we should be locked up.*"[370] In five

[367] "Socialism," spring–autumn 1930: HRSA, 3/3:186 ("not a lachrymose notion of compassion"), 235–36, 338, 355, 385, 388, 410. As with Fascism's alleged turn to the right in 1920–21, the 1928–29 adjustments to the Nazi message were surface makeup applied over a radical nationalist foundation.

[368] HRSA, 3/2:348–49.

[369] HRSA, 2/1:21–22, 167–68, 287, 291–93, 391–95; 2/2:442–47, 462–63, 490–95, 504–07, 538, 545, 553–54, 574–79, 614–17, 631–32, 636–37, 662 ("Kampf um das Lebensraum"), 730–36, 740, 758, 766, 814–15, 856 (conquest of land and soil is biologically cost-effective); 3/1:14–16, 136, 146–48 ("the blood-sacrifice of 200,000 [men] would perhaps secure the nation for a further fifty years"), 151, 154–61, 168–69, 184–87, 240, 309–10; 3/2:54–55 ("Germany's situation demands a decision by arms"); 207, 235–36, 261–62, 271–72, 347–49; 3/3:91, 99, 175, 184–85, 259; quotations: 2/1:21, 2/2:491, 3/1:168–69.

[370] HRSA, 3/3:335 (my emphasis).

of his twenty July–September 1930 campaign speeches he brought the gospel of *Lebensraum* in detail to audiences that totalled around 50,000 in the major cities of northwest Germany – Kiel, Essen, Cologne, Koblenz, Hamburg. Germany's 62 million were 20 million too many for the Reich's narrow borders. "Healthy nations adjust[ed] their soil [area] to their population numbers." Past German disunity had meant that "the earth was divided up, and we lost the world mastery that was our due."[371] National Socialism would obliterate disunity, and secure that due: "From the shambles of interest groups a German *Volk* must rise again."[372]

Hitler's morning-after analysis of the outcome was simple, and essentially correct: "What drew people [to us]? The *national idea!*"[373] For the first time in German politics, the Protestant nationalist majority culture had found a *single* credible political voice, and one with far greater ability than the monarchical-conservative *Vaterlandspartei* to gather to itself all segments of the *Volk*. The post-1919 international constraints that had deterred nationalist extremism were giving way, just as a movement capable of giving that extremism full-throated voice reached organizational maturity.[374] The NSDAP, by indefatigable low-level agitation and by Hitler's words and example, convinced voters that they could indeed *right now* at last abolish Weimar, unify German society, free Germany from its putative subjugation to the foreign yoke, and achieve the nation's imperial destinies.

But Hitler was not quite finished. The title of his post-election speech was a Japanese warrior proverb: "After victory, tighten your helmet-strap." Not content with enlightening the German people about their future throughout the summer, he gave two major speeches that November, at Mannheim and Erlangen, in which he expanded notably on his favored theme: "no *Volk* had a greater right than we to the concept of world domination. We had the right, and no other nation (stormy applause)." But that was also true for the future: "If any *Volk* has the right to have a say in the future shaping of the earth, then it is our own *Volk*." The laws of nature decreed it:

> [W]e know one thing: every living thing strives for expansion, and every *Volk* strives for world domination [*Weltherrschaft*]. Only he who keeps this final goal before his eyes finds the right road. And a *Volk* that is too gutless to set this goal for itself, or no longer has courage and strength enough to find this road, travels a second road, that of renunciation, of surrender, a road that ends at last in and with annihilation [*bei der Vernichtung und in der Vernichtung seinen Abschluss findet*].

---

[371] Saxon Landtag campaign, June: HRSA, 3/3:219–20, 223, 233–34; Reichstag campaign, July–September: HRSA, 3/3:311–19 ("world mastery": 312), 338, 347, 351–53, 364, 386; and a passing reference to Germany's "right to space," 296 (Frankfurt am Main).

[372] HRSA, 3/3:347.

[373] HRSA, 3/3:425 (emphasis in original: "*Die nationale Gedanke!*").

[374] Marks, *The Illusion of Peace: International Relations in Europe 1918–1933* (New York, 1976), 112–14, is insightful on the vital catalytic role of the Rhineland evacuation.

Hitler spelled out the consequences of these insights with unexpectedly gentle irony: "When today so many preach that we are entering the age of peace, I can only say: my dear fellows, *you have badly misinterpreted the horoscope of the age, for it points not to peace, but to war as never before.*"[375] That objective required the conversion of the NSDAP's commanding position in German politics into total power in Berlin.

4. TO ROME AND BERLIN, 1921–1922 / 1930–1933

The collapse of Giolitti's last government in June 1921 and of the Müller Grand Coalition cabinet in March 1930 inaugurated the final disintegration of constitutional order in both countries. In each case, the challengers had assembled the nation's most cohesive, militant, and powerful political force, seized the initiative, and claimed total domination. In each case, the governing elites faced unpromising and steadily narrowing options. In each case, incomprehension of the nature of the Fascist and Nazi movements and interlocking enmities precluded concerted resistance, and fostered the fatal delusion that the newcomers could be tamed and exploited.

I. Italy: Socialist Ruin, Liberal Capitulation

Liberal Italy's final collapse was swift. Bonomi, Giolitti's unlucky successor, lingered on uneasily after the collapse of the pact of pacification in August 1921 had deprived his government of any prospect of dominating Italy's civil war.[376] Giolitti's inclusion of the Fascists in the spring 1921 "national blocs" in retrospect marked the end of Liberal Italy. Liberalism had failed to house-train the Socialists through police action or "constitutionalize" them through the lure of office. Giolitti and his associates nevertheless confidently expected that the Fascists, as members of the national camp, would docilely subside once violence had broken Socialists and *popolari*, leaving Italy to its rightful and natural Liberal rulers. But what if the Fascists, as their rhetoric and deeds in the Po Valley and Tuscany increasingly proclaimed, sought to conquer total power and create a "Fascist state"? Liberal Italy, almost in its entirety, failed to imagine that outcome until it happened.

It also failed to offer an alternative. The political and parliamentary paralysis reaffirmed in the May 1921 election (Figure 4.10) derived from irreducible and interlocking fears and enmities. Virtually all Liberals sought, as always, to deny the two mass parties a voice in policy. Virtually all forces in parliament, Liberal

---

[375] HRSA, 3/3:420, 4/1:53, 95, 101 (5 and 13 November 1930) (my emphasis); crowds: 5,000–7,000 at Mannheim, 1,500 at Erlangen, including the rector of Erlangen university, the regional scholarly and social elites, and the student corps "in closed formations" (according to the *Monatsschrift für akademische Leben*, organ of the local Nazi student organization). Both speeches were widely reported in the local and regional press.

[376] De Felice, 2:201–08.

or otherwise, rejected collaboration with the PSI. The fiery line between clerical and anti-clerical divided *popolari* from both Socialists and Liberals. A PPI-PSI ruling coalition would have to overcome mutual ideological abhorrence; deep internal divisions within each party between moderates and *massimalisti* or clericals; fierce competition between their *leghe* in the northern countryside; fear of isolation, alongside a historic adversary, in taking responsibility for a decrepit, paralyzed, and predictably recalcitrant government machine; the impossible requirement of forty or more Liberal recruits in order to make up a bare majority; and Fascist threats of bloody reprisal. Parliamentary arithmetic, as after the 1919 election, required PPI participation in any Liberal-led cabinet. But the *popolari* were now determined that they would no longer allow the Liberals – and especially Giolitti – to patronize and exploit them. And the Communists, with fifteen seats, reviled all other forces on principle, and happily accepted the role of pariahs.

Bonomi's cabinet thus rested on *popolari* and the ambiguous support of *democratici* and other Liberals. But by late autumn 1921, Giolitti had determined that the time was coming to take back the power that was his by right. The recession deepened, driving unemployment upward toward its peak in January 1922 (Figure 4.2). At the end of December 1921 the *Banca Italiana di Sconto*, a vital link in Italy's financial network deeply compromised by the collapse of the Ansaldo steel and machine-building combine, suspended payment.[377] And Pope Benedict XV, who had permitted the formation of the *popolari* and had marginally distanced the Church from day-to-day Italian politics, died unexpectedly. His successor, Cardinal Achille Ratti (Pius XI), was by birth a member of the Lombard industrial elite, and had learned fear and abhorrence of Bolshevism firsthand as papal representative at Warsaw during the 1920 Soviet invasion. For the PPI his advent presaged nothing good.

Concentric attack from *democratici*, Fascists, Nationalists, and Salandra's right-Liberals over Bonomi's alleged failure to stand up to PPI encroachment, and his dilatory and ineffectual approach to the banking and industrial crisis, impelled his cabinet to resign on 2 February 1922. The ensuing interregnum, symptomatically, was the longest in united Italy's history. The PPI vetoed Giolitti in revenge for his conduct the previous spring and from fear of further exploitation. A royal effort to reinstall Bonomi, after all else had failed, received a mere 127 votes. Giolitti proposed to lead an emergency cabinet in defiance of the PPI and of the *Statuto*, equipped with the king's authorization to create a subservient Chamber of Deputies by decreeing a return to single-member constituencies. Yet making Italy governable again by smashing the mass parties required the support of reputable non-Giolittians. And the accomplices Giolitti sought to enlist, Orlando and Enrico De Nicola, the president of the Chamber, primly refused to share responsibility for breaking the constitution. In return, through the agency of his faithful Piedmontese lieutenant of many

---

[377] On the economic issues, see the lucid analysis of Forsyth, *Crisis of Liberal Italy*, 254–60.

years, Luigi Facta, Giolitti torpedoed Orlando and De Nicola. And at Bologna and Florence, Fascist-organized mass demonstrations with the participation of noteworthy Liberal figures demanded military dictatorship.[378]

The ultimate victor – Liberal Italy's last prime minister – was Facta, who took office on 25 February. Facta had the inestimable advantage of not being the *maestro* himself. His deficit in leadership qualities and inability to command deep loyalties in parliament commended him to all parties and factions. Giolitti grudgingly approved the new cabinet to keep warm the seat he himself proposed to reoccupy in due course. Despite an effort by Don Sturzo to veto even Facta, the *popolari* warily accepted office, as in previous postwar governments, in the hope of achieving at least some of their religious and social ambitions. Giolitti's exclusion soothed his Liberal rivals. And Nationalists and Fascists happily supported Facta as a means of keeping from office the one man deemed capable of barring their path to power.

Mussolini thus retained the initiative. He repeatedly and vociferously insisted that no force or coalition could rule Italy against Fascism.[379] No significant figure in the government majority dared disagree. But the Duce was fully aware that a democratic-PPI-reformist Socialist coalition might still emerge at the eleventh hour if Fascism overplayed its hand and alienated patriotic and middle-class opinion through excessive savagery. Giolitti, despite his almost eighty years, might yet return vengefully to government. Salandra might rise again, as a lesser evil in Liberal eyes than Mussolini or Giolitti. Or D'Annunzio, once again stirring in the background, might steal the Duce's militant followers.

Converting Fascism's precarious negative advantages into command of government required a carefully calibrated blend of violence, intimidation, and blandishment. The objective throughout 1922 was threefold. First, to keep Liberals and Nationalists persuaded that Fascist savagery was transitory, that only the Duce in person could muzzle the provincial *squadre*, and that only Fascist support could ensure the durable exclusion of *popolari* and Socialists from a major role in government, as Giolitti and "national bloc" Liberalism had sought since spring 1921. Second, to cow the *popolari* into submissiveness, should their parliamentary support be needed, and to deter a PPI-PSI alliance against Fascism. Third, to maintain within the Fascist movement a controlled and politically functional ferocity, and a keen awareness that the conquest of power in Rome depended on the obedience of the *squadre* to the Duce's leadership.[380]

Violence came first. In fall–winter 1921–22 Bonomi had directed police and prefects to disarm and dissolve Italy's armed bands. Police and prefects ignored instructions, applied them only to Communists and Socialists, or shamefacedly or disingenuously confessed helplessness in the face of Fascist might.[381] The almost invariable impunity of *squadrista* murderers and leaders (often the

[378] Veneruso, *Vigilia*, 61–63, 77–81, 91–92.
[379] OO, 18:8, 57, 215, 291–92 (to the Chamber of Deputies, 19 July 1922).
[380] See especially OO, 18:139.
[381] De Felice, 2:203–07; chronology of violence: Franzinelli, *Squadristi*, 347–81.

same individuals); the incessant daily acts of violence and intimidation; and the increasing ability of the Po Valley *squadre* to concentrate division-sized mobile forces made clear that only a coordinated offensive against the PNF all across northern and central Italy by police and army, amid predictable bloodshed and destruction, could restore order. But unlike their Weimar counterparts, neither the Italian state nor its army possessed the command machinery that such a task required. The corps commanders and units across the Po Valley and Tuscany had been so deeply complicit with the *squadre* for so long that their willingness and even ability to strike cleanly was in doubt. Above all else, the political will in Rome required to answer Fascist civil war with the full power of the Italian state, always minimal, had by early 1922 largely vanished. Mussolini summed up in May 1922 with cold precision: "The Liberal state is destined to perish as a victim of its own cowardice."[382]

The Po Valley *squadre*, now subordinated to Balbo as regional commander, prefigured the state's demise from March onward through a series of rehearsals: local seizures of power that established or demonstrated Fascist domination of cities, provinces, and regions. In late March some 30,000 provincial Fascists descended on Milan for an intimidating show of force. In mid-May Balbo occupied Ferrara for three days with militarily organized crowds of up to 40,000 agricultural laborers, demanding that the government fund the public works employment that recession and budgetary embarrassment had postponed. Rome surrendered to Fascist demands. A few days later came the turn of Rovigo; massed *squadre* devastated what remained of the city's PSI and Communist organizations while the police stood by submissively. At the end of May, some 20,000 armed *squadristi* occupied Bologna to secure the removal of the prefect, Cesare Mori, who had distinguished himself for resolve and personal courage in attempting to enforce the laws.[383] Rome surrendered, and transferred Mori to the South.

Fascism also expressed its contempt for the Liberal order in another way highly relevant to its eventual triumph. Between January 1921 and October 1922 *squadristi* assassinated one Socialist parliamentary deputy with pistols and a hand grenade, probably killed a second, and beat or publicly humiliated Socialist and Communist deputies on at least twenty-six occasions, while PPI deputies, including two ministers, suffered similar treatment on at least five.[384] Fascist violence in the Chamber of Deputies itself became routine; on one occasion in August 1922 only an alert police official and a Nationalist colleague restrained Arpinati from shooting a Communist speaker.[385] Yet

---

[382] OO, 18:208.

[383] Mori: de Grazia and Luzzatto, eds., *Dizionario del fascismo*, 2:169–71, and note 95.

[384] Franzinelli, *Squadristi*, 301, 303, 304, 309 (found dead after threats in the Fascist press), 318, 319, 320, 321, 323, 325, 336, 338, 341, 344, 353 (killed), 357, 359, 362, 372, 391, 392, 393, 394, 396; Facta to prefects, 30 June 1922, Répaci, 2:25–26.

[385] Giulia Albanese, *La Marcia su Roma* (Rome, 2006), 55; Albertini, *I giorni di un liberale. Diari 1907–1923*, ed. Luciano Monzali (Bologna, 2000), 392–93.

the intimidated tolerance and patriotic complicity of government and Liberal opinion only weakened, however briefly, in July 1922, after Farinacci orchestrated the occupation and final conquest of his fief, Cremona. After seizing city hall, forcing the prefect to remove the city government, and compelling Rome to acquiesce, Farinacci's men burned the houses of two PPI deputies, including that of Guido Miglioli, leader and theoretician of the Catholic *leghe*.[386]

The PPI reacted by deposing Facta on 19 July 1922. *Popolari*, Socialists, Communists, and even some Liberals voted against the government for failing to uphold order. Mussolini added his votes to the revolt, merrily spoiling the symmetry of what otherwise would have been an anti-Fascist majority. In announcing his Party's vote he openly explained Fascism's ostensible choice: to be a "legalitarian party, that is a party of government,... or rather an insurrectionary party." The second alternative, he implied, depended on Fascism's adversaries: "no Italian government can remain standing if its program includes machine guns against Fascism."[387] In the North, the *squadre* meanwhile conquered with customary savagery yet another PSI stronghold, the city of Novara. At the end of July Balbo led a second march on Ravenna that secured the Po Valley's southeast exit for Fascism. "Lofty columns of fire and smoke" throughout southeastern Romagna testified to the diligence of Fascist "reprisals."[388]

In Rome, Giolitti largely determined the final outcome. He took sweet revenge upon the *popolari* and upon Sturzo, whom he later famously described as a "loathsome underhanded little priest [*pretucolo intrigante*]."[389] As in February, to resolve the crisis it had created, the PPI must once more swallow a government enjoying the support of Fascists, Nationalists, and right-Liberals. The *popolari* completed the deadlock by refusing to join a government in which the Right once again played a role. Giolitti sabotaged bids by Orlando and Bonomi, and publicly denounced the prospect of a governing mésalliance [*connubio*] between the Socialists and Sturzo; the result, Giolitti predicted on this and other occasions that summer and autumn, would be a "genuine civil war." In the end, on 31 July, the king turned once more to Facta. The *popolari* swallowed their pride, in part because of pressure from the party's clerical conservatives and their Vatican sponsors. Facta, his authority and that of parliament diminished almost to the vanishing point, wearily assumed office again in the hope of securing a blessed escape through Giolitti's return to power.[390]

---

386 Veneruso, *Vigilia*, 354–59, 371–72 (*Corriere della Sera* misgivings).

387 De Felice, 2:268–69; OO, 18:291.

388 Italo Balbo, *Diario 1922* (Milan, 1932), 95–110 (quotation, 109).

389 Giolitti to Ambrosini, 1 January 1923, in Répaci, 2:152–53.

390 Giolitti to Malagodi, 20 July 1922 (published 26 July), in Répaci, 2:120–21, also 29, 122, 123; Veneruso, *Vigilia*, ch. 6, offers an admirable account of the intricacies of the parliamentary crisis; Facta's aspirations: Répaci, 2:26, 30, 36, 47, 49, 53, 57–58, 59, 61–62, 144–46 (letters to his wife and to Giolitti); for the PPI Right's celebration of Fascism's "incontestably useful results" and denunciation of alliance with the "godless" Socialists, ibid., 278–79 (19 September 1922).

But as Facta took office, the Socialist trade unions and their allies swept away Liberal qualms about the increasing scale and indiscriminate nature of Fascist violence. The "Labor Alliance," an amorphous confederation of Socialist, anarchist, syndicalist, and republican unions formed in February 1922 to resist Fascism, abruptly and imprudently launched a nationwide general strike that summoned up the specter of 1919. The Fascist reaction was immediate and decisive: an ultimatum to Facta to break the strike within forty-eight hours, or the *squadre* would take the place of a state that had "once more demonstrated its impotence."[391] Fascist mobilization began immediately and widespread combat continued until 8 August (see Figure 4.2). The *squadre* seized and operated stalled trains and trams, and attacked "anti-national" town and city councils, organizations, facilities, and individuals throughout northern and central Italy. The destruction of the Left's Milan-Genoa-Turin "strategic triangle," as Mussolini had described it, and the elimination of government authority throughout North and Center were the objectives. Milan and Genoa fell; Turin was too distant from the road to Rome to warrant a major effort. Elsewhere Fascist victory was general, except at Parma, where the "*Arditi* of the People," a Socialist-Communist-anarchist militia sporadically active since 1921, drove back Balbo and a force of 10,000 *squadristi* with well-directed rifle fire. An energetic prefect and a resolute local army commander, in striking exception to the general rule, separated the combatants and restored order.[392]

The Left's general strike opened Mussolini's road to Rome, and determined the conditions under which he ultimately assumed power. The two forces at united Italy's core – the Liberal parliamentary elite and the monarchy with its army – had since 1919 fiercely resisted the surrender of any scrap of sovereignty to the mass parties. Since May 1921 the entire governing class – from Giolitti to Nitti, from Albertini of the *Corriere della Sera* to the great industrialists of Milan and Turin – had achieved virtual unanimity on a second fundamental point: only Fascist participation in government would keep PPI and PSI from power.[393] And the third point of universal agreement was the imperative necessity of avoiding "a *genuine* civil war." The term's underlying meaning for the Liberals emerges from between the lines of Giolitti's summer 1922 letters.[394] The *maestro*, and the parliamentary elite of which he was the supreme expression, feared beyond all else the advent of an anti-Fascist governing majority dominated by Sturzo

[391] OO, 18:329.

[392] OO, 18:284; Mondini, *Politica delle armi*, 157–58.

[393] Simone Neri Serneri, "Partiti, parlamento e governo: dal liberalismo al fascismo," in Grassi Orsini and Quagliariello, eds., *Il partito politico*, 276–77 and note 40; De Felice, 2:282–87, 301–10, 327–33, 348–53; Répaci, 2:136–37, 140–42, 269–70 (Albertini, key industrialists, Orlando), 172–73 (Nitti), 321 (Giolitti, publicly); Répaci, 2:311–12 (Taddei, Facta's interior minister); and Albertini, *Diari*, 393. Also noteworthy are the "affectionate greetings" that De Nicola sent to Mussolini at the 24 October Naples PNF rally (Répaci, 2:322), and the insistence of Giovanni Amendola, Facta's minister of colonies and future anti-Fascist martyr, that Fascism's "reaction" against Socialism had been a "fact of indisputable merit [valore]" (ibid., 286).

[394] Note 390; my emphasis.

and the Left, and backed by Italy's "subversives" and popular classes. Fascist defiance of the state might indeed summon up conflict between *squadre* and army; internecine war among the "healthy forces of the nation" was to be avoided at almost any cost. But its alternative – or sequel – was a second and infinitely more menacing internal conflict: a war that pitted the national camp, perhaps deprived by its own hand of Fascist support, against a revived Left, in control through parliament of at least a fraction of state power, and even more bent on vengeance than the implacable masses of 1919–20.

That matrix of Liberal and royal ambitions and fears gave Mussolini the freedom of movement required to secure power largely on his own terms, if still within the constricting framework of the Italian state. He was as aware as Hitler the following November that a frontal clash with the army would prove suicidal. But the "March on Rome" foreseen since spring 1922 and prepared with increasing haste from August onward was no bluff, at least for Fascism's enemies, who in the event suffered grievously. Nor for its friends; to Mussolini and his closest associate, "Michelino" Bianchi, the announced objective was a "Fascist Revolution" to create a "Fascist state." Mussolini, although not Bianchi, was willing to envisage two fallback alternatives: participation – with five decisive portfolios in hand – in a Giolitti cabinet, or an immediate general election that Fascism would fight from a position of strength.[395] But only if the alternative was the army machine-gun fire with which Badoglio, whom Facta had consulted along with Diaz in early October, had reportedly promised to sweep the *squadre* away.[396]

It did not come to that. Mussolini had quietly put aside his enduring anti-clericalism, and solemnly assured the Vatican of Fascism's deep religiosity while mischievously playing on the Curia's horror of a PPI-PSI alliance. He soothed monarchy, army, Nationalists, Liberals, and the numerous monar-chists within Fascism's own ranks by declarations of loyalty to the king from August–September 1922 onward. Fascism's "republican inclination" was for the moment dead.[397] He wooed the industrialists with professions of faith in laissez-faire and a stringently orthodox fiscal program: drastic cuts in govern-ment expenditure and bureaucracy, extensive privatizations, tax reform, and limits on parliament's spending powers. He kept Giolitti, Facta, Salandra, and D'Annunzio in play personally or through intermediaries such as the pliant prefect of Milan, Lusignoli.[398] D'Annunzio removed himself from the game, first by injuries sustained in August by falling from a window after a dispute with his mistress, then out of pique, after Facta guilelessly sought to enlist the Poet for a public reconciliation with Giolitti, "the man of naval gunfire," at a

---

[395] OO, 18:262, 330, 349, 351, 384, 418–19, 423 (June–September 1922).

[396] Répaci, 2:88; Rochat, *Vittorio Veneto a Mussolini*, 404–03; OO, 18:443–44; Piero Pieri and Rochat, *Pietro Badoglio* (Milan, 2002), 333.

[397] OO, 18:418–19, 456; for Mussolini's mocking insincerity see especially Répaci, 1:443–44 (tes-timony of De Vecchi).

[398] See especially Lyttelton, *Seizure*, 84–85.

planned grand commemoration on 4 November of Italy's 1918 victory. Salandra, although fatuously expectant of the leading role until the end, was too far
to the right to assemble a governing majority easily. Giolitti, the king, and the
hapless Facta were thus the figures with the best chance of keeping Fascism
from "becoming the State."

Yet from July onward Giolitti followed events indolently from watering
places in France and Switzerland, before returning to his Piedmontese country retreat. The *maestro* also held adamantly to the line he had established:
his sixth ministry must have Fascist participation. Facta faithfully echoed that
line, which placed both Liberals and king at Mussolini's mercy so long as he
could wield the threat of "genuine civil war." Facta correspondingly took pride
in having averted "general conflagration."[399] And to avoid troubling Giolitti's
negotiations and to ensure an orderly transition, he sought desperately to hold
together a cabinet divided and on the verge of internal collapse almost from
its inception on 1 August.[400] For the same reasons he also swallowed a further
deep humiliation in early October: the necessity of dismissing, in response to the
violent Fascist occupation of Trento and Bolzano, appointees who had sought
to conciliate the newly annexed non-Italian populations – a policy as unacceptable to Fascism in the north as it was in the eastern borderlands. Fascist
publication on 3 October of regulations constituting the *squadre* as a "militia," in overt violation of the *Statuto* and of public security legislation, likewise
passed without challenge.

Under cover of his contacts with Giolitti and others, Mussolini announced
his decision for insurrection to his entourage on 12 October. Four days later
he appointed and briefed a committee of commanders soon to be known
grandiosely as the "Quadrumvirs of the Fascist Revolution": Bianchi; Balbo;
Cesare Maria De Vecchi, a choleric and murderous monarchical Fascist from
Turin with a distinguished war record; and an ambitious retired general, Emilio
De Bono. Mussolini, not for the last time, overruled military requests for more
time. The aim of the insurrection – although he was too canny to disclose it –
was not to storm Rome, parliament, and interior ministry, but to destroy the
flagging will of the Liberal regime. Speed was vital, for Mussolini consistently
overestimated the *maestro*: "If Giolitti returns to power, we're f[ucked] ... we
must get a move on." When parliament re-convened in November his rivals
might regain the initiative. Delay might cause the Fascist movement to fracture from impatience. And as Balbo pointed out, despite much intimidatory
talk of a march on Rome, "no one yet seriously believes in our insurrectionary
intentions"; action that autumn might still enjoy a degree of surprise.[401]

Mussolini's closing remarks at the Fascist mass meeting and leadership conference at Naples on 24 October provoked cries of "To Rome! To Rome!" Yet

399 Facta to his wife, 10 October 1922, Répaci, 2:47.
400 Factions within the cabinet: Mondini, *Politica delle armi*, 161.
401 Quotations: De Felice, 2:305; Balbo, *Diario*, 179; for the March's underlying concept, Mondini,
    Politica delle armi, 168–69, and Lyttelton, *Seizure*, 86–90.

that same evening Facta was still sufficiently deluded to telegraph the king at the royal hunting retreat in Tuscany that "the project [of a] march on Rome has definitely lapsed." The following day "some Fascist action" seemed possible. But not until the first hours of 27 October did the prime minister report impending "insurrectional movements" all across Italy, and request the royal presence in Rome; the monarch did not arrive until early evening.[402] By that point the "Quadrumvirs" had announced Fascism's insurrection – on the anniversary of Vittorio Veneto and to redeem the *vittoria mutilata* – while the *squadre* seized prefectures, city halls, and communications throughout northern and central Italy. Facta had informed the king, in urging his immediate return to Rome, that the cabinet had at last collapsed. Yet during the night of 27–28 October, as reports of Fascist local successes across the North and Center poured into the interior ministry, Facta and his colleagues showed remarkable backbone, and unanimously if most belatedly chose resistance. Insurrection was unacceptable, however urgent Fascist participation in government might be. The king concurred; Facta, apparently considering his duty done, then went to bed. The acting commander of the Rome garrison, General Emanuele Pugliese, assumed control of the city just after midnight; at 0600 Facta ordered the general to implement the plan prepared over the previous weeks to halt Fascist movements far from the capital with rail and road blocks manned by *Carabinieri* and troops. And at 0750 on 28 October, with full cabinet agreement, a top priority telegram informed Italy's prefects and military commanders that a state of siege would exist throughout Italy from noon onward, and directed them to take all necessary steps to restore order.[403]

Pugliese's blocking forces indeed halted the "March." Some 20,000 Tuscan and Po Valley *squadristi* massed at the army cordon at Civitavecchia, and remained there, under a pitiless rain, in notable logistical embarrassment. Blocking positions at Orte and Viterbo to the north and at Avezzano and Segni to the east and south of Rome proved equally effective, or unnecessary. Yet north of Pugliese's cordon, Fascist success was virtually total; corps commanders in Florence and Milan, and garrisons all across northern Italy stood aside or fraternized with the *squadre*, which characteristically celebrated with battery, murder, and arson.[404]

Around 0900 on 28 October the king, upon whose verbal authorization the cabinet had prepared the state of siege order, abruptly refused to sign it. Facta, discreet Piedmontese lawyer and monarchical loyalist, never revealed directly whether or how Victor Emmanuel III had justified that sudden and momentous change of heart. But Facta's family nevertheless came to believe that fear of a dynastic coup, in collaboration with the Fascists, by the Duke of Aosta, the king's tall, militarily distinguished, and ambitious cousin, had impelled the king's about-face. Yet the army had apparently offered a far weightier argument:

[402] Ibid., 195; OO, 18:459 note; Répaci, 2:66–68.
[403] Répaci, 2:337–41.
[404] Mondini, *Politica delle armi*, 169–71.

a guarded preference for Mussolini over Facta, and for avoiding a war within the national camp that might prove arduous given Fascist conquests across the North.[405] Diaz and General Guglielmo Pecori Giraldi, authoritative figures indeed among the "generals of victory," reportedly responded during the night of 27/28 October to a royal query about the army's stance with only superficially enigmatic words: "the army will do its duty, but it would be better not to put it to the test." Diaz had happily received enthusiastic greetings from the mobilized *squadre* in Florence on 27 October; he presumably spoke for himself as well as for the army.[406]

The situation thus offered reason enough for psychological collapse and capitulation, by a figure to whom the evasion of direct responsibility – with the sole exception of his decision to recall Salandra and take Italy to war in 1915 – was a fundamental principle. In January 1941, amid the far greater war and military disasters that his 1922 decision had helped bring upon Italy, the normally reticent monarch gave way to self-pity: "I had to call 'these people' [*questa gente*] to power because all the others, some in one way, some in another, had abandoned me."[407] Giolitti, whom the king esteemed but disliked, had not descended to the rescue from Piedmont. Facta had not detected or reported the insurrection in timely fashion. The cabinet had collapsed. The army lacked enthusiasm. Putting the Fascists down in blood throughout Italy was a daring course with unpredictable effects. Yet one consequence was certain: governments thereafter would be dependent on the despised *popolari* and PSI. Such a prospect would have terrified taller and more self-confident men than Victor Emmanuel. The king also shared with his political class a time horizon that made capitulation seem the least of numerous evils. Giolitti's two long prewar ministries had each lasted a mere three years. No government since had survived for more than twenty months.

Victor Emmanuel III's rejection of the state of siege delivered Italy to Mussolini. Prefects, police chiefs, and army commanders who had not yet made timely accommodation with the insurgents now took their cue from Rome. The Duce of Fascism, from the fortified offices of *Il Popolo d'Italia* in Milan, scorned participation in the Salandra government that the king initially sought and that Nationalists and monarchically inclined Fascists such as De Vecchi and Grandi were promoting. Mussolini instead serenely demanded a formal royal summons to form a government as his price for ending the crisis.[408] By the evening of 30 October the Duce of Fascism was in power, with a cabinet of six Fascists, a Nationalist, Diaz and the equally pro-Fascist Thaon di Revel as proud representatives of army and navy, and two *popolari* along with four

---

[405] Lyttelton, *Seizure*, 91, persuasively notes the likely importance to the king's decision of the drastic overnight deterioration of the situation in the North.

[406] Répaci, 1:594, 2:402, 386; De Felice, 2:360–63; Rochat, *Vittorio Veneto a Mussolini*, 406–07; Mondini, *Politica delle armi*, 169–72; Lyttelton, *Seizure*, 92.

[407] Puntoni, *Parla Vittorio Emanuele*, 40.

[408] See especially De Felice, 2:372–74.

Liberals of various stripes as hostages for their groups' good behavior. More than 30,000 bedraggled *squadristi* paraded through Rome, provoking clashes in the working-class neighborhoods that left at least twenty-two dead, before government-organized special trains bore them riotously homeward.[409] Yet as Mussolini remarked almost two years later, the Fascist triumph was not wholly gratifying. Despite the nascent regime's propaganda, its advent had not been the revolution Mussolini still sought: "The revolution comes later."[410]

II. "Genuine German Suffering," Reichswehr Imperatives, National Socialist Victory

If the Great Depression had less influence over Nazi emergence in 1930 than often supposed, Germany's subsequent descent into economic calamity created an atmosphere of apocalyptic crisis that made Hitler's apocalyptic remedies seem almost reasonable. That was very unlike Italy, where the 1921–22 recession and the resulting state deficits, although helpful to Mussolini's ascent, did not mandate a regime that was to be – in Gregor Strasser's words – "the opposite of everything that now exists."[411] The newly elected Reichstag's first meeting in October 1930 foreshadowed the coming chaos: Nazi deputies, brown-shirted in defiance of a Prussian edict against political uniforms, boisterously invaded the chamber *en masse* while the SA demonstrated outside. The representatives of the anti-system parties – 107 Nazis, 77 Communists, and 44 DNVP – did not yet constitute an anti-system majority. But their numbers and implacable hostility made the cabinet wholly reliant either on Article 48 decrees, or on the SPD's 143 votes – the precise opposite of what Brüning, Hindenburg, and the Reichswehr had sought.

Over the next two years, the Great Depression drove German politics and sustained Hitler's continuing rise. Germany and the United States, the two most advanced industrialized countries, suffered most. As the slump bottomed out in winter 1932, scarcely 44 percent of each country's working-age population had work, and millions had long since ceased to look (see Figure 4.12).[412] World trade shrank to a third of its 1928 volume, an exceptionally hard blow to the export-dependent German economy and an apparent confirmation of Hitler's diatribes against the world market.

Two forces determined Brüning's response. Fiscal orthodoxy – a body of age-encrusted superstition that even SPD experts shared – dictated drastic expenditure cuts as the sovereign remedy for recession. Brüning's ruling superstition was nevertheless different: a monomaniacal Bismarckian faith in the primacy of

---

[409] Albanese, *Marcia*, 115–20.

[410] De Felice, 2:780: "[S]i é compiuto un fatto rivoluzionario e un insurrezione vittoriosa non una rivoluzione. La rivoluzione viene dopo."

[411] Karl Dietrich Bracher, *Die Auflösung der Weimarer Republik* (Düsseldorf, 5th ed., 1984), 98 (Strasser speech, 20 October 1932).

[412] Balderston, *German Economic Crisis*, 11 (Britain's corresponding figures in 1930–33 were only slightly below 60 percent).

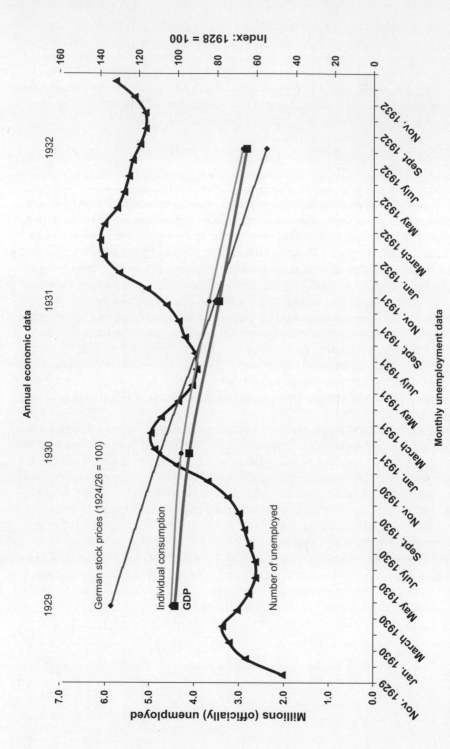

FIGURE 4.12. Catastrophe, 1929–1932.
Base data: Balderston, *German Economic Crisis*, 2; Wehler, DGG, 4:260.

foreign policy – the road to renewed central European hegemony and continental primacy. Yet Brüning also sought to imitate Bismarck's inspired domestic exploitation of foreign success. Had the 1930 electorate not thrilled to Nazi promises to free Germany from foreign domination? Government "national deeds" must therefore upstage Hitler, win over Hugenberg's wild men, consolidate Brüning's increasingly shaky place in Hindenburg's confidence, and rally behind the nation's natural leaders the same German population those leaders had calculatingly deprived of self-government.[413]

The end of reparations was Brüning's immediate and overriding objective. But the Western powers would only consent if Germany otherwise appeared on the brink of chaos and Bolshevism. To resuscitate the economy through government expenditure would demonstrate that Germany was still solvent. The "Hunger-Chancellor" therefore rejected the many pump-priming schemes presented to him by panicked advisors – or advocated by the National Socialists.[414] Germany *would not* pay reparations, therefore it could not *seem* able to pay them. Brüning described his policy eloquently in January 1932: it was "his assignment to call attention, in discussion with the foreign powers, to genuine German suffering [*wirkliche deutsche Not*], rather than working with bogus suffering [*fingierte Not*]."[415] As unemployment support expenses rose and revenues dropped, as each successive emergency package of tax increases and spending cuts failed to secure deliverance, Brüning tightened the spigot. Perhaps catastrophic deflation would impress the Western powers more readily than the catastrophic inflation of 1923.

Government remained possible because from fall 1930 to spring 1932 the Social Democrats stood loyally by the authoritarian nationalist Brüning, the "lesser evil." In bitter expiation of their earlier flight from responsibility in 1923 and of their part in Müller's downfall, they braved scurrilous Communist attacks and supported or tolerated the government whenever Brüning dared face the Reichstag. The party even disciplined SPD deputies who voted against Germany's second pocket battleship in March 1931. For if the SPD toppled

---

[413] For this motivation (accompanied by an astoundingly indulgent view of Brüning), William L. Patch, Jr., *Heinrich Brüning and the Dissolution of the Weimar Republic* (Cambridge, 1998), 130–31, 150–51; monomania: Winkler, *Weimar*, 443.

[414] Wehler, DGG, 4:521–29, offers incisive summary and detailed refutation of Knut Borchardt's much-debated contention that Brüning could not have acted otherwise in the face of rigid constraints that included Weimar's allegedly excessive social expenditure, the absence of theoretical backing for countercyclical government spending, and public terror of inflation; Ursula Büttner, "Politische Alternativen zum Brüningschen Deflationskurs," VfZ 37 (1989), 209–47, demonstrates the breadth of support for government action, and persuasively argues the exact converse of a key Borchardt thesis: Brüning, not public pressure, determined his policy of economic catastrophe, and only his suppression of the German people's right to self-government made that policy sustainable. The evidence that nationalist foreign policy goals were the primary driving force behind the 1930–32 "hunger-dictatorship" is in any case overwhelming, and would be decisively relevant even if Brüning *had* lacked alternatives to deflation.

[415] Hermann Weiss and Paul Hoser, eds., *Die deutschnationalen und die Zerstörung der Weimarer Republik. Aus dem Tagebuch von Reinhold Quaatz 1928–1933* (Munich, 1989), 174; human consequences: Winkler, *Weimar*, 482–83.

Brüning, the Center would surely retaliate by destroying the Weimar coalition government of Otto Braun in Prussia. The Right would secure control of the Prussian police. And what little remained of German democracy would perish.[416]

Brüning's nationalist monomania soon generated two other hare-brained initiatives that cut across his priority aim of ending reparations, and across one another. Along with increased expenditure, the Reichswehr's "second rearmament plan" dictated the breaking of the disarmament "shackles" imposed in 1919.[417] Foreign office and Reichswehr pursued that goal vigorously with Brüning's personal backing in the futile multilateral disarmament talks held at Geneva from early 1932. But "equality of rights," the German code-word for rearmament, was scarcely calculated to encourage Paris to surrender its reparations hold over Germany as it had surrendered the Rhineland. Especially since that surrender, in bitter foretaste of a later ritual, had increased rather than diminished German demands.

The foreign office, under Stresemann's amateurish successor Julius Curtius and a new and fiercely militant permanent undersecretary who was personally close to Brüning, offered a scheme of its own: a creeping *Anschluss* with Austria thinly disguised – an old Prussian tradition – as a customs union. The German-Austrian joint announcement in March 1931 of that bid for central European hegemony in massive violation of the 1919 settlement provoked Czech and French political and financial retaliation that coincided with the collapse from fraud and incompetence of a key Vienna bank, the Creditanstalt. By June Vienna had repudiated Curtius's project; only French loans could ward off state bankruptcy.[418] French anger and anxiety over the customs union, the launching in mid-May of the first pocket-battleship, and a dramatic Brüning denunciation of reparations as foreign "tribute" that implied that Germany would cease payments and perhaps also repudiate foreign debt led to crisis in Germany as well. The reparations manifesto, which accompanied an austerity decree even more draconian than previous editions, triggered a run on the Reichsmark that cut German gold reserves by 40 percent by mid-July, just as a number of poorly supervised German banks collapsed from fraud and mismanagement. Germany's downward economic trajectory accelerated decisively.[419]

The flight from the Reichsmark ceased when the SPD declined to topple the government over the new budget; Brüning ended the run on bank deposits by taking over the offending banks, imposing exchange controls, and in due

---

[416] Winkler, "Choosing the Lesser Evil: The German Social Democrats and the Fall of the Weimar Republic," JCH 25:2/3 (1990), 205–27.

[417] Geyer, *Aufrüstung*, especially 267–68 (the objectives of German "disarmament" negotiations); idem, "Zweite Rüstungsprogramm," 138–50.

[418] Iago Gil Aguado, "The Creditanstalt Crisis of 1931 and the Failure of the Austro-German Customs Union Project," HJ 44:1 (2001), 199–221.

[419] Most of the foregoing rests on the original and persuasive account of Thomas Ferguson and Peter Temin, "Made in Germany: The German Currency Crisis of July 1931," *Research in Economic History* 21 (2003), 1–53.

course promulgating the punitive capital flight tax that fleeced Germany's Jewish emigrants after 1933. Reparations ceased temporarily, thanks to the providential moratorium on reparations and war debt payments proposed by Herbert Hoover in mid-June 1931. Yet Brüning sought not ephemeral relief but German "freedom" for all time. At the end of August 1931 he issued new emergency decrees that empowered Germany's federal states and municipalities to disregard existing regulations, laws, and state constitutions as required to balance their budgets. That measure surpassed all previous abuses of Article 48, which taken literally served to protect "public security and order," not to avert financial or parliamentary embarrassment.

The Reich president's emergency powers had tempted Brüning and his Reichswehr backers into the abyss. Yet Brüning's dependence on the SPD and his failure to end the slump, eliminate reparations, and open the road to German rearmament gradually eroded the all-important relationship with the Reich president upon which the chancellor's power rested.[420] At his estate at Neudeck, on the Polish Corridor border, the "old gentleman" was exposed to the lobbying of the noble neighbors who had organized the estate's purchase in 1927 through public subscription by a grateful nation. His own class endlessly reproached him for having signed the Young Plan laws and for tolerating a cabinet led by a Catholic and supported by "Marxists." *Stahlhelm* and DNVP, with Schleicher's covert encouragement, agitated from December 1930 onward for a Prussian Landtag election to destroy the Weimar Coalition government under Otto Braun, which Hindenburg perceived as a standing affront to Prussia's essence, and the Reichswehr staffs viewed as insurmountable obstacle to their territorial defense preparations.[421]

The same logic gradually impelled Schleicher and the Reichswehr planners to accept that they must – and therefore could – have Hitler's support. His still-increasing electoral success, demonstrated in 1930–31 elections in the lesser states in which the NSDAP conquered up to 37 percent of the vote, was essential to creating the right-wing Reichstag majority that army and navy required to fund their programs.[422] And the Hitler movement sprang from and shared the armed forces' constituency, the German Protestant-nationalist majority culture. The more NSDAP and SA grew, the more vital Hitler's followers became to the future mass army. That even the supposedly rational Groener could describe Hitler, after meeting him in January 1932, as "a modest, decent chap, who wants the best" suggests the extent to which wish-fulfillment fantasy formed the basis of Reichswehr policy.[423]

---

[420] Patch, *Brüning*, 190, 199–200, 211, 246–47; Weiss and Hoser, eds., *Tagebuch Quaatz*, 155, 156, 158.

[421] Patch, *Brüning*, 185–86.

[422] NSDAP percentage of the popular vote: Bremen, 30 November 1930: 25.4; Schaumburg-Lippe, 3 May 1931: 27.0; Oldenburg, 17 May 1931: 37.2; Hamburg, 27 September 1931: 26.2; Hesse, 15 November 1931: 37.1.

[423] "Bescheidener, ordentlicher Mensch, der Bestes will": Ilse Maurer and Udo Wengst, eds., *Staat und NSDAP 1930–1932. Quellen zur Ära Brüning* (Düsseldorf, 1977), 271–72; similarly, Thilo

Schleicher nevertheless continued to back Brüning with diminishing conviction. In October 1931 the general counselled Hindenburg to accept the cabinet reconstruction that Curtius's disgrace and resignation necessitated, making Groener Reich interior minister in addition to his defense portfolio. Brüning and Groener were nevertheless sinking fast in the Reich president's esteem. The general, a widower, had contracted marriage with his housekeeper in October 1930; six months later a baby boy was born. That was behavior decidedly "not in accordance with *Stand*" – and Groener as a Württemberger was already low in the esteem of true Prussians.[424] But perhaps more dangerous to the Reichswehr minister was the growing estrangement within the army between "desk" and "front" deriving from many of the same causes as Brüning's estrangement from Hindenburg. Budgetary restraint, cooperation with the allegedly pacifist and "Wehrmacht-hostile" SPD, and antagonism to leading forces within the national camp such as the NSDAP were deeply abhorrent to the officer corps, and especially to its youthful enthusiasts.

Hitler exploited these needs and hopes with his customary unwavering focus upon the attainment of power. At the September 1930 treason trial of three young officers who had campaigned within the army for benevolent neutrality toward an eventual Nazi coup d'état, he stressed under oath his commitment to legality and his Party's innocence of any thought of seducing the armed forces from their allegiance. He also promised that once in power, and with perfect legality, "November 1918 will find its expiation, and heads would also roll."[425] The officer corps scarcely blinked; an elite whose members had cheerfully shot Communists "attempting to escape" could never regard the heads of the "November criminals" as sacred. The lure of the NSDAP's paramilitary formations for the army's mobilization and border defense planners proved irresistible; by mid-1931 the barriers between army and NSDAP erected after November 1923 were crumbling. Groener's sometimes grotesque efforts to persuade the officer corps that the Reichswehr must stand united behind the existing government increasingly met with "icy silence."[426] Hitler further dramatized the army's need of him by two displays of SA power in October 1931. In the first, he joined with *Stahlhelm* and Hugenberg in the so-called "Harzburg Front" demonstration against Brüning government and Weimar state – and departed the scene with conspicuous contempt for his partners once the SA had marched past. The following week the NSDAP staged its own triumphant rally at Brunswick, for which the SA mobilized and assembled a small field army: more than 100,000 uniformed men out of a total strength that reached 300,000 by December 1931.

Vogelsang, "Neue Dokumente zur Geschichte der Reichswehr 1930–1933," VfZ 2:4 (1954), 417.

[424] Patch, *Brüning*, 185; "unstandesgemäss": Bracher, *Auflösung*, 432 note 37.

[425] HRSA, 3/3:434–53 (quotation, 441).

[426] Vivid documents, including Groener's promise of presentation watches to informers: Ernst-Otto Schüddekopf, *Das Heer und die Republik* (Hannover, 1955), 288–307 (quotation, 306); Vogelsang, *Reichswehr, Staat und NSDAP* (Stuttgart, 1962), 419.

At this juncture the Weimar constitution intruded, with a deadline that notably hastened its own destruction: the Reich president's seven-year term expired on 5 May 1932. But the field marshal had celebrated his eighty-fourth birthday on 2 October 1931. He was weary of office and increasingly dismayed by the incessant personal attacks of his former constituency, "national" Germans generally and the old-Prussian Right in particular. Hugenberg and Hitler, despite assiduous Brüning and Schleicher efforts to woo them, spurned the government's proposal to prolong the president's term through a painless parliamentary two-thirds vote. The NSDAP in particular would only lend the additional votes Brüning required in return for the chancellorship, Reichswehr ministry, and foreign ministry.[427] A predictably riotous presidential election was thus the only option. The stakes were not merely the immediate prize of the presidency, but also the leading position when Hindenburg predictably passed from the scene.

The "old gentleman" nevertheless at first declined to run, then unhappily agreed to cooperate with his increasingly desperate backers on condition that, as in 1925, he need not campaign, and that he receive at least some support from the Right.[428] The *Stahlhelm* refused to endorse its most illustrious honorary member unless he agreed to destroy the Republic. The Kyffhäuser League of the *Kriegervereine*, after much vacillation, ultimately supported Germany's foremost veteran, and the field marshal allowed his candidacy to go forward. The "Harzburg Front" predictably disintegrated. *Stahlhelm* and Hugenberg feared Hitler's prowess, and instead supported the colorless Theodor Duesterberg, retired Prussian officer and co-leader of the *Stahlhelm*. Other forces on the Right opted unconditionally for the NSDAP.[429]

Hitler held back until all rivals were committed, secured the German citizenship that candidacy demanded through helpful Nazi officials in Brunswick, and mounted the usual frenetic campaign on the theme: "That's enough! Vote Hitler!"[430] Elated Nazi speakers, with Goebbels in the lead, scoffed at Hindenburg's new constituency: "Tell me who praises you, and I will tell you who you are! Hindenburg is praised by the Berlin gutter press [and] lauded by the party of deserters." Hitler likewise boasted of having "forced the SPD to the feet of the field marshal."[431] Hindenburg fell 172,662 votes short of the necessary absolute majority in the first round. Hitler instantly threw himself into the second, crisscrossing Germany in this and subsequent campaigns by aircraft – *Hitler über Deutschland* – in brilliant dramatization of the NSDAP claim to represent modernity and "the Germany of the future."[432] Hindenburg, deeply

[427] Göring, in Weiss and Hoser, eds., *Tagebuch Quaatz*, 178.

[428] Ibid., 171.

[429] See especially Larry Eugene Jones, "Hindenburg and the Conservative Dilemma in the 1932 Presidential Elections," GSR 20:2 (1997), 235–59.

[430] HRSA, 4:136–37; Rudolf Morsey, "Hitler als Braunschweiger Regierungsrat," VfZ 8 (1960), 419–48; Paul, *Aufstand*, 95–99.

[431] Quoted in Bracher, *Auflösung*, 409; HRSA, 4:169, 201; Hindenburg's new supporters: Falter, "The Two Hindenburg Elections of 1925 and 1932," 234–39.

[432] "Wir sind das Deutschland der Zukunft": HRSA, 4:181.

FIGURE 4.13. Last Victory of the "Lesser Evil," March–April 1932

	First Round (13 March)		Second Round (10 April)	
	Votes	% of Vote	Votes	% of Vote
Thälmann	4,984,341	13.24	3,706,759	10.16
Hindenburg	18,651,497	49.54	19,359,983	53.05
Duesterberg	2,557,729	6.79		
Hitler	11,339,446	30.12	13,418,547	36.77
Minor candidates	116,304	0.31	5,472	0.01

Note: Anti-system candidates in italics.
Data: Falter, WA, 46.

wounded by the slurs of his own people and by the votes of the SPD, nevertheless prevailed (see Figure 4.13).

Yet that outcome was no victory for the Republic. Hindenburg's reelection made Brüning's removal – and ultimately Hitler's advent – possible. In the increasingly violent run-up to the quadrennial Prussian Landtag election on 24 April, Groener silently and perhaps inadvertently broke with army policy. Public security and the defense of the German state took precedence over his duty to the Reichswehr rearmament agenda that he was still vigorously pressing on Brüning.[433] As interior minister he moved belatedly to ban the SA and SS over the resistance of Schleicher, who insisted vehemently on Nazi usefulness as a "counterweight" to the SPD.[434] Hindenburg, despite lobbying by Schleicher through a fellow alumnus of his old regiment, the president's notably dense son Oskar, approved the necessary decree on 12 April with extreme ill grace.[435] Then the Prussian elections, along with simultaneous balloting in lesser states, more than confirmed the NSDAP's indispensability to the army: 36.3 percent of the Prussian popular vote, and pluralities of up to 40.9 percent in other Landtage across Germany except Bavaria, where the BVP remained the largest party by a mere 0.1 percent. Goebbels was exultant, but also alarmed about "winning to death"; before exhaustion set in, "we must take power."[436] The Braun coalition remained lamely in office, thanks to a prescient pre-election change in parliamentary rules that required an absolute majority to elect a new prime minister. Weimar Prussia had nevertheless lost its democratic legitimacy to National Socialism.

---

[433] Bracher, *Auflösung*, 432 and note, quoting a Schleicher assistant, Eugen Ott; Groener to Brüning, 13 April 1932, in Geyer, "Zweite Rüstungsprogramm," 152–53.

[434] On the long prehistory of the SA ban, see Bracher, *Auflösung*, 425–31, and Hürter, *Groener*, 336–45.

[435] Hindenburg himself, Oskar von Hindenburg, Schleicher, and Kurt von Hammerstein-Equord, the army chief since 1930, had all served in the Imperial German Army's 3rd Foot Guards Regiment; Hitler not unreasonably judged Oskar "a rare specimen of imbecility [Doofheit]" (Goebbels, 2/3:114).

[436] Goebbels, 2/2:268, 271 ("Sie sind einig geworden").

Schleicher acted immediately. At the end of April he and the army chief of staff, Kurt von Hammerstein-Equord – yet another old Schleicher comrade from the Imperial German Army's 3rd Foot Guards Regiment – met with Hitler, and "reached agreement," apparently on the removal of both Braun and Brüning. That saved the Nazi leaders from the temptation and snare of settling for a mere share of power in Prussia and the Reich in coalition with the Center. On 8 May, Schleicher and Hitler reached an astonishing pact: Groener and Brüning would fall, the SA ban would end, and new elections would bring the Reichstag, like the Prussian Landtag, into line with the sentiments of the German *Volk*.[437] Schleicher and Hindenburg's entourage fatuously believed Hitler's vague and purely verbal suggestion that in return, the NSDAP would tolerate or support the new right-wing cabinet. The general later disclosed the logic behind agreement with Hitler: he had turned on Brüning because vigorous rearmament was only possible with NSDAP support.[438]

Groener hastened the government's downfall by lapsing into apparent incoherence under NSDAP heckling while defending the SA ban in the Reichstag on 10 May. Hindenburg was already determined to remove him; the *Junker* neighbors had erupted in outrage at the "agrarian Bolshevism" that allegedly characterized a modest government plan to settle the unemployed on bankrupt great estates. But the Reichswehr cast the decisive vote.[439] Schleicher threatened to resign, along with other generals, if Groener did not. The SPD and a parliamentary majority demonstratively voted confidence in the cabinet, forcing momentary delay. Brüning and Groener had nevertheless undertaken in March 1930 to rule Germany against the Left through Hindenburg's presidential powers. When Hindenburg frostily refused on 29 May to sign any more Article 48 decrees, Brüning duly resigned. The field marshal's parting shot, that his own "good name and honor" demanded Brüning's dismissal, was in retrospect not without humor.[440]

Schleicher, as the political chief of Germany's most powerful institution and the most decisive of Hindenburg's advisors, improvised the next step: a new presidential cabinet under a right-wing aristocrat and Center Party Landtag back-bencher, Franz von Papen, whom Schleicher had chosen for his malleability. Papen's other qualification for office appeared to be his extensive social connections and a certain rapport with Hindenburg. He also had other priorities than Schleicher's single-minded advocacy of the armed forces' overriding rearmament goals: a "'revolutionary-conservative' state leadership," that would curtail universal suffrage, remodel the Reichstag into a corporatist body, and add an upper chamber as a corrective to "exaggerated parliamentarism."[441]

[437] Ibid., 2/2:276.
[438] Otto Meissner, *Staatssekretär unter Ebert, Hindenburg, Hitler* (Hamburg, 1950), 224–25; for the later dispute over Hitler's promises, AdR Papen 1:392 note, 395 and note.
[439] Winkler, *Weimar*, 473.
[440] Brüning, *Memoiren*, 602 (a source often untrustworthy for Brüning's goals, but credible here).
[441] AdR Papen, 2:560, 736, 760; background: Hans Mommsen, "Entscheidung für den Präsidialstaat: Komplott der Machteliten oder Selbstpreisgabe der Demokratie?," in Heinrich

The new "cabinet of barons" contained seven nobles, including Schleicher, now forced to assume Groener's public role as Reichswehr minister. Only the DNVP offered parliamentary support. The cabinet – that is, Schleicher – then freely took the two critical decisions agreed with Hitler: to dissolve the Reichstag and to destroy Weimar Coalition Prussia.[442] The first decision launched the NSDAP campaigning machine into its most impressive performance. The second became possible when the Nazi-Communist street fighting that now invariably accompanied elections gave pretext to Papen, through a Hindenburg decree, to deploy on 20 July 1932 the machine guns and troops of *Generalleutnant* Gerd von Rundstedt's 3rd Infantry Division on the streets of Berlin, to arrest the SPD government's leaders, and to place Prussia under Reich control.[443]

Hitler cast the 31 July election (Figure 4.11) as a titanic struggle against Weimar's record and Germany's *Zersplitterung*. His enemies thought it "typically German to have thirty parties." His own "life's goal [was] to annihilate and exterminate [*zu vernichten und auszurotten*] these thirty parties" and to make the nation whole. His prophetic vein was also in evidence in other ways: "We have chosen for ourselves an objective, and to achieve it [will] do battle fanatically and ruthlessly right into the grave [*bis ins Grab hinein*] (applause)."[444] The election outcome confirmed Germany's transition from dictatorship based intermittently on parliamentary majorities to dictatorship erected against the expressed objections of the vast majority of the German people, and resting on Reichswehr and Reich president alone. The 230 NSDAP and 89 KPD seats gave the totalitarian parties an absolute majority of fourteen seats; the NSDAP's 13.7 million votes and local absolute majorities all across north Germany made clear its preponderance. The NSDAP press derided the "barons" as an affront to democracy and the career open to talent.

Schleicher met with Hitler and apparently promised the chancellorship.[445] And in a tense audience with Hindenburg on 13 August, Hitler demanded just that, invoking Victor Emmanuel's decision in 1922 as precedent. The field marshal however answered with an unexpected, categorical, and humiliating "No," and a deliberately insulting demand that Hitler conduct himself in "chivalric" fashion. Neither Papen nor Schleicher was resigned to the outcome. The general

---

August Winkler and Elizabeth Müller-Luckner, eds., *Die deutsche Staatskrise 1930–1933: Handlungsspielräume und Alternativen* (Munich, 1992), 1–18.

[442] Schleicher's role: AdR Papen, 1:3–4, 206, 211.

[443] Intensity of violence: seventy-two dead in Prussia in the fifty days preceding the 31 July election: Reichardt, *Kampfbünde*, 74.

[444] HRSA, 5/1:275–76, 249; similarly throughout spring–summer 1932 ("forty or fifty parties, associations, and petty groups"): HRSA, 5/1:3, 17, 22, 45, 89, 96, 180, 207, 218, 261, 278, 280, 285–86, 289, 293; for the campaign directives and themes of the party as a whole, Paul, *Aufstand*, 100–03.

[445] Goebbels, 2/2:333–34; Heinrich Muth, "Das 'Kölner Gespräch' am 4. Januar 1933," GWU 37:8, 9 (1986), 465–66; Schleicher's advocacy in cabinet: AdR Papen, 1:379–81 and note 7.

had apparently lost Hindenburg's trust by supporting a Hitler chancellorship; and Papen, on his own authority, had offered Hitler the vice-chancellorship – the beginning of a long personal quest to find a formula for participation in government acceptable to the Führer of the NSDAP.[446]

"Dictatorship against the entire *Volk* and a cabinet of national subjugation," as Goebbels wrathfully summarized Papen's course, was clearly not sustainable; Papen's justice minister had already told his colleagues that they could rule without NSDAP support only if Hindenburg set the constitution aside. Schleicher, fertile in expedients in earlier months, fell back on Prusso-German military wisdom: escalation in the face of failure, setting aside the constitution and preventing the new Reichstag from meeting.[447] But Hindenburg was unwilling to approve such a course, although he agreed to block a Hitler cabinet based on the BVP-Center-NSDAP "black-brown" parliamentary coalition that the NSDAP was exploring to force Papen and Schleicher to terms. He also, in a significant departure from his customary commitment to formal legality, gave Papen full powers to dissolve the new Reichstag, should it prove recalcitrant, and to delay the subsequent elections beyond the sixty-day limit the constitution required.[448] Hitler proclaimed his continued resolve: "I know they are convinced that they are all far cleverer than we are.... Let them be clever. We are the more determined. [And] I am the most unrelenting of all." On 8 September he briefed his chief subordinates to prepare for a desperate effort to prove the NSDAP unstoppable in yet another election.[449]

On 12 September the new Reichstag met for its first business session, with Hermann Göring in the chair as representative of the largest parliamentary group, duly elected with the votes of the BVP, Center, DNVP, and NSDAP.[450] A Communist no-confidence motion setting aside Papen's latest Article 48 decree passed by the devastating margin of 512 to 42. Göring triumphantly declared the cabinet deposed – while a discomfited Papen, presidential dissolution order in hand, proclaimed the Reichstag ended and its decisions null and void.[451] After further dithering and consultation with Hindenburg, the cabinet determined to hold new elections in accordance with the constitution, and set 6 November as the date. Schleicher again argued for avoiding elections altogether, or at least postponing them. But Papen and colleagues overruled him from "consideration for the position of the Reich president"; in recognition of the further weakening

---

[446] AdR Schleicher, 1:392–96, 398; Papen's quest, August 1932–January 1933: Muth, "Kölner Gespräch."

[447] Goebbels 2/2:340; AdR Papen, 1:385, 401.

[448] AdR Papen, 1:475–76; Goebbels, 2/2:348, 349.

[449] HRSA, 5/1:349; Goebbels, 2/2:359.

[450] For Göring's reemergence as a key figure, Tyrell, "Der Wegbereiter: Hermann Göring als politischer Beauftragter Hitlers in Berlin 1930–1932/33," in Manfred Funke, ed., *Demokratie und Diktatur* (Berlin, 1987), 178–97.

[451] Although badly outmaneuvered, Papen for once had law and Reichstag custom on his side: Huber, *Verfassungsgeschichte*, 7:1097–100.

of his cabinet's position, Hindenburg now insisted on respect for the sixty-day deadline.[452]

Germany's fourth national campaign in seven months began as the grimmest autumn of the Great Depression closed in. Papen sought futilely to woo a distrustful or enraged public, while he and his colleagues deliberated over a decree against "vilification of the state" and the circulation of "untrue or distorted facts." Like Brüning's "Reich flight tax," this was an idea with a future.[453] Hitler inevitably campaigned for democracy against "reaction": Papen's "rule by the grace of God" was "obsolete and no longer viable even in the days of our monarchs." *Leistung* not membership in Berlin's exclusive *Herrenklub* determined one's "divine calling." Fairness demanded his own summons to the chancellorship; nor was he a "drummer" for others.[454] A violent Berlin transport strike in which KPD and NSDAP combined against their common enemy, the German state, enlivened the campaign's closing days.

The outcome (Figure 4.11) was a stinging setback for all concerned except the KPD. The NSDAP's Reichstag seats dropped from 230 to 196, and Nazis and Center-BVP together no longer possessed a potential majority. But Hitler, despite the loss of 2 million votes and increasing strains within his movement, could wait for Papen and Schleicher to come to him, as they immediately did.[455] Even the rise in Communist votes and a post-election crisis within the NSDAP had their uses in persuading the German establishment to surrender the chancellorship before more of Hitler's voters chose "proletarian" over nationalist revolution. Hitler boasted that "*I can wait!*"; the cabinet by contrast faced an immediate emergency.[456] The voters had overwhelmingly repudiated it once more. Its previously derisory authority had wholly vanished. It was supposed to govern a society in economic collapse. Above all, it must by 6 December face a new Reichstag in which NSDAP and KPD together still possessed a majority of five votes, theoretically sufficient to overturn both cabinet and Article 48 decrees.

As the Great Depression hit bottom, the original Reichswehr and Hindenburg project of ruling against the parties had failed irreparably. It had clearly been a poor idea to attempt to govern primarily by decree, without majority support, yet without breaking a constitution that provided a Reichstag (i) elected by universal suffrage, that (ii) could invalidate Article 48 decrees

---

[452] AdR Papen, 2:576–83, 599.

[453] Ibid., 2:814–15.

[454] HRSA, 5/2:37, 39 (quotations in original), 59, 147, 151; Party campaign playbook: Paul, *Aufstand*, 104–08.

[455] Muth, "Kölner Gespräch," 472–74 (intermediary: Heinrich Himmler).

[456] HRSA, 5/2:163 (2 November 1932); Thomas D. Grant, *Stormtroopers and Crisis in the Nazi Movement* (London, 2004) documents the winter 1932–33 turmoil in the SA, and suggests that the NSDAP faced immediate "disintegration or victory." But war and political struggle are *relational* in nature: ongoing panic in government circles cancelled out NSDAP disarray – which was itself a further argument for accepting Hitler's terms, lest his supporters defect to the KPD.

and overturn cabinets by simple majority, that (iii) could not be dissolved without holding an election within sixty days, and that (iv) must meet within thirty days of each new election. In the course of the November election campaign the Reich supreme court at Leipzig had inflicted further damage on Papen by partially invalidating – as pretextual – his 20 July overthrow of the SPD-Center government of Prussia.

On 9 November Schleicher nevertheless again urged escalation: the cabinet must prevent the Reichstag from meeting, once the parties had predictably declined to offer the government a working majority. But as one of his colleagues sagely remarked, "a dictatorship without widespread support must of necessity collapse." The cabinet therefore agreed to offer its resignation to Hindenburg, while authorizing one more Papen-Schleicher effort to harness Hitler's supporters to their own purposes in a "concentration of the national forces." Hindenburg himself sought to reduce the corporal to obedience through a personal appeal to patriotism and *Kameradschaft*. But despite exhaustion and demoralization throughout the NSDAP and SA, and increasing restlessness and appetite for office on the part of key leaders such as Gregor Strasser, Hitler reaffirmed his demand for the chancellorship, and for the Article 48 powers accorded to Brüning and Papen.[457] Mussolini, who had at last received Göring after many vain NSDAP efforts to establish close contact, joined Goebbels in jovially advising "no compromises."[458]

That left the Reich president and his caretaker cabinet in straits far more dire than those of the NSDAP. Hindenburg had publicly announced his opposition to Hitler's evident aim of "party dictatorship." But no other type now seemed possible. Hitler refused to support or tolerate a cabinet led by Schleicher, should he replace Papen.[459] Papen was now leaning more than ever toward meeting Hitler's price, but could see no way to move Hindenburg. The Reich president himself was increasingly upset at the prospect of losing Papen: "They want to take away a man I trust, and force a chancellor on me." Schleicher initially advised patience; negotiations with Strasser and others were under way. But Hindenburg was feeling increasingly exposed: on 1 December he insisted to Schleicher and Papen that he must have a government. In cabinet the next day, the chief of the Reich president's secretariat, Otto Meissner, reported that Hindenburg's morale (*"geistige Zustand"*) was cracking under the strain, and that delay was unacceptable. With virtual unanimity the ministers then repudiated Papen on the grounds that he could neither tame the NSDAP nor avoid bloodshed.[460]

[457] AdR Papen, 2:902–03, 906–07, 952–56, 985–86, 988–1000, 1034–35.

[458] Goebbels, 2/3:63; Hans Woller, "Machtpolitisches Kalkül oder ideologisches Affinität? Zur Frage des Verhältnisses zwischen Mussolini und Hitler vor 1933," in Benz et al., eds., *Der Nationalsozialismus*, 57–58.

[459] AdR Papen, 2:1013, 1017.

[460] Meissner memorandum, 2 December 1932, in Vogelsang, "Zur Politik Schleichers gegenüber der NSDAP 1932," VfZ 6 (1958), 103–05; AdR Papen, 2:1025, 1026, 1034–38.

In response to a query about the Reichswehr's options in the event of civil disturbances, Schleicher called in a key assistant, Major Eugen Ott, to brief the cabinet on the large-scale planning exercise involving commanders, staffs, and civil authorities that the Reichswehr ministry had held on 25–26 November. The exercise scenario was a political statement; either consciously or unconsciously, it made clear what the Reichswehr did *not* want. The planners posited a drastic and improbable worst-case scenario that foreordained failure: a widely observed KPD-SPD – and possibly NSDAP – general strike and passive resistance campaign throughout the Reich on the model of March 1920; the likely paralysis of Germany's industrial infrastructure and urban food supplies due to NSDAP withdrawal from emergency services units; SA unhelpfulness in defending East Prussia against "Communist arson squads" and Polish incursions; and a very difficult "psychological situation" for the troops themselves. Ott's verdict and that of the commanders of the army's seven infantry divisions was an uncompromising rejection of the option of temporary military dictatorship: "the tension in the Reich must be solved without commitment of the Wehrmacht."[461] That "tension" stood in the way of what the Reichswehr *did* want: to rearm as swiftly and massively as possible.[462]

Hindenburg inexplicably liked and trusted Papen. But the cabinet's rejection of his preferred chancellor forced the field marshal, much against his will, to appoint Schleicher as head of a presidential cabinet on 2 December. The general assumed office with his usual ebullient confidence, in the hope that something would turn up; he sought anxiously to enlist the trade unions and above all Gregor Strasser, with or without "the blessing of the Messiah, Hitler."[463] But Strasser collapsed under the strain of the last of many conflicts with Hitler over whether the NSDAP should accept less than the chancellorship. On 8 December he unaccountably resigned all Party offices and departed on holiday to Italy, while Hitler summoned the customary leadership meetings to confirm his Führerdom by acclamation. The "traitor" Strasser failed to carry with him a significant following.[464] Schleicher's manifest inability to govern, Hitler's charisma, and continuing hope of victory and office held the battered NSDAP together. In the first half of January, a massive National Socialist propaganda

[461] Wolfram Pyta, "Vorbereitungen für den militärischen Ausnahmezustand unter Papen/ Schleicher," MGM 51 (1992), 389, 396, 407, 410–14; Carsten, *Reichswehr*, 378–83, compares the actual situation to the exercise assumptions, but implies that misperception was the source of the decision to choose the worst imaginable case. But operations staffs do not choose worst-case scenarios from masochism. Eberhard Kolb and Pyta, "Die Staatsnotstandsplanung unter den Regierungen Papen und Schleicher," in Winkler and Müller-Luckner, eds., *Die deutsche Staatskrise*, 155–82, offer much useful analysis, but fail to situate Reichswehr planning sufficiently within the context of the army's institutional objectives.

[462] Again, for the details, Geyer, "Zweite Rüstungsprogramm."

[463] Schleicher–François-Poncet conversation, 29 November 1932, Ministère des Affaires Étrangères, *Documents diplomatiques français 1932–1939*, series 1, vol. 2 (Paris, 1966), 89; Schleicher, in Vogelsang, "Neue Dokumente," 428.

[464] Goebbels, 2/3:75–79, 81; and the perceptive account of Kershaw, *Hitler, 1889–1936*, 396–403.

machine and the Party's leading speakers invaded the small state of Lippe in northwest Germany; a Landtag election on 15 January offered an ideal opportunity to prove that the NSDAP was "again on the march." Hitler spoke sixteen times in ten days, and the Party raised its share of the vote to 39.5 percent. Goebbels trumpeted the outcome as a cosmic victory: *"Signal Lippe!"* And Hitler reiterated his refusal to lend his votes to any government that he did not lead.[465]

Schleicher by contrast was now genuinely desperate. The new Reichstag had met from 6 to 9 November and had recessed without a no-confidence vote; all political forces feared yet another national election. But the chamber was due to reconvene at the end of January. In cabinet on 16 January Schleicher therefore advocated preemptive dissolution should a no-confidence vote on the model of the previous September seem likely, and an extra-constitutional postponement of new elections until the following autumn. Agreement with Hitler was nevertheless still possible – and even a "broad basis, perhaps from Strasser to the Center Party." No other minister offered more concrete prospects, although the foreign minister, Konstantin von Neurath, and Meissner both opposed on Hindenburg's behalf any solution resembling a "party cabinet."[466]

The DNVP helped bring the government crisis to a head by stridently attacking Schleicher's flirtations with trade unions and SPD, and by warning of the alleged threat of "Bolshevism in the countryside." Schleicher in desperation turned to Hindenburg for support on 23 January, asking for a dissolution order and permission to postpone elections for "several months." Ominously, Hindenburg insisted on reflecting further before conceding even the dissolution. And he flatly refused "at this time" to sanction Schleicher's unconstitutional plan to postpone the resulting elections. Absurdly and almost insultingly, the Reich president made eventual approval contingent on Schleicher gaining the agreement of the very party leaders whose power the postponement would destroy.[467]

Schleicher had definitively lost the confidence of the Reich president – and the NSDAP leadership was aware as early as 10 January that Hindenburg had not even authorized him to dissolve the Reichstag.[468] Still more decisively, Schleicher had lost the backing of the Reichswehr. It had now become the fundamental axiom of German politics that if cabinet and Reich president dissolved the Reichstag and postponed elections, the outcome would be strikes, riots, and a KPD-NSDAP quasi-alliance against the state, as in the Berlin transport strike.[469] But in removing Papen, Schleicher had himself largely foreclosed

[465] Goebbels, 2/3:107; Paul, *Aufstand*, 109–10; HRSA, 6:309; Muth, "Kölner Gespräch," 538.
[466] AdR Schleicher, 230–36.
[467] Ibid., 282–85; 304–06 for Schleicher's failure to enlist Kaas for the proposed unconstitutional course.
[468] Goebbels, 2/3:103.
[469] For instance: Ott ("Generalstreik *Aller*") (emphasis in original), in Pyta, "Militärischen Ausnahmezustand," 410; and note 476.

the option of martial law and temporary military dictatorship legitimized by Hindenburg's waning authority. As he had remarked to the Reichswehr's corps and division commanders in mid-December, the November planning exercise showed that the army could not cope with "sabotage and passive resistance." He had taken on the chancellorship because "in a few days Papen would have had the Wehrmacht in the streets with machine guns against nine-tenths of the *Volk*." An eventual conflict with the Nazis in the new year, he insisted paradoxically, would be fought out, but added significantly that "their destruction [*Zerschlagung*] does not lie in the interest of the state."[470] No record of what the commanding generals thought of Schleicher's contradictions survives. But as conflict with a recalcitrant Reichstag and with the NSDAP and SA seemingly approached in January 1933, the "front," it emerged, had strong views that Schleicher had ignored at his peril. As with Müller, and Brüning, and Papen, the imperatives of government increasingly conflicted with the priorities of the Reichswehr. The Reichswehr prevailed.

On 28 January 1933, as the Reichstag prepared to reconvene in four days, Schleicher confessed to the cabinet that Hindenburg would probably not concede a dissolution order. In that case, he advised, the cabinet should resign. No one disagreed. The chancellor, still touchingly faithful to the army's requirements, once again suggested as best option that Hindenburg, despite earlier reluctance, make Hitler chancellor. That course Schleicher likewise advised the following day in presenting the cabinet's resignation to Hindenburg – with the proviso that no NSDAP "party hack" be made Reichswehr minister.[471]

Schleicher got his wish. The December 1932–January 1933 intrigues of Papen, who still enjoyed Hindenburg's trust and burned with resentment over Schleicher's perceived *Dolchstoss*, figure prominently in the literature.[472] In the course of December and January Papen indeed procured, initially in deepest secrecy, Hitler's emergence as leader of the "cabinet of national concentration" that the Reich president's entourage and the army had in their various ways sought since 1930. But despite the conspiratorial details, the outcome was no accident, no sudden reversal of the order of things; Schleicher and Papen had intermittently sought precisely that result since summer 1932. And despite the distress of the NSDAP after the November election, no authoritative political figure capable of winning Hindenburg's trust was willing to put the Nazis down in blood. To govern Germany without giving Hitler power required breaking the constitution in some way, and might lead to open civil war.[473] Hindenburg had appeared willing to act unconstitutionally on Papen's behalf at the end of August 1932. But the cabinet had lost its nerve, once Papen's bungled dissolution of the Reichstag on 12 September demonstrated that he had the support of

---

[470] Schleicher, in Vogelsang, "Neue Dokumente," 427–28.

[471] AdR Schleicher, 306–11.

[472] Muth, "Kölner Gespräch," 529–41; Turner, *Hitler's Thirty Days to Power: January 1933* (London, 1996), chs. 5–6; Bracher, *Auflösung*, ch. 11.

[473] See the detailed army and interior ministry option papers, AdR Schleicher, 238–43, 267–69.

a mere 8 percent of the elected representatives of the German people. Now, in January 1933, Hindenburg was increasingly weary of the struggle. His reputation was being dragged in the mud over the inheritance tax evasion inherent in assigning ownership of Neudeck, from the beginning, to his son Oskar. State subsidies to feckless and needy *Junker* had inevitably led to scandals involving acquaintances, friends, and relatives. The eastern agrarian interest groups that represented "his people" remained deeply hostile both to government efforts to settle the unemployed on the land, and to Schleicher's flirtations with trade unions and SPD.

The breakdown in close succession of the Papen and Schleicher cabinets, and word of the army's decided judgment that a new "*Kampfkabinett*" meant civil war, led Hindenburg in late January to insist that any cabinet equipped with Article 48 powers must have "more of a following in the country than Papen." Hitler remained suspect "because he demanded the Reichswehr [ministry], aimed at dictatorship, and was a lunatic [*Phantast*]" who "felt bound by no given word." Papen, the one major political figure who still enjoyed the field marshal's trust, remained an essential component of any new government that included the Nazis, whose "following in the country" remained indispensable to *any* German-national government. The DNVP too must participate – and Hitler might even receive presidential decree powers if sufficiently "hemmed in [*eingerahmt*]."[474]

A Hitler cabinet with Papen as vice-chancellor therefore seemed the path of least resistance. No significant figure in government circles proposed a credible alternative to Hitler. The cabinet apparently believed that reappointing Papen to rule in defiance of the constitution would produce a catastrophic and generalized "state- and Reich-president-crisis." Even without war in the streets, a two-thirds majority of the Reichstag (NSDAP, DNVP, KPD, and a mere forty-two additional votes) could impeach the Reich president, placing his powers in abeyance until a popular referendum voted him out or confirmed him in office; a two-thirds majority could also ask the Reich supreme court to remove the president for unconstitutional behavior.[475] But generalized insurrection was the greatest fear of all. The finance minister, Lutz Schwerin von Krosigk, assumed a leading role in bringing down both Papen and Schleicher because he otherwise expected a KPD-NSDAP alliance against the German state that would force "the troops to fight against both Right *and* Left." The spectacle of the army "gunning down nationalist youth at the barricades" would force Hindenburg out.[476]

In his final audience with Hindenburg on 28 January, Schleicher too suggested that meeting Hitler's price remained the best option. Even the far from pro-Nazi army chief, Hammerstein-Equord, had come to view a Hitler chancellorship as the lesser evil. The domestic objectives that Hitler spelled out to a key

[474] Weiss and Hoser, eds., *Tagebuch Quaatz*, 224–25, 228 (21/28 January; source: Meissner).

[475] Huber, *Verfassungsgeschichte*, 6:313–14, with details on NSDAP preparations to impeach (December 1932).

[476] AdR Papen, 1030; AdR Schleicher, 308, 317.

army figure in early December 1932, the enthusiastic promotion of "technical rearmament" and of the "spiritual rearmament of the German people," and the "total extermination [*Ausrottung*] of Marxism," were infinitely alluring compared to a new Papen chancellorship and "the Wehrmacht in the streets with machine guns against nine-tenths of the *Volk*."[477] And all concerned had to consider what would happen when Hindenburg, now eighty-five, died or became unable to discharge his duties. If the Hitler experiment was unavoidable, it was best conducted while the "old gentleman" still had a potentially decisive influence over its course.

As Papen's persistent advocacy took effect, the safeguard that gave Hindenburg the most confidence was the Reichswehr; he brusquely reserved to himself as commander-in-chief the choice of Reichswehr minister. And the ideal man, in Hindenburg's naive judgment a "completely apolitical" general, was close to hand. Blomberg, whom Groener and Schleicher had sought to sideline with a temporary assignment as leader of Germany's unyielding delegation to the Geneva disarmament talks, had acquired in that capacity direct access to Hindenburg, to whom he had previously paid court at Neudeck during his service as commander in East Prussia. Blomberg's imposing presence, criticism of Brüning's allegedly feeble disarmament conference stance, and unwillingness to admit that Germany must provisionally abjure war with its neighbors (which had led Groener and Schleicher to remove him as chief of staff in 1929) apparently commended him to the field marshal.[478]

On 29 January Hindenburg secretly summoned Blomberg to Berlin as a further guarantee that Hitler would remain as "hemmed in" as Papen had promised. Yet Blomberg's ambitious, forward-looking, and highly professional former chief of staff, Walter von Reichenau, had been in close touch with Hitler since April 1932; Blomberg himself had first met Hitler in 1930, and greatly admired the Führer of the NSDAP. At some point in late December 1932 or January 1933, the general too had advised Hindenburg that a Hitler chancellorship was the only alternative to a civil war within the national camp that in turn might cause the army to disintegrate. That Reichenau was in Berlin during the final negotiations over the new cabinet, perhaps acting as liaison to Blomberg, suggests the extent to which Schleicher had lost control over Reichswehr policy.[479]

---

[477] AdR Schleicher, 307–08, 310–11; Vogelsang, *Reichswehr, Staat und NSDAP*, 388–89; idem, "Hitlers Brief an Reichenau vom 4. Dezember 1932," VfZ 7 (1959), 429–37, and HRSA, 5/2:236–47. The last portion of the letter (244–47) was in effect Hitler's exposition of what he could offer the Reichswehr; the letter's recipients were the individuals – Reichenau and Blomberg – who emerged the following month as the new Reichswehr leadership.

[478] Kershaw, *Hitler, 1889–1936*, 420; Post, *Civil-Military Fabric*, 154–57; Samuel W. Mitcham, Jr., "Generalfeldmarschall Werner von Blomberg," in Gerd R. Ueberschär, ed., *Hitlers militärische Elite*, 2 vols. (Darmstadt, 1998), 1:29–31.

[479] Vogelsang, "Hitlers Brief an Reichenau," 430; idem, *Reichswehr, Staat und NSDAP*, 387, 389 note; Blomberg's views and advocacy: ibid., 375; Meissner, *Staatssekretär*, 266; Mitcham, "Blomberg," 30–31.

On Monday, 30 January 1933, the field marshal administered the oath of office to Blomberg – behind Schleicher's back – just after 0900. Some of the remaining ministers-to-be initially had no clear idea why Hindenburg's office had summoned them for 1130. Neurath and Schwerin von Krosigk even agreed telephonically that they would refuse appointment to a new Papen *Kampf-kabinett*. But both readily joined the Hitler government – and served until 1938 and 1945 respectively. Hugenberg proved the most intractable recruit; the Reich president required his presence, but the DNVP leader quarreled with Hitler over the vital issue of control of the Prussian police. In the end, in what Hugenberg later reputedly described as "the greatest stupidity in my life," he allowed himself to be flattered and hustled into the cabinet. Papen's smooth patter assuaged or silenced conservative doubts, and Hitler and his new colleagues took the oath of office around noon.[480] The twenty-first and final cabinet of the Weimar Republic and of the German Reich contained only three Nazis: Hitler, the colorless bureaucrat Wilhelm Frick as Reich interior minister, and the ebullient Göring as Reich minister without portfolio and Prussian interior minister. The new Reich chancellor was nevertheless gloatingly confident that he could outwit his coalition partners and erect the same dictatorship over Germany that had long existed within the NSDAP. Benito Mussolini had shown the way.[481]

5. OUT OF THE NATIONAL PASTS . . .

In both Italy and Germany the temptation to ascribe a chain of events that ended in national ruin to some temporary "accident in the works" has been strong.[482] Contingency – the revolutionary impact of war on a scale as yet unsurpassed, and in the German case the roller coaster of hyperinflation and Great Depression – inevitably played a major role. Yet the founding of the two regimes in 1922 and 1933 and their subsequent trajectories also owed much to their respective national pasts, to powerful continuities in personnel, structures, attitudes, and myths. Why else did the two advanced capitalist countries most devastated in the Great Depression receive in 1933 leaders as different as Adolf Hitler and Franklin Delano Roosevelt?

Explaining the advent of the Fascist and Nazi regimes requires disassociating two complexes of processes that in reality were concurrent and interrelated: the collapse of Liberal Italy and of the German Republic on the one hand, and on the other the emergence of Fascist and Nazi parties, committed to total power, as each country's most powerful political force. In understanding the collapse,

---

[480] Larry Eugene Jones, "'The Greatest Stupidity of my Life': Alfred Hugenberg and the Formation of the Hitler Cabinet, January 1933," JCH 27:1 (1992), 63–87; AdR Schleicher, 321–23.

[481] Wolfgang Schieder, "Fascismo e nazionalsozialismo nei primi anni trenta," in Del Boca et al., eds, *Il regime fascista*, 46–51, documents the extent to which Hitler and his associates saw, and sometimes publicly invoked, the Italian dictatorship as a model before 1933.

[482] An archaeology of the concept (coined by Fritz Stern during the Fischer debate): Jürgen Steinle, "Hitler als 'Betriebsunfall in der Geschichte,'" GWU 45:5 (1994), 288–302; for Italy (Benedetto Croce's "parenthesis"), p. 3 in this volume.

and especially the difference in timing of up to a decade, structural analysis of the two societies' external and internal circumstances is the most promising course.[483]

External constraints or their absence played a major and usually unacknowledged role in differentiating the two cases. Italy, however humiliated by its putatively faithless allies and exposed to their "blackmail of grain and coal," preserved sufficient national independence after 1919 to make internal political experiments short of Bolshevism thinkable. It fell to Liberal Italy's Fascist successor to discover the policy consequences of financial and resource dependence.[484] Germany's defeat, partial occupation, reparations obligations, and disarmament deprived it from 1918 onward of enough sovereignty so that a radical nationalist cabinet or regime was too great a risk. Reparations, the consequent indispensability of American loans, the Reichswehr's impotence, and above all France's "watch on the Rhine" until 30 June 1930 prevented nationalist Germans from voting for "liberation," and prolonged Weimar's anemic existence.

The internal systemic crises that opened in 1918–19 and ended in 1922/33 derived from the long-delayed unadulterated impact of mass politics upon two profoundly fractured societies that shared a tripartite division: a "national *Lager*" that lacked its own mass party and faced both Catholic and Socialist mass forces. The storms of 1919 struck Liberal Italy with particular force, since its restricted franchise (Figure 2.6) had hitherto prevented Socialists and Catholics from converting their strength in "real Italy" into corresponding representation in Rome. In Germany, Bismarck's early decision for universal male suffrage allowed Socialists and Catholics together to command 51.2 percent of the popular vote by 1912 (Figure 2.7). But in neither country did the two mass parties threaten to wrest control of the state from the national camp, or succeed in doing so before 1918–19.

In Italy, PSI and PPI failed immediately and dramatically, despite a wafer-thin combined majority in the 1919–21 Chamber of Deputies (Figure 4.6). Their primordial and mutual ideological abhorrence, their local rivalries across the northern countryside, and the external magnetism that Kremlin and Vatican exercised over the majority of their cadres and adherents made a PSI-PPI coalition unattainable even in the bloody spring and summer of 1922. Parliamentary arithmetic prevented the Liberals from governing effectively so long as they rejected durable compromise with the least radical of the mass parties, the PPI. Italy's "two red years" thus presented in patriotic eyes a unique spectacle

---

[483] Detlev Junker, "Die letzte Alternative vor Hitler: Verfassungsbruch und Militärdiktatur," in Christoph Gradmann and Oliver von Mengersen eds., *Das Ende der Weimarer Republik und die nationalsozialistische Machtergreifung* (Heidelberg, 1994), 67–69, ironically notes the disorienting "over-abundant supply of explanations" of Weimar's collapse and Hitler's advent, and persuasively suggests that analysis of the "power-political situation" of 1932 should take priority, because only then did a Hitler government become inevitable. But structural analysis also offers the best explanation of the Italian and German roads from 1918 to 1922 and 1932/33.

[484] See Knox, *Common Destiny*, 126.

of untamed chaos at the periphery and paralysis at the center. Giovanni Giolitti, united Italy's greatest statesman after Cavour, had failed even before Fascism established its presence decisively.

Germany's violent transition in 1918–19 from monarchical authoritarian empire to democratic "party-state" was perhaps even more shocking to nationalist Germans than the electoral "Caporetto" of November 1919 had been to Italian Liberals and *interventisti*. Yet the German revolution of November 1918 nevertheless reordered Germany in ways that made provisional stability possible. Germany's lead in economic and social development over Italy was never more visible than in the good sense that the German urban working classes displayed in 1918–19. The majority Social Democrats managed to rally a majority – however transitory – of Germans for a democratic republic and against the disorder that might well unhinge Germany's advanced economy. The SPD's Italian counterpart by contrast opposed and vilified Italy's war, then voted lemming-like to join Lenin's Communist International in October 1919. Ebert, Noske, and many of their colleagues were men of a different stamp: patriots and men of common sense and prudence who "hated revolution as they hated sin."

Once provoked by armed uprisings, they brutally and effectively repressed Germany's *massimalisti* with the only tools at hand. That result ultimately recoiled upon the German Republic, which in the end died by the sword by which it had lived: the Reichswehr, lineal descendant of the *Freikorps*, and the emergency powers of the Reich president. But until March 1930, despite the fragmenting effects of the electoral law and the interminable querulous wrangling of Germany's "thirty parties," the SPD was Germany's preeminent force for parliamentary democracy. The working-class disunity so often lamented as an alleged source of ultimate collapse and surrender in 1932–33 was in reality a fundamental precondition of Weimar's relative longevity. The KPD's insistently affirmed monopoly over revolutionary extremism freed the majority Socialists to rule and support the "bourgeois" Republic.[485]

The two states' administrative structures and the character of their supreme executives also contributed to Liberal Italy's swift collapse and to Weimar's survival – and ultimate demise. Italy's French-Piedmontese centralization made government control of Italian society brittle and intermittent. The interior ministry directly commanded each of the seventy-odd provinces through its prefects. But in troubled times the large number of provinces that required day-to-day action made competent oversight impossible. Public order, already problematic by summer 1919, became far more so once Nitti had demoralized the peripheral authorities by failing to back them firmly against PSI violence. Giolitti evicted D'Annunzio from Fiume, but failed utterly closer to home.

The legacy of Germany's historic territorial fragmentation and of the *Kaiserreich*'s federal structure made Germany very different, in ways that on balance reinforced the Republic. In the aftermath of the Munich soviets, Germany's

---

[485] As Winkler, *Weimar*, 595, trenchantly observes.

second-largest federal state fatefully constituted itself as a playground for paramilitary leagues, nationalist assassins, and *völkisch* sects. That extreme form of Bavarian exceptionalism nevertheless did not last: after the 1923 Putsch the BVP government held the line at home against Bavaria's most conspicuous political export, National Socialism. By 1929–30 elections in the minor federal states offered Hitler a means of outflanking the center and building the momentum that made the NSDAP the second-largest German party in September 1930. But throughout, the "red Prussia" that true Bavarians so hated proved the strongest citadel of German democracy. Its SPD-Center-DDP government and SPD-controlled police dominated three-fifths of Germany until July 1932, when Papen's coup from above, partially legitimated by the Nazi Landtag election victory from below that spring, swept away the last major stronghold of Germany's democratic minority.

At the very center of power both states possessed structures with fatefully similar features, despite differences in origin. The Italian monarchy retained noteworthy powers over war, foreign policy, and domestic emergency. Victor Emmanuel III, mindful of his father's failure to coerce parliament in 1898–1900 and ensuing assassination, normally preferred to hide from political exposure behind his constitutional role. But in the three supreme crises – 1915, 1922, 1943 – that punctuated his reign, his compass was dynastic advantage, not the *Statuto*. The king's preeminent instrument, *ultima ratio regum*, was not prime minister and cabinet but the *Regio Esercito Italiano*. When parliament or ministers failed him, he fell back on the military core of the Piedmontese-Italian state. And the army's inclinations were inevitably authoritarian, nationalist, and congruent with its own institutional interests.

In the German case, the supreme executive helped to create Weimar and – under new management – destroy it. The Republic's founders revived many of the prerogatives of William II, "all-highest warlord," for the president and plebiscitary Führer of the German Reich. Election by all Germans; supreme command of the armed forces; and power to dissolve parliament, select the chancellor, and govern by decree made the office a formidable instrument for the Republic's preservation or destruction. The president's powers exacerbated the congenital irresponsibility of political parties born under Bismarck and excluded from government until 1918–19. But it also provided remedies. When the parties failed or refused to govern, Ebert could and did. In Hindenburg's aged authoritarian hands, those same powers constituted an enormous temptation to remake German politics so that the parties could never govern again.

Finally, the two military establishments played salient roles that help explain Italy's swift collapse and the timing and nature of Weimar's longer decline and end. The Italian army's overcommitment to domestic policing from 1919 onward, together with the perceived slights that Nitti visited upon an officer corps convinced that victory entitled it to respect and perquisites, helped widen the long-standing gap between *Regio Esercito* and Liberal parliamentary order. The army lacked an institutional agenda other than a senior officer corps as large as postwar austerity would permit, and perhaps a future war against the despised Yugoslav successor state. It also lacked, especially after the institution of the army council in January 1921, a functioning high command capable of political or military initiatives. Except for D'Annunzio's Garibaldian sedition at Fiume, military hostility to the Liberal order remained latent until Fascism's expansion as a mass movement gave local and regional commanders an ally through which to conduct a highly congenial proxy war against the "internal enemy." Despite formal loyalty to Italy's increasingly incoherent governments, the army's widespread support of the *squadre* at the periphery and its tacit option in October 1922 for a Mussolini government in Rome dictated the outcome.

The military instrument of the German Republic was very different from its Italian counterpart. The Reichswehr's shrinkage to fewer than 4,000 officers had effects not foreseen by the framers of the Versailles "shame-treaty": it gave Groener and Seeckt license to distill the very best from the debris of the "old army." The Treaty forbade a general staff; the Reichswehr officer corps as a whole was made up largely of general staff officers, competitively selected early in their careers as the army's best brains. The Treaty forbade universal military training; the army fostered as its reserves the paramilitary formations that formed a characteristic, pervasive, and profoundly anti-democratic feature of Weimar life. Most important, the war that Germany had allegedly lost only through blackest treachery gave the officer corps a cause that banished what little strategic sense its blinkered members possessed.

Defeat had deprived them of their rightful position at the summit of German society. Defeat had deprived Germany of its rightful domination of Europe. With all the precision and diligence fostered by generations of training and experience, under the protection of the commanding figure of Hans von Seeckt, mid-level officers such as Stülpnagel set about creating a military instrument that would overthrow the post-1919 world order by stages: first the domination of Europe, then the final confrontation with Anglo-America.[486] But the birth of that instrument presupposed, as a first stage, the overthrow of Weimar. For the SPD, while in its majority not pacifist, was sufficiently pacific that it presented a seemingly insuperable obstacle to rearmament – unless driven out of government.

The radical nationalist outcome of the two "state crises" was on one level a product of these structural configurations. Both societies were sufficiently advanced so that systemic change from the radical Left was not part of their repertoires. Turin was not and could not be Petrograd. A successful Spartacist or even USPD seizure of power in Berlin would merely have provoked total civil war: *Freikorps*, some of the SPD, and virtually all other segments of German society, heavily armed with war surplus equipment, would have exterminated the self-proclaimed vanguard of the proletariat with a zeal and thoroughness far surpassing anything seen in 1919–20. Military dissidents and

---

[486] Stülpnagel memorandum, 6 March 1926, ADAP B/1/1/144 (343, 345).

"old Right" were almost equally powerless, as D'Annunzio's misadventures and the pitiable failure of the Kapp Putsch demonstrated. In both countries the "national camp" had lost the dominant position that it saw as its right, lacked the unitary mass organization required to dominate Socialists and Catholics, and was bereft of leaders capable of reversing a situation that it perceived as unbearable.

War and aftermath in both Italy and Germany thus offered unique prospects for challengers from within the national camp. Power vacuums at the center of government mirrored organizational and leadership deficits within the preexisting non-Socialist and non-Catholic political forces.[487] In Italy the skills and ethos acquired in war and the coincidence in 1919 of external humiliation with the triumphant resurgence of the "internal enemy" gave Benito Mussolini his opening. The apprenticeship of *squadrismo* – race-war against the putative Slav menace in the eastern borderlands – appeared wholly legitimate to the harassed guardians of the Liberal state and to the army that furnished Francesco Giunta's warriors with rifles, hand grenades, gasoline, and vehicles. A similar legitimacy in Liberal and military eyes attended the subsequent explosion of "sacred violence" in Emilia and Tuscany that answered the red flags hoisted over northern Italy's town halls in autumn–winter 1920 (see Figure 4.9).

In Germany the removal of the monarchy and the subsequent failure of Kapp, Lüttwitz, and Ehrhardt likewise opened the road for a wholly new type of nationalist politics. Its godfathers were the Reichswehr on the one hand and the Pan-German League on the other – a lineage that suggests the power of at least *some* continuities in German history. The army, then and later, sought to apply what it innocently conceived to be a central strategic lesson of the Great War: the overriding need for radical nationalist "enlightenment" of troops and population. Germany had lost because it had lacked conviction: a notion only plausible in a nation for all its learning impervious to arithmetic, and abidingly devoted to the strategically preposterous notion that *Geist* must invariably triumph over mere materiel. The Pan-Germans added the racist and anti-Semitic cosmology that had played an increasing role in their wartime agitation. Their 1919 creation, the "German-Racist Defense and Defiance League," spread throughout German society its murderous slogans against "the Jews as lightning-rods for all injustice." The army took the already demonstrably nationalist *Gefreiter* Hitler, trained him in Pan-German lore and agitational technique, and happily set him loose upon Munich's *völkisch* beer-hall scene. The experience of the Munich "Jew-Soviets" of April 1919 had already inclined Bavaria's authorities to indulgence toward anti-Semitic fanaticism and nationalist armed bands. They beamed approvingly as Hitler deployed his unique gifts to build a political and paramilitary movement that aimed to "nationalize the masses" and reverse the verdict of 1918.[488]

---

[487] Distinctively: Bracher, *Auflösung*, passim on Weimar's "Machtverfall."

[488] A famous phrase (MK, 337–38) for the first stage in Hitler's self-assigned mission; the notion pervades the 6,000 pages of HSA and HRSA.

The 1923 Putsch nevertheless showed the limits of official tolerance; *Landespolizei* and Reichswehr stood firm behind their leaders. But Hitler had demonstrated his indispensability as the creator of a movement more militant and effective than the *Vaterlandspartei* of the late war or the now-dissolved *Schutz- und Trutz-Bund*. Above all, despite his eccentricities and his failure in November 1923, Hitler had proven himself the one German nationalist leader capable of deeds. His subsequent achievements through the "power of the spirit and of the spoken word" proved his "calling."[489] He re-founded and consolidated the NSDAP as a cohesive *Führerpartei* with formidable paramilitary auxiliaries, based on cadres steeled in war, indoctrinated in military-organizational technique, imbued with the Prussian military imperative of individual initiative, and increasingly structured to defeat democracy "with the weapon of democracy." With the instrument that he and his chosen band created, he then worked the "miracle" of Nazism's ascent from electoral insignificance to largest German party and undisputed champion of the national camp.

The crumbling of the Liberal state and the destruction of the German Republic thus coincided with the rise of challengers associated, both in personnel and in ethos, with the national armies and the radical nationalist cause. In both cases, the army's intervention – or reluctance to intervene – was decisive to the outcome. From the May 1921 elections onward, Liberal Italy's *Staatskrise* was insoluble through parliamentary means, as the deadlocks surrounding the formation of the two Facta governments demonstrated. Giolitti alone could still in theory dominate the situation. But he embodied Liberal rejection of the claims of the mass parties, and would tolerate no outcome that allowed even the PPI a policy role. The Fascist participation in government that virtually all Liberals had sought since 1921 was thus by July–August 1922 the only apparent option.

The one major figure who offered to put Mussolini's movement down in blood was Badoglio. But his price was the explicit political and royal backing that was supremely unlikely, and perhaps in addition his own reinstatement as army chief.[490] Quite apart from the mass "martyrdom" of youthful members of the national camp that Badoglio's option entailed, the probable strategic outcome was singularly daunting. The Liberal regime had already proven itself unable to govern or police Italy against the Socialists; if it now destroyed the *squadre*, who or what would protect it from PSI and Communist vengeance, and from the resentment of the PPI's "loathsome underhanded little priest"?[491] Mussolini, amply aware of his own indispensability, driven onward by an exaggerated fear of Giolitti's return to power and by the probably correct perception that his turbulent movement must seize power or disintegrate, placed king and army before an inescapable choice: his summons to power or "genuine civil war." The monarch's surrender because "all... some in one way, some in

---

[489] Weber on charisma, Lossow on Hitler: pp. 300–01, 345.
[490] See note 396.
[491] Giolitti's distasteful description of Don Sturzo offers unique insight into Liberal Italy's suicide; hence the repetition.

another, had abandoned me" was overdetermined above all by the army's dis-
inclination to put down an insurrection successful throughout northern Italy,
and its discreetly expressed partiality toward a Mussolini government.

In the German case the army's posture went far beyond the "benevolent neutrality" with which the *Regio Esercito Italiano* greeted the March on Rome.[492]
Generations of historians have sought to construct explanations of Weimar's
collapse and Nazism's triumph as a function of labor relations, class politics,
and the machinations of malefactors of great wealth both industrial and agrarian. But like Nazism's alleged lower-middle-class character, such constructs
derive primarily from the demands or implications of Marxist theory and sociological convention rather than from the empirical evidence.[493]

Weimar's demise had many authors. Hindenburg, Hugenberg, Papen,
Brüning, and a variety of other figures and organizations played greater or lesser
roles. The obduracy of the parties destroyed the Grand Coalition, last best hope
of German democracy. The KPD in accordance with its own inclinations and
in obeisance to strict instructions from Moscow, targeted the "social-fascist"
SPD as its main enemy throughout. Mussolini urged Hitler onward with avun-
cular advice and Fascist press support.[494] The traditional Right in general and
Hugenberg in particular so hated the Republic and its leading party, the Social
Democratic Party of Germany, that they committed *hara-kiri* in order to consummate their enemies' ruin.[495] The noble neighbors at Neudeck and an assortment of agricultural interest groups lobbied against Brüning and ultimately for
Hitler. Some minor business leaders also interceded for Hitler, even if Germany's
major corporations largely held aloof, in noteworthy disconfirmation of their
purported influence over Weimar's demise and its outcome.[496]

---

[492] Mondini, *Politica delle armi*, 160–71.

[493] See especially Matzerath and Turner, "Selbstfinanzierung der NSDAP"; Turner, *German Big
Business and the Rise of Hitler* (Oxford, 1985); and Turner's trenchant summary, "'Alliance
of Elites' as a Cause of Weimar's Collapse and Hitler's Triumph?," in Winkler and Müller-
Luckner, eds., *Die deutsche Staatskrise*, 205–14. For eloquent defense of the labor relations
thesis, and of the notion that Weimar's failure was preeminently a failure of democratic social
policy, see Feldman, "The Weimar Republic: A Problem of Modernization?," AfS 26 (1986),
1–26.

[494] For Stalin's rationale (a nationalist Germany would quarrel with the West, creating revolutionary opportunities for Soviet Russia), see Robert C. Tucker, "The Emergence of Stalin's Foreign
Policy," *Slavic Review* 36 (1977), 580–84; for the policy's later development, entry of 7 September 1939 in Ivo Banac, ed., *The Diary of Georgi Dimitrov, 1933–1949* (New Haven, CT, 2003),
115–16, and Stalin's remarks to Stafford Cripps, 1 July 1940, cited in Sir Llewellyn Woodward,
British Foreign Policy in the Second World War, vol. 1 (London, 1970), 470 note. Mussolini:
p. 383 in this volume; Knox, *Common Destiny*, 132, 136; and the many Hitler interviews with
the controlled Italian press in the later volumes of HRSA.

[495] For this felicitous image, Hans Mommsen, "Entscheidung für den Präsidialstaat," 14–15.

[496] On the disunity and relative lack of influence on the outcome of the interest lobbies, see
Wolfgang Zollitsch, "Adel und adlige Machteliten in der Endphase der Weimarer Republik.
Standespolitik und agrarische Interessen"; Jürgen John, "Zur politische Rolle der Grossindu-
strie in der Weimarer Staatskrise," and Turner, "Alliance of Elites," in Winkler and Müller-
Luckner, eds., *Die deutsche Staatskrise*, 205–14, 215–38, and 239–56 respectively.

Yet the aged Reich president had needed no encouragement to seize upon the SPD's exit from government in 1930 to exclude it permanently, lending his powers to Brüning's welcome experiment in nationalist moderate authoritarianism. Once Brüning's usefulness had ended, the field marshal placed his authority squarely behind Papen's "revolutionary-conservative" effort to destroy Weimar altogether, in the fatuous expectation that Hitler would lend his constituency to the "cabinet of barons." When nine-tenths of the German people damned Papen beyond rescue and Schleicher too failed, Hindenburg, his entourage, and Germany's inherited elites sought in desperation to harness Hitler to Papen.

But presidential grudges and preferences, and the intrigues of figures in the entourage such as Meissner and the president's asinine son Oskar ("whose position was not foreseen in the constitution") were not the primary source of movement by stages from ailing democracy in spring 1930 to Hitler on 30 January 1933. Even Papen, whose assiduous advocacy and fervent assurances finally overcame the Reich president's aversion to appointing the "Bohemian corporal" to the chancellorship, was not the prime mover. His role in December 1932–January 1933 was merely to find a way to accomplish at last what virtually everyone in authority in Germany had regarded as necessary and inevitable since spring–summer 1932 at the latest: to bring the NSDAP into government and thus end Germany's *Staatskrise* before it metastasized into a "state- and Reich-president-crisis" and a civil war that would seemingly benefit only the KPD.

The prime mover behind these events and the decisive force in their resolution was the Reichswehr as an institution. Schleicher, despite the widespread tendency in the literature to celebrate his purported un-military open-mindedness and to present his many intrigues as personal foibles, was not a Weimar *politician*. He acted throughout as the political agent of an institution driven by implacable goals that a plurality of the German people shared. Those goals burned through Weimar's insubstantial fabric in March 1930, even before "freedom" for the Rhineland and Nazism's organizational and electoral expertise and commitment paralyzed the parliamentary system. The struggles over the pocket-battleships and the approaching deadlines of the army's "second rearmament plan" had persuaded Groener and Schleicher that they must eject the SPD from government. The Reich president was similarly inclined. The presidential cabinets of Brüning and Papen were Schleicher inventions created to serve the army's overriding interests. Papen's destruction of "red Prussia" in July 1932 had long been an army goal.[497] "Taming" Hitler's movement for the cause of rearmament had been the most urgent need of the army, and of Groener and Schleicher, from autumn 1930. Hitler's ever-greater electoral successes made him ever more indispensable. And the disarray and despondency within his movement in autumn–winter 1932–33 was small indeed compared to the fear and despondency of Hindenburg, Schleicher, their advisors, and the

[497] Carsten, *Reichswehr*, 369.

cabinet. The Reichswehr itself foreclosed the option of presidential military dictatorship, while Hindenburg's mental rigidity, distress at political and personal attacks, and increasing terror of responsibility did the rest. Schleicher, at his wits' end, ultimately advocated a Hitler chancellorship. Blomberg suddenly emerged at Hindenburg's summons as the representative of the "front" and of the total war faction, the most modern, professional, and relentless group within the world's most professional and ideologically committed army. Hitler was the Reichswehr's choice. But not, it soon became clear, the Reichswehr's instrument.

CONCLUSION

Into the Radical Nationalist Future: Inheritances and Prospects of the New Regimes

The legacies that Mussolini, Hitler, and their followers assumed in 1922 and 1933 were difficult indeed. The interrelationships at the outset between two states' external and internal situations, their economic, military, and political instruments, and the dictators' goals demand painstaking analysis. For on them depended in large part the speed and extent of the regimes' subsequent radicalization and external success.

Economic and geopolitical constraints gripped both states, but with unequal force. Reparations, war debts, and the imperative need for foreign credit forced good behavior on both Rome and Berlin throughout the 1920s. But Hitler's arrival after the Great Depression touched bottom gave him a Germany freed in advance of the external financial tutelage that had helped preserve the Republic. Reparations ended in the first weeks of the Papen government; foreign lending had virtually ceased. The economy Hitler inherited was roughly equal in size to that of Britain and 39 percent of that of the United States; by 1938 the respective figures were 115 and 43 percent.[1] Germany's technological prowess gave its post-1933 armed forces synthetic fuel and rubber, the hardest armor plate of the coming war, and the first nerve gases, operational jet fighters, and ballistic missiles. Much of Versailles already lay in ruins; Hitler could express ironic approbation of the Stresemann diplomacy he had once vilified: "Of [all] my predecessors, he was not the worst."[2] And geography, ideology, and great-power politics – the strip of fragile *Saisonstaaten* from Baltic to Black Sea established in 1919, Soviet Russia's shared aim of destroying the post-1919 world order, and the absence from the scene until 1940–41 of the United States – smoothed the new Germany's path.

By contrast, financial dependence hobbled Mussolini throughout his first decade in power.[3] Thereafter the economic weakness deriving from Italy's

[1] GDP (PPP) base figures in these paragraphs: Maddison, 50–51; see also Figures 2.1–2.5.
[2] Hitler, *Monologe*, 87.
[3] See Knox, *Common Destiny*, 126.

relative poverty and forty-year lag behind Germany made Fascist Italy's road to its many wars hard indeed. With less than half of Germany's GDP in 1922 and 42 percent in 1938, a steel industry that produced between 8 (1922) and 10 percent (1938) of Germany's, an energy supply that was 73 percent (1938) imported, and the need for 5 million tons a year of seaborne supplies easily blockaded at Gibraltar and Suez, Italy remained effectively paralyzed until it found a mighty ally that could distract the Western powers. Italy's economy remained far less industrialized than Germany's, nor did that imbalance change in Italy's favor: industry produced 34 percent of GDP in 1925, against Germany's 56 percent, and 31 against 58 percent in 1938. Agriculture by contrast still made up 43 percent of Italy's GDP in 1922, and 30 percent in 1938.[4]

The two societies shared a number of common features. Both majority cultures demanded that the nation be "*one*, indivisible" and deplored any sign of *innere Zerrissenheit*, from parties and interest groups to the presence of the Jewish "race" – a notion fully developed in Germany although as yet embryonic in Italy. The thirst for the German national integration glimpsed in August 1914 and the continuing quest of Italy's *literati* for the seamless unity that the "fourth war of the *Risorgimento*" had failed to deliver inspired the cadres and adherents of the single parties of the new regimes. Conversely, both cultures assumed, if for different reasons, that treachery must be at the root of failure. The *Risorgimento* prophets had attributed foreign domination largely to Italian "Judas"-figures; Germany's poets, philosophers, theologians, and scientists had proclaimed the superiority of German *Geist* with such supreme confidence that only *Dolchstoss* could explain 1918.

Amid the fear, privation, and slaughter that led to "mutilated victory" and unacknowledgeable defeat in 1917–19, these presumptions generated the omnidirectional thirst for vengeance that PNF and NSDAP embodied and perpetuated until 1945. Generational divides accentuated by war likewise marked both societies and their radical nationalist movements. War and national humiliation stripped the "front generation," born from 1890 to 1900, of all respect for their elders. That generation provided the principal cadres of the two movements, from Grandi (1895) and Balbo (1896) to almost half the key *Gauleiter* of 1933.[5] War had taught them self-assertion and the skills required for command – and for revolution. Their immediate successors, the university and high school students of the era of *Freikorps* and *squadrismo*, were if anything even more terrifying, for they had yet to prove themselves. The German university system in particular incubated a cohort of ruthless young scholars and law graduates whose "unconditional will to deeds" powered such pivotal regime

4 Mitchell, *European Historical Statistics, 1750–1970*, 811; Vera Zamagni, "Un'analisi macroeconomica degli effetti della guerra," in idem, ed., *Come perdere la guerra e vincere la pace* (Bologna, 1997), 52.
5 Hüttenberger, *Die Gauleiter*, 213–20: sixteen of thirty long-serving and exemplary *Gauleiter* were born between 1890 and 1900, and two more in 1902.

institutions as the Reich Security Head Office (RSHA) of Heinrich Himmler (1900) and of the youthful Reinhard Heydrich (1904).[6]

A lesser capacity for mass fanaticism distinguished Italy. Despite the hatred of "the foreigner" lovingly cultivated in the *Risorgimento* and after, nineteenth-century Italian political culture largely derived, indirectly or through Napoleonic conquest, from Italy's more advanced French neighbor. Italy's small Jewish community, despite the persistence of clerical anti-Semitism, was in 1922 still widely considered part of the nation. Jews served in disproportionate numbers as officers in army and navy, joined the PNF, and marched on Rome.[7] Racialist theories had a limited foothold, and their proponents explicitly rejected the biopolitical and negative eugenic corollaries widespread in Germany. Italian Führer-myths, from Garibaldi to D'Annunzio, were feeble compared to their German counterparts. The wartime cult and Nationalist plots surrounding Cadorna stood little chance in the absence of battlefield victory. Mussolini's early invocations of dictatorship were correspondingly tentative; in the end, he largely invented his own role. And the monarchy stood enduringly in his way.

Yet the most significant of the many cultural characteristics that limited the penetration and effectiveness of new Fascist regime was the gulf between the 72 percent (1921) of the population over six years of age that could read, and the 28 percent that could not.[8] That cleavage largely coincided with the primordial divide between city and countryside: the historic domination over the *contado* of Italy's "hundred cities." That cleavage had divided Italy's 1915–18 *Frontgemeinschaft* against itself, and along with the military malpractice of the officer corps was the root cause of the disintegration of 2nd Italian Army after the Caporetto breakthrough. It had expressed itself through the rage of the landless peasantry, of their *leghe*, and of their womenfolk against the war – and the property – of the *signori* of the towns. Its consequences had driven even democratic *interventisti* such as Bissolati to despair: "We built on sand; the Italians were not ready."

In the aftermath of 1915–18 rural backwardness gave the war between the Fascist *superuomini* of literate urban Italy and the *contadini* and workers of Emilia, Tuscany, and Apulia its savage edge.[9] The Fascist mass movement of 1921–22 indeed recruited widely from the rural strata upon which the *leghe* had imprudently trampled. But Fascism's symbols and values, and its war against the postwar "internal enemy...more malignant, more loathsome, than before,"

---

[6] Wildt, *Generation des Unbedingten*, especially 848–49: over two-thirds of RSHA cadres were born after 1900, and roughly 60 percent between 1900 and 1910.

[7] Mondini, "L'identità negata," 154: as of 1938, 9,663 "Jews," as defined by the Fascist racial laws, were members of the PNF, and 220 possessed the coveted March on Rome certificate; for the army officer corps, ibid., 152, also pp. 70–71 in this volume.

[8] *Censimento 1921*, 19:221.

[9] See for instance Piazzesi, *Diario*, 62–62, 67 (Piazzesi on the enemy: "herd more than people"; the "reds," on the attack: "He wanted the war!").

were not rural. They were the continuation both in personnel and in concepts of the most militant strands of the prewar revolt against Giolitti, of the interventionist fanaticism in which that revolt culminated, and of the merciless 1917–18 *"fascio* of national defense." The violence that brought Fascism to power continued the Great War in a way that fatally undermined the very national cohesion that the new regime required for its future success. And the continuing literacy deficit throughout rural Italy limited Fascism's capacity to repair the damage, while the enforced immobility of 1922–32 in external policy and the doggedness and authority of Italy's preexisting institutions, above all monarchy, army, and Roman Church, limited Mussolini's ability to reward his faithful followers with careers.

Germany was inevitably very different, in ways that reinforced National Socialism and gave it uncommon driving force. The nation's modern high culture, founded in middle-class rejection of *ancien régime* France, had acquired a fierce anti-Western character through revolutionary and Napoleonic conquest. As early as the 1813–15 "war of liberation" and its aftermath, Germany's "German-Christian" majority came to define itself against Germany's oldest minority. Then came Jewish emancipation – and Darwin. Pseudo-scientific anti-Semitism, Haeckel's biopolitics, and Ratzel's biogeographic corollaries offered the ingredients for a theory of history that might serve, in other less inhibited hands, as the root of a powerful all-explanatory ideology. Its claim to be science and the links it purported to establish between race, nation, individual, and the very nature of the universe gave it an uncommon motivational force only paralleled in the "pleasant twentieth century" by Marxism-Leninism. And even nationalist Germans who rejected the anti-Christian overtones of biopolitics accepted many premises of pre-1914 *völkisch* thought. The leadership tradition drummed into Germany's schoolchildren throughout the long nineteenth century was likewise ready to hand: Arminius, slayer of Romans; Frederick Barbarossa rising from beneath the Kyffhäuser to save the German *Volk*; Luther, founder of Protestant Germany and of the language itself; Frederick, who made Prussia great; and Bismarck, booted and spurred, victor over German fragmentation and the French ancestral enemy. By 1900 virtually universal literacy made these ideas accessible in one form or another to every single German. And for a century Prussia's universal service army had instilled in much of the male population a leadership tradition – comparatively indifferent to hierarchical niceties and increasingly demanding of individual initiative in combat – that complemented and reinforced the charismatic elements in German political culture.

Nor was the notion of dictatorship so novel as in Italy. From 1912 onward Class had proposed and predicted it, with Bismarck as model, as sovereign remedy for the Hohenzollern monarchy's "persistent incompetence" and the national *"innere Zerrissenheit"* that defeat would necessarily accentuate. Tirpitz and associates had sought throughout the Great War to implement that ideal, despite the resistance of William II. But as with Cadorna, dictatorship required victory; Ludendorff offered strategic folly and the catastrophes of spring–autumn 1918.

November 1918 created a wholly new situation. By decapitating the German state, it freed from all restraint the radical nationalism that Class and others had pioneered. German Protestantism likewise graduated from the comforting embrace of the monarchy into a cold postwar world in which only a mighty national Führer could offer solace. In the final analysis, the German-national majority culture accepted the divided and divisive Weimar "party-state" only because France held the Rhine bridgeheads and resistance lacked even the grim prospects of *Endkampf* 1918. Those peculiar circumstances gave National Socialism its chance and much of its subsequent power. It answered the inherited yearning for mythic leadership and national integration. It proposed to heal at last the *innere Zerrissenheit* of 1915–33, and restore the *Volksgemeinschaft* of 1914 on a day-to-day basis. It could plausibly claim to represent the German people's free and democratic choice, against an old order that had tragically lost the war and had farcically returned in Papen's baronial "dictatorship against the entire *Volk*."

The NSDAP's modernity was constantly on display: from "Hitler over Germany" to the advanced technology and military organizational techniques that delivered its electoral triumphs.[10] And it promised, in its own twisted way, the freedom that modernity entailed. National Socialism not only undertook to break the shackles of Versailles and to give Germany its external biogeographic freedom. It also promised to free the individual German from the shackles of the old society, to at last deliver the equality earned on the battlefields of 1914–18 and denied by the *Kaiserreich* in law and by Weimar in social reality. The National Socialist "pursuit of happiness" through the career open to talent was no mere electoral promise.[11] The NSDAP, as the careers of its cadres demonstrate, already offered it before 1933. Hitler's advent as chancellor extended it to all throughout the nation who professed to be his faithful followers. And the tenacity of Germany's preexisting social divisions, legacy of the society of *Stände*, gave the National Socialist *Leistungsprinzip* an altogether uncommon magnetism. No other party could insist, with anything approaching Hitler's plausibility, that "[w]e are the Germany of the future."[12]

These claims and most other central features of National Socialism found a particularly eager reception in the German armed forces. The decapitation of the state had also set army and navy free from higher authority. Versailles had shrunk and twisted both services into force structures wholly incompatible with their self-conceived missions, and with the place in German society and politics they considered theirs by right. But the "shame-treaty" had also fashioned

[10] The impassioned continuing debate over National Socialism's modernity or atavism is too complex for summary here, and pertains above all to the deeds and misdeeds of the regime in power; Detlev J. K. Peukert, *Inside Nazi Germany* (New Haven, CT, 1982), offers a durable introduction to many of the issues.

[11] For the phrase, and valuable analysis: Geyer, "The Stigma of Violence, Nationalism, and War in Twentieth-Century Germany," GSR 15:1 (1992), 98.

[12] HRSA, 4:181.

a remedy of sorts: by forcing a massive reduction in force it had accentuated the army's already powerful drive toward quality – of a particularly dangerous kind. War had made the military specialists of the general staff, already on the attack in the last years before 1914, supreme over the *Junker* traditionalism embodied in the Kaiser's military cabinet and the war ministry. Great War, Versailles Treaty, and the efforts of Groener and Seeckt made the Reichswehr officer corps the concentrated essence of the new type: fanatical in both nationalism and professionalism. The leaders of the Reichswehr demanded the total commitment of German society to war, painfully aware that the army itself no longer possessed the required popular ascendancy. When Weimar failed them, they destroyed it. The ultimate result, whatever initial misgivings some generals may have harbored, was an answered prayer.

National Socialism and the German army shared a sacred past: the formative experience ("*Erleben*") of the Great War and of the pitiless postwar fighting against "Bolsheviks" and Poles.[13] Preparation for the total war of the future – the army's axiomatic goal – made Hitler's militant mass following and his promise to reintegrate German society indispensable. Hitler's increasing authority offered the prospect of the charismatic nationalist dictatorship that the army's total war theorists demanded. And in the interim, the army no longer needed to fear the civil disturbance nightmare its planners had perhaps disingenuously conjured up: SA, SS, and Göring's Prussian police ruled the streets from 30 January 1933.

The self-consciously modern professionals of which Reichenau, still more than Blomberg, was the exemplar saw the "National Socialist Idea" as indispensable reinforcement of the troops' fighting power: November 1918 would never recur. The officer corps as a whole greeted with "indescribable jubilation" the prospect of geometric expansion of the services' force structures, of the command of an ever-larger portion of Germany's male population, and of promotions of unprecedented speed.[14] The effects of the "shame-treaty" indeed gave the professionals a unique opportunity: to create a gigantic military instrument virtually from nothing, with a minimum of obsolete materiel and "human materiel." All except a few thousand of the future army's half-million regular and reserve officers thus owed their entire careers to the new regime and to its Führer. The National Socialist career open to talent in war, realm of "chance and probability within which the creative spirit is free to roam," would foreseeably foster a further massive increase in the aggressiveness and fighting power of the German armed forces.

Nothing similar existed or could exist in Italy. The monarchy stood in the way. The army by 1922 had of its own accord largely stripped away the innovations in weapons and tactics grudgingly learned in war. Its existing force

---

[13] Shared past ("gleichen Erleben des Grossen Krieges"): Jürgen Förster, DRZW, 9/1:487.
[14] "Ungeheurer Jubel": Hermann Ramcke, *Vom Schiffjungen zum Fallschirmjäger-General* (Berlin, 1943), 196; also the quiet professional satisfaction (July 1933) registered in Hürter, ed., *Ein deutscher General an der Ostfront*, 25.

structures and cadres fatally encumbered – as much as or more than Italy's economic weakness – efforts to create forces capable of realizing Mussolini's expansionist goals. The "generals of victory" exploited their tacit bargain with the new regime to checkmate a modest mid-1920s attempt at reform.[15] Fascist ideology coexisted uneasily with traditional monarchical loyalties, and did not find its way directly into training lesson plans for officers and troops, whereas Blomberg and Reichenau almost immediately decreed the propagation throughout the armed forces of the National Socialist idea.[16] The *Regio Esercito* also lacked the immediate spur to action that helped drive the Reichswehr. Its ancestral enemy, Austria-Hungary, had vanished. The army's planners soon realized that a punitive expedition against the Yugoslav successor state was foolhardy unless some outside force neutralized France. Above all, the army's dominant postwar corporate objective was the respect, the officer positions, and the perquisites that the Fascist regime offered, not the destruction of the post-1918 world order.

Yet that was precisely what both dictators sought. Mussolini's frequent geopolitical indiscretions before October 1922 gave way to a diplomatic prudence interrupted by outbursts such as his temporary seizure of Corfù from Greece in 1923. In private he developed a coherent program aimed at the total "fascistization" of Italian society, its demographic expansion, and the conquest of geopolitical freedom.[17] Hitler by contrast had already set forth his goals from 1921–22 onward, and until late 1930 had publicly emphasized his enduring commitment to seizing the world mastery at which Germany had all too consciously aimed in 1914–18.

Both programs, despite the merely regional character of Fascist ambitions, had a novel domestic corollary. Both claimed a total power over the individual unattainable within the boundaries of the existing Italian and German states. The House of Savoy, the Roman Church, and much of Italy's civil society stood in the way of the barbaric remolding of the Italian people that Mussolini proposed. The PNF alone, even had it enjoyed Mussolini's unalloyed trust, was inadequate to the task. It lacked the mission tactics tradition of its German counterpart, its cadres were unseasoned and extraordinarily uneven in quality, its internal structures dated from mid-1921 at the earliest, and it faced an establishment in far less disarray than did the NSDAP. The result was a slow-motion "seizure of power" that lasted until 1926 and beyond, and an enduring vulnerability to the royal coup d'état that finally felled Fascism in July 1943.

In Germany, by contrast, the National Socialist regime and its Party possessed from the outset massive advantages in all respects. But even Hitler and his associates faced an insuperable structural obstacle that imposed war as firmly

---

[15] Rochat, *Vittorio Veneto a Mussolini*, 517–51; and, in general, Knox, *Hitler's Italian Allies*, ch. 3, and Sema, "La cultura dell'esercito."

[16] See Jürgen Förster, DRZW, 9/1:484–505, who improves notably on the already excellent older literature on "Geistige Kriegführung."

[17] On all this, see Knox, *Common Destiny*, chs. 2–3.

as their fanatical commitment to adjust "soil [area] to population size." Only war could recreate August 1914. Only war could finally eliminate Germany's tenacious working-class and Catholic subcultures, erase Germany's inherited barriers of confession and *Stand*, exterminate the Jewish racial enemy, execute the "eugenic will of the nation," and create through the "National Socialist *Leistungsprinzip*" the elitist yet classless racist society of the "German future."

Mussolini's far weaker position enjoined similarly "heroic deeds." As he soon appreciated, his undeniable "power of the spirit and of the spoken word" alone was insufficient. Only a great victorious war could overthrow the monarchy and end the "dual power" established in 1922. Only war could drastically curtail the "Catholic totalitarianism" that remained Fascism's chief ideological rival.[18] Only war could achieve the national integration that neither 1915–18 nor the violence of the *squadre* had secured. Mussolini promised in 1924 that "the revolution comes later." That promise applied equally to the National Socialist regime that as yet existed only in the minds of Hitler and his followers – and whose alliance Italy required to escape from geopolitical servitude. When the flag of the National Socialist movement at last flew over Berlin, Mussolini's promise would come due. The "war as never before," latent since 1918–19, would reemerge to spread across Europe and the world. For war was "indispensable for consummating the Revolution."[19]

---

[18] For the phrase, used half-jokingly: Pius XI, in OO, 37:129.
[19] Hitler, Isnard, and Brissot de Warville: pp. 361 and 13.

Frequently Cited Works

A comprehensive source listing would be very long indeed, and unavoidably incomplete. What follows is a list of all works cited in the notes more than once, for use in conjunction with the abbreviation key. Readers should also note that given the vastness of the secondary literature, even footnote references not prefaced with "see especially" are often highly selective.

Afflerbach, Holger, *Falkenhayn: Politisches Denken und Handeln im Kaiserreich* (Munich, 1996).

Alatri, Paolo, *Nitti, D'Annunzio e la questione adriatica, 1919–1920* (Milan, 1959).

———, ed., *Scritti Politici di Gabriele D'Annunzio* (Milan, 1980).

———, et al., *Storia della società italiana*, vol. 21, *La disgregazione dello stato liberale* (Milan, 1982).

Albanese, Giulia, *La Marcia su Roma* (Rome, 2006).

Albertini, Luigi, *Epistolario 1911–1926*, 4 vols. (Milan, 1968).

———, *I giorni di un liberale. Diari 1907–1923*, ed. Luciano Monzali (Bologna, 2000).

———, *Venti anni di vita politica*, 5 vols. (Bologna, 1950–53).

Altrock, Constantin von, *Vom Sterben des deutschen Offizierkorps* (Berlin, 2nd rev. ed., 1922).

Ambrosoli, Luigi, *Né aderire né sabotare 1915–1918* (Milan, 1961).

Arbizzani, Luigi, "Lotte agrarie in provincia di Bologna nel primo dopoguerra," in Renato Zangheri, ed., *Le campagne emiliane nell'età moderna* (Milan, 1957), 283–332.

Arendt, Hannah, *The Origins of Totalitarianism* (New York, 1966 [1951]).

Arndt, Ernst Moritz, *Gedichte* (Halle, n.d.).

Ay, Karl Ludwig, *Die Entstehung einer Revolution. Die Volksstimmung in Bayern während des Ersten Weltkrieges* (Berlin, 1968).

Bajohr, Frank, Johe, Werner, and Lohalm, Uwe, eds., *Zivilisation und Barbarei. Die widersprüchlichen Potentiale der Moderne, Detlev Peukert zum Gedenken* (Hamburg, 1991).

Balbo, Italo, *Diario 1922* (Milan, 1932).

Baldassini, Cristina, "Fascismo e memoria. L'autorappresentazione dello squadrismo," *Contemporanea* 5:3 (2002), 475–505.

Balderston, Theo, *The Origins and Course of the German Economic Crisis* (Berlin, 1993).

Banti, Alberto Mario, *La nazione del Risorgimento. Parentela, santità e onore alle origini dell'Italia unita* (Turin, 2000).

———, *Il Risorgimento italiano* (Rome, 2005).

Barbadoro, Idomeneo, "La condotta della guerra: strategia, tattica e scelte politiche," in Paolo Alatri et al., *Storia della società italiana*, vol. 21, *La disgregazione dello stato liberale* (Milan, 1982), 35–70.

Barberi, Benedetto, *I consumi nel primo secolo dell'unità d'Italia (1861–1960)* (Milan, 1961).

Barberis, Walter, *Le armi del principe. La tradizione militare sabauda* (Turin, 1988).

Becker, Jean-Jacques, 1914. *Comment les français sont entrés dans la guerre* (Paris, 1977).

Behrens, C. B. A., *Society, Government and the Enlightenment. The Experiences of Eighteenth Century France and Prussia* (New York, 1985).

Benz, Wolfgang, Buchheim, Hans, and Mommsen, Hans, eds., *Der Nationalsozialismus. Studien zur Ideologie und Herrschaft* (Frankfurt am Main, 1993).

Berdahl, Robert M., *The Politics of the Prussian Nobility* (Princeton, NJ, 1988).

Berghahn, Volker, and Deist, Wilhelm, eds., *Rüstung im Zeichen der wilhelminischen Weltpolitik: grundlegende Dokumente 1890–1914* (Düsseldorf, 1988).

Blackbourn, David, *Populists and Patricians* (London, 1987).

Bobbio, Norberto, *Profilo ideologico del novecento italiano* (Turin, 1986).

Boemeke, Manfred F., Feldman, Gerald D., and Glaser, Elisabeth, eds., *The Treaty of Versailles: A Reassessment after 75 Years* (New York, 1998).

Bosworth, Richard J. B., *Italy, the Least of the Great Powers: Italian Foreign Policy Before the First World War* (Cambridge, 1979).

Bracher, Karl Dietrich, *Die Auflösung der Weimarer Republik* (Düsseldorf, 5th ed., 1984).

Brüning, Heinrich, *Memoiren 1918–1934* (Stuttgart, 1970).

Burchardt, Lothar, *Friedenswirtschaft und Kriegsvorsorge. Deutschlands wirtschaftliche Rüstungsbestrebungen vor 1914* (Boppard, 1968).

Burckhardt, Jacob, *Briefe*, ed. Max Burckhardt, 11 vols. (Munich, 1949–94).

Burleigh, Michael, *Death and Deliverance: "Euthanasia" in Germany, 1900–1945* (Cambridge, 1994).

Bussmann, Walter, "Treitschke als Politiker," HZ 177:2 (1954), 249–79.

Caciulli, Vincenzo, "La paga di Marte. Assegni, spese e genere di vita degli ufficiali italiani prima della Grande Guerra," *Rivista di storia contemporanea* 22:4 (1993), 569–95.

Cadorna, Luigi, *Lettere famigliari* (Milan, 1967).

Cafagna, Luciano, *Dualismo e sviluppo nella storia d'Italia* (Padua, 1989).

Caizzi, Bruno, *Storia dell'industria italiana dal XVIII secolo ai giorni nostri* (Turin, 1965).

Camera dei Deputati, *Comitati segreti sulla condotta della guerra* (Rome, 1967).

Capra, Carlo, "Nobili, notabili, élites: dal 'modello' francese al caso italiano," *Quaderni Storici* 13 (1978), 12–42.

Cardoza, Anthony L., *Agrarian Elites and Italian Fascism: The Province of Bologna, 1901–1926* (Princeton, NJ, 1982).

Carsten, F. L., *The Origins of Prussia* (Oxford, 1954).

———, *The Reichswehr and Politics, 1918 to 1933* (Berkeley, CA, 1973).

Cary, Noel D., "The Making of the Reich President, 1925: German Conservatism and the Nomination of Paul Von Hindenburg," CEH 23:2–3 (1990), 179–204.

Ceva, Lucio, "Il problema dell'alto comando in Piemonte durante la prima guerra d'indipendenza," *Il Risorgimento* 37:2/3 (1985), 1943–83.

———, "Riflessioni e notizie sui sottufficiali," NA 2182 (1992), 331–53.

Chabod, Federico, *Storia della politica estera italiana dal 1870 al 1896*, vol. I, *Le premesse* (Bari, pbk. ed., 1971).

Chickering, Roger, *We Men Who Feel Most German: A Cultural Study of the Pan-German League, 1886–1914* (Boston, 1984).

———, and Förster, Stig, eds., *Great War, Total War* (Cambridge, 2000).

Clark, Linda L., *Social Darwinism in France* (University, AL, 1984).

Class, Heinrich (pseud. Daniel Frymann), *Wenn ich der Kaiser wär'. Politische Wahrheiten und Notwendigkeiten* (Leipzig, 1914 [1912]).

———, *Wider den Strom* (Leipzig, 1932).

Clausewitz, Carl von, *On War*, ed. and trans. Michael Howard and Peter Paret (Princeton, NJ, 1989).

Colapietra, Raffaele, *Leonida Bissolati* (Milan, 1958).

Commissariato Generale dell'Emigrazione, *L'emigrazione italiana dal 1910 al 1923*, 2 vols. (Rome, 1926).

Conrad, J., "Die Latifundien im preussischen Osten," *Jahrbücher für Nationalöknomie und Statistik* 50 (1888), 121–70.

Coppola, Francesco, "Accademia sinistra," *Politica* 2:2 (1919), 223–57.

Cordova, Ferdinando, "Le origini dei sindacati fascisti," SC 1:4 (1970), 925–1009.

Corner, Paul, *Fascism in Ferrara, 1915–1925* (London, 1975).

Corradini, Enrico, *Discorsi politici* (Florence, 1923).

———, *L'ombra della vita. Costume-letteratura e teatro-arte* (Naples, 1908).

De Caprariis, Vittorio, "Partiti politici e opinione pubblica durante la Grande Guerra," in Istituto per la storia del Risorgimento italiano, *Atti del XLI congresso di storia del Risorgimento italiano* (Rome, 1963), 73–175.

De Felice, Renzo, "Ordine pubblico e orientamenti delle masse popolari italiane nella prima metà del 1919," RSS 6:20 (1963), 467–504.

———, *Storia degli ebrei italiani sotto il fascismo* (Turin, 1961).

De Maria, Luciano, ed., *Per conoscere Marinetti e il futurismo* (Milan, 1973).

De Stefano, Natalia, "Moti popolari in Emilia-Romagna e Toscana 1915–1917," RSS 32 (1967), 191–216.

Dehio, Ludwig, "Ranke and German Imperialism," in idem, *Germany and World Politics in the Twentieth Century* (New York, 1967).

Deist, Wilhelm, "Der militärische Zusammenbruch des Kaiserreichs. Zur Realität der 'Dolchstosslegende,'" in Ursula Büttner, ed., *Das Unrechtsregime*, vol. 1 (Hamburg, 1986), 101–29.

Del Boca, Angelo, Legnani, Massimo, and Rossi, Mario G., eds., *Il regime fascista. Storia e storiografia* (Rome, 1995).

Del Negro, Piero, "Ufficiali di carriera e ufficiali di complemento nell'esercito italiano della grande guerra: la provenienza regionale," in Gérard Canini, ed., *Les fronts invisibles: nourrir–fournir–soigner* (Nancy, 1984), 263–86.

Della Peruta, Franco, *Realtà e mito nell'Italia dell'ottocento* (Milan, 1996).

Demeter, Karl, *The German Officer-Corps in Society and State 1650–1945* (New York, 1965).

Deuerlein, Ernst, "Hitlers Eintritt in die Politik und der Reichswehr," VfZ 7 (1959), 177–227.

Dirks, Carl, and Janssen, Karl-Heinz, *Der Krieg der Generäle* (Munich, 2001).

Duggan, Christopher, *Francesco Crispi, 1818–1901: From Nation to Nationalism* (Oxford, 2002).

Dülffer, Jost, *Weimar, Hitler und die Marine. Reichspolitik und Flottenbau 1920–1939* (Düsseldorf, 1972).

Düppler, Jörg, and Gross, Gerhard P., eds., *Kriegsende 1918. Ereignis, Wirkung, Nachwirkung* (Munich, 1999).

Echternkamp, Jörg, *Der Aufstieg des deutschen Nationalismus (1770–1840)* (Frankfurt am Main, 1998).

Einaudi, Luigi, *La condotta economica e gli effetti sociali della guerra italiana* (Bari, 1933).

Engelmann, Roger, *Provinzfaschismus in Italien. Politische Gewalt und Herrschaftsbildung in der Marmorregion von Carrara 1921–1924* (Munich, 1992).

Epstein, Klaus, *Matthias Erzberger and the Dilemma of German Democracy* (Princeton, NJ, 1959).

Esercito e città dall'Unità agli anni trenta, 2 vols. (Rome, 1989).

Falter, Jürgen W., "The Two Hindenburg Elections of 1925 and 1932: A Total Reversal of Voter Coalitions," CEH 23:2–3 (1990), 225–41.

Farneti, Paolo, "La crisi della democrazia italiana e l'avvento del fascismo: 1919–1922," *Rivista Italiana di Scienze Politiche* 5:1 (1975), 45–82.

————, *Sistema politico e società civile* (Turin, 1971).

Fehrenbach, Elizabeth, *Traditionelle Gesellschaft und revolutionäres Recht* (Göttingen, 1974).

————, *Wandlungen des deutschen Kaisergedankens* (Munich, 1969).

Feldman, Gerald D., *Army, Industry and Labor in Germany 1914–1918* (Princeton, NJ, 1966).

Fischer, Fritz, *Germany's Aims in the First World War* (New York, 1967).

————, *War of Illusions: German Policies from 1911 to 1914* (New York, 1975).

Fischer, Wolfram, ed., *Handbuch der europäischen Wirtschafts- und Sozialgeschichte*, vol. 5 (Berlin, 1985).

Fletcher, Roger, *Revisionism and Empire. Socialist Imperialism in Germany 1897–1914* (London, 1984).

Forcella, Enzo, and Monticone, Alberto, *Plotone d'esecuzione. I processi della prima guerra mondiale* (Bari, 1968).

Förster, Stig, "Der Deutsche Generalstab und die Illusion des kurzen Krieges, 1871–1914: Metakritik eines Mythos," MGM 54 (1995), 61–95.

Forsyth, Douglas J., *The Crisis of Liberal Italy: Monetary and Financial Policy, 1914–1922* (Cambridge, 1993).

François, Etienne, "Alphabetisierung und Lesefähigkeit in Frankreich und Deutschland um 1800," in Helmut Berding, Etienne François, and Hans-Peter Ullmann, eds., *Deutschland und Frankreich im Zeitalter der Französischen Revolution* (Frankfurt am Main, 1989), 409–17.

Franzinelli, Mimmo, *Squadristi. Protagonisti e tecniche della violenza fascista 1919–1922* (Milan, 2003).

Franz-Willing, Georg, *Ursprung der Hitlerbewegung 1919–1922* (Preussisch Oldendorf, 1974).

French, David, "'Had We Known How Bad Things Were in Germany, We Might Have Got Stiffer Terms': Great Britain and the German Armistice," in Manfred F.

Boemeke, Gerald D. Feldman, and Elisabeth Glaser, eds., *The Treaty of Versailles: A Reassessment after 75 Years* (New York, 1998).

Frescura, Attilio, *Diario di un imboscato* (Milan, 1981 [1919]).

Frevert, Ute, *Ehrenmänner: das Duell in der bürgerlichen Gesellschaft* (Munich, 1991).

Fritzsche, Peter, *Germans into Nazis* (Cambridge, MA, 1998).

Gaeta, Franco, ed., *La crisi di fine secolo e l'età giolittiana* (Turin, 1982).

————, *La stampa nazionalista* (Rocca San Casciano, 1965).

Galasso, Giuseppe, "Le forme del potere, classi e gerarchie sociali," ESI 1:470–71.

Gasman, Daniel, *The Scientific Origins of National Socialism. Social Darwinism in Ernst Haeckel and the German Monist League* (London, 1971).

Gasser, Adolf, *Preussischer Militärgeist und Kriegsentfesselung 1914* (Frankfurt am Main, 1985).

Gatti, Angelo, *Caporetto. Dal diario di guerra inedito (maggio–dicembre 1917)*, ed. Alberto Monticone (Bologna, 1964).

Geibel, Emanuel, *Werke*, ed. Wolfgang Stammler (Leipzig, n.d.).

Gemzell, Carl-Axel, *Raeder, Hitler und Skandinavien. Der Kampf für einen maritimen Operationsplan* (Lund, 1965).

Gentile, Emilio, "Il futurismo e la politica. Dal nazionalismo modernista al fascismo (1909–1920)," in Renzo De Felice, ed., *Futurismo, cultura e politica* (Turin, 1988).

————, *Le origini dell'ideologia fascista* (Bari, 1975).

————, *Storia del partito fascista 1919–1922. Movimento e milizia* (Bari, 1989).

Geyer, Michael, *Aufrüstung oder Sicherheit: Die Reichswehr in der Krise der Machtpolitik 1924–1936* (Wiesbaden, 1980).

————, *Deutsche Rüstungspolitik 1960–1980* (Frankfurt am Main, 1984).

————, "Insurrectionary Warfare: The German Debate about a Levée en Masse in October 1918," JMH 73 (2001), 459–527.

————, "Rückzug und Zerstörung 1917," in Gerhard Hirschfeld, Gerd Krumeich, and Irina Renz, eds., *Die Deutschen an der Somme 1914–1918. Krieg, Besatzung, Verbrannte Erde* (Essen, 2006), 163–79.

————, "Das zweite Rüstungsprogramm (1930–34)," MGM 17 (1975), 125–72.

Ghisalberti, Carlo, *Storia costituzionale d'Italia, 1849–1948* (Bari, 1974).

Gibelli, Antonio, *L'officina della guerra. La Grande Guerra e le trasformazioni del mondo mentale* (Turin, 1991).

Giovannini, Elio, *L'Italia massimalista. Socialismo e lotta sociale e politica nel primo dopoguerra italiano* (Rome, 2001).

Giusti, Ugo, *Le correnti politiche italiane attraverso due riforme elettorali dal 1909 al 1921* (Florence, 1922).

Gooch, John, *Army, State and Society in Italy, 1870–1915* (New York, 1989).

Gordon, Harold J., Jr., *Hitler and the Beer Hall Putsch* (Princeton, NJ, 1972).

Granier, Gerhard, *Magnus von Levetzow, Seeoffizier, Monarchist und Wegbereiter Hitlers* (Boppard, 1982).

Grassi Orsini, Fabio, and Quagliariello, Gaetano, eds., *Il partito politico dalla grande guerra al fascismo* (Bologna, 1996).

Grazia, Victoria de, and Luzzatto, Sergio, eds., *Dizionario del fascismo*, 2 vols. (Turin, 2002–03).

Groener, Wilhelm, *Lebenserinnerungen: Jugend – Generalstab – Weltkrieg* (Göttingen, 1957).

Grosser, Dieter, *Vom monarchischen Konstitutionalismus zur parlamentarischen Demokratie. Die Verfassungspolitik der deutschen Parteien im letzten Jahrzehnt des Kaiserreiches* (The Hague, 1970).

Grosser Generalstab, *Kriegsbrauch im Landkriege* (Berlin, 1902).

Gudmundsson, Bruce I., *Stormtroop Tactics: Innovation in the German Army, 1914–1918* (Westport, CT, 1989).

Haeckel, Ernst, *The History of Creation* (New York, 1879).

Hagemann, Karen, "Occupation, Mobilization, and Politics: The Anti-Napoleonic Wars in Prussian Experience, Memory, and Historiography," CEH 39:4 (2006), 580–610.

Hansen, Ernst Willi, "Zum 'Militärisch-Industriellen-Komplex' in der Weimarer Republik," in Klaus-Jürgen Müller and Eckhardt Opitz, eds., *Militär und Militarismus in der Weimarer Republik* (Düsseldorf, 1978), 101–40.

Hastings, Derek, "How 'Catholic' Was the Early Nazi Movement? Religion, Race, and Culture in Munich, 1919–1924," CEH 36:3 (2003), 383–433.

Heinemann, Ulrich, *Die verdrängte Niederlage. Politische Öffentlichkeit und Kriegsschuldfrage in der Weimarer Republik* (Göttingen, 1983).

Herwig, Holger, "Admirals versus Generals: The War Aims of the Imperial German Navy, 1914–1918," CEH 5 (1972), 208–33.

Hewitson, Mark, "The Kaiserreich in Question: Constitutional Crisis in Germany before the First World War," JMH 73:4 (2004), 655–83.

Hintze, Otto, *The Historical Essays of Otto Hintze*, ed. Felix Gilbert (Oxford, 1975).

Hitler, Adolf, *Monologe im Führerhauptquartier 1941–1944*, ed. Werner Jochmann (Hamburg, 1980).

Hobohm, Martin, *Soziale Heeresmissstände als Teilursache des deutschen Zusammenbruchs von 1918* (Berlin, 1931).

Hoover, Arlie J., "God and Germany in the Great War: The View of the Protestant Pastors," *Canadian Review of Studies in Nationalism* 14:1 (1987), 65–81.

———, *God, Germany, and Britain in the Great War: A Study in Clerical Nationalism* (Westport, CT, 1989).

Horn, Wolfgang, *Führerideologie und Parteiorganization in der NSDAP (1919–1933)* (Düsseldorf, 1972).

Huber, Ernst Rudolf, *Deutsche Verfassungsgeschichte seit 1789*, 8 vols. (Stuttgart, 1957–91).

Hull, Isabel V., *Absolute Destruction: Military Culture and the Practices of War in Imperial Germany* (Ithaca, NY, 2004).

———, *The Entourage of Kaiser Wilhelm II 1888–1918* (Cambridge, 1982).

———, "Military Culture and the Production of 'Final Solutions' in the Colonies: The Example of Wilhelminian Germany," in Robert Gellately and Ben Kiernan, eds., *The Specter of Genocide: Mass Murder in Historical Perspective* (Cambridge, 2003), 141–62.

———, "Military Culture, Wilhelm II, and the End of the Monarchy in World War I," in Annika Mombauer and Wilhelm Deist, eds., *The Kaiser* (Cambridge, 2003), 235–58.

Hürten, Heinz, ed., *Das Krisenjahr 1923. Militär und Innenpolitik 1922–1924* (Düsseldorf, 1980).

———, ed., *Zwischen Revolution und Kapp-Putsch. Militär und Innenpolitik 1918–1920* (Düsseldorf, 1977).

Hürter, Johannes, ed., *Ein deutscher General an der Ostfront. Die Briefe und Tagebuchblätter des Gotthard Heinrici 1941/42* (Erfurt, 2001).

———, *Wilhelm Groener: Reichswehrminister am Ende der Weimarer Republik (1928–1932)* (Munich, 1993).

Hüttenberger, Peter, *Die Gauleiter. Studie zum Wandel des Machtgefüges in der NSDAP* (Stuttgart, 1969).

Ilari, Virgilio, *Storia del servizio militare in Italia*, 4 vols. (Rome, 1989–90).

Isnenghi, Mario, *Il mito della grande guerra da Marinetti a Malaparte* (Bari, 1970).

———, *I vinti di Caporetto nella letteratura di guerra* (Padua, 1967).

———, and Rochat, Giorgio, *La Grande Guerra 1914–1918* (Milan, 2000).

Jacobsen, Hans-Adolf, *Nationalsozialistische Aussenpolitik 1933–1938* (Frankfurt am Main, 1968).

Joachimsthaler, Anton, *Hitlers Weg begann in München 1913–1923* (Munich, 2000).

John, Hartmut, *Das Reserveoffizierkorps im deutschen Kaiserreich 1890–1914* (Frankfurt am Main, 1981).

Jones, Simon M., *Domestic Factors in Italian Intervention in the First World War* (New York, 1986).

Jünger, Ernst, *Der Kampf als inneres Erlebnis, in Sämtliche Werke*, 22 vols. (Stuttgart, 1978–2007), 7:9–103.

———, *In Stahlgewittern* (Berlin, 1920).

Jürgensen, Kurt, "Deutsche Abende – Flensburg 1914," GWU 20 (1969), 1–16.

Kaehler, Siegfried A., "Vier quellenkritische Untersuchungen zum Kriegsende 1918," in idem, *Studien zur Deutschen Geschichte des 19. und 20. Jahrhunderts* (Göttingen, 1961), 259–305.

Kaelble, Hartmut, "Der Mythos von der rapiden Industrialisierung in Deutschland," GG 9 (1983), 106–18.

Kampers, Franz, *Die Deutsche Kaiseridee in Prophetie und Sage* (Munich, 1969 [1896]).

Kater, Michael H., *The Nazi Party: A Social Profile of Members and Leaders, 1919–1945* (Cambridge, 1983).

Kedourie, Elie, *Nationalism* (London, 1960).

Kennedy, Paul, and Nicholls, Anthony, eds., *Nationalist and Racist Movements in Britain and Germany Before 1914* (London, 1981).

Kernig, C. D., ed., *Marxism, Communism, and Western Society*, 8 vols. (New York, 1972–73).

Kershaw, Ian, *Hitler, 1889–1936: Hubris* (London, 1998).

Klein, Fritz, "Between Compiègne and Versailles: The Germans from a Misunderstood Defeat to an Unwanted Peace," in Manfred F. Boemeke, Gerald D. Feldman, and Elisabeth Glaser, eds., *The Treaty of Versailles: A Reassessment after 75 Years* (New York, 1998), 337–70.

Knox, MacGregor, *Common Destiny: Dictatorship, Foreign Policy, and War in Fascist Italy and Nazi Germany* (Cambridge, 2000).

———, *Hitler's Italian Allies* (Cambridge, 2000).

Kocka, Jürgen, *Klassengesellschaft im Krieg. Deutsche Sozialgeschichte 1914–1918* (Göttingen, 1973).

Koselleck, Reinhart, *Preussen zwischen Reform und Revolution. Allgemeines Landrecht, Verwaltung und Soziale Bewegung von 1791 bis 1848* (Stuttgart, 2nd ed., 1975).

Koshar, Rudy, *Social Life, Local Politics and Nazism: Marburg 1880–1935* (Chapel Hill, NC, 1986).

Kramer, Alan, "Italienische Kriegsgefangene im Ersten Weltkrieg," in Hermann J. W. Kuprian and Oswald Überegger, eds., *Der Erste Weltkrieg im Alpenraum* (Innsbruck, 2006), 247–58.

Krieger, Leonard, *The German Idea of Freedom* (Chicago, 1972).

Krüger, Peter, "German Disappointment and Anti-Western Resentment, 1918–19," in Hans-Jürgen Schröder, ed., *Confrontation and Cooperation: Germany and the United States in the Era of World War I, 1900–1924* (Oxford, 1993), 323–35.

Labanca, Nicola, *In marcia verso Adua* (Turin, 1993).

Lange, Karl, "Der Terminus 'Lebensraum' in Hitlers 'Mein Kampf,'" VfZ 13 (1965), 426–37.

Leed, Eric J., *No Man's Land: Combat and Identity in World War I* (New York, 1979).

Lehnert, Detlev, "Propaganda des Bürgerkrieges? Politische Feindbilder in der Novemberrevolution als mentale Destabilisierung der Weimarer Demokratie," in idem and Klaus Megerle, eds., *Politische Teilkulturen zwischen Integration und Polarisierung* (Opladen, 1990), 61–101.

Lenin, Vladimir Ilyich, *Collected Works*, 45 vols. (Moscow, 1960–70).

Lepsius, Johannes, Bartholdy, Albrecht Mendelssohn, and Thimme, Friedrich, eds., *Die grosse Politik der europäischen Kabinette, 1871–1914*, 40 vols. (Berlin, 1922–27).

Liulevicius, Vejas Gabriel, *War Land on the Eastern Front: Culture, National Identity, and German Occupation in World War I* (Cambridge, 2000).

Lohalm, Uwe, *Völkischer Radikalismus. Die Geschichte des Deutschvölkischen Schutz-und Trutz-Bundes 1919–1923* (Hamburg, 1970).

Longerich, Peter, *Geschichte der SA* (Munich, 2nd rev. ed., 2003).

Lossberg, Fritz von, *Meine Tätigkeit im Weltkriege 1914–1918* (Berlin, 1939).

Lundeberg, Philip K., "The German Naval Critique of the U-Boat Campaign, 1915–18," *Military Affairs* 27:3 (1963), 105–18.

Lupfer, Timothy T., "The Dynamics of Doctrine: The Changes in German Tactical Doctrine During the First World War," *Leavenworth Papers* 4 (1981).

Lussu, Emilio, *Un anno sull'altipiano* (Milan, 1970 [1938]).

Lutz, Ralph H., ed., *The Fall of the German Empire, 1914–1918*, 2 vols. (Stanford, CA, 1932).

Lyttelton, Adrian, "Landlords, Peasants and the Limits of Liberalism," in John A. Davis, ed., *Gramsci and Italy's Passive Revolution* (London, 1979), 104–35.

Lyttelton, Adrian, *The Seizure of Power. Fascism in Italy, 1919–1929* (New York, 1973).

Maier, Charles S., *Recasting Bourgeois Europe: Stabilization in France, Germany, and Italy in the Decade after World War I* (Princeton, NJ, 1975).

Maiocchi, Roberto, *Scienza italiana e razzismo fascista* (Florence, 1999).

Malagodi, Olindo, *Conversazioni della guerra (1914–1919)*, 2 vols. (Milan, 1960).

Malia, Martin, *Comprendre la Révolution russe* (Paris, 1980).

Malinowski, Stephan, *Vom König zum Führer: Sozialer Niedergang und politische Radikalisierung im deutschen Adel zwischen Kaiserreich und NS-Staat* (Berlin, 2003).

Mann, Thomas, *Friedrich und der Grosse Koalition* (Berlin, 1915).

Maranini, Giuseppe, *Storia del potere in Italia 1848–1967* (Florence, 1967).

Marks, Sally, "Smoke and Mirrors: In the Smoke-Filled Rooms and the Galérie des Glaces," in Manfred F. Boemeke, Gerald D. Feldman, and Elisabeth Glaser, eds., *The Treaty of Versailles: A Reassessment after 75 Years* (New York, 1998), 203–20.

Martini, Ferdinando, *Diario 1914–1918* (Milan, 1966).

Matzerath, Horst, and Turner, Henry A., Jr., "Die Selbstfinanzierung der NSDAP 1930–32," GG 3:1 (1977), 59–92.

Max von Baden, *Erinnerungen und Dokumente* (Stuttgart, 1968).

Mazzini, Giuseppe, *Scritti politici*, ed. Franco Della Peruta, 3 vols. (Turin, 1976).

McAleer, Kevin, *Dueling: The Cult of Honor in Fin-de-Siècle Germany* (Princeton, NJ, 1994).

Meier-Welcker, Hans, *Seeckt* (Frankfurt am Main, 1967).

Meinecke, Friedrich, *Werke*, vol. 8, *Autobiographische Schriften* (Stuttgart, 1969).

Meissner, Otto, *Staatssekretär unter Ebert, Hindenburg, Hitler* (Hamburg, 1950).

Melograni, Piero, *Storia politica della grande guerra 1915/1918* (Bari, 1969).

Messerschmidt, Manfred, "Völkerrecht und 'Kriegsnotwendigkeit' in der deutschen militärischen Tradition seit den Einigungskriegen," GSR 6 (1983), 237–43.

Milatz, Alfred, *Wähler und Wahlen in die Weimarer Republik* (Bonn, 1968).

Miller, Susanne, *Burgfrieden und Klassenkampf. Die deutsche Sozialdemokratie im Ersten Weltkrieg* (Düsseldorf, 1974).

Missalla, Heinrich, *"Gott mit uns." Die deutsche katholische Kriegspredigt 1914–1918* (Munich, 1968).

Mitcham, Samuel W., Jr., "Generalfeldmarschall Werner von Blomberg," in Gerd R. Ueberschär, ed., *Hitlers militärische Elite*, 2 vols. (Darmstadt, 1998), 1:28–36.

Mitchell, Brian R., *European Historical Statistics, 1750–1970* (New York, 1976).

———, *European Historical Statistics, 1750–1975* (New York, 2nd rev. ed., 1981).

Moeller, Robert G., "Dimensions of Social Conflict in the Great War: The View from the German Countryside," CEH 14 (1981), 142–68.

Mombauer, Annika, *Helmuth von Moltke and the Origins of the First World War* (Cambridge, 2001).

———, "A Reluctant Military Leader? Helmuth Von Moltke and the July Crisis of 1914," WIH 6:4 (1999), 417–46.

Mommsen, Hans, "Entscheidung für den Präsidialstaat: Komplott der Machteliten oder Selbstpreisgabe der Demokratie?," in Heinrich August Winkler and Elizabeth Müller-Luckner, eds., *Die deutsche Staatskrise 1930–1933: Handlungsspielräume und Alternativen* (Munich, 1992), 1–18.

Mommsen, Wolfgang J., *Max Weber und die deutsche Politik 1890–1920* (Tübingen, 2nd rev. ed., 1974).

———, "The Social Consequences of World War I: The Case of Germany," in Arthur Marwick, ed., *Total War and Social Change* (New York, 1988), 25–44.

Mondini, Marco, "L'identità negata: materiali di lavoro su ebrei ed esercito dall'età liberale al secondo dopoguerra," in Ilaria Pavan and Guri Schwartz, eds., *Gli ebrei in Italia tra persecuzione fascista e reintegrazione postbellica* (Florence, 2001).

———, *La politica delle armi. Il ruolo dell'esercito nell'avvento del fascismo* (Rome, 2006).

———, *Veneto in armi. Tra mito della nazione e piccola patria* (Gorizia, 2002).

Monticone, Alberto, *Gli italiani in uniforme 1915–1918* (Bari, 1972).

———, "Salandra e Sonnino verso la decisione dell'intervento," in idem, *Gli italiani in uniforme 1915–1918* (Bari, 1972).

Mühlberger, Detlev, *The Social Bases of Nazism* (Cambridge, 2003).

Muth, Heinrich "Das 'Kölner Gespräch' am 4. Januar 1933," GWU 37:8, 9 (1986), 463–80, 529–41.

Namier, Lewis, *1848: The Revolution of the Intellectuals* (Garden City, NY, 1964).

Nipperdey, Thomas, "Nationalidee und Nationaldenkmal in Deutschland im 19. Jahrhundert," HZ 206 (1968), 567–73.

Noakes, Jeremy, and Pridham, Geoffrey, eds., *Nazism, 1919–45: A Documentary Reader*, 4 vols. (Exeter, 1988–98).

Noiret, Serge, *Massimalismo e crisi dello stato liberale: Nicola Bombacci (1879–1924)* (Milan, 1992).

———, *La nascita del sistema dei partiti nell'Italia contemporanea: La proporzionale del 1919* (Bari, 1994).

O'Brien, Paul, *Mussolini in the First World War: The Journalist, the Soldier, the Fascist* (Oxford, 2005).

Offer, Avner, *The First World War: An Agrarian Interpretation* (Oxford, 1989).

Omodeo, Adolfo, *Momenti della vita di guerra. Dai diari e dalle lettere dei caduti 1915– 1918* (Turin, 1968 [1934]).

Oriani, Alfredo, *Fino a Dogali* (Bari, 1918 [1889]).

———, *La rivolta ideale*, ed. and preface by Benito Mussolini (Bologna, 1926 [1906]).

Orlow, Dietrich, *The History of the Nazi Party, 1919–1933* (London, 1971).

Papafava dei Carraresi, Novello, *Appunti militari 1919–1921* (Ferrara, 1921).

Papini, Giovanni, and Prezzolini, Giuseppe, *Vecchio e nuovo nazionalismo* (Rome, 1967 [1914]).

Pastor, Ludwig von, *Leben des Freiherrn Max von Gagern 1810–1889* (Munich, 1912).

Patch, William L., Jr., *Heinrich Brüning and the Dissolution of the Weimar Republic* (Cambridge, 1998).

Paul, Gerhard, *Aufstand der Bilder. Die NS-Propaganda vor 1933* (Bonn, 1990).

Perfetti, Francesco, "La 'conversione' all'interventismo di Mussolini nel suo carteggio con Sergio Panunzio," SC 17:1 (1986), 139–70.

Peukert, Detlev J. K., *The Weimar Republic: The Crisis of Classical Modernity* (New York, 1992).

Pflanze, Otto, *Bismarck and the Development of Germany*, 3 vols. (Princeton, NJ, 1963–90).

Phelps, Reginald H., "'Before Hitler Came': Thule Society and Germanen Orden," JMH 25 (1963), 245–61.

Piazzesi, Mario, *Diario di uno squadrista toscano* (Rome, 1980).

Piretti, Maria Serena, *Le elezioni politiche in Italia dal 1848 a oggi* (Rome, 1995).

Pluviano, Marco, and Guerrini, Irene, *Le fucilazioni sommarie nella prima guerra mondiale* (Udine, 2004).

Poliakov, Léon, *The Aryan Myth. A History of Racist and Nationalist Ideas in Europe* (New York, 1974).

Post, Gaines, Jr., *The Civil-Military Fabric of Weimar Foreign Policy* (Princeton, NJ, 1973).

Pressel, Wilhelm, *Die Kriegspredigt 1914–1918 in der evangelischen Kirche Deutschlands* (Göttingen, 1967).

Preuss, Hugo, *Das deutsche Volk und die Politik* (Jena, 1915).

Prezzolini, Giuseppe, *Caporetto* (Rome, 1919).

Procacci, Giuliano, "Geografia e struttura del movimento contadino della Valle padana nel suo periodo formativo (1901–1906)," SSt 5:1 (1964).

Pulzer, Peter G. J., *The Rise of Political Anti-Semitism in Germany and Austria* (New York, 1964).

Puntoni, Paolo, *Parla Vittorio Emanuele III* (Milan, 1958).

Pyta, Wolfram, "Vorbereitungen für den militärischen Ausnahmezustand unter Papen/ Schleicher," MGM 51 (1992), 385–428.

Rainero, Romain H., ed., *Da Oriani a Corradini* (Milan, 2003).

Ratzel, Friedrich, *Der Lebensraum. Eine Biogeographische Studie* (Tübingen, 1901).

———, *Politische Geographie* (Munich, 1897).

Rauh, Manfred, *Die Parlamentarisierung des Deutschen Reiches* (Düsseldorf, 1977).

Reichardt, Sven, *"Faschistische Kampfbünde." Gewalt und Gemeinschaft im italienischen Squadrismus und in der deutschen SA* (Cologne, 2002).

Reichsarchiv, *Der Weltkrieg, 1914 bis 1918*, 14 vols. (Berlin, 1925–44).

Rietzler, Rudolf, *"Kampf in der Nordmark."* Das Aufkommen des Nationalsozialismus in Schleswig-Holstein (1919–1928) (Neumünster, 1982).

Riezler, Kurt, *Tagebücher, Aufsätze, Dokumente,* ed. Karl Dietrich Erdmann (Göttingen, 1972).

Ritter, Gerhard, *The Sword and the Scepter. The Problem of Militarism in Germany,* vol. 3 (Coral Gables, FL, 1972).

Rocca, Gianni, *Cadorna* (Milan, 1985).

Rocco, Alfredo, *Scritti e discorsi politici,* 3 vols. (Milan, 1938).

———, and Coppola, Francesco, "Manifesto," *Politica* 1:1 (December 1918), 1–17.

Rochat, Giorgio, *Gli Arditi della Grande Guerra. Origini, battaglie e miti* (Gorizia, 2nd exp. ed., 1990).

———, *L'esercito italiano da Vittorio Veneto a Mussolini* (Bari, 1967).

———, *L'esercito italiano in pace e in guerra. Studi di storia militare* (Milan, 1991).

———, "Gli ufficiali italiani nella prima guerra mondiale," in idem, *L'esercito italiano in pace e in guerra. Studi di storia militare* (Milan, 1991).

———, and Massobrio, Giulio, *Breve storia dell'esercito italiano dal 1861 al 1943* (Turin, 1968).

Röhl, John C. G., "Admiral von Müller and the Approach of War, 1911–1914," HJ 12:4 (1969), 651–73.

———, "An der Schwelle zum Weltkrieg. Eine Dokumentation über den 'Kriegsrat' vom 8. Dezember 1912," MGM 21 (1977), 77–134.

———, and Sombart, Nicolas, eds., *Kaiser Wilhelm II: New Interpretations* (Cambridge, 1982).

Rosenberg, Hans, *Bureaucracy, Aristocracy, and Autocracy: The Prussian Experience, 1660–1815* (Cambridge, MA, 1958).

Rossini, Giuseppe, ed., *Benedetto XV, i cattolici e la prima guerra mondiale* (Rome, 1963).

Rumi, Giorgio, *Alle origini della politica estera fascista (1918–1923)* (Bari, 1968).

———, "Il Popolo d'Italia (1918–1925)," in Brunello Vigezzi, ed., *1919–1925. Dopoguerra e fascismo. Politica e stampa in Italia* (Bari, 1965), 423–522.

Rusinow, Dennison, *Italy's Austrian Heritage* (Oxford, 1965).

Sabbatucci, Giovanni, "Il problema dell'irredentismo e le origini del movimento nazionalista in Italia," SC 1:3–4 (1970), 467–502, and 2:1 (1971), 53–106.

Salandra, Antonio, *Il diario di Salandra* (Milan, 1969).

Samuels, Martin, *Command or Control? Command, Training and Tactics in the British and German Armies, 1888–1918* (London, 1995).

Scheck, Raffael, "Politics of Illusion: Tirpitz and Right-Wing Putschism, 1922–24," GSR 18:1 (1995), 29–49.

Schmidt, Ernst-Heinrich, *Heimatheer und Revolution 1918. Die militärischen Gewalten im Heimatgebiet zwischen Oktoberreform und Novemberrevolution* (Stuttgart, 1981).

Schreiber, Gerhard, *Revisionismus und Weltmachtstreben. Marineführung und deutsch-italienische Beziehungen 1919/1944* (Stuttgart, 1978).

Schulte, Bernd F., *Die Verfälschung der Riezler-Tagebücher* (Frankfurt am Main, 1985).

Schulze, Hagen, *Freikorps und Republik, 1918–1920* (Boppard, 1969).

———, *Der Weg zum Nationalstaat. Die deutsche Nationalbewegung vom 18. Jahrhundert bis zur Reichsgründung* (Munich, 1985).

Scotti, Tommaso Gallarati, "Idee e orientamenti politici e religiosi al Comando Supremo: appunti e ricordi," in Giuseppe Rossini, ed., *Benedetto XV, i cattolici e la prima guerra mondiale* (Rome, 1963).

Sema, Antonio, "La cultura dell'esercito," in Gabriele Turi et al., *Cultura e società negli anni del fascismo* (Milan, 1987), 91–116.

Sereni, Emilio, *Il capitalismo nelle campagne (1860–1900)* (Turin, 1968 [1947]).

Serpieri, Arrigo, *La guerra e le classi rurali italiane* (Bari, 1930).

Sewell, William H., "Marc Bloch and the Logic of Comparative History," *History and Theory* 6 (1967), 208–18.

Sheehan, James J., ed., *Imperial Germany* (New York, 1976).

Silvestri, Mario, *Caporetto* (Milan, 1984).

——, *Isonzo 1917* (Milan, 2nd ed., 1971).

Snowden, Frank M., *The Fascist Revolution in Tuscany, 1919–1922* (Cambridge, 1989).

Sonnino, Sidney, *Carteggio 1914–1916* (Bari, 1974).

——, *Diario 1914–1916* (Bari, 1972).

Spriano, Paolo, *Torino operaia nella Grande Guerra* (Turin, 1960).

Squeri, Lawrence, "The Italian Local Elections of 1920 and the Outbreak of Fascism," *Historian* 3 (1983), 324–36.

Sternhell, Zeev, *La droite révolutionnaire. Les origines du fascisme français, 1885–1914* (Paris, 1978).

Stoltenberg, Gerhard, *Politische Strömungen im schleswig-holsteinischen Landvolk 1918–1933* (Düsseldorf, 1962).

Stumpo, Enrico, "I ceti dirigenti in Italia nell'età moderna. Due modelli diversi: Nobiltà piemontese e patriziato toscano," in Amelio Tagliaferri, ed., *I ceti dirigenti in Italia in età moderna e contemporanea* (Udine, 1984), 151–97.

Suval, Stanley, *Electoral Politics in Wilhelmine Germany* (Chapel Hill, NC, 1985).

Suzzi Valli, Roberta, "The Myth of Squadrismo in the Fascist Regime," JCH 35:2 (2000), 131–50.

SVIMEZ, *Un secolo di statistiche italiane. Nord e Sud 1861–1961* (Rome, 1961).

Talmon, Jacob L., *The Origins of Totalitarian Democracy* (London, 1952).

Tasca, Angelo, *Nascita e avvento del fascismo* (Florence, 2nd ed., 2002).

Thaer, Albrecht von, *Generalstabsdienst an der Front und in der OHL. Aus Briefen und Tagebuchaufzeichnungen 1915–1919* (Göttingen, 1958).

Thayer, John A., *Italy and the Great War: Politics and Culture* (Madison, WI, 1964).

Thoss, Bruno, "Nationale Rechte, militärische Führung, und Diktaturfrage in Deutschland 1913–1923," MGM 42 (1987), 27–77.

Turner, Henry Ashby, Jr., "'Alliance of Elites' as a Cause of Weimar's Collapse and Hitler's Triumph?," in Heinrich August Winkler and Elizabeth Müller-Luckner, eds., *Die deutsche Staatskrise 1930–1933: Handlungsspielräume und Alternativen* (Munich, 1992), 205–14.

——, *Hitler's Thirty Days to Power: January 1933* (London, 1996).

Tyrell, Albrecht, ed., *Führer befiehl ... Selbstzeugnisse aus der 'Kampfzeit' der NSDAP* (Düsseldorf, 1969).

——, *Vom "Trommler" zum "Führer." Der Wandel von Hitlers Selbstverständnis zwischen 1919 und 1924 und die Entwicklung der NSDAP* (Munich, 1975).

Veneruso, Danilo, *La vigilia del fascismo: Il primo ministero Facta nella crisi dello stato liberale in Italia* (Bologna, 1968).

Ventura, Angelo, "La svolta antiebraica nella storia del fascismo italiano," *Rivista Storica Italiana* 113:1 (2001), 36–65.

Verhey, Jeffrey, *The Spirit of 1914* (Cambridge, 2000).

Vigezzi, Brunello, *Da Giolitti a Salandra* (Florence, 1969).

———, *L'Italia di fronte alla prima guerra mondiale*, vol. I, *L'Italia neutrale* (Milan, 1966).

Vivarelli, Roberto, *Storia delle origini del fascismo. L'Italia dalla grande guerra alla marcia su Roma*, 2 vols. (Bologna, 1990).

Vogelsang, Thilo, "Hitlers Brief an Reichenau vom 4. Dezember 1932," VfZ 7 (1959), 429–37.

———, "Neue Dokumente zur Geschichte der Reichswehr 1930–1933," VfZ 2:4 (1954), 397–436.

———, *Reichswehr, Staat und NSDAP* (Stuttgart, 1962).

Volkmann, Erich Otto, *Soziale Heeresmissstände als Mitursache des deutschen Zusammenbruchs von 1918* (Berlin, 1929).

Volkov, Shulamit, "The Written Matter and the Spoken Word: On the Gap Between Pre-1914 and Nazi Anti-Semitism," in François Furet, ed., *Unanswered Questions* (New York, 1989), 33–53.

Vondung, Klaus, *Die Apokalypse in Deutschland* (Munich, 1988).

———, "Geschichte als Weltgericht: Genesis und Degradation einer Symbolik," in idem, ed., *Kriegserlebnis* (Göttingen, 1980), 62–84.

Wehler, Hans-Ulrich, *The German Empire 1871–1918* (Leamington Spa, 1985).

———, ed., *Moderne deutsche Sozialgeschichte* (Cologne, 1973).

Weindling, Paul, *Health, Race and German Politics between National Unification and Nazism, 1870–1945* (Cambridge, 1989).

Weiss, Hermann, and Hoser, Paul, eds., *Die deutschnationalen und die Zerstörung der Weimarer Republik. Aus dem Tagebuch von Reinhold Quaatz 1928–1933* (Munich, 1989).

Wildt, Michael, *Generation des Unbedingten: Das Führungskorps des Reichssicherheitshauptamtes* (Hamburg, 2001).

Williamson, George S., *The Longing for Myth in Germany: Religion and Aesthetic Culture from Romanticism to Nietzsche* (Chicago, 2004).

Winkler, Heinrich August, *Weimar, 1918–1933: Die Geschichte der ersten deutschen Demokratie* (Munich, 1993).

———, and Müller-Luckner, Elizabeth, eds., *Die deutsche Staatskrise 1930–1933: Handlungsspielräume und Alternativen* (Munich, 1992).

Wittfogel, Karl A., *Oriental Despotism: A Comparative Study of Total Power* (New York, rev. ed., 1981).

Wollstein, Günter, *Das "Grossdeutschland" der Paulskirche: Nationale Ziele in der bürgerlichen Revolution 1848–49* (Düsseldorf, 1977).

Zamagni, Vera, *Dalla periferia al centro. La seconda rinascita economica dell'Italia 1861–1990* (Bologna, exp. ed., 1993).

Zangheri, Renato, ed., *Lotte agrarie in Italia. La Federazione nazionale dei lavoratori della terra (1901–1926)* (Milan, 1960).

Zehnpfennig, Barbara, *Hitlers Mein Kampf: Eine Interpretation* (Munich, 2nd rev. ed., 2002).

Ziemann, Benjamin, "Enttäuschte Erwartung und kollektive Erschöpfung. Die deutschen Soldaten an der Westfront 1918 auf dem Weg zur Revolution," in Jörg Düppler and Gerhard P. Gross, eds., *Kriegsende 1918. Ereignis, Wirkung, Nachwirkung* (Munich, 1999), 165–82.

Index